Psychological Testing

PSYCHOLOGICAL
TESTING Third Edition

ANNE ANASTASI
Professor of Psychology, Graduate School, Fordham University

THE MACMILLAN COMPANY,
COLLIER-MACMILLAN LIMITED, LONDON

Seventh Printing, 1972

Earlier editions coyright 1954 and © 1961 by The Macmillan
Company.

Library of Congress catalog card number: 68:13818

The Macmillan Company
Collier-Macmillan Canada, Ltd., Toronto, Ontario

Printed in the United States of America

Preface

THE PRIMARY objective of this book is to enable the reader to evaluate psychological tests of any type and to interpret test results correctly. This objective is approached in three ways: (1) through an understanding of the principles of test construction, (2) through psychological knowledge about the behavior being measured, and (3) through familiarity with the field of available instruments. Although successive editions of this text have placed increasing emphasis on principles of test construction relative to the discussion of specific instruments, it is recognized that such principles cannot be adequately grasped in the abstract. Acquaintance with the major types of available tests, together with an understanding of their special contributions and limitations, is an essential component of knowledge about contemporary testing. To this end, outstanding examples of each type of test have again been discussed in the text of the third edition, although the number of specific tests thus discussed has been reduced. At the same time, Appendix C contains a classified list of over two hundred tests, including not only those cited in the text but also others added to provide a more representative sample. Except in the case of tests published too recently for inclusion in the *Mental Measurements Yearbooks*, the yearbook reference is also given for each test. Nearly half the tests discussed in this edition have been either initially published or revised since 1961 (when the second edition of this book appeared).

It has been a major aim of this revision to put more "psychology" into "psychological testing." Much of the current confusion about the meaning of test scores stems from inadequate knowledge about the *behavior* the tests are designed to assess. Throughout this book, therefore, special efforts have been made to provide information from behavioral science that should help in the interpretation of test scores. Among the topics introduced in this connection are the meaning of an IQ (Chapter 8), the nature of intelligence (Chapter 22), "culture-fair tests" (Chapter 10), testing the culturally disadvantaged (Chapter 21), adult intelligence (Chapter 11), problems in the diagnosis of organicity (Chapter 12), response styles (Chapter 17), recent research with projective techniques (Chapter 19), and the measurement of environments (Chapter 22). The newly added Part 5, comprising Chapters 21 and 22, focuses on current problems in the use of psychological tests. Chapter 21 is concerned with the "anti-test revolt"—its origins, misconceptions, and constructive implications. Chapter 22 deals specifically with typical contributions that available psychological knowledge can make to the interpretation of test results.

In line with the fuller treatment of test-construction principles incorporated into the present edition, the discussion of norms, reliability, and validity in Chapters 3 to 6 has been reorganized and expanded, and a new chapter on item analysis has been added. The interpretation of factor-analytic results has also been elaborated and clarified, with special reference to its applications to test scores (Chapter 13). Examples of specific new topics introduced in connection with test construction include the use of anchor tests in norming, nonnormative scales, moderator variables, synthetic validity, and the multitrait-multimethod matrix. More attention has also been given to ethical problems in the use of tests, such as confidentiality of test results and invasion of privacy (Chapters 2 and 21 and Appendix A).

Although intended primarily as a college text, this book will also prove useful to the practitioner in several fields. It provides a comprehensive view of current tests and testing problems for anyone who uses tests, such as the counselor, school psychologist, personnel psychologist, and clinical psychologist. Among the parts of special interest to clinical psychology, for example, are those dealing with individual intelligence tests, the measurement of intellectual impairment, projective techniques, and other personality tests. The book should likewise provide guidelines for the interpretation of test scores on the part of teachers, principals, social workers, psychiatrists, and others who utilize test results in reaching practical decisions. Educators will be particularly interested in the chapter on educational tests as well as the chapters on group intelligence and aptitude tests. The new chapter on occupational tests covers both procedures and instruments of particular relevance to the use of tests for personnel selection and classification in industrial, professional, and military contexts.

I am happy to acknowledge the gracious cooperation of many colleagues in the preparation of this revision. First, I wish to express my sincere appreciation to the many authors and test publishers who provided photographs of test materials, specimen tests, reprints, and unpublished manuscripts. I am especially grateful for the promptness, courtesy, and thoroughness with which my innumerable questions were answered by mail and telephone. For assistance extending far beyond the interests and responsibilities of any single publisher, I want to convey special thanks to Mrs. Blythe Mitchel of Harcourt, Brace & World. Acknowledgement is also made of the thoughtful recommendations submitted by course instructors in response to a questionnaire circulated among current users of the second edition. Special thanks in this connection are due to Dr. John T. Cowles for his numerous, constructive, and wide-ranging suggestions. To my colleagues in the Department of Psychology at Fordham University—particularly Dr. George Domino and Dr. Dorothea McCarthy—I am indebted for their enthusiastic cooperation and their willingness to discuss any questions I raised at any time. Mrs. Kathleen Mellor is to be complimented for the exceptional competence and responsibility of her secretarial services throughout the preparation of the book. Finally, it is a pleasure to record the contribution of my husband, Dr. John P. Foley, Jr., who participated in the solution of countless problems that arose at all stages, from the initial planning to the finished product.

A. A.

Contents

Part 2
TESTS OF GENERAL INTELLECTUAL DEVELOPMENT

PART 5
TESTING TODAY

PART 1

PRINCIPLES OF PSYCHOLOGICAL TESTING

CHAPTER **1**

Functions and Origins of Psychological Testing

ANYONE READING this book today could undoubtedly illustrate what is meant by a psychological test. It would be easy enough to recall a test the reader himself has taken in school, in college, in the armed services, in the counseling center, or in the personnel office. Or perhaps the reader has served as a subject in an experiment in which standardized tests were employed. This would certainly not have been the case fifty years ago. Psychological testing is a relatively young branch of one of the youngest of the sciences.

CURRENT USES OF PSYCHOLOGICAL TESTS

Basically, the function of psychological tests is to measure differences between individuals or between the reactions of the same individual on different occasions. One of the first problems that stimulated the development of psychological tests was the identification of the mentally retarded. To this day, the detection of intellectual deficiency remains an important application of certain types of psychological tests. Related clinical uses of tests include the examination of the emotionally maladjusted, the delinquent, and other types of subnormal deviants. A strong impetus to the early development of tests was likewise provided by problems arising in education. At present, schools are among the largest test users. The classification of children with reference to their ability to profit from different types of school instruction, the identification of the intellectually retarded on the one hand and the gifted on the other, the diagnosis of academic failures, the educational and vocational counseling of high school and college students, and the selection of applicants for professional and other special schools are some of the many educational uses to which tests are being put. In a somewhat different setting, the testing of children for adoption illustrates another specific way in which tests aid in practical decisions.

The selection and classification of industrial personnel represent relatively recent and rapidly expanding applications of psychological testing. From the assembly-line operator or filing clerk to top management, there is scarcely a type of job for which some kind of psychological test has not proved helpful in such matters as hiring, job assignment, transfer, promotion, or termination. To be sure, the effective employment of tests in many of these situations, especially in connection with high-level jobs, usually requires that the tests be used as an adjunct to skillful interviewing, so that test scores may be properly interpreted in the light of other background information about the individual. Nevertheless, testing constitutes an important part of the total personnel program. A closely related application of psychological testing is to be found in the selection and classification of military personnel. From simple beginnings in World War I, the scope and variety of psychological tests employed in military situations showed a phenomenal increase during World War II. Subsequently, research on test development has been continuing on a large scale in all branches of the armed services.

It is clearly evident that psychological tests are currently being employed in the solution of a wide range of practical problems. One should not, however, lose sight of the fact that such tests are also serving important functions in basic research. Nearly all problems in differential psychology, for example, require testing procedures as a means of gathering data. As illustrations, reference may be made to studies on the nature and extent of individual differences, the identification of psychological traits, the measurement of group differences, and the investigation of biological and cultural factors associated with behavioral differences. For all such areas of research—and for many others—the precise measurement of individual differences made possible by well-constructed tests is an essential prerequisite. Similarly, psychological tests provide standardized tools for investigating such varied problems as age changes within the individual, the effects of education, the outcome of psychotherapy, the impact of propaganda, and the influence of distraction on performance.

From the many different uses of psychological tests, it follows that some knowledge of such tests is needed for an adequate understanding of most fields of contemporary psychology. It is primarily with this end in view that the present book has been prepared. The book is not designed to make the individual either a skilled examiner and test administrator or an expert on test construction. It is directed, not to the test specialist, but to the general student of psychology. Some acquaintance with the leading current tests is necessary in order to understand references to the use of such tests in the psychological literature. And a proper evaluation and interpretation of test results must ultimately rest on a knowledge of how the tests were constructed, what they can be expected to accomplish, and what are their peculiar limitations. Today a familiarity with tests is required, not only by those who give. or construct tests, but by the general psychologist as well.

A brief overview of the historical antecedents and origins of psychological testing will provide perspective and should aid in the understanding of present-day tests.[1] The direction in which contemporary psychological testing has been progressing can be clarified when considered in the light of the precursors of such tests. The special limitations as well as the advantages that characterize current tests likewise become more intelligible when viewed against the background in which they originated.

The roots of testing are lost in antiquity. Dubois (1966) gives a provocative and entertaining account of the system of civil service examinations prevailing in the Chinese empire for some three thousand years. Among the ancient Greeks, testing was an established adjunct to the educational process. Tests were used to assess the mastery of physical as well as intellectual skills. The Socratic method of teaching, with its interweaving of testing and teaching, has much in common with today's programed learning. From their beginnings in the middle ages, European universities relied on formal examinations in awarding degrees and honors. To identify the major developments that shaped contemporary testing, however, we need go no farther than the nineteenth century. It is to these developments that we now turn.

EARLY INTEREST IN THE CLASSIFICATION AND TRAINING OF THE MENTALLY RETARDED

The nineteenth century witnessed a strong awakening of interest in the humane treatment of the mentally retarded and the insane. Prior to that time, neglect, ridicule, and even torture had been the common lot of these unfortunates. With the growing concern for the proper care of mental deviates came a realization that some uniform criteria for identifying and classifying these cases were required. The establishment of many special institutions for the care of the mentally retarded in both Europe and America made the need for setting up admission standards and an objective system of classification especially urgent. First it was necessary to differentiate between the insane and the mentally retarded. The former manifested emo-

---

[1] A more detailed account of the early origins of psychological tests can be found in Goodenough (1949) and Peterson (1926). See also Boring (1950) and Murphy (1949) for more general background and Anastasi (1958a, Ch. 1; 1965) for historical antecedents of the study of individual differences.

tional disorders that might or might not be accompanied by intellectual deterioration from an initially normal level; the latter were characterized essentially by intellectual defect that had been present from birth or early infancy. What is probably the first explicit statement of this distinction is to be found in a two-volume work published in 1838 by the French physician Esquirol (1838), in which over one hundred pages are devoted to mental retardation. Esquirol also pointed out that there are many degrees of mental retardation, varying along a continuum from normality to low-grade idiocy. In the effort to develop some system for classifying the different degrees and varieties of retardation, Esquirol tried several procedures but concluded that the individual's use of language provides the most dependable criterion of his intellectual level. It is interesting to note that current criteria of mental retardation are also largely linguistic and that present-day intelligence tests are heavily loaded with verbal content. The important part verbal ability plays in our concept of intelligence will be repeatedly demonstrated in subsequent chapters.

Of special significance are the contributions of another French physician, Seguin, who pioneered in the training of the mentally retarded. Having rejected the prevalent notion of the incurability of mental retardation, Seguin (1866) experimented for many years with what he termed the physiological method of training; and in 1837 he established the first school devoted to the education of mentally retarded children. In 1848 he emigrated to America, where his ideas gained wide recognition. Many of the sense-training and muscle-training techniques currently in use in institutions for the mentally retarded were originated by Seguin. By these methods, severely retarded children are given intensive exercise in sensory discrimination and in the development of motor control. Some of the procedures developed by Seguin for this purpose were eventually incorporated into performance or nonverbal tests of intelligence. An example is the Seguin Form Board, in which the individual is required to insert variously shaped blocks into the corresponding recesses as quickly as possible.

THE FIRST EXPERIMENTAL PSYCHOLOGISTS

The early experimental psychologists of the nineteenth century were not, in general, concerned with the measurement of individual differences. The principal aim of psychologists of that period was the formulation of generalized descriptions of human behavior. It was the uniformities rather than the differences in behavior that were the focus of attention. Individual differences were either ignored or were accepted as a necessary evil that limited the applicability of the generalizations. Thus, the fact that one individual reacted differently from another when observed under identical conditions was regarded as a form of error. The presence of such error, or individual variability, rendered the generalizations approximate rather than exact. This was the attitude toward individual differences that prevailed in such laboratories as that founded by Wundt at Leipzig in 1879, where many of the early experimental psychologists received their training.

In their choice of topics, as in many other phases of their work, the founders of experimental psychology reflected the influence of their backgrounds in physiology and physics. The problems studied in their laboratories were concerned largely with sensitivity to visual, auditory, and other sensory stimuli and with simple reaction time. This emphasis on sensory phenomena was in turn reflected in the nature of the first psychological tests, as will be apparent in subsequent sections.

Still another way in which nineteenth-century experimental psychology influenced the course of the testing movement may be noted. The early psychological experiments brought out the need for rigorous control of the conditions under which observations were made. For example, the wording of directions given to the subject in a reaction-time experiment might appreciably increase or decrease the speed of the subject's response. Or again, the brightness or color of the surrounding field could markedly alter the appearance of a visual stimulus. The importance of making observations on all subjects under standardized conditions was thus vividly demonstrated. Such standardization of procedure eventually became one of the special earmarks of psychological tests.

THE CONTRIBUTIONS OF FRANCIS GALTON

It was the English biologist Sir Francis Galton who was primarily responsible for launching the testing movement. A unifying factor in Galton's numerous and varied research activities was his interest in human heredity. In the course of his investigations on heredity, Galton realized the need for measuring the characteristics of related and unrelated persons. Only in this way could he discover, for example, the exact degree of resemblance between parents and offspring, brothers and sisters, cousins, or twins. With this end in view, Galton was instrumental in inducing a number of educational institutions to keep systematic anthropometric records on their students. He also set up an anthropometric laboratory at the International Exposition of 1884 where, by paying threepence, visitors could be measured in certain physical traits and could take tests of keenness of vision and hearing, muscular strength, reaction time, and other simple sensorimotor functions. When the exposition closed, the laboratory was transferred to South Kensington Museum, London, where it operated for six years. By such methods, the first large, systematic body of data on individual differences in simple psychological processes was gradually accumulated.

Galton himself devised most of the simple tests administered at his anthropometric laboratory, many of which are still familiar either in their original or in modified forms. Examples include the Galton bar for visual discrimination of length, the Galton whistle for determining the highest audible pitch, and graduated series of weights for measuring kinesthetic discrimination. It was Galton's belief that tests of sensory discrimination could serve as a means of gauging a person's intellect. In this respect, he was partly influenced by the theories of Locke. Thus Galton wrote: "The only information that reaches us concerning outward events appears to pass through the avenue of our senses; and the more perceptive the senses are of difference, the larger is the field upon which our judgment and intelligence can act" (Galton, 1883, p. 27). Galton had also noted that idiots tend to be defective in the ability to discriminate heat, cold, and pain—an observation that further strengthened his conviction that sensory discriminative capacity "would on the whole be highest among the intellectually ablest" (Galton, 1883, p. 29).

Galton also pioneered in the application of rating-scale and questionnaire methods, as well as in the use of the free association technique subsequently employed for a wide variety of purposes. A further contribution of Galton is to be found in his development of statistical methods for the analysis of data on individual differences. Galton selected and adapted a number of techniques previously derived by mathematicians. These techniques he put in such form as to permit their use by the mathematically untrained investigator who might wish to treat test results quantitatively. He thereby extended enormously the application of statistical procedures to the analysis of test data. This phase of Galton's work has been carried forward by many of his students, the most eminent of whom was Karl Pearson.

CATTELL AND THE EARLY "MENTAL TESTS"

An especially prominent position in the development of psychological testing is occupied by the American psychologist James McKeen Cattell. The newly established science of experimental psychology and the still newer testing movement merged in Cattell's work. For his doctorate at Leipzig, he completed a dissertation on individual differences in reaction time, despite Wundt's resistance to this type of investigation. While lecturing at Cambridge in 1888, Cattell's own interest in the measurement of individual differences was reinforced by contact with Galton. On his return to America, Cattell was active both in the establishment of laboratories for experimental psychology and in the spread of the testing movement.

In an article written by Cattell in 1890, the term "mental test" was used for the first time in the psychological literature. This article described a series of tests that were being administered annually to college students in the effort to determine their intellectual level. The tests, which had to be administered individually, included measures of muscular strength, speed of movement, sensitivity to pain, keenness of vision and of hearing, weight discrimination, reaction time, memory, and the like. In his choice of tests, Cattell shared Galton's view that a measure of intellectual functions could be obtained through tests of sensory discrimination and reaction time. Cattell's preference for such tests was also bolstered by the fact that simple functions could be measured with precision and accuracy, whereas the development of objective measures for the more complex functions seemed at that time a well-nigh hopeless task.

Cattell's tests were typical of those to be found in a number of test series developed during the last decade of the nineteenth century. Such test series were administered to schoolchildren, college students, and miscellaneous adults. At the Columbian Exposition held in Chicago in 1893, Jastrow set up an exhibit at which visitors were invited to take tests of sensory, motor, and simple perceptual processes and to compare their skill with the norms (Peterson, 1926; Philippe, 1894). A few attempts to evaluate such early tests yielded very discouraging results. The individual's performance showed little correspondence from one test to another (Sharp, 1898–1899; Wissler, 1901), and it exhibited little or no relation to independent estimates of intellectual level based on teachers' ratings (Bolton, 1891–92; Gilbert, 1894) or academic grades (Wissler, 1901).

A number of test series assembled by European psychologists of the period tended to cover somewhat more complex functions. Kraepelin (1895), who was interested primarily in the clinical examination of psychiatric patients, prepared a long series of tests to measure what he regarded as basic factors in the characterization of an individual. The tests, employing chiefly simple arithmetic operations, were designed to measure practice effects, memory, and susceptibility to fatigue and to distraction. A few years earlier, Oehrn (1889), a pupil of Kraepelin, had employed tests of perception, memory, association, and motor functions in an investigation on the interrelations of psychological functions. Another German psychologist, Ebbinghaus (1897), administered tests of arithmetic computation, memory span, and sentence completion to schoolchildren. The most complex of the three tests, sentence completion, was the only one that showed a clear correspondence with the children's scholastic achievement.

Like Kraepelin, the Italian psychologist Ferrari and his students were interested primarily in the use of tests with pathological cases (Guicciardi & Ferrari, 1896). The test series they devised ranged from physiological measures and motor tests to apprehension span and the interpretation of pictures. In an article published in France in 1895, Binet and Henri criticized most of the available test series as being too largely sensory and as concentrating unduly on simple, specialized abilities. They argued further that, in the measurement of the more complex functions, great precision is not necessary, since individual differences are larger in these functions. An extensive and varied list of tests was proposed, covering such functions as memory, imagination, attention, comprehension, suggestibility, aesthetic appreciation, and many others. In these tests we can recognize the trends that were eventually to lead to the development of the famous Binet intelligence scales.

BINET AND THE RISE OF INTELLIGENCE TESTS

Binet and his coworkers devoted many years to active and ingenious research on ways of measuring intelligence. Many approaches were tried, even including the measurement of physical traits, handwriting analysis, and palmistry! The results, however, led to a growing conviction that the direct, even though crude, measurement of complex intellectual functions was the best solution. Then a specific situation arose that brought Binet's efforts to immediate practical fruition. In 1904, the Minister of Public Instruction appointed a commission to study procedures for the education of subnormal children attending the Paris schools. It was to meet this practical demand that Binet, in collaboration with Simon, prepared the first Binet-Simon Scale (Binet & Simon, 1905).

This scale, known as the 1905 scale, consisted of 30 problems or tests arranged in ascending order of difficulty. The difficulty level was determined empirically by administering the tests to 50 normal children aged 3 to 11 years, and to some mentally retarded children. The tests were designed to cover a wide variety of functions, with special emphasis on judgment, comprehension, and reasoning, which Binet regarded as essential components of intelligence. Although sensory and perceptual tests were included, a much greater proportion of verbal content was found in this scale than in most test series of the time. The 1905 scale was presented as a preliminary and tentative instrument, and no precise objective method for arriving at a total score was formulated.

In the second, or 1908, scale, the number of tests was increased, some unsatisfactory tests from the earlier scale were eliminated, and all tests were grouped into age levels. Thus, in the 3-year level were placed all tests normal 3-year-olds could pass; in the 4-year level all tests passed by normal 4-year-olds; and so on to age 13. The child's score on the test could then be expressed as a *mental age*, i.e., the age of normal children whose performance he equaled. Since mental age is such a simple concept to grasp, its introduction undoubtedly did much to popularize intelligence testing.[2]

[2] Goodenough (1949, pp. 50–51) notes that in 1887, 21 years before the appearance of the 1908 Binet-Simon Scale, S. E. Chaille published in the *New Orleans Medical and*

A third revision of the Binet-Simon Scale appeared in 1911, the year of Binet's untimely death. In this scale, no fundamental changes were introduced. Minor revisions and relocations of specific tests were instituted. More tests were added at several year levels, and the scale was extended to the adult level.

Even prior to the 1908 revision, the Binet-Simon tests attracted wide attention among psychologists throughout the world. Translations and adaptations appeared in many languages. In America, a number of different revisions were prepared, the most famous of which is the one developed under the direction of L. M. Terman at Stanford University, and known as the Stanford-Binet (Terman, 1916). It was in this test that the intelligence quotient (IQ), or ratio between mental age and chronological age, was first used. The latest revision of this test is widely employed today and will be more fully considered in Chapter 8. Of special interest, too, is the first Kuhlmann-Binet revision, which extended the scale downward to the age level of 3 months (Kuhlmann, 1912). This scale represents one of the earliest efforts to develop preschool and infant tests of intelligence.

GROUP TESTING

The Binet tests, as well as all their revisions, are *individual scales* in the sense that they can be administered to only one person at a time. Many of the tests in these scales require oral responses from the subject or necessitate the manipulation of materials. Some call for individual timing of responses. For these and other reasons, such tests are not adapted to group administration. Another characteristic of the Binet type of test is that it requires a highly trained examiner. Such tests are essentially clinical instruments, suited to the intensive study of individual cases.

Group testing, like the first Binet scale, was developed to meet a pressing practical need. When the United States entered World War I in 1917, a committee was appointed by the American Psychological Association to consider ways in which psychology might assist in the conduct of the war. This committee, under the direction of Robert M. Yerkes, recognized the need for the rapid classification of the million and a half recruits with respect to general intellectual level. Such information was relevant to many administrative decisions, including rejection or discharge from military service, assignment to different types of service, or admission to officer-training camps. It was in this setting that the first group intelligence test was developed. In this task, the Army psychologists drew on all available

---

Surgical Journal a series of tests for infants arranged according to the age at which the tests are commonly passed. Partly because of the limited circulation of the journal and partly, perhaps, because the scientific community was not ready for it, the significance of this age-scale concept passed unnoticed at the time.

test materials, and especially on an unpublished group intelligence test prepared by Arthur S. Otis, which he turned over to the Army.

The tests finally developed by the Army psychologists have come to be known as the Army Alpha and the Army Beta. The former was designed for general routine testing; the latter was a nonlanguage scale employed with illiterates and with foreign-born recruits who were unable to take a test in English. Both were suitable for administration to large groups.

Shortly after the termination of World War I, the Army tests were released for civilian use. Not only did the Army Alpha and Army Beta themselves pass through many revisions, the latest of which are even now in use, but they also served as models for most group intelligence tests. The testing movement underwent a tremendous spurt of growth. Soon group intelligence tests were being devised for all ages and types of persons, from preschool children to graduate students. Large-scale testing programs, previously impossible, were now being launched with zestful optimism. Because group tests were designed as mass testing instruments, they not only permitted the simultaneous examination of large groups but also simplified the instructions and administration procedures so as to demand a minimum of training on the part of the examiner. Schoolteachers began to give intelligence tests to their classes. College students were routinely examined prior to admission. Extensive studies of special adult groups, such as prisoners, were undertaken. And soon the general public became IQ-conscious.

The application of such group intelligence tests far outran their technical improvement. That the tests were still crude instruments was often forgotten in the rush of gathering scores and drawing practical conclusions from the results. When the tests failed to meet unwarranted expectations, skepticism and hostility toward all testing often resulted. Thus, the testing boom of the twenties, based on the indiscriminate use of tests, may have done as much to retard as to advance the progress of psychological testing.

APTITUDE TESTING

Although intelligence tests were originally designed to sample a wide variety of functions in order to estimate the individual's general intellectual level, it soon became apparent that such tests were quite limited in their coverage. Not all important functions were represented. In fact, most intelligence tests were primarily measures of verbal ability and, to a lesser extent, of the ability to handle numerical and other abstract and symbolic relations. Gradually psychologists came to recognize that the term "intelligence test" was a misnomer, since only certain aspects of intelligence were measured by such tests.

To be sure, the tests covered abilities that are of prime importance in our culture. But it was realized that more precise designations, in terms of the type of information these tests are able to yield, would be preferable. For example, a number of tests that would probably have been called intelligence tests during the twenties later came to be known as scholastic aptitude tests. This shift in terminology was made in recognition of the fact that many so-called intelligence tests measure that combination of abilities demanded by academic work.

Even prior to World War I, psychologists had begun to recognize the need for tests of special aptitudes to supplement the global intelligence tests. These *special aptitude tests* were developed particularly for use in vocational counseling and in the selection and classification of industrial and military personnel. Among the most widely used are tests of mechanical, clerical, musical, and artistic aptitudes.

The critical evaluation of intelligence tests that followed their widespread and indiscriminate use during the twenties also revealed another noteworthy fact: an individual's performance on different parts of such a test often showed marked variation. This was especially apparent on group tests, in which the items are commonly segregated into subtests of relatively homogeneous content. For example, a person might score relatively high on a verbal subtest and low on a numerical subtest, or vice versa. To some extent, such internal variability is also discernible on a test like the Stanford-Binet, in which, for example, all items involving words might prove difficult for a particular individual, whereas items employing pictures or geometric diagrams may place him at an advantage.

Test users, and especially clinicians, frequently utilized such intercomparisons in order to obtain more insight into the individual's psychological make-up. Thus, not only the IQ or other global score but also scores on subtests would be examined in the evaluation of the individual case. Such a practice is not to be generally recommended, however, because intelligence tests were not designed for the purpose of differential aptitude analysis. Often the subtests being compared contain too few items to yield a stable or reliable estimate of a specific ability. As a result, the obtained difference between subtest scores might be reversed if the individual were retested on a different day or with another form of the same test. If such intraindividual comparisons are to be made, tests are needed that are specially designed to reveal differences in performance in various functions.

While the practical application of tests demonstrated the need for differential aptitude tests, a parallel development in the study of trait organization was gradually providing the means for constructing such tests. Statistical studies on the nature of intelligence had been exploring the interrelations among scores obtained by many persons on a wide variety of different tests. Such investigations were begun by the English psychologist Charles Spearman (1904, 1927) during the first decade of the present century. Subsequent methodological developments, based on the work of such American psychologists as T. L. Kelley (1928) and L. L. Thurstone (1935,

1947), as well as on that of other American and English investigators, have come to be known as "factor analysis."

The contributions that the methods of factor analysis have made to test construction will be more fully examined and illustrated in Chapter 13. For the present, it will suffice to note that the data gathered by such procedures have indicated the presence of a number of relatively independent factors, or traits. Some of these traits were represented, in varying proportions, in the traditional intelligence tests. Verbal comprehension and numerical reasoning are examples of this type of trait. Others, such as spatial, perceptual, and mechanical aptitudes, were found more often in special aptitude tests than in intelligence tests.

One of the chief practical outcomes of factor analysis was the development of *multiple aptitude batteries.* These batteries are designed to provide a measure of the individual's standing in each of a number of traits. In place of a total score or IQ, a separate score is obtained for such traits as verbal comprehension, numerical aptitude, spatial visualization, arithmetic reasoning, and perceptual speed. Such batteries thus provide a suitable instrument for making the kind of intraindividual analysis, or differential diagnosis, that clinicians had been trying for many years to obtain, with crude and often erroneous results, from intelligence tests. These batteries also incorporate into a comprehensive and systematic testing program much of the information formerly obtained from special aptitude tests, since the multiple aptitude batteries cover some of the traits not ordinarily included in intelligence tests.

Multiple aptitude batteries represent a relatively late development in the testing field. Nearly all have appeared since 1945. In this connection, the work of the military psychologists during World War II should also be noted. Much of the test research conducted in the armed services was based on factor analysis and was directed toward the construction of multiple aptitude batteries. In the Air Force, for example, special batteries were constructed for pilots, bombardiers, radio operators, range finders, and scores of other military specialists. A report of the batteries prepared in the Air Force alone occupies at least nine of the nineteen volumes devoted to the aviation psychology program during World War II (Army Air Forces, 1947–1948). Research along these lines is still in progress under the sponsorship of various branches of the armed services. A number of multiple aptitude batteries have likewise been developed for civilian use and are being widely applied in educational and vocational counseling and in personnel selection and classification. Examples of such batteries will be discussed in Chapter 13.

To avoid confusion, a point of terminology should be clarified. The term "aptitude test" has been traditionally employed to refer to tests measuring relatively homogeneous and clearly defined segments of ability; the term "intelligence test" customarily refers to more heterogeneous tests yielding a single global score such as an IQ. Special aptitude tests typically measure a single aptitude. Multiple aptitude batteries measure a number of aptitudes but provide a profile of scores, one for each aptitude.

STANDARDIZED ACHIEVEMENT TESTS

While psychologists were busy developing intelligence and aptitude tests, traditional school examinations were undergoing a number of technical improvements (Caldwell & Courtis, 1923; Ebel & Damrin, 1960). An important step in this direction was taken by the Boston public schools in 1845, when written examinations were substituted for the oral interrogation of students by visiting examiners. Commenting on this innovation, Horace Mann cited arguments remarkably similar to those used much later to justify the replacement of essay questions by objective multiple-choice items. The written examinations, Mann noted, put all students in a uniform situation, permitted a wider coverage of content, reduced the chance element in question choice, and eliminated the possibility of favoritism on the examiner's part.

After the turn of the century, the first standardized tests for measuring the outcomes of school instruction began to appear. Spearheaded by the work of E. L. Thorndike, these tests utilized measurement principles developed in the psychological laboratory. Examples include scales for rating the quality of handwriting and written compositions, as well as tests in spelling, arithmetic computation, and arithmetic reasoning. Still later came the achievement batteries, initiated by the publication of the first edition of the Stanford Achievement Test in 1923. Foreshadowing many characteristics of modern testing, this battery provided comparable measures of performance in different school subjects, evaluated in terms of a single normative group.

At the same time, evidence was accumulating regarding the lack of agreement among teachers in grading essay tests. By 1930 it was widely recognized that essay tests were not only more time-consuming for examiners and examinees, but also yielded less reliable results than the "new type" of objective items. As the latter came into increasing use in standardized achievement tests, there was a growing emphasis on the design of items to test the understanding and application of knowledge and other broad educational objectives. The decade of the 1930s also witnessed the introduction of test-scoring machines, for which the new objective tests could be readily adapted.

The establishment of statewide, regional, and national testing programs was another noteworthy parallel development. Probably the best known of these programs is that of the College Entrance Examination Board (CEEB). Established at the turn of the century to reduce duplication in the examining of entering college freshmen, this program has undergone profound changes in its testing procedures and in the number and nature of participating colleges—changes that reflect many intervening developments in both testing and education. In 1947, the testing functions of the CEEB were merged with those of the Carnegie Corporation and the American Council on Education to form Educational Testing Service (ETS). In subsequent years, ETS has assumed responsibility for a growing number of testing programs on behalf of universities, professional schools, government agencies, and other institutions.

Mention should also be made of the American College Testing Program, established in 1959 to screen applicants to colleges not included in the CEEB program, and of several national testing programs for the selection of highly talented students for scholarship awards. Among the latter, the largest is the testing program conducted by the National Merit Scholarship Corporation.

Achievement tests are used not only for educational purposes but also in the selection of applicants for industrial and government jobs. An important landmark in this connection was the development of the examination system in the United States civil service (Kavruck, 1956). Competitive examinations were established in a few government departments in 1872 but were not permanently installed as a regular procedure until 1883. Test-construction techniques developed during and prior to World War I were introduced into the civil service examination program with the appointment of L. J. O'Rourke as director of the newly established research division in 1922.

As more and more psychologists trained in psychometrics participated in the construction of standardized achievement tests, the technical aspects of achievement tests increasingly came to resemble those of intelligence and aptitude tests. Procedures for constructing and evaluating all these tests have much in common. The increasing efforts to prepare achievement tests that would measure the attainment of broad educational goals, as contrasted to the recall of factual minutiae, also made the content of achievement tests resemble more closely that of intelligence tests. Today the difference between these two types of tests is chiefly one of degree of specificity of content and extent to which the test presupposes a designated course of prior instruction.

MEASUREMENT OF PERSONALITY

Another area of psychological testing is concerned with the affective or nonintellectual aspects of behavior. Tests designed for this purpose are commonly known as personality tests, although some psychologists prefer to use the term personality in a broader sense, to refer to the entire individual. Intellectual as well as nonintellectual traits would thus be included under this heading. In the terminology of psychological testing, however, the designation "personality test" most often refers to measures of such characteristics as emotional adjustment, interpersonal relations, motivation, interests, and attitudes.

An early precursor of personality testing may be recognized in Kraepelin's use of the free association test with abnormal patients. In this test, the subject is given specially selected stimulus words and is required to respond to each with the first word that comes to mind. Kraepelin (1892) also employed this technique to study the psychological effects of fatigue, hunger, and drugs and concluded that all these agents increase the relative frequency of superficial associations. Sommer (1894), also writing during the last decade of the nineteenth century, suggested that the free association test might be used to differentiate between the various forms of mental disorder. The free association technique has subsequently been utilized for a variety of testing purposes and is still currently employed. Mention should also be made of the work of Galton, Pearson, and Cattell in the development of standardized questionnaire and rating-scale techniques. Although originally devised for other purposes, these procedures were eventually employed by others in constructing some of the most common types of current personality tests.

The prototype of the personality questionnaire, or *self-report inventory,* is the Personal Data Sheet developed by Woodworth during World War I (see Symonds, 1931, Ch. 5). This test was designed as a rough screening device for identifying seriously neurotic men who would be unfit for military service. The inventory consisted of a number of questions dealing with common neurotic symptoms, which the individual answered about himself. A total score was obtained by counting the number of symptoms reported. Immediately after the war, civilian forms of this questionnaire were prepared, including a special form for use with children. The Woodworth Personal Data Sheet, moreover, served as a model for most subsequent emotional adjustment inventories. In some of these questionnaires, an attempt was made to subdivide emotional adjustment into more specific forms, such as home adjustment, school adjustment, and vocational adjustment. Other tests concentrated more intensively on a narrower area of behavior or were concerned with more distinctly social responses, such as dominance-submission in interpersonal contacts. A later development was the construction of tests for quantifying the expression of interests and attitudes. These tests, too, were based essentially on questionnaire techniques.

Another approach to the measurement of personality is through the application of *performance* or *situational tests.* In such tests, the subject has a task to perform whose purpose is generally disguised. Most of these tests simulate everyday-life situations quite closely. The first extensive application of such techniques is to be found in the tests developed in the late twenties and early thirties by Hartshorne, May, and their associates (1928, 1929, 1930). This series, standardized on schoolchildren, was concerned with such behavior as cheating, lying, stealing, cooperativeness, and persistence. Objective, quantitative scores could be obtained on each of a large number of specific tests. A more recent illustration, for the adult level, is provided by the series of situational tests developed during World War II in the Assessment Program of the Office of Strategic Services (OSS, 1948). These tests were concerned with relatively complex and subtle social and emotional behavior and required rather elaborate facilities and trained personnel for their administration. The interpretation of the subject's responses, moreover, was relatively subjective.

Projective techniques represent a third approach to the study of personality and one that has shown phenomenal growth, especially among clinicians. In such tests, the subject is given a relatively unstructured task that permits wide latitude in its solution. The assumption underlying such methods is that the individual will project his characteristic modes of response into such a task. Like the performance and situational tests, projective techniques are more or less disguised in their purpose, thereby reducing the chances that the subject can deliberately create a desired impression. The previously cited free association test represents one of the earliest types of projective techniques. Sentence-completion tests have also been used in this manner. Other tasks commonly employed in projective techniques include drawing, arranging toys to create a scene, extemporaneous dramatic play, and interpreting pictures or inkblots.

All available types of personality tests present serious difficulties, both practical and theoretical. Each approach has its own special advantages and disadvantages. On the whole, personality testing lags far behind aptitude testing in its positive accomplishments. But such lack of progress is not to be attributed to insufficient effort. Research on the measurement of personality has reached impressive proportions since 1950, and many ingenious devices and technical improvements are under investigation. It is rather the special difficulties encountered in the measurement of personality that account for the slow advances in this area.

SOURCES OF INFORMATION ABOUT TESTS

Today psychological testing is in a state of rapid change and expansion. There is a constant stream of new tests, revised forms of old tests, and additional data that may refine or alter the interpretation of scores on existing tests. The rapidity of change, together with the vast number of available tests, makes it impracticable to survey specific tests in any single text. More intensive coverage of testing instruments and problems in special areas can be found in books dealing with the use of tests in such fields as counseling, clinical practice, education, and personnel selection. In order to keep abreast of current developments, however, anyone working with tests needs to be familiar with more direct sources of contemporary information about tests.

One of the most important sources is the series of *Mental Measurements Yearbooks* edited by Buros (1965). These yearbooks cover nearly all commercially available psychological, educational, and vocational tests published in English. The coverage is especially complete for paper-and-pencil tests. Each yearbook includes tests published during a specified period, thus supplementing rather than supplanting the earlier yearbooks. The *Sixth Mental Measurements Yearbook,* for example, is concerned principally with tests appearing between 1959 and 1964. Tests of continuing interest, however, may be reviewed repeatedly in successive yearbooks, as new data accumulate from pertinent research. The earliest publications in this series were merely bibliographies of tests. Beginning in 1938, however, the yearbook assumed its current form, which includes critical reviews of most of the tests by one or more test experts, as well as a complete list of published references pertaining to each test. Routine information regarding publisher, price, forms, and age of subjects for whom the test is suitable is also regularly given.

A comprehensive bibliography covering all types of published tests available in English-speaking countries is provided by *Tests in Print* (Buros, 1961). Information regarding early tests can be found in a bibliography prepared by Hildreth (1939), which covers a 50-year period. A later supplement (Hildreth, 1946) extended this list to 1945.

A number of psychological and educational journals represent additional sources of current information about tests. New tests are regularly abstracted in *Psychological Abstracts,* as are articles about tests. *Educational and Psychological Measurement* publishes articles dealing with the construction, use, and evaluation of tests, particularly articles reporting new data on test validity. Other journals publishing reviews of specific tests, new data on existing tests, or periodic surveys of current tests include the *Journal of Counseling Psychology, Personnel and Guidance Journal, Personnel Psychology,* and the *Review of Educational Research.*

Finally, it should be noted that the most direct source of information regarding specific current tests is provided by the catalogues of test publishers and by the manual that accompanies each test. A comprehensive list of test publishers, with addresses, can be found in the latest *Mental Measurements Yearbook.* For ready reference, the names and addresses of some of the larger American publishers and distributors of psychological tests are given in Appendix B. Catalogues of current tests can be obtained from most of these publishers on request. Manuals and specimen sets of tests can be purchased by qualified users.

The test manual should provide the essential information required for administering, scoring, and evaluating a particular test. In it should be found full and detailed instructions, scoring key, norms, and data on reliability and validity. Moreover, the manual should report the number and nature of subjects on whom norms, reliability, and validity were established, the methods employed in computing indices of reliability and validity, and the specific criteria against which validity was checked. In the event that the necessary information is too lengthy to fit conveniently into the manual, references to the printed sources in which such information can be readily located should be given. The manual should, in other words, enable the test user to evaluate the test before choosing it for his specific purpose. It might be added that many test manuals still fall short of this goal. But some of the larger and more professionally oriented test publishers are giving increasing attention to the preparation of manuals that meet adequate scientific standards. An enlightened public of test users provides the firmest assurance that such standards will be maintained and improved in the future.

A succinct but comprehensive guide for the evaluation of psychological tests is to be found in *Standards for Educational and Psychological Tests and Manuals* (1966), published by the American Psychological Association. These standards represent a summary of recommended practices in test construction, based on the current state of knowledge in the field. They are concerned with the information about validity, reliability, norms, and other test characteristics that ought to be reported in the manual. Relevant portions of the *Standards* will be discussed in the following chapters, in connection with the appropriate topics.

CHAPTER **2**

Nature and Use
of Psychological
Tests

THE HISTORICAL introduction presented in Chapter 1 has already revealed the variety of purposes for which psychological tests have been used, as well as the wide diversity of available tests. Although the general public may still associate psychological tests most closely with "IQ tests" and with tests designed to detect emotional disorders, these tests represent only a small proportion of the available types of instruments. The major categories of psychological tests will be discussed and illustrated in Parts 2, 3, and 4, which cover tests of general intellectual level, traditionally called intelligence tests; tests of separate abilities, including multiple aptitude batteries, tests of special aptitudes, and achievement tests; and personality tests, concerned with measures of emotional and motivational traits, interpersonal behavior, interests, attitudes, and other nonintellectual characteristics.

In the face of such diversity in nature and purpose, what are the common differentiating characteristics of psychological tests? How do psychological tests differ from other methods of gathering information about individuals? The answer is to be found in certain fundamental features of both the construction and use of tests. It is with these features that the present chapter is concerned.

WHAT IS A PSYCHOLOGICAL TEST?

A psychological test is essentially an objective and standardized measure of a sample of behavior. Psychological tests are like tests in any other science, insofar as observations are made on a small but carefully chosen *sample* of an individual's behavior. In this respect, the psychologist proceeds in much the same way as the chemist who tests a patient's blood or a community's water supply by analyzing one or more samples of it. If the psychologist wishes to test the extent of a child's vocabulary, a clerk's ability to perform arithmetic computations, or a pilot's eye-hand coordination, he examines their performance with a representative set of words, arithmetic problems, or motor tests. Whether or not the test adequately covers the behavior under consideration obviously depends on the number and nature of items in the sample. For example, an arithmetic test consisting of only five problems, or one including only multiplication items, would be a poor measure of the individual's computational skill. A vocabulary test composed entirely of baseball terms would hardly provide a dependable estimate of a child's total range of vocabulary.

The *diagnostic* or *predictive value* of a psychological test depends on the degree to which it serves as an indicator of a relatively broad and significant area of behavior. Measurement of the behavior sample directly covered by the test is rarely, if ever, the goal of psychological testing. The child's knowledge of a particular list of 50 words is not, in itself, of great interest. Nor is the job applicant's performance on a specific set of 20 arithmetic problems of much importance. If, however, it can be demonstrated that there is a close correspondence between the child's knowledge of the word list and his total mastery of vocabulary, or between the applicant's score on the arithmetic problems and his computational performance on the job, then the tests are serving their purpose.

It should be noted in this connection that the test items need not resemble closely the behavior the test is to predict. It is only necessary that an empirical correspondence be demonstrated between the two. The degree of similarity between the test sample and the predicted behavior may vary widely. At one extreme, the test may coincide completely with a part of the behavior to be predicted. An example might be a foreign vocabulary test in which the students are examined on 20 of the 50 new words they have studied; another example is provided by the road test taken prior to obtaining a driver's license. A lesser degree of similarity is illustrated by many vocational aptitude tests administered prior to job training, in which there is only a moderate resemblance between the tasks performed on the job and those incorporated in the test. At the other extreme one finds projective personality tests such as the Rorschach inkblot test, in which an attempt is made to predict from the subject's associations to inkblots how he will react to other people, to emotionally toned stimuli, and to other complex, everyday-life situations. Despite their superficial differences, all these tests consist of samples of the individual's behavior. And each must prove its worth by an empirically demonstrated correspondence between the subject's performance on the test and in other situations.

Whether the term "diagnosis" or the term "prediction" is employed in this connection also represents a minor distinction. Prediction commonly connotes a temporal estimate, the individual's future performance on a job, for example, being forecast from his present test performance. In a broader sense, however, even the diagnosis of present condition, such as mental retardation or emotional disorder, implies a prediction of what the individual will do in situations other than the present test. It is logically simpler to consider all tests as behavior samples from which predictions regarding other behavior can be made. Different types of tests can then be characterized as variants of this basic pattern.

Another point that should be considered at the outset pertains to the concept of *capacity*. It is entirely possible, for example, to devise a test for predicting how well an individual can learn French before he has even begun the study of French. Such a test would involve a sample of the types of behavior required to learn the new language, but would in itself presuppose no knowledge of French. It could then be said that this test measures the individual's "capacity" or "potentiality" for learning French. Such terms should, however, be used with caution in reference to psychological tests. Only in the sense that a present behavior sample can be used as an indicator of other, future behavior can we speak of a test measuring "capacity." No psychological test can do more than measure behavior. Whether such behavior can serve as an effective index of other behavior can be determined only by empirical try-out.

STANDARDIZATION.   It will be recalled that in the initial definition a psychological test was described as a standardized measure. Standardization implies *uniformity of procedure* in administering and scoring the test. If the scores obtained by different individuals are to be comparable, testing conditions must obviously be the same for all. Such a requirement is only a special application of the need for controlled conditions in all scientific observations. In a test situation, the single independent variable is usually the individual being tested.

In order to secure uniformity of testing conditions, the test constructor provides detailed directions for administering each newly developed test. The formulation of such directions is a major part of the standardization of a new test. Such standardization extends to the exact materials employed, time limits, oral instructions to subjects, preliminary demonstrations, ways of handling queries from subjects, and every other detail of the testing situation. Many other, more subtle factors may influence the subject's performance on certain tests. Thus, in giving instructions or presenting problems orally, consideration must be given to the rate of speaking, tone of voice, inflection, pauses, and facial expression. In a test involving the detection of absurdities, for example, the correct answer may be given away by smiling or pausing when the crucial word is read. Standardized testing procedure, from the examiner's point of view, will be discussed further in a later section of this chapter dealing with problems of test administration.

Another important step in the standardization of a test is the establishment of *norms*. Without norms, test scores cannot be interpreted. Psychological tests have no predetermined standards of passing or failing. An individual's score can be evaluated only by comparing it with the scores obtained by others. As its name implies, a norm is the normal or average performance. Thus, if normal 8-year-old children complete 12 out of 50 problems correctly on a particular arithmetic reasoning test, then the 8-year-old norm on this test corresponds to a score of 12. The latter is known as the raw score on the test. It may be expressed as number of correct items, time required to complete a task, number of errors, or some other objective measure appropriate to the content of the test. Such a raw score is meaningless until evaluated in terms of a suitable set of norms.

In the process of standardizing a test, it must be administered to a large, representative sample of the type of subjects for whom it is designed. This group, known as the standardization sample, serves to establish the norms. Such norms indicate not only the average performance but also the relative frequency of varying degrees of deviation above and below the average. It is thus possible to evaluate different degrees of superiority and inferiority. The specific ways in which such norms may be expressed will be considered in Chapter 3. All permit the designation of the individual's position with reference to the normative or standardization sample.

It might also be noted that norms are established for personality tests in essentially the same way as for aptitude tests. The norm on a personality test is not necessarily the most desirable or "ideal" performance, any more than a perfect or errorless score is the norm on an aptitude test. On both types of tests, the norm corresponds to the performance of typical or average individuals. On dominance-submission tests, for example, the norm falls at an intermediate point representing the degree of dominance or submission manifested by the average individual. Similarly, in an emotional adjustment inventory, the norm does not ordinarily correspond to a complete absence of unfavorable or maladaptive responses, since a few such responses occur in the majority of "normal" individuals in the standardization sample. It is thus apparent that psychological tests, of whatever type, are based on empirically established norms.

OBJECTIVE MEASUREMENT OF DIFFICULTY.   Reference to the definition of a psychological test with which this discussion opened will show that such a test was characterized as an objective as well as a standardized measure. In what specific ways are such tests objective? Some aspects of the objectivity of psychological tests have already been touched on in the discussion of standardization. Thus, the administration, scoring, and interpretation of scores are objective insofar as they are independent of the subjective judgment of the individual examiner. Any one individual should theoretically obtain the identical score on a test regardless of who happens to be his examiner. This is not entirely so, of course, since perfect standardization and objectivity have not been attained in practice. But at least such objectivity is the goal of test construction and has been achieved to a reasonably high degree in most tests.

There are other major ways in which psychological tests can be properly described as objective. The determination of the difficulty level of an item or of a whole test, and the measurement of test reliability and validity, are based on objective, empirical procedures. The concepts of reliability and validity will be considered in subsequent sections. We shall turn our attention first to the concept of difficulty.

When Binet and Simon prepared their original, 1905 scale for the measurement of intelligence, they arranged the 30 items of the scale in order of increasing difficulty. Such difficulty, it will be recalled, was determined by trying out the items on 50 normal and a few mentally retarded children. The items correctly solved by the largest number of children were, *ipso facto*, taken to be the easiest; those passed by relatively few children were regarded as more difficult items. By this procedure, an empirical order of difficulty was established. This early example typifies the objective measurement of difficulty level, which is now common practice in psychological test construction.

Not only the arrangement but also the selection of items for inclusion in a test can be determined by the proportion of subjects in the trial samples who pass each item. Thus, if there is a bunching of items at the easy or difficult end of the scale, some items can be discarded. Similarly, if items are sparse in certain portions of the difficulty range, new items can be added to fill the gaps. More technical aspects of item analysis will be considered in Chapter 7.

The difficulty level of the test as a whole is, of course, directly dependent on the difficulty of the items that make up the test. A comprehensive check of the difficulty of the total test for the population for which it is designed is provided by the distribution of total scores. If the standardization sample is a representative cross section of such a population, then it is generally expected that the scores will fall roughly into a *normal distribution curve*. In other words, there should be a clustering of individuals near the center of the range and a gradual tapering off as the extremes are approached. A theoretical normal curve, with all irregularities eliminated, is shown in Figure 1. In plotting such a frequency distribution, scores are indicated on the baseline, and frequencies, or number of persons obtaining each score, on the vertical axis. A smooth curve like the one illustrated is closely approximated when very large samples are tested.[1]

Let us suppose, however, that the obtained distribution curve is not normal but clearly skewed, as illustrated in Figures 2A and 2B. The first of these distributions, with a piling of scores at the low end, suggests that the

---

[1] For a fuller discussion of the implications of the normal curve, as well as for illustrations of obtained distributions of test scores, see Anastasi (1958a, Ch. 2).

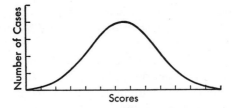

FIG. 1. A Normal Distribution Curve.

test has too high a floor for the group under consideration, lacking a suffi-cient number of easy items to discriminate properly at the lower end of the range. The result is that persons who would normally scatter over a con-siderable range obtain zero or near-zero scores on this test. A peak at the low end of the scale is therefore obtained. This artificial piling of scores is illus-trated schematically in Figure 3, in which a normally distributed group yields a skewed distribution on a particular test. The opposite skewness is illustrated in Figure 2B, with the scores piled up at the upper end, a finding that suggests insufficient test ceiling. Administering a test designed for the general population to selected samples of college or graduate students will usually yield such a skewed distribution, a number of students obtaining nearly perfect scores. With such a test, it is impossible to measure indi-vidual differences among the more able subjects in the group. If more difficult items had been included in the test, some individuals would un-doubtedly have scored higher than the present test permits.

When the standardization sample yields a markedly nonnormal distribu-tion on a test, the difficulty level of the test is ordinarily modified until a

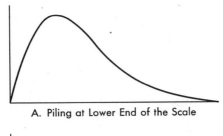

A. Piling at Lower End of the Scale

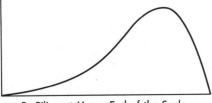

B. Piling at Upper End of the Scale

FIG. 2. Skewed Distribution Curves.

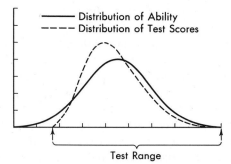

FIG. 3.   Skewness Resulting from Insufficient "Test Floor."

normal curve is approximated. Depending on the type of deviation from normality that appears, easier or more difficult items may be added, other items eliminated or modified, the position of items in the scale altered, or the scoring weights assigned to certain responses revised. Such adjustments are continued until the distribution becomes at least roughly normal. Under these conditions, the most likely score, obtained by the largest number of subjects, usually corresponds to about 50 percent correct items. To the layman who is unfamiliar with the methods of psychological test construction, a 50 percent score may seem shockingly low. It is sometimes objected, on this basis, that the examiner has set too low a standard of passing on the test. Or the inference is drawn that the group tested is a particularly poor one. Both conclusions, of course, are totally meaningless when viewed in the light of the procedures followed in developing psychological tests. Such tests are deliberately constructed and specifically modified so as to yield a mean score of approximately 50 percent correct. Only in this way can the maximum differentiation between individuals at all ability levels be obtained with the test. With a mean of approximately 50 percent correct items, there is the maximum opportunity for a normal distribution, with individual scores spreading widely at both extremes.[2]

RELIABILITY.   How good is this test? Does it really work? These questions could—and occasionally do—result in long hours of futile discussion. Subjective opinions, hunches, and personal biases may lead, on the one hand, to extravagant claims regarding what a particular test can accomplish and, on the other hand, to stubborn rejection. The only way in which questions such as these can be conclusively answered is by empirical trial. The *objective evaluation* of psychological tests involves primarily the de-

[2] Actually, the normal curve provides finer discrimination at the ends than at the middle of the scale. Equal discrimination at all points of the scale would require a rectangular distribution. The normal curve, however, has an advantage if subsequent statistical analyses of scores are to be conducted, because many current statistical techniques assume approximate normality of distribution. For this and other reasons, it is likely that most tests designed for general use will continue to follow a normal-curve pattern for some time to come. In the construction of custom-made tests to serve clearly defined purposes, however, the form of the distribution of scores should depend on the type of discrimination desired.

termination of the reliability and the validity of the test in specified situations.

As used in psychometrics, the term reliability always means consistency. Test reliability is the consistency of scores obtained by the same persons when retested with the identical test or with an equivalent form of the test. If a child receives an IQ of 110 on Monday and an IQ of 80 when retested on Friday, it is obvious that little or no confidence can be put in either score. Similarly, if in one set of 50 words an individual identifies 40 correctly, whereas in another, supposedly equivalent set he gets a score of only 20 right, then neither score can be taken as a dependable index of his verbal comprehension. To be sure, in both illustrations it is possible that only one of the two scores is in error, but this could be demonstrated only by further retests. From the given data, we can conclude only that both scores cannot be right. Whether one or neither is an adequate estimate of the individual's ability in vocabulary cannot be established without additional information.

Before a psychological test is released for general use, a thorough, objective check of its reliability must be carried out. The different types of test reliability, as well as methods of measuring each, will be considered in Chapter 4. Reliability can be checked with reference to temporal fluctuations, the particular selection of items or behavior sample constituting the test, the role of different examiners or scorers, and other aspects of the testing situation. It is essential to specify the type of reliability and the method employed to determine it, because the same test may vary in these different aspects. The number and nature of individuals on whom reliability was checked should likewise be reported. With such information, the test user can predict whether the test will be about equally reliable for the group with which he expects to use it, or whether it is likely to be more reliable or less reliable.

VALIDITY.   Undoubtedly the most important question to be asked about any psychological test concerns its validity, i.e., the degree to which the test actually measures what it purports to measure. Validity provides a direct check on how well the test fulfills its function. The determination of validity usually requires independent, external *criteria* of whatever the test is designed to measure. For example, if a medical aptitude test is to be used in selecting promising applicants for medical school, ultimate success in medical school would be a criterion. In the process of validating such a test, it would be administered to a large group of students at the time of their admission to medical school. Some measure of performance in medical school would eventually be obtained for each student on the basis of grades, ratings by instructors, success or failure in completing training, and the like. Such a composite measure constitutes the criterion with which each student's initial test score is to be correlated. A high correlation, or *validity coefficient,* would signify that those individuals who scored high on the test had been relatively successful in medical school, whereas those scoring low on the test had done poorly in medical school. A low correlation would indicate little correspondence between test score and criterion measure and hence poor validity for the test. The validity coefficient enables us to determine how closely the criterion performance could have been predicted from the test scores.

In a similar manner, tests designed for other purposes can be validated against appropriate criteria. A vocational aptitude test, for example, can be validated against on-the-job success of a trial group of new employees. A pilot aptitude battery can be validated against achievement in flight training. Tests designed for broader and more varied uses are validated against a number of criteria and their validity can be established only by the gradual accumulation of data from many different kinds of investigations.

The reader may have noticed an apparent paradox in the concept of test validity. If it is necessary to follow up the subjects or in other ways to obtain independent measures of what the test is trying to predict, why not dispense with the test? The answer to this riddle is to be found in the distinction between the validation group on the one hand and the groups on which the test will eventually be employed for operational purposes on the other. Before the test is ready for use, its validity must be established on a representative sample of subjects. The scores of these persons are not themselves employed for operational purposes but serve only in the process of testing the test. If the test proves valid by this method, it can then be used on other samples in the absence of criterion measures.

It might still be argued that we would only need to wait for the criterion measure to mature, or become available, on *any* group in order to obtain the information that the test is trying to predict. But such a procedure would be so wasteful of time and energy as to be prohibitive in most instances. Thus, we could determine which applicants will succeed on a job or which students will satisfactorily complete college by admitting all who apply and waiting for subsequent developments! It is the very wastefulness of such a procedure that tests are designed to reduce. By means of tests, the individual's eventual performance in such situations can be predicted with a determinable margin of error. The more valid the test, of course, the smaller will be this margin of error.

The special problems encountered in determining the validity of different types of tests, as well as the specific criteria and statistical procedures employed, will be discussed in Chapters 5 and 6. One further point, however, should be considered at this time. Validity tells us more than the degree to which the test is fulfilling its function. It actually tells us *what* the test is measuring. By examining the criterion data, together with the validity coefficients of the test, we can objectively determine what the test is measuring. It would thus be more accurate to define validity as the extent to which we know what the test measures. The interpretation of test scores would undoubtedly be clearer and less ambiguous if tests were regularly named in terms of the criteria against which they had been validated. A tendency in this direction can be recognized in such test labels as "scholastic aptitude test" and "personnel classification test" in place of the vague title "intelligence test."

REASONS FOR CONTROLLING THE USE OF PSYCHOLOGICAL TESTS

"May I have a Stanford-Binet blank? I'd like to find my little sister's IQ. The family think she's precocious."

"Last night I answered the questions in an intelligence test published in our newspaper and I got an IQ of 80—I think psychological tests are silly."

"I'd like to borrow the Ishihara color-blindness test to show my brother. He's applying for a Navy commission and would like some practice so he can pass that test."

"My roommate is studying psych. She gave me a personality test and I came out neurotic. I've been too upset to go to class ever since."

"I represent the school paper. We'd like a list of the IQ's of the entering freshmen to publish in our first Fall issue."

The above remarks are not imaginary. Each is based on a real incident, and the list could easily be extended by any psychologist. Such remarks illustrate potential misuses of psychological tests in such ways as to render the tests worthless or to hurt the individual. Like any scientific instrument or precision tool, psychological tests must be properly used to be effective. In the hands of either the unscrupulous or the well-meaning but uninformed user, such tests can cause serious damage.

There are two principal reasons for controlling the use of psychological tests: (a) to prevent general familiarity with test content, which would invalidate the test and (b) to ensure that the test is used by a qualified examiner. Obviously, if an individual were to memorize the correct responses on a test of color blindness, such a test would no longer be a measure of color vision for him. Under these conditions, the test would be completely invalidated. Test content clearly has to be restricted in order to forestall deliberate efforts to fake scores.

In other cases, however, the effect of familiarity may be less obvious, or the test may be invalidated in good faith by misinformed persons. A schoolteacher, for example, may give her class special practice in problems closely resembling those on an intelligence test, "so that the pupils will be well prepared to take the test." Such an attitude is simply a carry-over from the usual procedure of preparing for a school examination. When applied to an intelligence test, however, it is likely that such specific training or coaching will raise the scores on the test without appreciably affecting the broader area of behavior the test tries to sample. Under such conditions, the validity of the test as a predictive instrument is reduced.

The need for a qualified examiner is evident in each of the three major aspects of the testing situation—selection of the test, administration and scoring, and interpretation of scores. Tests cannot be chosen like lawn mowers, from a mail-order catalogue. They cannot be evaluated by name, author, or other easy marks of identification. To be sure, it requires no psychological training to consider such factors as cost, bulkiness and ease of transporting test materials, testing time required, and ease and rapidity of scoring. Information on these practical points can usually be obtained from a test catalogue and should be taken into account in planning a testing program. For the test to serve its function, however, an evaluation of its technical merits in terms of such characteristics as validity, reliability, difficulty level, and norms is essential. Only in such a way can the test user determine the appropriateness of any test for his particular purpose and its suitability for the type of persons with whom he plans to use it.

The introductory discussion of test standardization earlier in this chapter has already suggested the importance of a trained examiner. An adequate realization of the need to follow instructions precisely, as well as a thorough familiarity with the standard instructions, is required if the test scores obtained by different examiners are to be comparable or if any one individual's score is to be evaluated in terms of the published norms. Careful control of testing conditions is also essential. Similarly, incorrect or inaccurate scoring may render the test score worthless. In the absence of proper checking procedures, scoring errors are far more likely to occur than is generally realized.

The proper interpretation of test scores requires a thorough understanding of the test, the individual, and the testing conditions. What is being measured can be objectively determined only by reference to the specific procedures in terms of which the particular test was validated. Other information, pertaining to reliability, nature of the group on which norms were established, and the like, is likewise relevant. Some background data regarding the individual being tested are essential in interpreting any test score. The same score may be obtained by different persons for very different reasons. The conclusions to be drawn from such scores would therefore be quite dissimilar. Finally, some consideration must also be given to special factors that may have influenced a particular score, such as unusual testing conditions, temporary emotional or physical state of the subject, and extent of the subject's previous experience with tests.

TESTING AND PROFESSIONAL ETHICS

In order to circumvent the misuse of psychological tests, it has become necessary to erect a number of safeguards around both the tests themselves and the test scores. The distribution and use of psychological tests constitutes a major area in *Ethical Standards of Psychologists* (1963), the code of professional ethics officially adopted by the American Psychological Association. These standards have been reproduced completely in Appendix A. Principles 13, 14, and 15 are specifically directed to testing, being concerned with Test Security, Test Interpretation, and Test Publication. Other principles that, although broader in scope, are highly relevant to testing include 6 (Confidentiality), 7 (Client Welfare), and 9 (Impersonal Services). Some of the matters discussed in the *Ethical Standards* are closely related to points covered in the *Standards for Educational and Psychological Tests and Manuals* (1966), cited in Chapter 1. For a fuller and richer understanding of the principles set forth in the *Ethical Standards,* the reader should consult a later companion publication, the *Casebook on Ethical Standards of Psychologists* (1967). Highlights of ethical testing practices will be considered below.[3]

The first and most fundamental requirement is that the sale and distribution of tests be restricted to qualified users. The necessary qualifications will, of course, vary with the type of test. Thus, a relatively long period of intensive training and supervised experience is required for the proper use of individual intelligence tests and most personality tests, whereas a minimum of specialized psychological training is needed in the case of educational achievement or vocational proficiency tests. It should also be noted that students who take tests in class for instructional purposes are not usually equipped to administer the tests to others or to interpret the scores properly.

Test scores should likewise be released only to persons qualified to interpret them. When an individual is given his own score, not only should the score be interpreted by a properly qualified person, but facilities should also be available for counseling any individual who may become emotionally disturbed by a knowledge of his score. For example, a college student might become seriously discouraged when he learns of his poor performance on a scholastic aptitude test. A gifted schoolchild might develop habits of laziness and shiftlessness, or he might become uncooperative and unmanageable, if he discovers that he is much brighter than any of his associates. A severe personality disorder may be precipitated when a maladjusted individual is given his score on a personality test. Such detrimental effects may, of course, occur regardless of the correctness or incorrectness of the

[3] The ethics of psychological testing will be reexamined more intensively in Ch. 21, in the light of certain problems of contemporary interest.

score itself. Even when a test has been accurately administered and scored and properly interpreted, a knowledge of such a score without the opportunity to discuss it further may be detrimental to the individual. The possible harm is further compounded if the score itself is in error.

A question arising particularly in connection with personality tests is that of invasion of privacy. Insofar as some tests of emotional, motivational, or attitudinal traits are necessarily disguised, the subject may reveal characteristics in the course of such a test without realizing that he is so doing. Although there are few available tests whose approach is subtle enough to fall into this category, the possibility of developing such indirect testing procedures imposes a grave responsibility on the psychologist who uses them. For purposes of testing effectiveness it may be necessary to keep the examinee in ignorance of the specific ways in which his responses on any one test are to be interpreted. Nevertheless, a person should not be subjected to any testing program under false pretenses. Of primary importance in this connection is the obligation to have a clear understanding with the examinee regarding the use that will be made of his test results. The following statement contained in *Ethical Standards of Psychologists* (principle 7d) is especially relevant to this problem:

The psychologist who asks that an individual reveal personal information in the course of interviewing, testing, or evaluation, or who allows such information to be divulged to him, does so only after making certain that the responsible person is fully aware of the purposes of the interview, testing, or evaluation and of the ways in which the information may be used.

Still other professional problems concern the marketing of psychological tests by authors and publishers. Tests should not be released prematurely for general use. Nor should any claims be made regarding the merits of a test in the absence of sufficient objective evidence. When a test is distributed early for research purposes only, this condition should be clearly specified and the distribution of the test restricted accordingly. As already indicated in the preceding chapter, the test manual should provide adequate data to permit an evaluation of the test itself as well as full information regarding administration, scoring, and norms. The manual should be a factual exposition of what is known about the test rather than a selling device designed to put the test in a favorable light. It is the responsibility of the test author and publisher to revise tests and norms often enough to prevent obsolescence. The rapidity with which a test becomes outdated will, of course, vary widely with the nature of the test.

Tests or major parts of tests should not be published in a newspaper, magazine, or popular book, either for descriptive purposes or for self-evaluation. Under these conditions, self-evaluation would not only be subject to such drastic errors as to be well-nigh worthless, but it might also be detrimental to the individual for the reasons already discussed. Moreover, any publicity given to specific test items will tend to invalidate the future use of the test with other persons. It might also be added that presentation of test materials in this fashion tends to create an erroneous and distorted picture of psychological testing in general. Such publicity may foster either naïve credulity or indiscriminate resistance on the part of the public toward all psychological testing. Another unprofessional practice is testing by mail. An individual's performance on either aptitude or personality tests cannot be properly assessed by mailing test forms to him and having him return them by mail for scoring and interpretation. Not only does this procedure provide no control of testing conditions but usually it also involves the interpretation of test scores in the absence of other pertinent information about the individual. Under these conditions, test results may be worse than useless.

PROBLEMS OF RAPPORT

In psychometric parlance, the term "rapport" refers to the examiner's efforts to arouse the subject's interest in the test, elicit his cooperation, and ensure that he follows the standard test instructions. In ability tests, the instructions call for careful concentration on the given tasks and for putting forth one's best efforts to perform well; in personality inventories, they call for frank and honest responses to questions about one's usual behavior; in certain projective tests, they call for full reporting of associations evoked by the stimuli, without any censoring or editing of content. Still other kinds of tests may require other approaches. But in all instances, the examiner must motivate the subject to follow the instructions as fully and conscientiously as he can.

The training of examiners covers techniques for the establishment of rapport as well as those more directly related to test administration. In establishing rapport, as in other testing procedures, uniformity of conditions is essential for comparability of results. If a child is given a coveted prize whenever he solves a test problem correctly, his performance cannot be directly compared with the norms or with that of other children who are motivated only with the standard verbal encouragement or praise. Any unavoidable deviation from standard motivating conditions for a particular test should be noted and taken into account in interpreting performance.

Although rapport can be more fully established in individual testing, steps can also be taken in group testing to motivate the subjects and relieve their anxiety. Specific techniques for establishing rapport vary with the nature of the test and with the age and other characteristics of the subjects. In testing preschool children,[4] special factors to be considered include shy-

---

[4] A detailed description of recommended procedures for testing young children can be found in Goodenough (1949, pp. 298–304).

ness with strangers, distractability, and negativism. A friendly, cheerful, and relaxed manner on the part of the examiner helps to reassure the child. The shy, timid child needs more preliminary time to become familiar with his surroundings. For this reason it is better for the examiner not to be too demonstrative at the outset, but rather to wait until the child is ready to make the first contact. Test periods should be brief, and the tasks should be varied and intrinsically interesting to the child. The testing should be presented to the child as a game and his curiosity aroused before each new task is introduced. A certain flexibility of procedure is necessary at this age level because of possible refusals, loss of interest, and other manifestations of negativism.

Children in the first two or three grades of elementary school present many of the same testing problems as the preschool child. The game appeal is still the most effective way of arousing their interest in the test. The older schoolchild can usually be motivated through an appeal to his competitive spirit and his desire to do well on tests. When testing children from disadvantaged backgrounds or from different cultures, however, the examiner cannot assume they will be motivated to excel on academic tasks to the same extent as children in the standardization sample. This problem and others pertaining to the testing of persons with dissimilar experiential backgrounds will be considered further in Chapters 21 and 22.

It should be borne in mind that every test presents an implied threat to the individual's prestige. Some reassurance should therefore be given at the outset. It is helpful to explain, for example, that no one is expected to finish or to get all the items correct. The individual might otherwise experience a mounting sense of failure as he finds that he is unable to finish any part of the test within the time allowed.

It is also desirable to eliminate the element of surprise from the test situation as far as possible, because the unexpected and unknown are likely to produce anxiety. Many group tests provide a preliminary explanatory statement that is read to the group by the examiner. An even better procedure is to announce the tests a few days in advance and to give each subject a printed booklet that explains the purpose and nature of the tests, offers general suggestions on how to take tests, and contains a few sample items. Such explanatory booklets are regularly available to participants in large-scale testing programs such as those conducted by the College Entrance Examination Board (1967b, 1967c, 1967d). The United States Employment Service has likewise developed a booklet on how to take tests, as well as a more extensive pretesting orientation technique for use with culturally disadvantaged applicants unfamiliar with tests.

More general orientation booklets are also available. Examples include *Taking a Test* by Manuel (1956) and the more comprehensive treatment by Anderson, Katz, and Shimberg (1965) entitled *Meeting the Test*. A tape recording and two booklets are combined in *Test Orientation Pro-*

cedure (TOP), designed specifically for job applicants with little prior testing experience (Bennett & Doppelt, 1967). The first booklet, used together with the tape, provides general information on how to take tests; the second contains practice tests. In the absence of a tape recorder, the examiner may read the instructions from a printed script.

Adult testing presents some additional problems. Unlike the schoolchild, the adult is not so likely to work hard at a task merely because it is assigned to him. It therefore becomes more important to "sell" the purpose of the tests to the adult, although high school and college students also respond to such an appeal. Cooperation of the examinee can usually be secured by convincing him that it is in his own interests to obtain a valid score, i.e., a score correctly indicating what he can do rather than over-estimating or underestimating his abilities. Most persons can be made to understand that an incorrect decision, which might result from invalid test scores, would mean subsequent failure, loss of time, and frustration for them. This approach can serve not only to motivate the individual to try his best on ability tests but also to reduce cheating and to encourage frank reporting on personality inventories, because the examinee realizes that he himself would otherwise be the loser. It is certainly not in the best interests of the individual to be admitted to a course of study for which he is not qualified or assigned to a job he cannot perform or that he would find uncongenial.

PROBLEMS OF TEST ADMINISTRATION

A whole volume could easily be devoted to a discussion of desirable procedures of test administration. But such a survey falls outside the scope of the present book. Moreover, it is more practicable to acquire such techniques within specific settings, because no one individual would normally be concerned with all forms of testing, from the examination of infants to the clinical testing of psychotic patients or the administration of a mass testing program for military personnel. The present discussion will therefore deal principally with the common rationale of test administration rather than with specific questions of implementation.[5]

ADVANCE PREPARATION OF EXAMINERS. The most important requirement for good testing procedure is advance preparation. In testing there can be no emergencies. Special efforts must therefore be made to foresee and forestall emergencies. Only in this way can uniformity of procedure be assured.

[5] For detailed suggestions regarding testing procedure, the reader is referred to Goodenough (1949, Ch. 20) for the testing of preschool children; Terman and Merrill (1960, pp. 45–59) for individual testing of older children and adults; and Clemans (1971) for group testing. A helpful checklist of proper practices to follow in the group testing of schoolchildren can be found in *Test Administration Guide* (Prescott, undated).

Advance preparation for the testing session takes many forms. Memorizing the verbal instructions is essential in most individual testing. Even in a group test in which the instructions are read to the subjects, some previous familiarity with the statements to be read prevents misreading and hesitation and permits a more natural, informal manner during test administration. The preparation of test materials is another important preliminary step. In individual testing and especially in the administration of performance tests, such preparation involves the actual layout of the necessary materials to facilitate subsequent use with a minimum of search or fumbling. Materials should generally be placed on a table near the testing table so that they are within easy reach of the examiner but do not distract the subject. When apparatus is employed, frequent periodic checking and calibration may be necessary. In group testing, all test blanks, answer sheets, special pencils, or other materials needed should be carefully counted, checked, and arranged in advance of the testing day.

Rehearsal of procedure with one or more trial subjects is another essential prerequisite in both individual and group testing. In the case of group testing, and especially in large-scale projects, such preparation may include the advance briefing of examiners and proctors, so that each is thoroughly familiar with the functions he is to perform. In general, the examiner reads the instructions, takes care of timing, and is in charge of the group in any one testing room. The proctors hand out and collect test materials, make certain that subjects are following instructions, answer individual questions of subjects within the limitations specified in the manual, and prevent cheating.

TESTING CONDITIONS.   Standardized procedure applies not only to verbal instructions, timing, materials, and other aspects of the tests themselves but also to the testing environment. Some attention should be given to the selection of a suitable testing room. This room should be free from undue noise and distraction and should provide adequate lighting, ventilation, seating facilities, and working space for the subjects. Special steps should also be taken to prevent interruptions during the test. Posting a sign on the door to indicate that testing is in progress is effective, provided all personnel have learned that such a sign means no admittance under any circumstances. In the testing of large groups, locking the doors or posting an assistant outside each door may be necessary to prevent the entrance of late-comers.

It is important to realize the extent to which testing conditions may influence scores. Even apparently minor aspects of the testing situation may appreciably alter performance. Such a factor as the use of desks or of chairs with desk arms, for example, proved to be significant in a group testing project with high school students, the groups using desks tending to obtain higher scores (Kelley, 1943; Traxler & Hilkert, 1942). There is also evidence to show that the type of answer sheet employed may affect test scores (Bell, Hoff, & Hoyt, 1964). Because of the establishment of independent test-scoring and data-processing agencies that provide their own machine-scorable answer sheets, examiners today sometimes administer group tests with answer sheets other than those provided by the test publishers and used in the standardization sample. In the absence of empirical verification, the equivalence of these answer sheets cannot be assumed. Changes in the answer sheets may render timing, norms, and other standardization data inapplicable.

Many other, more subtle testing conditions have been shown to affect performance on ability tests as well as personality tests. Whether the examiner is a stranger or someone familiar to the subjects has been found to make a significant difference in test scores (Sacks, 1952; Tsudzuki, Hata, & Kuze, 1957). In another study, the general manner and behavior of the examiner, as illustrated by smiling, nodding, and making such comments as "good" or "fine," were shown to have a decided effect on test results (Wickes, 1956). In a projective test requiring the subject to write stories to fit given pictures, the presence of the examiner in the room tended to inhibit the inclusion of strongly emotional content in the stories (Bernstein, 1956). In the administration of a typing test, job applicants typed at a significantly faster rate when tested alone than when tested in groups of two or more (Kirchner, 1966). Examples could readily be multiplied. The implications are threefold. First, follow standardized procedures to the minutest detail, when these are described in the manual. Second, record any unusual testing conditions, however minor. Third, take testing conditions into account when interpreting test results.

CHAPTER 3

The Interpretation of Test Scores: Norms and Their Uses

IN THE absence of additional interpretive data, a raw score on any psychological test is meaningless. To say that an individual has correctly solved 15 problems on an arithmetic reasoning test, or identified 34 words in a vocabulary test, or successfully assembled a mechanical object in 57 seconds conveys little or no information about his standing in any of these functions. Nor do the familiar percentage scores provide a satisfactory solution to the problem of interpreting test scores. A score of 65 percent correct on one vocabulary test, for example, might be equivalent to 30 percent correct on another, and to 80 percent correct on a third. The difficulty level of the items making up each test will, of course, determine the meaning of the score. Like all raw scores, percentage scores can be interpreted only by reference to *norms*.

Essentially, psychological test norms represent the test performance of the standardization sample. The norms are thus empirically established by determining what a representative group of persons actually do on the test. Any individual's raw score is then referred to the distribution of scores obtained by the standardization sample, to discover where he falls in that distribution. Does his score coincide with the average performance of the standardization group? Is he slightly below average? Or does he fall near the upper end of the distribution?

In order to determine more precisely the individual's exact position with reference to the standardization sample, the raw score is converted into some relative measure. These derived scores are designed to serve a dual purpose. First, they indicate the individual's relative standing in the normative sample and thus permit an evaluation of his performance in reference to other persons. Second, they provide comparable measures that permit a direct comparison of the individual's performance on different tests. For example, if an individual has a raw score of 40 on a vocabulary test and a raw score of 22 on an arithmetic reasoning test, we obviously know nothing about his relative performance on the two tests. Is he better in vocabulary or in arithmetic, or equally good in both? Since raw scores on different tests are usually expressed in different units, a direct comparison of such scores is impossible. The difficulty level of the particular test would also affect such a comparison between raw scores. Derived scores, on the other hand, can be expressed in the same units and referred to the same or to closely similar normative samples for different tests. The individual's relative performance in many different functions can thus be compared.

There are various ways in which raw scores may be converted to fulfill the two objectives stated above.[1] Fundamentally, however, derived scores are of three major types: age scores, percentiles, and standard scores. These types, together with some of their common variants, will be considered in separate sections of this chapter. But first it will be necessary to examine a few elementary statistical concepts that underlie the development and utilization of norms. The following section is included simply to clarify the meaning of certain common statistical measures. Simplified computational examples are given only for this purpose and not to provide training in statistical methods. For computational details and specific procedures to be followed in the practical application of these techniques, the reader is referred to any recent textbook on psychological or educational statistics.

STATISTICAL CONCEPTS

A major object of statistical method is to organize and summarize quantitative data in order to facilitate their understanding. A list of 1,000 test scores can be an overwhelming sight. In that form, it conveys little meaning. A first step in bringing order into such a chaos of raw data is to tabulate the scores into a *frequency distribution,* as illustrated in Table 1. Such a distribution is prepared by grouping the scores into convenient class intervals and tallying each score in the appropriate interval. When all scores have been entered, the tallies are counted to find the frequency, or number of cases, in each class interval. The sums of these frequencies will equal N, the total number of cases in the group. Table 1 shows the scores of 1,000 college students in a code-learning test in which one set of artificial words, or nonsense syllables, was to be substituted for another. The raw scores, giving number of correct syllables substituted during a two-minute trial, ranged from 8 to 52. They have been grouped into class intervals of

[1] An exhaustive survey of different types of derived scores is given by Lyman (1963, Ch. 6).

TABLE 1   FREQUENCY DISTRIBUTION OF SCORES OF 1,000 COLLEGE STUDENTS ON A CODE-LEARNING TEST

(From Anastasi, 1934, p. 34)

Class Interval	Frequency
52–55	1
48–51	1
44–47	20
40–43	73
36–39	156
32–35	328
28–31	244
24–27	136
20–23	28
16–19	8
12–15	3
8–11	2
	1,000

4 points, from 52–55 at the top of the distribution down to 8–11. The frequency column reveals that two persons scored between 8 and 11, three between 12 and 15, eight between 16 and 19, and so on.

The information provided by a frequency distribution can also be presented graphically in the form of a distribution curve. Figure 4 shows the data of Table 1 in graphic form. On the baseline, or horizontal axis, are

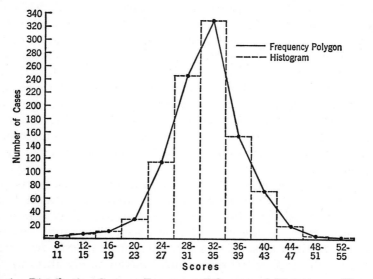

FIG. 4.   Distribution Curves: Frequency Polygon and Histogram. (Data from Table 1.)

the scores grouped into class intervals; on the vertical axis are the frequencies, or number of cases falling within each class interval. The graph has been plotted in two ways, both forms being in common use. In the *histogram,* the height of the column erected over each class interval corresponds to the number of persons scoring in that interval. We can think of each individual standing on another's shoulders to form the column. In the *frequency polygon,* the number of persons in each interval is indicated by a point placed in the center of the class interval and across from the appropriate frequency. The successive points are then joined by straight lines.

Except for minor irregularities, the distribution portrayed in Figure 4 resembles the bell-shaped *normal curve.* A mathematically determined, perfect normal curve is reproduced in Figure 6. This type of curve has important mathematical properties and provides the basis for many kinds of statistical analyses. For the present purpose, however, only a few features will be noted. Essentially, the curve indicates that the largest number of cases cluster in the center of the range and that the number drops off gradually in both directions as the extremes are approached. The curve is bilaterally symmetrical, with a single peak in the center. Most distributions of human traits, from height and weight to aptitudes and personality characteristics, approximate the normal curve. In general, the larger the group, the more closely will the distribution resemble the theoretical normal curve.

A group of scores can also be described in terms of some measure of *central tendency.* Such a measure provides a single, most typical or representative score to characterize the performance of the entire group. The most familiar of these measures is the average, more technically known as the *mean (M).* As is well known, this is found by adding all scores and dividing the sum by the number of cases *(N).* Another measure of central tendency is the *mode,* or most frequent score. In a frequency distribution, the mode is the midpoint of the class interval with the highest frequency. Thus, in Table 1, the mode falls midway between 32 and 35, being 33.5. It will be noted that this score corresponds to the highest point on the distribution curve in Figure 4. A third measure of central tendency is the *median,* or middlemost score when all scores have been arranged in order of size. The median is the point that bisects the distribution, half the cases falling above it and half below.

Further description of a set of test scores is given by measures of *variability,* or the extent of individual differences around the central tendency. The most obvious and familiar way of reporting variability is in terms of the *range* between the highest and lowest score. The range, however, is extremely crude and unstable, for it is determined by only two scores. A single unusually high or low score would thus markedly affect its size. A more precise method of measuring variability is based on the difference between each individual's score and the mean of the group.

At this point it will be helpful to look at the example in Table 2, in which the various measures under consideration have been computed on 10 cases. Such a small group was chosen in order to simplify the demonstration, although in actual practice we would rarely perform these computations on so few cases. Table 2 serves also to introduce certain standard

TABLE 2   ILLUSTRATION OF CENTRAL TENDENCY AND VARIABILITY

		Score (X)	Diff. (x)		Diff. Squared (x^2)
		48	+8		64
	50% of	47	+7		49
	cases	43	+3	+ 20	9
		41	+1		1
Median = 40.5 →		41	+1		1
		40	0		0
		38	−2		4
	50% of	36	−4	− 20	16
	cases	34	−6		36
		32	−8		64
		$\Sigma X = 400$	$\Sigma\ |x| = 40$		$\Sigma x^2 = 244$

$$M = \frac{\Sigma X}{N} = \frac{400}{10} = 40$$

$$AD = \frac{\Sigma\ |x|}{N} = \frac{40}{10} = 4$$

$$\text{Variance} = \sigma^2 = \frac{\Sigma x^2}{N} = \frac{244}{10} = 24.40$$

$$SD \text{ or } \sigma = \sqrt{\frac{\Sigma x^2}{N}} = \sqrt{24.40} = 4.9$$

statistical symbols that should be noted for future reference. Original raw scores are conventionally designated by a capital X, and a small x is used to refer to deviations of each score from the group mean. The Greek letter Σ means "sum of." It will be seen that the first column in Table 2 gives the data for the computation of mean and median. The mean is 40; the median is 40.5, falling midway between 40 and 41—five cases (50 percent) are above the median and five below. There is little point in finding a mode in such a small group, since the cases do not show clear-cut clustering on any one score. Technically, however, 41 would represent the mode, because two persons obtained this score, while all other scores occur only once.

The second column shows how far each score deviates above or below the mean of 40. The sum of these deviations will always equal zero, because the positive and negative deviations around the mean necessarily balance, or cancel each other out ($+20 - 20 = 0$). If we ignore signs, of course, we can average the absolute deviations, thus obtaining a measure known as the *average deviation* (*AD*). The symbol $|x|$ in the *AD* formula indicates that absolute values were summed, without regard to sign. Although of some descriptive value, the *AD* is not suitable for use in further mathematical analyses because of the arbitrary discarding of signs.

A much more serviceable measure of variability is the *standard deviation* (symbolized by either *SD* or σ), in which the negative signs are legitimately eliminated by squaring each deviation. This procedure has been followed in the last column of Table 2. The sum of this column divided by the number of cases $\left(\dfrac{\Sigma x^2}{N}\right)$ is known as the *variance*, or *mean square deviation*, and is symbolized by σ^2. The variance has proved extremely useful in sorting out the contributions of different factors to individual differences in test performance. For the present purposes, however, our chief concern is with the *SD*, which is the square root of the variance, as shown in Table 2. This measure is commonly employed in comparing the variability of different groups. In Figure 5, for example, are two distributions having the same

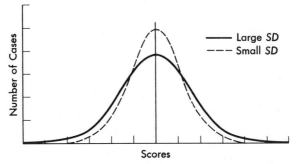

FIG. 5.   Frequency Distributions with the Same Mean but Different Variability.

mean but differing in variability. The distribution with wider individual differences yields a larger *SD* than the one with narrower individual differences.

The *SD* also provides the basis for expressing an individual's scores on different tests in terms of norms, as will be shown in the section on standard scores. The interpretation of the *SD* is especially clear-cut when applied to a normal or approximately normal distribution curve. In such a distribution, there is an exact relationship between the *SD* and the proportion of cases, as shown in Figure 6. On the baseline of this normal curve have been marked distances representing one, two, and three standard deviations above and below the mean. For instance, in the example given in Table 2, the mean would correspond to a score of 40, $+1\sigma$ to 44.9 (40 + 4.9), $+2\sigma$ to 49.8 (40 + 2 × 4.9), and so on. The percentage of cases that fall between the mean and $+1\sigma$ in a normal curve is 34.13. Because the curve is symmetrical, 34.13 percent of the cases are likewise found between the mean and -1σ, so that between $+1\sigma$ and -1σ on both sides of the mean there are 68.26 percent of the cases. Nearly all the cases (99.72 percent) fall within $\pm 3\sigma$ from the mean. These relationships are particularly relevant in the interpretation of standard scores and percentiles, to be discussed in later sections.

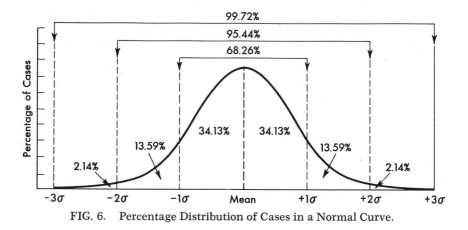

FIG. 6.   Percentage Distribution of Cases in a Normal Curve.

AGE SCORES

The concept of mental age, it will be recalled, was introduced in the 1908 revision of the Binet-Simon Scales. In age scales such as the Binet and its revisions, individual items are grouped into year levels. For example, those items passed by the majority of 7-year-olds in the standardization sample are placed at the 7-year level, those passed by the majority of 8-year-olds are assigned to the 8-year level, and so forth.[2] A child's score on this test will then correspond to the highest year level that he can successfully complete. If, for example, a 10-year-old child can satisfactorily complete the 12-year items, his mental age (MA) is 12 although his chronological age (CA) is 10. He is thus two years accelerated, because he equals the performance of an average child two years his senior.

In actual practice, the individual's performance on age scales such as the Binet shows a certain amount of *scatter*. In other words, the subject fails some tests below his mental age level and passes some above it. For this reason, it is customary to compute the *basal age*, i.e., the highest age at and below which all tests are passed. Partial credits, in months, are then added to this basal age for all tests passed at higher year levels. The

[2] The exact percentage who must pass an item varies somewhat at different year levels. This percentage must decrease from the lower to the upper year levels if the IQ is to remain constant. The reason for this requirement will be explained in Ch. 8, in connection with the construction of the Stanford-Binet.

child's mental age on the test is the sum of the basal age and the additional months of credit earned at higher age levels.

Mental age norms may also be employed with tests that are not divided into year levels. In such a case, the subject's raw score is first determined. Such a score may be the total number of correct items on the whole test; or it may be based on time, on number of errors, or on some combination of such measures. The mean raw scores obtained by the children in each year group within the standardization sample constitute the age norms for such a test. The mean raw score of the 8-year-old children, for example, would represent the 8-year norm. If an individual's raw score is equal to the mean 8-year-old raw score, then his mental age on the test is 8 years. All raw scores on such a test would be transformed in a similar manner by reference to the age norms.

It should be noted that the mental age unit does not remain constant with age, but tends to shrink with advancing years. For example, a child who is one year retarded at age 4 will be approximately three years retarded at age 12. One year of mental growth from ages 3 to 4 is equivalent to three years of growth from ages 9 to 12. Since intellectual development progresses more rapidly at the earlier ages and gradually decreases as the individual approaches his mature limit, the mental age unit shrinks correspondingly with age. This relationship may be more readily visualized if we think of the individual's height as being expressed in terms of "height age." The difference, in inches, between a height age of 3 and 4 years would be greater than that between a height age of 10 and 11. Owing to the progressive shrinkage of the MA unit, one year of acceleration or retardation at, let us say, age 5 represents a larger deviation from the norm than does one year of acceleration or retardation at age 10.

In order to provide a measure that, unlike mental age, permits a uniform interpretation regardless of the age of the subject, the intelligence quotient (IQ) was introduced. Although the need for such a ratio measure had been previously indicated by Stern and by Kuhlmann, the IQ was first employed in the 1916 form of the Stanford-Binet. The IQ is the ratio of mental age to chronological age, the fraction being customarily multiplied by 100 in order to avoid the use of decimals, as shown below:

$$IQ = 100\frac{MA}{CA}$$

If a child's mental age equals his chronological age, his IQ will be exactly 100. An IQ of 100 thus represents normal or average performance. IQ's below 100 indicate retardation, and those above 100, acceleration. The shrinkage in the mental age unit is automatically adjusted by the use of the ratio. For example, if a 4-year-old has a mental age of 3, his IQ will be 75 ($100 \times 3/4 = 75$). The same child at age 12 will probably have a mental age of 9, and his IQ will still be 75 ($100 \times 9/12 = 75$). Such an IQ indicates the same relative standing in the group, whether obtained by a 4-year-old or by a 12-year-old. The IQ is thus comparable at different ages, in the sense that the interpretation of a particular IQ remains the same regardless of the age of the subject. If every individual's MA falls three times as far from the mean at age 12 as it did at age 4, then the standard deviation of mental ages will be three times as large at age 12 as it was at age 4. Under these conditions, each individual's IQ will fall just as far above or below the mean at age 12 as it did at age 4. Hence, the standard deviation of the IQ will be equal at both ages.

To recapitulate, for IQ's to be directly comparable at different ages, their *SD*'s must remain the same with age. With ratio IQ's, this implies that the *SD*'s of the mental ages increase proportionately with age. This condition was met closely enough in the 1937 Stanford-Binet (McNemar, 1942; Terman & Merrill, 1937) to make the IQ applicable to this test. Figure 7 shows the spread of Stanford-Binet mental ages from ages 6 to 18, as indicated by the range of approximately the middle 68 percent of the cases at each age. It will be recalled that this is the approximate per-

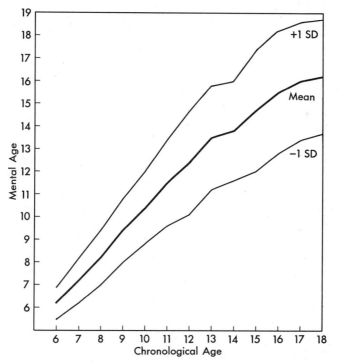

FIG. 7. Means and Standard Deviations of Stanford-Binet Mental Ages. (Data from McNemar, 1942, pp. 32–33.)

centage of cases falling between $+1$ SD and -1 SD from the mean in a normal curve. The trend toward greater variability in mental age with increasing chronological age is clearly apparent in Figure 7. Even in such a carefully constructed test as the Stanford-Binet, however, some inequalities remained in the SD's of the IQ at different ages. This difficulty was handled in the 1937 Stanford-Binet by the preparation of a correction table to be used with IQ's at certain age levels (McNemar, 1942, pp. 173–174). In the 1960 revision of the Stanford-Binet (Terman & Merrill, 1960), the problem was circumvented by replacing the ratio IQ with a deviation IQ, to be discussed later in this chapter.

In several other intelligence tests that provide age norms, however, the conditions for IQ constancy are not met. In such tests, the same ratio IQ may signify different degrees of superiority or inferiority at different ages. Thus, an IQ of 115 at one age may indicate the same degree of superiority as an IQ of 125 at another age. This discrepancy would occur if the SD of the IQ proved to be 15 at one age and 25 at the other. Despite its apparent logical simplicity, the ratio IQ is not directly applicable to most psychological tests. Its use should be preceded by a thorough check of variability at different ages, to ensure that the condition of uniform IQ variability, or proportionately increasing MA variability, has been met.

A further limitation in the applicability of the ratio IQ is to be found in adult testing. A consideration of the very concept of age norms will indicate that their usefulness is largely restricted to children. To say that a 10-year-old child has a mental age of 12 conveys a vivid and objectively definable picture. It is one of the chief advantages of the mental age concept that it can be clearly grasped by the layman. Such an advantage is greatly reduced, however, with adult mental ages. On such a test as the Stanford-Binet, for example, the average adult does not improve much beyond the 15-year level. Hence, the average adult mental age on this test is under 16 (actually 15 years-9 months). To be sure, superior adult levels have been added to give the test adequate ceiling, and mental ages above 15-9 may thus be obtained. But to say that a particular adult received a mental age of 20 on such a test does not permit the same clear-cut interpretation as would be possible with a mental age of 8 or 10. Certainly a mental age of 20 cannot be defined as what the average 20-year-old can do, for the average 20-year-old obtains a mental age of 15-9. In testing a mentally retarded adult whose mental age is below 15-9, of course, the mental age concept is as applicable as with children. With normal and superior adults, however, other types of scores, such as percentiles or standard scores, are now commonly employed.

Still another limitation of age scores arises from the fact that they can be employed only with functions that show a clear and consistent change with age. Traits that exhibit little relation to age obviously do not lend themselves to measurement in terms of age units. Most personality characteristics, for example, would fall into this category.

PERCENTILES

Percentile scores are expressed in terms of the percentage of persons in the standardization sample who fall below a given raw score. For example, if 28 percent of the subjects obtain fewer than 15 problems correct on an arithmetic reasoning test, then a raw score of 15 corresponds to the 28th percentile (P_{28}). A percentile indicates the individual's relative position in the standardization sample. Percentiles can also be regarded as ranks in a group of 100, except that in ranking it is customary to start counting at the top, the best person in the group receiving a rank of one. With percentiles, on the other hand, we begin counting at the bottom, so that the lower the percentile, the poorer the individual's standing.

The 50th percentile (P_{50}) corresponds to the median, already discussed as a measure of central tendency. Percentiles above 50 represent above-average performance; those below 50 signify inferior performance. The 25th and 75th percentile are known as the first and third quartile points (Q_1 and Q_3), because they cut off the lowest and highest quarters of the distribution. Like the median, they provide convenient landmarks for describing a distribution of scores and comparing it with other distributions.

Percentiles should not be confused with the familiar percentage scores. The latter are raw scores, expressed in terms of the percentage of correct items; percentiles are derived scores, expressed in terms of percentage of persons. A raw score lower than any obtained in the standardization sample would have a percentile rank of zero (P_0); one higher than any score in the standardization sample would have a percentile rank of 100 (P_{100}). These percentiles, however, do not imply a zero raw score and a perfect raw score.

In test manuals, percentile norms are sometimes reported in the form of a graph, as illustrated in Figure 8. Such a graph, known as an *ogive,* shows the cumulative percentage of cases falling below each score. As in the previously discussed frequency graphs, scores are given on the baseline, frequencies (i.e., cumulative percentages) on the vertical axis. Figure 8 was plotted from the data of Table 3, which shows the same 1,000 scores given in Table 1. The first two columns of Table 3, giving class intervals and frequencies, are identical with those of Table 1. In the third column are the cumulative frequencies, found by adding frequencies from the bottom up. Thus, the number of cases falling at or below a score of 11 is 2; the number at or below 15 is 5 (3 + 2); the number at or below 19 is 13

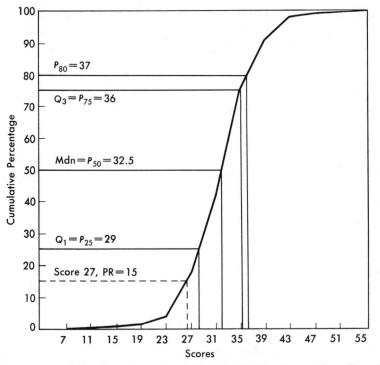

FIG. 8.   Cumulative Frequency Graph Used in Finding Percentiles. (Data from Table 3.)

(8 + 5). In the fourth column, these cumulative frequencies have been changed to percentages by dividing each by 10 (since $N = 1,000$).

The ogive in Figure 8 shows the cumulative percentage frequency below the upper limit of each class interval.[3] Such an ogive can be read in either direction. For example, if we wish to find the median, we locate the 50 percent point on the vertical axis, draw a horizontal line from this point to the graph, and at the point where the line meets the graph drop a perpendicular to the baseline. This has been done in Figure 8, showing that the median is 32.5. Similarly, Q_1 is found to be approximately 29 and Q_3 approximately 36. The raw score corresponding to any other percentile can be found in the same manner; for the 80th percentile, for example, it is 37. Working in the opposite direction, we can start with an individual's raw score and locate the percentile rank corresponding to it. Thus, for a raw score of 27, we raise a perpendicular above 27 on the baseline until it

[3] The observant reader may have noticed that the points on the graph have been plotted slightly to the right of the score values on the baseline. In a continuous scale, the numbers 11, 15, etc., correspond to the *midpoints* of scores. The *upper limits* of the scores, at which cumulative percentage frequencies have been plotted, fall on 11.5, 15.5, etc.

TABLE 3   CUMULATIVE FREQUENCY DISTRIBUTION

Class Interval	Frequency	Cumulative Frequency	Cumulative Percentage Frequency
52–55	1	1,000	100.0
48–51	1	999	99.9
44–47	20	998	99.8
40–43	73	978	97.8
36–39	156	905	90.5
32–35	328	749	74.9
28–31	244	421	42.1
24–27	136	177	17.7
20–23	28	41	4.1
16–19	8	13	1.3
12–15	3	5	0.5
8–11	2	2	0.2

meets the curve; a horizontal line drawn from that point to the vertical axis shows the percentile rank to be 15.

Percentile scores have several advantages. They are easy to compute and can be readily understood, even by relatively untrained persons. More-over, percentiles are universally applicable. They can be used equally well with adults and children and are suitable for any type of test, whether it measures aptitude or personality variables.

The chief drawback of percentile scores arises from the marked in-equality of their units, especially at the extremes of the distribution. If the distribution of raw scores approximates the normal curve, as is true of most test scores, then raw score differences near the median or center of the distribution are exaggerated in the percentile transformation, whereas raw score differences near the ends of the distribution are greatly shrunk. This distortion of distances between scores can be seen in Figure 9. In a normal curve, it will be recalled, cases cluster closely at the center and scatter more widely as the extremes are approached. Consequently, any given percentage of cases near the center covers a shorter distance on the baseline than the same percentage near the ends of the distribution. In Figure 9, this discrepancy in the gaps between percentile ranks (*PR*) can readily be seen if we compare the distance between a *PR* of 40 and a *PR* of 50 with that between a *PR* of 10 and a *PR* of 20. Even more striking is the discrepancy between these distances and that between a *PR* of 10 and a *PR* of 1. (In a mathematically derived normal curve, zero percentile is not reached until infinity and hence cannot be shown on the graph.)

The same relationship can be seen from the opposite direction if we ex-amine the percentile ranks corresponding to equal σ-distances from the

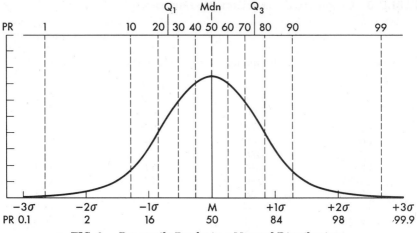

FIG. 9.   Percentile Ranks in a Normal Distribution.

mean of a normal curve. These percentile ranks are given under the graph in Figure 9. Thus, the percentile difference between the mean and $+1\sigma$ is 34 $(84 - 50)$. That between $+1\sigma$ and $+2\sigma$ is only 14 $(98 - 84)$.

It is apparent that percentiles show each individual's *relative position* in the normative sample but not the *amount* of difference between scores. If plotted on arithmetic probability paper, however, percentile scores can also provide a correct visual picture of the differences between scores. Arithmetic probability paper is a cross-section paper in which the vertical lines are spaced in the same way as the percentile points in a normal distribution (see Figure 9), whereas the horizontal lines are uniformly spaced, or vice versa. Such normal percentile charts can be used to plot the scores of different persons on the same test or the scores of the same person on different tests. In either case, the actual interscore difference will be correctly represented. A number of aptitude and achievement batteries now utilize this technique in their score profiles, which show the individual's performance in each test. An example is the Individual Report Form of the Differential Aptitude Tests, reproduced in Figure 10.

STANDARD SCORES

Current tests are making increasing use of standard scores, which are the most satisfactory type of derived score from most points of view. Standard scores express the individual's distance from the mean in terms of the standard deviation of the distribution.

LINEAR STANDARD SCORES.   Standard scores may be obtained by either linear or nonlinear transformations of the original raw scores. When found by a linear transformation, they retain the exact numerical relations of the

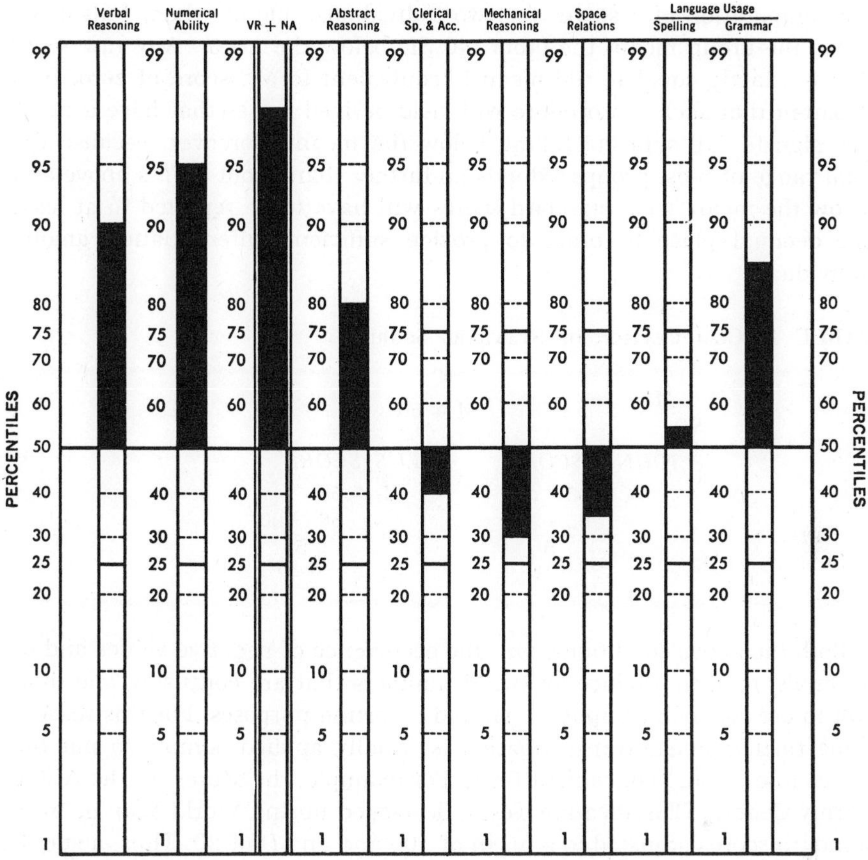

| Verbal Reasoning | Numerical Ability | VR + NA | Abstract Reasoning | Clerical Sp. & Acc. | Mechanical Reasoning | Space Relations | Language Usage Spelling | Grammar |

PERCENTILES: 99, 95, 90, 80, 75, 70, 60, 50, 40, 30, 25, 20, 10, 5, 1

FIG. 10. Individual Report Form for Use with the Differential Aptitude Tests. Vertical bars show distance above or below norm on each test. Percentiles are spaced so as to correspond to equal distances in a normal distribution. (Report Form reproduced by permission. Copyright © 1963, The Psychological Corporation, New York, N.Y. All rights reserved.)

original raw scores, because they are computed by subtracting a constant from each raw score and then dividing the result by another constant. The relative magnitude of differences between standard scores derived by such a linear transformation corresponds exactly to that between the raw scores. All properties of the original distribution of raw scores are duplicated in the distribution of these standard scores. For this reason, any computations that can be carried out with the original raw scores can also be carried out with linear standard scores, without any distortion of results.

Linearly derived standard scores are often designated simply as "standard scores" or "z scores." To compute a z score, we find the difference between the individual's raw score and the mean of the normative group and then divide this difference by the SD of the normative group. Table 4 shows the computation of z scores for two individuals, one of whom falls 1 SD above the group mean, the other .40 SD below the mean. Any raw score that is exactly equal to the mean is equivalent to a z score of zero. It is apparent that such a procedure will yield derived scores that have a negative sign for all subjects falling below the mean. Moreover, because the total range of most groups extends no farther than about 3 SD's above and below the mean, such standard scores will have to be reported to at least one decimal place in order to provide sufficient differentiation among individuals.

TABLE 4 COMPUTATION OF STANDARD SCORES

$$z = \frac{X - M}{SD} \qquad M = 60 \qquad SD = 5$$

JOHN'S SCORE
$X_1 = 65$
$z_1 = \dfrac{65 - 60}{5}$
$= +1.00$

BILL'S SCORE
$X_2 = 58$
$z_2 = \dfrac{58 - 60}{5}$
$= -0.40$

Both the above conditions, viz., the occurrence of negative values and of decimals, tend to produce awkward numbers that are confusing and difficult to use for both computational and reporting purposes. For this reason, some further linear transformation is usually applied, simply to put the scores into a more convenient form. For example, the scores on the AGCT (Army General Classification Test), developed during World War II, were standard scores adjusted to a mean of 100 and an SD of 20. Thus, a standard score of -1 on this test would be expressed as 80 ($100 - 20 = 80$). Similarly, a standard score of $+1.5$ would correspond to 130 ($100 + 1.5 \times 20 = 130$). To convert an original standard score to the new scale, it is simply necessary to multiply the standard score by the desired SD (20) and add it to or subtract it from the desired mean (100).

Any other convenient values can be arbitrarily chosen for the new mean and SD. The College Entrance Examination Board employs a mean of 500 and an SD of 100. Scores on the separate subtests of the Wechsler Intelligence Scales are converted to a distribution with a mean of 10 and an SD of 3. All such measures are examples of linearly transformed standard scores.

NORMALIZED STANDARD SCORES. It will be recalled that one of the reasons for transforming raw scores into any derived scale is to render scores on different tests comparable. The linearly derived standard scores discussed in the preceding section will be comparable only when found from distributions that have approximately the same form. Under such conditions, a score corresponding to 1 SD above the mean, for example, signifies that the individual occupies the same position in relation to both groups. His score exceeds approximately the same percentage of persons in both distributions, and this percentage can be determined if the form of the distribution is known. If, however, one distribution is markedly skewed and the other normal, a z score of +1.00 might exceed only 50 percent of the cases in one group but would exceed 84 percent in the other.

In order to achieve comparability of scores from dissimilarly shaped distributions, nonlinear transformations may be employed to fit the scores to any specified type of distribution curve. The mental age and percentile scores described in earlier sections represent nonlinear transformations, but they are subject to other limitations already discussed. Although under certain circumstances another type of distribution may be more appropriate, the normal curve is usually employed for this purpose. One of the chief reasons for this choice is that most raw score distributions approximate the normal curve more closely than they do any other type of curve. Moreover, physical measures such as height and weight, which use equal-unit scales derived through physical operations, generally yield normal distributions.[4] Another important advantage of the normal curve is that it has many useful mathematical properties, which facilitate further computations.

Normalized standard scores are standard scores expressed in terms of a distribution that has been transformed to fit a normal curve. Such scores can be computed by reference to tables giving the percentage of cases falling at different SD distances from the mean of a normal curve. First, the percentage of persons in the standardization sample falling at or above each raw score is found. This percentage is then located in the normal curve frequency table, and the corresponding normalized standard score is obtained. Normalized standard scores are expressed in the same form as linearly derived standard scores, viz., with a mean of zero and an SD of 1. Thus, a normalized score of zero indicates that the individual falls at the mean of a normal curve, excelling 50 percent of the group. A score of −1.00 means that he surpasses approximately 16 percent of the group; and a score of +1.00, that he surpasses 84 percent. These percentages correspond to a distance of 1 SD below and 1 SD above the mean of a normal curve, respectively, as can be seen by reference to the bottom line of Figure 9.

Like linearly derived standard scores, normalized standard scores can be put into any convenient form. If the normalized standard score is multiplied by 10 and added to or subtracted from 50, it is converted into a T score, a type of score first proposed by McCall (1922). On this scale, a

---

[4] Partly for this reason and partly as a result of other theoretical considerations, it has frequently been argued that, by normalizing raw scores, an equal-unit scale could be developed for psychological measurement similar to the equal-unit scales of physical measurement. This, however, is a debatable point that involves certain questionable assumptions.

score of 50 corresponds to the mean, a score of 60 to 1 *SD* above the mean, and so forth. Another well-known transformation is represented by the *stanine* scale, developed by the United States Air Force during World War II. This scale provides a single-digit system of scores with a mean of 5 and an *SD* of approximately 2.[5] The name *stanine* (a contraction of "standard *nine*") is based on the fact that the scores run from 1 to 9. The restriction of scores to single-digit numbers has certain computational advantages, for each score requires only a single column on computer punched cards.

Raw scores can readily be converted to stanines by arranging the original scores in order of size and then assigning stanines in accordance with the normal curve percentages reproduced in Table 5. For example, if the

TABLE 5 NORMAL CURVE PERCENTAGES FOR USE IN STANINE CONVERSION

Percentage	4	7	12	17	20	17	12	7	4
Stanine	1	2	3	4	5	6	7	8	9

group consists of exactly 100 persons, the 4 lowest-scoring persons receive a stanine score of 1, the next 7 a score of 2, the next 12 a score of 3, and so on. When the group contains more or fewer than 100 cases, the number corresponding to each designated percentage is first computed, and these numbers of cases are then given the appropriate stanines. Thus, out of 200 cases, 8 would be assigned a stanine of 1 (4 percent of 200 = 8). With 150 cases, 6 would receive a stanine of 1 (4 percent of 150 = 6). For any group containing from 10 to 100 cases, Bartlett and Edgerton (1966) have prepared a table whereby ranks can be directly converted to stanines. Because of their practical as well as theoretical advantages, stanines are being used increasingly, especially with aptitude and achievement tests.

Although normalized standard scores are the most satisfactory type of score for the majority of purposes, there are nevertheless certain technical objections to normalizing all distributions routinely. Such a transformation should be carried out only when the sample is large and representative and when there is reason to believe that the deviation from normality results from defects in the test rather than from characteristics of the sample or from other factors affecting the behavior under consideration. It should also be noted that when the original distribution of raw scores approximates normality, the linearly derived standard scores and the normalized standard scores will be very similar. Although the methods of deriving

[5] Kaiser (1958) proposed a modification of the stanine scale that involves slight changes in the percentages and yields an *SD* of exactly 2, thus being easier to handle quantitatively. Other variants are the *C* scale (Guilford, 1965, Ch. 19), consisting of 11 units and also yielding an *SD* of 2, and the 10-unit *sten* scale, with 5 units above and 5 below the mean (Canfield, 1951).

these two types of scores are quite different, the resulting scores will be nearly identical under such conditions. Obviously, the process of normalizing a distribution that is already virtually normal will produce little or no change. Whenever feasible, it is generally more desirable to obtain a normal distribution of raw scores by proper adjustment of the difficulty level of test items rather than by subsequently normalizing a markedly nonnormal distribution. With an approximately normal distribution of raw scores, the linearly derived standard scores will serve the same purposes as normalized standard scores.

THE DEVIATION IQ.   Another variant of standard scores is the deviation IQ. These so-called IQ's are actually standard scores with a mean of 100 and an *SD* that approximates the *SD* of the familiar Stanford-Binet IQ distribution. Although the *SD* of the 1937 Stanford-Binet IQ was not exactly constant at all ages, it fluctuated around a median value slightly greater than 16 (Terman & Merrill, 1937, p. 40). Hence, if an *SD* close to 16 is chosen in reporting standard scores on a newly developed test, the resulting scores can be interpreted in the same way as Stanford-Binet IQ's. Since Stanford-Binet IQ's have been in use for many years, testers and clinicians have become accustomed to interpreting and classifying test performance in terms of such IQ levels. They have learned what to expect from individuals with IQ's of 40, 70, 90, 130, and so forth. There are therefore certain practical advantages in the use of a derived scale that corresponds to the familiar distribution of Stanford-Binet IQ's. Such a correspondence of score units can be achieved by the selection of numerical values for the mean and *SD* that agree closely with those in the Stanford-Binet distribution.

It should be added that the use of the term "IQ" to designate such standard scores may at first be somewhat misleading. Such IQ's are not derived by the same methods employed in finding traditional ratio IQ's. They are not ratios of mental ages and chronological ages. For this reason, some criticism of the practice of calling such scores IQ's has been expressed. The justification lies in the general familiarity of the term "IQ," and in the fact that such scores *can* be interpreted as IQ's provided that their *SD* is approximately equal to that of previously known IQ's. Among the first tests to express scores in terms of deviation IQ's were the Wechsler Intelligence Scales. In these tests, the mean is 100 and the *SD* 15. Deviation IQ's are also used in a number of current group tests of intelligence and in the 1960 revision of the Stanford-Binet.

With the increasing use of deviation IQ's, it is important to remember that deviation IQ's from different tests are comparable only when they employ the same or closely similar values for the *SD*. This value should always be reported in the manual and carefully noted by the test user. If a test maker chooses a different value for the *SD* in making up his deviation IQ scale, the meaning of any given IQ on his test will be quite different from its meaning on other tests. These discrepancies are illustrated in Table 6, which shows the percentage of cases in normal distributions with SD's from 12 to 18 who would obtain IQ's at different levels. These SD values have actually been employed in the IQ scales of published tests. Table 6 shows, for example, that an IQ of 70 cuts off the lowest 3.1 percent when the SD is 16 (as in the 1960 Stanford-Binet); but it may cut off as few as 0.7 percent (SD = 12) or as many as 5.1 percent (SD = 18). An IQ of 70 has been used traditionally as a cutoff point for identifying mental retardation. The same discrepancies, of course, apply to IQ's of 130 and above, which might be used in selecting children for special classes for the gifted. The IQ range between 90 and 110, generally described as normal, may include as few as 42 percent or as many as 59.6 percent of the population, depending on the test chosen. To be sure, test publishers are making efforts to adopt the uniform SD of 16 in new tests and in new editions of earlier tests. There are still enough variations among currently available tests, however, to make the checking of the SD imperative.

TABLE 6 PERCENTAGE OF CASES AT EACH IQ INTERVAL IN NORMAL DISTRIBUTIONS WITH MEAN OF 100 AND GIVEN STANDARD DEVIATIONS

(Courtesy Test Department, Harcourt, Brace & World)

IQ Interval	Percentage Frequency			
	SD = 12	SD = 14	SD = 16	SD = 18
130 and above	0.7	1.6	3.1	5.1
120–129	4.3	6.3	7.5	8.5
110–119	15.2	16.0	15.8	15.4
100–109	29.8 } 59.6	26.1 } 52.2	23.6 } 47.2	21.0 } 42.0
90– 99	29.8	26.1	23.6	21.0
80– 89	15.2	16.0	15.8	15.4
70– 79	4.3	6.3	7.5	8.5
Below 70	0.7	1.6	3.1	5.1
Total	100.0	100.0	100.0	100.0

INTERRELATIONSHIPS OF DERIVED SCORES

At this stage in our discussion of derived scores, the reader may have become aware of a rapprochement among the various types of scores. Percentiles have gradually been taking on at least a graphic resemblance to normalized standard scores. Linear standard scores are indistinguishable from normalized standard scores if the original distribution of raw scores closely approximates the normal curve. Finally, standard scores have become IQ's and vice versa. In connection with the last point, a reexamination of the meaning of a ratio IQ on such a test as the Stanford-Binet will show that these IQ's can themselves be interpreted as standard scores. If we know that the 1937 Stanford-Binet IQ distribution had a mean of 100 and an *SD* of approximately 16, we can conclude that an IQ of 116 falls at a distance of 1 *SD* above the mean and represents a standard score of +1.00. Similarly, an IQ of 132 corresponds to a standard score of +2.00, an IQ of 76 to a standard score of −1.50, and so forth. Moreover, a Stanford-Binet ratio IQ of 116 corresponds to a percentile rank of approximately 84, because in a normal curve 84 percent of the cases fall below +1.00 *SD* (Figure 9).

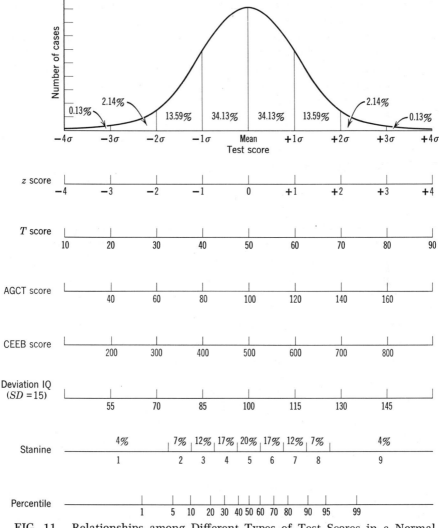

FIG. 11.   Relationships among Different Types of Test Scores in a Normal Distribution.

In Figure 11 are summarized the relationships that exist in a normal distribution among the types of scores so far discussed in this chapter. These include z scores, AGCT scores, College Entrance Examination Board (CEEB) scores, Wechsler deviation IQ's ($SD = 15$), T scores, stanines, and percentiles. Ratio IQ's on any test will coincide with the given deviation IQ scale if they are normally distributed and have an SD of 15. Any other normally distributed IQ could be added to the chart, provided we know its SD. If the SD is 20, for instance, then an IQ of 120 corresponds to $+1\ SD$, an IQ of 80 to $-1\ SD$, and so on.

In conclusion, the exact form in which scores are reported is dictated largely by convenience, familiarity, and ease of developing norms. Standard scores in any form (including the deviation IQ) have been widely replacing other types of scores because of certain advantages they offer with regard to test construction and statistical treatment of data. Most types of derived scores, however, are fundamentally similar if carefully derived and properly interpreted. When certain statistical conditions are met, each of these scores can be readily translated into any of the others.

EDUCATIONAL NORMS

It is customary to interpret scores on educational achievement tests in terms of *grade norms*. This practice is understandable, because the tests are employed within an academic setting. To describe a pupil's achievement as equivalent to seventh-grade performance in spelling, eighth-grade in reading, and fifth-grade in arithmetic has the same popular appeal as the use of mental age in the traditional intelligence tests. Such grade equivalents may also be employed to plot an achievement profile for the child.

Grade norms are found by computing the mean raw score obtained by children in each grade. Thus, if the average number of problems solved correctly on an arithmetic test by the fourth graders in the standardization sample is 23, then a raw score of 23 corresponds to a grade equivalent of 4. Intermediate grade equivalents, representing fractions of a grade, are usually found by interpolation, although theoretically they could be obtained directly by testing children at different times within the school year. Because the school year covers ten months, successive months can be expressed as decimals. For example, 4.0 refers to average performance at the beginning of the fourth grade (September testing), 4.5 refers to average performance at the middle of the grade (February testing), and so forth.

Despite their popularity, grade norms have several shortcomings. First, the content of instruction varies somewhat from grade to grade. Hence, grade norms are appropriate only for common subjects taught throughout the grade levels covered by the test. They are not generally applicable at the high school level, where many subjects may be studied for only one or two years. Even with subjects taught in each grade, however, the emphasis placed on different subjects may vary from grade to grade, and progress may therefore be more rapid in one subject than in another during a particular grade. In other words, grade units are obviously unequal and these inequalities occur irregularly in different subjects.

Grade norms are also subject to misinterpretation unless the test user keeps firmly in mind the manner in which they were derived. For example, if a fourth-grade child obtains a grade equivalent of 6.9 in arithmetic, it does *not* mean that he has mastered the arithmetic processes taught in the sixth grade. He undoubtedly obtained his score largely by superior performance in fourth-grade arithmetic. It certainly could not be assumed that he has the prerequisites for seventh-grade arithmetic. Finally, grade norms tend to be incorrectly regarded as performance standards. A sixth-grade teacher, for example, may assume that all pupils in her class should fall at or close to the sixth-grade norm in achievement tests. This misconception is certainly not surprising when grade norms are used. Yet individual differences within any one grade are such that the range of achievement test scores will inevitably extend over several grades.

Achievement test scores can also be interpreted in terms of *educational age norms*, analogous to mental age norms, but this practice is now rarely followed. The mean scores of children of a given chronological age are virtually identical with those of children in the corresponding grade. When differences exist, they may reflect only variations in promotion policy, which may be limited to the standardization sample employed. In establishing grade norms, moreover, it is customary to eliminate children whose ages are very atypical for their grades, in order to avoid such possible distortions. Under these conditions, age and grade norms would be closely similar. Because grade norms are educationally more meaningful, they would usually be preferred. The computation of a so-called educational quotient (EQ) by dividing educational age (EA) by CA meets with the additional type of difficulty described in connection with the IQ, and is not recommended. It is likely that the relationship between changes in EA and CA is such as to produce unequal variability of the EQ at different ages. No uniform interpretation could therefore be attached to a given EQ when obtained by children of different ages.

For the majority of testing purposes, the most satisfactory types of norms for educational achievement tests are those showing the child's position *within his own grade level*. Percentiles and stanines are commonly employed for this purpose. Computed by the procedures described earlier in this chapter, these norms are reported separately for each grade within the standardization sample. The individual's raw score is then converted into a percentile or a stanine by reference to the appropriate table for his own grade.

Most well-standardized achievement tests provide several kinds of norms, usually including grade equivalents, percentiles-within-grades, and stanines-within-grades. Table 7 illustrates the application of these three types of norms to the arithmetic computation test of the Stanford Achievement Test (1964) for the fifth-grade level. Percentile and stanine norms are reported for the beginning, middle, and end of each grade. Those reproduced in Table 7 are for the end of the fifth grade, applicable to tests administered in May or June.

TABLE 7 NORMS FOR ARITHMETIC COMPUTATION TEST OF STANFORD ACHIEVEMENT TEST, INTERMEDIATE II BATTERY, FORM W, 1964 EDITION
(Reproduced by permission of Harcourt, Brace & World)

Raw Score	Grade Equiv.	Percentile Rank[a]	Stanine[a]	Raw Score	Grade Equiv.	Percentile Rank[a]	Stanine[a]
39	12.9			19	6.0	58	
38	12.6			18	5.9	50	5
37	12.2			17	5.8	46	
36	11.7			16	5.6	42	
35	11.2			15	5.4	36	
34	10.5		9	14	5.2	30	4
33	9.9			13	5.0	24	
32	9.4						
31	8.8	99+		12	4.8	20	
30	8.5	99		11	4.6	16	3
29	8.2	96		10	4.4	11	
28	7.9	94		9	4.1	8	
27	7.7	92	8	8	3.8	6	
26	7.4	90		7	3.7	6	2
				6	3.5	4	
25	7.1	88					
24	6.8	84	7	5	3.3	2	
23	6.6	80		4	2.9	1	
				3	2.6	1−	1
22	6.5	76		2	2.2		
21	6.3	70	6	1	2.0 −		
20	6.2	64					

[a] End of grade 5: May–June

SPECIFICITY OF NORMS

THE NORMATIVE SAMPLE. Any norm, however expressed, is restricted to the particular normative population from which it was derived. The test user should never lose sight of the way in which norms are established.

Psychological test norms are in no sense absolute, universal, or permanent. They merely represent the test performance of the subjects constituting the standardization sample. In choosing such a sample, an effort is usually made to obtain a representative cross section of the population for which the test is designed.

In statistical terminology, a distinction is made between *sample* and *population*. The former refers to the group of individuals actually tested. The latter designates the larger, but similarly constituted, group from which the sample is drawn. For example, if we wish to establish norms of test performance for the population of 10-year-old, urban, public school boys, we might test a carefully chosen sample of 500 10-year-old boys attending public schools in several American cities. The sample would be checked with reference to geographical distribution, socioeconomic level, ethnic composition, and other relevant characteristics to ensure that it was truly representative of the defined population.

In the development and application of test norms, considerable attention should be given to the standardization sample. It is apparent that the sample on which the norms are based should be large enough to provide stable values. Another, similarly chosen sample of the same population should not yield norms that diverge appreciably from those obtained. Norms with a large sampling error would obviously be of little value in the interpretation of test scores.

Equally important is the requirement that the sample be representative of the population under consideration. Subtle selective factors that might make the sample unrepresentative should be carefully investigated. A number of such selective factors are illustrated in institutional samples. Because such samples are usually large and readily available for testing purposes, they offer an alluring field for the accumulation of normative data. The special limitations of these samples, however, should be carefully analyzed. Testing subjects in school, for example, will yield an increasingly superior selection of cases in the successive grades, owing to the progressive dropping out of the less able pupils. Nor does such elimination affect different subgroups equally. For example, the rate of selective elimination from school is greater for boys than for girls, and it is greater in lower than in higher socioeconomic levels.

Selective factors likewise operate in other institutional samples, such as prisoners, patients in mental hospitals, or institutionalized mental retardates. Because of many special factors that determine institutionalization itself, such groups are not representative of the entire population of criminals, psychotics, or mental retardates. For example, mental retardates with physical handicaps are more likely to be institutionalized than are the physically fit. Similarly, the relative proportion of lower-grade retardates will be much greater in institutional samples than in the total population.

Closely related to the question of representativeness of sample is the need for defining the specific population to which the norms apply. Obviously, one way of ensuring that a sample is representative is to restrict the population to fit the specifications of the available sample. For example, if the population is defined to include only 14-year-old schoolchildren rather than all 14-year-old children, then a school sample would be representative. Ideally, of course, the desired population should be defined in advance in terms of the objectives of the test. Then a suitable sample should be assembled. Practical obstacles in obtaining subjects, however, may make this goal unattainable. In such a case, it is far better to redefine the population more narrowly than to report norms on an ideal population which is not adequately represented by the standardization sample. In actual practice, very few tests are standardized on such broad populations as is popularly assumed. No test provides norms for the human species! And it is doubtful whether any tests give truly adequate norms for such broadly defined populations as "adult American men," "10-year-old American children," and the like. Consequently, the samples obtained by different test constructors often tend to be unrepresentative of their alleged populations and biased in different ways. Hence, the resulting norms are not comparable.

INTERTEST COMPARISONS.   An IQ, or any other score, should always be accompanied by the name of the test on which it was obtained. Test scores cannot be properly interpreted in the abstract; they must be referred to particular tests. If the school records show that Bill Jones received an IQ of 94 and Tom Brown an IQ of 110, such IQ's cannot be accepted at face value without further information. The positions of these two students might have been reversed by exchanging the particular tests that each was given in his respective school.

Similarly, an individual's relative standing in different functions may be grossly misrepresented through lack of comparability of test norms. Let us suppose that a student has been given a verbal comprehension test and a spatial aptitude test to determine his relative standing in the two fields. If the verbal ability test was standardized on a random sample of high school students, while the spatial test was standardized on a selected group of boys attending elective shop courses, the examiner might erroneously conclude that the individual is much more able along verbal than along spatial lines, when the reverse may actually be the case.

Still another example involves longitudinal comparisons of a single individual's test performance over time. If a schoolchild's cumulative record shows IQ's of 118, 115, and 101 at the fourth, fifth, and sixth grades, the first question to ask before interpreting these changes is, "What tests did he take on these three occasions?" The apparent decline may reflect no more than the differences among the tests. In that case, he would have obtained these scores even if the three tests had been administered within a week of each other.

There are three principal reasons to account for systematic variations among the scores obtained by the same individual on different tests. First, tests may differ in *content* despite their similar labels. So-called intelligence tests provide many illustrations of this confusion. Although commonly described by the same blanket term, one of these tests may include only verbal content, another may tap predominantly spatial aptitudes, and still another may cover verbal, numerical, and spatial content in about equal proportions. Second, the *scale units* may not be comparable. As explained earlier in this chapter, if IQ's on one test have an *SD* of 12 and IQ's on another have an *SD* of 18, then an individual who received an IQ of 112 on the first test is most likely to receive an IQ of 118 on the second. Third, the composition of the *standardization samples* used in establishing norms for different tests may vary. Obviously, the same individual will appear to have performed better when compared with an inferior group than when compared with a superior group.

Lack of comparability of either test content or scale units can usually be detected by reference to the test itself or to the test manual. Differences in the respective normative samples, however, are more likely to be overlooked. Such differences probably account for many otherwise unexplained discrepancies in test results.

There is considerable evidence to indicate that scores on many tests that are commonly used interchangeably do in fact differ materially. These discrepancies can be demonstrated whenever the same group of persons takes several tests. The results of different studies can also be combined if all groups have taken at least one common test, which serves as an *anchor test* in establishing equivalence of scores. Goldman (1961), for example, brought together the results of four separate studies, each of which had included an Otis intelligence test. Scores on this test were compared with scores on each of eight other tests that had been administered along with the Otis in one or more of the investigations. Through these comparisons, it was demonstrated that an IQ of 100 on the Otis might correspond to an IQ as low as 91 on one test and as high as 113 on another. Similar discrepancies were found in other portions of the IQ distribution.

NATIONAL ANCHOR NORMS.   One solution for the lack of comparability of norms is to use an anchor test to work out equivalency tables for scores on different tests. This was roughly approximated in the Goldman survey cited above, but the results were too crude for use in actual conversion of scores (Goldman, 1961, pp. 297–301). The separate investigators included in that survey had employed different levels and forms of the Otis as anchor tests, as well as different statistical procedures for finding score equivalence. Under better controlled conditions, however, it is possible to prepare tables showing what score in Test A is equivalent to each score in Test B. This can be done by the *equipercentile method,* in which scores are considered equivalent when they have equal percentiles in a given group. For example, if the 80th percentile in the same group corresponds to an IQ of 115 on Test A and to an IQ of 120 on Test B, then Test-A-IQ 115 is considered to be equivalent to Test-B-IQ 120. This approach has been followed to a limited extent by some test publishers, who have prepared equivalency tables for a few of their own tests (see, e.g., Lennon, 1966a).

A more direct approach is to employ an anchor test during the standardization of a new test, so that its norms will be adjusted to those of the anchor test in the first place. This procedure, too, has been utilized by some test publishers to ensure comparability of scores among their own tests. One example is provided by the Evaluation and Adjustment Series of high school achievement tests, published by Harcourt, Brace & World, which uses the Otis Quick-Scoring Mental Ability Tests as an anchor test (Maberly, 1966). Another example is to be found in the achievement testing program of the College Entrance Examination Board, in which the Scholastic Aptitude Test is the anchor test (Dyer & King, 1955; Angoff, 1968).

More ambitious proposals have been made from time to time for calibrating each new test against a single anchor test, which has itself been administered to a highly representative, national normative sample (Lennon, 1966b). No single anchor test, of course, could be used in establishing norms for *all* tests, regardless of content. What is required is a battery of anchor tests, all administered to the same national sample. Each new test could then be checked against the most nearly similar anchor test in the battery.

The data gathered in Project TALENT (Flanagan *et al.,* 1964) so far come closest to providing such an anchor battery for a high school population. Using a random sample of about 5 percent of the high schools in this country, the investigators administered a two-day battery of specially constructed aptitude, achievement, interest, and temperament tests to approximately 400,000 students in grades 9 through 12. Even with the availability of anchor data such as these, however, it must be recognized that independently developed tests can never be regarded as completely interchangeable.[6] At best, the use of national anchor norms would appreciably *reduce* the lack of comparability among tests, but it would not eliminate it.

Thus far the Project TALENT battery has been employed to calibrate several test batteries in use by the Navy and Air Force (Dailey, Shaycoft, & Orr, 1962; Shaycoft, Neyman, & Dailey, 1962). The general procedure is to administer both the Project TALENT battery and the tests to be calibrated to the same sample. Through correlational analysis, a composite of

---

[6] For an excellent analysis of some of the technical difficulties involved in efforts to achieve score comparability with different tests, see Angoff (1964, 1966, 1971).

Project TALENT tests is identified that is most nearly comparable to each test to be normed. By means of the equipercentile method, tables are then prepared giving the corresponding scores on the Project TALENT composite and on the particular test. For several other batteries, data have been gathered to identify the Project TALENT composite corresponding to each test in the battery (Cooley, 1965; Cooley & Miller, 1965). These batteries include the General Aptitude Test Battery of the United States Employment Service, the Differential Aptitude Tests, and the Flanagan Aptitude Classification Tests.

SPECIALIZED NORMS. Another approach to the nonequivalence of existing norms—and probably a more realistic one—is to standardize tests on more narrowly defined populations, so chosen as to suit the specific purposes of each test. In such cases, the limits of the normative population should be clearly reported with the norms. Thus, the norms might be said to apply to "employed clerical workers in large business organizations" or to "first-year engineering students." For many testing purposes, highly specific norms are desirable. Even when representative norms are available for a broadly defined population, it is often helpful to have separately reported *subgroup norms.* This is true whenever recognizable subgroups yield appreciably different scores on a particular test. The subgroups may be formed with respect to age, grade, type of curriculum, sex, geographical region, urban or rural environment, socioeconomic level, and many other factors. The use to be made of the test determines the type of differentiation that is most relevant, as well as whether general or specific norms are more appropriate.

Mention should also be made of *local norms,* often developed by the test users themselves within a particular setting. The groups employed in deriving such norms are even more narrowly defined than the subgroups considered above. Thus, an employer may accumulate norms on applicants for a given type of job within his company. A college admissions office may develop norms on its own student population. Or a single elementary school may evaluate the performance of individual pupils in terms of its own score distribution. These local norms are more appropriate than broad national norms for many testing purposes, such as the prediction of subsequent job performance or college achievement, the comparison of a child's relative achievement in different subjects, or the measurement of an individual's progress over time.

NONNORMATIVE SCALES

FIXED REFERENCE GROUP. Although most derived scores are computed in such a way as to provide an immediate normative interpretation of test performance, there are some notable exceptions. One type of nonnormative scale utilizes a fixed reference group in order to ensure *comparability and continuity* of scores, without providing normative evaluation of performance. With such a scale, normative interpretation requires reference to independently collected norms from a suitable population. Local or other specialized norms are often used for this purpose.

One of the clearest examples of scaling in terms of a fixed reference group is provided by the score scale of the College Board Scholastic Aptitude Test (Angoff, 1962, 1968; Dyer & King, 1955). Between 1926 (when this test was first administered) and 1941, SAT scores were expressed on a normative scale, in terms of the mean and *SD* of the candidates taking the test at each administration. As the number and variety of College Board member colleges increased and the composition of the candidate population changed, it was concluded that scale continuity should be maintained. Otherwise, an individual's score would depend on the characteristics of the group tested during a particular year. An even more urgent reason for scale continuity stemmed from the observation that students taking the SAT at certain times of the year performed more poorly than those taking it at other times, owing to the differential operation of selective factors. After 1941, therefore, all SAT scores were expressed in terms of the mean and *SD* of the approximately 11,000 candidates who took the test in 1941. These candidates constitute the fixed reference group employed in scaling all subsequent forms of the test. Thus, a score of 500 on any form of the SAT corresponds to the mean of the 1941 sample; a score of 600 falls 1 *SD* above that mean, and so forth.

To permit translation of raw scores on any form of the SAT into these fixed-reference-group scores, a short anchor test (or set of common items) is included in each form. Each new form is thereby linked to one or two earlier forms, which in turn are linked with other forms by a chain of items extending back to the 1941 form. These nonnormative SAT scores can then be interpreted by comparison with any appropriate distribution of scores, such as that of a particular college, a type of college, a region, etc. These specialized norms are more useful in making college admission decisions than would be annual norms based on the entire candidate population. Any changes in the candidate population over time, moreover, can be detected only with a fixed score scale. It will be noted that the principal difference between the fixed-reference-group scales under consideration and the previously discussed scales based on national anchor norms is that the latter require the choice of a single group that is accepted as *the* appropriate normative sample for all testing purposes. Apart from the practical difficulties in obtaining such a group, the assumption that any one group can serve this function satisfactorily is debatable.

Scales built from a fixed reference group are analogous in one respect to scales employed in physical measurement. In this connection, Angoff (1962, pp. 32–33) writes:

There is hardly a person here who knows the precise original definition of the length of the foot used in the measurement of height or distance, or which king it was whose foot was originally agreed upon as the standard; on the other hand, there is no one here who does not know how to evaluate lengths and distances in terms of this unit. Our ignorance of the precise original meaning or derivation of the foot does not lessen its usefulness to us in any way. Its usefulness derives from the fact that it remains the same over time and allows us to familiarize ourselves with it. Needless to say, precisely the same considerations apply to other units of measurement—the inch, the mile, the degree of Fahrenheit, and so on. In the field of psychological measurement it is similarly reasonable to say that the original definition of the scale is or should be of no consequence. What is of consequence is the maintenance of a constant scale—which, in the case of a multiple-form testing program, is achieved by rigorous form-to-form equating—and the provision of supplementary normative data to aid in interpretation and in the formation of specific decisions, data which would be revised from time to time as conditions warrant.

CONTENT MEANING.   A different kind of nonnormative scale attempts to give content meaning to scores by interpreting the individual's performance in terms of *what* he can do. In this type of scale, the frame of reference is not a population of persons but a content domain. Ebel (1962, p. 15) proposed the term *content standard score* [7] for this type of score, which he defines as "a number that indicates the percent of a systematic sample from a defined domain of tasks which an individual has performed correctly." Examples would be the kinds of arithmetic operations a person can perform and the size of his vocabulary. Although this type of score shares a content reference with the traditional "percentage correct" score, it differs from the latter in its use of a systematic sample and a uniformly defined content domain. Without such controls, content scores are uninterpretable, since they vary with the number and nature of items constituting any particular test.

The development of objective, interpretable content scores is admittedly difficult. Only exploratory efforts in this direction have been made thus far. But the approach is well worth considering and may be encountered increasingly in tests of the future. Ebel (1962) suggests two ways in which content-meaningful scores might be developed. The first is by means of "scale books" of carefully chosen representative items. An individual's score on a test could then be translated into the most probable percentage of these scale items that he could correctly complete.

The second proposed method is to build content meaning into the test by a systematic definition and sampling of item content. With sufficiently full and precise test specifications, it should prove possible for two test constructors to develop tests independently that would yield approximately the same raw scores. These raw scores would have direct content meaning by virtue of the way in which the tests were constructed. At this point we

[7] The term "standard" may be somewhat confusing in this context since it does not refer to a standard deviation, as it does in the more familiar standard scores.

would have come full circle and would have attained meaningful raw scores requiring no further conversion.

Flanagan (1962) describes several procedures followed in developing tests for Project TALENT, which were designed to facilitate the interpretation of scores in terms of content meaning. For example, literature items were selected in such a way as to permit an estimate of the portion of commonly recommended books that the individual had read. In a spelling test, scores could be expressed as the proportion of words in a 5,000-word list that the students were expected to spell correctly. Through a sampling of words from a group of dictionaries, a word-meaning test was developed that could provide an estimate of the student's vocabulary. A reading test was equated to samples of reading content at various difficulty levels, ranging from the works of Louisa Mae Alcott to those of Dostoevski, and from movie magazines to the *Saturday Review*.

Although content-meaning scores have been considered predominantly with regard to achievement tests, they are theoretically applicable to any kind of test. Scores on aptitude or personality tests could also be interpreted in terms of a defined content domain. It is interesting to speculate on the effects that this approach might have on the interpretation of intelligence test scores. To describe a child's intelligence test performance in terms of the specific intellectual skills and knowledge he has mastered might help to counteract the confusions and misconceptions that have become attached to the IQ.

CHAPTER **4**

Reliability

RELIABILITY REFERS to the consistency of scores obtained by the same individuals when re-examined with the same test on different occasions, or with different sets of equivalent items, or under other variable examining conditions. This concept of reliability underlies the computation of the *error of measurement* of a single score, whereby we can predict the range of fluctuation likely to occur in a single individual's score as a result of irrelevant, chance factors.

The concept of test reliability has been used to cover several aspects of score consistency. In its broadest sense, test reliability indicates the extent to which individual differences in test scores are attributable to "true" differences in the characteristics under consideration and the extent to which they are attributable to chance errors. To put it in more technical terms, measures of test reliability make it possible to estimate what proportion of the total variance of test scores is *error variance*. The crux of the matter, however, lies in the definition of error variance. Factors that might be considered error variance for one purpose would be classified under true variance for another. For example, if we are interested in measuring fluctuations of mood, then the day-by-day changes in scores on a test of cheerfulness-depression would be relevant to the purpose of the test and would hence be part of the true variance of the scores. If, on the other hand, the test is designed to measure more permanent personality characteristics, the same daily fluctuations would fall under the heading of error variance.

Essentially, any condition that is irrelevant to the purpose of the test represents error variance. Thus, when the examiner tries to maintain uniform testing conditions by controlling the testing environment, instructions, time limits, rapport, and other similar factors, he is reducing error variance and making the test scores more reliable. Despite optimum testing conditions, however, no test is a perfectly reliable instrument. Hence, every test should be accompanied by a statement of its reliability. Such a measure of reliability characterizes the test when administered under standard conditions and given to subjects similar to those constituting the normative sample.

The characteristics of this sample should therefore be specified, together with the type of reliability that was measured.

There could, of course, be as many varieties of test reliability as there are conditions affecting test scores, since any such conditions might be irrelevant for a certain purpose and would thus be classified as error variance. The types of reliability computed in actual practice, however, are relatively few. In this chapter, the principal techniques for measuring the reliability of test scores will be examined, together with the sources of error variance identified by each. Since all types of reliability are concerned with the degree of consistency or agreement between two independently derived sets of scores, they can all be expressed in terms of a *correlation coefficient*. Accordingly, the next section will consider some of the basic characteristics of correlation coefficients, in order to clarify its use and interpretation. More technical discussion of correlation, as well as more detailed specifications of computing procedures, can be found in any elementary textbook of educational or psychological statistics (e.g., Blommers & Lindquist, 1960; Guilford, 1965; Peatman, 1963).

THE CORRELATION COEFFICIENT

MEANING OF CORRELATION.   Essentially, a correlation coefficient (r) expresses the degree of correspondence, or *relationship,* between two sets of scores. Thus, if the top-scoring individual in variable 1 also obtains the top score in variable 2, the second-best individual in variable 1 is second best in variable 2, and so on down to the poorest individual in the group, then there would be a perfect correlation between variables 1 and 2. Such a correlation would have a value of $+1.00$.

A hypothetical illustration of a perfect positive correlation is shown in Figure 12. In this figure will be found a scatter diagram, or bivariate distribution. Each tally mark in this diagram indicates the score of one individual in both variable 1 (horizontal axis) and variable 2 (vertical axis). It will be noted that all of the 100 cases in the group are distributed along the diagonal running from the lower left- to the upper right-hand corner of the diagram. Such a distribution indicates a perfect positive correlation $(+1.00)$, since it shows that each individual occupies the same relative position in both variables. The closer the bivariate distribution of scores approaches this diagonal, the higher will be the positive correlation.

Figure 13 illustrates a perfect negative correlation (-1.00). In this case, there is a complete reversal of scores from one variable to the other. The best individual in variable 1 is the poorest in variable 2 and vice versa, this reversal being consistently maintained throughout the distribution. It will be noted that, in this scatter diagram, all individuals fall on the diagonal

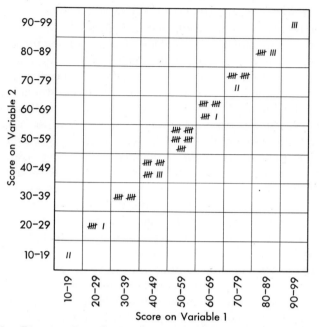

FIG. 12.   Bivariate Distribution for a Hypothetical Correlation of +1.00.

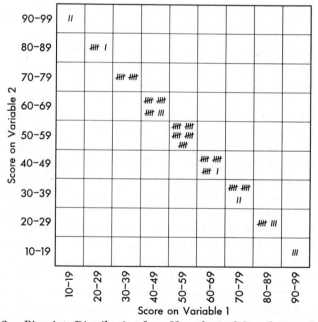

FIG. 13.   Bivariate Distribution for a Hypothetical Correlation of −1.00.

extending from the upper left- to the lower right-hand corner. This diagonal runs in the reverse direction from that in Figure 12.

A zero correlation indicates complete absence of relationship, such as might occur by chance. If each individual's name were pulled at random out of a hat to determine his position in variable 1, and if the process were repeated for variable 2, a zero or near-zero correlation would result. Under these conditions, it would be impossible to predict an individual's relative standing in variable 2 from a knowledge of his score in variable 1. The top-scoring subject in variable 1 might score high, low, or average in variable 2. Some individuals might by chance score above average in both variables, or below average in both; others might fall above average in one variable and below in the other; still others might be above the average in one and at the average in the second, and so forth. There would be no regularity in the relationship from one individual to another.

The coefficients found in actual practice generally fall between these extremes, having some value higher than zero but lower than 1.00. Correlations between measures of abilities are nearly always positive, although frequently low. When a negative correlation is obtained between two such variables, it usually results from the way in which the scores are expressed. For example, if time scores are correlated with amount scores, a negative correlation will probably result. Thus, if each subject's score on an arithmetic computation test is recorded as the number of seconds required to complete all items, while his score on an arithmetic reasoning test represents the number of problems correctly solved, a negative correlation can be expected. In such a case, the poorest (i.e., slowest) individual will have the numerically highest score on the first test, while the best individual will have the highest score on the second.

Correlation coefficients may be computed in various ways, depending on the nature of the data. The most common is the *Pearson Product-Moment Correlation Coefficient*. This correlation coefficient takes into account not only the individual's position in the group, but also the amount of his deviation above or below the group mean. It will be recalled that when each individual's standing is expressed in terms of standard scores, persons falling above the average receive positive standard scores, while those below the average receive negative scores. Thus, an individual who is superior in both variables to be correlated would have two positive standard scores; one inferior in both would have two negative standard scores. If, now, we multiply each individual's standard score in variable 1 by his standard score in variable 2, all of these products will be positive, provided that each individual falls on the same side of the mean on both variables. The Pearson correlation coefficient is simply the mean of these products. It will have a high positive value when corresponding standard scores are of equal sign and of approximately equal amount in the two variables. When subjects above the average in one variable are below the average in the other, the corresponding cross-products will be negative. If the sum of the cross-products is negative, the correlation will be negative. When some products are positive and some negative, the correlation will be close to zero.

In actual practice, it is not necessary to convert each raw score to a standard score before finding the cross-products, since this conversion can be made once for all after the cross-products have been added. There are many shortcuts for computing the Pearson correlation coefficient. The method demonstrated in Table 8 is not the quickest, but it illustrates the

TABLE 8 COMPUTATION OF PEARSON PRODUCT-MOMENT CORRELATION COEFFICIENT

Pupil	Arithmetic X	Reading Y	x	y	x^2	y^2	xy
Bill	41	17	+1	−4	1	16	− 4
Carol	38	28	−2	+7	4	49	−14
Geoffrey	48	22	+8	+1	64	1	8
Ann	32	16	−8	−5	64	25	40
Bob	34	18	−6	−3	36	9	18
Jane	36	15	−4	−6	16	36	24
Ellen	41	24	+1	+3	1	9	3
Ruth	43	20	+3	−1	9	1	− 3
Dick	47	23	+7	+2	49	4	14
Mary	40	27	0	+6	0	36	0
Σ	400	210	0	0	244	186	86
M	40	21					

$$\sigma_x = \sqrt{\frac{244}{10}} = \sqrt{24.40} = 4.94 \qquad \sigma_y = \sqrt{\frac{186}{10}} = \sqrt{18.60} = 4.31$$

$$r_{xy} = \frac{\Sigma xy}{N\,\sigma_x\,\sigma_y} = \frac{86}{(10)\,(4.94)\,(4.31)} = \frac{86}{212.91} = .40$$

meaning of the correlation coefficient more clearly than other methods that utilize computational shortcuts. Table 8 shows the computation of a Pearson r between the arithmetic and reading scores of 10 children. Next to each child's name are his scores in the arithmetic test (X) and the reading test (Y). The sums and means of the 10 scores are given under the respective columns. The third column shows the deviation (x) of each arithmetic score from the arithmetic mean; and the fourth column, the deviation (y) of each reading score from the reading mean. These deviations are squared in the next two columns, and the sums of the squares are used in computing the standard deviations of the arithmetic and reading scores by the method described in Chapter 3. Rather than dividing each x and y by its corresponding σ to find standard scores, we perform this division only once at the end, as shown in the correlation formula in Table 8.

The cross-products in the last column (xy) have been found by multiplying the corresponding deviations in the x and y columns. To compute the correlation (r), the sum of these cross-products is divided by the number of cases (N) and by the product of the two standard deviations $(\sigma_x \sigma_y)$.

STATISTICAL SIGNIFICANCE. The correlation of .40 found in Table 8 indicates a moderate degree of positive relationship between the arithmetic and reading scores. There is some tendency for those children doing well in arithmetic also to perform well on the reading test and vice versa, although the relation is not close. If we are concerned only with the performance of these 10 children, we can accept this correlation as an adequate description of the degree of relation existing between the two variables in this group. In psychological research, however, we are usually interested in generalizing beyond the particular *sample* of individuals tested to the larger *population* which they represent. For example, we might want to know whether arithmetic and reading ability are correlated among American schoolchildren of the same age as those we tested. Obviously, the 10 cases actually examined would constitute a very inadequate sample of such a population. Another comparable sample of the same size might yield a much lower or a much higher correlation.

There are statistical procedures for estimating the probable fluctuation to be expected from sample to sample in the size of correlations, means, standard deviations, and any other group measures. The question usually asked about correlations, however, is simply whether the correlation is significantly greater than zero. In other words, if the correlation in the population is zero, could a correlation as high as that obtained in our sample have resulted from sampling error alone? When we say that a correlation is "significant at the 1 percent (.01) level," we mean the chances are no greater than one out of 100 that the population correlation is zero. Hence, we conclude that the two variables are truly correlated. Significance levels refer to the risk of error we are willing to take in drawing conclusions from our data. If a correlation is said to be significant at the .05 level, the probability of error is 5 out of 100. Most psychological research applies either the .01 or the .05 levels, although other significance levels may be employed for special reasons.

The correlation of .40 found in Table 8 fails to reach significance even at the .05 level. As might have been anticipated, with only 10 cases it is difficult to establish a general relationship conclusively. With this size of sample, the smallest correlation significant at the .05 level is .63. Any correlation below that value simply leaves unanswered the question of whether the two variables are correlated in the population from which the sample was drawn.

The minimum correlations significant at the .01 and .05 levels for groups of different sizes can be found by consulting tables of the significance of correlations in any statistics textbook. For interpretive purposes in this book, however, only an understanding of the general concept is required. Parenthetically, it might be added that significance levels can be interpreted in a similar way when applied to other statistical measures. For example, to say that the difference between two means is significant at the .01 level indicates that we can conclude, with only one chance out of 100 of being wrong, that a difference in the obtained direction would be found if we tested the whole population from which our samples were drawn. For instance, if in the sample tested the boys had obtained a significantly higher mean than the girls on a mechanical comprehension test, we could conclude that the boys would also excel in the total population.

THE RELIABILITY COEFFICIENT.   Correlation coefficients have many uses in the analysis of psychological data. The measurement of test reliability represents one application of such coefficients. An example of a reliability coefficient, computed by the Pearson Product-Moment method, is to be found in Figure 14. In this case, the scores of 104 persons on two equiva-

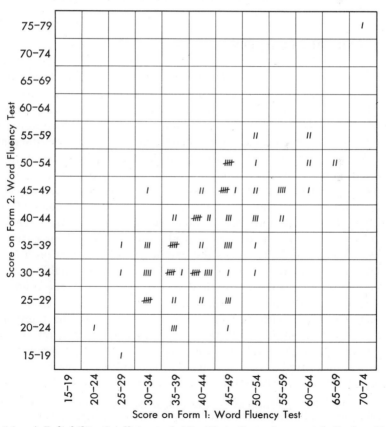

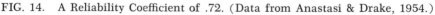

FIG. 14.   A Reliability Coefficient of .72. (Data from Anastasi & Drake, 1954.)

lent forms of a Word Fluency test [1] were correlated. In one form, the subjects were given five minutes to write as many words as they could that began with a given letter. The second form was identical, except that a different letter was employed. The two letters were chosen by the test authors as being approximately equal in difficulty for this purpose.

The correlation between the number of words written in the two forms of this test was found to be .72. This correlation is high and significant at the .01 level. With 104 cases, any correlation of .25 or higher is significant at this level. Nevertheless, the obtained correlation is somewhat lower than is desirable for reliability coefficients, which usually fall in the .80's or .90's. An examination of the scatter diagram in Figure 14 shows a typical bivariate distribution of scores corresponding to a high positive correlation. It will be noted that the tallies cluster close to the diagonal extending from the lower left- to the upper right-hand corner; the trend is definitely in this direction, although there is a certain amount of scatter of individual entries. In the following section, the use of the correlation coefficient in computing different measures of test reliability will be considered.

TYPES OF RELIABILITY

TEST-RETEST RELIABILITY.   The most obvious method for finding the reliability of test scores is by repeating the identical test on a second occasion. The reliability coefficient (r_{11}) in this case is simply the correlation between the scores obtained by the same persons on the two administrations of the test. The error variance corresponds to the random fluctuations of performance from one test session to the other. These variations may result in part from uncontrolled testing conditions, such as extreme changes in weather, sudden noises and other distractions, or a broken pencil point. To some extent, however, they arise from changes in the condition of the subject himself, as illustrated by illness, fatigue, emotional strain, worry, recent experiences of a pleasant or unpleasant nature, and the like. Retest reliability shows the extent to which scores on a test can be generalized over different occasions; the higher the reliability, the less susceptible the scores are to the random daily changes in the condition of the subject or of the testing environment.

When retest reliability is reported in a test manual, the interval over which it was measured should always be specified. Since retest correlations decrease progressively as this interval lengthens, there is not one but an infinite number of retest reliability coefficients for any test. It is also desirable to give some indication of relevant intervening experiences

[1] One of the subtests of the SRA Tests of Primary Mental Abilities for Ages 11 to 17. The data were obtained in an investigation by Anastasi and Drake (1954).

of the subjects on whom reliability was measured, such as educational or job experiences, counseling, psychotherapy, and so forth.

Apart from the desirability of reporting length of interval, what considerations should guide the choice of interval? Illustrations could readily be cited of tests showing high reliability over periods of a few days or weeks, but whose scores reveal an almost complete lack of correspondence when the interval is extended to as long as ten or fifteen years. Many preschool intelligence tests, for example, yield moderately stable measures within the preschool period, but are virtually useless as predictors of late childhood or adult IQ's. In actual practice, however, a simple distinction can usually be made. Short-range, random fluctuations that occur during intervals ranging from a few hours to a few months are generally included under the error variance of the test score. Thus, in checking this type of test reliability, an effort is made to keep the interval short. In testing young children, the period should be even shorter than for older subjects, since at early ages progressive developmental changes are discernible over a period of a month or even less. For any type of subject, the interval between retests should rarely exceed six months.

Any additional changes in the relative test performance of individuals that occur over longer periods of time are apt to be cumulative and progressive rather than entirely random. Moreover, they are likely to characterize a broader area of behavior than that covered by the test performance itself. Thus, an individual's general level of scholastic aptitude, mechanical comprehension, or artistic judgment may have altered appreciably over a ten-year period, owing to unusual intervening experiences. The individual's status may have either risen or dropped appreciably in relation to others of his own age, because of circumstances peculiar to his own home, school, or community environment, or for other reasons such as illness or emotional disturbance.

The extent to which such factors can affect an individual's psychological development provides an important problem for investigation. This question, however, should not be confused with that of the reliability of a particular test. When we measure the reliability of the Stanford-Binet, for example, we do not ordinarily correlate retest scores over a period of ten years, or even one year, but over a few weeks. To be sure, long-range retests have been conducted with such tests, but the results are generally discussed in terms of the "constancy of the IQ" or the predictability of adult intelligence from childhood performance, rather than in terms of the reliability of a particular test. The concept of reliability is generally restricted to short-range, random changes that characterize the test performance itself rather than the entire behavior domain that is being tested.

It should be noted that different behavior functions may themselves vary in the extent of daily fluctuation they exhibit. For example, steadiness of delicate finger movements is undoubtedly more susceptible to slight changes in the subject's condition than is verbal comprehension. If we wish to obtain an over-all estimate of the individual's habitual finger steadiness, we would probably require repeated tests on several days, whereas a single test session would suffice for verbal comprehension. Again we must fall back on an analysis of the purposes of the test and on a thorough understanding of the behavior the test is designed to predict.

Although apparently simple and straightforward, the test-retest technique presents difficulties when applied to most psychological tests. Practice will probably produce varying amounts of improvement in the retest scores of different individuals. Moreover, if the interval between retests is fairly short, the subjects may recall many of their former responses. In other words, the same pattern of right and wrong responses is likely to recur through sheer memory. Thus, the scores on the two administrations of the test are not independently obtained and the correlation between them will be spuriously high. The nature of the test itself may also change with repetition. This is especially true of problems involving reasoning or ingenuity. Once the subject has grasped the principle involved in the problem, or once he has worked out a solution, he can reproduce the correct response in the future without going through the intervening steps. Only tests that are not appreciably affected by repetition lend themselves to the retest technique. A number of sensory discrimination and motor tests would fall into this category. For the large majority of psychological tests, however, the retest technique is inappropriate.

ALTERNATE-FORM RELIABILITY. One way of avoiding the difficulties encountered in test-retest reliability is through the use of alternate forms of the test. The subjects can then be tested with one form on the first occasion and with another, comparable form on the second. The correlation between the scores obtained on the two forms represents the reliability coefficient of the test. It will be noted that such a reliability coefficient is a measure of both temporal stability and consistency of response to different item samples (or test forms). This coefficient thus combines two types of reliability. Since both types are important for most testing purposes, however, alternate-form reliability provides a useful measure for evaluating many tests.

The concept of item sampling, or *content sampling*, underlies not only alternate-form reliability but also other types of reliability to be discussed shortly. It is therefore appropriate to examine it more closely. Everyone has probably had the experience of taking a course examination in which he felt he had a "lucky break" because many of the items covered the very topics he happened to have studied most carefully. On another occasion, he may have had the opposite experience, finding an unusually large number of items on areas he had failed to review. This familiar situation illustrates error variance resulting from content sampling. To what extent do scores on this test depend on factors *specific* to the particular selection of items? If a different investigator, working independently, were to prepare another test in accordance with the same specifications, how much would an individual's score differ on the two tests?

Let us suppose that a 40-item vocabulary test has been constructed as a measure of general verbal comprehension. Now suppose that a second list of 40 different words is assembled for the same purpose, and that the items are constructed with equal care to cover the same range of difficulty as the first test. The differences in the scores obtained by the same individuals on these two tests illustrate the type of error variance under consideration. Owing to fortuitous factors in the past experience of different subjects, the relative difficulty of the two lists will vary somewhat from person to person. Thus, the first list might contain a larger number of words unfamiliar to individual A than does the second list. The second list, on the other hand, might contain a disproportionately large number of words unfamiliar to individual B. If the two individuals are approximately equal in their over-all word knowledge (i.e., in their "true scores"), B will nevertheless excel A on the first list, while A will excel B on the second. The relative standing of these two subjects will therefore be reversed on the two lists, owing to chance differences in the selection of items.

Like test-retest reliability, alternate-form reliability should always be accompanied by a statement of the length of the interval between test administrations, as well as a description of relevant intervening experiences. If the two forms are administered *in immediate succession,* the resulting correlation shows reliability across forms only, not across occasions. The error variance in this case represents fluctuations in performance from one set of items to another, but not fluctuations over time.

In the development of alternate forms, care should of course be exercised to ensure that they are truly parallel. Fundamentally, parallel forms of a test should be independently constructed tests designed to meet the same specifications. The tests should contain the same number of items, and the items should be expressed in the same form and should cover the same type of content. The range and level of difficulty of the items should also be equal. Instructions, time limits, illustrative examples, format, and all other aspects of the test must likewise be checked for comparability.

It should be added that the availability of parallel test forms is desirable for other reasons besides the determination of test reliability. Alternate forms are useful in follow-up studies or in investigations of the effects of some intervening experimental factor on test performance. The use of several alternate forms also provides a means of reducing the possibility of coaching or cheating.

Although much more widely applicable than test-retest reliability, alternate-form reliability also has certain limitations. In the first place, if the behavior functions under consideration are subject to a large practice effect, the use of alternate forms will reduce but not eliminate such an effect. To be sure, if all subjects were to show the same improvement with repetition, the correlation between their scores would remain unaffected, since adding a constant amount to each score does not alter the correlation coefficient. It is much more likely, however, that individuals will differ in amount of improvement, owing to extent of previous practice with similar material, motivation in taking the test, and other factors. Under these conditions, the practice effect represents another source of variance that will tend to reduce the correlation between the two test forms. If the practice effect is small, reduction will be negligible.

Another related question to be considered is the degree to which the nature of the test will change with repetition. In certain types of ingenuity problems, for example, any item involving the same principle can be readily solved by most subjects once they have worked out the solution to the first. In such a case, changing the specific content of the items in the second form would not suffice to eliminate this carry-over from the first form. Finally, it should be added that alternate forms are unavailable for many tests, because of the practical difficulties of constructing comparable forms. For all these reasons, other techniques for estimating test reliability are often required.

SPLIT-HALF RELIABILITY.   From a single administration of one form of a test it is possible to arrive at a measure of reliability by various split-half procedures. In such a way, two scores are obtained for each individual by dividing the test into comparable halves. It is apparent that split-half reliability provides a measure of consistency with regard to content sampling. Temporal stability of the scores does not enter into such reliability, because only one test session is involved. This type of reliability coefficient is sometimes called a coefficient of internal consistency, since only a single administration of a single form is required.

To find split-half reliability, the first problem is how to split the test in order to obtain the most nearly comparable halves. Any test can be divided in many different ways. In most tests, the first half and the second half would not be comparable, owing to differences in nature and difficulty level of items, as well as to the cumulative effects of warming up, practice, fatigue, boredom, and any other factors varying progressively from the beginning to the end of the test. A procedure that is adequate for most purposes is to find the scores on the odd and even items of the test. If the items were originally arranged in an approximate order of difficulty, such a division yields very nearly equivalent half-scores. One precaution to be observed in making such an odd-even split pertains to groups of items dealing with a single problem, such as questions referring to a particular mechanical diagram or to a given passage in a reading test. In this case, a whole group of items should be assigned intact to one or the other half. Were the items in such a group to be placed in different halves of the test, the similarity of the half-scores would be spuriously inflated, since any single error in understanding of the problem might affect items in both halves.

Once the two half-scores have been obtained for each subject, they may be correlated by the usual method. It should be noted, however, that this correlation actually gives the reliability of only a half-test. For example, if the entire test consists of 100 items, the correlation is computed between two sets of scores each of which is based on only 50 items. In both test-retest and alternate-form reliability, on the other hand, each score is based on the full number of items in the test.

Other things being equal, the longer a test, the more reliable it will be.[2] It is reasonable to expect that, with a larger sample of behavior, we can arrive at a more adequate and consistent measure. The effect that lengthening or shortening a test will have on its reliability coefficient can be estimated by means of the Spearman-Brown formula, given below:

$$r_{11} = \frac{nr'_{11}}{1 + (n-1)r'_{11}}$$

in which r_{11} is the estimated coefficient, r'_{11} the obtained coefficient, and n is the number of times the test is lengthened or shortened. Thus, if the number of test items is increased from 25 to 100, n is 4; if it is decreased from 60 to 30, n is 1/2. The Spearman-Brown formula is widely used in determining reliability by the split-half method, many test manuals reporting reliability in this form. When applied to split-half reliability, the formula always involves doubling the length of the test. Under these conditions, it can be simplified as follows:

$$r_{11} = \frac{2r'_{11}}{1 + r'_{11}}$$

A shortcut method for finding spit-half reliability was developed by Rulon (1939). It requires only the variance of the *differences* between each person's scores on the two half-tests (σ^2_d) and the variance of total scores (σ^2_x); these two values are substituted in the following formula:

$$r_{11} = 1 - \frac{\sigma^2_d}{\sigma^2_x}$$

It is interesting to note the relationship of this formula to the definition of error variance. Any difference between a person's scores on the two half-tests represents chance error. The variance of these differences, divided by the variance of total scores, gives the proportion of error variance in the

---

[2] Lengthening a test, however, will increase only its consistency in terms of content sampling, not its stability over time (see Cureton, 1965).

scores. When this error variance is subtracted from 1.00, it gives the proportion of "true" variance, which is equal to the reliability coefficient.

KUDER-RICHARDSON RELIABILITY. A fourth method for finding reliability, also utilizing a single administration of a single form, is based on the consistency of subjects' responses to all items in the test. This *interitem consistency* is influenced by two sources of error variance: 1) content sampling (as in alternate-form and split-half reliability); and 2) heterogeneity of the behavior domain sampled. The more homogeneous the domain, the higher the interitem consistency. For example, if one test includes only multiplication items, while another comprises addition, subtraction, multiplication, and division items, the former test will probably show more interitem consistency than the latter. In the latter, more heterogeneous test, one subject may perform better in subtraction than in any of the other arithmetic operations; another subject may score relatively well on the division items, but more poorly in addition, subtraction, and multiplication; and so on. A more extreme example would be represented by a test consisting of 40 vocabulary items, in contrast to one containing 10 vocabulary, 10 spatial relations, 10 arithmetic reasoning, and 10 perceptual speed items. In the latter test, there might be little or no relationship between a subject's performance on the different types of items.

It is apparent that test scores will be less ambiguous when derived from relatively homogeneous tests. Suppose that in the highly heterogeneous, 40-item test cited above, individuals A and B both obtain a score of 20. Can we conclude that the performances of the two subjects on this test were equal? Not at all. Subject A might have correctly completed 10 vocabulary items, 10 perceptual speed items, and none of the arithmetic reasoning and spatial relations items. In contrast, Subject B could have received a score of 20 by the successful completion of 5 perceptual speed, 5 spatial relations, and 10 arithmetic reasoning items.

Many other combinations could obviously produce the same total score of 20. This score would have a very different meaning when obtained through such dissimilar combinations of items. In the relatively homogeneous vocabulary test, on the other hand, a score of 20 would probably mean that the subject had succeeded with approximately the first 20 words, if the items were arranged in ascending order of difficulty. He might have failed two or three easier words and correctly responded to two or three more difficult items beyond the 20th, but such individual variations are slight in comparison with those found in a more heterogeneous test.

A highly relevant question in this connection is whether the criterion that the test is trying to predict is itself relatively homogeneous or heterogeneous. Although homogeneous tests are to be preferred because their scores permit fairly unambiguous interpretation, a single homogeneous test is obviously not an adequate predictor of a highly heterogeneous criterion. Moreover, in the prediction of a heterogeneous criterion, the heterogeneity of test items would not necessarily represent error variance. Traditional intelligence tests provide a good example of heterogeneous tests designed to predict heterogeneous criteria. In such a case, however, it may be desirable to construct several relatively homogeneous tests, each measuring a different phase of the heterogeneous criterion. Thus, unambiguous interpretation of test scores could be combined with adequate criterion coverage.

The most common procedure for finding interitem consistency is that developed by Kuder and Richardson (1937). As in the split-half methods, inter-item consistency is found from a single administration of a single test. Rather than requiring two half-scores, however, such a technique is based on an examination of performance on each item. Of the various formulas derived in the original article, the most widely applicable, commonly known as "Kuder-Richardson formula 20," is the following: [3]

$$r_{11} = \left(\frac{n}{n-1} \right) \frac{\sigma^2_t - \Sigma pq}{\sigma^2_t}$$

In this formula, r_{11} is the reliability coefficient of the whole test, n is the number of items in the test, and σ_t the standard deviation of total scores on the test. The only new term in this formula, Σpq, is found by tabulating the proportion of persons who pass (p) and the proportion who do not pass (q) each item. The product of p and q is computed for each item, and these products are then added for all items, to give Σpq. Since in the process of test construction p is often routinely recorded in order to find the difficulty level of each item, this method of determining reliability involves little additional computation.

It can be shown mathematically that the Kuder-Richardson reliability coefficient is actually the mean of all split-half coefficients resulting from different splittings of a test (Cronbach, 1951). The ordinary split-half coefficient, on the other hand, is based on a planned split designed to yield equivalent sets of items. Hence, unless the test items are highly homogeneous, the Kuder-Richardson coefficient will be lower than the split-half reliability. An extreme example will serve to highlight the difference. Suppose we construct a 50-item test out of 25 different kinds of items such that items 1 and 2 are vocabulary items, items 3 and 4 arithmetic reasoning, items 5 and 6 spatial orientation, and so on. The odd and even scores on this test could theoretically agree quite closely, thus yielding a high split-half reliability coefficient. The homogeneity of this test, however, would be very low, since there would be little consistency of performance among the entire set of 50 items. In this example, we would expect the Kuder-Richardson reliability to be much lower than the split-half reliability. It can be seen that the difference between Kuder-Richardson and split-

[3] A simple derivation of this formula can be found in Ebel (1965, pp. 320–327).

half reliability coefficients may serve as a rough index of the heterogeneity of a test.

SCORER RELIABILITY. It should now be apparent that the different types of reliability vary in the factors they subsume under error variance. In one case, error variance covers temporal fluctuations; in another, it refers to differences between sets of parallel items; and in still another, it includes any interitem inconsistency. On the other hand, the factors *excluded* from measures of error variance are broadly of two types: (*a*) those factors whose variance should remain in the scores, since they are part of the true differences under consideration; and (*b*) those irrelevant factors that can be experimentally controlled. For example, it is not customary to report the error of measurement resulting when a test is administered under distracting conditions or with a longer or shorter time limit than that specified in the manual. Timing errors and serious distractions can be empirically eliminated from the testing situation. Hence, it is not necessary to report special reliability coefficients corresponding to "distraction variance" or "timing variance."

Similarly, most tests provide such highly standardized procedures for administration and scoring that error variance attributable to these factors is negligible. This is particularly true of group tests designed for mass testing and machine scoring. With such instruments, we need only to make certain that the prescribed procedures are followed carefully. With clinical instruments employed in intensive individual examinations, on the other hand, there is evidence of considerable "examiner variance." Through special experimental designs, it is possible to separate this variance from that attributable to temporal fluctuations in the subject's condition or to the use of alternate test forms.

One source of error variance that can be checked quite simply is scorer variance. Certain types of tests—notably tests of creativity and projective tests of personality—leave a good deal to the judgment of the scorer. With such tests, there is as much need for a measure of scorer reliability as there is for the more usual reliability coefficients. Scorer reliability can be found by having a sample of test papers independently scored by two examiners. The two scores thus obtained by each subject are then correlated in the usual way, and the resulting correlation coefficient is a measure of scorer reliability. This type of reliability is commonly computed when subjectively scored instruments are employed in research. Test manuals should also report it when appropriate; a few already do so, and it is anticipated that the number will grow.

OVERVIEW. The different types of reliability coefficients discussed in this section are summarized in Tables 9 and 10. In Table 9 the operational procedures followed in obtaining each type of reliability are classified with regard to number of test forms and number of testing sessions required.

TABLE 9 Techniques for Measuring Reliability, in Relation to Test Form and Testing Session

Testing Sessions Required	Test Forms Required	
	One	Two
One	Split-Half Kuder-Richardson Scorer	Alternate-Form (Immediate)
Two	Test-Retest	Alternate-Form (Delayed)

Table 10 shows the sources of variance treated as error variance by each procedure.

Any reliability coefficient may be interpreted directly in terms of the *percentage of score variance* attributable to different sources. Thus, a reliability coefficient of .85 signifies that 85 percent of the variance in test scores depends on true variance in the trait measured and 15 percent depends on error variance (as operationally defined by the specific procedure followed). The statistically sophisticated reader may recall that it is the *square* of a correlation coefficient that represents proportion of common variance. Actually, the proportion of true variance in test scores is the square of the correlation between scores on a single form of the test

TABLE 10 Sources of Error Variance in Relation to Reliability Coefficients

Type of Reliability Coefficient	Error Variance
Test-Retest	Time sampling
Alternate-Form (Immediate)	Content sampling
Alternate-Form (Delayed)	Time sampling and Content sampling
Split-Half	Content sampling
Kuder-Richardson	Content sampling and Content heterogeneity
Scorer	Interscorer differences

and true scores, free from chance errors. This correlation, known as the index of reliability,[4] is equal to the square root of the reliability coefficient ($\sqrt{r_{11}}$). When the index of reliability is squared, the result is the reliability

[4] Derivations of the index of reliability, based on two different sets of assumptions, are given by Gulliksen (1950c, Chs. 2 and 3).

coefficient (r_{11}), which can therefore be interpreted directly as the percentage of true variance.

Experimental designs that yield more than one type of reliability coefficient on the same subjects permit the analysis of total score variance into different components. Let us consider the following hypothetical example. Forms A and B of a creativity test have been administered with a two-month interval to 100 sixth-grade children. The resulting alternate-form reliability is .70. From the responses on either form, a split-half reliability coefficient can also be computed.[5] This coefficient, stepped up by the Spearman-Brown formula, is .80. Finally, a second scorer has rescored a random sample of 50 papers, from which a scorer reliability of .92 is obtained. The three reliability coefficients can now be analyzed to yield the error variances shown in Table 11 and Figure 15. It will be noted that by subtracting the error variance attributable to content sampling alone (split-half reliability) from the error variance attributable to both content and

TABLE 11   ANALYSIS OF SOURCES OF ERROR VARIANCE IN A HYPOTHETICAL TEST

From delayed alternate-form reliability:	$1 - .70 = .30$ (time sampling plus content sampling)
From split-half, Spearman-Brown reliability:	$1 - .80 = .20*$ (content sampling)
Difference	$.10*$ (time sampling)
From scorer reliability:	$1 - .92 = .08*$ (interscorer difference)

Total Measured Error Variance* $= .20 + .10 + .08 = .38$
True Variance $= 1 - .38 = .62$

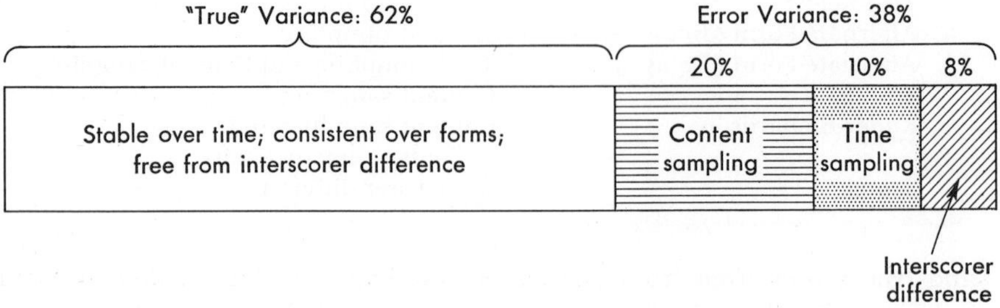

FIG. 15.   Percentage Distribution of Score Variance in a Hypothetical Test.

[5] For a better estimate of the coefficient of internal consistency, split-half correlations could be computed for each form and the two coefficients averaged by the appropriate statistical procedures.

time sampling (alternate-form reliability), we find that .10 of the variance can be attributed to time sampling alone. Adding the error variances attributable to content sampling (.20), time sampling (.10), and interscorer difference (.08) gives a total error variance of .38 and hence a true variance of .62. These proportions, expressed in the more familiar percentage terms, are shown graphically in Figure 15.

RELIABILITY OF SPEEDED TESTS

Both in test construction and in the interpretation of test scores, an important distinction is that between the measurement of speed and of power. A pure *speed test* is one in which individual differences depend entirely on speed of performance. Such a test is constructed from items of uniformly low difficulty, all of which are well within the ability level of the persons for whom the test is designed. The time limit is made so short that no one can finish all the items. Under these conditions, each person's score reflects only the speed with which he worked. A pure *power test,* on the other hand, has a time limit long enough to permit everyone to attempt all items. The difficulty of the items is steeply graded, and the test includes some items too difficult for anyone to solve, so that no one can get a perfect score. It will be noted that both speed and power tests are designed to prevent the achievement of perfect scores. The reason for such a precaution is that perfect scores are indeterminate, since it is impossible to know how much higher the individual's score would have been if more items, or more difficult items, had been included. To enable each individual to show fully what he is able to accomplish, the test must provide adequate ceiling, either in number of items or in difficulty level.

In actual practice, the distinction between speed and power tests is one of degree, most tests depending on both power and speed in varying proportions. Information about these proportions is needed for each test in order not only to understand what the test measures but also to choose the proper procedures for evaluating its reliability. Single-trial reliability coefficients, such as those found by odd-even or Kuder-Richardson techniques, are inapplicable to speeded tests. To the extent that individual differences in test scores depend on speed of performance, reliability coefficients found by these methods will be spuriously high. An extreme example will help to clarify this point. Let us suppose that a 50-item test depends entirely on speed, so that individual differences in score are based wholly on number of items attempted, rather than on errors. Then, if individual A obtains a score of 44, he will obviously have 22 correct odd items and 22 correct even items. Similarly, individual B, with a score of 34, will have odd and even scores of 17 and 17, respectively. Consequently, except for accidental careless errors on a few items, the correlation between odd and even scores would be perfect, or +1.00. Such a correlation, however, is entirely spurious and provides no information about the reliability of the test.

An examination of the procedures followed in finding both split-half and Kuder-Richardson reliability will show that both are based on the consistency in *number of errors* made by the subject. If, now, individual differences in test scores depend, not on errors, but on speed, the measure of reliability must obviously be based on consistency in *speed of work*. When test performance depends on a combination of speed and power, the single-trial reliability coefficient will fall below 1.00, but it will still be spuriously high. As long as individual differences in test scores are appreciably affected by speed, single-trial reliability coefficients cannot be properly interpreted.

What alternative procedures are available to determine the reliability of significantly speeded tests? If the test-retest technique is applicable, it would be appropriate. Similarly, equivalent-form reliability may be properly employed with speed tests. Split-half techniques may also be used, provided that the split is made in terms of time rather than in terms of items. In other words, the half-scores must be based on separately timed parts of the test. One way of effecting such a split is to administer two equivalent halves of the test with separate time limits. For example, the odd and even items may be separately printed on different pages, and each set of items given with one-half the time limit of the entire test. Such a procedure is tantamount to administering two equivalent forms of the test in immediate succession. Each form, however, is half as long as the test proper, while the subjects' scores are normally based on the whole test. For this reason, either the Spearman-Brown or some other appropriate formula should be used to find the reliability of the whole test.

If it is not feasible to administer the two half-tests separately, an alternative procedure is to divide the total time into quarters, and to find a score for each of the four quarters. This can easily be done by having the subjects mark the item on which they are working whenever the examiner gives a prearranged signal. The number of items correctly completed within the first and fourth quarters can then be combined to represent one half-score, while those in the second and third quarters can be combined to yield the other half-score. Such a combination of quarters tends to balance out the cumulative effects of practice, fatigue, and other factors. This method is especially satisfactory when the items are not steeply graded in difficulty level.

When is a test appreciably speeded? Under what conditions must the special precautions discussed in this section be observed? Obviously, the mere employment of a time limit does not signify a speed test. If all subjects finish within the given time limit, speed of work plays no part in determining the scores. Percentage of subjects who fail to complete the test might be taken as a crude index of speed versus power. Even when no one finishes the test, however, the role of speed may be negligible. For example, if every subject completes exactly 40 items of a 50-item test, individual differences with regard to speed are entirely absent, although no one had time to attempt all the items.

The essential question, of course, is: "To what extent are individual differences in test scores attributable to speed?" In more technical terms, we want to know what proportion of the total variance of test scores is speed variance. This proportion can be estimated roughly by finding the variance of number of items completed by different persons and dividing it by the variance of total test scores (σ^2_c/σ^2_t). In the example cited above, in which every individual finishes 40 items, the numerator of this fraction would be zero, since there are no individual differences in number of items completed ($\sigma^2_c = 0$). The entire index would thus equal zero in a pure power test. On the other hand, if the total test variance (σ^2_t) is attributable to individual differences in speed, the two variances will be equal and the ratio will be 1.00. Several more refined procedures have been developed for determining this proportion, but their detailed consideration falls beyond the scope of this book.[6]

An example of the effect of speed on single-trial reliability coefficients is provided by data collected in an investigation of the first edition of the SRA Tests of Primary Mental Abilities for Ages 11 to 17 (Anastasi & Drake, 1954). In this study, the reliability of each test was first determined by the usual odd-even procedure. These coefficients, given in the first row of Table 12, are closely similar to those reported in the test manual. Reliability coefficients were then computed by correlating scores on separately timed halves. These coefficients are shown in the second row of Table 12. Calculation of speed indexes showed that the Verbal Meaning

TABLE 12   RELIABILITY COEFFICIENTS OF FOUR OF THE SRA TESTS OF PRIMARY MENTAL ABILITIES FOR AGES 11 TO 17 (1ST EDITION)
(Data from Anastasi & Drake, 1954)

Reliability Coefficient Found by:	Verbal Meaning	Reasoning	Space	Number
Single-trial odd-even method	.94	.96	.90	.92
Separately timed halves	.90	.87	.75	.83

test is primarily a power test, while the Reasoning test is somewhat more dependent on speed. The Space and Number tests proved to be highly speeded. It will be noted in Table 12 that, when properly computed, the reliability of the Space test is .75, in contrast to a spuriously high odd-even

[6] See, e.g., Cronbach & Warrington, 1951; Gulliksen, 1950b, 1950c; Guttman, 1955; Helmstadter & Ortmeyer, 1953.

coefficient of .90. Similarly, the reliability of the Reasoning test drops from .96 to .87, and that of the Number test drops from .92 to .83. The reliability of the relatively unspeeded Verbal Meaning test, on the other hand, shows a negligible difference when computed by the two methods.

DEPENDENCE OF RELIABILITY COEFFICIENTS ON THE SAMPLE TESTED

HETEROGENEITY.   An important factor influencing the size of a reliability coefficient is the nature of the group on which reliability is measured. In the first place, any correlation coefficient is affected by the range of individual differences in the group. If every member of a group were alike in spelling ability, then the correlation of spelling with any other ability would be zero in that group. It would obviously be impossible, within such a group, to predict an individual's standing in any other ability from a knowledge of his spelling score.

Another, less extreme, example is provided by the correlation between two aptitude tests, such as a verbal comprehension and an arithmetic reasoning test. If these tests were administered to a highly homogeneous sample, such as a group of 300 college sophomores, the correlation between the two would probably be close to zero. There is little relationship, within such a selected sample of college students, between any individual's verbal ability and his numerical reasoning ability. On the other hand, were the tests to be given to a heterogeneous sample of 300 persons, ranging from institutionalized mentally retarded persons to college graduates, a high correlation would undoubtedly be obtained between the two tests. The mentally retarded would obtain poorer scores than the college graduates on *both* tests, and similar relationships would hold for other subgroups within this highly heterogeneous sample.

Examination of the hypothetical scatter diagram given in Figure 16 will further illustrate the dependence of correlation coefficients on the variability, or extent of individual differences, within the group. This scatter diagram shows a high positive correlation in the entire, heterogeneous group, since the entries are closely clustered about the diagonal extending from lower left- to upper right-hand corners. If, now, we consider only the subgroup falling within the small rectangle in the upper right-hand portion of the diagram, it is apparent that the correlation between the two variables is close to zero. Individuals falling within this restricted range in both variables represent a highly homogeneous group, as did the college sophomores mentioned above.

Like all correlation coefficients, reliability coefficients depend on the variability of the sample within which they are found. Thus, if the reliability coefficient reported in a test manual was determined in a group rang-

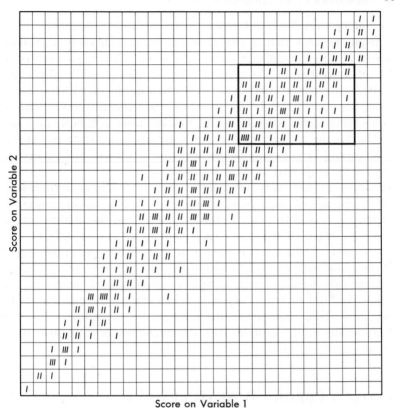

FIG. 16.   The Effect of Restricted Range upon a Correlation Coefficient.

ing from fourth-grade children to high school students, it cannot be assumed that the reliability would be equally high within, let us say, an
eighth-grade sample. When a test is to be used to discriminate individual
differences within a more homogeneous sample than the standardization
group, the reliability coefficient should be redetermined on such a sample.
Formulas for estimating the reliability coefficient to be expected when
the standard deviation of the group is increased or decreased are available
in elementary statistics textbooks. It is preferable, however, to recompute
the reliability coefficient empirically on a group comparable to that on
which the test is to be used. For tests designed to cover a wide range of
age or ability, the test manual should report separate reliability coefficients
for relatively homogeneous subgroups within the standardization sample.

ABILITY LEVEL.   Not only does the reliability coefficient vary with the
extent of individual differences in the sample, but it may also vary between
groups differing in average ability level. These differences, moreover, cannot usually be predicted or estimated by any statistical formula, but can
be discovered only by empirical tryout of the test on groups differing in

age or ability level. Such differences in the reliability of a single test may arise from the fact that a slightly different combination of abilities is measured at different difficulty levels of the test. Or it may result from the statistical properties of the type of score employed, as in the Stanford-Binet IQ's (McNemar, 1942, Ch. 6; Terman & Merrill, 1960). Thus, for different ages and for different IQ levels, the reliability coefficient of the Stanford-Binet varies from .83 to .98. In other tests, reliability may be relatively low for the younger and less able groups, since their scores are unduly influenced by guessing. Under such circumstances, the particular test should not be employed at these levels.

It is apparent that every reliability coefficient should be accompanied by a full description of the type of group on which it was determined. Special attention should be given to the variability and the ability level of the sample. The reported reliability coefficient is applicable only to samples similar to that on which it was computed. A desirable and growing practice in test construction is to fractionate the standardization sample into more homogeneous subgroups, with regard to age, sex, grade level, occupation, and the like, and to report separate reliability coefficients for each subgroup. Under these conditions, the reliability coefficients are more likely to be applicable to the samples with which the test is to be used in actual practice.

STANDARD ERROR OF MEASUREMENT

INTERPRETATION OF INDIVIDUAL SCORES. The reliability of a test may be expressed in terms of the standard error of measurement ($\sigma_{meas.}$), also called the standard error of a score. This measure is particularly well suited to the interpretation of individual scores. For many testing purposes, it is therefore more useful than the reliability coefficient. The standard error of measurement can be easily computed from the reliability coefficient of the test, by the following formula:

$$\sigma_{meas.} = \sigma_1\sqrt{1 - r_{11}}$$

in which σ_1 is the standard deviation of the test scores and r_{11} the reliability coefficient, both computed on the same group. For example, if deviation IQ's on a particular intelligence test have a standard deviation of 15 and a reliability coefficient of .89, the $\sigma_{meas.}$ of an IQ on this test is: $15\sqrt{1 - .89} = 15\sqrt{.11} = 15(.33) = 5$.

To understand what the $\sigma_{meas.}$ tells us about a score, let us suppose that we had a set of 100 IQ's obtained with the above test by a single boy, Jim. Because of the types of chance errors discussed in this chapter, these scores will vary, falling into a normal distribution around Jim's true score.

The mean of this distribution of 100 scores can be taken as the true score and the standard deviation of the distribution can be taken as the $\sigma_{meas.}$· Like any standard deviation, this standard error can be interpreted in terms of the normal curve frequencies discussed in Chapter 3 (see Figure 6). It will be recalled that between the mean and $\pm 1\sigma$ there are approximately 68 percent of the cases in a normal curve. Thus, we can conclude that the chances are roughly 2:1 (or 68:32) that Jim's IQ on this test will fluctuate between $\pm 1\sigma_{meas.}$ or 5 points on either side of his true IQ. If his true IQ is 110, we would expect him to score between 105 and 115 about two-thirds (68 percent) of the time.

If we want to be more certain of our prediction, we can choose higher odds than 2:1. Reference to Figure 6 in Chapter 3 shows that $\pm 3\sigma$ covers 99.7 percent of the cases. It can be ascertained from normal curve frequency tables that a distance of 2.58σ on either side of the mean includes exactly 99 percent of the cases. Hence, the chances are 99:1 that Jim's IQ will fall within $2.58\sigma_{meas.}$, or $(2.58)(5) = 13$ points, on either side of his true IQ. We can thus state at the 99 percent confidence level (with only one chance of error out of 100) that Jim's IQ on any single administration of the test will lie between 97 and 123 ($110 - 13$ and $110 + 13$). If Jim were given 100 equivalent tests, his IQ would fall outside this band of values only once.

In actual practice, of course, we do not have the true scores, but only the scores obtained in a single test administration. Under these circumstances, we could try to follow the above reasoning in the reverse direction. If an individual's obtained score is unlikely to deviate by more than $2.58\sigma_{meas.}$ from his true score, we could argue that his *true* score must lie within $2.58\sigma_{meas.}$ of his *obtained* score. Although we cannot assign a probability to this statement for any given obtained score, we *can* say that the statement would be correct for 99 percent of all the cases. On the basis of this reasoning, Gulliksen (1950c, pp. 17–20) proposed that the standard error of measurement be used as illustrated above to estimate the reasonable limits of the true score for persons with any given obtained score. It is in terms of such "reasonable limits" that the error of measurement is customarily interpreted in psychological testing and it will be so interpreted in this book.

The standard error of measurement and the reliability coefficient are obviously alternative ways of expressing test reliability. Unlike the reliability coefficient, the error of measurement is independent of the variability of the group on which it is computed. Expressed in terms of individual scores, it remains unchanged when found in a homogeneous or a heterogeneous group. On the other hand, being reported in score units, the error of measurement will not be directly comparable from test to test. The usual problems of comparability of units would thus arise when errors of measurement are reported in terms of arithmetic problems, words in a vocabulary test, and the like. Hence, if we want to compare the reliability of *different tests,* the reliability coefficient is the better measure. To interpret *individual scores,* the standard error of measurement is more appropriate.

INTERPRETATION OF SCORE DIFFERENCES. It is particularly important to consider test reliability and errors of measurement when evaluating the *differences* between two scores. Thinking in terms of the range within which each score may fluctuate serves as a check against overemphasizing small differences between scores. Such caution is desirable both when comparing test scores of different persons and when comparing the scores of the same individual in different abilities. Similarly, changes in scores following instruction or other experimental variables need to be interpreted in the light of errors of measurement.

A frequent question about test scores concerns the individual's relative standing in different areas. Is Jane more able along verbal than along numerical lines? Does Tom have more aptitude for mechanical than for verbal activities? If Jane scored higher on the verbal than on the numerical subtests on an aptitude battery and Tom scored higher on the mechanical than on the verbal, how sure can we be that they would still do so on a retest with another form of the battery? In other words, could the score differences have resulted merely from the chance selection of specific items in the particular verbal, numerical, and mechanical tests employed?

Because of the growing interest in the interpretation of score profiles, test publishers have been developing report forms that permit the evaluation of scores in terms of their errors of measurement. Outstanding examples are provided by the Sequential Tests of Educational Progress (STEP) and the School and College Ability Tests (SCAT), both of which will be discussed in later chapters. Tables of norms and individual profiles for these tests are constructed in terms of percentile bands, based on the obtained score and its standard error. Each band covers a distance of approximately one standard error of measurement on either side of the obtained score. An example of a SCAT profile plotted with such percentile bands is given in Figure 17. In interpreting the profiles, the test user is advised to attach no importance to differences between scores whose percentile bands overlap, as they do for the verbal and quantitative scores in Figure 17.

Another way of handling the problem of reliability in intraindividual comparisons is illustrated by the Differential Aptitude Tests (DAT), one of whose score profiles was reproduced in Chapter 3 (Figure 10). In this case, the standard error of the difference between each pair of scores was computed, and it was found that a difference of about 10 standard score points between any two DAT subtests is significant at the .05 level. The report form was so designed that such a difference corresponded to a distance of 1 inch. Hence, the test user can assume that differences of 1 inch or more on the profile are significant at the .05 level or better.

SCAT STUDENT PROFILE
SCHOOL AND COLLEGE ABILITY TESTS

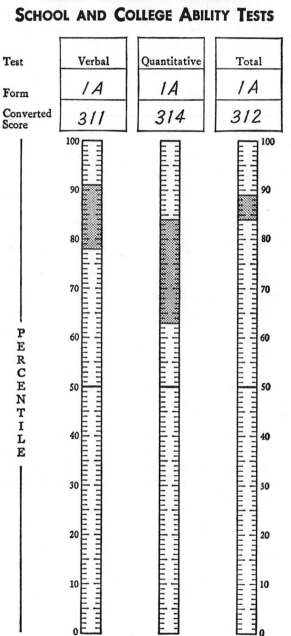

Test	Verbal	Quantitative	Total
Form	*1A*	*1A*	*1A*
Converted Score	*311*	*314*	*312*

FIG. 17. SCAT Student Profile, Illustrating Use of Percentile Bands. (Reproduced by permission of Cooperative Test Division, Educational Testing Service.)

It is well to bear in mind that the standard error of the difference between two scores is larger than the error of measurement of either of the two scores. This follows from the fact that this difference is affected by the chance errors present in *both* scores. The standard error of the difference between two scores can be found from the standard errors of measurement of the two scores by the following formula:

$$\sigma_{diff.} = \sqrt{\sigma^2_{meas._1} + \sigma^2_{meas._2}}$$

in which $\sigma_{diff.}$ is the standard error of the difference between the two scores, and $\sigma_{meas._1}$ and $\sigma_{meas._2}$ are the standard errors of measurement of the separate scores. By substituting $SD\sqrt{1 - r_{11}}$ for $\sigma_{meas._1}$ and $SD\sqrt{1 - r_{2II}}$ for $\sigma_{meas._2}$, we may rewrite the formula directly in terms of reliability coefficients, as follows:

$$\sigma_{diff.} = SD\sqrt{2 - r_{1I} - r_{2II}}$$

In this substitution, the same *SD* was used for tests 1 and 2, since their scores would have to be expressed in terms of the same scale before they could be compared.

We may illustrate the application of the above procedure to two of the DAT subtests, Verbal Reasoning and Mechanical Reasoning, whose split-half reliabilities are .88 and .85, respectively. DAT scores are reported as standard scores with a mean of 50 and an *SD* of 10. Hence, the standard error of the difference between the scores on these two tests can be found as follows:

$$\sigma_{diff.} = 10\sqrt{2 - .88 - .85} = 5.20$$

To determine how large a score difference could be obtained by chance at the .05 level, we multiply the standard error of the difference (5.20) by 1.96. The result is approximately 10. Thus the difference between an individual's Verbal and Mechanical scores must be 10 points or greater to be significant at the .05 level.

CHAPTER 5

Validity:
Basic Concepts

THE VALIDITY of a test concerns *what* the test measures and *how well* it does so. In this connection, we should guard against accepting the test name as an index of what the test measures. Test names provide short, convenient labels for identification purposes. Most test names are far too broad and vague to furnish meaningful clues to the behavior area covered, although increasing efforts are being made to use more specific and operationally definable test names. The trait measured by a given test can be defined only through an examination of the objective sources of information and empirical operations utilized in establishing its validity (Anastasi, 1950). Moreover, the validity of a test cannot be reported in general terms. No test can be said to have "high" or "low" validity in the abstract. Its validity must be determined with reference to the particular use for which the test is being considered.

Fundamentally, all procedures for determining test validity are concerned with the relationships between performance on the test and other independently observable facts about the behavior characteristics under consideration. The specific methods employed for investigating these relationships are numerous and have been described by various names. In the *Standards for Educational and Psychological Tests and Manuals* (1966), these procedures are classified under three principal categories: content, criterion-related, and construct validity. Each of these types of validation procedures will be considered in one of the following sections, and the relations among them will be examined in a concluding section. Techniques for analyzing and interpreting validity data with reference to practical decisions will be discussed in Chapter 6.

CONTENT VALIDITY

NATURE.   Content validity involves essentially the systematic examination of the test content to determine whether it covers a representative sample of the behavior domain to be measured. Such a validation procedure is commonly used in evaluating achievement tests. This type of test is designed to measure how well the individual has mastered a specific skill or course of study. It might thus appear that mere inspection of the content of the test should suffice to establish its validity for such a purpose. A test of multiplication, spelling, or American history would seem to be valid by definition if it consists of multiplication, spelling, or American history items, respectively.

The solution, however, is not so simple as it appears to be.[1] One difficulty is presented by the problem of content sampling. The content area to be tested must be systematically analyzed to make certain that all major aspects are adequately covered by the test items, and in the correct proportions. For example, a test can easily become overloaded with those aspects of the field that lend themselves more readily to the preparation of objective items. The content area under consideration should be fully described in advance, rather than being defined after the test has been prepared. A well-constructed achievement test should cover the objectives of instruction, not just its subject matter. Content must therefore be broadly defined to include major objectives, such as the application of principles and the interpretation of data, as well as factual knowledge. Moreover, content validity depends on the relevance of the individual's test responses to the behavior area under consideration, rather than on the apparent relevance of item content. Mere inspection of the test may fail to reveal the processes actually used by subjects in taking the test.

It is also important to guard against any tendency to overgeneralize regarding the content sampled by the test. For instance, a multiple-choice spelling test may measure the ability to recognize correctly and incorrectly spelled words. But it cannot be assumed that such a test also measures ability to spell correctly from dictation, frequency of misspellings in written compositions, and other aspects of spelling ability (Ahlström, 1964; Knoell & Harris, 1952). Still another difficulty arises from the possible inclusion of irrelevant factors in the test scores. For example, a test designed to measure the effects of instruction in such areas as mathematics or mechanics may be unduly influenced by the ability to understand verbal directions or by speed of performing simple, routine tasks.

SPECIFIC PROCEDURES.   Content validity is built into a test from the outset through the choice of appropriate items. The preparation of test

---

[1] Further discussions of content validity from several angles can be found in Ebel (1956), Gulliksen (1950), Huddleston (1956), and Lennon (1956).

items is preceded by a thorough and systematic examination of relevant course syllabi and textbooks, as well as by consultation with subject-matter experts. On the basis of the information thus gathered, *test specifications* are drawn up for the item writers. These specifications should show the topics to be covered, the kinds of learning to be tested (in terms of objectives), and the relative importance of individual topics and objectives. On this basis, the number of items of each kind to be prepared on each topic can be established. The most systematic way of setting up such specifications is in terms of a two-way table, with objectives across the top and topics in the left-hand column. Not all cells in such a table, of course, need to have items, since certain kinds of learning may be unsuitable or irrelevant for certain topics. It might be added that such a specification table will also prove helpful in the preparation of teacher-made examinations for classroom use in any subject.

In listing objectives to be covered in an achievement test, the test constructor can be guided by an unusually thorough survey of educational objectives given in the *Taxonomy of Educational Objectives* (Bloom et al., 1956; Krathwohl et al., 1964). Prepared by a group of specialists in educational measurement, this handbook also provides examples of many types of items designed to test each objective. Two volumes are currently available, covering cognitive and affective domains, respectively. A third will extend the taxonomy to psychomotor skills. The major categories given in the cognitive domain include knowledge (in the sense of remembered facts, terms, methods, principles, etc.), comprehension, application, analysis, synthesis, and evaluation. The classification of affective objectives, concerned with the modification of attitudes, interests, values, and appreciation, includes five major categories: receiving, responding, valuing, organization, and characterization.

The discussion of content validity in the manual of an achievement test should include information on the subject-matter areas and the learning skills or objectives covered by the test, with some indication of the number of items in each category. In addition, the procedures followed in selecting categories and classifying items should be described. If subject-matter experts participated in the test-construction process, their number and professional qualifications should be stated. If they served as judges in classifying items, the directions they were given should be reported, as well as the extent of agreement among judges. Because curricula and course content change over time, it is particularly desirable to give the dates when subject-matter experts were consulted. Information should likewise be provided about number and nature of course syllabi and textbooks surveyed, including publication dates.

A number of empirical procedures may also be followed in order to supplement the content validation of an achievement test. Both total scores and performance on individual items can be checked for *grade progress*.

In general, those items are retained that show the largest gains in the percentages of children passing them from the lower to the upper grades. Figure 18 shows a portion of a table included in the *Teachers Guide* accompanying the Sequential Tests of Educational Progress (STEP). For every item in each test in this achievement battery, the information provided includes its classification with regard to learning skill and type of material, as well as the percentage of children in the normative sample who gave the right answer to the item in each of the grades for which that level of the test is designed. The 35 items included in Figure 18 represent one part of the Reading test for Form A, Level 4, which covers grades 4 to 6.

Other supplementary procedures that may be employed, when appropriate, include analyses of types of errors commonly made on a test and observation of the work methods employed by subjects. The latter could be done by testing subjects individually with instructions to "think aloud" while solving each problem. The contribution of speed can be checked by noting how many subjects fail to finish the test or by one of the more refined methods discussed in Chapter 4. To detect the possible irrelevant influence of ability to read instructions on test performance, scores on the test can be correlated with scores on a reading comprehension test. On the other hand, if the test is designed to measure reading comprehension, giving the questions without the reading passage on which they are based will show how many could be answered simply from the subjects' prior information or other irrelevant cues.

LIMITATIONS.   Especially when bolstered by such empirical checks as those illustrated above, content validity provides an adequate technique for evaluating achievement tests. It permits us to answer two questions that are basic to the validity of an achievement test: (1) Does the test cover a representative sample of curricular content? (2) Is test performance reasonably free from the influence of irrelevant variables?

For aptitude and personality tests, on the other hand, content validity is usually inappropriate and may, in fact, be misleading. Although considerations of relevance and effectiveness of content must obviously enter into the initial stages of constructing any test, eventual validation of aptitude or personality tests requires empirical verification by the procedures to be described in the following sections. These tests bear less intrinsic resemblance to the behavior domain they are trying to sample than do achievement tests. Consequently, the content of aptitude and personality tests can do little more than reveal the hypotheses that led the test constructor to choose a certain type of content for measuring a specified trait. Such hypotheses need to be empirically confirmed to establish the validity of the test.

Unlike achievement tests, aptitude and personality tests are not based on a specified course of instruction or uniform set of prior experiences from which test content can be drawn. Hence, in the latter tests, individuals are

| | | | | | SKILL | | | | | TYPE OF MATERIAL | | | | | | |
ITEM NUMBER	RIGHT ANSWER	GRADE 4 - % RIGHT (NORMS)	GRADE 5 - % RIGHT (NORMS)	GRADE 6 - % RIGHT (NORMS)	REPRODUCE IDEAS	TRANSLATE; MAKE INFERENCES	ANALYZE MOTIVATION	ANALYZE PRESENTATION	CRITICIZE	DIRECTIONS; ANNOUNCEMENT INFORMATION; EXPLANATION	LETTER	STORY	POETRY	OPINION; INTERPRETATION	PLAY	ITEM NUMBER
PART ONE																PART ONE
1	B	38	52	61			*				*					1
2	H	54	68	77		*					*					2
3	A	72	86	95	*						*					3
4	G	10	24	33			*				*					4
5	D	46	60	69				*			*					5
6	E	62	76	85	*							*				6
7	B	45	59	68	*							*				7
8	G	63	77	86	*							*				8
9	D	47	61	70		*	*					*				9
10	E	65	79	88			*					*				10
11	B	50	64	73	*					*						11
12	E	49	63	72	*					*						12
13	D	46	60	69	*					*						13
14	E	55	69	78		*				*						14
15	C	56	70	79				*		*						15
16	G	22	36	45		*					*					16
17	B	72	86	95	*						*					17
18	H	49	63	72	*						*					18
19	A	63	77	86			*				*					19
20	F	61	75	84			*				*					20
21	C	52	66	75	*				*					*		21
22	F	22	36	45		*			*					*		22
23	C	39	53	62	*				*					*		23
24	E	28	42	51				*	*					*		24
25	D	40	54	63		*			*					*		25
26	E	55	69	78	*										*	26
27	C	24	38	47				*							*	27
28	F	34	48	57		*									*	28
29	A	33	47	56			*								*	29
30	H	45	59	68		*									*	30
31	B	24	38	47				*	*	*						31
32	A	23	37	46			*		*	*						32
33	C	17	31	40	*				*	*						33
34	H	24	38	47		*			*	*						34
35	B	20	34	43	*			*	*	*						35

FIG. 18. Data on Content Validity, as Illustrated by a Portion of Item Table from STEP Reading Test, Form A, Level 4. (Reproduced by permission of Educational Testing Service.)

likely to vary more in the work methods or psychological processes employed in responding to the same test items. The identical test might thus measure different functions in different persons. Under these conditions, it would be virtually impossible to determine the psychological functions measured by the test from an inspection of its content. For example, college graduates might solve a problem in verbal or mathematical terms, while a mechanic would arrive at the same solution in terms of spatial visualization. Or a test measuring arithmetic reasoning among high school freshmen might measure only individual differences in speed of computation when given to college students. A specific illustration of the dangers of relying on content analysis of aptitude tests is provided by a study conducted with a digit-symbol substitution test (Burik, 1950). This test, generally regarded as a typical "code-learning" test, was found to measure chiefly motor speed in a group of high school students.

FACE VALIDITY. Content validity should not be confused with face validity. The latter is not validity in the technical sense; it refers, not to what the test actually measures, but to what it appears superficially to measure. Face validity pertains to whether the test "looks valid" to the subjects who take it, the administrative personnel who decide on its use, and other technically untrained observers. Fundamentally, the question of face validity concerns rapport and public relations. Although common usage of the term validity in this connection may make for confusion, face validity itself is a desirable feature of tests. Certainly if test content appears irrelevant, inappropriate, silly, or childish, the result will be poor cooperation, regardless of the actual validity of the test. When tests originally designed for children and developed within a classroom setting were first extended for adult use, they frequently met with resistance and criticism because of their lack of face validity. Especially in adult testing, it is not sufficient for a test to be objectively valid. It also needs face validity to function effectively in practical situations.

Face validity can often be improved by merely reformulating test items in terms that appear relevant and plausible in the particular setting in which they will be used. For example, if a test of simple arithmetic reasoning is constructed for use with machinists, the items should be worded in terms of machine operations rather than in terms of "how many oranges can be purchased for 36 cents" or other traditional schoolbook problems. Similarly, an arithmetic test for naval personnel can be expressed in naval terminology, without necessarily altering the functions measured. To be sure, face validity should never be regarded as a substitute for objectively determined validity. It cannot be assumed that improving the face validity of a test will improve its objective validity. Nor can it be assumed that when a test is modified so as to increase its face validity, its objective validity remains unaltered. The validity of the test in its final form will always need to be directly checked.

CRITERION-RELATED VALIDITY

Criterion-related validity indicates the effectiveness of a test in predicting an individual's behavior in specified situations. For this purpose, performance on the test is checked against a *criterion*, i.e., a direct and independent measure of that which the test is designed to predict. Thus, for a mechanical aptitude test, the criterion might be subsequent job performance as a machinist; for a scholastic aptitude test, it might be college grades; and for a neuroticism test, it might be associates' ratings or other available information on the subjects' behavior in various life situations.

LONG-TERM PREDICTION VERSUS DIAGNOSIS. The criterion measure against which test scores are validated may be obtained at approximately the same time as the test scores or after a stated interval. In an earlier version of the APA test *Standards,* a distinction was made between concurrent and predictive validity on the basis of these time relations between criterion and test. In the revised edition, this distinction has been de-emphasized, although the terms will undoubtedly remain for some time in test manuals. The term prediction can be used in the broader sense, to refer to prediction from the test to any criterion situation, or in the more limited sense of prediction over a time interval. It is in the latter sense that it is used in the expression predictive validity. The information provided by predictive validity is most relevant to tests used in the selection and classification of personnel. Hiring job applicants, selecting students for admission to college or professional schools, and assigning enlisted men to different military specialties represent examples of the sort of decisions requiring a knowledge of the predictive validity of tests. Other examples include the use of tests to screen out men likely to develop emotional disorders under military stress and the use of tests to identify psychiatric patients most likely to benefit from a particular therapy.

In a number of instances, concurrent validity is found merely as a substitute for predictive validity. It is frequently impracticable to extend validation procedures over the time required for predictive validity or to obtain a suitable preselection sample for testing purposes. As a compromise solution, therefore, tests are administered to a group on whom criterion data are already available. Thus, the test scores of college students may be compared with their cumulative grade-point average at the time of testing, or those of employees compared with their current job success.

For certain uses of psychological tests, on the other hand, concurrent validity is the most appropriate type and can be justified in its own right. The logical distinction between predictive and concurrent validity is based, not on time, but on the objectives of testing. Concurrent validity is relevant to tests employed for *diagnosis* of existing status, rather than prediction of future outcomes. The difference can be illustrated by asking: "Is Smith neurotic?" (concurrent validity) and "Is Smith likely to become neurotic?" (predictive validity).

Because the criterion for concurrent validity is always available at the time of testing, we might ask what function is served by the test in such situations. Basically, such tests provide a simpler, quicker, or less expensive substitute for the criterion data. For example, if the criterion consists of continuous observation of a patient during a two-week hospitalization period, a test that could sort out normals from neurotic and doubtful cases would appreciably reduce the number of persons requiring such extensive observation.

CRITERION CONTAMINATION. An essential precaution in finding the validity of a test is to make certain that the test scores do not themselves influence any individual's criterion status. For example, if a college instructor or a foreman in an industrial plant knows that a particular individual scored very poorly on an aptitude test, such knowledge might influence the grade given to the student or the rating assigned to the worker. Or a high-scoring individual might be given the benefit of the doubt when academic grades or on-the-job ratings are being prepared. Such influences would obviously raise the correlation between test scores and criterion in a manner that is entirely spurious or artificial.

This possible source of error in test validation is known as criterion contamination, since the criterion ratings become "contaminated" by the rater's knowledge of the test scores. To prevent the operation of such an error, it is absolutely essential that no person who participates in the assignment of criterion ratings have any knowledge of the subjects' test scores. For this reason, test scores employed in "testing the test" must be kept strictly confidential. It is sometimes difficult to convince teachers, employers, military officers, and other line personnel that such a precaution is essential. In their urgency to utilize all available information for practical decisions, such persons may fail to realize that the test scores must be put aside until the criterion data mature and validity can be checked.

COMMON CRITERIA. Any test may be validated against as many criteria as there are specific uses for it. Any method for assessing behavior in any situation could provide a criterion measure for some particular purpose. The criteria employed in finding the validities reported in test manuals, however, fall into a few common categories. Among the criteria most frequently employed in validating intelligence tests is some index of *academic achievement*. It is for this reason that such tests have often been more precisely described as measures of scholastic aptitude. The specific indices used as criterion measures include school grades, achievement test scores, promotion and graduation records, special honors and awards, and teachers' or instructors' ratings for "intelligence." Insofar as such ratings given within an academic setting are likely to be heavily colored by the individual's scholastic performance, they may be properly classified with the criterion of academic achievement.

The various indices of academic achievement have provided criterion data at all educational levels, from the primary grades to college and graduate school. Although employed principally in the validation of general intelligence tests, they have also served as criteria for certain multiple-aptitude and personality tests. In the validation of any of these types of tests for use in the selection of college students, for example, a common criterion is freshman grade-point average. This measure is the average grade in all courses taken during the freshman year, each grade being weighted by the number of course points for which it was received.

A variant of the criterion of academic achievement frequently employed with out-of-school adults is the amount of education the individual completed. It is expected that in general the more intelligent individuals continue their education longer, while the less intelligent drop out of school earlier. The assumption underlying this criterion is that the educational ladder serves as a progressively selective influence, eliminating those incapable of continuing beyond each step. Although it is undoubtedly true that college graduates, for example, represent a more highly selected group than elementary school graduates, the relation between amount of education and scholastic aptitude is far from perfect. Especially at the higher educational levels, economic, social, motivational, and other nonintellectual factors may influence the continuation of the individual's education. Moreover, with such concurrent validation, it is difficult to disentangle cause-and-effect relations. To what extent are the obtained differences in intelligence test scores simply the result of the varying amount of education? And to what extent could the test have predicted individual differences in subsequent educational progress? These questions can be answered only when the test is administered before the criterion data have matured, as in predictive validation.

In the development of special aptitude tests, a frequent type of criterion is based on *performance in specialized training*. For example, mechanical aptitude tests may be validated against final achievement in shop courses. Various business school courses, such as stenography, typing, or bookkeeping, provide criteria for aptitude tests in these areas. Similarly, performance in music or art schools has been employed in validating music or art aptitude tests. Several professional aptitude tests have been validated in terms of achievement in schools of law, medicine, dentistry, engineering, and other areas. In the case of custom-made tests, designed for use within a specific testing program, training records are a frequent source of criterion data. An outstanding illustration is the validation of Air Force pilot selection tests against performance in basic flight training.

Among the specific indices of training performance employed for criterion purposes may be mentioned achievement tests administered on completion of training, formally assigned grades, instructors' ratings, and successful completion of training versus elimination from the program. Multiple aptitude batteries have often been checked against grades in specific high school or college courses, in order to determine their validity as differential predictors. For example, scores on a verbal comprehension test may be compared with grades in English courses, spatial visualization scores with geometry grades, and so forth.

In connection with the use of training records in general as criterion measures, a useful distinction is that between intermediate and ultimate criteria. In the development of an Air Force pilot-selection test or a medical aptitude test, for example, the ultimate criteria would be combat performance and eventual achievement as a practicing physician, respectively. Obviously it would require a long time for such criterion data to mature. It is doubtful, moreover, whether a truly ultimate criterion is ever obtained in actual practice. Finally, even were such an ultimate criterion available, it would probably be subject to many uncontrolled factors that would render it relatively useless. For example, it would be difficult to evaluate the relative degree of success of physicians practicing different specialties and in different parts of the country. For these reasons, such intermediate criteria as performance records at some stage of training are frequently employed as criterion measures.

For many purposes, the most satisfactory type of criterion measure is that based on follow-up records of actual *job performance*. This criterion has been used to some extent in the validation of general intelligence as well as personality tests, and to a large extent in the validation of special aptitude tests. It is a common criterion in the validation of custom-made tests for specific jobs. The "jobs" in question may vary widely in both level and kind, including work in business, industry, the professions, the armed forces, and any other field. Most measures of job performance, although probably not representing ultimate criteria, at least provide good intermediate criteria for many testing purposes. In this respect they are to be preferred to training records. On the other hand, the measurement of job performance does not permit as much uniformity of conditions as is possible during training. Moreover, since it usually involves a longer follow-up, the criterion of job performance is likely to entail a loss in the number of available subjects. Because of the variation in the nature of nominally similar jobs in different organizations, test manuals reporting validity data against job criteria should describe not only the specific criterion measures employed but also the job duties performed by the workers.[2]

Validation by the method of *contrasted groups* generally involves a com-

---

[2] More detailed treatment of specific criterion measures that can be used as indices of job performance will be given in Chapter 16, in connection with the occupational use of tests.

posite criterion that reflects the cumulative and uncontrolled selective influences of everyday life. This criterion is ultimately based on survival within a particular group versus elimination therefrom. For example, in the validation of an intelligence test, the scores obtained by institutionalized mentally retarded children may be compared with those obtained by schoolchildren of the same age. In this case, the multiplicity of factors determining commitment to an institution for the mentally retarded constitutes the criterion. Similarly, the validity of a musical aptitude or a mechanical aptitude test may be checked by comparing the scores obtained by students enrolled in a music school or an engineering school, respectively, with the scores of unselected high school or college students.

To be sure, contrasted groups can be selected on the basis of any criterion, such as school grades, ratings, or job performance, by simply choosing the extremes of the distribution of criterion measures. The contrasted groups included in the present category, however, are distinct groups that have gradually become differentiated through the operation of the multiple demands of daily living. The criterion under consideration is thus more complex and less clearly definable than those previously discussed.

The method of contrasted groups is used quite commonly in the validation of personality tests. Thus, in validating a test of social traits, the test performance of salesmen or executives, on the one hand, may be compared with that of clerks or engineers, on the other. The assumption underlying such a procedure is that, with reference to many social traits, individuals who have entered and remained in such occupations as selling or executive work will as a group excel persons in such fields as clerical work or engineering. Similarly, college students who have engaged in many extracurricular activities may be compared with those who have participated in none during a comparable period of college attendance. Occupational groups have frequently been used in the development and validation of interest tests, such as the Strong Vocational Interest Blank, as well as in the preparation of attitude scales. Other groups sometimes employed in the validation of attitude scales include political, religious, geographical, or other special groups generally known to represent distinctly different points of view on certain issues.

A number of personality tests concerned with the measurement of emotional or social adjustment are validated on such groups as institutionalized delinquents versus nondelinquents, or on neurotics versus normals. During World War II, for example, comparisons were made between the scores obtained on certain personality tests by the general selectee population and the scores obtained by individuals discharged from service because of neuropsychiatric disability. The criterion in such a case is inability to remain in military service because of personality difficulties.

In the development of certain personality tests, psychiatric diagnosis is used both as a basis for the selection of items and as evidence of test validity. Psychiatric diagnosis may serve as a satisfactory criterion provided that it is based on prolonged observation and detailed case history, rather than on a cursory psychiatric interview or examination. In the latter case, there is no reason to expect the psychiatric diagnosis to be superior to the test score itself as an indication of the individual's emotional condition. Such a psychiatric diagnosis could not be regarded as a criterion measure, but rather as an indicator or predictor whose own validity would have to be determined.

Mention has already been made, in connection with other criterion categories, of certain types of *ratings* by school teachers, instructors in specialized courses, and job supervisors. To these can be added ratings by officers in military situations, ratings of students by school counselors, and ratings by coworkers, classmates, fraternity brothers or sorority sisters, and other groups of associates. The ratings discussed earlier represented merely a subsidiary technique for obtaining information regarding such criteria as academic achievement, performance in specialized training, or job success. We are now considering the use of ratings as the very core of the criterion measure. Under these circumstances, the ratings themselves define the criterion. Moreover, such ratings are not restricted to the evaluation of specific achievement, but involve a personal judgment by an observer regarding any of the variety of traits that psychological tests attempt to measure. Thus, the subjects in the validation sample might be rated on such characteristics as dominance, mechanical ingenuity, originality, leadership, or honesty.

Ratings have been employed in the validation of almost every type of test. They are particularly useful in providing criteria for personality tests, since objective criteria are much more difficult to find in this area. This is especially true of distinctly social traits, in which ratings based on personal contact may constitute the most logically defensible criterion. Although ratings may be subject to many judgmental errors, when obtained under carefully controlled conditions they represent a valuable source of criterion data. Techniques for improving the accuracy of ratings and for reducing common types of errors will be considered in Chapter 16.

Finally, correlations between a new test and *previously available tests* are frequently cited as evidence of validity. When the new test is an abbreviated or simplified form of a currently available test, the latter can properly be regarded as a criterion measure. Thus, a paper-and-pencil test might be validated against a more elaborate and time-consuming performance test whose validity had previously been established. Or a group test might be validated against an individual test. The Stanford-Binet, for example, has repeatedly served as a criterion in validating group tests. In such a case, the new test may be regarded at best as a crude approximation of the earlier one. It should be noted that unless the new test represents a simpler or shorter substitute for the earlier test, the use of the latter as a criterion is indefensible.

SPECIFICITY OF CRITERIA.   Criterion-related validity is most appropriate for local validation studies, in which the effectiveness of a test for a specific program is to be assessed. This is the approach followed, for example, when a given company wishes to evaluate a test for selecting applicants for one of its jobs or when a given college wishes to determine how well an academic aptitude test can predict the course performance of its students. Criterion-related validity can be best characterized as the practical validity of a test in a specified situation (Campbell, 1960; Dunnette, 1963b). This type of validation represents applied research, as distinguished from basic research, and as such it provides results that are less generalizable than the results of other procedures.

That criterion-related validity may be quite specific has been demonstrated repeatedly. Figure 19 gives examples of the wide variation in the correlations of a single type of test with criteria of job proficiency. The first graph shows the distribution of 72 correlations found between intelligence test scores and measures of the job proficiency of general clerks; the second graph summarizes in similar fashion 191 correlations between finger dexterity tests and the job proficiency of benchworkers. Although in both instances the correlations tend to cluster in a particular range of validity,

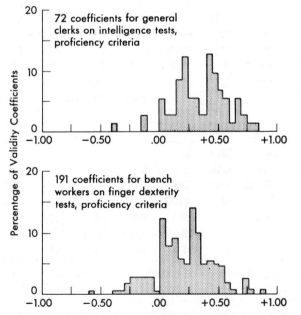

FIG. 19.   Examples of Variation in Validity Coefficients of Given Tests for Particular Jobs. (Adapted from Ghiselli, 1966, p. 29.)

the variation among individual studies is considerable. The validity coefficient may be high and positive in one study and negligible or even substantially negative in another.

Similar variation with regard to the prediction of course grades is illustrated in Figure 20. This figure shows the distribution of correlations obtained between course grades in English and scores on each of the subtests of the Differential Aptitude Tests. Thus, for the Verbal Reasoning test (VR), the largest number of validity coefficients fell between .50 and .59 among boys and between .60 and .69 among girls; but for both sexes, the correlations between VR and English grades in different courses or different schools ranged from .19 and below to .70 and above. Equally wide variations were found with the other subtests and, it might be added, with grades in other courses not included in Figure 20.

Some of the variation in validity coefficients against job criteria reported in Figure 19 results from differences among the specific tests employed in different studies to measure intelligence or finger dexterity. In the results of both Figures 19 and 20, moreover, some variation is attributable to differences in homogeneity and level of the groups tested. The range of validity coefficients found, however, is far wider than could be explained in

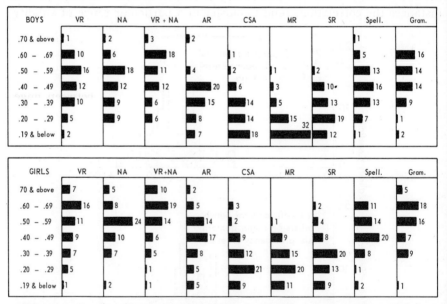

FIG. 20.   Graphic Summary of Validity Coefficients of the Differential Aptitude Tests (Forms L and M) for Course Grades in English. The bars and accompanying numbers in each column indicate the number of coefficients in the ranges given at the left. (From Fourth Edition Manual of the Differential Aptitude Tests, Forms L and M, 1966, p. 5–3. Reproduced by permission. Copyright © 1966, The Psychological Corporation, New York, N.Y. All rights reserved.)

these terms. Differences in the criteria themselves are undoubtedly a major reason for the variation observed among validity coefficients. Thus, the duties of office clerks or benchworkers may differ widely among companies or among departments in the same company. Similarly, courses in the same subject may differ in content, teaching method, instructor characteristics, bases for evaluating student achievement, and numerous other ways. Consequently, what appears to be the same criterion may represent a very different combination of traits in different situations.

Criteria may also vary over time in the same situation. For example, the validity coefficient of a test against job training criteria often differs from its validity against job performance criteria (Ghiselli, 1966). There is evidence that the traits required for successful performance of a given job or even a single task vary with the amount of practice or job experience of the individual (Fleishman & Hempel, 1954, 1955; Ghiselli & Haire, 1960). There is also abundant evidence to show that job criteria change over time for other reasons, such as changing nature of jobs, shifts in organizational goals, individual advancement in rank, and other temporal conditions (MacKinney, 1967; Prien, 1966). It is well known, of course, that educational curricula and course content change over time. In other words, the criteria most commonly used in validating intelligence and aptitude tests—namely, job performance and educational achievement—are dynamic rather than static. It follows that criterion-related validity is itself subject to temporal changes.

SYNTHETIC VALIDITY.   Criteria not only differ across situations and over time, but they are also likely to be complex (see, e.g., Richards et al., 1965). Success on a job, in school, or in other activities of daily life depends not on one trait but on many traits. Hence, practical criteria are likely to be multifaceted. Several different indicators or measures of job proficiency or academic achievement could thus be used in validating a test. Since these measures may tap different traits or combinations of traits, it is not surprising to find that they yield different validity coefficients for any given test. When different criterion measures are obtained for the same individuals, their intercorrelations are often quite low. For instance, accident records or absenteeism may show virtually no relation to productivity or error data for the same job (Seashore, Indik, & Georgopoulos, 1960). These differences, of course, are reflected in the validity coefficients of any given test against different criterion measures. Thus, a test may fail to correlate significantly with supervisors' ratings of job proficiency and yet show appreciable validity in predicting who will resign and who will be promoted at a later date (Albright, Smith, & Glennon, 1959).

Because of criterion complexity, validating a test against a composite criterion of job proficiency, academic achievement, or other similar accomplishments may be of questionable value and is certainly of limited generality. If different subcriteria are relatively independent, a more effective procedure is to validate each test against that aspect of the criterion it is best designed to measure. An analysis of these more specific relationships lends *meaning* to the test scores in terms of the multiple dimensions of criterion behavior (Dunnette, 1963; Ebel, 1961; Wallace, 1965). For example, one test might prove to be a valid predictor of a clerk's perceptual speed and accuracy in handling detail work, another of her ability to spell correctly, and still another of her ability to resist distraction.

If, now, we return to the practical question of evaluating a test or combination of tests for effectiveness in predicting a complex criterion such as success on a given job or in a given educational institution, we are faced with the necessity of conducting a separate validation study in each local situation and repeating it at frequent intervals. This is admittedly a desirable procedure and one that is often recommended in test manuals. In many situations, however, it is not feasible to follow this procedure because of insufficient number of available cases, lack of adequately trained personnel or time to carry out the investigation, difficulty of controlling conditions properly, or other practical limitations. For these reasons, personnel psychologists have shown increasing interest in a technique known as synthetic validity. First introduced by Lawshe (1952), the concept of synthetic validity has been defined by Balma (1959, p. 395) as "the inferring of validity in a specific situation from a systematic analysis of job elements, a determination of test validity for these elements, and a combination of elemental validities into a whole." Several procedures have been developed for gathering the needed empirical data and for combining these data to obtain an estimate of synthetic validity for a particular complex criterion (see, e.g., Fine, 1963; Guion, 1965; Lawshe & Balma, 1966, Ch. 14; McCormick, 1959; Primoff, 1959). Essentially, the process involves three steps: (1) detailed job analysis to identify the job elements and their relative weights; (2) analysis and empirical study of each test to determine the extent to which it measures proficiency in performing each of these job elements; and (3) finding the validity of each test for the given job synthetically from the weights of these elements in the job and in the test. Synthetic validity offers a promising tool for generalizing validity data from one job, academic program, or other complex criterion situation to another without actually conducting a separate validity study in each situation.

CONSTRUCT VALIDITY

The construct validity of a test is the extent to which the test may be said to measure a theoretical construct or trait. Examples of such constructs are intelligence, mechanical comprehension, verbal fluency, speed of walking, neuroticism, and anxiety. Focusing on a broader, more enduring, and more abstract kind of behavioral description than the previously discussed types of validity, construct validation requires the gradual accumulation of information from a variety of sources. Any data throwing light on the nature of the trait under consideration and the conditions affecting its development and manifestations are grist for this validity mill. Illustrations of specific techniques suitable for construct validation will be considered below.

AGE DIFFERENTIATION. A major criterion employed in the validation of a number of intelligence tests is age. Such tests as the Stanford-Binet and most preschool tests are checked against chronological age to determine whether the scores show a progressive increase with advancing age. Since abilities are expected to increase with age during childhood, it is argued that the test scores should likewise show such an increase, if the test is valid. The very concept of an age scale of intelligence, as initiated by Binet, is based on the assumption that "intelligence" increases with age, at least until maturity.

The criterion of age differentiation, of course, is inapplicable to any functions that do not exhibit clear-cut and consistent age changes. In the area of personality measurement, for example, it has found limited use. Moreover, it should be noted that age differentiation is essentially a negative rather than a positive criterion. Thus, if the test scores fail to improve with age, such a finding probably indicates that the test is not a valid measure of the abilities it was designed to sample. On the other hand, to prove that a test measures something that increases with age does not define the area covered by the test very precisely. A measure of height or weight would also show regular age increments, although it would obviously not be designated as an intelligence test.

A final point should be emphasized regarding the interpretation of the age criterion. A psychological test validated against such a criterion measures behavior characteristics that increase with age *under the conditions existing in the type of environment in which the test was standardized.* Because different cultures may stimulate and foster the development of dissimilar behavior characteristics, it cannot be assumed that the criterion of age differentiation is a universal one. Like all other criteria, it is circumscribed by the particular cultural setting in which it is derived.

CORRELATIONS WITH OTHER TESTS. Correlations between a new test and similar earlier tests are sometimes cited as evidence that the new test measures approximately the same general area of behavior as other tests designated by the same name, such as "intelligence tests" or "mechanical aptitude tests." Unlike the correlations found in criterion-related validity, these correlations should be moderately high, but not too high. If the new test correlates too highly with an already available test, without such added advantages as brevity or ease of administration, then the new test represents needless duplication.

Correlations with other tests are employed in still another way to demonstrate that the new test is relatively free from the influence of certain irrelevant factors. For example, a special aptitude test or a personality test should have a negligible correlation with tests of general intelligence or scholastic aptitude. Similarly, reading comprehension should not appreciably affect performance on such tests. Thus, correlations with tests of general intelligence, reading, or verbal comprehension are sometimes reported as indirect or negative evidence of validity. In these cases, high correlations would make the test suspect. Low correlations, however, would not in themselves insure validity. It will be noted that this use of correlations with other tests is similar to one of the supplementary techniques described under content validity.

FACTOR ANALYSIS. Of particular relevance to construct validity is factor analysis, a statistical procedure for the identification of psychological traits. Essentially, factor analysis is a refined technique for analyzing the interrelationships of behavior data. For example, if 20 tests have been given to 300 persons, the first step is to compute the correlations of each test with every other. An inspection of the resulting table of 190 correlations may itself reveal certain clusters among the tests, suggesting the location of common traits. Thus, if such tests as vocabulary, analogies, opposites, and sentence completion have high correlations with each other and low correlations with all other tests, we could tentatively infer the presence of a verbal comprehension factor. Because such an inspectional analysis of a correlation table is difficult and uncertain, however, more precise statistical techniques have been developed to locate the common factors required to account for the obtained correlations. These techniques of factor analysis will be examined further in Chapter 13, together with multiple aptitude tests developed by means of factor analysis.

In the process of factor analysis, the number of variables or categories in terms of which each individual's performance can be described is reduced from the number of original tests to a relatively small number of factors, or common traits. In the example cited above, five or six factors might suffice to account for the intercorrelations among the 20 tests. Each individual might thus be described in terms of his scores in the five or six factors, rather than in terms of the original 20 scores. A major purpose of factor analysis is to simplify the description of behavior by reducing the number of categories from an initial multiplicity of test variables to a few common factors, or traits.

After the factors have been identified, they can be utilized in describing the factorial composition of a test. Each test can thus be characterized in terms of the major factors determining its scores, together with the weight or loading of each factor. Such factor loadings also represent the correlations of the test with each factor, a correlation known as the *factorial va-*

lidity of the test. Thus, if the verbal comprehension factor has a weight of .66 in a vocabulary test, the factorial validity of this vocabulary test as a measure of the trait of verbal comprehension is .66. It should be noted that factorial validity is essentially the correlation of the test with whatever is common to a group of tests or other indices of behavior. The set of variables analyzed can, of course, include both test and nontest data. Ratings and other criterion measures can thus be utilized, along with other tests, to explore the factorial validity of a particular test and to define the common traits it measures.

INTERNAL CONSISTENCY.   In the published descriptions of certain tests, especially in the area of personality, the statement is made that the test has been validated by the method of internal consistency. The essential characteristic of this method is that the criterion is none other than the total score on the test itself. Sometimes an adaptation of the contrasted group method is used, extreme groups being selected on the basis of the total test score. The performance of the upper criterion group on each test item is then compared with that of the lower criterion group. Items that fail to show a significantly greater proportion of "passes" in the upper than in the lower criterion group are considered invalid, and are either eliminated or revised. Correlational procedures may also be employed for this purpose. For example, the biserial correlation between "pass-fail" on each item and total test score can be computed. Only those items yielding significant item-test correlations would be retained. A test whose items were selected by this method can be said to show internal consistency, since each item differentiates in the same direction as the entire test.

Another application of the criterion of internal consistency involves the correlation of subtest scores with total score. Many intelligence tests, for instance, consist of separately administered subtests (such as vocabulary, arithmetic, picture completion, etc.) whose scores are combined in finding the total test score. In the construction of such tests, the scores on each subtest are often correlated with total score and any subtest whose correlation with total score is too low is eliminated. The correlations of the remaining subtests with total score are then reported as evidence of the internal consistency of the entire instrument.

It is apparent that internal consistency correlations, whether based on items or subtests, are essentially measures of homogeneity. Because it helps to characterize the behavior domain or trait sampled by the test, the degree of homogeneity of a test has some relevance to its construct validity. Nevertheless, the contribution of internal consistency data to test validation is very limited. In the absence of data external to the test itself, little can be learned about what a test measures.

EFFECT OF EXPERIMENTAL VARIABLES ON TEST SCORES.   A further source of data for construct validation is provided by experiments on the effect of selected variables on test scores. Whether pitch discrimination as measured by a particular test is or is not susceptible to practice, for instance, can be checked by administering the test to the same subjects before and after a period of intensive practice. A test designed to measure anxiety-proneness can be administered to subjects who are subsequently put through a situation designed to arouse anxiety, such as taking an examination under distracting and stressful conditions. The initial anxiety test scores can then be correlated with physiological and other indices of anxiety expression during and after the examination. A different hypothesis regarding an anxiety test could be evaluated by administering the test before and after an anxiety-arousing experience and seeing whether test scores rise significantly on the retest. Positive findings from such an experiment would indicate that the test scores reflect current anxiety level. In a similar way, experiments can be designed to test any other hypothesis regarding the trait measured by a given test.

CONVERGENT AND DISCRIMINANT VALIDATION.   In a thoughtful analysis of construct validation, Campbell (1960) points out that in order to demonstrate construct validity we must show not only that a test correlates highly with other variables with which it should theoretically correlate, but also that it does not correlate significantly with variables from which it should differ. In an earlier article, Campbell and Fiske (1959) described the former process as convergent validation and the latter as discriminant validation. Correlation of a mechanical aptitude test with subsequent grades in a shop course would be an example of convergent validation. For the same test, discriminant validity would be illustrated by a low and insignificant correlation with scores on a reading comprehension test, since the latter would be an irrelevant variable in a test designed to measure mechanical aptitude.

It will be recalled that the requirement of low correlation with irrelevant variables was discussed in connection with supplementary and precautionary procedures followed in content validation. Such discriminant validation is especially relevant to the validation of personality tests, in which irrelevant variables may affect scores in a variety of ways.

Campbell and Fiske (1959) proposed a systematic experimental design for the dual approach of convergent and discriminant validation, which they called the *multitrait-multimethod matrix*. Essentially, this procedure requires the assessment of two or more traits by two or more methods. A hypothetical example provided by Campbell and Fiske will serve to illustrate the procedure. Table 13 shows all possible correlations among the scores obtained when three traits are each measured by three methods. The three traits could represent three personality characteristics, such as (A) dominance, (B) sociability, and (C) achievement motivation. The three methods could be (1) a self-report inventory, (2) a projective technique, and (3) associates' ratings. Thus, A_1 would indicate dominance scores on the self-report inventory, A_2 dominance scores on the projective test, C_3 associates' ratings on achievement motivation, and so forth.

The hypothetical correlations given in Table 13 include reliability coefficients (in parentheses) and validity coefficients (in italics). In the latter, the scores obtained for the same trait by different methods are correlated; each measure is thus being checked against other, independent measures of the same trait, as in the familiar validation procedure. The table also includes correlations between *different* traits measured by the *same* method (in solid-line triangles) and correlations between *different* traits measured

TABLE 13   A HYPOTHETICAL MULTITRAIT-MULTIMETHOD MATRIX
(From Campbell & Fiske, 1959, p. 82)

Traits	Method 1			Method 2			Method 3		
	A_1	B_1	C_1	A_2	B_2	C_2	A_3	B_3	C_3
Method 1 A_1	(.89)								
B_1	.51	(.89)							
C_1	.38	.37	(.76)						
Method 2 A_2	.57	.22	.09	(.93)					
B_2	.22	.57	.10	.68	(.94)				
C_2	.11	.11	.46	.59	.58	(.84)			
Method 3 A_3	.56	.22	.11	.67	.42	.33	(.94)		
B_3	.23	.58	.12	.43	.66	.34	.67	(.92)	
C_3	.11	.11	.45	.34	.32	.58	.58	.60	(.85)

Note: The validity diagonals are the three sets of italicized values. The reliability diagonals are the three sets of values in parentheses. Each heterotrait-monomethod triangle is enclosed by a solid line. Each heterotrait-heteromethod triangle is enclosed by a broken line.

by *different* methods. For satisfactory construct validity, the validity coefficients should obviously be higher than the correlations between different traits measured by different methods; they should also be higher than the correlations between different traits measured by the same method. For example, the correlation between dominance scores from a self-report inventory and dominance scores from a projective test should be higher than the correlation between dominance and sociability scores from a self-report inventory. If the latter correlation, representing common method variance, were high, it might indicate, for example, that a person's scores on this inventory are unduly affected by some irrelevant common factor such as ability to understand the questions or desire to make oneself appear in a favorable light on all traits.

It might be noted that within the framework of the multitrait-multimethod matrix, reliability represents agreement between two measures of the same trait obtained through maximally similar methods, such as parallel forms of the same test; validity represents agreement between two measures of the same trait obtained by maximally different methods, such as test scores and supervisor's ratings. Since similarity and difference of methods are matters of degree, theoretically reliability and validity can be regarded as falling along a single continuum. Ordinarily, however, the techniques actually employed to measure reliability and validity correspond to easily identifiable regions of this continuum.

OVERVIEW

We have considered several ways of asking, "How valid is this test?" To point up the distinctive features of the different types of validity, let us apply each in turn to a test consisting of 50 assorted arithmetic problems. Four ways in which this test might be employed, together with the type of validation procedure appropriate to each, are illustrated in Table 14. This

TABLE 14   VALIDATION OF A SINGLE ARITHMETIC REASONING TEST FOR DIFFERENT PURPOSES

Testing Purpose	Illustrative Question	Type of Validity
Achievement test in elementary school arithmetic	How much has Dick learned in the past?	Content
Aptitude test to predict performance in high school mathematics	How well will Jim learn in the future?	Criterion-related: predictive
Technique for diagnosing brain damage	Does Bill belong in the brain-damaged or in the normal group?	Criterion-related: diagnostic
Measure of logical reasoning	How can we describe Henry's psychological functioning?	Construct

example highlights the fact that the choice of validation procedure depends on the use to be made of the test scores. The same test, when employed for different purposes, should be validated in different ways. If an achievement test is used to predict subsequent performance at a higher educational level, as when selecting high school students for college admission, it needs to be evaluated against the criterion of subsequent college performance rather than in terms of its content validity.

The examples given in Table 14 focus on the differences among the various types of validation procedures. Further consideration of these procedures, however, shows that content, criterion-related, and construct validity do not correspond to distinct or logically coordinate categories. On the contrary, construct validity is a comprehensive concept, which includes the other types. All the specific techniques for establishing content and criterion-related validity, discussed in earlier sections of this chapter, could have been listed again under construct validity. Comparing the test performance of contrasted groups, such as neurotics and normals, is one way of checking the construct validity of a test designed to measure emotional adjustment, anxiety, or other postulated traits. Comparing the test scores of institutionalized mental defectives with those of normal schoolchildren is one way to investigate the construct validity of an intelligence test. The correlations of a mechanical aptitude test with performance in shop courses and in a wide variety of jobs contribute to our understanding of the construct measured by the test. Validity against various practical criteria is commonly reported in test manuals to aid the potential user in understanding what a test measures. Although he may not be directly concerned with the prediction of any of the specific criteria employed, by examining such criteria the test user is able to build up a concept of the behavior domain sampled by the test.

Content validity likewise enters into both the construction and the subsequent evaluation of all tests. In assembling items for any new test, the test constructor is guided by hypotheses regarding the relations between the type of content he chooses and the behavior he wishes to measure. All the techniques of criterion-related validation, as well as the other techniques discussed under construct validation, represent ways of testing such hypotheses. As for the test user, he too relies in part on content validity in evaluating any test. For example, he may check the vocabulary in an emotional adjustment inventory to determine whether some of the words are too difficult for the subjects he plans to test; he may choose a nonverbal rather than a verbal test of intelligence for examining children with reading disabilities; he may conclude that the scores on a particular test depend too much on speed for his purposes; or he may notice that an intelligence test developed twenty years ago contains many obsolescent items unsuitable for use today. All these observations about content are relevant to the construct validity of a test. In fact, there is no information provided by any validation procedure that is *not* relevant to construct validity.

The term construct validity was officially introduced into the psychometrist's lexicon in 1954 in the *Technical Recommendations for Psychological Tests and Diagnostic Techniques*, which constituted the first version of the current test *Standards* (1966). Although the validation procedures subsumed under construct validity were not new at the time, the discussions of construct validation that followed served to make the implications of these procedures more explicit and to provide a systematic rationale for their use. Construct validation has focused attention on the role of psychological theory in test construction and on the need to formulate hypotheses that can be proved or disproved in the validation process. Construct validation has also stimulated the search for novel ways of gathering validity data. Although the principal techniques employed in investigating construct validity have long been familiar, the field of operation has been expanded to admit a wider variety of procedures.

This very multiplicity of data-gathering techniques, however, presents certain hazards. It is possible for a test constructor to try a large number of different validation procedures, a few of which will yield positive results by chance. If these confirmatory results were then to be reported without mention of all the validity probes that yielded negative results, a very misleading impression about the validity of a test could be created. Another possible danger in the application of construct validation is that it may open the way for subjective, unverified assertions about test validity. Since construct validity is such a broad and loosely defined concept, it has been widely misunderstood. Some textbook writers and test constructors seem to perceive it as content validity expressed in terms of psychological trait names. Hence, they present as construct validity purely subjective accounts of what they believe (or hope) the test measures.

A further source of confusion arises from a statement that construct validation "is involved whenever a test is to be interpreted as a measure of some attribute or quality which is not 'operationally defined'" (Cronbach & Meehl, 1955, p. 282). Appearing in the first detailed published analysis of the concept of construct validity, this statement served to foster loose thinking about test scores and what they measure. Actually, the theoretical construct, trait, or behavior domain measured by any test can be defined in terms of the operations performed in establishing the validity of the test. Such a definition would take into account the variables with which the test correlated significantly, as well as the conditions found to affect its scores and the groups that differ significantly in such scores. These procedures are entirely in accord with the positive contributions made by the concept of construct validity. It is only through the empirical investigation of the relationships of test scores to other external data that we can discover what a test measures.

CHAPTER 6

Validity:
Measurement
and Interpretation

CHAPTER 5 was concerned with different concepts of validity and their appropriateness for various testing functions; this chapter deals with quantitative expressions of validity and their interpretation. The test user is concerned with validity at either or both of two stages. First, when considering the suitability of a test for his purposes, he examines available validity data reported in the test manual or other published sources. Through such information, he arrives at a tentative concept of what psychological functions the test actually measures, and he judges the relevance of such functions to his proposed use of the test. In effect, when a test user relies on published validation data, he is dealing with construct validity, regardless of the specific procedures used in gathering the data. As we have seen (Chapter 5), the criteria employed in published studies cannot be assumed to be identical with those the test user wants to predict. Jobs bearing the same title in two different companies are rarely identical. Two courses in freshman English taught in different colleges may be quite dissimilar.

Because of the specificity of each criterion, test users are usually advised to check the validity of any chosen test against local criteria whenever possible. Although published data may strongly suggest that a given test should have high validity in a particular situation, direct corroboration is always desirable. The determination of validity against specific local criteria represents the second stage in the test user's evaluation of validity. The techniques to be discussed in this chapter are especially relevant to the analysis of validity data obtained by the test user himself. Most of them are also useful, however, in understanding and interpreting the validity data reported in test manuals.

EXPECTANCY TABLES

The relation between test scores and criterion status can be analyzed in a number of ways. A simple device for expressing this relation is provided by the expectancy table. Basically, an expectancy table gives the probability of different criterion outcomes for persons who obtain each test score. For example, if a student obtains a score of 530 on the CEEB Scholastic Aptitude Test, what are the chances that his freshman grade-point average in a specific college will fall in the A, B, C, D, or F category? This type of information can be obtained by examining the bivariate distribution of predictor scores (SAT) plotted against criterion status (freshman grade-point average). It is from this bivariate distribution that the validity coefficient of the test is computed—that is, the correlation between test and criterion.

The bivariate distribution in the above example would show the freshman grade distribution of students in each score interval on the SAT. If the number of cases in each cell of such a bivariate distribution is changed to a percentage, the result is an expectancy table, such as the one illustrated in Table 15. The data from which this table was prepared were obtained from 111 students in a watch-repair course. The predictor was the Space Relations test of the Differential Aptitude Tests, administered at the time of admission. The criterion was end-of-course grades. The correlation between test scores and criterion was .69.

The first column of Table 15 shows the test scores, divided into five class intervals; the number of students whose scores fall into each interval is given in the second column. The remaining entries in each row of the table indicate the percentage of cases within each test-score interval who re-

TABLE 15   EXPECTANCY TABLE SHOWING RELATION BETWEEN DAT SPACE RELATIONS TEST AND TERMINAL GRADES FOR 111 STUDENTS IN THE AMERICAN INSTITUTE OF SPECIALIZED WATCH REPAIR

(From Fourth Edition Manual of the Differential Aptitude Tests, Forms L and M, 1966, p. 5–58. Reproduced by permission. Copyright 1947, 1952, © 1959, 1963, 1966. Published by The Psychological Corporation, New York, N.Y. All rights reserved.)

Test Score	Number of Cases	Percentage Receiving Each Criterion Grade				
		E	D	C	B	A
80–99	9				33	67
60–79	33			21	58	21
40–59	43	2	18	40	40	
20–39	14	21	36	29	14	
0–19	12	33	25	33	9	

ceived each grade at the end of the course. Thus, of the 9 students scoring between 80 and 99 on the Space Relations test, 33 percent received a grade of B and 67 percent a grade of A. At the other extreme, of the 12 students scoring between 0 and 19, 33 percent received a grade of E, 25 percent D, 33 percent C, 9 percent B, and none A. Within the limitations of the available data, these percentages represent the best estimates of the probability that an individual will receive a given criterion grade. For example, if a new student receives a test score of 65 (in the 60–79 interval), we would conclude that the probability of his obtaining an A grade is 21 out of 100; the probability of his obtaining B, 58 out of 100; and the probability of his obtaining C, 21 out of 100.

In many practical situations, criteria can be dichotomized into "success" and "failure" in a job, course of study, or other undertaking. Under these conditions, an *expectancy chart* can be prepared, showing the probability of success or failure corresponding to each score interval. Figure 21 is an example of such an expectancy chart. Based on a pilot selection battery developed by the Air Force, this expectancy chart shows the percentage of men scoring within each stanine on the battery who failed to complete primary flight training. It can be seen that 77 percent of the men receiv-

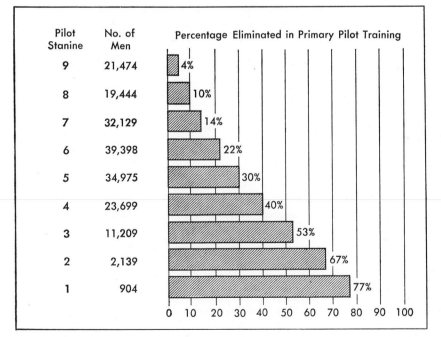

FIG. 21.   Expectancy Chart Showing Relation between Performance on Pilot Selection Battery and Elimination from Primary Flight Training. (From Flanagan, 1947, p. 58.)

ing a stanine of 1 were eliminated in the course of training, while only 4 percent of those at stanine 9 failed to complete the training satisfactorily. Between these extremes, the percentage of failures decreases consistently over the successive stanines. On the basis of this expectancy chart, it could be predicted, for example, that approximately 40 percent of pilot cadets who obtain a stanine score of 4 will fail and approximately 60 percent will satisfactorily complete primary flight training. Similar statements regarding the probability of success and failure could be made about individuals who receive each stanine. Thus, an individual with a stanine of 4 has a 60:40 or 3:2 chance of completing primary flight training.

Figures 22 and 23 illustrate two other types of expectancy charts (Lawshe & Balma, 1966, pp. 357–372). Both are based on the job performance of 51 hosiery seamers who had been tested for visual acuity on the Ortho-Rater. The job-performance criterion was dichotomized at the midpoint, so that those individuals were considered "superior" who had seamed at least

Test scores	Chances in a 100 of being superior
10-11	90
9	70
7-8	50
3-6	30
0-2	10

0 10 20 30 40 50 60 70 80 90 100

FIG. 22.   Individual Expectancy Chart Showing Relation between Ortho-Rater Near-Point Visual Acuity and Job Performance of Hosiery Seamers. (From Lawshe & Balma, 1966, p. 367.)

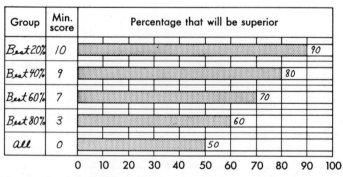

Group	Min. score	Percentage that will be superior
Best 20%	*10*	90
Best 40%	*9*	80
Best 60%	*7*	70
Best 80%	*3*	60
all	*0*	50

0 10 20 30 40 50 60 70 80 90 100

FIG. 23.   Institutional Expectancy Chart Showing Relation between Ortho-Rater Near-Point Visual Acuity and Job Performance of Hosiery Seamers. (From Lawshe & Balma, 1966, p. 366.)

as many pairs of hose as the average worker in a 40-hour period. Scores on the Ortho-Rater were divided into fifths of the group, rather than in terms of equal score intervals. Thus, the top 20 percent of the group obtained a score of 10 or 11 in visual acuity, the next 20 percent obtained a score of 9, and so on down to the lowest 20 percent who scored between 0 and 2. The percentage of workers whose job performance was superior (as defined above) in each Ortho-Rater score group is shown by the horizontal bars in Figure 22.

In Figure 23, the same data are plotted in terms of cumulative percentages. Thus, the best 20 percent in terms of visual acuity scored above 10 on the Ortho-Rater; of these, 90 percent were superior job performers. Among the best 40 percent, scoring above 9 in visual acuity, 80 percent were superior on the job. Among the best 60 percent, scoring above 7 in visual acuity, 70 percent were superior on the job, and so forth. Figure 23 is designed for *institutional* prediction and is relevant to the establishment of suitable cutoff scores for a given job. With such an expectancy chart, an employer could predict what proportion of workers would reach or exceed a specified level of job performance if the minimum test score for hiring applicants were set at different points. Figure 22, on the other hand, is designed for *individual* prediction and is relevant to decisions made in counseling and in assessing an individual applicant for a job.

The expectancy charts reproduced in Figures 22 and 23 illustrate still another procedural feature. The percentages given on these charts are theoretical rather than empirical values. Rather than representing the actual percentage of superior workers found within each test-score interval, these percentages were found from the correlation coefficient between test and criterion. On the assumption that the relationship between the two variables is linear and uniform throughout the range, it is possible to find the percentage falling into each category by consulting tables of normal bivariate surfaces. A simplified and abbreviated set of such tables, arranged so as to facilitate the preparation of expectancy charts, is provided by Lawshe and Balma (1966, pp. 368–372). The advantages of using theoretical percentages, particularly with small samples, is that they tend to reduce the chance irregularities arising when percentages are computed in categories containing very few cases. However, if there is reason to believe that the relation between predictor and criterion is curvilinear or that this relation varies in different portions of the score range, empirical expectancy tables and charts should be prepared.

VALIDITY COEFFICIENTS

MEASUREMENT OF RELATIONSHIP.   A validity coefficient is a correlation between test score and criterion measure. Because it provides a single numerical index of test validity, it is commonly used in test manuals to report the validity of a test against each criterion for which data are available. A correlation coefficient can be found for any set of data that can be represented by an expectancy table. When both predictor and criterion are continuous variables, as in Table 15, the familiar Pearson Product-Moment Correlation Coefficient is applicable.

When the criterion is dichotomized, as in the situations represented by Figures 21 and 22, a *biserial correlation* may be computed. Such a correlation is based on the difference in mean test scores obtained by the two criterion groups, as well as on the standard deviation of test scores and the proportion of individuals who fall into the two criterion groups. Other types of correlation coefficients are available for expressing the relationship between test scores and criterion under still different circumstances, as when both variables are dichotomized, or when the relationship varies at different parts of the range. The specific procedures for computing these different kinds of correlations can be found in any standard statistics text.

CONDITIONS AFFECTING VALIDITY COEFFICIENTS. As in the case of reliability, it is essential to specify the *nature of the group* on which a validity coefficient is found. The same test may measure different functions when given to individuals who differ in age, sex, educational level, occupation, or any other relevant characteristic. As illustrated in Chapter 5, in connection with content validity, the work methods employed to arrive at the same solution of a test problem may vary widely from group to group. Consequently, a test could have high validity in predicting a particular criterion in one population, and little or no validity in another. Or it might be a valid measure of different functions in the two populations. Thus, unless the validation sample is representative of the population on which the test is to be used, validity should be redetermined on a more appropriate sample.

The question of *sample heterogeneity* is relevant to the measurement of validity, as it is to the measurement of reliability; both characteristics are commonly reported in terms of correlation coefficients. It will be recalled that, other things being equal, the wider the range of scores, the higher will be the correlation. This fact should be kept in mind when interpreting the validity coefficients given in test manuals.

A special difficulty encountered in many validation samples arises from *preselection*. For example, a new test that is being validated for job selection may be administered to a group of newly hired employees on whom criterion measures of job performance will eventually be available. It is likely, however, that such employees represent a superior selection of all those who applied for the job. Hence, the range of such a group in both test scores and criterion measures will be curtailed at the lower end of the distribution. The effect of such preselection will therefore be to lower the validity coefficient. In the subsequent use of the test, when it is administered to all applicants for selection purposes, the validity can be expected to be somewhat higher.

Validity coefficients may also change over time because of changing selection standards. An example is provided by a comparison of validity coefficients computed over a 30-year interval with Yale students (Burnham, 1965). Correlations were found between a predictive index based on College Entrance Examination Board tests and high school records, on the one hand, and average freshman grades, on the other. This correlation dropped from .71 to .52 over the 30 years. An examination of the bivariate distributions clearly reveals the reason for this drop. Because of higher admission standards, the later class was more homogeneous than the earlier class in both predictor and criterion performance. Consequently, the correlation was lower in the later group, although the accuracy with which individuals' grades were predicted showed little change. In other words, the observed drop in correlation did *not* indicate that the predictors were less valid than they had been 30 years earlier. Had the differences in group homogeneity been ignored, it might have been wrongly concluded that this was the case.

For the proper interpretation of a validity coefficient, attention should also be given to the *form of the relationship* between test and criterion. The computation of a Pearson correlation coefficient assumes that the relationship is linear and uniform throughout the range. There is evidence that in certain situations, however, these conditions may not be met (Fisher, 1959; Kahneman & Ghiselli, 1962). Thus, a particular job may require a minimum level of reading comprehension, to enable employees to read instruction manuals, labels, and the like. Once this minimum is exceeded, however, further increments in reading ability may be unrelated to degree of job success. This would be an example of a nonlinear relation between test and job performance. An examination of the bivariate distribution or scatter diagram obtained by plotting reading comprehension scores against criterion measures would show a rise in job performance up to the minimal required reading ability and a leveling off beyond that point. Hence, the entries would cluster around a curve rather than a straight line.

In other situations, the line of best fit may be a straight line, but the individual entries may deviate farther around this line at the upper than at the lower end of the scale. Suppose that performance on a scholastic aptitude test is a necessary but not a sufficient condition for successful achievement in a course. That is, the low-scoring students will perform poorly in the course; but among the high-scoring students, some will perform well in the course and others will perform poorly because of low motivation. In this situation, there will be wider variability of criterion performance among the high-scoring than among the low-scoring students. This condition in a bivariate distribution is known as heteroscedasticity.

The Pearson correlation assumes homoscedasticity or equal variability throughout the range of the bivariate distribution. In the present example, the bivariate distribution would be fan-shaped—wide at the upper end and narrow at the lower end.

Still other circumstances may produce differently shaped bivariate distributions, some of them combining a curvilinear relationship with heteroscedasticity in a pattern resembling a twisted pear (Fisher, 1959; Storms, 1960). This pattern is most likely to occur when a predictor correctly identifies only one of several causal factors that can lead to a given result. In all such instances, the use of a single correlation coefficient to report validity will be misleading, since the relationship varies at different portions of the range. An examination of the bivariate distribution itself would give a better indication of the nature of the relationship between test and criterion. Expectancy tables and expectancy charts would also correctly reveal the relative effectiveness of the test at different levels.

MAGNITUDE OF A VALIDITY COEFFICIENT.   How high should a validity coefficient be? No general answer to this question is possible, since the interpretation of a validity coefficient must take into account a number of concomitant circumstances. The obtained correlation, of course, should be high enough to be *statistically significant* at some acceptable level, such as the .01 or .05 levels discussed in Chapter 4. In other words, before drawing any conclusions about the validity of a test, we should be reasonably certain that the obtained validity coefficient could not have arisen through chance fluctuations of sampling from a true correlation of zero.

Having established a significant correlation between test scores and criterion, however, we need to evaluate the size of the correlation in the light of the uses to be made of the test. If we wish to predict an individual's exact criterion score, such as the grade-point average a student will receive in college, the validity coefficient may be interpreted in terms of the *standard error of estimate,* which is analogous to the error of measurement discussed in connection with reliability. It will be recalled that the error of measurement indicates the margin of error to be expected in an individual's score as a result of the unreliability of the test. Similarly, the error of estimate shows the margin of error to be expected in the individual's predicted criterion score, as a result of the imperfect validity of the test.

The error of estimate is found by the following formula:

$$\sigma_{est.} = \sigma_y\sqrt{1 - r^2_{xy}}$$

in which r^2_{xy} is the square of the validity coefficient and σ_y is the standard deviation of the criterion scores. It will be noted that if the validity were perfect ($r_{xy} = 1.00$), the error of estimate would be zero. On the other hand, with a test having zero validity, the error of estimate is as large as the standard deviation of the criterion distribution ($\sigma_{est.} = \sigma_y\sqrt{1 - 0} = \sigma_y$).

Under these conditions, the prediction is no better than a guess; and the range of prediction error is as wide as the entire distribution of criterion scores. Between these two extremes are to be found the errors of estimate corresponding to tests of varying validity.

Reference to the formula for $\sigma_{est.}$ will show that the term $\sqrt{1 - r^2_{xy}}$ serves to indicate the size of the error *relative to the error that would result from a mere guess*, i.e., with zero validity. In other words, if $\sqrt{1 - r^2_{xy}}$ is equal to 1.00, the error of estimate is as large as it would be if we were to guess the subject's score. The predictive improvement attributable to the use of the test would thus be nil. If the validity coefficient is .80, then $\sqrt{1 - r^2_{xy}}$ is equal to .60, and the error is 60 percent as large as it would be by chance. To put it differently, the use of such a test enables us to predict the individual's criterion performance with a margin of error that is 40 percent smaller than it would be if we were to guess.

It would thus appear that even with a validity of .80, which is unusually high, the error of predicted scores is considerable. If the primary function of psychological tests were to predict each individual's exact position in the criterion distribution, the outlook would be quite discouraging. When examined in the light of the error of estimate, most tests do not appear very efficient. In most testing situations, however, it is not necessary to predict the specific criterion performance of individual cases, but rather to determine which individuals will exceed a certain minimum standard of performance, or cutoff point, in the criterion. Who will successfully complete medical school, primary flight training, or officer candidate school? Who will prove to be a satisfactory clerk, salesman, or machine operator? Such information is useful not only in group selection but also in individual guidance. For example, it is advantageous to be able to predict that a given person has a good chance of passing all courses in law school, even if we are unable to estimate with certainty whether his grade average will be 74 or 81.

A test may appreciably improve predictive efficiency if it shows *any* significant correlation with the criterion, however low. Under certain circumstances, even validities as low as .20 or .30 may justify inclusion of the test in a selection program. For many testing purposes, evaluation of tests in terms of the error of estimate is unrealistically stringent. Consideration must be given to other ways of evaluating the contribution of a test, which take into account the types of decisions to be made from the scores. Some of these procedures will be illustrated in the following section.

TEST VALIDITY AND DECISION THEORY

Let us suppose that 100 applicants have been given an aptitude test and followed up until each could be evaluated for success on a certain job.

Figure 24 shows the bivariate distribution of test scores and measures of job success for the 100 subjects. The correlation between these two variables is slightly below .70. The minimum acceptable job performance, or criterion cutoff point, is indicated in the diagram by a heavy horizontal line. The 40 cases falling below this line would represent job failures; the 60 above the line, job successes. If all 100 applicants are hired, therefore, 60 percent will succeed on the job. Similarly, if a smaller number were

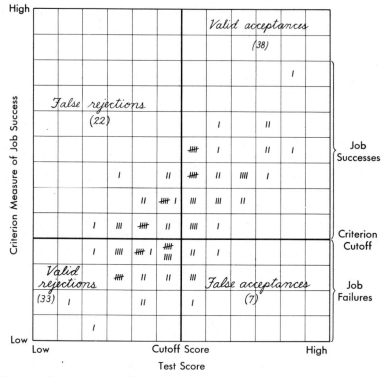

FIG. 24.   Increase in the Proportion of "Successes" Resulting from the Use of a Screening Test.

hired at random, without reference to test scores, the proportion of successes would probably be close to 60 percent. Suppose, however, that the test scores are used to select the 45 most promising applicants out of the 100 (selection ratio = .45). In such a case, the 45 individuals falling to the right of the heavy vertical line would be chosen. Within this group of 45, it can be seen that there are 7 job failures, or *false acceptances*, falling below the heavy horizontal line, and 38 job successes. Hence, the percentage of job successes is now 84 rather than 60 (i.e., 38/45 = .84). This increase is attributable to the use of the test as a screening instrument. It will be noted that errors in predicted criterion score that do not affect the decision can be ignored. Only those prediction errors that cross the cutoff line and hence place the individual in the wrong category will reduce the selective effectiveness of the test.

For a complete evaluation of the effectiveness of the test as a screening instrument, another category of cases in Figure 24 must also be examined. This is the category of *false rejections*, comprising the 22 individuals who score below the cutoff point on the test but above the criterion cutoff. From these data we would estimate that 22 percent of the total applicant sample are potential job successes who will be lost if the test is used as a screening device with the present cutoff point. These false rejects in a personnel selection situation correspond to the *false positives* in clinical evaluations. The latter term has been adopted from medical practice, in which a test for a pathological condition is reported as positive if the condition is present and negative if the patient is normal. A false positive thus refers to a case in which the test erroneously indicates the presence of a pathological condition, as when brain damage is indicated in an individual who is actually normal. This terminology is likely to be confusing unless we remember that in clinical practice a positive result on a test denotes pathology and unfavorable diagnosis, whereas in personnel selection a positive result conventionally refers to a favorable prediction regarding job performance, academic achievement, and the like.

In setting a cutoff score on a test, attention should be given to the percentage of false rejects (or false positives) as well as to the percentages of successes and failures within the selected group. In certain situations, the cutoff point should be set sufficiently high to exclude all but a few possible failures. This would be the case when the job is of such a nature that a poorly qualified worker could cause serious loss or damage. An example would be a commercial airline pilot. Under other circumstances, it may be more important to admit as many qualified persons as possible, at the risk of including more failures. In the latter case, the number of false rejects can be reduced by the choice of a lower cutoff score. Other factors that normally determine the position of the cutoff score include the available personnel supply, the number of job openings, and the urgency or speed with which the openings must be filled.

In the terminology of decision theory, the example given in Figure 24 illustrates a simple *strategy*, or plan for deciding which applicants to accept and which to reject. In more general terms, a strategy is a technique for utilizing information in order to reach a decision about individuals. In this case, the strategy was to accept the 45 persons with the highest test scores. The increase in percentage of successful employees from 60 to 84 could be used as a basis for estimating the *payoff*, or net benefit to the company resulting from the use of the test.

Statistical decision theory was developed by Wald (1950) with special reference to the decisions required in the inspection and quality control of industrial products. Many of its implications for the construction and interpretation of psychological tests have been systematically worked out by Cronbach and Gleser (1965). Essentially, decision theory is an attempt to put the decision-making process into mathematical form, so that available information may be used to arrive at the most effective decision under specified circumstances. The mathematical procedures employed in decision theory are often quite complex, and few are in a form permitting their immediate application to practical testing problems. Some of the basic concepts of decision theory, however, are proving helpful in the reformulation and clarification of certain questions about tests. A few of these ideas were introduced into testing before the formal development of statistical decision theory and were later recognized as fitting into that framework.

An example of such a precursor of decision theory in psychological testing is to be found in the Taylor-Russell tables (1939), which permit a determination of the net gain in selection accuracy attributable to the use of the test. The information required includes the validity coefficient of the test, the selection ratio or proportion of applicants who must be accepted, and the proportion of successful applicants selected without the use of the test. A change in any of these three factors can alter the predictive efficiency of the test.

For purposes of illustration, one of the Taylor-Russell tables has been reproduced in Table 16. This table is designed for use when the percentage of successful applicants selected prior to the use of the test is 60. Other tables are provided by Taylor and Russell for other percentages of successful applicants. Across the top of the table are given different values of the selection ratio, and along the side are the test validities. The entries in the body of the table indicate the proportion of successful persons selected after the use of the test. Thus, the difference between .60 and any one table entry shows the increase in proportion of successful selections attributable to the test.

Obviously if the selection ratio were 100 percent, that is, if all applicants had to be accepted, no test, however valid, could improve the selection process. Reference to Table 16 shows that, when as many as 95 percent of applicants must be admitted, even a test with perfect validity ($r = 1.00$) would raise the proportion of successful persons by only 3 percent (.60 to .63). On the other hand, when only 5 percent of applicants need to be chosen, a test with a validity coefficient of only .30 can raise the percentage of successful applicants selected from 60 to 82. The rise from 60 to 82 represents the *incremental validity* of the test, or the increase in predictive validity attributable to the test. It indicates the contribution the test makes to the selection of individuals who will meet the minimum standards in criterion performance. In applying the Taylor-Russell tables, of course, test validity should be computed on the same sort of group used to estimate percentage of prior successes. In other words, the contribution of the test is

TABLE 16 PROPORTION OF "SUCCESSES" EXPECTED THROUGH THE USE OF TESTS
OF GIVEN VALIDITY, WHEN PROPORTION OF "SUCCESSES" PRIOR TO USE OF TEST
WAS .60

(From Taylor and Russell, 1939, p. 576)

Validity	Selection Ratio										
	.05	.10	.20	.30	.40	.50	.60	.70	.80	.90	.95
.00	.60	.60	.60	.60	.60	.60	.60	.60	.60	.60	.60
.05	.64	.63	.63	.62	.62	.62	.61	.61	.61	.60	.60
.10	.68	.67	.65	.64	.64	.63	.63	.62	.61	.61	.60
.15	.71	.70	.68	.67	.66	.65	.64	.63	.62	.61	.61
.20	.75	.73	.71	.69	.67	.66	.65	.64	.63	.62	.61
.25	.78	.76	.73	.71	.69	.68	.66	.65	.63	.62	.61
.30	.82	.79	.76	.73	.71	.69	.68	.66	.64	.62	.61
.35	.85	.82	.78	.75	.73	.71	.69	.67	.65	.63	.62
.40	.88	.85	.81	.78	.75	.73	.70	.68	.66	.63	.62
.45	.90	.87	.83	.80	.77	.74	.72	.69	.66	.64	.62
.50	.93	.90	.86	.82	.79	.76	.73	.70	.67	.64	.62
.55	.95	.92	.88	.84	.81	.78	.75	.71	.68	.64	.62
.60	.96	.94	.90	.87	.83	.80	.76	.73	.69	.65	.63
.65	.98	.96	.92	.89	.85	.82	.78	.74	.70	.65	.63
.70	.99	.97	.94	.91	.87	.84	.80	.75	.71	.66	.63
.75	.99	.99	.96	.93	.90	.86	.81	.77	.71	.66	.63
.80	1.00	.99	.98	.95	.92	.88	.83	.78	.72	.66	.63
.85	1.00	1.00	.99	.97	.95	.91	.86	.80	.73	.66	.63
.90	1.00	1.00	1.00	.99	.97	.94	.88	.82	.74	.67	.63
.95	1.00	1.00	1.00	1.00	.99	.97	.92	.84	.75	.67	.63
1.00	1.00	1.00	1.00	1.00	1.00	1.00	1.00	.86	.75	.67	.63

not evaluated against chance success unless applicants were previously selected by chance—a most unlikely circumstance. Since applicants are ordinarily selected on the basis of previous job history, letters of recommendation, interviews, and the like, the contribution of the test should be evaluated on the basis of what the test adds to these previous selection procedures.

In many practical situations, what is wanted is an estimate of the effect of the selection test, not on percentage of persons exceeding the minimum performance, but on over-all *output* of the selected persons. How does the actual level of job proficiency or criterion achievement of the workers hired on the basis of the test compare with that of the total applicant sample that would have been hired without the test? Following the work of Taylor and Russell, several investigators addressed themselves to this question (Brogden, 1946; Brown & Ghiselli, 1953; Jarrett, 1948; Richardson, 1944).

Brogden (1946) first demonstrated that the expected increase in output is directly proportional to the validity of the test. Thus, the improvement resulting from the use of a test of validity .50 is 50 percent as great as the improvement expected from a test of perfect validity.

The relation between test validity and expected rise in criterion achievement can be readily seen in Table 17. Expressing criterion scores as standard scores with a mean of zero and an SD of 1.00, this table gives the expected mean criterion score of workers selected with a test of given validity and with a given selection ratio. It will be noted, for example, that when 20 percent of the applicants are hired and the validity coefficient is .50, the mean criterion performance is .70 SD above the mean of the unselected population of applicants. With the same selection ratio and a perfect test (validity coefficient $= 1.00$), the mean criterion score of the selected applicants would be 1.40, just twice what it would be with the test of validity .50. Similar direct linear relations will be found if other mean criterion performances are compared within any row of Table 17. For instance, with a selection ratio of 60 percent, a validity of .25 yields a mean criterion score of .16, while a validity of .50 yields a mean of .32. Again, doubling the validity doubles the output rise.

Such an evaluation of test validity is obviously much more favorable than that based on the previously discussed error of estimate. The reason for the difference is that prediction errors that do not affect decisions are irrelevant to the selection situation. For example, if Smith and Jones are both superior workers and are both hired on the basis of the test, it does not matter if the test shows Smith to be better than Jones while in job performance Jones excels Smith.

In decision theory, the mathematical payoff function derived for any given strategy incorporates a number of parameters not traditionally considered in evaluating the predictive effectiveness of tests. One such parameter is the previously mentioned selection ratio, or the proportion of applicants who can (or must) be accepted in a job, educational institution, clinic, etc. Another is the cost of administering the test. Thus, a test of low validity is more likely to be retained if it is short, inexpensive, easily administered by relatively untrained personnel, and suitable for group administration. An individual test requiring a trained examiner or expensive equipment would need a higher validity to justify its use. A further consideration is whether the test assesses an area of criterion-related behavior not otherwise covered by available techniques.

Another major aspect of decision theory is the evaluation of outcomes. The payoff, or expected benefit of a decision strategy, is based on the probability of each outcome (such as job success or failure), together with estimates of the relative value of such outcomes. The lack of adequate systems for assigning values to outcomes is one of the chief obstacles to the wide application of decision theory. In industrial decisions, a dollar-and-cents

TABLE 17 MEAN STANDARD CRITERION SCORE OF SELECTED CASES IN RELATION TO TEST VALIDITY AND SELECTION RATIO

(From Brown and Ghiselli, 1953, p. 342)

Selection Ratio	Validity Coefficient																				
	.00	.05	.10	.15	.20	.25	.30	.35	.40	.45	.50	.55	.60	.65	.70	.75	.80	.85	.90	.95	1.00
.05	.00	.10	.21	.31	.42	.52	.62	.73	.83	.94	1.04	1.14	1.25	1.35	1.46	1.56	1.66	1.77	1.87	1.98	2.08
.10	.00	.09	.18	.26	.35	.44	.53	.62	.70	.79	.88	.97	1.05	1.14	1.23	1.32	1.41	1.49	1.58	1.67	1.76
.15	.00	.08	.15	.23	.31	.39	.46	.54	.62	.70	.77	.85	.93	1.01	1.08	1.16	1.24	1.32	1.39	1.47	1.55
.20	.00	.07	.14	.21	.28	.35	.42	.49	.56	.63	.70	.77	.84	.91	.98	1.05	1.12	1.19	1.26	1.33	1.40
.25	.00	.06	.13	.19	.25	.32	.38	.44	.51	.57	.63	.70	.76	.82	.89	.95	1.01	1.08	1.14	1.20	1.27
.30	.00	.06	.12	.17	.23	.29	.35	.40	.46	.52	.58	.64	.69	.75	.81	.87	.92	.98	1.04	1.10	1.16
.35	.00	.05	.11	.16	.21	.26	.32	.37	.42	.48	.53	.58	.63	.69	.74	.79	.84	.90	.95	1.00	1.06
.40	.00	.05	.10	.15	.19	.24	.29	.34	.39	.44	.48	.53	.58	.63	.68	.73	.77	.82	.87	.92	.97
.45	.00	.04	.09	.13	.18	.22	.26	.31	.35	.40	.44	.48	.53	.57	.62	.66	.70	.75	.79	.84	.88
.50	.00	.04	.08	.12	.16	.20	.24	.28	.32	.36	.40	.44	.48	.52	.56	.60	.64	.68	.72	.76	.80
.55	.00	.04	.07	.11	.14	.18	.22	.25	.29	.32	.36	.40	.43	.47	.50	.54	.58	.61	.65	.68	.72
.60	.00	.03	.06	.10	.13	.16	.19	.23	.26	.29	.32	.35	.39	.42	.45	.48	.52	.55	.58	.61	.64
.65	.00	.03	.06	.09	.11	.14	.17	.20	.23	.26	.28	.31	.34	.37	.40	.43	.46	.48	.51	.54	.57
.70	.00	.02	.05	.07	.10	.12	.15	.17	.20	.22	.25	.27	.30	.32	.35	.37	.40	.42	.45	.47	.50
.75	.00	.02	.04	.06	.08	.11	.13	.15	.17	.19	.21	.23	.25	.27	.30	.32	.33	.36	.38	.40	.42
.80	.00	.02	.04	.05	.07	.09	.11	.12	.14	.16	.18	.19	.21	.22	.25	.26	.28	.30	.32	.33	.35
.85	.00	.01	.03	.04	.05	.07	.08	.10	.11	.12	.14	.15	.16	.18	.19	.20	.22	.23	.25	.26	.27
.90	.00	.01	.02	.03	.04	.05	.06	.07	.08	.09	.10	.11	.12	.13	.14	.15	.16	.17	.18	.19	.20
.95	.00	.01	.01	.02	.02	.03	.03	.04	.04	.05	.05	.06	.07	.07	.08	.08	.09	.09	.10	.10	.11

value can frequently be assigned to different outcomes. Even in such cases, however, certain outcomes pertaining to good will, public relations, and employee morale are difficult to assess in monetary terms. Educational decisions must take into account institutional goals, social values, and other relatively intangible factors. Individual decisions, as in counseling, must consider the individual's preferences and value system. It has been repeatedly pointed out, however, that decision theory did not introduce the problem of values into the decision process, but merely made it explicit. Value systems have always entered into decisions, but they were not heretofore clearly recognized or systematically handled.

Whether a psychological test is to be used in making terminal or sequential decisions also influences its effectiveness. For instance, instead of sorting applicants into accepted and rejected categories only, we might introduce a third category for uncertain cases who are to be examined further with more intensive techniques. Another strategy, suitable for the diagnosis of psychological disorders, would be to use only two categories but to test further *all* cases classified as positives (i.e., possibly pathological) by the preliminary screening test. It should also be noted that many personnel decisions are in effect sequential, although they may not be so perceived. Incompetent employees hired because of prediction errors can usually be discharged after a probationary period; failing students can be dropped from college at several stages. In such situations, it is only adverse selection decisions that are terminal. To be sure, incorrect selection decisions that are later rectified may be costly in terms of several value systems. But they are often less costly than terminal wrong decisions.

Still another condition that may alter the effectiveness of a psychological test is the availability of alternative treatments and the possibility of adapting treatments to individual characteristics. An example would be the utilization of different training procedures for workers at different aptitude levels, or the introduction of compensatory educational programs for students with certain educational disabilities. Under these conditions, the decision strategy followed in individual cases should take into account available data on the interaction of initial test score and differential treatment.

In assessing the contribution of a psychological test to the decision process, clinical psychologists use the concept of *base rate*, or the frequency of a given condition in the population to which the test is applied (Buchwald, 1965; Cureton, 1957a; Meehl & Rosen, 1955). For example, if 5 percent of the intake population of a particular clinic has organic brain damage, then 5 percent is the base rate of brain damage in this population. It will be noted that base rate corresponds to one of the terms employed in the Taylor-Russell tables, namely, the proportion of applicants who succeed (or fail) prior to the use of the test. In both contexts, extreme base rates permit little improvement in prediction by means of a test. Let us consider an example in which test validity is .60 and the selection ratio is 70 percent. Under these conditions, reference to the appropriate Taylor-Russell table (1939) shows that, if 90 percent of those hired prior to the use of the test were satisfactory on the job, introduction of the test raises this percentage to 99 (9 percent improvement). Similarly, with 10 percent initially satisfactory employees, the percentage rises to 21 (11 percent improvement). On the other hand, when the percentage of initially satisfactory employees is 50, the percentage rises to 75 (25 percent improvement).

In evaluating the incremental validity of any test for clinical diagnosis, the same restrictions imposed by the base rate must be taken into account. Although the introduction of any valid test will improve predictive or diagnostic accuracy, the improvement is greatest when base rates are closest to 50 percent. Moreover, with extreme base rates, the improvement may be negligible. Under these conditions, the use of a test may prove to be unjustified when the cost of its administration and scoring is taken into account. In a clinical situation, this cost would include the time of professional personnel that might otherwise be spent on the treatment of additional cases (Buchwald, 1965). The number of false positives, or normal individuals incorrectly classified as pathological, would of course increase this over-all cost in a clinical situation.

When the seriousness of a rare condition makes its diagnosis urgent, tests of moderate validity may be employed in an early stage of sequential decisions. For example, all cases might first be screened with an easily administered test of moderate validity. If the cutoff score is set high enough (high scores being favorable), there will be few false negatives but many false positives, or normals diagnosed as pathological. The latter can then be detected through a more intensive individual examination given to all cases diagnosed as positive by the test. This solution would be appropriate, for instance, when available facilities make the intensive individual examination of all cases impracticable.

In many personnel decisions, the selection ratio is determined by the practical demands of the situation. Because of supply and demand in filling job openings, for example, it may be necessary to hire the top 40 percent of applicants in one case and the top 75 percent in another. Most of the techniques discussed thus far, such as the Taylor-Russell tables, assume a given selection ratio. When the selection ratio is not externally imposed, as in a counseling situation, the cutting score on a test can be set at that point giving the maximum differentiation between criterion groups. This can be done roughly by comparing the distribution of test scores in the two criterion groups. More precise mathematical procedures for setting optimal cutting scores have also been worked out (Darlington & Stauffer, 1966; Guttman & Raju, 1965; Rorer et al., 1966). These procedures make it possible to take into account other relevant parameters, such as the relative seriousness of false positives and false negatives.

The examples cited illustrate some of the ways in which the concepts and rationale of decision theory can assist in the evaluation of psychological tests for specific testing purposes. Essentially, decision theory has served to focus attention on the complexity of factors that determine the contribution a given test can make in a particular situation. The validity coefficient alone cannot indicate whether or not a test should be used, since it is only one of the factors to be considered in evaluating the impact of the test on the efficacy of the total decision process.[1]

MODERATOR VARIABLES

DIFFERENTIALLY PREDICTABLE SUBSETS OF PERSONS. The validity of a test for a given criterion may vary among subgroups differing in personal characteristics. The classic psychometric model assumed that prediction errors were characteristic of the test rather than of the person and that these errors were randomly distributed among persons. With the flexibility of approach ushered in by decision theory, there has been increasing exploration of prediction models involving interaction between persons and tests. Such interaction implies that the same test may be a better predictor for certain classes or subsets of persons than it is for others. For example, a given test may be a better predictor of criterion performance for men than for women, or a better predictor for applicants from a lower than for applicants from a higher socioeconomic level. In these examples, sex and socioeconomic level are known as *moderator variables*, since they moderate the validity of the test (Saunders, 1956).

When computed in a total group, the validity coefficient of a test may be too low to be of much practical value in prediction. But when recomputed in subsets of individuals differing in some identifiable characteristic, validity may be high in one subset and negligible in another. The test could thus be used effectively in making decisions regarding persons in the first group but not in the second. Perhaps another test or some other assessment device can be found that is an effective predictor in the second group.

A moderator variable is some characteristic of persons that makes it possible to predict the predictability of different individuals with a given instrument. It may be a demographic variable, such as sex, age, educational level, or socioeconomic background; or it may be a score on another test. Interests and motivation often function as moderator variables. Thus, if an applicant has little interest in a job, he will probably perform poorly regardless of his scores on relevant aptitude tests. Among such persons, the correlation between aptitude test scores and job performance would be low.

[1] For further discussion of the concepts of decision theory, see Adams (1960), Bross (1953), Chernoff & Moses (1959), and Cronbach & Gleser (1965).

For individuals who are interested and highly motivated, on the other hand, the correlation between aptitude test score and job success may be quite high.

EMPIRICAL EXAMPLES OF MODERATOR VARIABLES.   Evidence for the operation of moderator variables comes from a variety of sources. In a survey of several hundred correlation coefficients between aptitude test scores and academic grades, Seashore (1962) found higher correlations for women than for men in the large majority of instances. The same trend was found in high school and college, although the trend was more pronounced at the college level. The data do not indicate the reason for this sex difference in the predictability of academic achievement, but it may be interesting to speculate about it in the light of other known sex differences. If women students in general tend to be more conforming and more inclined to accept the values and standards of the school situation, their class achievement will probably depend largely on their abilities. If, on the other hand, men students tend to concentrate their efforts on those activities (in or out of school) that arouse their individual interests, these interest differences would introduce additional variance in their course achievement and would make it more difficult to predict achievement from test scores. Whatever the reason for the difference, sex does appear to function as a moderator variable in the predictability of academic grades from aptitude test scores.

A number of investigations have been specially designed to assess the role of moderator variables in the prediction of academic achievement. Several studies (Frederiksen & Gilbert, 1960; Frederiksen & Melville, 1954; Stricker, 1966) tested the hypothesis that the more compulsive students, identified through two tests of compulsivity, would put a great deal of effort into their course work, regardless of their interest in the courses, but that the effort of the less compulsive students would depend on their interest. Since effort will be reflected in grades, the correlation between the appropriate interest test scores and grades should be higher among noncompulsive than among compulsive students. This hypothesis was confirmed in several groups of male engineering students, but not among liberal arts students of either sex.

In another study (Grooms & Endler, 1960), the college grades of the more anxious students correlated higher ($r = .63$) with aptitude and achievement test scores than did the grades of the less anxious students ($r = .19$). A different approach is illustrated by Berdie (1961), who investigated the relation between intraindividual variability on a test and the predictive validity of the same test. It was hypothesized that a given test will be a better predictor for those individuals who perform more consistently in different parts of the test—and whose total scores are thus more reliable. This hypothesis was confirmed in a group of engineering freshmen whose grades were predicted from a mathematics test.

Ghiselli (1956, 1960a, 1960b, 1963) has extensively explored the role of moderator variables in industrial situations. In a study of taxi drivers (Ghiselli, 1956), the correlation between an aptitude test and a job-performance criterion in the total applicant sample was only .220. The group was then sorted into thirds on the basis of scores on an occupational interest test. When the validity of the aptitude test was recomputed within the third whose occupational interest level was most appropriate for the job, it rose to .664. In an investigation of the prediction of managerial effectiveness, Hobert and Dunnette (1967) analyzed the operation of moderator variables separately among underpredicted and overpredicted cases. By these procedures, it proved possible to increase the validity of a predictor battery even though the original validity was unusually high. Other occupational data are provided by a series of studies suggesting different relationships between predictors and job performance criteria among Negro and white employees of the Port of New York Authority, including female toll collectors and maintenance men (Lopez, 1966).[2]

In a still different context, there is evidence that self-report personality inventories may have higher validity for some types of neurotics than for others (Fulkerson, 1959). The characteristic behavior of the two types tends to make one type careful and accurate in reporting symptoms, the other careless and evasive. The individual who is characteristically precise and careful about details, who tends to worry about his problems, and who uses intellectualization as a primary defense is likely to provide a more accurate picture of his emotional difficulties on a self-report inventory than is the impulsive, careless individual who tends to avoid expressing unpleasant thoughts and emotions and who uses denial as a primary defense.

SELECTION STRATEGY: A HYPOTHETICAL EXAMPLE.   The predictive validity of tests can be improved if moderator variables are incorporated into the appropriate selection strategy. In its simplest form, this strategy calls for the sequential use of two tests (or two scores derived from a single test). The first test is used to screen out those individuals for whom the second test is likely to have low validity in predicting a particular criterion. Then, from among the remaining cases, those scoring high on the second test are selected. More complex selection strategies can be applied when different tests prove to have high validity in different subgroups (Ghiselli, 1960a, 1963).

The identification and use of moderator variables in a simple selection strategy can be illustrated with the following hypothetical example (Dunnette, 1966, pp. 106–112). Figure 25 shows a bivariate distribution or

[2] Supplemented by unpublished reports of later studies—courtesy of Dr. Felix M. Lopez, Jr., April, 1967.

scatterplot of criterion (job output) and predictor (perceptual speed and accuracy test) for 48 beer-bottle inspectors in a fictitious bottle manufacturing plant. Considered as a whole, this scatterplot is neither rectilinear nor homoscedastic. The individuals in the lower right-hand portion of the scatterplot deviate from a straight-line relationship; and variability is wider at the upper end of the score range than at the lower end. To identify moderator variables, we need to compare the individuals falling along the principal diagonal, for whom the test is a good predictor of the criterion, with

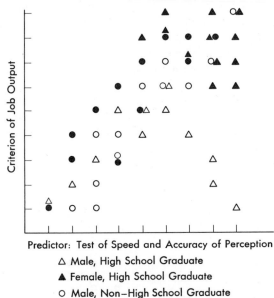

Predictor: Test of Speed and Accuracy of Perception

△ Male, High School Graduate

▲ Female, High School Graduate

○ Male, Non–High School Graduate

● Female, Non–High School Graduate

FIG. 25. Multidimensional Scatterplot Showing Relation between Test and Criterion in Subsets of Individuals Differing in Sex and Educational Level: Initial Validation Sample. (From PERSONNEL SELECTION AND PLACEMENT by Marvin D. Dunnette. © 1966 by Wadsworth Publishing Company, Inc., Belmont, California. Used by permission of the publisher.)

the deviant cases for whom the test fails to predict. This comparison is facilitated if we employ a *multidimensional scatterplot,* as proposed by Rimland (1960). All that is required is the use of a different color or symbol for individuals in different subgroups. In the present example, the possible moderator variables under investigation are sex and educational level. Accordingly different symbols have been employed in Figure 25 for males, females, high school graduates, and non–high school graduates.

Examination of Figure 25 reveals several interesting facts about the four subsets of persons. For the nongraduates of both sexes, job performance is well predicted from test scores; the validity coefficient in this group is .87.

High school graduates, on the other hand, show no linear relation between test and criterion. Among the women graduates, all perform well on this job, regardless of test score. Thus, for women applicants, high school graduation would be a sufficient qualification for employment, without the test. For the men graduates, the relation between test and criterion is clearly curvilinear, the best job performers being those with test scores in the middle of the range. In this subset, both high and low scorers should be rejected. This relationship, incidentally, is not unusual in relatively routine jobs, in which an optimum ability level is required. Individuals falling below this level fail for lack of the minimum requisite skill; those above this level are overqualified and are likely to be dissatisfied with the job, a state that may be reflected in poorer performance.

Before the results of the above study are put into practice, it is essential to *cross-validate* the observed relationships in a new sample. Since the identification of moderator variables may capitalize on chance errors, it is particularly important to verify the results in a second group. Data on moderator variables are likely to be quite unstable from one sample to another (Ghiselli, 1963; Hakel, 1966; Stricker, 1966). In the present example, it is possible that the deviations from a straight-line relation in Figure 25 resulted from chance variations of sampling. In that case, the deviant individuals in the second sample might differ in sex or education from those in

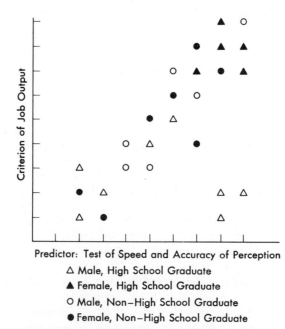

Predictor: Test of Speed and Accuracy of Perception

△ Male, High School Graduate
▲ Female, High School Graduate
○ Male, Non–High School Graduate
● Female, Non–High School Graduate

FIG. 26.   Multidimensional Scatterplot Showing Relation between Test and Criterion in Subsets of Individuals Differing in Sex and Educational Level: Cross-Validation Sample. (From PERSONNEL SELECTION AND PLACEMENT by Marvin D. Dunnette. © 1966 by Wadsworth Publishing Company, Inc., Belmont, California. Used by permission of the publisher.)

the first sample. Figure 26 presents the results of cross validation in a second sample of 26 employees. Such results could be obtained by repeating the investigation at a later date with a new group of applicants. If that procedure is not feasible, the original sample can be subdivided at random into two groups; the analysis is then conducted independently in each group.

Since the relationships found in the sample analyzed in Figure 26 corroborate the trends identified in Figure 25, we are ready to apply the results in selecting subsequent job applicants. Figure 27 shows a set of selection strategies that might be established as a result of this investigation.

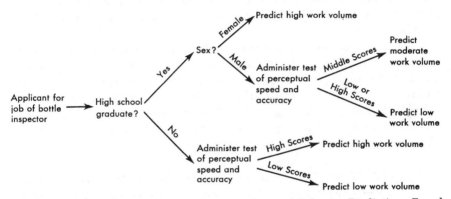

FIG. 27.   Selection Strategies, Decision Rules, and Behavior Predictions Based on Hypothetical Investigation of Bottle Inspectors. (From PERSONNEL SELECTION AND PLACEMENT by Marvin D. Dunnette. © 1966 by Wadsworth Publishing Company, Inc., Belmont, California. Used by permission of the publisher.)

It will be noted that different screening routes are followed for subsets of individuals prior to the prediction of criterion output, from which the decision to hire or reject would be made. The first item to be ascertained pertains to education. Applicants who are high school graduates would be hired without testing if female, but would be tested if male. Both high- and low-scoring applicants in the latter group would be rejected; those scoring in the middle range might be held in reserve and hired if needed to fill a job quota, since their output would at best be expected to reach a moderate level. All non–high school graduates would be tested, regardless of sex, and the higher-scoring applicants would be hired from this subset.

It should be noted, of course, that the above example is oversimplified for purposes of illustration. In actual practice, it is likely that more than one test would be tried and that more potential moderator variables would be explored. For higher-level jobs, moreover, intensive interviews, reference checkups, and other assessment procedures would probably be used with any subsets for which the tests are predicted to be of low validity.[3]

[3] For further discussion of these more complex selection strategies, see Dunnette (1963a; 1966, Ch. 8).

COMBINING INFORMATION FROM DIFFERENT TESTS

For the prediction of practical criteria, not one but several tests are generally required. Most criteria are complex, the criterion measure depending on a number of different traits. A single test designed to measure such a criterion would thus have to be highly heterogeneous. It has already been pointed out, however, that a relatively homogeneous test, measuring largely a single trait, is more satisfactory because it yields less ambiguous scores (Ch. 4). Hence, it is usually preferable to use a combination of several relatively homogeneous tests, each covering a different aspect of the criterion, rather than a single test consisting of a hodgepodge of many different kinds of items.

When a number of specially selected tests are employed together to predict a single criterion, they are known as a *test battery*. The chief problem arising in the use of such batteries concerns the way in which scores on the different tests are to be combined in arriving at a decision regarding each individual. The procedures followed for this purpose may be subsumed under three major headings: (*a*) multiple regression equation, (*b*) multiple cutoff scores, and (*c*) clinical judgment.

MULTIPLE REGRESSION EQUATION. The multiple regression equation yields a predicted criterion score for each individual on the basis of his scores on all the tests in the battery. The following regression equation illustrates the application of this technique to predicting a student's achievement in high school mathematics courses from his scores on verbal (V), numerical (N), and reasoning (R) tests:

$$\text{Mathematics Achievement} = .21\,V + .21\,N + .32\,R + 1.35$$

In this equation, the student's stanine score on each of the three tests is multiplied by the corresponding weight given in the equation. The sum of these products, plus a constant (1.35), gives the student's predicted stanine position in mathematics courses.

Suppose that Bill Jones receives the following stanine scores:

Verbal	6
Numerical	4
Reasoning	8

The estimated mathematics achievement of this student is found as follows:

$$\text{Mathematics Achievement} = (.21)(6) + (.21)(4) + (.32)(8) + 1.35 = 6.01$$

Bill's predicted stanine is approximately 6. It will be recalled (Ch. 3) that a stanine of 5 represents average performance. Bill would thus be expected to do somewhat better than average in mathematics courses. His very superior performance in the reasoning test $(R = 8)$ and his above-average score on the verbal test $(V = 6)$ compensate for his poor score in speed and accuracy of computation $(N = 4)$.

Specific techniques for the computation of regression equations can be found in texts on psychological statistics (cf., e.g., Guilford, 1965). Essentially, such an equation is based on the correlation of each test with the criterion, as well as on the intercorrelations among the tests. Obviously, those tests that correlate higher with the criterion should receive more weight. It is equally important, however, to take into account the correlation of each test with the other tests in the battery. Tests correlating highly with each other represent needless duplication, since they cover to a large extent the same aspects of the criterion. The inclusion of two such tests will not appreciably increase the validity of the entire battery, even though both tests may correlate highly with the criterion. In such a case, one of the tests would serve about as effectively as the pair; only one would therefore be retained in the battery.

Even after the most serious instances of duplication have been eliminated, however, the tests remaining in the battery will correlate with each other to varying degrees. For maximum predictive value, tests that make a more nearly unique contribution to the total battery should receive greater weight than those that partly duplicate the functions of other tests. In the computation of a multiple regression equation, each test is weighted in direct proportion to its correlation with the criterion and in inverse proportion to its correlations with the other tests. Thus, the highest weight will be assigned to the test with the highest validity and the least amount of overlap with the rest of the battery.

The validity of the entire battery can be found by computing the multiple correlation (R) between the criterion and the battery. This correlation indicates the highest predictive value that can be obtained from the given battery, when each test is given optimum weight for predicting the criterion in question. The optimum weights are those determined by the regression equation.

It should be noted that these weights are optimum only for the particular sample in which they were found. Because of chance errors in the correlation coefficients used in deriving them, the regression weights may vary from sample to sample. Hence, the battery should be cross-validated by correlating the predicted criterion scores with the actual criterion scores in a new sample. Formulas are available for estimating the amount of shrinkage in a multiple correlation to be expected when the regression equation is applied to a second sample, but empirical verification is preferable whenever possible. The larger the sample on which regression weights were derived, the smaller the shrinkage will be.

Under certain conditions the predictive validity of a battery can be improved by including in the regression equation a test having a zero correlation with the criterion but a high correlation with another test in the battery. This curious situation arises when the test that is uncorrelated with the criterion acts as a *suppressor variable* to eliminate or suppress the irrelevant variance in the other test. For example, reading comprehension might correlate highly with scores on a mathematical or a mechanical aptitude test, because the test problems require the understanding of complicated written instructions. If reading comprehension is irrelevant to the job behavior to be predicted, the reading comprehension required by the tests introduces error variance and lowers the predictive validity of the tests. Administering a reading comprehension test and including scores on this test in the regression equation will eliminate this error variance and raise the validity of the battery. The suppressor variable appears in the regression equation with a negative weight. Thus, the higher an individual's score on reading comprehension, the more is deducted from his score on the mathematical or mechanical test.

Although situations requiring suppressor variables are not common, when they do arise the introduction of suppressor variables effects appreciable improvement in predictive validity. An example is provided by an investigation of 63 industrial mechanics (Sorenson, 1966). The most effective battery for predicting job performance in this group included: (1) a questionnaire covering education, previous mechanical experience, and other background data (criterion correlation = .30); (2) a mechanical insight test stressing practical mechanics of the "nuts-and-bolts" type (criterion correlation = .22); and (3) a test of mechanical comprehension oriented toward the academic understanding of mechanical principles (criterion correlation = −.04; correlation with test 2 = .71). The third test functioned as a suppressor variable, as can be seen from the following regression equation:

$$C = 17T_1 + 10T_2 - 6T_3 + 866$$

Without the suppressor variable the test battery would "overpredict" the job performance of individuals who obtain high scores on the practical mechanics test through an application of mechanical principles but who lack the practical mechanical know-how required on the job. The irrelevant contribution of academic knowledge of mechanical principles to scores on the practical mechanics tests was thus ruled out by the suppressor variable.

Parenthetically, it should be noted that the units in which scores are expressed in a regression equation are arbitrary and chosen for convenience. Usually raw scores on each test are entered and the weights and constant in the equation automatically adjust for differences in units. The final predicted score is expressed in the units of the criterion scale.

MULTIPLE CUTOFF SCORES. An alternative strategy for combining test scores utilizes multiple cutoff points. Briefly, this procedure involves the establishment of a minimum cutoff score on each test. Every individual who falls below such a minimum score on *any one* of the tests is rejected. Only those persons who reach or exceed the cutoff scores in all tests are accepted. An example of this technique is provided by the General Aptitude Test Battery (GATB) developed by the United States Employment Service for use in the occupational counseling program of its State Employment Service offices (USES, 1962). Of the nine aptitude scores yielded by this battery, those to be considered for each occupation were chosen on the basis of criterion correlations as well as means and standard deviations of workers in that occupation.

The development of GATB occupational standards for machine cutters in the food-canning and preserving industry is illustrated in Table 18. In terms of standard scores with a mean of 100 and an *SD* of 20, the cutoff scores for this occupation were set at 75 in Motor Coordination (*K*), Finger Dexterity (*F*), and Manual Dexterity (*M*). Table 18 gives mean, standard deviation, and correlation with the criterion (supervisory ratings) for each of the nine scores in a group of 57 women workers. On the basis of criterion

TABLE 18 ILLUSTRATIVE DATA USED TO ESTABLISH CUTOFF SCORES ON GATB

(From USES, 1958, p. 10)

	Aptitude	Mean	SD	Criterion Correlation
G	Intelligence	75.1	14.2	−.094
V	Verbal	80.1	11.3	−.085
N	Numerical	73.2	18.4	−.064
S	Spatial	78.9	15.9	.041
P	Form Perception	80.1	23.5	−.012
Q	Clerical Perception	86.3	16.6	.088
K	Motor Coordination	89.3	20.7	.316*
F	Finger Dexterity	92.4	18.1	.155
M	Manual Dexterity	88.2	18.6	.437**

* significant at .05 level.
** significant at .01 level.

correlations, Manual Dexterity and Motor Coordination appeared promising. Finger Dexterity was added because it yielded the highest mean score in the battery, even though individual differences within the group were not significantly correlated with criterion ratings. It would seem that women who enter or remain in this type of job are already selected with regard to Finger Dexterity.[4]

[4] The data have been somewhat simplified for illustrative purposes. Actually, the final choice of aptitudes and cutting scores was based on separate analyses of three groups of workers on related jobs, on the results obtained in a combined sample of 194 cases, and on qualitative job analyses of the operations involved.

The validity of the composite *KFM* pattern of cutting scores in a group of 194 workers is shown in Table 19. It will be seen that, of 150 good workers, 120 fell above the cutting scores in the three aptitudes and 30 were false re-

TABLE 19   EFFECTIVENESS OF GATB CUTOFF SCORES ON APTITUDES *K*, *F*, AND *M* IN IDENTIFYING GOOD AND POOR WORKERS

(From USES, 1958, p. 14)

Criterion Rating	Score Pattern		Total
	Non-Qualifying	Qualifying	
Good	30	120	150
Poor	30	14	44
Total	60	134	194

jects, falling below one or more cutoffs. Of the 44 poor workers, 30 were correctly identified and 14 were false acceptances. The over-all efficacy of this cutoff pattern is indicated by a tetrachoric correlation of .70 between predicted status and criterion ratings.

If only scores yielding significant validity coefficients are taken into account, one or more essential abilities in which all workers in the occupation excel might be overlooked. Hence the need for considering also those aptitudes in which workers excel as a group, even when individual differences beyond a certain minimum are unrelated to degree of job success. The multiple cutoff method is preferable to the regression equation in situations such as these, in which test scores are not linearly related to the criterion. In some jobs, moreover, workers may be so homogeneous in a key trait that the range of individual differences is too narrow to yield a significant correlation between test scores and criterion.

The strongest argument for the use of multiple cutoffs rather than a regression equation centers around the question of compensatory qualifications. With the regression equation, an individual who rates low in one test may receive an acceptable total score because he rates very high in some other test in the battery. A marked deficiency in one skill may thus be compensated for by outstanding ability along other lines. It is possible, however, that certain types of activity may require essential skills for which there is no substitute. In such cases, individuals falling below the required minimum in the essential skill will fail, regardless of their other abilities. An opera singer, for example, cannot afford to have poor pitch discrimination, regardless of how well he meets the other requirements of such a career. Similarly, operators of sound-detection devices in submarines need good auditory discrimination. Those men incapable of making the necessary discriminations cannot succeed in such an assignment, regardless of superior mechanical aptitude, general intelligence, or other traits in which they may excel. With a multiple cutoff strategy, individuals lacking any essential skill would always be rejected, while with a regression equation they might be accepted.

When the relation between tests and criterion is linear and additive, on the other hand, a higher proportion of correct decisions will be reached with a regression equation than with multiple cutoffs. Another important advantage of the regression equation is that it provides an estimate of each person's criterion score, thereby permitting the relative evaluation of all individuals. With multiple cutoffs, no further differentiation is possible among those accepted or among those rejected. In many situations, the best strategy may involve a combination of both procedures. Thus, the multiple cutoff may be applied first, in order to reject those falling below minimum standards on any test, and predicted criterion scores may then be computed for the remaining acceptable cases by the use of a regression equation. If enough is known about the particular job requirements, the preliminary screening may be done in terms of only one or two essential skills, prior to the application of the regression equation.

CLINICAL JUDGMENT. When tests are employed in the intensive study of individual cases, as in clinical diagnosis, counseling, or the selection of high-level personnel, it is a common practice for scores on separate tests to be utilized by the examiner in arriving at a decision without further statistical manipulation. To be sure, the individual's scores are interpreted with reference to any available general or local norms; but no statistical formula or other automatic procedure is applied in combining scores from different tests or in evaluating the individual's score pattern. Through a relatively subjective process, the examiner interprets the individual's scores in terms of his own past experience with similar cases, his familiarity with particular job requirements, or his knowledge of psychological theory and relevant published research. The result may be presented in the form of a detailed description of personality dynamics, a specific prediction (e.g., Mr. Brown will make a good executive vice-president for this company; Miss Peterson will not respond well to psychotherapy), or both.

In a provocative book entitled *Clinical Versus Statistical Prediction*, Meehl (1954) discussed the process of clinical judgment and surveyed some 20 investigations comparing the two types of prediction. The criteria predicted in these studies included principally success in some kind of schooling or training (college, Air Force pilot training, etc.), response to therapy on the part of psychotic or neurotic patients, and criminal recidivism as well as institutional adjustment of reformatory inmates. Predictions were made by clinical psychologists, counselors, psychiatrists, and other professional persons with varying amounts of experience in the use of clinical procedures. Focusing only on the process of combining data, rather than on differences in the kind of data obtained, Meehl showed that, with only one questionable exception, the routine application of statistical procedures yielded at least as many correct predictions as clinical analysis, and frequently more. In this connection, Meehl also called attention to the much greater cost of clinical predictions, in terms of both time and level of personnel required. Once a regression equation or other statistical strategy has been developed, it can be applied by a clerk or even a machine.

The publication of Meehl's book stimulated a lively controversy regarding the relative merits of clinical judgment and statistical predictions.[5] Several penetrating analyses of the process of clinical judgment appeared (Donahoe, 1960; Hoffman, 1960; Holtzman, 1960; Kahn, 1960; McArthur, 1954; Miller & Bieri, 1963; Richards, 1963; Sarbin, Taft, & Bailey, 1960; Thorne, 1960). Additional and better-controlled empirical comparisons of clinical and statistical predictions were conducted, with the weight of the evidence shifting somewhat in favor of the clinical approach (Albrecht, Glaser, & Marks, 1964; Alexakos, 1966; Dicken & Black, 1965; Holt, 1958; Lindzey, 1965; McHugh & Apostolakos, 1959; Meehl, 1959; Meehl, 1965; Sydiaha, 1959; Trankell, 1959). An important methodological point is that the optimum situations for the application of clinical judgment and statistical prediction differ. Each method performs better than the other within its own proper domain. Hence, comparisons of the two methods under identical conditions are likely to favor one or the other, but the results cannot be generalized to all applications of either method.

When statistical formulas of known validity are available for combining test scores, they should certainly be used in preference to subjective clinical judgment. The clinician's chief contributions to diagnosis and prediction are in areas in which satisfactory tests are unavailable. Systematic interviewing, case histories, and direct observation of behavior are still the principal sources of information on many aspects of personality. Clinical methods also lend themselves better than tests to the evaluation of rare and idiosyncratic events that occur too infrequently to permit the establishment of statistical strategies. Similarly, the clinician can give due consideration to the context in which events occur. For example, the same physical disability may have very different effects on the personality development of two children because of other concomitant traits or circumstances. To be sure, this is a problem of pattern analysis, which theoretically can be handled by appropriate statistical procedures; but when the modifying variables are numerous and each occurs infrequently, the statistical procedures may become too complex to be practicable. The ideal procedure, when time and available facilities permit, is probably a combination of clinical and statistical approaches. The clinician should utilize all the objective test data, norms, and regression equations applicable to the particular situation, while

---

[5] For a survey of much of the pertinent literature appearing since the publication of Meehl's book, see Sawyer (1966).

supplementing this information with facts and inferences attainable only through clinical procedures.

The validity of clinical predictions against actual outcomes should be systematically investigated whenever feasible. More data are also needed on the consistency of predictions about the same subjects made by different clinicians and by the same clinicians at different times. Insofar as possible, the process and cues on which clinical predictions are based should be made explicit in clinical records. Such a practice would not only facilitate research and training, but would also serve to encourage reliance on sound data and defensible interpretations. Finally, the "clinician as instrument" is an important concept in this connection. Undoubtedly the objectivity and skill with which data are gathered and interpreted—and the resulting accuracy of predictions—vary widely with the abilities, personality, professional training, and experience of individual clinicians.

USE OF TESTS FOR CLASSIFICATION DECISIONS

Psychological tests may be used for purposes of selection, placement, or classification. In *selection*, each individual is either accepted or rejected. Deciding whether or not to admit a student to college, to hire a job applicant, or to accept an Army recruit for officer training are examples of selection decisions. When selection is done sequentially, the earlier stages are often called "screening," the term "selection" being reserved for the more intensive final stages. "Screening" may also be used to designate any rapid, rough selection process even when not followed by further selection procedures.

Both placement and classification differ from selection in that no one is rejected, or eliminated from the program. All individuals are assigned to appropriate "treatments" so as to maximize the effectiveness of outcomes. In *placement*, the assignments are based on a single score. This score may be derived from a single test, such as an intelligence test. If a battery of tests has been administered, a composite score computed from a single regression equation would be employed. Examples of placement decisions include the sectioning of college freshmen into different mathematics classes on the basis of their scores on mathematical aptitude tests, assigning applicants to clerical jobs requiring different levels of skill and responsibility, and placing psychiatric patients into "more disturbed" and "less disturbed" wards. It is evident that in each of these decisions only one criterion is employed and that placement is determined by the individual's position along a single predictor scale.

Classification, on the other hand, always involves two or more criteria. In a military situation, for example, classification is a major problem, since each man in an available manpower pool must be assigned to the military specialty where he can serve most effectively. Classification decisions are likewise required in industry, when new employees are assigned to training programs for different kinds of jobs. Other examples include the assignment of students to different curricula in college (science, liberal arts, etc.), as well as the choice of a field of concentration by the student. Counseling is based essentially on classification, since the client is told his chances of succeeding in different kinds of work. Clinical diagnosis is likewise a classification problem, the major purposes of each diagnosis being a decision regarding the most appropriate type of therapy.

Although placement can be done with either one or more predictors, classification requires multiple predictors whose validity is individually determined against each criterion. A classification battery requires a different regression equation for each criterion. Some of the tests may have weights in all the equations, although of different values; others may be included in only one or two equations, having zero or negligible weights for some of the criteria. Thus, the combination of tests employed out of the total battery, as well as the specific weights, differs with the particular criterion. An example of such a classification battery is that developed by the Air Force for assignment of personnel to different training programs (DuBois, 1947). This battery, consisting of both paper-and-pencil and apparatus tests, provided stanine scores for pilots, navigators, bombardiers, and a few other air-crew specialties. By finding an individual's estimated criterion scores from the different regression equations, it was possible to predict whether, for example, he was better qualified as a pilot than as a navigator.

Such differential prediction of criteria with a battery of tests permits a fuller utilization of available human resources than is possible with a single general test or with a composite score from a single regression equation. As we saw in the Taylor-Russell tables and elsewhere in this chapter, the effectiveness of any test in selecting personnel for a given job depends on the selection ratio. In classification decisions, we work with a smaller selection ratio and are thus able to assign better qualified persons to each job. If out of 100 applicants, 10 are needed to fill each of two different jobs, the selection ratio is 10 percent for each job, when separate predictors are employed for each. If a single predictor (such as a general intelligence test) were used to select applicants for both jobs, the selection ratio would be 20 percent, since we could do no better than take the top 20 applicants.

Even when predictors for the two jobs are highly correlated, so that some of the same applicants will qualify for both jobs, there is considerable gain from the use of separate predictors. This situation is illustrated in Table 20, which shows the mean standard criterion score of workers selected for each of two jobs by a selection strategy (single predictor) and by a classification strategy involving two different predictors, each validated against its own job criterion. If workers were assigned by chance, with no selection, the mean standard score in this scale would be zero. This would be the case if the selection ratio were 50 percent for each job, so that 100 percent of the applicants would have to be hired. Note that even under these conditions, job performance would be improved by the use of two predictors, as shown in the last row of the table. With two uncorrelated predictors, mean job performance would be .31 (approximately ⅓ of a standard deviation above the chance value). As the correlation between the predictors increases, the job effectiveness of the selected employees decreases; but it remains better

TABLE 20 MEAN STANDARD CRITERION SCORE OF PERSONS PLACED ON TWO JOBS BY SELECTION OR CLASSIFICATION STRATEGIES

(Adapted from Brogden, 1951, p. 182)

Selection Ratio for Each Job	Selection: Single Predictor	Classification: Two predictors whose intercorrelation is				
		0	.20	.40	.60	.80
5%	.88	1.03	1.02	1.01	1.00	.96
10	.70	.87	.86	.84	.82	.79
20	.48	.68	.67	.65	.62	.59
30	.32	.55	.53	.50	.46	.43
40	.18	.42	.41	.37	.34	.29
50	.00	.31	.28	.25	.22	.17

than chance even when the correlation is .80. With lower selection ratios, we can of course obtain better qualified personnel. As can be seen in Table 20, however, for each selection ratio, mean job performance is better when applicants are chosen through classification than through selection strategies.

A practical illustration of the advantages of classification strategies is provided by the use of Aptitude Area scores in the assignment of personnel to military occupational specialties in the U. S. Army (Helme, 1960; Helme & Fitch, 1962). Each Aptitude Area corresponds to a group of Army jobs requiring common qualifications. From an 11-test classification battery, two-test combinations are employed to find the individual's score in each Aptitude Area. Figure 28 shows the results of an investigation of 1,800 enlisted men in which the use of Aptitude Area scores was compared to the use of a global screening test (AFQT). It will be noted that only 56 percent of this group reached or exceeded the 50th percentile on the AFQT, while 91 percent reached or exceeded the average standard score of 100 on their best Aptitude Area. Thus, if men were allocated to specific jobs on the basis of the aptitudes required by each job, nearly everyone could be assigned to a type of work in which his performance was as good as the average performance of the entire sample or better. This apparent impossibility, in which nearly everyone is above average, can be attained by capitalizing on the fact that nearly everyone excels in *some* aptitude.

The data of Figure 28 were based on the utilization of only two test scores for predicting achievement in each Aptitude Area or type of job. This procedure was followed for many years because of the practical difficulties of utilizing the entire battery with appropriate regression equations for each job area. Although the use of the full regression equations provides a more effective way to allocate men to different jobs (Sorenson, 1965), the

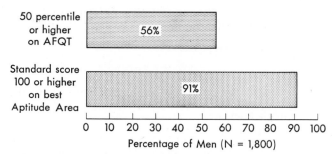

FIG. 28.   Percentages of Enlisted Men Scoring Above Average on AFQT and on Best Aptitude Area. (Courtesy of J. E. Uhlaner, U.S. Army Behavioral Science Research Laboratory, 1967.)

excessive hand computation required by this procedure made it impracticable. With the increasing availability of modern computer facilities, however, plans are under way to change over to the use of full regression equations on the entire test battery (Boldt, 1964). Under these conditions, the effectiveness of the classification procedures will be even greater than it was with the relatively crude approximation represented by the Aptitude Area scores.

The *differential validity* of a classification test depends on the difference between its correlations with the separate criteria to be predicted. In a two-criterion classification problem, for example, the ideal test would have a high correlation with one criterion and a zero correlation (or preferably a negative correlation) with the other criterion. General intelligence tests are relatively poor for classification purposes, since they predict success about equally well in most areas. Hence, their correlations with the criteria to be differentiated would be too similar. An individual scoring high on such a test would be classified as successful for either assignment, and it would be impossible to predict in which he would do better. In a classification battery, we need some tests that are good predictors of criterion A and poor predictors of criterion B, and other tests that are poor predictors of A and good predictors of B. Statistical procedures have been developed for selecting tests so as to maximize the differential validity of a classification battery (Brogden, 1951; Cronbach & Gleser, 1965; Horst, 1954; Mollenkopf,

1950b). When the number of criteria is greater than two, such procedures become quite complex.

An alternative way of handling classification decisions is by means of the *multiple discriminant function* (French, 1966). Essentially, this is a mathematical procedure for determining how closely the individual's scores on a whole set of tests approximate the scores typical of persons in a given occupation, curriculum, psychiatric syndrome, or other category. A person would then be assigned to the particular group he resembles most closely. Although the regression equation permits the prediction of degree of success in each field, the multiple discriminant function treats all persons in one category as of equal status. Group membership is the only criterion data utilized by this method. The discriminant function is useful when criterion scores are unavailable and only group membership can be ascertained. Some tests, for instance, are validated by administering them to persons in different occupations, although no measure of degree of vocational success is available for individuals within each field.

The discriminant function is also appropriate when there is a nonlinear relation between the criterion and one or more predictors. For example, in certain personality traits there may be an optimum range for a given occupation. Individuals having either more or less of the trait in question would thus be at a disadvantage. It seems reasonable to expect, for instance, that salesmen showing a moderately high amount of social dominance would be most likely to succeed, and that the chances of success would decline as scores move in either direction from this region. With the discriminant function, we would tend to select individuals falling within this optimum range. With the regression equation, on the other hand, the more dominant the score, the more favorable would be the predicted outcome. If the correlation between predictor and criterion were negative, of course, the regression equation would yield more favorable predictions for the low scorers. But there is no way whereby an intermediate score would receive maximum credit. Although in many instances the two techniques would lead to the same choices, there are situations in which persons would be differently classified by regression equations and discriminant functions. For most psychological testing purposes, regression equations provide a more effective technique. Under certain circumstances, however, the discriminant function is better suited to yield the required information.

7

Item Analysis

FAMILIARITY WITH the basic concepts and techniques of item analysis, like knowledge about other phases of test construction, can help the test user in his evaluation of published tests. In addition, item analysis is particularly relevant to the construction of informal, local tests, such as the quizzes and examinations prepared by teachers for classroom use. Some of the general guidelines for effective item writing, as well as the simpler statistical techniques of item analysis, can materially improve classroom tests and are worth using even with small groups.

Items can be analyzed qualitatively, in terms of their content and form, and quantitatively, in terms of their statistical properties. Qualitative analysis includes the consideration of content validity, discussed in Chapter 5, and the evaluation of items in terms of effective item-writing procedures, to be discussed in the next section. Quantitative analysis includes principally the measurement of item difficulty and item validity. Both the validity and the reliability of any test depend ultimately on the characteristics of its items. High reliability and validity can be built into a test in advance through item analysis. Tests can be improved through the selection, substitution, or revision of items.

Item analysis makes it possible to shorten a test, and at the same time increase its validity and reliability. Other things being equal, a longer test is more valid and reliable than a shorter one. The effect of lengthening or shortening a test on the reliability coefficient was discussed in Chapter 4, where the Spearman-Brown formula for estimating this effect was also presented. These estimated changes in reliability occur when the discarded items are equivalent to those that remain, or when equivalent new items

are added to the test. Similar changes in validity will result from the dele-
tion or addition of items of equivalent validity. All such estimates of change
in reliability or validity refer to the lengthening or shortening of tests
through a *random* selection of items, without item analysis. When a test is
shortened by eliminating the least satisfactory items, however, the short
test may be more valid and reliable than the original, longer instrument.

ITEM CONTENT AND FORM

The principles of effective item writing are essentially the same for different types of tests, although they have been most frequently discussed
with reference to the construction of achievement tests. This type of test
is used widely in education, as well as in the selection and classification of
personnel for civil service and the armed services. Since it is characteristic
of achievement tests that they measure the effects of a clearly defined
course of training, coverage can be specified more clearly for this type of
test than for other types.

PLANNING THE TEST. The test constructor who plunges directly into
item writing is likely to produce a lopsided test. Without an advance plan,
some areas will be overrepresented while others may remain untouched. It
is generally easier to prepare objective items on some topics than on others.
And it is easier to prepare items that require the recall of simple facts than
to devise items calling for critical evaluation, integration of different facts,
or application of principles to new situations. Yet follow-up studies have
shown that the factual details learned in a course are most likely to be
forgotten, while the understanding of principles and their application to
new situations show either no retention loss or an actual gain with time
after completion of a course. Thus, the test constructed without a blueprint
is likely to be overloaded with relatively impermanent and less important
material. Many of the popular criticisms of objective tests stem from the
common overemphasis of rote memory and trivial details in poorly constructed tests.

To guard against these fortuitous imbalances and disproportions of item
coverage, *test specifications* should be drawn up before any items are prepared. For classroom examinations, such specifications should begin with
an outline of the objectives of the course as well as of the subject matter to
be covered. In listing objectives, the test constructor should ask himself
what changes in behavior the course was designed to produce. Such changes
may pertain to attitudes, interests, interpersonal relations, and other emotional or motivational characteristics, as well as to the acquisition of knowledge and the development of intellectual skills.

Table 21 illustrates a well-planned two-way table of specifications for a

300-item examination on the history of civilization (Dressel *et al.*, 1949). Across the top are listed 12 content categories or topics to be covered. In the left-hand column are 8 educational objectives or types of learning to be tested. The entries in the body of the table represent the desired number of items, classified by content and objective. These numbers should reflect the relative importance and scope of each topic and objective. When a particular objective or type of learning is inapplicable to a given topic, no items are listed in the corresponding cell. Column and row totals show the over-all weight of each topic and type of learning in the entire examination.

It should be noted that the planned weights may not always correspond closely to the actual weights in the total test score, since the latter are influenced by the ability of items to discriminate among individuals. In an extreme example, if all examinees obtain the same score on a particular group of items, the effect of these items will be simply to add a constant to everyone's score; they will thus contribute nothing to individual differences in total score. Such nondiscriminating items can be identified through statistical item analysis, as we shall see in a later section.

ITEM WRITING. The test constructor must first decide on the most appropriate item form for his material. The advantages traditionally cited in favor of essay questions are that they test the individual's ability to select, relate, and organize material, as well as his ability to express ideas clearly and accurately. Unfortunately, the time available to the examinee in answering essay questions is usually too short to measure these particular skills. It is possible, in fact, that essay examinations may be partly responsible for the habits of unclear and careless writing developed by many students. Apart from lack of time for effective organization and good writing, the student answering essay questions writes for an instructor who knows more about the subject than he does. Confident in the expectation that even obscure answers will be understood and duly credited, the student rarely takes the trouble to communicate clearly.

With small groups, it may not be worthwhile to prepare objective items, especially in an area that is rapidly changing and would require frequent item revision. Under such circumstances, essay questions that are carefully formulated and scored may provide the most practicable solution. Or a combination of essay and objective items may be chosen. Essay items can be improved by full and explicit formulation of the question and by systematic scoring procedures. A common weakness of essay examinations arises from subjectivity of scoring. It has been repeatedly demonstrated that the same answer may receive very different grades from different examiners or even from the same examiner at different times. To minimize these sources of error variance, it is advisable to list in advance the points to be covered by the answer and the credit to be assigned to each. Preparing sample answers also helps, especially when several persons are to do the scoring.

TABLE 21 TWO-WAY SPECIFICATION TABLE FOR AN EXAMINATION IN THE HISTORY OF CIVILIZATION

(From Dressel et al., 1949, p. 91)

CONTENT / OBJECTIVES	I Nature of Civilization	II Hellenic Civilization	III Hellenistic Civilization	IV Roman Civilization	V Medieval Civilization, the Church	VI Medieval Civilization, Feudalism	VII The Medieval Mind	VIII The Renaissance	IX The Reformation	X The 18th Century	XI The French Revolution	XII The Last Century	TOTAL
Knowledge and Understanding of													
1. Historical Terms	—	2	1	1	3	—	1	2	1	5	5	4	25
2. Cause-Effect Relationships	1	1	—	3	2	3	4	1	6	3	3	3	30
3. Motivating Ideals	—	1	—	1	6	5	6	1	10	3	1	7	41
4. Miscellaneous	9	11	4	6	4	6	12	9	5	8	11	13	98
Ability to													
5. Recognize Chronological Relationships	—	5	1	3	5	—	3	1	1	1	2	3	25
6. Use Historical Maps	—	—	2	1	2	1	—	2	1	6	3	5	23
7. Evaluate Differences in Civilizations	1	4	1	1	1	1	6	—	—	5	6	6	32
8. Read Historical Materials	—	—	—	5	—	6	—	5	—	—	—	10	26
TOTAL	11	24	9	21	23	22	32	21	24	31	31	51	300

As the art of item writing develops, more and more of the abilities formerly believed to be amenable only to essay questions are proving to be testable by objective items. Among the chief advantages of objective items are ease, rapidity, and objectivity of scoring. Since each objective item requires much less of the examinee's time than does a typical essay question, objective items also permit a fuller coverage of content and hence reduce an important source of chance errors in total scores.

Among objective items, there is a choice of several specific forms, such as true-false, multiple-choice, completion, matching, and arrangement (in order of magnitude, chronological order, etc.). The content and type of learning to be tested would largely determine the most appropriate item form. Multiple-choice items have proved to be the most widely applicable. They are also easier to score than certain other forms, and reduce the chances of correct guessing by presenting several alternative responses.

Many practical rules for effective item writing have been formulated on the basis of years of experience in preparing items and empirical evaluation of responses. Anyone planning to prepare objective items would do well to consult one of the books summarizing these suggestions (e.g., Ebel, 1965, Chs. 3–6; Gronlund, 1965, Chs. 6–11; Stanley, 1964, Chs. 6–8; Wesman, 1971; Wood, 1960). The *Taxonomy of Educational Objectives* (Bloom *et al.*, 1956; Krathwohl *et al.*, 1964), discussed in Chapter 5, contains many illustrations of items designed to test different learning skills. Of considerable help, too, are published collections of items. Gerberich (1956) provides a detailed classification of items designed for different purposes and illustrates his discussion with over 200 items. References to published item collections in special fields, ranging from accounting and art appreciation to world history and zoology, can be found in Furst (1958) and Gerberich (1956).

To add one more summary of item-writing "rules" to the many already available would be redundant. However, a few examples will be given to illustrate the kind of pitfalls that await the unwary item writer. Ambiguous or unclear items are a familiar difficulty. Misunderstandings are likely to occur because of the necessary brevity. It is difficult to write a single sentence that can stand alone with clarity and precision. In ordinary writing, any obscurity in one sentence can be cleared away by the sentences that follow; but it requires unusual skill to compose isolated sentences that can carry the whole burden unaided. The best test of clarity under these circumstances is to have the statement read by someone else. The writer, who knows the context within which he framed the item, may find it difficult to perceive other meanings in it. If he reads it a later time, however, the writer himself may be able to spot ambiguities.

While students who feel they may have been cheated out of one or two score points by ambiguous items are quick to call it to the instructor's attention, the opposite type of error is less likely to be publicized. Yet many poorly constructed items give an advantage to the observant guesser. For example, one item may give away the answer to another occurring in a different part of the examination. Thus, one item may require the student to identify the name of the psychologist who developed the tests of primary mental abilities, while another begins with the words, "In Thurstone's tests of primary mental abilities. . . ." Grammatical cues, such as differences in number or tense of verbs or the use of the indefinite article "a" instead of "an," may reveal the correct alternative in a multiple-choice item or may at least permit the student to eliminate at once one of the wrong alternatives.

In the effort to be clear, the inexperienced item writer frequently makes the correct alternative longer or qualifies it more fully than the other alternatives. Examinees soon learn that the odds are in their favor if they choose such an alternative when they do not know the correct answer. A final example is provided by clang, or alliterative associations, as in the following vocabulary item:

(poor) illicit: secret illegal sexual ignorant daring
(good) illicit: secret unlawful sexual illiterate daring

In the first example, the individual who does not know the meaning of *illicit* could get the item right by choosing the word that sounds most nearly like it. Substituting *unlawful* for *illegal* in the second version has eliminated this cue. In addition, the alliterative cue in this version would mislead the guesser, since on this basis he would choose a wrong alternative, *illiterate*.

ITEM DIFFICULTY

PERCENTAGE PASSING. In test construction, the difficulty of an item is based on the percentage of persons who answer it correctly. The easier the item, the larger will this percentage be. A word that is correctly defined by 70 percent of the standardization sample ($p = .70$) is regarded as easier than one that is correctly defined by only 15 percent ($p = .15$). It is customary to arrange items in order of difficulty, so that examinees begin with relatively easy items and proceed to items of increasing difficulty. This arrangement gives the individual confidence in approaching the test and also reduces the likelihood of his wasting much time on items beyond his ability to the neglect of easier items he can correctly complete.

A major reason for measuring item difficulty is to discard items of unsuitable difficulty level. Obviously if no one passes an item, it is excess baggage in the test. The same is true of items that everyone passes. Neither of these types of items provides any information about individual differences. Since such items do not affect the variability of test scores, they contribute nothing to the reliability or validity of the test. The closer the difficulty of an item approaches 1.00 or 0, the less differential information about examinees it contributes. Conversely, the closer the difficulty level approaches .50, the more differentiations the item can make. Suppose out of 100 persons, 50 pass an item and 50 fail it ($p = .50$). This item enables us to differentiate between each of those who passed it and each of those who failed it. We thus have 50×50 or 2500 bits of differential information. An item passed by 70 percent of the persons provides 70×30 or 2100 bits of information; one passed by 90 percent provides 90×10 or 900; one passed by 100 percent provides 100×0 or 0. The same relationships would hold for harder items, passed by fewer than 50 percent.

For maximum differentiation, then, it would seem that one should choose all items at the .50 difficulty level. The decision is complicated, however, by the fact that items within a test tend to be intercorrelated. The more homogeneous the test, the higher will these intercorrelations be. In an extreme case, if all items were perfectly intercorrelated and all were of .50 difficulty level, the same 50 persons out of 100 would pass each item. Consequently, half of the examinees would obtain perfect scores and the other half zero scores.

Because of item intercorrelations, it is best to choose items with a moderate spread of difficulty level, but whose average difficulty is .50. The fact that this choice yields wider differentiation in total scores than is obtained with items that are themselves widely distributed in difficulty level is illustrated in Figure 29. The three distributions of total scores given in Figure 29 were obtained by Ebel (1965) with three 16-item tests assembled for this purpose. The items in Test C were chosen so as to cluster close to the .50 difficulty level; those in Test D are widely distributed over the entire difficulty range; and those in Test E fall at the two extremes of difficulty. It will be noted that the widest spread of total test scores was obtained with the items concentrated around .50. The reliability coefficient was also highest in this case, and it was particularly low in the test composed of items with extreme difficulty values (Test E). This simple demonstration serves only to clarify the point; similar conclusions have been reached in more technical analyses of the problem, with both statistical and experimental techniques (Cronbach & Warrington, 1952; Lord, 1952a, 1952b).

Although items clustering around .50 difficulty are to be preferred for maximum differentiation among individuals, tests designed for special screening purposes should utilize items whose difficulty values come closest to the desired selection ratio (Lord, 1953). For example, to select the upper 20 percent of the cases, the best items are those clustering around a p of .20. Since in a screening test no differentiation is required *within* the accepted or rejected groups, the most effective use of testing time is obtained when items cluster near the critical cutoff. It follows, for instance, that if a test were to be used to screen scholarship applicants from a college population, the difficulty level of items should be considerably higher

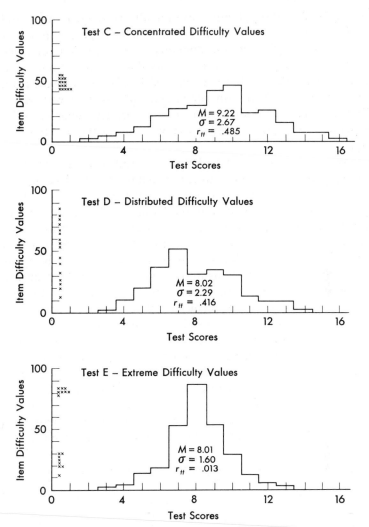

FIG. 29. Relation between Distribution of Test Scores and Distribution of Item Difficulty Values. (From Ebel, 1965, p. 363.)

than the average for that population. Similarly, if poor learners were being selected for a remedial training program, items of much lower than average difficulty values would be desirable.

INTERVAL SCALES. The percentage of persons passing an item expresses item difficulty in terms of an *ordinal scale;* that is, it correctly indicates the rank order or relative difficulty of items. For example, if Items 1, 2, and 3 are passed by 30, 20, and 10 percent of the cases, respectively, we can conclude that Item 1 is the easiest and Item 3 is the hardest of the three. But we cannot infer that the difference in difficulty between Items 1 and 2 is equal to that between Items 2 and 3. Equal percentage differences would correspond to equal differences in difficulty only in a rectangular distribution, in which the cases were uniformly distributed throughout the range. This problem is similar to that encountered in connection with percentile scores, which are also based on percentages of cases. It will be recalled from Chapter 3 that percentile scores do not represent equal units, but differ in magnitude from the center to the extremes of the distribution (Fig. 9, Ch. 3).

If we assume a normal distribution of the trait measured by any given item, the difficulty level of the item can be expressed in terms of an equal-unit interval scale by reference to a table of normal curve frequencies. In Chapter 3 we saw, for example, that approximately 34 percent of the cases in a normal distribution fall between the mean and a distance of 1σ in either direction (Fig. 6, Ch. 3). With this information, we can examine Figure 30, which shows the difficulty level of an item passed by 84 percent of the cases. Since it is the persons in the upper part of the distribution who pass and those in the lower part who fail, this 84 percent includes the upper half (50%) plus 34 percent of the cases from the lower half ($50 + 34 = 84$). Hence, the item falls 1σ *below* the mean, as shown in Figure 30. An item passed by 16 percent of the cases would fall 1σ *above* the mean, since above this point there are 16 percent of the cases ($50 - 34 = 16$). An item passed by exactly 50 percent of the cases falls at the mean and would thus have a 0 value on this scale. The more difficult items have plus values, the easier items minus values. The difficulty value corresponding to any percentage passing can be found by reference to a normal curve frequency table, given in any standard statistics text.

Because item difficulties expressed in terms of normal curve σ-units

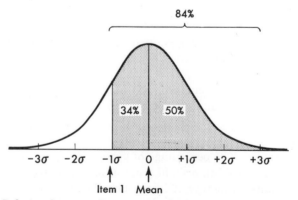

FIG. 30. Relation between Percentage of Persons Passing an Item and Item Difficulty in Normal Curve Units.

involve negative values and decimals, they are usually converted into a more manageable scale. One such scale, employed by Educational Testing Service in its test development, uses a unit designated by the Greek letter *delta* (Δ). The relation between Δ and normal curve σ-values (x) is shown below:

$$\Delta = 13 + 4x$$

The constants 13 and 4 were chosen arbitrarily in order to provide a scale that eliminates negative values and yields a range of integers broad enough to permit the dropping of decimals. An item passed by nearly 100 percent of the cases (99.87%), falling at -3σ, would have a Δ of: $13 + (4)(-3) = 1$. This is the lowest value likely to be found in most groups. At the other extreme, an item passed by less than 1 percent (0.13%) of the cases, will have a value of $+3\sigma$ and a Δ of: $13 + (4)(3) = 25$. An item falling at the mean will have a 0 σ-value and a Δ of: $13 + (4)(0) = 13$. The Δ scale is thus a scale in which practically all items will fall between 1 and 25, and the mean difficulty value within any given group corresponds to 13.

An important practical advantage of the Δ scale over other possible conversions is that a table is available (Fan, 1952) from which Δ can be found by simply entering the value of p (proportion of persons passing the item). The table eliminates the necessity of looking up normal curve σ-values and transforming these values to Δ's. For most practical purposes, an ordinal measure of item difficulty, such as percentage passing, is adequate. For more precise statistical analyses, requiring the measurement of difficulty on an interval scale, Δ values can be obtained with little additional effort.

ITEM VALIDITY

ITEM-CRITERION RELATIONSHIPS. All indices of item validity are based on the relationship between item response and criterion performance. Any criterion employed for test validation is also suitable for item validation. Since item responses are generally recorded as pass or fail, the measurement of item validity usually involves a dichotomous variable (the item) and a continuous variable (the criterion). In certain situations, the criterion too may be dichotomous, as in graduation versus nongraduation from college or success versus failure on a job. Moreover, a continuous criterion may be dichotomized for purposes of analysis. The basic relationship between item and criterion is illustrated by the three item characteristic curves reproduced in Figure 31. Using fictitious data, each of these curves shows the percentages of persons in each class-interval of criterion score who pass the item. It can be seen that Item 1 has a low validity, since it is

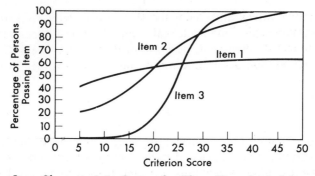

FIG. 31.   Item Characteristic Curves for Three Hypothetical Items. (Adapted from Lord, 1953, p. 520.)

passed by nearly the same proportion of persons throughout the criterion range. Items 2 and 3 are better, showing a closer correspondence between percentage passing and criterion score. Of these two, 3 is the more valid item, since its curve rises more steeply.

Although item characteristic curves can provide a vivid graphic representation of differences in item validities, decisions about indivdual items can be made more readily if validity is expressed by a single numerical index for each item. Over fifty different indices of item validity have been developed and used in test construction. One difference among them pertains to their applicability to dichotomous or continuous measures. Among those applicable to dichotomous variables, moreover, some assume a continuous and normal distribution of the underlying. trait, on which the dichotomy has been artificially imposed; others assume a true dichotomy. Another difference concerns the relation of item difficulty to item validity. Certain indices measure item validity independently of item difficulty. Others yield higher validities for items close to the .50 difficulty level than for those at the extremes of difficulty.

Despite differences in procedure and assumptions, most item validity indices provide closely similar results. Although the numerical values of the indices may differ, the items that are retained and those that are rejected on the basis of different validity indices are largely the same. In fact, the variation in item validity data from sample to sample is generally greater than that among different methods. For this reason, the choice of method is often based on the amount of computational labor required and the availability of special computational aids. Among the published computational aids are a number of abacs or nomographs. These are computing diagrams with which, for example, the value of an item-criterion correlation can be read directly if the percentages of persons passing the item in high and low criterion groups are known (Guilford, 1954, Ch. 15; Guilford, 1965, pp. 493–506; Henrysson, 1971).

USE OF EXTREME GROUPS. A common practice in item analysis is to compare the proportion of cases who pass an item in contrasting criterion groups. When the criterion is measured along a continuous scale, as in the case of course grades, job ratings, or output records, upper (U) and lower (L) criterion groups are selected from the extremes of the distribution. Obviously, the more extreme the groups the sharper will be the differentiation. But the use of very extreme groups, such as upper and lower 10 percent, would reduce the reliability of the results because of the small number of cases utilized. In a normal distribution, the optimum point at which these two conditions balance is reached with the upper and lower 27 percent (Kelley, 1939). When the distribution is flatter than the normal curve, the optimum percentage is slightly greater than 27 and approaches 33 (Cureton, 1957b). With small groups, as in an ordinary classroom, the sampling error of item statistics is so large that only rough results can be obtained. Under these conditions, therefore, we need not be too concerned about the exact percentage of cases in the two contrasted groups. Any convenient number between 25 percent and 33 percent will serve satisfactorily.

With the large and normally distributed samples employed in the development of standardized tests, it is customary to work with the upper and lower 27 percent of the criterion distribution. Many of the tables and abacs prepared to facilitate the computation of item validity indices are based on the assumption that the "27 percent rule" has been followed. It might be added that if the total sample contains 370 cases, the U and L groups will each include exactly 100 cases, thus obviating the necessity of computing percentages. For this reason, it is desirable in large-scale investigations to use a sample of 370 persons for purposes of item analysis.

SIMPLE ANALYSIS WITH SMALL GROUPS. Because item analysis is frequently conducted with small groups, such as the students who have taken a classroom quiz, we shall consider first a simple procedure especially suitable for this situation. Let us suppose that in a class of 60 students we have chosen the 20 students (33 percent) with the highest and the 20 with the lowest scores. We now have three groups of papers which we may call the Upper (U), Middle (M), and Lower (L) groups. First we need to tally the correct responses to each item given by students in the three groups. This can be done most readily if we list the item numbers in one column and prepare three other columns headed U, M, and L. As we come to each student's paper, we simply place a tally next to each item he answered correctly. This is done for each of the 20 papers in the U group, then for each of the 20 in the M group, and finally for each of the 20 in the L group. We are now ready to count up the tallies and record totals for each group as shown in Table 22. For illustrative purposes, the first seven items have been entered. A rough index of the validity or discriminative value of each item can be found by subtracting the number of persons answering it correctly in the L group from the number answering it correctly in the U group. These U-L differences are given in the last column of Table 22. A measure of item difficulty can be obtained with the same data by adding the number passing each item in all three criterion groups (U + M + L).

Examination of Table 22 reveals four questionable items that have been identified for further consideration or for class discussion. Two items, 2

TABLE 22 SIMPLE ITEM ANALYSIS PROCEDURE: NUMBER OF INDIVIDUALS GIVING CORRECT RESPONSE IN EACH CRITERION GROUP

Item	U (20)	M (20)	L (20)	Difficulty (U + M + L)	Discrimination (U − L)
1	15	9	7	31	8
2	20	20	16	56*	4
3	19	18	9	46	10
4	10	11	16	37	− 6*
5	11	13	11	35	0*
6	16	14	9	39	7
7	5	0	0	5*	5
.					
.					
.					
.					
75					

* Items chosen for discussion.

and 7, have been singled out because one seems to be too easy, having been passed by 56 out of 60 students, and the other too difficult, having been passed by only 5. Items 4 and 5, while satisfactory with regard to difficulty level, show a negative and zero discriminative value, respectively. We would also consider in this category any items with a very small positive U–L difference, of roughly three or less when groups of approximately this size are being compared. With larger groups, we would expect larger differences to occur by chance in a nondiscriminating item.

The purpose of item analysis in a teacher-made test is to identify deficiencies either in the test or in the teaching. Discussing questionable items with the class is often sufficient to diagnose the problem. If the wording of the item was at fault, it can be revised or discarded in subsequent testing. Discussion may show, however, that the item was satisfactory, but the point being tested had not been properly understood. In that case, the topic may be reviewed and clarified. In narrowing down the source of the difficulty, it is often helpful to carry out a supplementary analysis, as shown in Table 23, with at least some of the items chosen for discussion. This tabulation gives the number of students in the U and L groups who chose each *option* in answering the particular items.

TABLE 23 RESPONSE ANALYSIS OF INDIVIDUAL ITEMS

Item		Response Options [a]				
		1	2	3	4	5
2	Upper	0	0	0	*20*	0
	Lower	2	0	1	*16*	1
4	Upper	0	*10*	9	0	1
	Lower	2	*16*	2	0	0
5	Upper	2	3	2	*11*	2
	Lower	1	3	3	*11*	2
7	Upper	5	3	5	4	3
	Lower	0	5	8	3	4
.						
.						
.						

[a] Correct options have been italicized.

Although Item 2 has been included in Table 23, there is little more we can learn about it by tabulating the frequency of each wrong option, since only 4 persons in the L group and none in the U group chose wrong answers. Discussion of the item with the students, however, may help to determine whether the item as a whole was too easy and therefore of little intrinsic value, whether some defect in its construction served to give away the right answer, or whether it is a good item dealing with a point that happened to have been effectively taught and well remembered. In the first case, the item would probably be discarded, in the second it would be revised, and in the third it would be retained unchanged.

The data on Item 4 suggest that the third option had some unsuspected implications that led 9 of the better students to prefer it to the correct alternative. The point could easily be settled by asking those students to explain why they chose it. In Item 5, the fault seems to lie in the wording either of the stem or of the correct alternative, because the students who missed the item were uniformly distributed over the four wrong options. Item 7 is an unusually difficult one, which was answered incorrectly by 15 of the U and all of the L group. The slight clustering of responses on incorrect option

3 suggests a superficial attractiveness of this option, especially for the more easily misled L group. Similarly, the lack of choices of the correct response (option 1) by any of the L group suggests that this alternative was so worded that superficially, or to the uninformed, it seemed wrong. Both of these features, of course, are desiderata of good test items. Class discussion might show that Item 7 is a good item dealing with a point that few class members had actually learned.

THE INDEX OF DISCRIMINATION.   If the numbers of persons passing each item in U and L criterion groups are expressed as proportions,[1] the difference between these two proportions provides an index of item validity that can be interpreted independently of the size of the particular sample in which it was obtained. This index has been repeatedly described in the psychometric literature (see, e.g., Ebel, 1965; Johnson, 1951; Mosier & McQuitty, 1940) and has been variously designated as ULI, ULD, or simply D. Despite its simplicity, it has been shown to agree quite closely with other, more elaborate measures of item validity (Engelhart, 1965). The computation of D can be illustrated by reference to the data previously reported in Table 22. First, the numbers of persons passing each item in the U and L groups are changed to proportions. Because the number of cases in each group is 20, we could divide each number by 20. It is easier, however, to divide 1 by 20, which gives .05, and then multiply each number by that constant. Thus, for Item 1, $15 \times .05 = .75$ (U group) and $7 \times .05 = .35$ (L group). For this item, then, D, is: $.75 - .35 = .40$. The same value can be obtained if we first subtract the numbers passing the item in the U and L groups and then multiply the difference by .05 (from Table 22, $8 \times .05 = .40$). Even minor computational savings such as this mount up in item analysis, because the process must be repeated for each item.

D can have any value between $+1.00$ and -1.00. If all members of the U group and none of the L group pass an item, D equals 1.00. Conversely, if all members of the L and none of the U group pass it, D equals -1.00. If the proportions of both groups passing an item are equal, D will be zero.

D has several interesting properties. It has been demonstrated (Findley, 1956) that D is directly proportional to the difference between the numbers of correct and incorrect discriminations made by an item. This relationship is illustrated in Table 24, which is based on a group of 37 cases, thus yielding 10 cases in the upper and 10 in the lower 27 percent. Looking at Item 1, in the first row of Table 24, we see that it was passed by 9 U and 6 L cases and hence has a D of .30 ($9 - 6 = 3$; $3 \times .10 = .30$). The number of correct discriminations refers to the bits of differential information discussed earlier in this chapter. Again considering Item 1, we find that it enables us to differentiate correctly between the 9 U cases who passed it and the 4 L

[1] A proportion is simply a percentage reported as a decimal (e.g., $38\% = .38$).

TABLE 24 RELATION OF D TO THE NET NUMBER OF CORRECT DISCRIMINATIONS
(Adapted from Ebel, 1965, p. 355.)

	Number of Correct Responses		Number of Discriminations				
Item No.	U (10 cases)	L (10 cases)	Correct (C)	Neutral (N)	Incorrect (I)	Net Correct (C − I)	D
1	9	6	36	58	6	30	.30
2	8	5	40	50	10	30	.30
3	8	4	48	44	8	40	.40
4	7	3	49	42	9	40	.40
5	6	2	48	44	8	40	.40
6	4	2	32	56	12	20	.20
7	3	1	27	66	7	20	.20
8	2	0	20	80	0	20	.20

cases who failed it (from 2nd column of Table 24, $10 - 6 = 4$). Hence, the number of *correct* discriminations is $9 \times 4 = 36$ (3rd column).

Looking again at the first two columns, we see that 1 U case failed the item and 6 L cases passed it. Hence, there were 6 *incorrect* discriminations ($1 \times 6 = 6$). The net number of correct discriminations is thus $36 - 6 = 30$ (column 6). The number of neutral discriminations refers to the cases in which the item failed to make any discrimination, i.e., between the 9 U and 6 L cases who passed and between the 1 U and 4 L cases who failed [$(9 \times 6) + (1 \times 4) = 58$]. To return to our original point: It will be noted that, for Item 1, D (.30) is exactly equal to the proportion of net correct discriminations [2] ($30 \div 100 = .30$). The same relationship holds for the remaining items in Table 24. This has been shown to be a direct and completely generalizable relationship (Findley, 1956).

Another noteworthy characteristic of D is one it shares with several other indices of item validity. The values of D are not independent of item difficulty but are biased in favor of intermediate difficulty levels. Table 25 shows the maximum possible value of D for items with different percentages of correct responses. If either 100 percent or 0 percent of the cases in the total sample pass an item, there can be no difference in percentage passing in U and L groups; hence D is zero. At the other extreme, if 50 percent pass an item, it would be possible for all the U cases and none of the L cases to pass it, thus yielding a D of 1.00 ($1.00 - 0 = 1.00$). If 70 percent pass, the maximum value that D could take can be found as follows: (U) $50/50 = 1.00$; (L) $20/50 = .40$; $D = 1.00 - .40 = .60$. It will be recalled that, for most testing purposes, items closer to the .50 difficulty level

[2] With 10 cases in U and 10 in L group, the total number of possible discriminations is: $10 \times 10 = 100$.

TABLE 25   RELATION OF MAXIMUM VALUE OF D TO ITEM DIFFICULTY

Percentage Passing Item	Maximum Value of D
100	.00
90	.20
70	.60
50	1.00
30	.60
10	.20
0	.00

are preferable. Hence, item validity indices that favor this difficulty level are often appropriate for item selection.

PHI COEFFICIENT.   Many indices of item validity report the relationship between item and criterion in the form of a correlation coefficient. One of these is the phi coefficient (ϕ). Computed from a fourfold table, ϕ is based on the proportions of cases passing and failing an item in U and L criterion groups. Like all correlation coefficients, it yields values between +1.00 and −1.00. The ϕ coefficient assumes a genuine dichotomy in both item response and criterion variable. Consequently, it is strictly applicable only to the dichotomous conditions under which it was obtained and cannot be generalized to any underlying relationship between the traits measured by item and criterion. Like the D index, ϕ is biased toward the middle difficulty levels—that is, it yields the highest possible correlations for dichotomies closest to a 50–50 split.

Several computational aids are available for finding ϕ coefficients. When the number of cases in U and L criterion groups is equal, ϕ can be found with the Jurgensen tables (1947) by simply entering the percentages passing the item in U and L groups. Since in conducting an item analysis it is usually feasible to select U and L groups of equal size, the Jurgensen tables are widely used for this purpose. When the two criterion groups are unequal, ϕ can be found with another set of tables, prepared by Edgerton (1960), although their application is slightly more time consuming.

The significance level of a ϕ coefficient can be readily computed through the relation of ϕ to both Chi Square and the Normal Curve Ratio. Applying the latter, we can identify the minimum value of ϕ that would reach statistical significance at the .05 or .01 levels with the following formulas:

$$\phi_{.05} = \frac{1.96}{\sqrt{N}}$$

$$\phi_{.01} = \frac{2.58}{\sqrt{N}}$$

In these formulas, N represents the total number of cases in both criterion groups combined. Thus, if there were 50 cases in U and 50 in L groups, N would be 100 and the minimum ϕ significant at the .05 level would be $1.96 \div 100 = .196$. Any item whose ϕ reached or exceeded .196 would thus be significant at the .05 level.

BISERIAL CORRELATION. As a final example of a commonly used measure of item validity, we may consider the biserial correlation coefficient (r_{bis}), which contrasts with ϕ in two major respects. First, r_{bis} assumes a continuous and normal distribution of the trait underlying the dichotomous item response. Second, it yields a measure of item-criterion relationship that is independent of item difficulty. To compute r_{bis} directly from the data, we would need the mean criterion score of those who pass and those who fail the item, as well as the proportion of cases passing and failing the item in the entire sample and the standard deviation of the criterion scores.

Computing all the needed terms and applying the r_{bis} formula for each item can be quite time consuming. Tables have been prepared from which r_{bis} can be estimated by merely entering the percentages passing the item in the upper and lower 27 percent of the criterion group (Fan, 1952; 1954). These are the previously mentioned tables obtainable from Educational Testing Service. With these tables it is possible by entering the percentage passing in U and L groups to find three values: an estimate of p, the percentage who pass the item in the entire sample; the previously described Δ, a measure of item difficulty on an interval scale; and r_{bis} between item and criterion. These tables are only applicable when exactly 27 percent of the cases are placed in U and L groups.

There is no way of computing exact significance levels for these estimated biserial correlations, but it has been shown that their standard errors are somewhat larger than those of biserial correlations computed from all the data in the usual way. That is, the r_{bis} estimated from the Fan tables fluctuates more from sample to sample than does the r_{bis} computed by formula. With this information, one could use the standard error of r_{bis} to estimate approximately how large the correlation should be for statistical significance.[3]

SPECIAL PROBLEMS IN ITEM ANALYSIS

INTERNAL CONSISTENCY. Item analysis is frequently conducted against total score on the test itself. As was noted in Chapter 5, this procedure yields a measure of internal consistency, not external validity. Under cer-

[3] The formula for $\sigma_{r_{bis}}$ can be found in any standard statistics text, such as Guilford (1965, pp. 317–319).

tain conditions, the two approaches may lead to opposite results, the items chosen on the basis of external validity being the very ones rejected on the basis of internal consistency. Let us suppose that the preliminary form of a scholastic aptitude test consists of 100 arithmetic items and 50 vocabulary items. In order to select items from this initial pool by the method of internal consistency, the biserial correlation between performance on each item and total score on the 150 items may be used.[4] It is apparent that such biserial correlations would tend to be higher for the arithmetic than for the vocabulary items, since the total score is based on twice as many arithmetic items. If it is desired to retain the 75 "best" items in the final form of the test, it is likely that most of these items will prove to be arithmetic problems. In terms of the criterion of scholastic achievement, however, the vocabulary items might have been more valid predictors than the arithmetic items. If such is the case, the item analysis will have served to lower rather than raise the validity of the test.

The practice of rejecting items that have low correlations with total score provides a means of purifying or homogenizing the test. By such a procedure, the items with the highest average intercorrelations will be retained. This method of selecting items will increase test validity only when the original pool of items measures a single trait and when this trait is present in the criterion. Most tests developed in actual practice, however, measure a combination of traits required by a complex criterion. Purifying the test in such a case may reduce its criterion coverage and thus lower validity.

The selection of items to maximize test validity may be likened to the selection of tests that will yield the highest validity for a battery. It will be recalled (Ch. 6) that the test contributing most toward battery validity is one having the highest correlation with the criterion and the lowest correlation with the other tests in the battery. If this principle is applied to the selection of items, it means that the most satisfactory items are those with the highest item validities and the lowest coefficients of internal consistency. On this basis, it is possible to determine the *net effectiveness* of an item—that is, the net increase in test validity that accrues from the addition of that particular item. Thus, an item that has a high correlation with the external criterion but a relatively low correlation with total score would be preferred to one correlating highly with both criterion and test score, since the first item presumably measures an aspect of the criterion not adequately covered by the rest of the test.

It might seem that items could be selected by the same methods used in choosing tests for inclusion in a battery. Thus, each item could be correlated with the criterion and with every other item. The best items chosen by this method could then be weighted by means of a regression equation.

[4] Such part-whole correlations will be somewhat inflated by the common specific and error variance in the item and the test of which it is a part. Formulas have been developed to correct for this effect (Guilford, 1965, p. 503; Henrysson, 1963).

Such a procedure, however, is neither feasible nor theoretically defensible. Not only would the computation labor be prohibitive, but interitem correlations are also subject to excessive sampling fluctuation and the resulting regression weights would be too unstable to provide a basis for item selection. For these reasons, several approximation procedures have been developed for selecting items in terms of their net contribution to test validity. Some of these methods involve an empirical build-up process, whereby items are added to an ever-growing pool, and the validity of each successive composite is recomputed. Others begin with the complete set of items and reduce the pool by successive elimination of the poorest items until the desired test validity is attained. Because even these techniques require considerable computational labor, their use is practicable only when computer facilities are available.

It should be noted that all techniques for selecting items in terms of their net effectiveness represent the opposite approach from that followed when items are chosen on the basis of internal consistency. In the former procedure, a high item-test correlation increases the probability that the item will be rejected; in the latter, a high item-test correlation increases the probability of its acceptance. The objectives of the two procedures are, of course, unlike. One aims to increase the breadth of criterion coverage and reduce duplication; the other attempts to raise the homogeneity of the test. Both are desirable objectives of test construction.

Probably the best way to reconcile these objectives is to sort the relatively homogeneous items into separate tests, or subtests, each of which will cover a different aspect of the criterion. Thus, breadth of coverage is achieved through a variety of tests, each yielding a relatively unambiguous score, rather than through heterogeneity of items within a single test. By such a procedure, items with low indices of internal consistency would not be discarded, but would be segregated. Within each subtest or item group, fairly high internal consistency could thus be attained. At the same time, internal consistency would not be accepted as a substitute for item validity, and some attention would be given to adequacy of coverage and to the avoidance of excessive concentration of items in certain areas.

GROUP DIFFERENCES. Items are sometimes chosen so as to minimize certain group differences that are considered irrelevant to the purposes of the test. Thus, items passed by a significantly greater proportion of one group would be discarded, regardless of their general validity, difficulty level, or other characteristics. In the construction of the Stanford-Binet, for example, an effort was made to exclude any item that favored either sex significantly, on the assumption that such items might reflect purely fortuitous and irrelevant differences in the experiences of the two sexes (McNemar, 1942, Ch. 5). Owing to the limited number of items available for each age level, however, it was not possible to eliminate all sex-differentiating items. In order to rule out sex differences in total score, therefore, the remaining sex-differentiating items were balanced, approximately the same number favoring boys and girls.

No generalization can be made regarding the elimination of sex differences, or any other group differences, in the selection of test items. While certain tests, like the Stanford-Binet, have sought to equalize the performance of the two sexes, others have retained such differences and report separate norms for the two sexes. This practice is relatively common in the case of special aptitude tests, in which fairly large differences in favor of one or the other sex have been consistently found.

Under certain circumstances, moreover, items may be chosen, not to minimize, but to maximize, sex differentiation. An example of the latter procedure is to be found in the masculinity-femininity scales developed for use with several personality inventories (to be discussed in Chs. 17 and 18). Since the purpose of these scales is to measure the degree to which an individual's responses agree with those characteristic of men or of women in our culture, only those items that differentiate significantly between the sexes are retained.

A similar diversity of procedure can be found with reference to other group differences in item performance. In the development of a status scale for the Minnesota Multiphasic Personality Inventory, only those items were retained that differentiated significantly between the responses of high school students in two contrasted socioeconomic groups (Gough, 1948). Cross validation of this status scale on a new sample of high school students yielded a correlation of .50 with objective indices of socioeconomic status. The object of this test is to determine the degree to which an individual's emotional and social responses resemble those characteristic of persons in upper or lower socioeconomic levels, respectively. Hence, those items showing the maximum differentiation between social classes were included in the scale, and those showing little or no differentiation were discarded. This procedure is similar to that followed in the development of masculinity-femininity scales. It is apparent that in both types of tests the group differentiation constitutes the criterion in terms of which the test is validated. In such cases, socioeconomic level and sex, respectively, represent the most relevant variables on the basis of which items can be chosen.

Examples of the opposite approach to socioeconomic or cultural differentials in test responses can also be found. An extensive project on such cultural differentials in intelligence test items was conducted at the University of Chicago (Eells et al., 1951). These investigators believed that most intelligence tests might be unfair to children from lower socioeconomic levels, since many of the test items presuppose information, skills, or interests typical of middle-class children. To obtain evidence for such a hypothesis, a detailed item analysis was conducted on eight widely used group intelligence tests. For each item, the frequencies of correct responses by children in higher and lower socioeconomic levels were compared. Following this investigation, two members of the research team prepared a special test designed to be "fair" to lower-class urban American children. In the construction of this test, an effort was made to exclude the types of items previously found to favor middle-class children.[5]

As in the case of sex differences, no rigid policy can be laid down regarding items that exhibit cultural differentiation. Certain basic facts of test construction and interpretation should, however, be noted. First, whether items that differentiate significantly between certain groups are retained or discarded should depend on the purpose for which the test is designed. If the criteria to be predicted show significant differences between the sexes, socioeconomic groups, or other categories of persons, then it is to be expected that the test items will also exhibit such group differences. To eliminate items showing these differences might serve only to lower the validity of the test for predicting the given criteria (see Anastasi, 1966). In the second place, tests designed to measure an individual's resemblance to one or another group should obviously magnify the differentiation between such groups. For these tests, items showing the largest group differences in response should be chosen, as in the case of the masculinity-femininity and social status scales cited above.

The third point is of primary concern, not to the test constructor, but to the test user and the general student of psychology who wishes to interpret test results properly. Tests whose items have been selected with reference to the responses of any special groups cannot be used to compare such groups. For example, the statement that boys and girls do not differ significantly in Stanford-Binet IQ provides no information whatever regarding sex differences. Since sex differences were deliberately eliminated in the process of selecting items for the test, their absence from the final scores merely indicates that this aspect of test construction was successfully executed. Similarly, lack of socioeconomic differences on a test constructed so as to eliminate such differences would provide no information on the relative performance of socioeconomic classes.

Tests designed to maximize group differentiation, such as the masculinity-femininity and social status scales, are equally unsuitable for group comparisons. In these cases, the sex or socioeconomic differentiation in personality characteristics would be artificially magnified. To obtain an unbiased estimate of the existing group differences, the test items must be selected without reference to the responses of such groups. The principal conclusion to be drawn from the present discussion is that proper interpretation of scores on any test requires a knowledge of the basis on which items were selected for that test.

[5] Known as the Davis-Eells Games, this test has been discontinued because it proved unsatisfactory in a number of ways, including low validity in predicting academic achievement and other practical criteria. Moreover, the anticipated advantage of lower-class children on this test did not hold up in other samples.

SPEEDED TESTS.   Whether or not speed is relevant to the function being measured, item indices computed from a speeded test may be misleading. Except for items that all or nearly all subjects have had time to attempt, the item indices found from a speed test will reflect the *position* of the item in the test rather than its intrinsic difficulty or validity. Items that appear late in the test will be passed by a relatively small percentage of the total sample, because only a few persons have time to reach these items. Regardless of how easy the item may be, if it occurs late in a speeded test, it will appear difficult. Even if the item merely asked for the subject's name, the percentage of persons who pass it might be very low when the item is placed toward the end of a speeded test.

Similarly, item validities tend to be overestimated for those items that have not been reached by all subjects. Because the more proficient individuals tend to work faster, they are more likely to reach one of the later items in a speed test (Mollenkopf, 1950a). Thus, regardless of the nature of the item itself, some correlation between the item and the criterion would be obtained if the item occurred late in a speed test.

To avoid some of these difficulties, we could limit the analysis of each item to those persons who have reached the item. This is not a completely satisfactory solution, however, unless the number of persons failing to reach the item is small. Such a procedure would involve the use of a rapidly shrinking number of cases, and would thus render the results on the later items quite unreliable. Moreover, the sample on which the later items are analyzed would probably be selected, and hence not comparable to the larger samples used for the earlier items. As has already been pointed out, the faster subjects tend also to be the more proficient. The later items would thus be analyzed on a superior sample of individuals. One effect of such a selective factor would be to lower the apparent difficulty level of the later items, since the percentage passing would be greater in the selected superior group than in the entire sample. It will be noted that this is the opposite error from that introduced when the percentage passing is computed in terms of the entire sample. In that case, the apparent difficulty of items is spuriously raised.

The effect of the above procedure on indices of item validity is less obvious, but nonetheless real. It has been observed, for example, that some low-scoring subjects tend to hurry through the test, marking items almost at random in their effort to try all items within the time allowed. This tendency is much less common among high-scoring subjects. As a result, the sample on which a late-appearing item is analyzed is likely to consist of some very poor subjects, who will perform no better than chance on the item, and a larger number of very proficient and fast subjects, who are likely to answer the item correctly. In such a group, the item-criterion correlation will probably be higher than it would be in a more representative sample. Thus, the effect of speed on item validity is generally in the same direction, whether the item analysis includes the entire sample or only those who reach the item. In both cases, item validity is likely to be overestimated when an item occurs relatively late in a speeded test.

The anticipated effects of speed on indices of item difficulty and item validity have been empirically verified, both when item statistics are computed with the entire sample (Wesman, 1949) and when they are computed with only those persons who attempt the item (Mollenkopf, 1950a). In the latter study, comparable groups of high school students were given two forms of a verbal test and two forms of a mathematics test. Each of the two forms contained the same items as the other, but items occurring early in one form were placed late in the other. Each form was administered with a short time limit (speed conditions) and with a very liberal time limit (power conditions). Various intercomparisons were thus possible between forms and timing conditions. The results clearly showed that the position of an item in the speed tests affected its indices of difficulty and validity. When the same item occurred later in a speeded test, it was passed by a greater percentage of those attempting it, and it yielded a higher item-criterion correlation. This is to be expected when item statistics are limited to those persons reaching the item.

The difficulties encountered in the item analysis of speeded tests are fundamentally similar to those discussed in Chapter 4 in connection with the reliability of speeded tests. Various solutions, both empirical and statistical, have been developed for meeting these difficulties. One empirical solution is to administer the test with a longer time limit to the group on which item analysis is to be carried out. This solution is satisfactory provided that speed itself is not an important aspect of the ability to be measured by the test. Apart from the technical problems presented by specific tests, however, it is well to keep in mind that item-analysis data obtained with speeded tests are suspect and call for careful scrutiny.

CROSS VALIDATION

MEANING OF CROSS VALIDATION. It is essential that test validity be computed on a different sample of persons from that on which the items were selected. This independent determination of the validity of the entire test is known as cross validation (Mosier, 1951). Any validity coefficient computed on the same sample that was used for item-selection purposes will capitalize on chance errors within that particular sample and will consequently be spuriously high. In fact, a high validity coefficient could result under such circumstances even when the test has no validity at all in predicting the particular criterion.

Let us suppose that out of a sample of 100 medical students, the 30 with the highest and the 30 with the lowest medical school grades have been chosen to represent contrasted criterion groups. If, now, these two groups are compared in a number of traits actually irrelevant to success in medical school, certain chance differences will undoubtedly be found. Thus, there might be an excess of private-school graduates and of red-haired persons within the upper criterion group. If we were to assign each individual a score by crediting him with one point for private-school graduation and one point for red hair, the mean of such scores would undoubtedly be higher in the upper than in the lower criterion group. This is not evidence for the validity of the predictors, however, since such a validation process is based on a circular argument. The two predictors were chosen in the first place on the basis of the chance variations that characterized this particular sample. And the *same* chance differences are operating to produce the mean differences in total score. When tested in another sample, however, the chance differences in frequency of private-school graduation and red hair are likely to disappear or be reversed. Consequently, the validity of the scores will collapse.

AN EMPIRICAL EXAMPLE. A specific illustration of the need for cross validation is provided by an investigation conducted with the Rorschach inkblot test (Kurtz, 1948). In an attempt to determine whether the Rorschach could be of any help in selecting sales managers for life insurance agencies, this test was administered to 80 such managers. These managers had been carefully chosen from several hundred employed by eight life insurance companies, so as to represent an upper criterion group of 42 considered very satisfactory by their respective companies, and a lower criterion group of 38 considered unsatisfactory. The 80 test records were studied by a Rorschach expert, who selected a set of 32 signs, or response characteristics, occurring more frequently in one criterion group than in the other. Signs found more often in the upper criterion group were scored +1 if present and 0 if absent; those more common in the lower group were scored −1 or 0. Since there were 16 signs of each type, total scores could range theoretically from −16 to +16.

When the scoring key based on these 32 signs was reapplied to the original group of 80 persons, 79 of the 80 were correctly classified as being in the upper or lower group. The correlation between test score and criterion would thus have been close to 1.00. However, when the test was cross-validated on a second comparable sample of 41 managers, 21 in the upper and 20 in the lower group, the validity coefficient dropped to a negligible .02. It was thus apparent that the key developed in the first sample had no validity for selecting such personnel.

AN EXAMPLE WITH CHANCE DATA. That the use of a single sample for item selection and test validation can produce a completely spurious validity coefficient under pure chance conditions was vividly demonstrated by Cureton (1950). The criterion to be predicted was the grade-point average of 29 students registered in a particular course. The "items" consisted of 85 tags, numbered from 1 to 85 on one side. To obtain a score for each subject, the 85 tags were thoroughly shaken in a container and dropped on the table. All tags that fell with numbered side up were recorded as indicating the presence of that particular item in the student's test performance. Twenty-nine throws of the 85 tags thus provided complete records for each student, showing the presence or absence of each item or response sign. An item analysis was then conducted, with each student's grade-point average as the criterion. On this basis, 24 "items" were selected out of the 85, 9 of which occurred more frequently among the students with higher grades, and 15 among those with lower grades. The former received a +1 weight, the latter −1. The sum of these item weights constituted the total score for each student. Despite the known chance derivation of these "test scores," their correlation with the grade criterion in the original group of 29 students proved to be .82. Such a finding is similar to that obtained with the Rorschach scores in the previously cited study. In both instances, the apparent correspondence between test score and criterion resulted from the utilization of the same chance differences both in selecting items and in determining validity of total test scores.

CONDITIONS AFFECTING VALIDITY SHRINKAGE.   The amount of shrinkage of a validity coefficient in cross validation depends in part on the size of the original item pool and the proportion of items retained. When the number of original items is large and the proportion retained is small, there is more opportunity to capitalize on chance differences and thus obtain a spuriously high validity coefficient. Another condition affecting amount of shrinkage in cross validation is size of sample. Since spuriously high validity in the initial sample results from an accumulation of sampling errors, smaller groups (which yield larger sampling errors) will exhibit greater validity shrinkage.

If items are chosen on the basis of previously formulated hypotheses, derived from psychological theory or from past experience with the criterion, validity shrinkage in cross validation will be minimized. For example, if a particular hypothesis required that the answer "Yes" be more frequent among successful students, then the item would *not* be retained if a significantly larger number of "Yes" answers were given by the *unsuccessful* students. The opposite "shotgun" approach would be illustrated by assembling a miscellaneous set of questions with little regard to their relevance to the criterion behavior, and then retaining all items yielding significant positive or negative correlations with the criterion. Under the latter circumstances, we would expect much more shrinkage than under the former.

In summary, shrinkage of test validity in cross validation will be greatest when samples are small, the initial item pool is large, the proportion of items retained is small, and items are assembled without previously formulated rationale.

PART 2

TESTS OF GENERAL INTELLECTUAL DEVELOPMENT

CHAPTER 8

The Stanford-Binet
and the Measurement
of Intelligence

IN PART 1, we were concerned with the major principles of psychological testing. We are now ready to apply these principles to the evaluation of specific tests. We now know what questions to ask about each test and where to look for the answers. The test manuals, the *Mental Measurements Yearbooks*, appropriate journals, and other sources described in Chapter 1 may be consulted to obtain information regarding any of the tests cited.

The purpose of the remaining parts of the book is twofold. One objective is to afford an opportunity to observe the application of testing principles to a wide variety of tests. Another is to acquaint the reader with a few outstanding tests in each of the major areas. No attempt will be made to provide a comprehensive survey of available tests within any area. Such a survey would be outside the scope of this book. Moreover, it would probably be outdated before publication, because of the rapidity with which new tests appear. For these reasons, the discussion will concentrate on a few representative tests in each category, chosen either because of their widespread use or because they illustrate important developments in testing procedure. We shall consider tests of general intellectual development in Part 2, tests of separate abilities in Part 3, and personality tests in Part 4.

A classified list of representative tests in all areas covered in this text will be found in Appendix C. This list includes not only all currently available tests cited in the text, but also some additional examples of well-known tests in each category. With each test, the table gives the name of the publisher and the entry number in the *Sixth Mental Measurements Yearbook* where information about the test can be located. Unless otherwise indicated, all data about tests discussed in the text are taken from the test manual or technical supplements supplied by the test publishers.

THE MEASUREMENT OF GENERAL INTELLECTUAL DEVELOPMENT

Traditionally called "intelligence tests," the types of tests to be discussed in Part 2 are the direct descendants of the original Binet scales. Such tests are designed for use in a wide variety of situations and are validated against relatively broad criteria. They characteristically provide a single score, such as an IQ, indicating the individual's general intellectual level. An effort is made to arrive at this global estimate of intellectual performance by "the sinking of shafts at critical points" (Terman & Merrill, 1937, p. 4). In other words, a wide variety of tasks is presented to the subject in the expectation that an adequate sampling of all important intellectual functions will thus be covered. In actual practice, the tests are usually overloaded with certain functions, such as verbal ability, and completely omit others.

Because so many intelligence tests are validated against measures of academic achievement, they are often designated as tests of scholastic aptitude. Intelligence tests are frequently employed as preliminary screening instruments, to be followed by tests of special aptitudes. This practice is especially prevalent in the testing of normal adolescents or adults for counseling, personnel selection, and similar purposes. Another common use of general intelligence tests is to be found in clinical testing, especially in the identification and classification of the mentally retarded. For clinical purposes, individual tests such as the Stanford-Binet or Wechsler scales are generally employed.

This chapter will be concerned with the Stanford-Binet Intelligence Scale, as well as certain common problems regarding the interpretation of intelligence test scores. Chapter 9 will consider the principal types of group tests available for different ages and educational levels. Nonlanguage and performance scales will be treated in Chapter 10, together with other tests designed for special populations. Chapter 11 will be devoted to the Wechsler scales, including both the adult form and the forms for children. Although they are used for many of the same purposes as the Stanford-Binet, the Wechsler scales include performance as well as verbal tests. Moreover, although administered as individual scales, they share many technical features with group tests. For these reasons, the Wechsler scales can be most effectively considered after a discussion of other types of intelligence tests. Finally, Chapter 12 will examine the clinical use of tests in detecting intellectual impairment associated with brain damage and psychotic deterioration.

DEVELOPMENT OF STANFORD-BINET SCALES

EVOLUTION OF THE SCALES. The original Binet-Simon Scales have already been described briefly in Chapter 1. It will be recalled that the 1905 scale consisted simply of 30 short tests, arranged in ascending order of difficulty. The 1908 scale was the first age scale; and the 1911 scale introduced minor improvements and additions. The age range covered by the 1911 revision extended from 3 years to the adult level. Among the many translations and adaptations of the early Binet tests were a number of American revisions,[1] of which the most viable has been the Stanford-Binet. The first Stanford revision of the Binet-Simon Scales, prepared by Terman and his associates at Stanford University, was published in 1916 (Terman, 1916). This revision introduced so many changes and additions as to represent virtually a new test. Over one-third of the items were new, and a number of old items were revised, reallocated to different age levels, or discarded. The entire scale was restandardized on an American sample of approximately one thousand children and four hundred adults. Detailed instructions for administering and scoring each test [2] were provided, and the IQ was employed for the first time in any psychological test.

The second Stanford revision, appearing in 1937, consisted of two equivalent forms, L and M (Terman & Merrill, 1937). In this revision, the scale was greatly expanded and completely restandardized on a new and carefully chosen sample of the American population. The 3,184 subjects employed for this purpose included approximately one hundred children at each half-year interval from 1½ to 5½ years, two hundred at each age from 6 to 14, and one hundred at each age from 15 to 18. All subjects were within one month of a birthday (or half-year birthday) at the time of testing, and every age group contained an equal number of boys and girls. From age 6 up, most subjects were tested in school, although a few of the older subjects were obtained outside of school in order to round out the sampling. Preschool children were contacted in a variety of ways, many of them being siblings of the school children included in the sample. In order to obtain an adequate geographical distribution, testing was conducted in 17 communities located in 11 widely separated states. Several indices of socioeconomic level were checked in the effort to include a representative cross section of socioeconomic groups. Despite such precautions, the sampling was somewhat higher in socioeconomic level than the general population, and contained an excess of urban as contrasted to rural subjects. Both of these sampling inadequacies would tend to make the intel-

---

[1] An account of these early American revisions, together with a detailed description of the original Binet-Simon Scales, can be found in Peterson (1926).

[2] The items in the Binet scales are commonly called "tests," since each is separately administered and may contain several parts.

ligence test performance of the standardization group higher than that of the general population. To allow for this condition, adjustments were made such that the mean IQ of the standardization sample was in fact above 100.[3] It should also be noted that the population sampled was limited to native-born, white subjects.

A third revision, published in 1960, provided a single form (L-M) in which were incorporated the best items from the two 1937 forms (Terman & Merrill, 1960). Without introducing any new content, it was thus possible to eliminate obsolescent items and to relocate items whose difficulty level had altered during the intervening years owing to cultural changes. In preparing the 1960 Stanford-Binet, the authors were faced with a common dilemma of psychological testing. On the one hand, frequent revisions are desirable in order to profit from technical advances and refinements in test construction and from prior experience in the use of the test, as well as to keep test content up to date. The last-named consideration is especially important for information items and for pictorial material which may be affected by changing fashions in dress, household appliances, cars, and other common articles. The use of obsolete test content may seriously undermine rapport and may alter the difficulty level of items. On the other hand, revision may render much of the accumulated data inapplicable to the new form. Tests that have been widely used for many years have acquired a rich body of interpretive material which should be carefully weighed against the need for revision. It was for these reasons that the authors of the Stanford-Binet chose to condense the two earlier forms into one, thereby steering a course between the twin hazards of obsolescence and discontinuity. The loss of a parallel form was not too great a price to pay for accomplishing this purpose. As the authors point out, by 1960 there was less need for an alternate form than there had been in 1937 when no other well-constructed individual intelligence scale was available.

ITEM ANALYSIS.   Because the 1960 revision is made up entirely of items from the 1937 forms, any evaluation of the 1960 Stanford-Binet requires an examination of the procedures followed in developing the earlier forms (McNemar, 1942; Terman & Merrill, 1937, Ch. 2). The construction of the 1937 Stanford-Binet required nearly ten years of research. Much preliminary work went into the assembling of promising new items and their tryout on small groups of children who had taken the 1916 form of the test, thereby ensuring a certain minimum of similarity in the general area measured by the earlier and later forms.

The major step in the development of the 1937 Stanford-Binet included the administration of the provisional forms to the standardization sample of 3,184 subjects, and the final selection and allocation of items. All sub-

---

[3] Actually, this represented an overcorrection which was further corrected in later revisions of the normative tables (Pinneau, 1961).

jects were given both forms of the test, one-half taking Form L first, the other half Form M first. The interval between the two tests ranged from one day to one week. In this step, the criteria for item analysis were chronological age and composite total score on both provisional forms. The latter is an internal consistency criterion which serves to increase the homogeneity of the test. Three specific measures were employed in the analysis of each item: (*a*) curve of percentages of subjects passing the item in successive chronological ages; (*b*) curve of percentages of subjects passing the item in successive intervals of total score on the two forms; (*c*) biserial correlation of each item with total score on the two forms.

An illustration of the first of these three procedures is to be found in Figure 32, which shows the percentage of subjects at each age who passed two of the items retained in the final forms.[4] It will be noted that for the 3-year test the curve rises more steeply than for the 10-year test. Related to this difference is the fact that the percentage of 3-year-olds who pass the 3-year test (73 percent) is greater than the percentage of 10-year-olds who pass the 10-year test (59 percent). These differences in percentages pass-

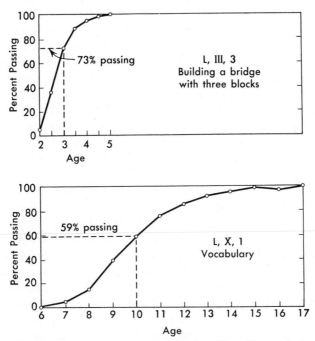

FIG. 32. Distribution of Percentages Passing Two Tests of the 1937 Stanford-Binet. (From Terman and Merrill, 1960, p. 15.)

[4] In the standard citation of Stanford-Binet items, the letter indicates the form (L or M), the Roman numeral designates the year level, and the Arabic numeral specifies the test or item number within that year level. Thus L,III,4 is the fourth item in the 3-year level of Form L.

ing an item are a necessary requirement of an age scale (McNemar, 1942, p. 9 and Ch. 8). In the discussion of age scores in Chapter 3, it was seen that the standard deviation of mental age must increase with age if that of the IQ is to remain constant. Now, if variability of MA is greater in older groups, it means that there must be a greater spread in the performance of older subjects over adjacent year levels. Hence, with increasing age, fewer and fewer subjects will pass a test that corresponds to their own age level. This relationship can be visualized if we consider a simplified illustration. Suppose that among 5-year-olds, 40 percent obtain an MA of 5, while 30 percent perform above and 30 percent below this level. Because anyone with an MA of 5 or higher should theoretically pass an item at the 5-year level, 70 percent (40% + 30%) of the 5-year-olds can be expected to pass the 5-year items. Suppose, on the other hand, that among 10-year-olds only 20 percent obtain an MA of 10, while 40 percent perform above and 40 percent below this level. This sort of distribution could be expected if the variability of MA is greater at 10 than at 5 years of age. Among the 10-year-olds, therefore, the percentage expected to pass 10-year items would be: 20 + 40 = 60. In this example, then, the percentage of at-age passes among 5-year-olds would be 70, while among 10-year-olds it would be 60.

In the 1937 Stanford-Binet, the percentage of at-age passes dropped from 77 at age 2 to slightly below 50 at the average adult level. Still lower percentages passing were used in selecting items for the superior adult levels, in order to provide adequate ceiling for the test. In the final selection of items, consideration was given not only to age differentiation and internal consistency, but also to the reduction and balancing of sex differences in percentage passing. An effort was made to exclude items passed by a significantly greater percentage of either sex, on the assumption that such items might reflect purely fortuitous and irrelevant differences in the experiences of the two sexes (see Ch. 7).

In the preparation of the 1960 Stanford-Binet, items were selected from forms L and M on the basis of the performance of 4,498 subjects, aged 2½ to 18 years, who had taken either or both forms of the test between 1950 and 1954. The subjects were examined in six states situated in the Northeast, in the Midwest, and on the West Coast. Although these cases did not constitute a representative sampling of American school children, care was taken to avoid the operation of major selective factors. The group also included two stratified samples of California children, used in special statistical analyses. These samples consisted of 100 6-year-olds stratified with regard to father's occupation and 100 15-year-olds stratified with regard to both father's occupation and grade distribution.

The 1960 Stanford-Binet did not involve a restandardization of the scale. The new samples were utilized only to check changes in item difficulty over the intervening period. Accordingly, the difficulty of each item was redetermined by finding the percentage of children passing it at successive *mental ages* on the 1937 forms. Some items were checked for possible regional and socioeconomic differences through subgroup comparisons within the total sample. No new material was introduced, but in a few items obsolescent drawings of common articles had to be altered. In these instances, the items were pretested on special groups before including them in the scale. Apart from these minor modifications in drawings, the only content changes in the 1960 Stanford-Binet include elimination of items, rescoring of a few items, and relocation of items in different year levels.

ADMINISTRATION AND SCORING

DESCRIPTION OF THE SCALE. The materials needed to administer the Stanford-Binet are shown in Figure 33. They include a box of standard toy objects for use at the younger age levels, two booklets of printed cards, a record booklet for recording responses, and a test manual. The tests are grouped into age levels extending from age II to superior adult. Between

FIG. 33. Test Materials Employed in Administering the Stanford-Binet. (Courtesy Houghton Mifflin Company.)

the ages of II and V, the test proceeds by half-year intervals. Thus, there is a level corresponding to age II, one to age II-6, one to age III, and so forth. Because progress is so rapid during these early ages, it proved feasible and desirable to measure change over six-month intervals. Between V and XIV the age levels correspond to yearly intervals. The remaining levels are designated as Average Adult and Superior Adult levels I, II, and III. Each age level contains six tests, with the exception of the Average Adult level, which contains eight.

The tests within any one age level are of approximately uniform difficulty and are arranged without regard to such residual differences in difficulty as may be present. An *alternate* test is also provided at each age level. Being of approximately equivalent difficulty, the alternate may be substituted for any of the tests in the level. Alternates are used if one of the regular tests must be omitted because special circumstances make it inappropriate for the individual or because some irregularity interfered with its standardized administration.

Four tests in each year level were selected on the basis of validity and representativeness to constitute an *abbreviated scale* for use when time does not permit the administration of the entire scale. These tests are marked with an asterisk on the record booklets. Comparisons between full-scale and abbreviated-scale IQ's on a variety of groups show a close correspondence between the two, the correlations being approximately as high as the reliability coefficient of the full scale (Himelstein, 1966; Terman & Merrill, 1960, pp. 61–62). The mean IQ, however, tends to run slightly lower on the short scale. This discrepancy is also found when the numbers of persons scoring higher on each version are compared. Over 50 percent of the subjects receive lower IQ's on the short version, while only 30 percent score higher.

ADMINISTRATION. In common with most individual intelligence tests, the Stanford-Binet requires a highly trained examiner. Both administration and scoring are fairly complicated for many of the tests. Considerable familiarity and experience with the scale are therefore required for a smooth performance. Hesitation and fumbling may be ruinous to rapport. Slight inadvertent changes in wording may alter the difficulty of items. A further complication is presented by the fact that tests must be scored as they are administered, since the subsequent conduct of the examination depends on the child's performance on previously administered levels.

Many clinicians regard the Stanford-Binet not only as a standardized test, but also as a clinical interview. The very characteristics that make this scale so difficult to administer also create opportunities for interaction between examiner and subject, and provide other sources of clues for the experienced clinician. Even more than most other individual tests, the Stanford-Binet makes it possible to observe the subject's work methods, his approach to a problem, and other qualitative aspects of performance. The examiner may also have an opportunity to judge certain personality characteristics, such as activity level, self-confidence, persistence, and ability to concentrate. Any qualitative observations made in the course of Stanford-Binet administration should, of course, be clearly recognized as such and ought not to be interpreted in the same manner as objective test scores. The value of such qualitative observations depends to a large extent on the skill, experience, and psychological sophistication of the examiner, as well as on his awareness of the pitfalls and limitations inherent in this type of observation. The types of clinical observations that can be made during an individual intelligence examination are richly illustrated by Moriarty (1960, 1961, 1966), who sees in the testing session an opportunity to investigate the child's behavior in meeting a challenging, demanding, difficult, or frustrating situation.

In taking the Stanford-Binet, no one subject tries all items. Each individual is tested only over a range of age levels suited to his own intellectual level. Testing usually requires no more than thirty to forty minutes for younger children and not more than one hour and a half for older subjects. The standard procedure is to begin testing at a level slightly below the expected mental age of the subject. Thus, the first tests given should be easy enough to arouse confidence, but not so easy as to cause boredom and annoyance. If the subject fails any test within the year level first administered, the next lower level is given. This procedure continues until a level is reached at which all tests are passed. This level is known as the *basal age*. Testing is then continued upward to a level at which all tests are failed, designated as the *ceiling age*. When this level is reached, the test is discontinued.

SCORING. Individual Stanford-Binet items, or tests, are scored on an all-or-none basis. For each test, the minimal performance that constitutes "passing" is specified in the manual. For example, in identifying objects by use at year level II-6, the child passes if he correctly identifies three out of six designated objects; in repeating five digits from memory at year level VII, correct response on any one of three series is counted as a pass; in answering comprehension questions at year level VIII, any four correct answers out of six represent a passing performance. Certain tests appear in identical form at different year levels, but are scored with a different standard of passing. Such tests are administered only once, the subject's performance determining the year level at which they are credited. The vocabulary test, for example, may be scored anywhere from level VI to Superior Adult III, depending on the number of words correctly defined.

The items passed and failed by any one individual will show a certain amount of *scatter* among adjacent year levels. We do not find that individuals pass all tests at or below their mental age level and fail all tests above such a level. Instead, the successfully passed tests are spread over several year levels, bounded by the subject's basal age at one extreme and his ceiling age at the other. The subject's mental age on the Stanford-Binet is found by crediting him with his basal age and adding to that age further months of credit for every test passed beyond the basal level. In the half-year levels between II and V, each of the six tests counts as one month; between VI and XIV, each of the six tests corresponds to two months of credit. Since each of the adult levels (AA, SA I, SA II, and SA III) covers more than one year of mental age, the months of credit for each test are adjusted accordingly. For example, the Average Adult level includes eight tests, each of which is credited with two months; the Superior Adult I level contains six tests, each receiving four months.

The highest mental age theoretically attainable on the Stanford-Binet is 22 years and 10 months. Such a score is not, of course, a true mental age, but a numerical score indicating degree of superiority above the Average Adult performance. It certainly does not correspond to the achievement of the average 22-year-old, since the latter would receive a mental age of 15-9. For any adult over 18 years of age, a mental age of 15-9 yields an IQ of 100 on this scale. In fact, above 13 years, mental ages cease to have the same significance as they do at lower levels, since it is just beyond 13 that the mean MA begins to lag behind CA on this scale. The Stanford-Binet is not suitable for adult testing, especially within the normal and superior range. Despite the three Superior Adult levels, there is insufficient ceiling for most superior adults or even for very superior adolescents (Kennedy et al., 1960). In such cases, it is often impossible to reach a ceiling age level at which all tests are failed. Moreover, most of the Stanford-Binet tests have more appeal for children than for adults, the content being of relatively little interest to most adults.

A major innovation introduced in the 1960 Stanford-Binet was the substitution of deviation IQ's for the ratio IQ's used in the earlier forms. These deviation IQ's are standard scores with a mean of 100 and an SD of 16. As explained in Chapter 3, the principal advantage of this type of IQ is that it provides comparable scores at all age levels, thus eliminating the vagaries of ratio IQ's. Despite the care with which the 1937 scales were developed in the effort to obtain constant IQ variability at all ages, the SD's of ratio IQ's on these scales fluctuated from a low of 13 at age VI to a high of 21 at age II-6. Thus, an IQ of 113 at age VI corresponded to an IQ of 121 at age II-6. Special correction tables were developed to adjust for the major IQ variations in the 1937 scales (McNemar, 1942, pp. 172–174). All these difficulties were circumvented in the 1960 form through the use of deviation IQ's, which automatically have the same SD throughout the age range. To facilitate procedure, Pinneau developed tables in which deviation IQ's can be looked up by entering MA and CA in years and months. These Pinneau tables are reproduced in the Stanford-Binet manual (Terman & Merrill, 1960).

A further change introduced in the 1960 form stems from the recognition that improvement on the test continues to age 18, rather than ceasing at age 16 as was assumed in the 1937 revision. Several major longitudinal studies conducted by different investigators over the intervening quarter-century strongly suggested that the abilities measured by intelligence tests continue to improve longer than had been supposed. The most direct evidence that improvement on the Stanford-Binet continues beyond age 16 was provided by Bradway, Thompson, and Cravens (1958), who retested subjects from the 1937 standardization sample after intervals of 10 and 25 years. When first tested, these subjects had been from 2 to 5½ years old. Mean IQ's remained virtually unchanged from first to second testings, but showed a significant rise of 11.3 points between second and third testings. The latter increase resulted from the fact that the subjects had continued to improve beyond age 16, while the computation of 1937 IQ's assumed termination of growth at that age.

The specific procedure followed in finding MA and IQ on the 1960 Stanford-Binet is illustrated in Table 26. In the upper part of this table is the

TABLE 26   COMPUTATION OF STANFORD-BINET MENTAL AGES AND INTELLIGENCE
QUOTIENTS

Year Level	Number of Tests Passed	Months Credit per Test	Total Credit	
		6-YEAR-OLD CHILD		
IV	6	Basal age	4 yrs.	0 mos.
IV-6	5	1		5
V	3	1		3
VI	3	2		6
VII	2	2		4
VIII	1	2		2
IX	0	Ceiling age		
			4 yrs. + 20 mos.	
	MA = 5-8	CA = 6-4	IQ = 88	
		35-YEAR-OLD ADULT		
XIII	6	Basal age	13 yrs.	0 mos.
XIV	5	2		10
AA	6	2		12
SA I	3	4		12
SA II	2	5		10
SA III	0	Ceiling age		
			13 yrs. + 44 mos.	
	MA = 16-8	CA = 18-0	IQ = 106	

record of a child whose chronological age is 6 years and 4 months (CA = 6-4). It will be noted that the basal age is IV and the ceiling age IX. Additional credits total to 20 months, or 1 year and 8 months. The MA is thus 5-8. By reference to the Pinneau tables, this child's IQ is found to be 88. In the lower part of Table 26 will be found the record of a 35-year-old adult. As for anyone whose age is 18 or over, CA is taken as 18 in looking up the IQ. This subject's basal age is XIII, and he earns 44 additional months credit, giving him an MA of 16-8 and an IQ of 106.

Although the deviation IQ is the most convenient index for evaluating an individual's standing in his age group, the MA itself can serve a useful function. To say that a 6-year-old child performs as well as a typical 8-year-old usually conveys more meaning to a layman than saying he has an IQ of 137. A knowledge of the child's MA level also facilitates an understanding of what can be expected of him in terms of educational achievement and other developmental norms of behavior.

NORMATIVE INTERPRETATION.   One of the advantages of the Stanford-Binet derives from the mass of interpretive data and clinical experience that have been accumulated regarding this test. For many clinicians, educators, and others concerned with the evaluation of general ability level, the Stanford-Binet IQ has become almost synonymous with intelligence. Much has been learned about what sort of behavior can be expected from a child with an IQ of 50 or 80 or 120 on this test. The distributions of IQ's in the standardization samples for the 1916 Stanford-Binet, and later for the 1937 revision, have provided a common frame of reference for the interpretation of IQ's.

Figure 34 presents this frame of reference, with the slightly modified values corresponding to the 1960 deviation IQ's (Pinneau, 1961). The figure shows the familiar normal curve turned sideways, with σ-units laid off on the baseline. Since the Stanford-Binet deviation IQ's have a mean of 100 and a σ of 16, IQ's of 116 and 84 are shown at $+1\sigma$ and -1σ, respectively; IQ's of 132 and 68 are at $+2\sigma$ and -2σ, and so on. The next three columns give some commonly used categories, with the corresponding deviation IQ's and the percentage of the general population falling into each category. For example, a deviation IQ above 148 is likely to occur in 1 out of 1,000 cases (.1%); 6.5 percent of the population fall between 124 and 148, and so on. Slightly over half (54.7%) score within $\pm.75\sigma$ of the mean, corresponding to deviation IQ's between 88 and 112. For many years it has been customary to use an IQ of 70 as an approximate cutoff point for possible mental retardation. This category corresponds to the lowest 1 or 2 percent of the population. In Figure 34, the cutoff is placed at -2.25σ, which corresponds to an IQ of 64 and below which are 1.2 percent of the cases.

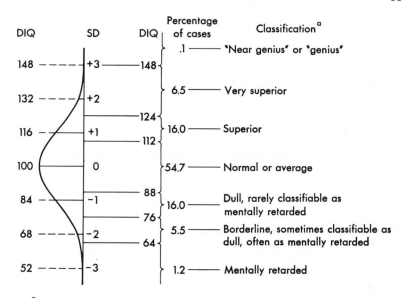

DIQ	SD	DIQ	Percentage of cases	Classification[a]
148	+3	148	.1	"Near genius" or "genius"
132	+2		6.5	Very superior
		124		
116	+1		16.0	Superior
		112		
100	0		54.7	Normal or average
84	−1	88	16.0	Dull, rarely classifiable as mentally retarded
		76		
68	−2		5.5	Borderline, sometimes classifiable as dull, often as mentally retarded
		64		
52	−3		1.2	Mentally retarded

[a] Terms slightly modified for closer conformity with current usage

FIG. 34. Theoretical Distribution and Classification of Deviation IQ's for the Stanford-Binet Scales. (From Pinneau, 1961, p. 70.)

The widespread use of such a classification of IQ levels, although of unquestionable help in standardizing the interpretation of test performance, carries certain dangers. Like all classifications of persons, it should not be rigidly applied, nor used to the exclusion of other data about the individual. There are, of course, no sharp dividing lines between the "mentally retarded" and the "borderline," or between the "superior" and the "very superior." Individuals with IQ's of 60 have been known to make satisfactory adjustments to the demands of daily living, while some with IQ's close to 100 require institutional care. Persons with IQ's of 160 do occasionally lead undistinguished lives, while some with IQ's much closer to 100 make outstanding contributions. Decisions regarding institutionalization, parole, discharge, or special training of mental retardates must take into account not only IQ but also social maturity, emotional adjustment, physical condition, and other circumstances of the individual case. Nor is high IQ synonymous with genius. High-level achievement may require in addition originality, special talents, persistence, singleness of purpose, and other propitious emotional and motivational factors.

From still another angle, it should be noted that Stanford-Binet IQ's differ considerably with different geographical regions, socioeconomic levels, educational institutions, and other cultural subgroups. For many purposes, therefore, local norms would provide a helpful supplement to the broad national norms. Furthermore, since the 1960 revision of the Stanford-Binet was *not* a restandardization, an IQ of 100 represents the population mean as of 1937. The 1937 standardization sample is thus employed as a fixed reference group in much the same way that the students taking the College Board Scholastic Aptitude Test in 1941 provided a fixed reference group for that test (see Ch. 3). In the light of intervening cultural and educational progress, as well as on the basis of empirical results obtained with other tests over the 30-year interval, it is to be expected that the mean Stanford-Binet IQ of the general population of the country would be above 100 today (see Anastasi, 1958a, pp. 209–211).

RELIABILITY

The reliability of the 1937 Stanford-Binet was determined by correlating IQ's on Forms L and M administered to the standardization group within an interval of one week or less. Such reliability coefficients are thus measures of both short-term temporal stability and equivalence of content across the two item samples. An exceptionally thorough analysis of the reliability of this test was carried out with reference to age and IQ level of subjects (McNemar, 1942, Ch. 6). In general, the Stanford-Binet tends to be more reliable for the older than for the younger ages, and for the lower than for the higher IQ's. Thus, at ages 2½ to 5½, the reliability coefficients range from .83 (for IQ 140–149) to .91 (for IQ 60–69); for ages 6 to 13, they range from .91 to .97, respectively, for the same IQ levels; and for ages 14 to 18, the corresponding range of reliability coefficients extends from .95 to .98.

The increasing reliability of scores with increasing age is characteristic of tests in general. It results in part from the better control of conditions that is possible with older subjects (especially in comparison with the preschool ages). Another factor is the slowing down of developmental rate with age. When reliability is measured by retesting, individuals who are undergoing less change are also likely to exhibit less random fluctuation over short periods of time (Pinneau, 1961, Ch. 5).

The higher reliability obtained with lower IQ levels at any given CA, on the other hand, appears to be associated with the specific structural characteristics of the Stanford-Binet. It will be recalled that because of the difference in number of items available at different age levels, each item receives a weight of 1 month at the lowest levels, a weight of 2 months at the intermediate levels, and weights of 4, 5, or 6 months at the highest levels. This weighting tends to magnify the error of measurement at the upper levels, because the chance passing or failure of a single item makes a larger difference in total score at these levels than it does at lower levels. Since at any given CA, individuals with higher IQ's are tested with higher age levels on the scale, their IQ's will have a larger error of measurement and lower reliability (Pinneau, 1961, Ch. 5). The relationship between IQ level and reliability of the Stanford-Binet is also illustrated graphically in Figure 35, showing the bivariate distribution of IQ's obtained by 7-year-old children on Forms L and M. It will be observed that the individual entries fall close to the diagonal at lower IQ levels and spread farther apart at the higher levels. This indicates closer agreement between L and M IQ's at lower levels and wider discrepancies between them at upper levels. With such a fan-shaped scatter diagram, a single correlation coefficient is misleading. For this reason, separate reliability coefficients have been reported for different portions of the IQ range.

On the whole, the data indicate that the Stanford-Binet is a highly reli-

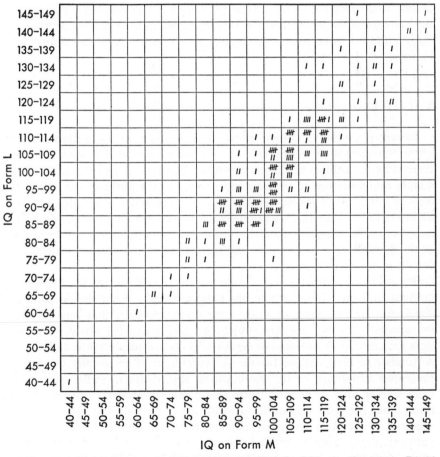

FIG. 35. Parallel-Form Reliability of the Stanford-Binet: Bivariate Distribution of IQ's Obtained by Seven-Year-Old Children on Forms L and M. (From Terman and Merrill, 1937, p. 45; reproduced by permission of Houghton Mifflin Company.)

able test, most of the reported reliability coefficients for the various age and IQ levels being over .90. Such high reliability coefficients were obtained despite the fact that they were computed separately within each age group. It will be recalled in this connection that all subjects in the standardization sample were tested within a month of a birthday or half-year birthday. This narrowly restricted age range would tend to produce lower reliability coefficients than found for most tests, which employ more heterogeneous samples. Translated in terms of individual IQ's, a reliability coefficient of .90 and an *SD* of 16 give an error of measurement of approximately 5 IQ points (see Ch. 4). In other words, the chances are about 2:1 that a child's true Stanford-Binet IQ differs by 5 points or less from the IQ obtained in a single testing, and the chances are 99:1 that it varies by no more than 13 points. Reflecting the same differences found in the reliability coefficients, these errors of measurement will be somewhat higher for younger than for older children, and somewhat higher for brighter than for duller individuals.

VALIDITY

CONTENT VALIDITY.   Some information bearing on the content validity of the Stanford-Binet is provided by an examination of the tasks to be performed by the subject in the various tests. These tasks run the gamut from simple manipulation to abstract reasoning. At the earliest age levels, the tests require chiefly eye-hand coordination, perceptual discrimination, and ability to follow directions, as in block building, stringing beads, comparing lengths, and matching geometric forms. A relatively large number of tests at the lower levels also involve the identification of common objects presented in toy models or in pictures.

Several tests occurring over a wide age range call for practical judgment or common sense. For example, the child is asked, "What should you do if you found on the streets of a city a three-year-old baby that was lost from its parents?" In other tests the subject is asked to explain why certain practices are commonly followed or certain objects are employed in daily living. A number of tests calling for the interpretation of pictorially or verbally presented situations, or the detection of absurdities in either pictures or brief stories, also seem to fall into this category. Memory tests are found throughout the scale and utilize a wide variety of materials. The subject is required to recall or recognize objects, pictures, geometric designs, bead patterns, digits, sentences, and the content of passages. Several tests of spatial orientation occur at widely scattered levels. These include maze-tracing, paper-folding, paper-cutting, rearrangement of geometric figures, and directional orientation. Skills acquired in school, such as reading and arithmetic, are required for successful performance at the upper year levels.

The most common type of test, especially at the upper age levels, is that employing verbal content. In this category are to be found such well-known tests as vocabulary, analogies, sentence completion, disarranged sentences, defining abstract terms, and interpreting proverbs. Some stress verbal fluency, as in naming unrelated words as rapidly as possible, giving rhymes, or building sentences containing three given words. It should also be noted that many of the tests that are not predominantly verbal in content nevertheless require the understanding of fairly complex verbal instructions. That the scale as a whole is heavily weighted with verbal ability is indicated by the correlations obtained between the 45-word vocabulary test and mental ages on the entire scale. These correlations were found to be .71, .83, .86, and .83 for groups of subjects aged 8, 11, 14, and 18 years, respectively (McNemar, 1942, pp. 139–140; see also Edwards, 1963).[5] The correlations are at least as high as those normally found between tests designed to measure the same functions, and they fall within the range of common reliability coefficients.

Insofar as all the functions listed are relevant to what is commonly regarded as "intelligence," the scale may be said to have content validity. The preponderance of verbal content at the upper levels is defended by the test authors on theoretical grounds. Thus, they write:

At these levels the major intellectual differences between subjects reduce largely to differences in the ability to do conceptual thinking, and facility in dealing with concepts is most readily sampled by the use of verbal tests. Language, essentially, is the shorthand of the higher thought processes, and the level at which this shorthand functions is one of the most important determinants of the level of the processes themselves (Terman & Merrill, 1937, p. 5).

CRITERION-RELATED VALIDITY. Data on the criterion-related validity of the Stanford-Binet, both concurrent and predictive, have been obtained chiefly in terms of academic achievement. Since the publication of the original 1916 Scale, many correlations have been computed between Stanford-Binet IQ and school grades, teachers' ratings, and achievement test scores. Most of these correlations fall between .40 and .75. School progress was likewise found to be related to Stanford-Binet IQ, children who were accelerated by one or more grades averaging considerably higher in IQ than those at normal age-grade location, and children who were retarded by one or more grades averaging considerably below (McNemar, 1942, Ch. 3).

[5] Since these are part-whole correlations, they are spuriously raised by the inclusion of the vocabulary test in the determination of MA. This effect is slight, however, since the vocabulary test constitutes less than 5 percent of the total number of test items (McNemar, 1942, p. 140).

Like most intelligence tests, the Stanford-Binet correlates highly with performance in nearly all academic courses, but its correlations are highest with the predominantly verbal courses, such as English and history. Correlations with achievement test scores show the same pattern. In a study of high school sophomores, for example, Form L IQ's correlated .73 with Reading Comprehension scores, .54 with Biology scores, and .48 with Geometry scores (Bond, 1940). Correlations in the .50's and .60's have been found with college grades. Among college students, both selective factors and insufficient test ceiling frequently lower the correlations.

There have been relatively few validation studies with the 1960 Form L-M (see Himelstein, 1966). Kennedy, Van de Reit, and White (1963) report a correlation of .69 with total score on the California Achievement Test in a large sample of Negro elementary school children. Correlations with scores on separate parts of the same battery were: Reading, .68; Arithmetic, .64; and Language, .70.

In interpreting the IQ, it should be borne in mind that the Stanford-Binet—like most so-called intelligence tests—is largely a measure of scholastic aptitude and that it is heavily loaded with verbal functions, especially at the upper levels. Individuals with a language handicap, as well as those whose strongest abilities lie along nonverbal lines, will thus score relatively low on such a test. Similarly, there are undoubtedly a number of fields in which scholastic aptitude and verbal comprehension are not of primary importance. Obviously, to apply any test to situations for which it is inappropriate will only reduce its effectiveness. Because of the common identification of Stanford-Binet IQ with the very concept of intelligence, there has been a tendency to expect too much from this one test.

CONSTRUCT VALIDITY.   Data on the construct validity of the Stanford-Binet come from many sources. *Continuity* in the functions measured in the 1916, 1937, and 1960 scales was ensured by retaining in each version only those items that correlated satisfactorily with mental age on the preceding form. Hence, the information that clinicians have accumulated over the years regarding typical behavior of individuals at different MA and IQ levels can be utilized in their interpretation of scores on this scale.

Age differentiation represents the major criterion in the selection of Stanford-Binet items. Thus, there is assurance that the Stanford-Binet measures abilities that increase with age during childhood and adolescence in our culture. In each form, *internal consistency* was a further criterion for item selection. That there is a good deal of functional homogeneity in the Stanford-Binet, despite the apparent variety of content, is indicated by a mean item-scale correlation of .66 for the 1960 revision. The predominance of verbal functions in the scale is shown by the higher correlation of verbal than nonverbal items with performance on the total scale (Terman & Merrill, 1960, pp. 33–34).

Further data pertaining to construct validity are provided by several independent *factor analyses* of Stanford-Binet items. If IQ's are to be comparable at different ages, the scale should have approximately the same factorial composition at all age levels. For an unambiguous interpretation of IQ's, moreover, the scale should be highly saturated with a single common factor. The latter point has already been discussed in connection with homogeneity in Chapter 4. If the scores were heavily weighted with two group factors, such as verbal and numerical aptitudes, an IQ of, let us say, 115 obtained by different persons might indicate high verbal ability in one case and high numerical ability in the other.

McNemar (1942, Ch. 9) conducted separate factorial analyses of Stanfor-Binet items at 14 age levels, including half-year groups from 2 to 5 and year groups at ages 6, 7, 9, 11, 13, 15, and 18. The number of subjects employed in each analysis varied from 99 to 200, and the number of items ranged from 19 to 35. In each of these analyses, tetrachoric correlations were computed between the items, and the resulting correlations were factor analyzed. By including items from adjacent year levels in more than one analysis, some evidence was obtained regarding the identity of the common factor at different ages. The examination of tests that recur at several age levels provided further data on this point. In general, the results of these analyses indicated that performance on Stanford-Binet items is largely explicable in terms of a single common factor. Evidence of additional group factors was found at a few age levels, but the contribution of these factors was small. It was likewise demonstrated that the common factor found at adjacent age levels was essentially the same, although this conclusion may not apply to more widely separated age levels. In fact, there was some evidence to suggest that the common factor becomes increasingly verbal as the higher ages are approached. The common factor loading of the vocabulary test, for example, rose from .59 at age 6 to .91 at age 18.

In a more intensive search for the contribution of group factors, Jones (1949, 1954) factor analyzed Stanford-Binet items separately in four groups of children aged 7, 9, 11, and 13 years. Each group consisted of 100 boys and 100 girls. At each age level, the results revealed a number of distinct but correlated abilities. Among them were several verbal, memory, reasoning, spatial visualization, and perceptual factors. Moreover, both the factors identified and their relative weights varied somewhat from one age level to another. The statistical techniques employed by McNemar and by Jones were such as to emphasize the role of a general factor in the first study, while focusing on the contributions of different group factors in the second. Combining the findings of the two studies suggests that there is, in fact, much in common in the scale as a whole—a characteristic that is largely built into the Stanford-Binet by selecting items that have high correlations with total scores. At the same time, performance is also influenced by a number of special abilities whose composition varies with the age level tested.

LONGITUDINAL STUDIES OF INTELLIGENCE

An important approach to the understanding of the construct, "intelligence," is through longitudinal studies of the same individuals over long periods of time. Although such investigations may be regarded as contributing to the long-term predictive validation of specific tests, they have broader implications for the nature of intelligence and the meaning of an IQ. When intelligence was believed to be largely an expression of hereditary potential, each individual's IQ was expected to remain very nearly constant throughout life. Any observed variation on retesting was attributed to weaknesses in the measuring instrument— either inadequate reliability or poor selection of functions tested. With increasing research on the nature of intelligence, however, has come the realization that intelligence itself is both complex and dynamic. In the following sections, we shall examine typical findings of longitudinal studies of intelligence and shall inquire into the conditions making for both stability and instability of the IQ.

STABILITY OF THE IQ. An extensive body of data has accumulated showing that, over the elementary, high school, and college period, intelligence test performance is quite stable (see Anastasi, 1958a, pp. 232–238). In a Swedish study of a relatively unselected population, for example, Husén (1951) found a correlation of .72 between the test scores of 613 third-grade school boys and the scores obtained by the same persons 10 years later on their induction into military service. Even preschool tests show remarkably high correlations with later retests. In a longitudinal study of 140 children conducted at Fels Research Institute (Sontag, Baker, & Nelson, 1958), Stanford-Binet scores obtained at 3 and at 4 years of age correlated .83. The correlation with the 3-year tests decreased as the interval between retests increased, but by age 12 it was still as high as .46. Of special relevance to the Stanford-Binet is the follow-up conducted by Bradway, Thompson, and Cravens (1958) on children originally tested between the ages of 2 and 5½ as part of the 1937 Stanford-Binet standardization sample. Initial IQ's correlated .65 with 10-year retests and .59 with 25-year retests. The correlation between the 10-year retest (Mean age = 14 years) and 25-year retest (Mean age = 29 years) was .85.

As would be expected, retest correlations are higher, the shorter the interval between tests. With a constant interval between tests, moreover, retest correlations tend to be higher the older the children. The effects of age and retest interval on retest correlations exhibit considerable regularity and are themselves highly predictable (Thorndike, 1933, 1940). One explanation for the increasing stability of the IQ with age is provided by the cumulative nature of intellectual development. The individual's intellectual skills and knowledge at each age include all his earlier skills and knowledge plus an increment of new acquisitions. Even if the annual increments bear no relation to each other, a growing consistency of performance level would emerge, simply because earlier acquisitions constitute an increasing proportion of total skills and knowledge as age increases. Predictions of IQ from age 10 to 16 would thus be more accurate than from 3 to 9, because scores at 10 include over half of what is present at 16, while scores at 3 include a much smaller proportion of what is present at 9.

Anderson (1940) described this relationship between successive scores as the *overlap hypothesis*. He maintained that, "Since the growing individual does not lose what he already has, the constancy of the IQ is in large measure a matter of the part-whole or overlap relation" (p. 394). In support of this hypothesis, Anderson computed a set of correlations between initial and terminal "scores" obtained with shuffled cards and random numbers. These correlations, which depended solely on the extent of overlap between successive measures, agreed closely with empirical test-retest correlations in intelligence test scores found in three published longitudinal studies. In fact, the test scores tended to give somewhat *lower* correlations, a difference Anderson attributed to such factors as errors of measurement and change in test content with age.

Although the overlap hypothesis undoubtedly accounts for some of the increasing stability of the IQ in the developing individual, annual increments are not random. On the contrary, the initially brighter children tend to make larger annual gains in mental age than do the initially duller (e.g., Pinneau, 1961). This tendency in turn yields an increasing variability in the mental age distribution with age and hence a constant IQ, as explained in Chapter 3. Such findings suggest two additional reasons for the general stability of the IQ. The first is the *environmental stability* characterizing the developmental years of most individuals. Children tend to remain in the same family, the same socioeconomic level, and the same cultural milieu as they grow up. They are not typically shifted at random from intellectually stimulating to intellectually handicapping environments. Hence, whatever intellectual advantages or disadvantages they had at one stage in their development tend to persist in the interval between retests.

A second reason for IQ stability pertains to the role of *prerequisite learning skills* on subsequent learning. Not only does the individual retain prior learning, but much of his prior learning provides tools for subsequent learning. Hence, the more progress he has made in the acquisition of intellectual skills and knowledge at any one point in time, the better able he is to profit from subsequent learning experiences. The concept of readiness in education is an expression of this general principle. Applications of the same principle underlie Project Head Start and other compensatory educational programs for culturally disadvantaged preschool children (Bloom, Davis, & Hess, 1965; Gordon & Wilkerson, 1966). Insofar as children from disadvantaged backgrounds lack some of the essential prerequisites for effective school learning, they would only fall farther and farther behind in academic achievement as they progressed through the school grades. It should be added that learning prerequisites cover not only such intellectual skills as the acquisition of language and of quantitative concepts, but also attitudes, interests, motivation, problem-solving styles, reactions to frustration, self-concepts, and other personality characteristics. The object of compensatory educational programs is to provide the learning prerequisites that will enable children to profit from subsequent schooling. In so doing, of course, these programs hope to disrupt the "stability" of IQ's that would otherwise have remained low. Compensatory education programs provide one example of the interaction between initial score and treatment in the prediction of subsequent score, discussed in Chapter 6.

INSTABILITY OF THE IQ.   Correlational studies on the stability of the IQ provide actuarial data, applicable to group predictions. For the reasons given above, IQ's tend to be quite stable in this actuarial sense. Studies of individuals, on the other hand, reveal large upward or downward shifts in IQ.[6] Sharp rises or drops in IQ may occur as a result of major environmental changes in the child's life. Drastic changes in family structure or home conditions, adoption into a foster home, severe or prolonged illness, and therapeutic or remedial programs are examples of the type of events that may alter the child's subsequent intellectual development. Even children who remain in the same environment, however, may show large increases or decreases in IQ on retesting. These changes mean, of course, that the child is developing at a faster or a slower rate than that of the normative population on which the test was standardized. In general, children in culturally disadvantaged environments tend to lose and those in superior environments to gain in IQ with age. Investigations of the specific characteristics of these environments and of the children themselves are of both theoretical and practical interest.

Typical data on the magnitude of individual IQ changes is provided by the California Guidance Study. In an analysis of retest data from

----

[6] See, e.g., Bayley, 1955; Bayley & Schaefer, 1964; Bradway, 1945a; Haan, 1963; Honzik, Macfarlane, & Allen, 1948; Kagan & Freeman, 1963; Kagan, Sontag, Baker, & Nelson, 1958; Sontag, Baker, & Nelson, 1958; Wiener, Rider, & Oppel, 1963.

Pinneau (1961) has prepared tables showing the median and range of individual IQ changes found in the Berkeley Growth Study for each age at test and retest from 1 month to 17 years.

222 cases in this study, Honzik, Macfarlane, and Allen (1948) reported individual IQ changes of as much as 50 points. Over the period from 6 to 18 years, when retest correlations are generally high, 59 per percent of the children changed by 15 or more IQ points, 37 percent by 20 or more points, and 9 percent by 30 or more. Nor are most of these changes random or erratic in nature. On the contrary, children exhibit consistent upward or downward trends over several consecutive years; and these changes are related to environmental characteristics. In the California Guidance Study, detailed investigation of home conditions and parent-child relationships indicated that large upward or downward shifts in IQ were associated with the cultural milieu and emotional climate in which the child was reared. In the previously mentioned follow-up of the 1937 Stanford-Binet standardization sample, Bradway (1945a) selected for special study the 50 children showing the largest IQ changes from the preschool to the junior high school period. Results of home visits and interviews with parents again indicated that significant rises or drops in IQ over the 10-year period were related to various familial and home characteristics.

Some investigators have concentrated more specifically on the personality characteristics associated with intellectual acceleration and deceleration. At the Fels Research Institute, 140 children were included in an intensive longitudinal study extending from early infancy to adolescence and beyond (Kagan & Freeman, 1963; Kagan, Sontag, Baker, & Nelson, 1958; Sontag, Baker, & Nelson, 1958). Within this group, those children showing the largest gains and those showing the largest losses in IQ between the ages of 4½ and 6 were compared in a wide variety of personality and environmental measures; the same was done with those showing the largest IQ changes between 6 and 10. During the preschool years, emotional dependency on parents was the principal condition associated with IQ loss. During the school years, IQ gains were associated chiefly with high achievement drive, competitive striving, and curiosity about nature. Suggestive data were likewise obtained regarding the role of parental attitudes and child-rearing practices in the development of these traits. It is also interesting to note that sibling resemblance in the pattern of IQ changes was significantly greater than the resemblance among unrelated children—a finding that provides further evidence that these changes are not random or haphazard.

Another approach to an understanding of IQ changes is illustrated by Haan's (1963) follow-up study of 49 men and 50 women who had participated in a long-term growth study. IQ's were obtained with a group test administered when the subjects were about 12 years old and again when they were in their middle or late 30's. Personality characteristics were investigated through a self-report inventory and a series of intensive interviews conducted at the time of the adult follow-up. The upper and lower 25 percent of the group in terms of IQ change, designated as accelerators and decelerators, were compared with special reference to their reliance on coping or defense mechanisms. These mechanisms refer to contrasting personality styles in dealing with problems and frustrations. Coping mechanisms in general represent an objective, constructive, realistic approach; defense mechanisms are characterized by withdrawal, denial, rationalization, and distortion. The results confirmed the hypothesis that accelerators made significantly more use of coping mechanisms and decelerators of defense mechanisms.

Similar results are reported by Moriarty (1966), from a longitudinal study of 65 children tested from two to four times between infancy and the early teens. On the basis of IQ changes, the children were classified into four categories: (a) relatively constant—40 percent; (b) accelerative spurts in one or more areas of functioning—25 percent; (c) slow, delayed, or inhibited development—9 percent; (d) erratic score changes, inconsistent performance in different functions, or progressive IQ decline—26 percent. Intensive case studies of the individual children in these four categories led Moriarty to hypothesize that characteristic differences in coping mechanisms constitute a major factor in the observed course of IQ over time.

Research on the factors associated with increases and decreases in IQ throws light on the conditions determining intellectual development in general. It also suggests that prediction of subsequent intellectual status can be improved if measures of the individual's emotional and motivational characteristics and of his environment are combined with initial test scores. From still another viewpoint, the findings of this type of research point the way to the kind of intervention programs that can effectively alter the course of intellectual development in the desired directions.

MEANING OF AN IQ

To the layman, the IQ is not identified with a particular type of score on a particular test, but is often a shorthand designation for intelligence. So prevalent has this usage become in our culture, that it cannot be merely ignored or deplored as a popular misconception. To be sure, when considering the numerical value of a given IQ, we should always specify the test from which it was derived. Different intelligence tests that yield an IQ do in fact differ in content and in other ways that affect the interpretation of their scores. Some of these differences among tests sharing the common label of "intelligence test" will become apparent in the next few chapters. Nonetheless, there is a need to reexamine the general connotations of the construct "intelligence," as symbolized by the IQ. It might be added that the prevalent conception of intelligence has been shaped to a considerable degree by the characteristics of the Stanford-Binet scale, which for many years provided the only instrument for the intensive measurement of intelligence and which was often used as a criterion for validating new tests.

First, intelligence should be regarded as a descriptive rather than an explanatory concept.[7] An IQ is an expression of an individual's ability level at a given point in time, in relation to his age norms. No intelligence test can indicate the reasons for his performance. To attribute inadequate performance on a test or in everyday-life activities to "inadequate intelligence" is a tautology and in no way advances our understanding of the individual's handicap. In fact, it may serve to halt efforts to explore the causes of the handicap in the individual's history.

Second, the IQ is not fixed and unchanging; and it is amenable to modification by environmental interventions. Some evidence for this conclusion was examined in the preceding section in connection with longitudinal studies. Other evidence comes from a variety of investigations dealing with the effects of education, special training programs, and major environmental changes (see Anastasi, 1958a). An individual's intelligence at any one point in time is the end product of a vast and complex sequence of interactions between hereditary and environmental factors. At any stage in this causal chain, there is opportunity for interaction with new factors; and because each interaction in turn determines the direction of subsequent interactions, there is an ever-widening network of possible outcomes. The connection between the genes an individual inherits and any of his behavioral characteristics is thus highly indirect and devious (see Anastasi, 1958b; Hebb, 1953).

Still another characteristic of intelligence has been foreshadowed by some of the findings regarding the construct validity of the Stanford-Binet. Intelligence is not a single, unitary ability, but a composite of several functions. The term is commonly used to cover that combination of abilities required for survival and advancement within a particular culture. It follows that the specific abilities included in this composite, as well as their relative weights, will vary with time and place. In different cultures and at different historical periods within the same culture, the qualifications for successful achievement will differ. The changing composition of intelligence can also be recognized within the life of the individual, from infancy to adulthood. An individual's relative ability will tend to increase with age in those functions whose value is emphasized by his culture or subculture; and his relative ability will tend to decrease in those functions whose value is deemphasized (see, e.g., Levinson, 1959, 1961).

[7] A good discussion of this point and of the need for a reexamination of the concept of intelligence can be found in Liverant (1960).

Typical intelligence tests designed for use in our culture with school-age children or adults measure largely verbal abilities; to a lesser degree, they also cover abilities to deal with numerical and other abstract symbols. These are the abilities that predominate in school learning. Most intelligence tests can therefore be regarded as measures of scholastic aptitude. The IQ is both a reflection of prior educational achievement and a predictor of subsequent educational performance. Because the functions taught in the educational system are of basic importance in our culture, the IQ is also an effective predictor of performance in many occupations and other activities of adult life. On the other hand, there are many other important functions that intelligence tests have never undertaken to measure.

CHAPTER 9

Group Tests

WHILE INDIVIDUAL scales such as the Stanford-Binet find their principal application in the clinic, group tests are used primarily in the educational system, civil service, industry, and the military services. It will be recalled that mass testing began during World War I with the development of the Army Alpha and the Army Beta for use in the United States Army (Ch. 1). The former was a verbal test designed for general screening and placement purposes. The latter was a nonlanguage test for use with individuals who could not properly be tested with the Alpha owing to foreign-language background or illiteracy. The pattern established by these tests was closely followed in the subsequent development of a large number of group tests for civilian application.

In this chapter, some of the outstanding examples of group tests in current use will be examined. First we shall consider the principal differences between group and individual tests. Then we shall discuss the characteristics of multilevel batteries designed for use over a wide age or grade range. Finally, the type of tests employed at different levels will be illustrated with reference to tests for primary school children, for the elementary and high school levels, for unselected adults, and for the college level and beyond.

GROUP TESTS VERSUS INDIVIDUAL TESTS

Group tests are designed primarily as instruments for mass testing. In comparison with individual tests, they have both advantages and disadvantages. On the positive side, group tests can be administered simultaneously to as many persons as can be fitted comfortably into the available space and reached through a microphone. Large-scale testing programs were made possible by the development of group testing techniques. By utilizing only printed items and simple responses that can be recorded on a test booklet or answer sheet, the need for a one-to-one relationship between examiner and examinee was eliminated.

A second way in which group tests facilitated mass testing was by greatly simplifying the examiner's role. In contrast to the extensive training and experience required to administer the Stanford-Binet, most group tests require only the ability to read simple instructions to the subjects and to keep accurate time. Some preliminary training sessions are desirable, of course, since inexperienced examiners are likely to deviate inadvertently from the standardized procedure in ways that may affect test results. Because the examiner's role is minimized, however, group testing can provide more uniform conditions than does individual testing. The use of tapes, records, and film in test administration offers further opportunities for standardizing procedure in large-scale testing.

Scoring is typically more objective in group testing and can usually be done by a clerk. Many group tests can also be scored by machine. Moreover, whether hand-scored or machine-scored, most group tests provide separate answer sheets and reusable test booklets. Since in these tests all responses are written on the answer sheet, the test booklets can be used indefinitely until they wear out, thereby effecting considerable economy. Answer sheets also take up less room than test booklets and hence can be more conveniently filed for large numbers of examinees.

From another angle, group tests usually provide better established norms than do individual tests. Because of the relative ease and rapidity of gathering data with group tests, it is customary to test very large, representative samples in the standardization process. In the most recently standardized group tests, it is not unusual for the normative samples to number between 100,000 and 500,000, in contrast to the 2,000 to 4,000 cases laboriously accumulated in standardizing the most carefully developed individual intelligence scales.

Group tests necessarily differ from individual tests in form and arrangement of items. Although open-ended questions calling for free responses could be used—and were used in the early group tests—today the typical group test employs *multiple-choice items*. This change was obviously required for uniformity and objectivity of scoring, whether by hand or machine. With regard to arrangement of items, whereas the Binet-type of scale groups items into age levels, group tests characteristically group items of similar content into *separately timed subtests*. Within each subtest, items are usually arranged in increasing order of difficulty. This arrangement ensures that each subject has an opportunity to try each type of item (such as vocabulary, arithmetic, spatial, etc.) and to complete the easier items of each type before trying the more difficult ones on which he might otherwise waste a good deal of time.

A practical difficulty encountered with separate subtests, however, is that the less experienced or less careful examiners may make timing errors. Such errors are more likely to occur and are relatively more serious with several short time limits than with a single long time limit for the whole test. To reconcile the use of a single time limit with an arrangement permitting all subjects to try all types of items at successively increasing difficulty levels, some tests utilize the *spiral-omnibus format*. One of the earliest tests to introduce this format was the Otis Self-Administering Tests of Mental Ability which, as its name implies, endeavored to reduce the examiner's role to a minimum. The same arrangement is followed in the 1967 edition of the Otis-Lennon Mental Ability Test, from the fourth-grade level up. In a spiral-omnibus test, the easiest items of each type are presented first, followed by the next easiest of each type, and so on in a rising spiral of difficulty level, as illustrated below:

1. The opposite of hate is: Answer
   1. enemy, 2. fear, 3. love, 4. friend, 5. joy .... ( )
2. If 3 pencils cost 5 cents, how many pencils can be bought for 50
   cents?.. ( )
3. A bird does not always have:
   1. wings, 2. eyes, 3. feet, 4. a nest, 5. a bill .... ( )
4. The opposite of honor is:
   1. glory, 2. disgrace, 3. cowardice, 4. fear, 5. defeat .... ( )

In order to avoid the necessity of repeating instructions in each item and to reduce the number of shifts in instructional set required of the subject, some tests apply the spiral-omnibus arrangement not to single items but to blocks of 5 to 10 items. This practice is followed, for example, in the Army General Classification Test (AGCT), to be discussed later in the chapter.

Although group tests have several desirable features and serve a well-nigh indispensable function in present-day testing, their limitations should also be noted. In group testing, the examiner has much less opportunity to establish rapport, obtain cooperation, and maintain the interest of subjects. Any temporary condition of the subject, such as illness, fatigue, worry, or anxiety, that may interfere with test performance is less readily detected in group than in individual testing. In general, individuals unaccustomed to testing may be somewhat more handicapped on group than on individual tests. Finally, unlike individual tests, group tests provide little or no opportunity for supplementary observations of the subject's behavior or for identifying the causes of poor performance on particular items. For all these reasons, when important decisions about individuals are to be made, it is often desirable to supplement group tests either with individual examination of doubtful cases or with additional information from other sources.

MULTILEVEL BATTERIES

In individual tests such as the Binet scales, the examiner selects the appropriate difficulty level at which to begin and the subject's own performance determines the range of item difficulties covered in his test. In a group test, on the other hand, all subjects are exposed to the same items. For this reason, any given group test covers a relatively restricted range of difficulty, suitable for the particular age, grade, or ability level for which it is designed. To provide comparable measures of intellectual development over a broader range, series of overlapping multilevel batteries have been constructed. Thus, any one individual is examined only with the level appropriate to him, but other levels can be used for retesting him in subsequent years or for comparative evaluations of different age groups. The fact that successive batteries overlap provides adequate floor and ceiling for individuals at the extremes of their own age or grade distributions.

Multilevel batteries are especially suitable for use in the schools, where comparability over several years is highly desirable. For this reason the levels are typically described in terms of grades. Most multilevel batteries provide a reasonable degree of continuity with regard to content or intellectual functions covered. Scores are expressed in terms of the same scale of units throughout. The normative samples employed at different levels are also more nearly equivalent than would be true of independently standardized tests.

Table 27 contains a list of representative multilevel batteries, together with the range of grades covered by each level. It will be noted that the individual ranges are quite narrow, most levels covering two to three grades. The total range that can be uniformly tested with a given multilevel battery, on the other hand, may extend from kindergarten to college.

The names of the batteries are also of interest. The terms "intelligence," "general ability," "mental ability," "mental maturity," "learning potential," "school-and-college ability," and "educational ability," are used to designate essentially the same type of test. In the psychometrician's vocabulary, these terms are synonymous and interchangeable. The most recent of the batteries listed in Table 27, entitled "Analysis of Learning Potential," is explicitly directed toward the prediction of academic performance. Utilizing several ingenious new item types, the development of this battery began with a detailed analysis of the abilities required by school learning tasks. It thus reflects a growing emphasis on the measurement of prerequisite intellectual skills for schoolwork and other activities of daily life. Its pri-

TABLE 27 REPRESENTATIVE MULTILEVEL BATTERIES

Battery	Grade Levels
Analysis of Learning Potential (ALP)	K, 1, 2–3, 4–6, 7–9, 9–12, College
California Test of Mental Maturity, 1963 Revision (CTMM)	4–6, 7–9, 9–12, 12–16, and adult
Cooperative School and College Ability Tests (SCAT) [a]	4–6, 6–8, 8–10, 10–12, 12–14, 15–16
Henmon-Nelson Tests of Mental Ability, Revised Edition	3–6, 6–9, 9–12, 13–17
Kuhlmann-Anderson Intelligence Tests, Seventh Edition	K, 1, 2, 3–4, 4–5, 5–7, 7–9, 9–12
Lorge-Thorndike Intelligence Tests	K–1, 2–3, 4–6, 7–9, 10–12 (also available in single booklet, multilevel edition of overlapping batteries A-H for grades 3–13)
Otis-Lennon Mental Ability Test [b]	K–1.5, 1.6–3.9, 4–6.9, 7–9.9, 10–12
Pintner General Ability Tests — Revised	K–2, 2–4, 4–9
SRA Short Test of Educational Ability (STEA)	K–1, 2–3, 4–6, 7–8, 9–12
SRA Tests of Educational Ability, 1962 Edition (TEA)	4–6, 6–9, 9–12

[a] Highest level (15–16) is restricted; four levels covering grades 4–14 also available in Series II, a shorter version published in 1968.
[b] Forms for kindergarten and for first grade are identical in content but differ in the way the child records his responses.

mary function is to assess the individual's readiness for school learning at each stage in the educational process.

Most of the batteries listed in Table 27 provide deviation IQ's or similar standard scores; the only exceptions are SCAT and the college level of the Henmon-Nelson, for which only percentiles are given. Some batteries provide several types of norms, including percentiles, stanines, or grade equivalents, as well as deviation IQ's. In addition to a total, global score, most batteries also yield separate verbal and quantitative, or linguistic and nonlinguistic scores. This breakdown is in line with the finding that an individual's performance in verbal and in other types of subtests may be quite dissimilar, especially at the upper levels. Attempts have also been made (e.g., CTMM) to report norms for the interpretation of scores on separate subtests, or combinations of subtests, representing narrower breakdowns. This practice is not to be recommended, however, because these part scores are usually too unreliable and too highly intercorrelated to permit meaningful interpretation of intraindividual differences. In general, the types of tests discussed in this chapter are suitable for assessing general intellectual development rather than relative standing in different aptitudes.

Some batteries provide parallel forms for testing readers and nonreaders. In the parts for nonreaders, instructions are given orally by the examiner and the test items use pictorial or numerical materials. The parallel batteries may be limited to certain critical levels, where the number of children who cannot read well enough to be properly tested with the usual type of material is relatively large. The Pintner series, for example, provides parallel batteries at the Elementary Level, designed for grades 2 to 4. Other batteries provide parallel verbal and nonverbal forms for all levels except the very lowest (which are always necessarily nonverbal). The Lorge-Thorndike, for example, contains separately scored verbal and nonverbal batteries from the fourth grade to college. These alternate batteries may be used singly or they may be administered in combination to permit a comparison of the individual's performance on the two types of tests.

Since persons with severe reading disabilities cannot be adequately assessed with tests that presuppose functional reading ability, nonverbal batteries are needed. Nonetheless, scores on verbal and nonverbal batteries cannot be regarded as alternate measures of the same intellectual functions. In the interpretation of nonverbal scores from such batteries, therefore, it is important to take into account the correlations between verbal and nonverbal scores, as well as the validity of the nonverbal scores in predicting academic achievement and other relevant criteria. It should also be noted that the use of parallel batteries for readers and nonreaders represents a different approach from that followed in reporting, for example, separate verbal and quantitative scores on a battery. Parallel batteries are designed to measure as nearly as possible the same traits; hence, the two scores should correlate as high as possible. In contrast, when separate scores are reported on verbal and quantitative tests, all of which require reading, the two scores are intended to differentiate between an individual's performance in different functions; hence, these scores should not correlate highly with each other.

TESTS FOR THE PRIMARY LEVEL

The youngest age at which it has proved feasible to employ group tests is the kindergarten and first-grade level. At the preschool ages, individual testing is required in order to establish and maintain rapport, as well as to administer the oral and performance type of items suitable for such children. By the age of 5 or 6, however, it is possible to administer printed tests to small groups of no more than 10 or 15 children. In such testing, the examiner must still give considerable individual attention to the subjects to make sure that directions are followed, see that pages are turned properly in the test booklets, and supervise other procedural details. With one or two assistant examiners, somewhat larger groups may be tested if necessary.

Group tests for the primary level generally cover kindergarten and the first two or three grades of elementary school. In such tests, each child is provided with a booklet on which are printed the pictures and diagrams constituting the test items. All instructions are given orally and are usually accompanied by demonstrations. Fore-exercises are frequently included in which subjects try one or two sample items and the examiner or proctor checks the responses to make certain that the instructions were properly understood. The child marks his responses on the test booklet with a crayon or soft pencil. Most of the tests require only marking the correct picture out of a set. A few call for simple motor coordination, as in drawing lines that join two dots.

Obviously tests for the primary level can require no reading or writing on the part of the subject. For this reason, they are sometimes described as "nonverbal tests," a term also used to refer to the tests for older nonreaders, discussed in the preceding section. This category should not be confused with the nonlanguage tests to be considered in the next chapter. Nonlanguage tests require no language at all, either written or spoken, and are suitable for foreign-speaking and deaf as well as for illiterate subjects. Nonlanguage tests for the primary level have also been developed for testing special groups of children, but the usual primary group test involves extensive use of spoken language. The designation "nonverbal" for these tests, although commonly employed, may be somewhat misleading, since it can be properly applied only to the test content and not to the subject's behavior. For example, tests of verbal comprehension can be administered at these age levels through the use of pictorial content. Thus, the child's vocabulary or his sentence comprehension can be tested by means of pictures. For this reason, it would seem more accurate to refer to these tests by such terms as "pictorial" or "nonreading," rather than "nonverbal."

Reference to Table 27 shows that several of the batteries listed have tests suitable for the primary level. To illustrate the nature of tests at this level, we shall examine the Primary Level of the Otis-Lennon Mental Ability Test. The current edition of this test, published in 1967–1968, is available in two equivalent forms (J and K) at all levels. The Primary Level actually consists of two levels, Primary I for kindergarten and Primary II for the first half of grade one. These two levels are identical in content and differ only in the way the child indicates his responses. In Primary I, responses are recorded by encircling the correct alternative; for this reason, the test must be hand scored. In Primary II, a machine-scorable booklet is used, on which responses are indicated by filling in a small oval under the correct alternative (see Fig. 36).

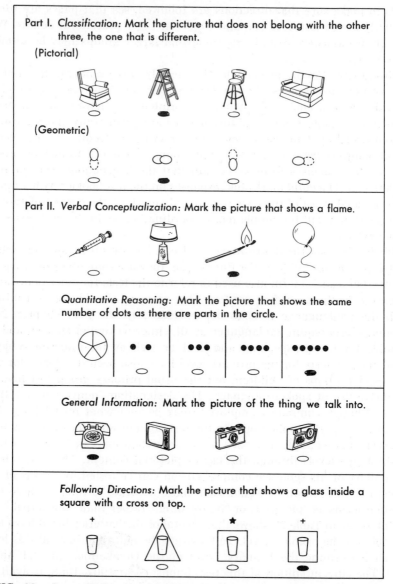

Part I. *Classification:* Mark the picture that does not belong with the other three, the one that is different.
(Pictorial)

(Geometric)

Part II. *Verbal Conceptualization:* Mark the picture that shows a flame.

Quantitative Reasoning: Mark the picture that shows the same number of dots as there are parts in the circle.

General Information: Mark the picture of the thing we talk into.

Following Directions: Mark the picture that shows a glass inside a square with a cross on top.

FIG. 36.　Items Illustrative of the Otis-Lennon Mental Ability Test, Primary I and Primary II Levels. (Copyright, 1967, Harcourt, Brace & World, Inc.)

For each item in the entire test, the examiner gives the instructions orally. By so doing, the examiner also controls the amount of time available to complete each item (about 15 seconds). The whole test requires approximately 25 to 30 minutes and is administered in two parts with a short rest period in between. Part I consists of 23 classification items; Part II contains a total of 32 items, designed to measure verbal conceptualization, quantitative reasoning, general information, and ability to follow directions. Typical items in each of these categories are shown in Figure 36.

Norms for all levels of the Otis-Lennon battery were obtained on a carefully chosen representative sample of over 200,000 pupils in 100 school systems drawn from all 50 states. Scores can be expressed as deviation IQ's with a σ of 16. Percentile ranks and stanines can also be found with reference to both age and grade norms. Well-constructed tests for the primary level have generally been found to have satisfactory reliability and criterion-related validity. The Otis-Lennon Primary II yielded an alternate-form reliability of .87 in a sample of 1,047 first-grade children, over an interval of two weeks. Split-half reliability in the total sample of 14,044 first-grade children was .90. Plans are under way to obtain validity data in terms of correlations with other ability tests, achievement tests, and school grades.

TESTS FOR THE ELEMENTARY AND HIGH SCHOOL LEVELS

Group intelligence tests designed for use from the fourth grade of elementary school through high school have much in common in both content and general design. Since functional literacy is presupposed at these levels, the tests are predominantly verbal in content; most also include arithmetic problems or other numerical tests. As noted in an earlier section, a few batteries provide parallel nonreading tests designed to assess the same abstract reasoning abilities in children with reading disabilities or other educational handicaps.

A TYPICAL ELEMENTARY SCHOOL TEST.   As an example of a test for the middle elementary-school grades, we shall consider Level B of the Lorge-Thorndike Multi-Level Battery (1964 edition). This level is suitable for children in the fourth and fifth grades.[1] Like other levels in the series, Level B is available in two equivalent forms, 1 and 2, each containing five verbal and three nonverbal tests. The verbal tests include Vocabulary, Sentence Completion, Arithmetic Reasoning, Verbal Classification, and Verbal Analogies. The nonverbal tests include Figure Classification, Number Series, and Figure Analogies. Typical items illustrating each of the eight tests are shown in Figures 37A and 37B. The authors recommend that both verbal and nonverbal parts be routinely administered to each child for a more comprehensive picture of his abilities. Total working time required is 35 minutes for the verbal and 27 minutes for the nonverbal parts. Although

[1] It is recommended, however, that this level be used in the sixth grade in educationally retarded schools and in the fourth grade in educationally accelerated schools. A similar flexibility characterizes the use of all other levels.

1. *Vocabulary:* choose the word which has the same meaning, or most nearly the same meaning, as the word in dark type at the beginning of the line.

   javelin   A. bleach   B. coffee   C. jacket   D. rifle   E. spear

---

2. *Sentence Completion:* choose the word that will make the best, the truest, and the most sensible sentence.

   There's no book so _____ but something good may be found in it.

   A. good   B. true   C. beautiful   D. bad   E. excellent

---

3. *Arithmetic Reasoning*

   A man has to take a 300-mile trip by car. If he goes 40 miles each hour, how many miles does he still have to travel after driving $5\frac{1}{2}$ hours?

   A. 180 mi.   B. 100 mi.   C. 60 mi.   D. 2 mi.   E. none of these

---

4. *Verbal Classification:* think in what way the words in dark type go together. Then find the word on the line below that belongs with them.

   cotton   wool   silk

   A. dress   B. sew   C. fibre   D. linen   E. cloth

---

5. *Verbal Analogies:* look at the first two words and figure out how they are related to each other. Then, from the five words on the line below, choose the word that is related to the third word in the same way.

   then ⟶ now : yesterday ⟶

   A. tomorrow   B. time   C. today   D. here   E. past

FIG. 37A.   Typical Items from the Lorge-Thorndike Intelligence Tests, Level B: Verbal Battery. (Reproduced by courtesy of Irving Lorge and Robert L. Thorndike.)

all subtests have time limits, they are said to be largely power tests.

Within each subtest, items were selected so as to yield an appropriate range of difficulty, as well as high internal consistency. Average item-subtest correlations in Level B range from .46 to .66 for the eight subtests. Norms for the complete battery (including all levels) were established by testing over 180,000 children in 70 school systems distributed over 42 states. To increase the representativeness of this standardization sample, the communities were selected on the basis of a composite of socioeconomic and educational variables previously found to be related to the intelligence test performance of children within a community. Scores are ex-

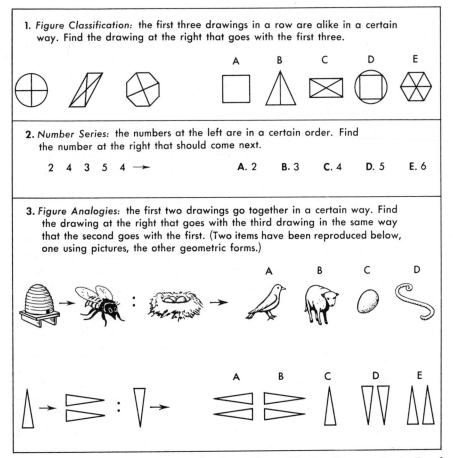

1. *Figure Classification:* the first three drawings in a row are alike in a certain way. Find the drawing at the right that goes with the first three.

A   B   C   D   E

2. *Number Series:* the numbers at the left are in a certain order. Find the number at the right that should come next.

2 4 3 5 4 →   **A.** 2   **B.** 3   **C.** 4   **D.** 5   **E.** 6

3. *Figure Analogies:* the first two drawings go together in a certain way. Find the drawing at the right that goes with the third drawing in the same way that the second goes with the first. (Two items have been reproduced below, one using pictures, the other geometric forms.)

A   B   C   D

A   B   C   D   E

FIG. 37B.   Typical Items from the Lorge-Thorndike Intelligence Tests, Level B: Nonverbal Battery. (Reproduced by courtesy of Irving Lorge and Robert L. Thorndike.)

pressed as deviation IQ's, with a mean of 100 and a σ of 16. Age, grade, and percentile norms are also provided.

Alternate-form reliability coefficients, found by administering Forms 1 and 2 of Level B within a week to 155 fourth-grade pupils, were .93 for the verbal battery and .85 for the nonverbal. Odd-even reliabilities in a group of 1,590 fourth graders were .95 for the verbal and .92 for the nonverbal battery. These reliabilities yield errors of measurement of about 3 to 4 IQ points. Apart from a priori choice of test content designed to measure the ability to handle abstract concepts, symbols, and relationships, evidence of validity centers around correlations with other intelligence tests and with tests of educational achievement. On the whole, these correlations are high, falling largely between .60 and .80. Investigations of predictive validity over intervals of one to two years have yielded correlations between .50 and .70 with achievement tests. Quite consistently, however, the correlations with the nonverbal battery run lower than those with the verbal battery.

The nonverbal and verbal batteries do nevertheless have much in common. A typical correlation between the two batteries, found in a group of 1,590 fourth graders, was .74. A factor analysis of the eight tests revealed a general factor that accounts for the largest proportion of the variance in each test. A smaller group factor was identified through four of the five tests in the verbal battery, and another group factor through the two number tests (cutting across verbal and nonverbal batteries). The Lorge-Thorndike verbal and nonverbal batteries thus appear to be more nearly comparable than is generally true of verbal and nonverbal tests.

A TYPICAL HIGH SCHOOL TEST.   An example of a group intelligence test for the high school level is provided by Level 2 of the School and College Ability Tests (SCAT), designed for grades 10 to 12. At all levels of the SCAT series, tests are available in two equivalent forms, A and B. Oriented specifically toward the prediction of academic achievement, all levels yield a verbal, a quantitative, and a total score. The verbal score is based on two tests, Sentence Understanding (I) and Word Meanings (III); the numerical score, on Numerical Computation (II) and Numerical Problem Solving (IV). Figure 38 shows a sample item from each of the four parts at Level 2. Administration of any one level requires approximately two class periods.[2]

In line with current trends in testing theory, SCAT undertakes to measure "developed abilities." This is simply an explicit admission of what is more or less true of all intelligence tests, namely that test scores reflect the nature and amount of schooling the individual has received rather than measuring "capacity" independently of relevant prior experiences. Accordingly, SCAT draws freely on word knowledge and arithmetic processes learned in the appropriate school grades. In this respect, SCAT does not really differ from other intelligence tests, especially those designed for the high school and college levels; it only makes overt a condition sometimes unrecognized in other tests.

Verbal, quantitative, and total scores from all SCAT levels are expressed on a common scale which permits direct comparison from one level to another. These scores can in turn be converted into percentiles for the appropriate grade, derived from a carefully chosen nationwide standardization sample. A particularly desirable feature of SCAT scores is the provision of a *percentile band* rather than a single percentile for each obtained score (see Fig. 17, Ch. 4). Representing a distance of approximately one stand-

---

[2] A shorter version, Series II, published in 1968, can be administered in a single class period. Series II contains only two tests, verbal analogies and quantitative comparisons; it is available in four levels, covering grades 4–14.

Part I. Sentence Understanding.
Select the missing word by deciding which one of the five words *best* fits
in with the meaning of the sentence.

To make you understand my point I must go back a bit and seem
to change the subject, but the (   ) will soon be plain.

A correction   B effect   C origin   D controversy   E connection

---

Part II. Numerical Computation
Choose the correct answer, using scratch paper if necessary.

$\frac{.7}{.05}$ is equal to which of the following?

F $\frac{7}{50}$
G $\frac{7}{5}$
H 14
J 35
K None of these

Part III. Word Meanings.
Pick the word or phrase whose meaning is closest to the word in large letters.

induce

A grant
B prolong
C mix
D persuade
E convict

Part IV. Numerical Problem Solving.
Choose the correct answer, using scratch paper if necessary.

A woman weighed 125 pounds. After she had gained $4\frac{1}{2}$ pounds,
lost 6 pounds, and gained $2\frac{1}{2}$ pounds, how many pounds did she weigh?

F 124
G 125
H 126
J 137
K 138

FIG. 38.   Typical Items from SCAT, Level 2, for Grades 10–12. (Reproduced
by permission of Cooperative Test Division, Educational Testing Service.)

ard error of measurement on either side of the corresponding percentile,
the percentile band gives the 68 percent confidence interval, or the range
within which are found 68 percent of the cases in a normal curve. In other
words, if we conclude that an individual's true score lies within the given

percentile band, we can expect to be correct for 68 cases out of every 100 (roughly 2 : 1 ratio). As explained in Chapter 4, the error of measurement provides a concrete way of taking the reliability of a test into account when interpreting an individual's score.

If two percentile bands overlap, the difference between the scores can be ignored; if they do not overlap, the difference can be regarded as significant. Thus, if two students were to obtain total SCAT scores that fall in the percentile bands 55–68 and 74–84, we could conclude with fair confidence that the second actually excels the first and would continue to do so on a retest. Percentile bands likewise help in comparing a single individual's relative standing on verbal and quantitative parts of the test. If a student's verbal and quantitative scores correspond to the percentile bands 78–91 and 63–84, respectively, we would conclude that he is *not* significantly better in verbal than in quantitative abilities, because his percentile bands for these two scores overlap.

Reliability coefficients for verbal, quantitative, and total scores were separately computed within single grade groups by the Kuder-Richardson technique. It will be recalled that this is a measure of interitem consistency within a single form administered once. The reported reliabilities are uniformly high. For the separate grade groups investigated, from grade 5 to grade 13, total score reliabilities are all .95 or .96; verbal and quantitative reliabilities vary between .88 and .94. These reliabilities may be spuriously high because the tests are somewhat speeded. It is reported that, in some of the samples tested, the numbers of subjects completing all items were as low as 65 percent and 80 percent for the two verbal tests and as low as 48 percent and 60 percent for the two quantitative tests. Under these circumstances, equivalent-form reliability would seem more appropriate. If the reliability coefficients are in fact spuriously high, the errors of measurement are underestimated; and hence the percentile bands should be wider.

A variety of sources provide information about what SCAT measures. Through preliminary experimentation, the four subtests illustrated in Figure 38 were chosen from nine subtests, each representing a different item type designed to sample abilities required for academic success. This selection was based on the correlations of each subtest with total grade averages, English grades, and mathematics grades in groups of ninth- and twelfth-grade students. Intercorrelations among the subtests were also considered, in order to maximize differences between verbal and quantitative measures. Items for the four types of subtests finally chosen were next selected on the basis of item-subtest correlations and appropriateness of difficulty level. This item analysis was conducted on large samples of students representative of the population for which the test was being developed. In the final forms, correlations between verbal and quantitative scores dropped from .71 in the fifth grade to .53 in the thirteenth. Such evidence for increasing differentiation of abilities with increasing age and educational level is consistent with findings on the organization of abilities (Anastasi, 1958a, Ch. 11).

In view of the stated purpose for which SCAT was developed, its predictive validity against academic achievement is of prime relevance. A number of studies at elementary, high school, and college levels have yielded fairly high correlations with grades and achievement test scores. The correlations tend to be higher with achievement tests than with grades, and higher for the lower than for the upper levels. Among high school groups, correlations with average grades cluster in the .50's; with grades in individual subjects, the correlations fall largely between .40 and .60. The effectiveness of the verbal and quantitative scores as differential predictors of grades in specific courses remains uncertain. English grades tend to correlate higher with verbal than with quantitative scores, and mathematics grades higher with quantitative than with verbal; but the differences are small and not entirely consistent. Moreover, total scores often yield the highest correlations with all types of courses.

TESTS FOR UNSELECTED ADULTS

The high school levels of multilevel batteries, as well as other tests designed for high school students, are suitable for testing general, unselected adult groups. Another source of adult tests is provided by the tests developed for military personnel during World Wars I and II and subsequently published in civilian editions.

CONTRIBUTIONS OF MILITARY TESTING. It will be recalled that the Army Alpha of World War I initiated the group testing movement. The original military forms of the Army Alpha (Yerkes, 1921, Part II, Ch. 1–4) were validated in terms of such criteria as amount of schooling and ratings of intelligence by officers. Additional validity data were obtained by administering preliminary forms of the test to a number of other groups. For example, the criterion of contrasted groups was applied by comparing the distributions of Alpha scores obtained by college students, officers, enlisted men, and mentally retarded adults. For schoolchildren, Alpha scores were checked against such criteria as Stanford-Binet MA, chronological age, school grades, and teachers' ratings of pupils' intelligence. Most of the indices of validity showed the Alpha to correlate fairly well with the criteria employed. For example, a correlation of .82 was found between a preliminary form of Alpha and school grades within a group of unselected 13-year-olds, and a correlation of .86 within a group of unselected 14-year-olds. Correlations with the Stanford-Binet ranged from .58 to .88. Correlations of the final form with ratings of intelligence by officers ranged from .45 to .67, and correlations with amount of schooling were in the .60's and .70's.

After World War I, the Army Alpha was released for general use. Several revisions were subsequently developed for civilian purposes and were widely administered, especially in testing applicants for industrial jobs. One of the current adaptations of this test is the Alpha Examination, Modified Form 9. Commonly known as "Alpha 9," this test consists of four numerical and four verbal subtests, from which can be obtained separate N and V scores, as well as a total score. Percentile norms are provided for boys and girls in each year of high school, separate norms being given for N, V, and total scores. The manual also includes supplementary norms based on smaller samples of special adult populations, such as engineers employed in a single large airplane company and men applying for executive positions. Total score reliabilities of about .90 were obtained when Alpha 9 was correlated with comparable earlier forms.

During World War II, the Army General Classification Test (AGCT) was developed to serve many of the functions for which the Army Alpha had been used in the earlier war. The AGCT was administered to over ten million inductees. In 1945, when this test was replaced by a revised edition, the earlier form was released for civilian use. The AGCT contains an equal number of vocabulary, arithmetic reasoning, and block-counting items. The inclusion of equal proportions of verbal, numerical, and spatial content in this test reflects the influence of the intervening research on factor analysis. The different types of items are arranged in spiral-omnibus form, with blocks of 5 or 10 items of each type following each other in order of increasing difficulty. This layout permits the administration of the entire test with a single time limit. The test proper is preceded by three pages of practice items, including 10 items of each type. Some of these practice items are given in Figure 39.

AGCT norms were derived from data obtained during the military application of the test. Both percentiles and AGCT standard scores are given. It will be recalled that the latter were adjusted so as to yield a mean of 100 and a σ of 20 points (Ch. 3). Retest reliability is .82; split-half and Kuder-Richardson reliabilities cluster about .95. It is possible that the latter value is spuriously high because of the influence of speed on test scores, although it is stated in the manual that the time limit allowed is sufficient for most subjects to reach their upper limit of difficulty.

Several measures of validity were found on the basis of the military samples tested. AGCT scores correlated .73 with amount of schooling. Correlations with many other tests are reported, some of which are extremely high. For example, a correlation of .90 was found with Army Alpha, and one of .83 with the Otis Higher Mental Ability Examination. Further data on validity were provided by correlations with performance in military training

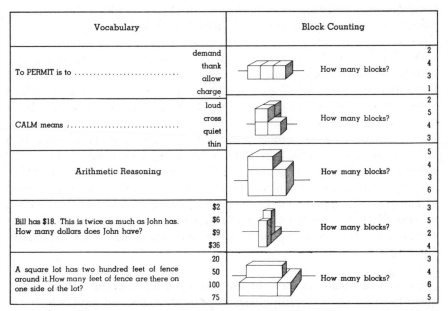

Vocabulary		Block Counting	
To PERMIT is to	demand thank allow charge	How many blocks?	2 4 3 1
CALM means :...........................	loud cross quiet thin	How many blocks?	2 5 4 3
Arithmetic Reasoning		How many blocks?	5 4 3 6
Bill has $18. This is twice as much as John has. How many dollars does John have?	$2 $6 $9 $36	How many blocks?	3 5 2 4
A square lot has two hundred feet of fence around it. How many feet of fence are there on one side of the lot?	20 50 100 75	How many blocks?	3 4 6 5

FIG. 39. Demonstration Items Illustrating the Three Types of Content in the Army General Classification Test. (From ARMY GENERAL CLASSIFI-CATION TEST: First Civilian Edition, Form AH by Science Research Associates, Inc. Copyright 1947, by Science Research Associates, Inc. Reprinted by permission of the publisher.)

schools for various occupational specialties, such as that of clerk, radio operator, and mechanic, as well as by correlations with performance in officer candidate schools. The median AGCT scores of men who had been employed in different civilian occupations are likewise given. All these data, as well as the principal norms given in the 1960 manual, are based on the original military samples tested during World War II. Subsequent data are meager. For this reason, the AGCT might best be used with local norms and following local validation studies. Comparability of the World War II military population with the current civilian population is questionable.

For military purposes, the AGCT has been replaced by the Armed Forces Qualification Test (AFQT). This test was prepared cooperatively by all the armed services, originally for the purpose of screening recruits and providing each service with an equitable distribution of ability among its quota of available manpower (Uhlaner, 1952). The AFQT included vocabulary, arithmetic reasoning, and spatial relations items, the last-named involving the recognition, perception, manipulation, and analysis of relations in two and three dimensions. Items were selected on the basis of difficulty level, as well as on the basis of their correlations with subtests and total test scores. The AFQT is employed in lieu of the AGCT as well as other screening tests formerly used by the different services. Following the general preliminary screening by means of the AFQT, each service now administers its own classification batteries, on the basis of which the inductees are assigned to particular specialties within that service.

In its original form, the AFQT was quite similar to the earlier AGCT, with which it correlated .90 in a sample of 4,000 cases. AFQT scores also correlated .69 with number of years of education in a sample of 929 cases. Performance on the AFQT was first reported in terms of Army Standard Scores. This score system employs the AGCT standard score scale, with a mean of 100 and a σ of 20. It also utilizes as a fixed reference group (see Ch. 3) a representative sample of the United States male population aged 20–29 who took the AGCT in 1940. With a previous form of the AGCT serving as anchor test, all scores on subsequent forms of AGCT and AFQT can be expressed in terms of the mean and σ of this fixed reference group (Uhlaner, 1952, pp. 5–6). Later forms have been somewhat modified, principally by the addition of a set of mechanical aptitude items; and scores are now reported as percentiles rather than standard scores (Karpinos, 1967).

SHORT SCREENING TESTS. In the testing of adult groups, there is frequent need for short screening tests of general intellectual level, which can be followed up with more specialized tests, interviews, and other selection or classification techniques. An example of such a brief testing instrument is the Quick Word Test. Utilizing the common finding that general intelligence tests correlate very highly with vocabulary tests,[3] this test consists of 100 multiple-choice vocabulary items in each of four equivalent forms. The items were selected on the basis of difficulty level and discriminative value against both total score and an external criterion of grade level. In the final forms, items are arranged so that difficulty ranges from low to high within each block of 5 items. Thus, approximately the same difficulty range is encountered in the last block as in the first. This arrangement was followed in an effort to maintain the subjects' interest and to reduce progressive discouragement.

The Quick Word Test is virtually self-administering; and it is untimed, most subjects requiring from 15 to 20 minutes to finish. Percentile and stanine norms are available on over 20,000 high school students in grades 9 to 12 from 14 school systems distributed in 13 states. Kuder-Richardson and split-half reliabilities for the four forms are .90 or slightly higher; alternate-form reliabilities are .88 and .89. Because the Quick Word Test is designed as a short substitute for more time-consuming group intelligence tests, the use of the latter tests as criteria in concurrent validation is appropriate. Correlations of Quick Word Test with total scores on such common group tests as the SCAT, Lorge-Thorndike (verbal battery), CTMM (short form), and Otis [4] range from .72 to .84. Since the Quick Word Test

---

[3] See, e.g., the results obtained with the Stanford-Binet (Ch. 8).
[4] An earlier edition of the Otis-Lennon Mental Ability Test.

was administered as an anchor test to groups of high school students who also took one or more of the above tests, tables of equivalent scores were prepared by the equipercentile method. With these tables, one can identify the score on each of these longer tests that corresponds to each score on the Quick Word Test.

On the whole, the Quick Word Test shows considerable promise for the purposes for which it was designed. It is also available in a more difficult level suitable for college and professional groups, as well as in a more recently developed elementary school level. In this connection, we should also note that several short screening tests of general intellectual level have been specially developed for use with industrial personnel. These will be considered in the chapter on occupational tests (Ch. 16).

TESTS FOR THE COLLEGE LEVEL AND BEYOND

COLLEGE ADMISSION. A number of tests have been developed for use in the admission, placement, and counseling of college students. An outstanding example is the Scholastic Aptitude Test (SAT) of the College Entrance Examination Board (Angoff, 1968). Several new forms of this test are prepared each year, a different form being employed in each administration. Separate scores are reported for the Verbal and Mathematics sections of the test. A shorter comparable form, known as the Preliminary SAT, has also been administered since 1959. Generally taken at an earlier stage, this test provides a rough estimate of the high school student's aptitude for college work and has been employed for educational counseling and other special purposes. Both tests are restricted to the testing program administered by the College Entrance Examination Board on behalf of member colleges. All applicants to these colleges take the SAT. Some colleges also require one or more achievement tests in special fields, likewise administered by CEEB.

Another nationwide program, launched in 1959, is the American College Testing Program (ACT). This program is limited largely to state university systems, but includes among its members one or more colleges in over half of the states. The ACT examination includes four parts: English Usage, Mathematics Usage, Social Studies Reading, and Natural Sciences Reading. Reflecting the point of view of its founder, E. F. Lindquist, the examination provides a set of work samples of college work. It overlaps traditional aptitude and achievement tests, focusing on the basic intellectual skills required for satisfactory performance in college.

In addition to the above restricted tests, a number of tests designed for college-bound high school students and for college students are commercially available to counselors and other qualified users. An example is the Ohio State University Psychological Test (OSUPT). This is a pure power test, administered with no time limit, but usually requiring from 1½ to 2 hours. The OSUPT is entirely verbal in content, including Same-Opposites, Verbal Analogies, and Reading Comprehension in four areas (natural science, mathematics, social science, literary description). With regard to reliability and predictive validity, OSUPT compares very favorably with other college admission tests. In 1964, new norms for Form 23 were obtained in a carefully stratified national sample of 3,000 high school students in grades 10 to 12.

A more recently developed test for the same general purpose is the College Qualification Test. It offers six possible scores: verbal, numerical, science information, social studies information, total information, and a total score on the entire test. The information demanded in the various fields is of a fairly general and basic nature and is not dependent on technical aspects of particular courses. Reliability and normative data compare favorably with those of similar tests. Validity data are promising but understandably less extensive than for tests that have been in use much longer.

It will be noted that, with the exception of the College Board's SAT (which can be supplemented with achievement tests), all these tests sample a combination of general aptitudes and knowledge about (or ability to handle) subject matter in major academic fields. When separate scores are available, their differential validity in predicting achievement in different fields is questionable. It would seem that total score provides the best predictor of performance in nearly all college courses. Among the part-scores, verbal scores are usually the best single predictors. Another important point to bear in mind is that scores on any of these tests are not intended as substitutes for high school grades in the prediction of college achievement. High school grades can predict college achievement as well as most tests or better. When test scores are combined with high school grades, however, the prediction of college performance is considerably improved.

GRADUATE SCHOOL ADMISSION.   The practice of testing applicants for admission to college has subsequently been extended to include graduate and professional schools.[5] Most of the tests designed for this purpose represent a combination of general intelligence and achievement tests. A well-known example is the Graduate Record Examinations (GRE), administered to applicants or entering students in a large number of graduate schools. This series of tests originated in 1936 in a joint project of the Carnegie Foundation for the Advancement of Teaching and the graduate schools of four eastern universities. In 1948, the GRE project was transferred to Educational Testing Service. Currently, the GRE are administered in two types of testing programs. The National Program for Graduate Student Selection is concerned with the testing of students at designated

---

[5] The testing of applicants to professional schools will be discussed in Chapter 16, in connection with occupational tests.

centers prior to their admission to graduate school. The test records are used by the universities for admission purposes, as well as for selecting recipients of scholarships, fellowships, and special appointments. The GRE are also employed in an Institutional Testing Program, in which colleges and universities administer the tests to their own students. In this case, the test records may be utilized as aids in such functions as student guidance, admission of students to candidacy for a degree, and evaluation of the effectiveness of instruction. In both programs, the tests are scored and retained by ETS.

In the Selection Program, the GRE include an Aptitude Test and an Advanced Test in the student's field of specialization. The latter is available in many specific fields, such as biology, government, philosophy, psychology, Spanish, and speech. The Aptitude Test is essentially a general intelligence or scholastic aptitude test suitable for advanced undergraduates or graduate students. Like many such tests, it yields separate verbal and quantitative scores. The Institutional Program provides not only Aptitude and Advanced Tests, but also three Area Tests, covering social science, humanities, and natural science. These tests emphasize the understanding of basic concepts and the ability to apply knowledge, rather than the recall of specific facts. Longitudinal studies of college students taking alternate forms of the Area Tests in their freshman, sophomore, and senior years revealed significant gains in mean scores (Lannholm & Pitcher, 1959).

Scores on all GRE tests are reported in terms of a single standard score scale with a mean of 500 and a σ of 100. These scores are directly comparable for all tests, having been anchored to the Aptitude Test scores of a fixed reference group of 2,095 seniors examined in 1952 at 11 colleges. A score of 500 on an Advanced Physics Test, for example, is the score expected from physics majors whose Aptitude Test score equals the mean Aptitude Test score of the reference group. Since graduate school applicants are a selected sample with reference to academic aptitude, the means of most groups actually taking each Advanced Test in the Graduate Student Selection Program will be considerably above 500. Moreover, there are consistent differences in the intellectual caliber of students majoring in different subjects. For normative interpretation, therefore, the percentiles given for individual groups are more relevant and local norms are still better.

The reliability and validity of the GRE have been investigated in a number of different student samples. Kuder-Richardson and odd-even reliability coefficients of the separate tests range from .84 to .95. Retests after an interval of one year yielded reliabilities of .85 to .97; after two years, the reliability coefficients ranged from .71 to .93. Predictive validity has been checked in terms of such criteria as graduate school grades, success versus failure in graduate school, instructors' ratings, and performance on Ph.D. qualifying examinations. Studies conducted in a number of universities indicate that the GRE are not appreciably superior to undergraduate grades as predictors of graduate school performance. But when combined with grades, they permit more effective prediction than can be obtained when grades alone are used. The multiple correlations found with such a combination of predictors were usually in the middle .60's.

It should be noted, moreover, that the GRE are designed to serve other functions besides the prediction of graduate school performance. They are employed partly as a measure of the candidate's breadth of cultural background, verbal comprehension, quantitative reasoning, and other qualifications considered important in the selection of graduate students. To the extent that the tests are used for these purposes, their effectiveness is more a matter of content validity than of predictive validity.

Another widely used test for the selection of graduate students is the Miller Analogies Test. Consisting of complex analogies items whose subject matter is drawn from many academic fields, this test has an unusually high ceiling. Although a 50-minute time limit is imposed, the test is primarily a power test. The Miller Analogies Test was first developed for use at the University of Minnesota, but later forms were made available to other graduate schools. Its administration, however, is restricted to licensed centers, and rigid controls are exercised over the test materials in order to prevent coaching and protect the security of the test.

Percentile norms on the Miller Analogies Test are given for several groups of graduate students in different fields and different universities, as well as for a few professional school groups. Marked variations in test performance are found among these different samples. The median of one group, for example, corresponds to the 90th percentile of another. Odd-even reliability coefficients of .92 to .94 were found with different groups of graduate students, and alternate-form reliabilities ranged from .85 to .89. Correlations with graduate course grades and with performance on comprehensive examinations vary widely in different institutions and departments, but more than half fall at or above .40, several being in the .60's and .70's. In general, its validity appears to be as good as that of other longer tests, or better. Correlations in the .70's and .80's have been reported between the Miller Analogies Test and the various parts of the GRE, which requires several hours to administer.

SUPERIOR ADULTS.   Any test designed for college or graduate students is also likely to be suitable for examining superior adults for occupational evaluation, research, or other purposes. The Miller Analogies Test, for example, is used for the selection and evaluation of high-level industrial personnel. Percentile norms on this test are available for groups of business executives, engineers, and other industrial personnel.

Another test that provides sufficient ceiling for the examination of highly superior adults is the Concept Mastery Test. Originating as a by-product of Terman's extensive longitudinal study of gifted children, Form A of the

Concept Mastery Test was developed for testing the intelligence of the gifted group in early maturity (Terman & Oden, 1947). For a still later follow-up, when the gifted subjects were in their mid-forties, Form T was prepared (Terman & Oden, 1959). This form, which is somewhat easier than Form A, was subsequently released for more general use. The Concept Mastery Test consists of both analogies and synonym-antonym (same-opposite) items. Like the Miller Analogies Test, it draws on concepts from many fields, including physical and biological sciences, mathematics, history, literature, music, and others. Although predominantly verbal, the test incorporates some numerical content in the analogies items.

Percentile norms are provided for graduate students, college seniors applying for fellowships, and selected adult groups, but the samples are small and such norms must be regarded as tentative. Alternate-form reliabilities range from .86 to .94. Scores show consistent rise with increasing educational level and moderately high correlations with other intelligence tests in superior adult groups. Available evidence of predictive validity, however, is meager.

CHAPTER 10

Performance, NonLanguage, and Other Special Tests

THE TESTS brought together in this chapter include both individual and group scales. They have been developed primarily for use with persons who cannot be properly or adequately examined with such instruments as the Binet scales or the group tests considered in the preceding chapter. Among the groups for which special testing instruments have been constructed are infants and preschool children, speech defectives, the physically handicapped, the foreign-speaking, the illiterate, the culturally disadvantaged, and those with markedly dissimilar experiential backgrounds. In clinical testing, performance and nonlanguage tests may also be employed to supplement the verbal type of intelligence test, in order to obtain a fuller picture of the individual's intellectual functioning.

Following an overview of the types of situations that led to the development of performance tests, we shall examine a typical example of a performance scale. We shall then consider the characteristic problems encountered in three major situations requiring performance tests or other special adaptations of testing techniques, namely: (1) cross-cultural testing, (2) infant and preschool testing, and (3) testing the physically handicapped. Specific instruments employed in these testing situations will be illustrated.

PERFORMANCE TESTS

HISTORICAL OVERVIEW. One of the earliest performance tests was the formboard developed by Seguin (1866) for use with mentally retarded children. Originally devised in connection with Seguin's program for the sensory and motor training of the mentally retarded, this formboard was subsequently incorporated into a number of performance scales. A photograph of the Seguin Form Board, as used in a current series of performance tests, is included in Figure 40. In administering this test, the examiner removes the ten pieces from the board and stacks them in a standard arrangement, instructing the subject to put them back as fast as he can. Three trials are allowed, the subject's score being the time required for the fastest of the three. The Seguin Form Board is one of the simplest formboards employed in performance scales, being suitable for relatively low mental ages. Many other formboards of increasing complexity have subsequently been developed for higher levels.

A number of other performance tests were developed to meet special testing requirements, following the early application of the Binet scales. In his pioneer psychological work with delinquent children, Healy recognized the need for performance tests to supplement the more verbal type of task which predominated in the Binet scales. As a result, the Healy-Fernald test series was assembled (Healy & Fernald, 1911). Several of the Healy-Fernald performance tests have found their way into later scales. We shall encounter a couple of picture-completion tests from this series later in the chapter.

Another early series of performance tests was developed by Knox (1914) for testing foreign-speaking immigrants on arrival in the United States. All tests in this series were of the performance type and were administered without the use of language. Among the tests included in the series was a set of formboards of increasing difficulty, as well as the Ship Test and the Knox Cube Test. In the Ship Test, ten rectangular pieces were to be arranged within a wooden frame to make a picture of a ship at sea. Undoubtedly this particular picture was chosen because of its appropriateness for testing immigrants who had just disembarked from an ocean liner. The Knox Cube Test is essentially a test of immediate memory for a series of movements. The examiner taps each of four cubes in a predetermined order and then indicates that the subject is to do likewise. The procedure is repeated with successive series of taps, increasing in length and in complexity of sequence.

The Pintner-Paterson Scale of Performance Tests (Pintner & Paterson, 1917) represented the first major attempt to develop a standardized series of performance tests with general norms. A number of tests included in this scale were taken from the work of Seguin, Healy, Knox, and others. The entire scale consisted of 15 tests, although for most testing purposes a shorter scale, including the 10 most satisfactory tests, was employed. Originally developed for use in Pintner's pioneer psychological research with the deaf, the Pintner-Paterson scale was used widely for a variety of other testing purposes. Several tests from the Pintner-Paterson scale have been incorporated in subsequent performance scales, from the Army Performance Scale of World War I to performance scales in use today. Although the Pintner-Paterson scale represented a considerable advance over earlier performance tests with regard to scope of tasks, standardization of procedure, and size of normative samples, it still lagged far behind the test-construction standards set by the Stanford-Binet and early group tests. Progress in the development of performance tests has always been relatively slow, these tests being relatively crude in comparison with most verbal tests of the same period.

The Kohs Block Design (Kohs, 1923) was originally developed as an adjunct to or a substitute for the Stanford-Binet in the identification of the mentally retarded. It has been widely used by clinical psychologists for a number of diagnostic purposes. The test is relatively easy to administer and requires little or no language. It utilizes a set of identical one-inch blocks whose six sides are painted red, blue, yellow, white, yellow-and-blue, and red-and-white, respectively. A set of cards containing colored designs are presented one at a time, the subject being required to reproduce each design by assembling the proper blocks. The number of blocks required from

FIG. 40.   Test Materials Employed in the Arthur Point Scale of Performance Tests, Revised Form II. (Courtesy The Psychological Corporation.)

the simplest to the most complex designs varies from 4 to 16. The score depends on both time and correctness of response.

Still another type of early performance test is illustrated by the Porteus Maze Tests. First developed in 1914, this test has undergone continuing research (Porteus, 1924, 1950, 1959). It consists of a series of printed line mazes, steeply graded in difficulty. The mazes can be administered with no verbal instructions by using the easier mazes for demonstration purposes. They range from the 3-year to the adult level. The standard procedure is to have the subject trace with a pencil the shortest path from the entrance to the exit of the maze, without ever lifting the pencil from the paper. There is no time limit, and subjects are not hurried in any way. As soon as an "error" is made, by either crossing a line or entering a wrong pathway, the subject is stopped and given a second trial on an identical maze. If an error is made on the second trial, a failure is recorded for that level. At the higher levels, four trials are allowed. Scoring takes into account the trial in which each maze was successfully completed. No spontaneous correction of errors is permitted, the maze being removed as soon as any error is made. In his presentation of this test series, Porteus has repeatedly described it as a measure of foresight and planning capacity. He maintains that it excels verbal tests in measuring those aspects of intelligence most important in practical social sufficiency. The Porteus Mazes have been used in investigations on a wide variety of subjects, including normals, mental defectives, patients with organic brain damage, delinquents, and many different ethnic and cultural groups.

ARTHUR POINT SCALE OF PERFORMANCE TESTS.   Combining the most promising performance tests then available, Form I of the Arthur Point Scale of Performance Tests was first released in 1930. The scale consists of the following nine tests, four of which have already been described:

1. *Knox Cube.*

2. *Seguin Form Board.*

3. *Two-Figure Form Board:* A more difficult formboard, in which a square and a cross are each divided into four pieces to be fitted together.

4. *Casuist Form Board:* This formboard is rendered more difficult by the close similarity of various pieces, which necessitates finer discriminations.

5. *Manikin:* A crude wooden figure of a man is to be assembled from arms, legs, head, and trunk.
   Feature Profile: Wooden pieces are to be assembled to form a face in profile.

6. *Male and Foal:* A relatively easy picture-completion test in which each piece, being of a different shape, fits only in its proper recess.

7. *Healy Picture Completion I:* From a large number of identical square cutouts, subject must choose the most appropriate piece to insert in each space in the picture.

FIG. 41.   Arthur Stencil Design Test I. (Courtesy The Psychological Corporation.)

8. *Porteus Mazes.*

9. *Kohs Block Design.*

All but the last two tests were taken from the Pintner-Paterson series. The nine tests were restandardized on a single sample of approximately 1,100 school children between the ages of 5 and 15, including about 100 at each age level. The raw score on each test is translated into a point score that weights each test in proportion to its ability to discriminate between successive age levels. Thus, tests that show marked progress between successive age levels receive higher weights than those exhibiting smaller age differences in performance. The sum of the point scores is converted into an MA, from which a ratio IQ is computed.

In 1947, a Revised Form II of the Arthur performance scale was issued. This form, which is pictured in Figure 40, consists of only five tests, including slightly modified versions of the Knox Cube, Seguin Form Board, and Porteus Mazes; another picture completion test from the Healy-Fernald series (Healy Picture Completion II); and a new test, the Arthur Stencil Design Test I. The new test, shown in Figure 41, is somewhat similar to the Kohs Block Design insofar as the subject must reproduce designs of increasing complexity which are presented singly on cards. In the Stencil Design Test, however, the design is reproduced by superimposing cut-out stencils in different colors on a solid card; several overlapping stencils are required for the more complex designs.

Revised Form II of the Arthur scale was prepared chiefly as an alternate for Form I, to be used in retesting. Norms on Form II were derived on 968 pupils from the same "middle-class American district" used in standardizing Form I. Special efforts were made in the development of Revised Form II to prepare directions suitable for deaf children; hence the use of language is reduced to a minimum in its administration.

The data on reliability and validity reported by Arthur are meager, although some pertinent information has been obtained by other investigators. A test-retest correlation of .85 was found when Form I was administered over a 2-year interval to a small group of mentally defective boys (Patterson, 1946). Since considerable practice effect was observed over this period, retests with the same form should be given only when the interval is very long. In reference to validity, the major criterion employed was that of age differentiation, a criterion on the basis of which tests were both selected and weighted.

CROSS-CULTURAL TESTING

THE PROBLEM.   The testing of persons with highly dissimilar cultural backgrounds has received increasing attention since midcentury. Tests are needed for the maximum utilization of human resources in the newly developing nations in Africa and elsewhere. The rapidly expanding educational facilities in these countries require testing for effective educational planning and individual guidance. With increasing industrialization, there is a mounting demand for tests to aid in the job selection and placement of personnel, particularly in mechanical, clerical, and professional fields.

In America the practical problems of cross-cultural testing have been associated chiefly with subcultures or minority cultures within the dominant culture. There is widespread concern regarding the applicability of available tests to culturally disadvantaged groups. It should be noted parenthetically that cultural disadvantage is a relative concept. Objectively there is only cultural difference between any two cultures or subcultures. Each culture fosters and encourages the development of behavior that is adapted to its values and demands. When an individual must adjust to and compete within a culture or subculture other than that in which he was reared, then cultural difference is likely to become cultural disadvantage.

Although concern with cross-cultural testing has been greatly stimulated by recent social and political developments, the problem was recognized at least as early as 1910. Some of the earliest cross-cultural tests were developed for testing the large waves of immigrants coming to the United States at the turn of the century. Other early tests originated in basic research on the comparative abilities of relatively isolated cultural groups. These cultures were often quite primitive and had had little or no contact with Western civilization within whose framework most psychological tests had been developed.

Basically, cross-cultural tests endeavor to rule out one or more parameters along which cultures vary. A well-known example of such a parameter is *language*. If the cultural groups to be tested speak different languages, the test should require no language on the part of either examiner or subjects. When educational backgrounds differ widely and illiteracy may be prevalent, *reading* must be ruled out (as in the nonreading group tests discussed in Chapter 9). Oral language was not eliminated from these tests because they were designed for persons speaking a common language. Another parameter in which cultures or subcultures differ is that of *speed*. Not only the tempo of daily life, but also the motivation to hurry and the value attached to rapid performance vary widely among national cultures, among ethnic minority groups within a single nation, and between urban and rural subcultures (see, e.g., Klineberg, 1928; Knapp, 1960). Accordingly, cross-cultural tests have often—though not always—tried to eliminate the influence of speed by allowing long time limits and giving no premium for faster performance.

Still other parameters along which cultures differ pertain to *test content*. Most nonlanguage and nonreading tests, for example, call for items of information that are specific to certain cultures. Thus they may require the examinee to understand the function of such objects as violin, postage stamp, gun, pocketknife, telephone, piano, or mirror. Obviously persons reared in relatively isolated cultures would lack the experiential background to respond correctly to such items. It was chiefly to control this type of cultural parameter that the classic "culture-free" tests were first developed. Following a brief examination of typical tests designed to eliminate one or more of the above parameters, we shall turn to a general evaluation of cross-cultural testing and an analysis of alternative approaches.

NONLANGUAGE GROUP TESTS.   The first nonlanguage group test was the Army Examination Beta developed for testing foreign-speaking and illiterate soldiers during World War I (Yerkes, 1921). In this test, no language was used at all by either examiner or examinees. Instructions were given by means of gesture, pantomime, and demonstrations. In addition, the procedure required the services of a trained demonstrator who performed before the group what the examinees were later expected to do in their test booklets. Responses were recorded by drawing lines or making simple marks, except in one test which required the writing of numbers.

In subsequent civilian editions of the Army Beta, the procedure for administration and scoring was considerably simplified. A currently available form is the 1946 restandardization known as the Revised Beta Examination. This form consists of six subtests, including: (a) Mazes, (b) Symbol-digit Substitution, (c) Pictorial Absurdities, (d) Paper Formboard, (e) Picture Completion, and (f) Perceptual Speed. Some language is used in giving the instructions, although the explanations rely principally on the practice exercises that precede each subtest. Total scores are converted to deviation IQ's. One of the chief uses of the Revised Beta and similar nonlanguage scales is to be found in mass industries employing many persons with foreign background or with little education. Nonlanguage scales have also been developed for use in bilingual or multilingual countries, such as Canada and India.

For most current testing purposes, it is not necessary to eliminate all language from the instructions, since the examinees usually have some knowledge of a common language. Moreover, short, simple instructions can generally be translated or given successively in two languages without appreciably altering the nature or difficulty of the test. None of these tests, however, require the examinee himself to use either written or spoken language. Nor do they require him to respond to the precise oral instructions that are typically given with each item in the previously discussed nonreading tests. Although a bilingual person may have sufficient mastery of English to communicate on ordinary matters and even to attend an English-speaking school, he may be handicapped when taking a verbal test in English. Such a person may lack the monolingual's vocabulary range, verbal fluency, or facility in handling verbal relations in English. Studies on American-born school children of foreign parentage, for example, often indicate a special deficiency in verbal tests.

The effects of bilingualism are varied and complex. They cannot be adequately summarized in any simple generalization (see Anastasi, 1958a, pp. 558–561; Darcy, 1963; Macnamara, 1967). Under certain conditions, intellectual development may be aided by bilingualism; under other conditions, it may be seriously retarded. Emotional as well as intellectual factors probably contribute to the specific effects of bilingualism in particular cases. In testing any bilingual groups, such as immigrants or children of immigrants, however, the possible influence of language handicap on test performance must be given serious consideration. It cannot be generally assumed that such individuals can be adequately measured with a verbal test, despite their apparent mastery of English.

CULTURE-FAIR TESTS. So-called culture-fair tests are characteristically designed to rule out several major cultural parameters, including not only language but also knowledge and intellectual skills specific to any given culture. Such tests follow a variety of approaches to achieve their objectives. The Leiter International Performance Scale is an individual performance scale. It was developed through several years of use with different ethnic groups in Hawaii, including elementary and high school pupils. The scale was subsequently applied to several African groups by Porteus and to a few other national groups by other investigators. A later revision, issued in 1948, was based on further testing of American children, high school students, and Army recruits during World War II. A distinctive feature of the Leiter scale is the almost complete elimination of instructions, either spoken or pantomime. Each test begins with a very easy task of the type to be encountered throughout that test. The comprehension of the task is treated as part of the test. The materials consist of a response frame, illustrated in Figure 42, with an adjustable card holder. All tests are administered by attaching the appropriate card, containing printed pictures, to the frame. The examinee chooses the blocks with the proper response pictures and inserts them into the frame.

The Leiter scale was designed to cover a wide range of functions, similar to those found in verbal scales. Among the tasks included may be mentioned: matching identical colors, shades of gray, forms, or pictures; copying a block design; picture completion; number estimation; analogies; series completion; recognition of age differences; spatial relations; footprint recognition; similarities; memory for a series; and classification of animals according to habitat. Administered individually, with no time limit, these

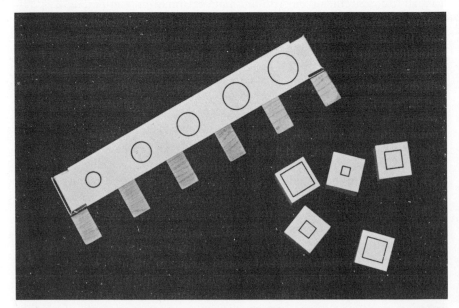

FIG. 42. Typical Materials for Use in the Leiter International Performance Scale. The test illustrated is the Analogies Progression Test from the Six-Year Level. (Courtesy C. H. Stoelting Company.)

tests are arranged into year levels from 2 to 18.[1] The scale is scored in terms of MA and ratio IQ, although there is no assurance that such an IQ retains the same meaning at different ages. In fact, the published data show considerable fluctuation in the standard deviation of the IQ's at different age levels. Split-half reliabilities of .91 to .94 are reported from several studies, but the samples were quite heterogeneous in age and probably in other characteristics. Validation data are based principally on age differentiation and internal consistency. Some correlations are also reported with teachers' ratings of intelligence and with scores on other tests, chiefly the Stanford-Binet. These correlations range from .64 to .81 but were obtained on rather heterogeneous groups.

The Culture Fair Intelligence Test, developed by Cattell and published by the Institute for Personality and Ability Testing (IPAT), is a paper-and-pencil test. This test is available in three levels: Scale 1, for ages 4 to 8 and mentally retarded adults; Scale 2, for ages 8 to 13 and average adults; and Scale 3, for grades 10 to 16 and superior adults. Each scale has been prepared in two parallel forms, A and B. Scale 1 requires individual administration for at least some of the tests; the other scales may be given either as individual or as group tests. Scale 1 comprises eight tests, only four of which are described by the author as culture-fair. The other four involve both verbal comprehension and specific cultural information. It is suggested that the four culture-fair tests can be used as a sub-battery, separate norms being provided for this abbreviated scale. Scales 2 and 3 are alike, except for difficulty level. Each consists of the following four tests, sample items from which are shown in Figure 43.

1. *Series:* Select the item that completes the series.

2. *Classification:* Mark the one item in each row that does not belong with the others.

3. *Matrices:* Mark the item that correctly completes the given matrix, or pattern.

4. *Conditions:* Insert a dot in one of the alternative designs so as to meet the same conditions indicated in the sample design. Thus, in the example reproduced in Figure 43, the dot must be in the two rectangles, but not in the circle. This condition can be met only in the third response alternative, which has been marked.

For Scale 1, only ratio IQ's are provided. In Scales 2 and 3, scores can be converted into deviation IQ's with σ's of either 24 or 16 points. The latter conversion was added later in order to ensure more comparability with IQ's obtained on other familiar tests. In interpreting IQ's from the Cattell test,

[1] The tests in year levels 2 to 12 are also available as the Arthur Adaptation of the Leiter International Performance Scale, standardized as a point scale by Dr. Grace Arthur. This scale is considered suitable for testing children between the ages of 3 and 8 years.

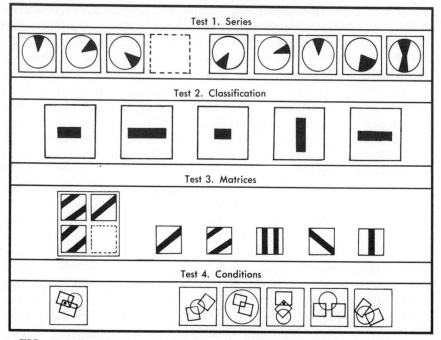

FIG. 43.   Sample Items from Culture Fair Intelligence Test, Scale 2. (Copyright by Institute of Personality and Ability Testing.)

it is thus important to note which conversion was used. Scale 2 has been standardized on larger samples than either of the other two scales, but the representativeness of the samples and the number of cases at some age levels still fall short of desirable test-construction standards. Although the tests are highly speeded, some norms are provided for an untimed version. Fairly extensive verbal instructions are required, but the author asserts that giving these instructions in a foreign language or in pantomime will not affect the difficulty of the test.

Reliability and validity data appear to have been gathered largely on Scale 2, although some data are also available on Scales 1 and 3. Split-half and Kuder-Richardson reliabilities cluster in the .70's. Retest reliabilities with alternate forms are lower, dropping to the .50's in some samples. Validity is discussed chiefly in terms of saturation with Spearman's general ability factor (g). Factorial validity of the Cattell test was accordingly determined from its correlations with a pool of intelligence tests, including both verbal and performance types. Data on concurrent and predictive validity in terms of non-test criteria are meager. The Cattell tests have been administered in several European countries, in America, and in certain African and Asiatic cultures. Norms tended to remain unchanged in cultures moderately similar to that in which the tests were developed; in other cultures, however, performance fell considerably below the original norms.

The Progressive Matrices, developed in Great Britain by Raven, were also designed as a measure of Spearman's g factor. Requiring chiefly the eduction of relations among abstract items, this test is regarded by most British psychologists as the best available measure of g. It consists of 60 matrices, or designs, from each of which a part has been removed. The subject chooses the missing insert from six or eight given alternatives. The items are grouped into five series, each containing 12 matrices of increasing difficulty but similar in principle. The earlier series require accuracy of discrimination; the later, more difficult series involve analogies, permutation and alternation of pattern, and other logical relations. Two sample items are reproduced in Figure 44. The test is administered with no time limit, and can be given individually or in groups. Very simple oral instructions are required.

Percentile norms are provided for each half-year interval between 8 and 14 years, and for each five-year interval between 20 and 65 years. These norms are based on British samples, including 1,407 children, 3,665 men in military service tested during World War II, and 2,192 civilian adults. Closely similar norms were obtained by Rimoldi (1948) on 1,680 children in Argentina. Use of the test in several European countries likewise indicated the applicability of available norms. Studies in a number of non-European cultures, however, have raised doubts about the suitability of this test for groups with very dissimilar backgrounds. In such groups, moreover, the test was found to reflect amount of education and to be susceptible to considerable practice effect.

The manual for the Progressive Matrices is quite inadequate, giving little

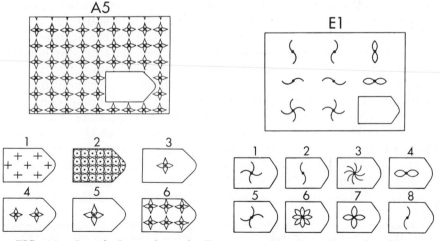

FIG. 44. Sample Items from the Progressive Matrices. (Reproduced by permission of J. C. Raven.)

information on reliability and none on validity. Many investigations have been published, however, that provide relevant data on this test. In a review of publications appearing prior to 1957, Burke (1958) lists over 50 studies appearing in England, 14 in America, and 10 elsewhere. Since that time, research has continued at a rapid pace, especially in America where this test has received growing recognition.[2]

Retest reliability in groups of older children and adults that were moderately homogeneous in age varies approximately between .70 and .90. At the lower score ranges, however, reliability falls considerably below these values. Correlations with both verbal and performance tests of intelligence range between .40 and .75, tending to be higher with performance than with verbal tests. Studies with the mentally retarded and with different occupational and educational groups indicate fair concurrent validity. Predictive validity coefficients against academic criteria run somewhat lower than those of the usual verbal intelligence tests. Several factorial analyses suggest that the Progressive Matrices are heavily loaded with a factor common to most intelligence tests (identified with Spearman's g by British psychologists), but that spatial aptitude, inductive reasoning, perceptual accuracy, and other group factors also influence performance (Burke, 1958).

A still different approach is illustrated by the Goodenough Draw-a-Man Test, in which the individual is simply instructed to "make a picture of a man; make the very best picture that you can." This test was in use without change from its original standardization in 1926 until 1963. An extension and revision was published in 1963 under the title of Goodenough-Harris Drawing Test (see Harris, 1963). In the revision, as in the original test, emphasis is placed on the child's accuracy of observation and on the development of conceptual thinking, rather than on artistic skill. Credit is given for the inclusion of individual body parts, clothing details, proportion, perspective, and similar features. A total of 73 scorable items were selected on the basis of age differentiation, relation to total scores on the test, and relation to group intelligence test scores. Data for this purpose were obtained by testing samples of 50 boys and 50 girls at each grade level from kindergarten through the ninth grade in urban and rural areas of Minnesota and Wisconsin, stratified according to father's occupation.

In the revised scale, subjects are also asked to draw a picture of a woman and of themselves. The Woman Scale is scored in terms of 71 items similar to those in the Man Scale. The Self Scale was developed as a projective test of personality, although available findings from this application are not promising. Norms on both Man and Woman Scales were established on new samples of 300 children at each year of age from 5 to 15, selected so as to

[2] An easier form, the Coloured Progressive Matrices, is available for children between 5 and 11 years and mentally retarded adults. A more advanced form has also been developed for superior adults, but its distribution is restricted to approved and registered users.

Man: Raw Score 7	Woman: Raw Score 31	Man: Raw Score 66
CA 5-8	CA 8-8	CA 12-11
Standard Score 73	Standard Score 103	Standard Score 134

FIG. 45.   Specimen Drawings Obtained in Goodenough-Harris Drawing Test. (Courtesy Dale B. Harris.)

be representative of the United States population with regard to father's occupation and geographical region. Point scores on each scale are transmuted into standard scores [3] with a mean of 100 and a σ of 15. In Figure 45 will be found three illustrative drawings produced by children aged 5-8, 8-8, and 12-11, together with the corresponding raw point scores and standard scores.

The reliability of the Draw-a-Man Test has been repeatedly investigated by a variety of procedures. In one carefully controlled study of the earlier form administered to 386 third- and fourth-grade school children, the retest correlation after a one-week interval was .68, and split-half reliability was .89 (McCarthy, 1944). Rescoring of the identical drawings by a different scorer yielded a scorer reliability of .90, and rescorings by the same scorer correlated .94. Studies with the new form (Dunn, 1967; Harris, 1963) have yielded similar results. Readministration of the test to groups of kindergarten children on consecutive days revealed no significant difference in performance on different days. Examiner effect was also found to be negligible, as was the effect of art training in school. The old and new scales

[3] The observant reader will have noticed that these standard scores use the same scale as the common deviation IQ. The term IQ is not used in this test in order to avoid many of the surplus meanings that have become associated with IQ.

are apparently quite similar; their scores correlate between .91 and .98 in homogeneous age groups. The correlation of the Man and Woman Scales is about as high as the split-half reliability of the Man Scale found in comparable samples. On this basis, Harris recommends that the two scales be regarded as alternate forms and that the mean of their standard scores be used for greater reliability.

Apart from the item-analysis data gathered in the development of the scales, information regarding the construct validity of the test is provided by correlations with other intelligence tests. These correlations vary widely, but the majority are over .50. In a study with 100 fourth-grade children, correlations were found between the Draw-a-Man Test and a number of tests of known factorial composition (Ansbacher, 1952). Such correlations indicated that, within the ages covered, the Draw-a-Man Test correlates highest with tests of reasoning, spatial aptitude, and perceptual accuracy. Motor coordination plays a negligible role in the test at these ages. For kindergarten children, the Draw-a-Man Test correlated higher with numerical aptitude and lower with perceptual speed and accuracy than it did for fourth-grade children (Harris, 1963). Such findings suggest that the test may measure somewhat different functions at different ages.

The original Draw-a-Man Test has been administered widely in clinics as a supplement to the Stanford-Binet and other verbal scales. It has also been employed in a large number of studies on different cultural and ethnic groups, including several American Indian samples. Such investigations have indicated that performance on this test is more dependent on differences in cultural background than was originally assumed. In a review of studies pertaining to this test, Goodenough and Harris (1950, p. 399) expressed the opinion that "the search for a culture-free test, whether of intelligence, artistic ability, personal-social characteristics, or any other measurable trait is illusory." This view was reaffirmed by Harris in his 1963 book. More recently, Dennis (1966) analyzed comparative data obtained with this test in 40 widely different cultural groups, principally from 6-year-old children. Mean group scores appeared to be most closely related to the amount of experience with representational art within each culture. In the case of groups with little indigenous art, it was hypothesized that test performance reflects degree of acculturation to Western civilization.

EVALUATION.   When psychologists began to develop instruments for cross-cultural testing in the first quarter of this century, they hoped it would be at least theoretically possible to measure hereditary intellectual potential independently of the impact of cultural experiences. The individual's behavior was thought to be overlaid with a sort of cultural veneer whose penetration became the objective of what were then called "culture-free" tests. Subsequent developments in genetics and psychology have demonstrated the fallacy of this concept. We now recognize that hereditary and environmental factors interact at all stages in the organism's development and that their effects are inextricably intertwined in the resulting behavior. For man, culture permeates nearly all environmental contacts. Since all behavior is thus affected by the cultural milieu in which the individual is reared and since psychological tests are but samples of behavior, cultural influences will and should be reflected in test performance. It is therefore futile to try to devise a test that is *free* from cultural influences. The present objective in cross-cultural testing is rather to construct tests that presuppose only experiences that are *common* to different cultures. For this reason, such terms as "culture-common," "culture-fair," and "cross-cultural" have replaced the earlier "culture-free" label.

A second point is that no one test can be universally applicable or equally "fair" to all cultures. There are as many varieties of culture-fair tests as there are parameters in which cultures differ. A nonreading test may be culture-fair in one situation, a nonlanguage test in another, a performance test in a third, and a translated adaptation of a verbal test in a fourth. The varieties of cross-cultural tests illustrated in this chapter are not interchangeable but are useful in different types of cross-cultural comparisons.

In the third place, it is unlikely that any test can be equally "fair" to more than one cultural group, especially if the cultures are quite dissimilar. While reducing cultural differentials in test performance, cross-cultural tests cannot completely eliminate such differentials. Every test tends to favor persons from the culture in which it was developed. The mere use of paper and pencil or the presentation of abstract tasks having no immediate practical significance will favor some cultural groups and handicap others. Emotional and motivational factors likewise influence test performance. Among the many relevant conditions differing from culture to culture may be mentioned the intrinsic interest of the test content, rapport with the examiner, drive to do well on a test, desire to excel others, and past habits of solving problems individually or cooperatively (see Anastasi, 1958a, pp. 561–568).

Each culture encourages and fosters certain abilities and ways of behaving, and discourages or suppresses others. It is therefore to be expected that, on tests developed within the American culture, Americans will generally excel. If a test were constructed by the same procedures within a culture differing markedly from ours, Americans would probably appear deficient in terms of test norms. Data bearing on this type of cultural comparison are meager. What evidence is available, however, suggests that persons from our culture may be just as handicapped on tests prepared within other cultures as members of those cultures are on our tests (see Anastasi, 1958a, pp. 566–568).

A fourth point pertains to the role of language in cross-cultural testing. Most cross-cultural tests utilize nonverbal content in the hope of obtaining a more nearly culture-fair measure of the same intellectual functions measured by verbal intelligence tests. Both assumptions underlying this approach are questionable. First, it cannot be assumed that nonverbal tests measure the same functions as verbal tests, however similar they may appear. A spatial analogies test is not merely a nonverbal version of a verbal analogies test. Some of the early nonlanguage tests, such as the Army Beta, were heavily loaded with spatial visualization and perceptual abilities, which are quite unrelated to verbal and numerical abilities. Even in tests like the Progressive Matrices and other nonlanguage tests deliberately designed to tap reasoning and abstract conceptualization, factorial analyses have revealed a large contribution of nonverbal factors to the variance of test scores (e.g., Das, 1963).

From a different angle, there is a growing body of evidence suggesting that nonlanguage tests may be more culturally loaded than language tests. Investigations with a wide variety of cultural groups in many countries have found larger group differences in performance and other nonverbal tests than in verbal tests (see Anastasi, 1961; Higgins & Sivers, 1958; Jensen, 1968; Ortar, 1963; Vernon, 1965). In a provocative analysis of the problem, Ortar (1963, pp. 232–233) writes:

On the basis of our results it appears that, both from the practical point of view and on theoretical grounds, the verbal tests and items are better suited as intercultural measuring instruments than any other kind. They must, of course, be translated and adapted, but this adaptation is infinitely easier and more reliable than the well-nigh impossible task of "translating" and adapting a performance test. The "language" of performance is the cultural perception, but its "words" and grammar and syntax are not even completely understood, let alone organized in national entities. We do not know how to "translate" a picture into the representational language of a different culture, but we are thoroughly familiar with the technique and requirements of translating verbal contents. . . . A concept that is non-existent in a certain language simply cannot be translated into this language, a factor which acts as a safeguard against mechanical use of a given instrument when adapting it for a different culture.

Among the examples cited by Ortar is the observation that, when presented with a picture of a head from which the mouth was missing, Oriental immigrant children in Israel said the body was missing. Unfamiliar with the convention of considering the drawing of a head as a complete picture, these children regarded the absence of the body as more important than the omission of a mere detail like the mouth. For a different reason, an item requiring that the names of the seasons be arranged in the proper sequence would be more appropriate in a cross-cultural test than would an item using pictures of the seasons. The seasons would not only look different in different countries for geographical reasons, but they would also probably be represented by means of conventionalized pictorial symbols which would be unfamiliar to persons from another culture.

Finally, the most basic question to ask about any culture-fair test pertains to its validity. A test constructed entirely from elements that are equally familiar in many cultures might measure trivial functions and possess little theoretical or practical validity in *any* culture. If intelligence is that combination of abilities important within a given culture, eliminating cultural differences from a test is likely to eliminate intelligence from it. The value systems of a particular culture are an integral component of its concept of intelligence.[4] Within our culture, the construct "intelligence" presupposes linguistic and numerical symbol systems whereby ideas are not only communicated but also generated. The use of verbal mediators greatly enhances the individual's ability to solve problems, whether the problems themselves be formulated in verbal or nonverbal terms. Ultimately both the theoretical meaning of a score on any culture-fair test and its practical value as a predictor of "real-life" criteria must be established by empirical investigation of its validity.

APPROACHES TO CROSS-CULTURAL TESTING. In the light of the methodological and theoretical problems presented by cross-cultural testing, we may examine three alternative approaches to the testing of persons in different cultures or subcultures. The first approach involves the choice of items common to many cultures and the validation of the resulting test against local criteria in many different cultures. This is the basic approach of the culture-fair tests, although their repeated validation in different cultures has often been either neglected altogether or inadequately executed. Without such a step, however, we cannot be sure that the test is relatively free from culturally restricted elements, nor that it possesses satisfactory validity in terms of practical criteria within each culture. On theoretical grounds, moreover, it appears unlikely that any single test could be designed that would meet these requirements across a wide range of cultures or subcultures.

A second major approach is to make up a test within one culture and administer it to individuals with different cultural backgrounds. Such a procedure would be followed when the object of testing is prediction of a local criterion within a particular culture. In such a case, if the specific cultural loading of the test is reduced, the test validity may also drop, since the criterion itself is culturally loaded. On the other hand, we should avoid the mistake of regarding any test developed within a single cultural framework as a universal yardstick for measuring "intelligence." Nor should we assume that a low score on such a test has the same causal explanation when obtained by a member of another culture as when obtained by a member of the test culture. What *can* be ascertained by such an approach is the cultural distance between groups, as well as the individual's degree of ac-

---

[4] For a delightful parody of attempts to develop culture-fair tests for cultures with sharply different value systems, the reader is urged to read "A culture fair test for the Ugh, No, and Oo-La-La cultures," by Bernardoni (1964).

culturation and his readiness for educational and vocational activities that are culture-specific.

As a third approach, different tests may be developed within each culture and validated against local criteria only. This approach is exemplified by the many revisions of the original Binet scales for use in different European, Asian, and African cultures, as well as by the development of tests for industrial and military personnel within particular cultures. A current example is provided by the test-development program conducted in several West African nations by the American Institutes for Research, under the sponsorship of the United States Agency for International Development (Schwarz, 1964a, 1964b). In such instances, the tests are validated against the specific educational and vocational criteria they are designed to predict, and performance is evaluated in terms of local norms. Each test is applied only within the culture in which it was developed and no cross-cultural comparisons are attempted. If the criteria to be predicted are technological, however, "Western-type intelligence" is likely to be needed, and the tests will reflect the direction in which the particular culture is evolving rather than its prevalent cultural characteristics at the time.

INFANT AND PRESCHOOL TESTS

All tests designed for infants and preschool children require individual administration. Some kindergarten children can be tested in small groups with the types of tests constructed for the primary grades. In general, however, group tests are not applicable until the child has reached school age. Most tests for children below the age of 6 are either performance or oral tests. A few involve rudimentary manipulation of paper and pencil.

It is customary to subdivide the first five years of life into the infant period and the preschool period. The first extends from birth to the age of approximately 18 months; the second, from 18 to 60 months. From the viewpoint of test administration, it should be noted that the infant must be tested while he is either lying down or supported on a person's lap. Little or no speech is possible during this period. Most of the tests deal with sensory and motor development. The preschool child, on the other hand, can walk, sit at a table, use his hands in manipulating test objects, and communicate by language. At the preschool level, the child is also much more responsive to the examiner as a person, while for the infant the examiner serves primarily as a means of providing specific objects. Preschool testing is a more highly interpersonal process—a feature that augments both the opportunities and the difficulties presented by the test situation.

DEVELOPMENTAL SCALES. Following a series of longitudinal studies of the normal course of behavior development in the infant and preschool child, Gesell and his associates at Yale prepared the Gesell Developmental Schedules (Gesell & Amatruda, 1947). These schedules are employed in assessing the level of behavior development attained in four major areas:

1. *Motor behavior:* both gross bodily control and finer motor coordination. This category includes postural reactions, head balance, sitting, standing, creeping, walking, reaching for and grasping objects, and manipulation of objects.

2. *Adaptive behavior:* eye-hand coordination in reaching for and handling objects, solution of practical problems, and exploration and manipulation of objects. Examples include reactions to such stimuli as toy cubes, a ringing bell, and a dangling ring, as well as drawing and the solution of simple formboards.

3. *Language behavior:* includes all means of communication, such as facial expression, gesture, postural movements, prelinguistic vocalizations, and speech. Comprehension of communication by others is also included.

4. *Personal-social behavior:* "the child's personal reactions to the social culture in which he lives." Among the types of behavior in this category are feeding, toilet-training and response to training in other socially imposed situations, play, development of a "sense of property," smiling and other responses to persons, and responses to mirror.

The Gesell Developmental Schedules represent a standardized procedure for observing and evaluating the course of behavior development in the child's daily life. Although a few may be properly described as tests, most of the items in these schedules are purely observational. Data are obtained through the direct observation of the child's responses to standard toys and other stimulus objects (see Fig. 46) and are supplemented by information provided by the mother. In evaluating the child's responses, the

FIG. 46.   Test Objects Employed with the Gesell Developmental Schedules. (Courtesy The Psychological Corporation.)

examiner is aided by very detailed verbal descriptions of the behavior typical of different age levels, together with drawings such as those reproduced in Figure 47. While extending from the age of 4 weeks to 6 years, the Gesell schedules typify the approach followed in infant testing. Items from these schedules have been incorporated in several other developmental scales designed for the infant level.

Although both observational and scoring procedures are less highly standardized in the Gesell schedules than in the usual psychological test, there is evidence that, with adequate training, examiner reliabilities over .95 can be attained (Knobloch & Pasamanick, 1960). In general, these schedules may be regarded as a refinement and elaboration of the qualitative observations routinely made by pediatricians and other specialists concerned with infant development. They appear to be most useful as a supplement to medical examinations for the identification of neurological defect and organically caused behavioral abnormalities in early life (Donofrio, 1965; Knobloch & Pasamanick, 1960).

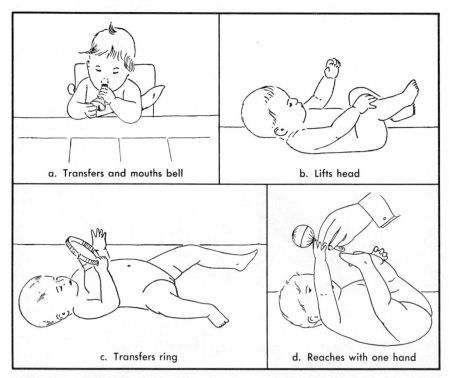

a. Transfers and mouths bell   b. Lifts head

c. Transfers ring   d. Reaches with one hand

FIG. 47. Drawings Employed with the Gesell Developmental Schedules to Illustrate Typical Behavior at 28 Weeks of Age. (From *Developmental Diagnosis,* by Arnold Gesell and Catherine S. Amatruda. Copyright 1941, 1947, by Arnold Gesell. By permission of Paul B. Hoeber, Inc., publisher.)

Two other types of developmental scales may be considered in this connection: the Oseretsky Tests of Motor Proficiency and the Vineland Social Maturity Scale. Both of these scales extend well beyond the preschool level, through later childhood and adolescence. They are of special relevance to the present discussion, however, because of certain similarities to the Gesell scales in content and in general approach. They are also more suitable for use at the lower age or intellectual levels than at higher levels.

The Oseretsky Tests of Motor Proficiency were originally published in Russia in 1923. They were subsequently translated into several languages and used in a number of European countries. In 1946, Doll (1946), then Director of Research for the Vineland Training School, sponsored and edited an English translation of the Portuguese adaptation of these tests. A scale of motor development is especially useful in testing the mentally retarded, who are also frequently retarded in motor functions. Other applications of the Oseretsky tests are found in the testing of children with motor disorders, in connection with the administration of therapeutic and training programs. The age range covered by the original Oseretsky tests extended from 4 to 16 years, the tests being arranged into year levels as in the Stanford-Binet. The Oseretsky scale was designed to cover all major types of motor behavior, from postural reactions and gross bodily movements to finger coordination and control of facial muscles. Administration of these tests requires only simple and easily obtainable materials, such as matchsticks, wooden spools, thread, paper, rope, boxes, rubber ball, and the like. Directions are given orally and by demonstration.

In 1955, the Lincoln-Oseretsky Motor Development Scale (Sloan, 1955) was issued as a revision and restandardization of the Oseretsky tests with simplified instructions and improved scoring procedures. Covering only ages 6 to 14, this revision includes 36 of the original 85 items. The tests, which in this revision are arranged in order of difficulty, were chosen on the basis of age correlation, reliability, and certain practical considerations. Tentative percentile norms were found on a standardization sample of 380 boys and 369 girls attending public schools in central Illinois. Split-half reliabilities computed for single age and sex groups fell mostly in the .80's and .90's. A one-year retest yielded a correlation of .70. A factor analysis of a slightly longer, earlier version indicated a single common factor identified as motor development.

The Vineland Social Maturity Scale (Doll, 1953, 1965) is a developmental schedule concerned with the individual's ability to look after his practical needs and to take responsibility. Although covering a range from birth to over 25 years, this scale has been found most useful at the younger age levels, and particularly with the mentally retarded. The entire scale consists of 117 items grouped into year levels. The information required for each item is obtained, not through test situations, but through an interview with an informant or with the subject himself. The scale is based on what the subject has actually done in his daily living. The items fall into eight categories: general self-help, self-help in eating, self-help in dressing, self-direction, occupation, communication, locomotion, and socialization. A social age (SA) and a social quotient (SQ) can be computed from the subject's record on the entire scale.

The Vineland Scale was standardized on 620 subjects, including 10 males and 10 females at each year from birth to 30 years. Validity of this scale was determined chiefly on the basis of age differentiation, comparison of normals and mental retardates, and correlation of scores with judgments of observers who knew the subjects well. A retest reliability of .92 has been reported for 123 cases, the retest intervals varying from one day to 9 months. The use of different examiners or informants did not appreciably affect results in this group, as long as all informants had had an adequate opportunity to observe the subjects.

Correlations between the Vineland Scale and the Stanford-Binet vary widely, but are sufficiently low, in general, to indicate that different facets of behavior are being tapped by the two scales. The Vineland Social Maturity Scale has proved helpful to clinicians in diagnosing mental retardation and in reaching decisions regarding institutionalization. For example, an individual who is intellectually deficient in terms of the Stanford-Binet may be able to adjust satisfactorily outside an institution if his social age on the Vineland scale is adequate. Discrepancies between MA and SA may likewise contribute to an understanding of certain cases manifesting behavior problems or delinquency.

On the other hand, the available norms must be regarded as tentative and probably require updating. The standardization sample obviously included too few cases at each age to ensure desirable stability and representativeness of norms. Moreover, the subjects came chiefly from middle-class American homes. It is apparent that many items, such as those relating to going out alone, use of spending money, and the like, would have a different significance for children in different socioeconomic levels or in certain minority groups. Cultural differences in child-rearing customs, rather than the child's ability level, might in such cases account for deviations from the norms. Similarly, a considerable number of items are unsuitable for children reared in institutions.

DOWNWARD EXTENSIONS OF THE BINET SCALES. Another type of measuring instrument suitable for the infant and preschool level is provided by several special revisions and downward extensions of the Binet scales. Kuhlmann's 1922 revision of the Binet extended the scales down to a 3-month level. This represents one of the earliest attempts to develop a standardized test for infants. The 1939 revision of the Kuhlmann-Binet likewise covers most of the infant period, the easiest tests being designed for the age of 4 months (Kuhlmann, 1939).

A scale that many psychologists consider one of the most satisfactory instruments for infant testing is the Cattell Infant Intelligence Scale. This scale was developed as a downward extension of the 1937 Stanford-Binet, Form L. In addition to Stanford-Binet items, the Cattell scale utilizes material from the Gesell Developmental Schedules and from other available infant tests, together with some original items. The items are grouped into age levels, and the MA and ratio IQ are computed by the same procedures followed in the 1937 Stanford-Binet. The Cattell scale extends from 2 to 30 months. During the first year, age levels are spaced at intervals of one month; during the second year, at two-month intervals; and during the first half of the third year, at three-month intervals.

If the child passes any test at the 30-month level, testing is continued with the Stanford-Binet, beginning at Year Level III. Between 22 and 30 months, Stanford-Binet items are intermingled with other items in the Cattell scale. Each age level contains five items, with one or two alternates. The small intervals between age levels, as well as the relatively large number of tests at each level, permit more precise measurement with this scale than is possible with most other available infant tests. Continuity and comparability with the Stanford-Binet are further advantages. In order to ensure close comparability of scores on the two scales, certain groups within the standardization samples were retested at the age of 3 years with Form L of the Stanford-Binet. The placement of items in the Cattell scale was then adjusted so as to yield approximately the same median IQ as that obtained by each group on the Stanford-Binet.

The Cattell scale was standardized on a total group of 274 children, varying numbers within this sample being retested at the ages of 3, 6, 9, 12, 18, 24, 30, and 36 months. As is nearly always true in longitudinal studies, the entire group was not available for all retests. Nor did it prove possible to administer all preliminary items suitable for a particular age to all children of that age. The children came from lower-middle-class families, as judged by income level and father's occupation, and were of north-European extraction. Like other groups employed in longitudinal studies, this sample was somewhat selected in terms of stability of residence and willingness of parents to cooperate in the study.

The principal statistical criterion employed for item selection was increase in percentage of children passing an item from one age to the next. Several other practical criteria, however, were applied in retaining or discarding items. Thus, items were eliminated if they were difficult to administer or score, involved an undue amount of subjectivity on the part of the examiner, required cumbersome apparatus, or failed to hold the attention of young children. An effort was also made to minimize the number of items testing primarily muscular coordination or depending unduly on specific home training.

All items in the Cattell scale are administered without a time limit. The author points out that timed tests are undesirable in testing infants or pre-school children. Not only do younger children often fail to understand the need for hurrying, but a timed test may penalize the bright child who is talkative and imaginative in his use of test materials, as well as the slow, deliberate child who plans carefully before he acts. For most children, the Cattell scale requires no more than twenty to thirty minutes. The order of administration of the tests is not prescribed, but is modified to suit the interests of the child and other specific circumstances.

The standardized materials required to administer these tests are very similar to those employed with the Gesell Developmental Schedules and at the lower levels of the Stanford-Binet. At the youngest ages, the tests are largely perceptual, comprising such activities as attending to a voice or bell, following a dangling ring or a moving person with the eyes, looking at a spoon or a cube, and inspecting own fingers. A few motor items, such as lifting head, manipulating fingers, or transferring objects from hand to hand, are also included. With increasing age, more complex manipulatory tasks are introduced and increasing use is made of verbal functions. Blocks, pegboards, formboards, cups, spoons, dolls, and other toy objects are employed at these levels. At the higher ages, the child follows oral instructions in using these materials. Naming objects or pictures of objects and identifying or pointing to objects named by the examiner are among the more highly verbal tasks utilized.

OTHER TESTS FOR YOUNG CHILDREN. The decades of 1950 and 1960 witnessed an upsurge of interest in tests for infants and preschool children. One contributing factor was the rapid expansion of educational programs for mentally retarded children. Another was the establishment of extensive preschool programs of compensatory education for culturally disadvantaged children, such as Head Start. To meet these pressing practical needs, new tests have appeared and well-known tests have been undergoing revision. An outstanding example at the infant level is the Bayley Infant Scales of Development. Available for about ten years in a preliminary research form, this test was released for general use in 1968. The Bayley scales represent a revision and standardization of the California First-Year Mental Scale, originally developed for use in the early stages of the Berkeley Growth Study. Combining new items with items borrowed from the Gesell, Cattell, and other infant and preschool tests, the Bayley scales are applicable from birth to 15 months. The norms are based on a carefully selected sample tested at each age level and are supplemented with extensive longitudinal data on other groups of infants.

Among tests for the preschool level, the Merrill-Palmer Scale of Mental Tests (Fig. 48) has been in use since 1931 and is currently in process of extensive revision (Stutsman, 1931). Being primarily a performance test,

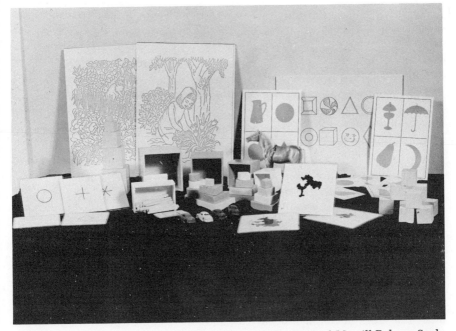

FIG. 48. Materials for Use in Administering the Revised Merrill-Palmer Scale at ages 3 and 4. (Courtesy Rachel S. Ball & Leland H. Stott—revision in preparation.)

the Merrill-Palmer has been employed widely as a supplement to the more highly verbal Stanford-Binet. From the practical standpoint of test administration, it has several advantages. Although the tests are grouped into 6-month age levels from 18 months to 6 years, the order of administration within each level is flexible. The examiner begins with a particularly appealing test and lets the child's interest influence the course of testing. The tests themselves are quite varied and intrinsically interesting to preschoolers. In addition, the tests are presented in individual, gaily colored, and differently shaped boxes—a procedure that stimulates curiosity and enhances the appeal of the tests for young children. Another feature of the Merrill-Palmer scale that increases its usefulness at the preschool level is a scoring system that makes provision for refusals and omissions.

A major weakness of the Merrill-Palmer scale in its original form stems from its emphasis on speed. For the preschool child, speed has not yet become an important goal. The large proportion of timed tests in this scale may handicap the slow, deliberate child, or the bright child who engages in animated conversation with the examiner while performing the tasks. Other technical deficiencies of the scale pertain to the form in which norms are expressed, the inadequate size and questionable representativeness of the original standardization sample, and the obvious need for updating norms. These are all problems that the ongoing revision can undoubtedly solve satisfactorily.[5]

EVALUATION OF INFANT AND PRESCHOOL TESTS. The testing of infants and preschool children presents many problems in *administration and scoring*.[6] Such testing requires a specially trained and experienced examiner who is alert to signs of fatigue, drowsiness, fear, inattention, and other adverse conditions and who knows how to adjust his procedure accordingly. The young child is not motivated to "do his best on the test." Intrinsic appeal of the task and rapport with the examiner must be relied on to provide motivation. With the infant, oral directions cannot be given; the examiner simply provides stimuli and sets the stage for the desired responses. Although oral communication can be used at the preschool level, new testing problems emerge as the child's sphere of activity widens and he reacts increasingly to the interpersonal aspects of the testing situation. Shyness, distractability, and negativism are among the major behavior characteristics that complicate test administration at these ages.

Scoring of infant and preschool tests is often difficult and relatively subjective because of the lack of any permanent record of performance. This difficulty is particularly characteristic of infant testing, in which the test record usually depends on the examiner's observation of relatively fleeting behavior. Did the child lift his head? Did his eyes actually follow a moving object? Few infant responses leave an objective record that may be studied at leisure or rescored.

The *normative samples* employed in standardizing infant and preschool scales are typically smaller and less representative than those used in developing tests for school-age children. Several infant and preschool scales have obtained their norms through follow-up testing of a single group of children. Notable examples are the Gesell and Cattell scales. An advantage of this longitudinal approach is that it permits an analysis of age changes within the individual that is impossible with cross-sectional approaches. On the other hand, shrinkage in sample size and selective dropping out of cases seriously limit the generalizability of such longitudinal data.

The *reliability* of infant and preschool tests is generally lower than that of tests for older children. This finding is not surprising in the light of the

---

[5] An excellent survey and evaluation of available tests for infant and preschool levels is provided by Stott and Ball (1965). Other new tests suitable for the preschool level include the Wechsler Preschool and Primary Scale of Intelligence, to be discussed in Chapter 11 together with the other scales in the Wechsler series, and the School Readiness Behavior Tests developed at the Gesell Institute, to be discussed in Chapter 15 with other educational tests.

[6] The manuals of infant and preschool tests are often a good source of information about effective procedures for obtaining rapport and handling special testing problems at these ages (see, e.g., P. Cattell, 1947; Gesell & Amatruda, 1947; Goodenough, Maurer, & Van Wagenen, 1940; Stutsman, 1931).

previously mentioned difficulties in test administration and scoring. Except for the lowest age levels, however, the more carefully constructed scales show satisfactory reliability. Split-half reliability coefficients of the Cattell scale, found at different age levels within the standardization sample, are given in Table 28. With the exception of the 3-month level, at which the

TABLE 28 SPLIT-HALF RELIABILITY OF THE CATTELL INFANT INTELLIGENCE SCALE

(Adapted from P. Cattell, 1947, p. 49)

Age in Months	Number of Cases	Reliability Coefficient
3	87	.56
6	100	.88
9	85	.86
12	101	.89
18	100	.90
24	80	.85
30	56	.71

reliability coefficient is only .56, all reliabilities fall between .71 and .90. Closely similar results were obtained by Bayley (1933) with the California First-Year Mental Scale. For the ages of 1, 2, and 3 months, the reliabilities were only .63, .51, and .74, respectively. Beyond 4 months, however, the coefficients ranged from .75 to .95, with a median value of .86. It should be noted that items for infant scales are usually selected so as to sample a wide variety of functions. Such heterogeneous content is unlikely to yield comparable halves for the computation of split-half reliability. If closely comparable forms had been available, the obtained reliability coefficients would probably have been still higher.

The determination of *validity* for infant and preschool tests is hampered by a dearth of suitable criteria. Independent estimates of the intelligence of young children are not readily available. We do not have school grades, records of job achievement, or officers' ratings on infants! To be sure, for extreme deviants, independent evidence of ability level can sometimes be obtained. This is especially true of mentally retarded children falling into clinical types that have clearly recognizable physical symptoms, such as Down's syndrome (mongolism). For less extreme deviants, however, and especially for the superior deviant, few criterion data can be found.

As a result, the validation of infant tests has been based largely on two criteria: age differentiation and prediction of subsequent status. The first of these criteria is generally employed in the original selection of items, although it is also used to check both item performance and total scores on the final forms. In terms of this criterion, infant tests in general show good validity. Clear-cut and progressive age changes in performance are found, even over as short a time as a month.

With regard to the second criterion, evidence for validity is much less satisfactory. This criterion has aroused considerable interest, since one of the practical uses of infant tests is the prediction of later intellectual level in children considered for adoption. Let us examine some typical retest correlations. In Bayley's longitudinal study with the California First-Year Mental Scale, correlations between tests administered under the age of 1 year and retests at 18 months were close to zero (Bayley, 1933, 1955; Pinneau, 1961). With subsequent retests, negative correlations as high as —.21 were obtained. The results for the first year are only slightly better with the Cattell Infant Intelligence Scale. Table 29 shows the correlations between Cattell IQ's obtained at the ages of 3, 6, 9, 12, 18, 24, and 30

TABLE 29 VALIDITY COEFFICIENTS OF THE CATTELL INFANT INTELLIGENCE
SCALE

(Adapted from P. Cattell, 1947, p. 49)

Age in Months	Number of Cases	Correlation with Stanford-Binet IQ at Age of 3 Years
3	42	.10
6	49	.34
9	44	.18
12	57	.56
18	52	.67
24	52	.71
30	42	.83

months, respectively, with the Stanford-Binet IQ subsequently obtained by the same children at the age of 3 years. It will be noted that below the age of 12 months the predictive correlations are only .10, .34, and .18. These correlations are little better than chance and indicate that such tests had virtually no validity in predicting the 3-year Stanford-Binet IQ. This lack of predictive validity of Cattell IQ's obtained prior to the age of 1 year has been confirmed by other investigators (Cavanaugh et al., 1957).

Beginning with the age of 12 months, however, the correlations are considerably higher, rising steadily from .56 to .83. Predictive validity over still longer intervals was investigated by Bradway (1944, 1945b) in retests of children from the Stanford-Binet standardization sample. Correlations ranging from .58 to .67 were found between Stanford-Binet IQ's obtained at the preschool level (ages 2 to 5) and at the junior high school level (ages 12–15).

The conclusion that emerges from such longitudinal studies is that preschool tests have moderate validity in predicting subsequent intelligence test performance, but that infant tests have virtually none. Several points should be noted in connection with the latter finding. First, a number of clinicians have argued that infant tests *do* improve the prediction of subsequent development, but only if interpreted in the light of concomitant clinical observations (Donofrio, 1965; Escalona, 1950; Knoblock & Pasamanick, 1960). Prediction might also be improved by a consideration of developmental trends through repeated testing, a procedure originally proposed by Gesell with reference to his Developmental Schedules.

In the second place, infant tests appear to be most useful in the diagnosis of defective development resulting from organic pathology. In the absence of organic pathology, the child's subsequent development is determined largely by the environment in which he is reared. This the test cannot be expected to predict. In fact, parental education and other characteristics of the home environment are better predictors of subsequent IQ than are infant test scores (Bayley, 1955; Pinneau, 1961).

Another reason for the negligible correlations between infant tests and subsequent tests is to be found in the changing nature and composition of intelligence with age. Intelligence in infancy is qualitatively different from intelligence at school age; it consists of a different combination of abilities (Bayley, 1955; Stott & Ball, 1965). This difference is analogous to the previously discussed difference in the nature of intelligence in different cultures and subcultures.

There is still another way in which infant and preschool testing resembles cross-cultural testing. Unlike the schoolchild, the infant and preschooler have not been exposed to the standardized series of experiences represented by the school curriculum. In developing tests for school-age children or for adults who have completed a prescribed amount of schooling, the test constructor has a large fund of common experiential material from which he can draw test items. Prior to school entrance, on the other hand, the individual's experiences are far less standardized, despite certain broad cultural uniformities in child-rearing practices. Under these conditions, the interpretation of test performance is much more difficult.

TESTING THE PHYSICALLY HANDICAPPED

DEAFNESS. Owing to their general retardation in linguistic development, deaf children are usually handicapped on verbal tests, even when the verbal content is presented visually. The testing of deaf children has already been noted as the primary object in the development of the original Pintner-Paterson Performance Scale. Similarly, deaf children represent one of the special groups for which the Arthur Performance Scale was prepared. In the Revised Form II of this scale, the verbal instructions required in

Form I were further reduced in order to increase the applicability of the test to deaf children. Several other tests discussed in this chapter, such as the Army Beta and other nonlanguage tests, can be used with the deaf.

Although adapted to the testing of the deaf, all of these tests have been standardized primarily on hearing subjects. For many purposes it is of course desirable to compare the performance of the deaf with general norms established on hearing persons. At the same time, norms obtained on deaf children are also useful in a number of situations pertaining to the educational development of such children.

To meet this need, the Hiskey-Nebraska Test of Learning Aptitude was developed and standardized on deaf and hard-of-hearing children (Hiskey, 1966). This is an individual test suitable for ages 3 to 16. Speed was eliminated, since it is difficult to convey the idea of speed to young deaf children. An attempt was also made to sample a wider variety of intellectual functions than those covered by most performance tests. Pantomime and practice exercises to communicate the instructions, as well as intrinsically interesting items to establish rapport, were considered important requirements for such a test. All items were chosen with special reference to the limitations of deaf children, the final item selection being based chiefly on the criterion of age differentiation.

The Hiskey-Nebraska Test consists of twelve subtests:

1. Bead Patterns
2. Memory for Color
3. Picture Identification
4. Picture Associations
5. Paper Folding (Patterns)
6. Visual Attention Span

7. Block Patterns
8. Completion of Drawings
9. Memory for Digits
10. Puzzle Blocks
11. Picture Analogies
12. Spatial Reasoning

Norms were derived separately from 1,079 deaf and 1,074 hearing children between the ages of 3 and 17 years, tested in 10 states. Split-half reliabilities in the .90's are reported for deaf and hearing groups. Intercorrelations of the 12 subtests range from the .30's to the .70's among younger children (ages 3 to 10) and from the .20's to the .40's among older children (ages 11 to 17). Correlations of .78 to .86 were found between the Hiskey-Nebraska and either the Stanford-Binet or the Wechsler Intelligence Scale for Children in small groups of hearing children. Further evidence of validity was provided by substantial correlations with achievement tests among deaf children. The manual contains a discussion of desirable practices to be followed in testing deaf children.

BLINDNESS.   Testing the blind presents a very different set of problems from those encountered with the deaf. Oral tests can be most readily adapted for blind persons, while performance tests are least likely to be applicable. A good introduction to procedures for testing the blind—together with a summary of the principal intelligence, special aptitude, achievement, and personality tests prepared for this purpose—may be found in a manual prepared by Bauman and Hayes (1951) and in a survey by Rawls (1954).

In addition to the usual oral presentation by the examiner, other suitable testing techniques have been utilized, such as phonograph records and tape or wire recordings. Some tests are also available in braille. The latter technique is somewhat limited in its applicability, however, by the greater bulkiness of materials printed in braille as compared with inkprint, by the slower reading rate for braille, and by the number of blind persons who are not facile braille readers. The subject's responses may likewise be recorded in braille or on a typewriter. Specially prepared embossed answer sheets or cards are also available for use with true-false, multiple-choice, and other objective-type items. In many individually administered tests, of course, oral responses can be obtained.

Among the principal examples of general intelligence tests that have been adapted for blind subjects are the Binet and the Wechsler. The first Hayes-Binet revision for testing the blind was based on the 1916 Stanford-Binet. In 1942, the Interim Hayes-Binet [7] was prepared from the 1937 Stanford-Binet (Hayes, 1942, 1943). All items that could be administered without the use of vision were selected from both Form L and Form M. This procedure yielded six tests for each year level from VII to XIV, and eight tests at the Average Adult level. In order to assemble enough tests for year levels III to VI, it was necessary to draw on some of the special tests devised for use in the earlier Hayes-Binet. Most of the tests in the final scale are oral, a few requiring braille materials. A retest reliability of .90 and a split-half reliability of .91 are reported by Hayes. Correlations with braille editions of standard achievement tests ranged from .82 to .93. The validity of this test was also checked against school progress.

The Wechsler scales, to be discussed in Chapter 11, have also been adapted for blind subjects. These adaptations consist essentially in using the verbal tests and omitting the performance tests. A few items inappropriate for blind subjects have also been replaced by alternates. When tested under these conditions, blind subjects as a group have been found to equal or excel the general seeing norms. A number of the group intelligence tests discussed in Chapter 9 have likewise been adapted for use with the blind. Among them may be mentioned the Kuhlmann-Anderson, Otis, Pintner Verbal Series, and the Scholastic Aptitude Test of the College Entrance Examination Board. Research with a tactual form of the Progressive Matrices has shown it to have promise as a nonverbal intelligence test for blind children between the ages of 9 and 15 years (Rich & Anderson, 1965).

[7] Originally designated as an interim edition because of the tentative nature of its standardization, this revision has come to be known by this name in the literature.

An adaptation of the Vineland Social Maturity Scale for blind preschool children has been developed and standardized by Maxfield and Buchholz (1957).

ORTHOPEDIC HANDICAPS. Although usually able to receive auditory and visual stimulation, the orthopedically handicapped may have such severe motor disorders as to make either oral or written responses impracticable. The manipulation of formboards or other performance materials would likewise meet with difficulties. Working against a time limit or in strange surroundings often increases the motor disturbance in the orthopedically handicapped. Their greater susceptibility to fatigue makes short testing sessions necessary.

Some of the severest motor handicaps are found among the cerebral palsied. Yet surveys of these cases have frequently employed common intelligence tests such as the Stanford-Binet or the Arthur Performance Scale. In such studies, the most severely handicapped were usually excluded as untestable. Frequently, informal adjustments in testing procedure are made in order to adapt the test to the child's response capacities. Both of these procedures, of course, are makeshifts.

A more satisfactory approach lies in the development of testing instruments suitable for even the most severely handicapped individuals. A number of new tests or adaptations of existing tests are now available for this purpose, although their normative and validity data are usually meager. Adaptations of the Leiter International Performance Scale and the Porteus Mazes, suitable for administration to cerebral-palsied children, have been prepared (Allen & Collins, 1955; Arnold, 1951). In both adapted tests, the examiner manipulates the test materials, while the subject responds only by appropriate head movements. A similar adaptation of the Stanford-Binet has been worked out (Katz, 1958). The previously cited Progressive Matrices provide a promising tool for this purpose. Since this test is given with no time limit, and since the response may be indicated orally, in writing, or by pointing or nodding, it appears to be especially appropriate for the orthopedically handicapped. Despite the flexibility and simplicity of its response indicator, this test covers a wide range of difficulty and provides a fairly high test ceiling. Successful use of this test has been reported in studies of cerebral-palsied children and adults (Allen & Collins, 1955; Holden, 1951; Tracht, 1948).

Another type of test that permits the utilization of a simple pointing response is the *picture vocabulary test.* These tests provide a rapid measure of "use" vocabulary, especially applicable to persons unable to vocalize well (such as the cerebral palsied) and to the deaf. Since they are easy to administer and can be completed in about 15 minutes or less, they are also useful as a rapid screening device in situations where no trained examiner is available but individual testing is needed. It was for these reasons, for example, that a pictorial vocabulary test was employed in a nationwide survey of the effectiveness of Project Head Start.

The Peabody Picture Vocabulary Test (PPVT)—used in the Head Start research—is typical of these instruments. It consists of a series of 150 plates, each containing four pictures, as illustrated in Figure 49. As each plate is presented, the examiner provides a stimulus word orally; the subject responds by pointing to or in some other way designating the picture on the plate that best illustrates the meaning of the stimulus word. Although the entire test covers a range from 2½ to 18 years, each indi-

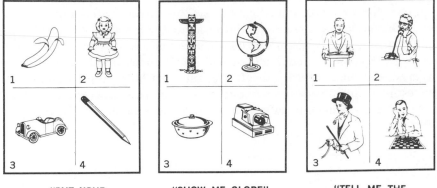

"PUT YOUR   "SHOW ME GLOBE"   "TELL ME THE
FINGER ON BANANA"   NUMBER OF INCERTITUDE"

FIG. 49.   The Peabody Picture Vocabulary Test: Testing Procedure and Typical Items. (Reproduced by permission of Lloyd M. Dunn and American Guidance Service, Inc.)

vidual is given only the plates appropriate to his own performance level, as determined by a specified run of successes at one end and failures at the other. Raw scores can be converted to mental ages, deviation IQ's, or percentiles. The PPVT is untimed and is available in two parallel forms which utilize the same set of cards but different stimulus words.

The standardization sample for the PPVT included a total of 4,012 cases between the ages of 2½ and 18 years tested in Nashville, Tennessee, and its environs. Alternate form reliability coefficients for different age levels within the standardization sample ranged from .67 to .84. Reliability coefficients within the same range were subsequently found in several mentally retarded or physically handicapped groups. Validity was originally established in terms of age differentiation. Since its publication, the test has been employed in a number of studies with normal, mentally retarded, emotionally disturbed, or physically handicapped subjects. These studies have yielded validity coefficients in the .60's with individual and group intelligence scales within relatively homogeneous age groups. Understandably, these correlations were higher with verbal than with performance tests. There is also some evidence of moderate concurrent and predictive validity against academic achievement tests.

Similar procedures of test administration have been incorporated in *pictorial classification tests,* as illustrated by the Columbia Mental Maturity Scale (CMMS). Originally developed for use with cerebral-palsied children, this scale comprises 100 items, each consisting of a set of three, four, or five drawings printed on a large card. The subject is required to identify the drawing that does not belong with the others, indicating his choice by pointing or nodding. To heighten interest and appeal, the cards and drawings are varicolored. Scores are expressed as mental ages and ratio IQ's. Norms were established by administering the CMMS to approximately 1,000 normal East Coast children, aged 3 to 10 years, who also took either the Stanford-Binet or a group intelligence test. Correlations with Stanford-Binet IQ's in homogeneous age groups cluster around .65. Split-half reliability is approximately .90. Moderate to high correlations with other intelligence tests have also been found in a variety of small groups of mentally retarded or physically handicapped cases. In general, the CMMS appears promising for testing children with severe motor or hearing handicaps, but more data are needed to evaluate its effectiveness with such handicapped persons.

CHAPTER **11**

The Wechsler Scales
and the Measurement
of Adult Intelligence

THIS CHAPTER is concerned with the intelligence scales prepared by David Wechsler. Although administered as individual tests and designed for many of the same uses as the Stanford-Binet, these scales differ in several important ways from the earlier test. Rather than being organized into age levels, all items of a given type are grouped into subtests and arranged in increasing order of difficulty within each subtest. In this respect the Wechsler scales follow the pattern established for group tests, rather than that of the Stanford-Binet. Another characteristic feature of these scales is the inclusion of verbal and performance subtests, from which separate verbal and performance IQ's are computed.

Because of their basic similarity, the Wechsler scales for adults, for school-age children, and for preschool and primary levels have been kept together in this chapter. Nevertheless, it is in the individual clinical examination of adults that Wechsler has made his most distinctive contribution. It is therefore appropriate that this chapter focus on the conceptual and procedural problems peculiar to the intelligence testing of adults; these problems will be considered in the last section of this chapter.

Besides their use as measures of general intelligence, the Wechsler scales have been investigated as a possible aid in psychiatric diagnosis. Beginning with the observation that brain damage, psychotic deterioration, and emotional difficulties may affect some intellectual functions more than others, Wechsler and other clinical psychologists argued that an analysis of the individual's relative performance on different subtests should reveal specific psychiatric disorders. The problems and results pertaining to such a profile analysis of the Wechsler scales will be analyzed in Chapter 12, where other types of tests designed to detect intellectual impairment will also be examined.

The interest aroused by the Wechsler scales and the extent of their use is attested by the more than 1,300 publications appearing to date about these scales. In addition to the usual test reviews in the *Mental Measurements Yearbooks,* research pertaining to the Wechsler scales has been surveyed periodically in the *Psychological Bulletin* (Guertin *et al.,* 1962, 1966; Guertin, Frank, & Rabin, 1956; Littell, 1960; Rabin & Guertin, 1951). A bibliography on the Wechsler scales, issued in 1961 in Czechoslovakia, lists publications in all languages, the large majority being in English (Hoskovec & Kanka, 1961).

WECHSLER ADULT INTELLIGENCE SCALE

ANTECEDENTS. The first form of the Wechsler scales, known as the Wechsler-Bellevue Intelligence Scale, was published in 1939. One of the primary objectives in its preparation was to provide an intelligence test suitable for adults. In first presenting this scale, Wechsler pointed out that previously available intelligence tests had been designed primarily for schoolchildren and had been adapted for adult use by adding more difficult items of the same kinds. The content of such tests was often of little interest to adults. Unless the test items have a certain minimum of face validity, rapport cannot be properly established with adult subjects. Many intelligence test items, written with special reference to the daily activities of the schoolchild, clearly lack face validity for most adults. As Wechsler (1939, p. 17) expressed it, "Asking the ordinary housewife to furnish you with a rhyme to the words, 'day,' 'cat,' and 'mill,' or an ex-army sergeant to give you a sentence with the words, 'boy,' 'river,' 'ball,' is not particularly apt to evoke either interest or respect."

The overemphasis on speed in most tests also tends to handicap the older person. Similarly, Wechsler believed that relatively routine manipulation of words received undue weight in the traditional intelligence test. He likewise called attention to the inapplicability of mental age norms to adults, and pointed out that few adults had previously been included in the standardization samples for individual intelligence tests.

It was to meet these various objections that the original Wechsler-Bellevue was developed. In form and content, this scale was closely similar to the more recent Wechsler Adult Intelligence Scale (WAIS) which has now supplanted it. The earlier scale had a number of technical deficiencies, particularly with regard to size and representativeness of normative sample and reliability of subtests, which were largely corrected in the later revision.

DESCRIPTION. Published in 1955, the WAIS comprises eleven subtests. Six subtests are grouped into a Verbal Scale and five into a Performance Scale. These subtests are listed and briefly described below, in the order of their administration.

VERBAL SCALE

1. *Information:* 29 questions covering a wide variety of information that adults have presumably had an opportunity to acquire in our culture. An effort was made to avoid specialized or academic knowledge. It might be added that questions of general information have been used for a long time in informal psychiatric examinations to establish the individual's intellectual level and his practical orientation.

2. *Comprehension:* 14 items, in each of which the subject explains what should be done under certain circumstances, why certain practices are followed, the meaning of proverbs, etc. Designed to measure practical judgment and common sense, this test is similar to the Stanford-Binet Comprehension items; but its specific content was chosen so as to be more consonant with the interests and activities of adults.

3. *Arithmetic:* 14 problems similar to those encountered in elementary school arithmetic. Each problem is orally presented and is to be solved without the use of paper and pencil.

4. *Similarities:* 13 items requiring the subject to say in what way two things are alike.

5. *Digit Span:* Orally presented lists of three to nine digits are to be orally reproduced. In the second part, the subject must reproduce lists of two to eight digits backwards.

6. *Vocabulary:* 40 words of increasing difficulty are presented both orally and visually. The subject is asked what each word means.

PERFORMANCE SCALE

7. *Digit Symbol:* This is a version of the familiar code-substitution test which has often been included in nonlanguage intelligence scales. The key contains 9 symbols paired with the 9 digits. With this key before him, the subject has 1½ minutes to fill in as many symbols as he can under the numbers on the answer sheet.

8. *Picture Completion:* 21 cards, each containing a picture from which some part is missing. Subject must tell what is missing from each picture.

9. *Block Design:* This test is similar to the previously described Kohs Block Design Test (Ch. 10). In the Wechsler adaptation, however, the blocks have only red, white, and red-and-white sides. Subject reproduces designs of increasing complexity requiring from four to nine cubes (see Fig. 50).

10. *Picture Arrangement:* Each item consists of a set of cards containing pictures to be rearranged in the proper sequence so as to tell a story. Figure 51 shows one set of cards in the order in which they are presented to the subject. This set shows the easiest of 8 items making up the test.

11. *Object Assembly:* Modeled after the Pintner-Paterson and Arthur Manikin and Feature Profile, this test includes improved versions of both of these objects, together with two additional objects to be assembled.

Both speed and accuracy of performance are taken into account in scoring Arithmetic, Digit Symbol, Block Design, Picture Arrangement, and Object Assembly.

Since the publication of the original Wechsler-Bellevue scale, a large

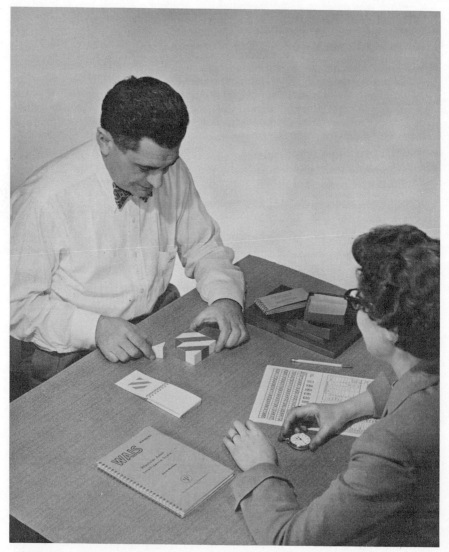

FIG. 50. The Block Design Test of the Wechsler Adult Intelligence Scale. (Courtesy of The Psychological Corporation.)

FIG. 51. Easy Item from the WAIS Picture Arrangement Test. (Reproduced by permission. Copyright © 1955, The Psychological Corporation, New York, N.Y. All rights reserved.)

number of *abbreviated scales* have been proposed. These scales are formed simply by omitting some of the subtests and prorating scores to obtain a Full Scale IQ comparable to the published norms. The fact that several subtest combinations, while effecting considerable saving in time, correlate over .90 with Full Scale IQ's has encouraged the development and use of abbreviated scales for rapid screening purposes. It is possible that the most effective combination of subtests varies for different intellectual levels or other special populations.

Applying a formula developed by McNemar (1950) to the intercorrelations of subtests found for the 25–34 year group of the WAIS standardization sample, Maxwell (1957) computed the correlations of every possible combination of two, three, four, and five subtests with Full Scale IQ. On this basis, she chose the ten best combinations for each of these battery sizes. It is noteworthy that the variations in the correlations with Full Scale IQ among the reported combinations are slight, all given combinations yielding correlations of .90 or higher. The best two-test combination consists of Vocabulary and Block Design. For three tests, the best combination includes Information, Vocabulary, and Block Design; for four tests, Information, Vocabulary, Block Design, and Picture Arrangement; and for five tests, Information, Similarities, Vocabulary, Block Design, and Picture Arrangement. Other combinations were as good or nearly as good as these. In a comparative analysis of a single four-test combination (one of Maxwell's best ten for this size of battery), Doppelt (1956) found correlations of .95 to .97 with Full Scale IQ's at different age levels from 18–19 to 75 and over. Equally close correspondences have been found in several investigations of abbreviated scales formed by reducing the number of items within subtests (see Guertin *et al.*, 1966, pp. 388–389).

Although an excessive amount of energy seems to have been expended in assembling and checking short forms of the Wechsler scales, it is probably inadvisable to use such abbreviated versions except as rough screening devices. Many of the qualitative observations made possible by the administration of an individual scale are lost when abbreviated scales are used. Moreover, the assumption that the original Full Scale norms are applicable to prorated total scores on short scales may not always be justified.

NORMS AND SCORING PROCEDURES. The WAIS standardization sample was chosen with exceptional care to insure its representativeness. The principal normative sample consisted of 1,700 cases, including an equal number of men and women distributed over seven age levels between 16 and 64 years. Subjects were selected so as to match as closely as possible the proportions in the 1950 United States census with regard to part of the country, urban-rural residence, race (white versus nonwhite), occupational level, and education. At each age level, one man and one woman from an institution for mental defectives were also included. Supplementary norms for older persons were established by testing an "old-age sample" of 475 persons, aged 60 years and over, in a typical Midwestern city (Doppelt & Wallace, 1955). It is admittedly difficult to obtain a representative sample of the population over 60. Although the WAIS sample is probably more nearly representative than any other elderly sample tested to date, there is evidence to suggest that significant regional differences occur in the relative magnitude of Verbal and Performance scores at these age levels (Eisdorfer & Cohen, 1961).

Raw scores on each WAIS subtest are transmuted into standard scores with a mean of 10 and a σ of 3. These scaled scores were derived from a reference group of 500 cases which included all persons between the ages of 20 and 34 in the standardization sample. All subtest scores are thus expressed in comparable units. Verbal, Performance, and Full Scale scores are found by adding the scaled scores on the six Verbal subtests, the five Performance subtests, and all eleven subtests, respectively. By reference to appropriate tables provided in the manual, these three scores can be expressed as deviation IQ's with a mean of 100 and a σ of 15. Such IQ's, however, are found with reference to the individual's own age group. They therefore show the individual's standing in comparison with persons of his own age level.

As can be seen in Figure 52, in the WAIS standardization sample Full Scale scores rise until the late twenties or early thirties and then decline slowly until 60. A sharper rate of decline was found beyond age 60 in the old-age sample. By deriving IQ's separately for each age level, individuals are thus compared with a declining norm beyond the peak age. The age decrement is greater in Performance than in Verbal scores and also varies from one subtest to another (Doppelt & Wallace, 1955). Thus, Digit Symbol, with its heavy dependence on speed and visual perception, shows the maximum age decline. In the other Performance subtests, however, speed may not be an important factor in the observed decline. In a special study

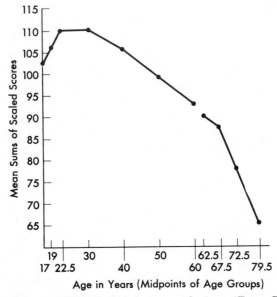

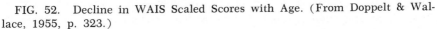

FIG. 52. Decline in WAIS Scaled Scores with Age. (From Doppelt & Wallace, 1955, p. 323.)

of this point, subjects in the old-age sample were given these tests under both timed and untimed conditions. Not only were the differences in scores under these two conditions slight, but the decrements from the 60–64 to the 70–74 age group were virtually the same under timed and untimed conditions (Wechsler, 1958, p. 137).

In the interpretation of WAIS IQ's, the relative magnitude of IQ's obtained on the Wechsler scales and on other intelligence tests should also be taken into account. It has been repeatedly found that brighter subjects tend to score higher on the Stanford-Binet than on the Wechsler scales, while duller subjects score higher on the Wechsler than on the Stanford-Binet. For example, studies of college freshmen show significantly higher mean IQ's on the Stanford-Binet than on the Wechsler, while the reverse is generally found among the mentally retarded. To some extent, the difference in standard deviation of Wechsler and Stanford-Binet IQ's may account for the differences between the IQ's obtained with the two scales. It will be recalled that the σ of the Stanford-Binet IQ is 16 (actually fluctuating around this value in the 1937 form), while that of the Wechsler IQ is 15. The discrepancies in individual IQ's, however, are larger than would be expected on the basis of such a difference. Another difference between the two scales is that the Wechsler has less floor and ceiling than the Stanford-Binet and hence does not discriminate as well at the extremes of the IQ range.

The relationship between Stanford-Binet and Wechsler IQ's depends not only on IQ level, but also on age. Other things being equal, older subjects tend to obtain higher IQ's on the Wechsler than on the Stanford-Binet, while the reverse is true of younger subjects. One explanation for such a trend is obviously provided by the use of a declining standard in the computation of the Wechsler IQ's of older persons. On the Stanford-Binet, on the other hand, all adults are evaluated in terms of the average peak age on that scale, viz., 18 years (16 years on the earlier form). It is also possible that, since the Stanford-Binet was standardized primarily on children and the Wechsler on adults, the content of the former tends to favor children while that of the latter favors older persons. It will be recalled that in the construction of the original Wechsler-Bellevue a special effort was made to choose material appropriate for adults.

RELIABILITY.   For each of the eleven subtests, as well as for Verbal, Performance, and Full Scale IQ's, reliability coefficients were computed within the 18–19, 24–34, and 45–54 year samples. These three groups were chosen as being representative of the age range covered by the standardization sample. Odd-even reliability coefficients (corrected for full test length by the Spearman-Brown formula) were employed for every subtest except Digit Span and Digit Symbol. The reliability of Digit Span was estimated from the correlation between Digits Forward and Digits Backward scores. No split-half technique could be utilized with Digit Symbol, which is a highly speeded test. The reliability of this test was therefore determined by parallel-form procedures in a group specially tested with WAIS and Wechsler-Bellevue Digit Symbol subtests.

Full Scale IQ's yielded reliability coefficients of .97 in all three age samples. Verbal IQ's had identical reliabilities of .96 in the three groups, and Performance IQ's had reliabilities of .93 and .94. All three IQ's are thus highly reliable in terms of internal consistency. As might be expected, the individual subtests yield lower reliabilities, ranging from a few coefficients in the .60's found with Digit Span, Picture Arrangement, and Object Assembly, to coefficients as high as .96 for Vocabulary. It is particularly important to consider these subtest reliabilities when evaluating the significance of differences between subtest scores obtained by the same individual, as in profile analysis.

The WAIS manual also reports standard errors of measurement for the three IQ's and for subtest scores. For Verbal IQ, such errors were 3 points in each group, for Performance IQ, just under 4 points, and for Full Scale IQ, 2.60. We could thus conclude, for example, that the chances are roughly 2:1 that an individual's true Verbal IQ falls within 3 points of his obtained Verbal IQ. The above values compare favorably with the 5-point error of measurement found for the Stanford-Binet. It should be remembered, however, that the Stanford-Binet reliabilities were based on parallel forms administered over intervals of one week or less; under such conditions we would anticipate somewhat lower reliability coefficients and greater fluctuation of scores.

VALIDITY. Any discussion of validity of the WAIS must draw on research done with the earlier Wechsler-Bellevue as well. Because it has been available much longer, the Wechsler-Bellevue has been used in many more investigations than the WAIS. Since all changes introduced in the WAIS represent improvements over the Wechsler-Bellevue (in reliability, ceiling, normative sample, etc.) and since the nature of the test has remained substantially the same, it is reasonable to suppose that validity data obtained on the Wechsler-Bellevue will underestimate rather than overestimate the validity of the WAIS.

The WAIS manual itself contains no validity data, but several aspects of validity are covered in a subsequent book by Wechsler (1958). Chapter 5 of that book is devoted to a discussion of the content validity of the Wechsler scales. Wechsler argues that the psychological functions tapped by each of the 11 chosen subtests fit the definition of intelligence, that similar tests have been successfully employed in previously developed intelligence scales, and that such tests have proved their worth in clinical experience. The test author himself places the major emphasis on this approach to validity.

Some empirical data on concurrent validity are summarized in a chapter on the use of the scales in counseling and guidance (Wechsler, 1958, Ch. 14). These data include mean IQ differences among various educational and occupational groups, as well as a few correlations with job-performance ratings and academic grades. Most group differences, though small, are in the expected directions. Persons in white-collar jobs of different kinds and levels averaged higher in Verbal than in Performance IQ, but skilled workers averaged higher in Performance than in Verbal. Verbal IQ correlated in the .30's with over-all performance ratings in studies of industrial executives and psychiatric residents. Both groups, of course, were already selected in terms of the abilities measured by these tests. Correlations in the .40's and .50's have been found between Verbal IQ and college or engineering school grades. In all these groups, the Verbal Scale yielded somewhat higher correlations than the Full Scale; correlations with the Performance Scale were much lower. Even the correlations with the Verbal Scale, however, were not appreciably higher than those obtained with the Stanford-Binet and with well-known group tests. In studies of mental retardates, WAIS IQ's have proved to be satisfactory predictors of institutional release rate and subsequent work adjustment (see Guertin et al., 1966).

The Wechsler scales have been repeatedly correlated with the Stanford-Binet as well as with other well-known tests of intelligence. Correlations with the Stanford-Binet in unselected adolescent or adult groups and among mental retardates cluster around .80. Within more homogeneous samples, such as college students, the correlations tend to be considerably lower. Group tests yield somewhat lower correlations with the Wechsler scales, such correlations ranging from about .40 to about .80. For both Stanford-Binet and group scales, correlations are nearly always higher with the Wechsler Verbal Scale than with the Full Scale, while correlations with the Performance Scale are much lower than either. On the other hand, Performance IQ's correlate more highly than Verbal IQ's with tests of spatial abilities. For example, a correlation of .72 was found between Performance IQ and the Minnesota Paper Form Board Test in a group of 16-year-old boys and girls (Janke & Havighurst, 1945). In other studies, Performance IQ's correlated .70 with Raven's Progressive Matrices (Hall, 1957) and .35 with the Bennett Mechanical Comprehension Test (Wechsler, 1958, p. 228).

Of some relevance to the construct validity of the Wechsler scales are the intercorrelations of subtests and of Verbal and Performance IQ's, as well as factorial analyses of the scales. In the process of standardizing the WAIS, intercorrelations of Verbal and Performance Scales and of the 11 subtests were computed on the same three age groups on which reliability coefficients had been found, namely, 18–19, 25–34, and 45–54. Verbal and Performance Scale scores correlated .77, .77, and .81, respectively, in these three groups. Intercorrelations of separate subtests were also similar in the three age groups, running higher among Verbal than among Performance subtests. Correlations between Verbal and Performance subtests, although still lower on the whole, were substantial. For example, in the 25–34 year group, correlations among Verbal subtests ranged from .40 to .81, among Performance subtests from .44 to .62, and between Performance and Verbal subtests from .30 to .67. Both individual subtest correlations and correlations between total Verbal and Performance Scale scores suggest that the two scales have much in common and that the allocation of tests to one or the other scale may be somewhat arbitrary.

Factorial analyses of the Wechsler scales have been conducted with a variety of subjects ranging from eighth-grade pupils to the old-age standardization sample (aged 60–75+) and including both normal and abnormal groups. They have also employed different statistical procedures and have approached the analysis from different points of view. Some have been directly concerned with age changes in the factorial organization of the Wechsler subtests, but the findings of different investigators are inconsistent in this regard. As an example, we may examine the factorial analyses of the WAIS conducted by Cohen (1957a, 1957b) with the intercorrelations of subtests obtained on four age groups in the standardization sample (18–19, 25–34, 45–54, and 60–75+). The major results of this study are in line with those of other investigations using comparable procedures (see Guertin et al., 1962, 1966).

That all 11 subtests have much in common was demonstrated in Cohen's study by the presence of a single general factor that accounted for about 50 percent of the total variance of the battery. In addition, three major group factors were identified. One was a *verbal comprehension* factor, with large weights in the Vocabulary, Information, Comprehension, and Similarities subtests. A *perceptual organization* factor was found chiefly in Block Design and Object Assembly. This factor may actually represent a combination of the perceptual speed and spatial visualization factors repeatedly found in factorial analyses of aptitude tests. The results of an earlier investigation by Davis (1956), in which "reference tests" measuring various factors were included with the Wechsler subtests, support this composite interpretation of the perceptual organization factor.

The third major group factor identified by Cohen was described as a *memory* factor. Found principally in Arithmetic and Digit Span, it apparently includes both immediate rote memory for new material and recall of previously learned material. Ability to concentrate and to resist distraction may be involved in this factor. Of special interest is the finding that the memory factor increased sharply in prominence in the old-age sample. At that age level it had significant loadings, not only in Arithmetic and Digit Span, but also in Vocabulary, Information, Comprehension, and Digit Symbol. Cohen points out that during senescence memory begins to deteriorate at different ages and rates in different persons. Individual differences in memory thus come to play a more prominent part in intellectual functioning than had been true at earlier ages. Many of the WAIS subtests require memory at all ages. Until differential deterioration sets in, however, individual differences in the retentive ability required in most of the subtests are insignificant.

It should be noted that the results of Cohen's study fail to support the standard practice of grouping tests into Verbal and Performance Scales, each yielding a separate IQ. Although the use of a Full Scale IQ is justified by the large general factor content of all subtests, the verbal comprehension factor occurs in only four of the six Verbal Scale subtests. The memory factor is found in the two remaining Verbal subtests, as well as in other subtests from both Scales in the case of older subjects. And the perceptual organization factor has significant loadings in only two of the five Performance Scale subtests. The remaining Performance subtests seem to have largely specific variance, not shared with other subtests in this battery.

Working with normal samples and using item intercorrelations and other procedural variations, Saunders (1959, 1960a, 1960b, 1961) found evidence of at least 10 identifiable factors in WAIS performance. There was not, however, a one-to-one correspondence between these factors and the WAIS subtests. Several subtests proved to be factorially complex, and certain factors cut across more than one subtest.

GENERAL EVALUATION.   The WAIS is unquestionably an improvement over its predecessor, the Wechsler-Bellevue. The care with which a representative nationwide normative sample was assembled is a particularly noteworthy feature of the WAIS standardization. The increase in length and difficulty range of subtests has raised reliabilities, although some subtest reliabilities are still too low for the type of intertest analyses often attempted with this scale. The availability of well-established norms for adults of different ages represents a special contribution of the WAIS. In view of the rapidly improving educational and cultural level of the population, however, such norms need frequent rechecking, especially with reference to the expected age decrement. WAIS IQ's vary systematically from Stanford-Binet IQ's, such differences being associated with both intellectual level and age of subjects. These differences need to be considered in interpreting IQ's on the two tests.

More empirical data on WAIS validity would be desirable. It might be noted that nearly all validity data have so far been gathered somewhat incidentally by investigators not directly concerned with the development or distribution of this scale. More systematic investigation of validity would strengthen the interpretation of test scores. Factorial analyses support the use of Full Scale IQ's, because of the large general factor in the test scores. But the grouping of particular tests into Verbal and Performance IQ's is not well substantiated by the results of such research. Abbreviated scales. though plentiful and correlating highly with Full Scale IQ's, should be used sparingly because they sacrifice much of the qualitative information that an individual clinical instrument should provide.

WECHSLER INTELLIGENCE SCALE FOR CHILDREN

DESCRIPTION.   The Wechsler Intelligence Scale for Children (WISC) was prepared as a downward extension of the original Wechsler-Bellevue (Seashore, Wesman, & Doppelt, 1950). Many items were taken from the Wechsler-Bellevue, easier items of the same types being added to each test. The WISC consists of twelve subtests, of which two are to be used either as alternates or as supplementary tests if time permits. As in the other Wechsler scales, the subtests are grouped into a Verbal and a Performance Scale, as follows (see Fig. 53):

VERBAL SCALE	PERFORMANCE SCALE
1. General Information	6. Picture Completion
2. General Comprehension	7. Picture Arrangement
3. Arithmetic	8. Block Design
4. Similarities	9. Object Assembly
5. Vocabulary	10. Coding (or Mazes)
(Digit Span)	

FIG. 53. Materials Used with the Wechsler Intelligence Scale for Children. (Courtesy The Psychological Corporation.)

The tests listed as alternates were those giving the lowest correlations with the rest of the scale. In the Verbal Scale, Digit Span proved to be the least satisfactory test and was therefore designated as alternate. In the Performance Scale, either Coding or Mazes may be omitted, the decision being left to the examiner. Coding requires less time than Mazes, however, and may be generally preferred for this reason. The Coding Test corresponds to the Digit Symbol Test of the adult scale, with an easier part added. The only subtest that does not appear in the adult scale is the Mazes. This test consists of eight paper-and-pencil mazes of increasing difficulty, performance being scored in terms of both time and errors. If all 12 tests are administered, the total scores must be prorated before the IQ is computed. Figure 54 shows a child working on one of the easier items of the Object Assembly Test.

As in the case of the WAIS, there has been considerable experimentation with abbreviated scales of the WISC. The correlations of these short forms with Full Scale IQ's, however, run lower than in the WAIS. With scales consisting of five or six subtests from both Verbal and Performance sets, correlations in the .80's have been found with Full Scale IQ's. The subtests

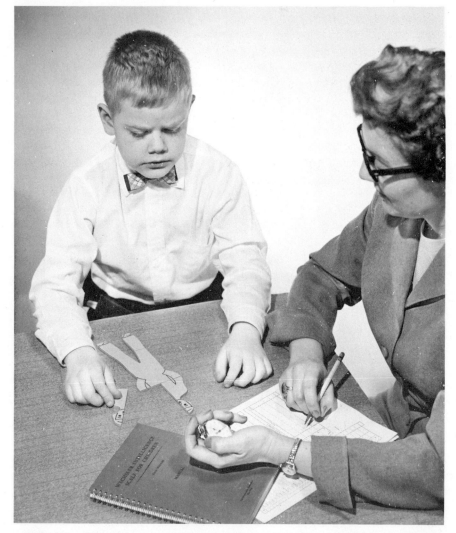

FIG. 54.   The Object Assembly Test of the Wechsler Intelligence Scale for Children. (Courtesy The Psychological Corporation.)

chosen most frequently for this purpose, in order of popularity, include Block Design, Information, Picture Completion, Picture Arrangement, and Coding.

NORMS AND SCORING PROCEDURES.   The treatment of scores on the WISC follows the procedures used in the adult scale, with minor differences. Raw scores on each subtest are first transmuted into normalized standard scores within the subject's own age group. Tables of such scaled scores are provided for every 4-month interval between the ages of 5 and 15 years. As in the adult scales, the subtest scaled scores are expressed in terms of a distribution with a mean of 10 and a σ of 3 points. The scaled subtest scores are added and converted into a deviation IQ with a mean of 100 and a σ of 15. Verbal, Performance, and Full Scale IQ's can be found by the same method. Wechsler (1951) subsequently described methods for finding mental age equivalents of WISC scores. Although not required for the computation of IQ's, these mental ages were provided to meet practical demands. Tables to facilitate the conversion of WISC raw scores into mental ages have also been prepared by Pinneau (1961, pp. 107–111).

The standardization sample for the WISC included 100 boys and 100 girls at each age from 5 through 15 years, giving a total of 2,200 cases. Each child was tested within 1½ months of his midyear. For example, the 5-year-olds ranged in age from 5-years–4-months–15-days to 5-years–7-months–15-days. Only white children were included. All subjects were obtained in schools, with the exception of 55 mental retardates tested in institutions. Testing was carried out in 85 communities located in 11 states, as well as in three institutions for the mentally retarded. The distribution of subjects conformed closely to the 1940 United States census for the country at large, in terms of geographical area, urban-rural proportion, and parental occupation. In many respects, the WISC standardization sample is more representative of the country at large than any other sample employed in standardizing individual tests.

As in the adult scales, normal and superior children tend to score higher on Stanford-Binet than on WISC (see Littell, 1960). The discrepancy in favor of the Binet is greater for brighter and for younger subjects. For the mentally retarded, the WISC yields a significantly higher mean IQ than the Binet.

RELIABILITY. Split-half reliability coefficients are reported for each subtest of the WISC, as well as for Verbal, Performance, and Full Scale scores. These reliabilities were computed separately within the 7½-, 10½-, and 13½-year samples, each age group consisting of 200 cases. Since the odd-even technique was inapplicable to Coding and Digit Span, scores on two parts of these tests were correlated. Owing to the lack of complete comparability of the two parts, however, the coefficients obtained for these two tests probably underestimate their reliabilities. The Full Scale reliability coefficients for the three age levels were .92, .95, and .94, respectively. The corresponding reliabilities for the Verbal Scale were .88, .96, and .96; for the Performance Scale, they were .86, .89, and .90. Thus, both the Full Scale and the Verbal and Performance IQ's appear to be sufficiently reliable for most testing purposes. Standard errors of measurement of the three IQ's, at the three age levels investigated, range from 3.00 to 5.61 IQ points.

A different picture is presented by the subtest reliabilities. A few of these coefficients are in the .50's. Most are evenly distributed in the .60's, .70's, and 80's. Only one test, Vocabulary, yielded any coefficients in the .90's; and even this test had a reliability of only .77 in the 7½-year group. It might be added that most of the subtests had lower reliability coefficients in the youngest age group than in the other two groups. The test manual rightly cautions the users of this scale against interpreting differences between subtest scores without due reference to the reliability coefficients of the particular subtests.

A four-year follow-up indicated that WISC IQ's are about as stable as Stanford-Binet IQ's over such an interval (Gehman & Matyas, 1956). When 60 fifth-grade pupils were retested in the ninth grade, their Stanford-Binet IQ's correlated .78. On the WISC, the Full Scale, Verbal, and Performance IQ's correlated .77, .77, and .74, respectively.

VALIDITY. No discussion of validity is included in the WISC manual. To be sure, the normative tables of standard score equivalents for each subtest provide evidence of age differentiation, but no evaluation of the data in terms of this criterion is given. It is also relevant to observe that, of the 55 institutionalized mental retardates tested in the standardization sample, only 4 obtained Full Scale IQ's above 70, the mean IQ of this group being 57 (Seashore, Wesman, & Doppelt, 1950, p. 109). A number of independent investigators have found concurrent validity coefficients between WISC scores and achievement tests or other academic criteria of intelligence clustering around .60 (Littell, 1960). As would be expected, the Verbal Scale tended to correlate higher than the Performance Scale with such criteria.

Comparisons of WISC and Stanford-Binet IQ's have yielded results very similar to those obtained with the adult scales. Such comparisons have utilized a variety of groups, including both preschool and school-age children and ranging from mentally retarded to gifted children (Littell, 1960). Correlations between WISC and Stanford-Binet vary widely with the age, intellectual level, and heterogeneity of the samples, but the majority are in the .80's. The Verbal Scale again correlates more highly with the Stanford-Binet than does the Performance Scale. With such a test as the Arthur Performance Scale, on the other hand, the reverse is true, the WISC Performance IQ yielding a higher correlation than the WISC Verbal IQ (Pastovic & Guthrie, 1951).

The WISC manual reports intercorrelations among the individual subtests, as well as the correlation of each subtest with Verbal, Performance, and Full Scale scores, and of these three composite scores with each other. All correlations are given separately for the 200 cases at each of three age levels in the standardization sample, viz., 7½, 10½, and 13½ years. The correlations between total Verbal and Performance scores were .60, .68, and .56, respectively, in these three age groups. Thus, the two parts of the scale have much in common, although the correlations between them are low enough to justify the retention of both parts. Factorial analyses of WISC subtests have identified factors quite similar to those found in the adult scales, namely, general, verbal comprehension, perceptual-spatial, and memory factors (see Littell, 1960). There is only a rough correspondence between the verbal comprehension factor and the subtests in the Verbal Scale, and between the perceptual-spatial factor and the subtests in the Performance Scale.

An analysis of occupational differences in Verbal, Performance, and Full Scale IQ is also relevant to the construct validity of the WISC. When the children in the standardization sample were classified into eight categories in terms of father's occupation, the usual hierarchy of mean IQ's was obtained. In Table 30 will be found the mean IQ of each occupational

TABLE 30 MEAN IQ's ON THE WECHSLER INTELLIGENCE SCALE FOR CHILDREN IN RELATION TO PATERNAL OCCUPATION

(Adapted from Seashore, Wesman, and Doppelt, 1950, pp. 107–109)

Occupational Category	Mean IQ		
	Verbal	Performance	Full Scale
Professional and semiprofessional workers	110.9	107.8	110.3
Proprietors, managers, and officials	105.9	105.3	106.2
Clerical, sales, and kindred workers	105.2	104.3	105.2
Craftsmen, foremen, and kindred workers	100.8	101.6	101.3
Operatives and kindred workers	98.9	99.5	99.1
Domestic, protective, and other service workers	97.6	96.9	97.0
Farmers and farm managers	96.8	98.6	97.4
Farm laborers and foremen, laborers	94.6	94.9	94.2

group on the Verbal, Performance, and Full Scales. It will be noted that a difference of 16 points was found between the means of the extreme groups in both Verbal and Full Scale IQ's, and a difference of 13 points between mean Performance IQ's. As in all such comparisons, however, the overlapping of distributions for different occupational categories was very large. Individual cases in the lowest category who excel individual cases in the highest category can easily be found. There is also some evidence indicating that these class differences decline with age, possibly because of exposure to relatively uniform schooling (Estes, 1953, 1955).

An analysis of the discrepancies between Verbal and Performance scores for each individual throws further light on these group comparisons (Seashore, 1951). For the entire standardization sample, the mean difference between Verbal and Performance IQ was, of course, zero. This follows from the procedure employed in computing deviation IQ's on the WISC. Each age group likewise yielded mean Verbal-Performance differences of practically zero. About half of the individual cases showed Verbal-Performance discrepancies of 8 points or more. In a breakdown with reference to occupational categories, all group differences were small and statistically insignificant, with one exception. The professional and semiprofessional category contains a significantly greater proportion of children with higher Verbal than Performance IQ's. In this group, 62 percent had a positive V-P difference, 35 percent a negative difference, and 3 percent had identical IQ's on both scales. In all other categories, the proportions of positive and negative discrepancies were approximately equal. The differences that did occur, however, were in the expected direction, viz., a greater tendency for rural children and children from lower socioeconomic levels to obtain higher scores on the Performance than on the Verbal Scale.

GENERAL EVALUATION. On the whole, the WISC compares favorably with other individual intelligence scales in the quality of its test-construction procedures. The size and representativeness of its normative sample and the careful procedures followed in determining reliability set a particularly high standard in test development. The dearth of validity data remains its principal weakness. More attention should also be given to the consistent discrepancies between WISC and Stanford-Binet IQ's at different ages and intellectual levels. Finally, there seems to be something of a paradox in the underlying rationale of the WISC. It will be recalled that a major reason for the development of the original Wechsler-Bellevue was the need for an adult intelligence test that would not be a mere upward extension of available children's scales. Having presumably achieved this objective, the author then proceeded to prepare a children's scale that was simply a downward extension of the adult scale. Subsequently, he carried the paradox farther by extending the scale to the preschool and primary level.

WECHSLER PRESCHOOL AND PRIMARY SCALE OF INTELLIGENCE

DESCRIPTION. In more than one sense, the Wechsler Preschool and Primary Scale of Intelligence (WPPSI) is the baby of the series. Published in 1967, this scale is designed for ages 4 to 6½ years. The scale includes 11 subtests, only 10 of which are used in finding the IQ. Eight of the subtests are downward extensions and adaptations of WISC subtests; the other three were newly constructed to replace WISC subtests that proved unsuitable for a variety of reasons. As in the WISC and WAIS, the subtests are grouped into a Verbal and a Performance scale, from which Verbal, Performance, and Full Scale IQ's are found. In the WPPSI, however, the administration of Verbal and Performance subtests is alternated in order to enhance variety and help to maintain the young child's interest and cooperation. Total testing time ranges from 50 to 75 minutes, in one or two testing sessions. Abbreviated scales are *not* recommended.

In the following list, the new subtests have been starred:

VERBAL SCALE	PERFORMANCE SCALE
Information	*Animal House
Vocabulary	Picture Completion
Arithmetic	Mazes
Similarities	*Geometric Design
Comprehension	Block Design
*Sentences (Supplementary Test)	

"Sentences" is a memory test, substituted for the WISC Digit Span. The child repeats each sentence immediately after oral presentation by the examiner. This test can be used as an alternate for one of the other verbal tests; or it can be administered as an additional test to provide further information about the child, in which case it is not included in the total score in calculating the IQ. "Animal House" is basically similar to the WAIS Digit-Symbol and the WISC Coding test. A key at the top of the board has pictures of dog, chicken, fish, and cat, each with a differently colored cylinder (its "house") under it. The child is to insert the correctly colored cylinder in the hole beneath each animal on the board (see Fig. 55). Time, errors, and omissions determine the score. "Geometric Design" requires the copying of 10 simple designs with a colored pencil.

TECHNICAL CHARACTERISTICS. The WPPSI was standardized on a national sample of 1,200 children—100 boys and 100 girls in each of six ½-year age groups from 4 to 6½. Children were tested within six weeks of the required birthday or midyear date. The sample was stratified against 1960 census data with reference to geographical region, urban-rural residence, proportion of whites and nonwhites, and father's occupational level. Raw scores on each subtest are converted to normalized standard scores with a mean of 10 and a σ of 3 within each ¼-year group. The sum of the scaled scores on the Verbal, Performance, and Full Scale are then converted to deviation IQ's with a mean of 100 and a σ of 15. Although Wechsler argues against the use of mental age scores because of their possible misinterpretations, the manual provides a table for converting raw scores on each subtest to "test ages" in ¼-year units.

For every subtest except Animal House, reliability was found by correlating odd and even scores and applying the Spearman-Brown formula. Since scores on Animal House depend to a considerable extent on speed, its re-

FIG. 55.   The Animal House Test of the Wechsler Preschool and Primary Scale of Intelligence. (Courtesy The Psychological Corporation.)

liability was found by a retest at the end of the testing session. Reliability coefficients were computed separately within each ½-year age group in the standardization sample. While varying with subtest and age level, these reliabilities fell mostly in the .80's. Reliability of the Full Scale IQ varied between .92 and .93; for Verbal IQ, it varied between .87 and .90; and for Performance IQ, between .84 and .91. Standard errors of measurement are also provided in the manual, as well as tables for evaluating the significance of the difference between scores. From these data it is suggested that a difference of 15 points or more between Verbal and Performance IQ's is sufficiently important to be investigated. Stability over time was also checked in a group of 50 kindergarten children retested after an average interval of 11 weeks. Under these conditions, reliability of Full Scale IQ was .92; for Verbal IQ it was .86; and for Performance IQ, .89.

Intercorrelations of the 11 subtests within each age level in the standardization sample fall largely between .40 and .60. Correlations between Verbal and Performance subtests are nearly as high as those within each scale. The overlap between the two scales is also indicated by an average correlation of .66 between Verbal and Performance IQ's. The manual reports a correlation of .75 with Stanford-Binet IQ in a group of 98 children aged 5 to 6 years. As in the case of the WISC, the Stanford-Binet correlates higher with the Verbal IQ (.76) than with the Performance IQ (.56). This group, which was somewhat below average in ability, had approximately the same mean IQ on Stanford-Binet and WPPSI (91.3 vs. 89.6). Similar comparisons at different ability levels are needed.

Owing to the recency of publication, little can be concluded at this time about the validity and the practical usefulness of the WPPSI. The procedures followed in standardizing the scale and estimating reliability are of a high technical quality. Both the size and composition of the normative sample represent a considerable advance over the preschool tests discussed in the preceding chapter and clearly reflect the improvements in test construction that have occurred in the interval.

PROBLEMS IN THE TESTING OF ADULT INTELLIGENCE

Having examined the full range of the currently available Wechsler scales, we may now return to Wechsler's initial objective, the measurement of adult intelligence. Two basic questions in adult testing concern: (1) the interpretation of the observed age decrement in test performance, and (2) the nature of adult intelligence. Both questions are closely related to broad methodological problems in the development and use of tests.

AGE DECREMENT. A distinctive feature introduced by the Wechsler adult scales was the use of a declining norm to compute deviation IQ's. Figure

52, presented in the first section of this chapter, shows the course of the total scaled scores from the youngest to the oldest groups in the WAIS standardization sample. It is apparent that the peak is reached between the ages of 20 and 34; beyond that age, scores decline slowly until the 60's and drop more sharply thereafter. The deviation IQ is found by referring an individual's total scaled score to the norm for his own age group. Thus, if he shows the same decline in performance with age as the normative sample, his IQ will remain constant. The underlying assumption is that it is "normal" for an individual's tested ability to decline with age beyond the 30's.

Two facts from the Wechsler standardization data are relevant to the interpretation of age changes. First, since the standardization sample is a *normative* sample, it should reflect existing population characteristics at each age level (see Anastasi, 1956). Because of the rising educational level of the general population, older groups at any one point in time will have received less education than younger groups. This educational difference is clearly reflected in the WAIS standardization sample, in which the maximum years of schooling are found at the 20–34 year levels and educational level drops consistently in the older groups. These age differences in amount of education are inevitable if the standardization sample is to be truly representative of the population of the country at the time the norms were established. Nevertheless, the educational differences complicate the interpretation of the observed score decrements. The older groups in the standardization sample may have performed more poorly on the test, not because they were growing old, but because they had received less education than the younger groups.

A second pertinent fact emerges from a comparison of the WAIS with the Wechsler-Bellevue, which was standardized approximately 15 years earlier. In the Wechsler-Bellevue standardization sample, improvement in score ceased at an earlier age and the decline set in earlier than in the WAIS sample. An examination of the educational distributions of the two samples reveals that the changes in the age curves parallel the educational changes that have occurred in the general population during the intervening period. Persons in the WAIS standardization sample had received more education on the average than persons in the corresponding age in the Wechsler-Bellevue sample, since the latter were educated 15 years earlier.

Cross-sectional studies of adult intelligence, in which persons of different ages are tested simultaneously, are likely to show an apparent age decrement because their results are confounded with cultural changes. Longitudinal studies, based on retests of the same persons over periods of 5 to 40 years, have generally shown the opposite trend, the scores tending to improve with age. Although most of these longitudinal data have been obtained with superior adults (Bayley & Oden, 1955; Burns, 1966; Campbell, 1965; Nisbet, 1957; Owens, 1953, 1966), similar results have been reported for normal and mentally retarded adults (Baller, Charles, & Miller, 1967; Bell & Zubek, 1960; Charles, 1953; Charles & James, 1964; Eisdorfer, 1963).

Neither cross-sectional nor longitudinal studies alone can provide a conclusive interpretation of observed age changes. Several excellent analyses of the methodological difficulties inherent in each approach, together with the required experimental designs, have been published (Damon, 1965; Kuhlen, 1963; Schaie, 1965). Basically, what is needed in order to tease out the effect of cultural changes is a combination of cross-sectional and longitudinal approaches. On the one hand, age differences in educational level may produce a spurious age decrement in test performance in cross-sectional studies. On the other hand, as the individual grows older, he is himself exposed to cultural changes that may improve his performance on intelligence tests. The expansion of mass media of communication would be an example of such cultural changes occurring within the lifetime of adults living in our society today.

A few studies provide data that permit at least a partial analysis of the contributing factors. Owens (1966) in his 40-year retest of Iowa State University students and Campbell (1965) in his 30-year retest of University of Minnesota students also tested *present* freshmen in the respective colleges. Thus, multiple comparisons could be made between the two groups tested at the same age 30 or 40 years apart, and the performance of a single group tested before and after the same time intervals. In both studies, the initial group improved over its own earlier performance, but performed about on a par with the younger group tested at the later date. Such findings suggest that it is cultural changes and other experiential factors, rather than age per se, that produce both the rises and declines in scores obtained with the more limited experimental designs.

NATURE OF ADULT INTELLIGENCE.   In our earlier discussion of the construct "intelligence" we noted that the term characteristically designates that combination of abilities required for survival or advancement within a particular culture or subculture. It was further observed that the nature and relative weights of these abilities differ among cultural groups and undergo change in the course of the individual's own lifetime. Some of the problems encountered in the construction of cross-cultural and infant tests are also encountered in the construction of tests for older adults.

Within the life span, testing has been oriented chiefly toward the schoolchild and college student. At these levels, the test constructor can draw on the large common pool of experiences that have been organized into academic curricula. Most intelligence tests measure how well the individual has acquired the intellectual skills taught in our schools; and they can in turn predict how well he is prepared for the next level in the educational hierarchy. Tests for adults, including the Wechsler scales, draw largely on this identifiable common fund of experience. As the individual grows older and his own formal educational experiences recede farther into the past, this fund of common experience may become increasingly less appropriate to assess his intellectual functioning. Adult occupations are more diversified than childhood schooling. The cumulative experiences of adulthood may thus stimulate a differential development of abilities in different persons.

Because intelligence tests are closely linked to academic abilities, it is not surprising to find that longitudinal studies of adults show larger age increments in score among those individuals who have continued their education longer (Campbell, 1965; Husén, 1951; Lorge, 1945; Owens, 1953). Similarly, persons whose occupations are more "academic" in content, calling into play verbal and numerical abilities, are likely to maintain their performance level or show improvement in intelligence test scores over the years, while those engaged in occupations emphasizing mechanical activities or interpersonal relations may show a loss. Some suggestive data in support of this hypothesis are reported by Williams (1960), who compared the performance of 100 persons, ranging in age from 65 to over 90, on a series of verbal and nonverbal tests. Rather striking correspondences were found between the individual's occupation and his relative performance on the two types of tasks. Longitudinal investigations of adults have also found suggestive relationships between total IQ changes and certain biographical inventory items (Charles & James, 1964; Owens, 1966).

Each time and place fosters the development of skills appropriate to its characteristic demands. Within the life span, these demands differ for the infant, the schoolchild, the adult in different occupations, and the retired septuagenarian. An interesting demonstration of the implications of this fact for intelligence testing was provided by Demming and Pressey (1957). These investigators began with a task analysis of typical adult functions, conducted through informal surveys of reading matter and of reported daily activities and problems. On this basis, they prepared preliminary forms of some 20 tests "indigenous" to the older years. The tests emphasized practical information, judgment, and social perception. Results with three of these tests, administered together with standard verbal and nonverbal tests to samples of different ages, showed that the older persons excelled the younger on the new tests while the reverse relationship held for the traditional tests. All these types of research suggest that whether intelligence test scores rise or decline with increasing age in adulthood depends largely on what experiences the individual undergoes during those years and on the relationship between these experiences and the functions covered by the tests.

CHAPTER **12**

Measurement of Intellectual Impairment

BESIDES ASCERTAINING an individual's general level of intellectual functioning, clinical psychologists are also concerned with the patterning of test scores. Marked irregularities in performance on different tests may be diagnostic of several pathological conditions. We can recognize at least two types of clinical problems in which performance patterns have been explored. The first problem pertains to the diagnosis of *intellectual deterioration* resulting from brain damage, psychotic disorders, or other pathological conditions. In this connection, a distinction must be made between mental retardation on the one hand, and mental deterioration on the other. In the former condition, the individual fails to reach a normal level of intellectual functioning; while in the latter, he declines from a formerly higher level. Most diagnostic procedures are based on the expectation that intellectual deterioration occurs in varying amounts in different intellectual functions. Thus, some functions are believed to remain relatively unaffected by psychotic and other disturbances. Others are considered to be much more sensitive to such pathological conditions. Similarly, it is expected that neurotic anxiety and other emotional disturbances will interfere with performance on certain types of tests, which require careful observation and concentration, while leaving performance on other tests unimpaired.

A second problem concerns the differentiation between mental retardation resulting from organic disorders and mental retardation resulting from experiential deprivation. There is a growing body of evidence suggesting that many cases of mental retardation are of the cultural-familial variety, in which there is no organic brain damage. In programs of special education and other remedial activities, it is especially important to identify the nature of the mental retardation. The diagnosis of *organicity*, or organic brain damage as a basis for mental retardation, has thus become another major application of pattern analysis. The hypothesis is that the cultural-familial retardate will show a different pattern of deficiencies in test performance than is found in the organically impaired mental retardate.

The two problems have much in common; but their differences should also be noted. The first approach is concerned not only with organic damage but also with the effects of emotional disorders on test performance. A second important distinction, with regard to the role of organicity in the two approaches, pertains to the time when brain damage occurs. It cannot be assumed that organic impairment in late childhood or adulthood will have the same behavioral effects as when it occurs prenatally or in early infancy.

PATTERN ANALYSIS WITH THE WECHSLER SCALES

TECHNIQUES OF PATTERN ANALYSIS. In addition to yielding an IQ, the Wechsler scales have been extensively investigated as possible diagnostic instruments for a wide variety of pathological conditions. Wechsler first discussed the diagnostic use of his scales in the second edition of the Wechsler-Bellevue manual, published in 1941. The 1958 edition of this book, dealing with the WAIS (Wechsler, 1958), contains a revised and expanded treatment of such a diagnostic use of the scales. Another similar system for clinical interpretation of Wechsler scores was proposed by Rapaport et al. (1945). Still other clinicians have recommended other techniques and modifications (see Guertin et al., 1962, 1966; Guertin, Frank, & Rabin, 1956; Littell, 1960; Rabin & Guertin, 1951). All these techniques are based essentially on the individual's relative performance on different subtests. The fact that raw scores on all Wechsler subtests are transmuted into standard scores permits direct comparisons among them and has undoubtedly encouraged the development of an overabundance of diagnostic indices. Specifically, these indices utilize any one of three procedures: measuring amount of scatter, analyzing score patterns, and computing a deterioration index.

Scatter is simply the extent of variation among the individual's scores on all the subtests. Wechsler (1958, p. 162) proposes that it be measured by finding the average deviation (*AD*) of the subtest scores around the individual's own mean. The underlying rationale of scatter indices implies that the *AD* should be larger in pathological than in normal cases. Wechsler illustrates this hypothesis with data on small matched groups of schizophrenics and normals, the former showing significantly greater *AD*'s.

Both Wechsler (1958, Ch. 11) and Rapaport et al. (1945) have described what they consider characteristic *score patterns* for various clinical syndromes. Wechsler provides such patterns for organic brain disorders, schizophrenia, anxiety states, juvenile delinquency, and mental deficiency. Each pattern is expressed in terms of the position of each subtest with reference to the individual's mean on all subtests. These patterns are supplemented with a number of special diagnostic signs associated with each syndrome. For example, some of the characteristic signs of schizophrenia listed by Wechsler (1958, p. 171) are:

Sum of Picture Arrangement plus Comprehension less than Information and Block Design
Object Assembly much below Block Design
Very low Similarities with high Vocabulary and Information

Obviously, a question that must be answered prior to the application of such a system of score patterns and diagnostic signs pertains to the minimum score difference required for statistical significance. With the reliability coefficients obtained in the standardization sample, it is possible to compute for every pair of WAIS subtests the smallest difference that would be significant at any desired probability level. A table giving these differences at the 15 percent level is reproduced by Wechsler (1958, p. 164). The minimum values found in this table for different test pairs vary from 2 to 4 scaled score points, most comparisons requiring 3 points for a significant difference. It should be noted, however, that this level of significance permits a much greater probability of error (15 percent) than the customary 5 percent or 1 percent levels. Other tables have subsequently been prepared to permit a fuller evaluation of intertest differences on both WAIS and WISC (Alimena, 1951; Field, 1960; Fisher, 1960; Hopkins & Michael, 1961).

Another type of intertest comparison proposed by Wechsler (1958, Ch. 12) requires the computation of a *deterioration index*. This index was suggested by the observation that in the standardization sample the amount of age decrement varied with the subtest. Tests requiring the utilization of past learning showed less decline than those involving speed, new learning, and the perception of new relations in verbal or spatial content. On the basis of such findings, Wechsler selected a set of "Hold" tests exhibiting little or no age decline and a set of "Don't Hold" tests manifesting relatively steep decline. These tests are listed below:

"HOLD" TESTS	"DON'T HOLD" TESTS
Vocabulary	Digit Span
Information	Similarities
Object Assembly	Digit Symbol
Picture Completion	Block Design

The deterioration index is found by subtracting the sum of the scaled scores on the four Don't Hold tests from the sum of the scaled scores on the four Hold tests, and dividing this difference by the sum of the Hold tests, as shown below:

$$DI = \frac{\text{Hold} - \text{Don't Hold}}{\text{Hold}}$$

Wechsler maintains that at any age individuals with mental disorders show the same differential loss on WAIS subtests found in the general population with advancing age. To allow for normal age decline, the scaled scores used in computing the deterioration index are found by reference to special normative tables for each age level. Hence, the individual's relative performance on each subtest is compared with that of his age peers.

CRITICAL EVALUATION OF PROFILE ANALYSIS. The diagnostic interpretation of Wechsler profiles by any of the above procedures has been widely criticized from a number of angles. The reliabilities of subtests, although higher in the WAIS than in the earlier Wechsler-Bellevue, are still not high enough to permit confident interpretation of any but the largest differences. For instance, to be significant at the .01 level, the difference between Arithmetic and Comprehension must be at least 5 points (McNemar, 1957).

A related question concerns the frequency of intertest differences in the normal population. The "abnormality" of any given magnitude of intertest differences must be evaluated in terms of these frequencies (Field, 1960). Differences that are statistically significant may nevertheless occur so frequently in the general population as to have no pathological significance. McNemar (1957), for example, showed that in the above comparison between Arithmetic and Comprehension subtests, 10 percent of the standardization sample yielded differences of 5 points or more, which are statistically significant at the .01 level. If we substitute the .15 level proposed by Wechsler, the percentage of differences above the minimum value in the normal population would be far greater.

If the Wechsler scales were to be used as a differential aptitude battery with normal subjects—to compare the individual's relative standing in different abilities—the subtests should have high reliabilities and very low intercorrelations. On the other hand, the rationale underlying the proposed diagnostic interpretations of profile irregularities requires high reliabilities and *high* subtest intercorrelations *in the normal population*. In an abnormal sample, of course, the subtests should have high reliabilities and lower intertest correlations because of the hypothesized increase in scatter of scores.

That the differences regarded as diagnostic by Wechsler do in fact occur frequently in the normal population has been further noted by Jones (1956), in reference to a statement in the WAIS manual (Wechsler, 1955, p. 18). There the number of intertest differences exceeding 3 points and those exceeding 5 points in the normal population is estimated from the results obtained in the standardization sample. As Jones points out, however, the eleven subtests in any one individual's record yield 55 possible intertest comparisons. Hence, a difference expected in, let us say, 10 percent of the cases in any one intertest comparison will actually occur about 5 times in a single individual's record (10 percent of $55 = 5.5$). Rather than occurring in only 10 percent of normal persons, therefore, differences of such magnitude would be found, on the average, 5 times in *every* normal person's record.

In individual cases, scatter greater than that found in the normative sample may result, not from pathological conditions, but from differences in educational, occupational, cultural, or other background factors. Language handicap may account for lower Verbal than Performance scores. It will be recalled that skilled laborers tend to score higher on Performance than on Verbal Scales, unlike white-collar groups (Ch. 11). Socioeconomic and urban-rural differences in subtest pattern have likewise been noted. There is also evidence that education affects relative standing on Verbal and Performance Scales. In a study of psychiatric patients (Smith, 1966), as schooling decreased from over 12 years to under 5 years, the percentage of cases with higher Performance than Verbal IQ's increased from 21 to 64. Sex differences in subtest scores may also confound the interpretation of WAIS patterns. In an investigation of the Wechsler Deterioration Index, for example, Norman (1966) showed that the choice of subtests is such as to indicate more deterioration among males than among females. This follows artificially from the inclusion of more tests in which males excel among the Hold tests, and more tests in which females excel among the Don't Hold tests.

As an example of the role of subcultural differences may be cited the research of Levinson (1959), who administered the WISC and WAIS to several Jewish groups in America. Not only was there a significant tendency for Verbal to exceed Performance IQ in these groups, but the difference also increased with age. Levinson attributes these findings to the cumulative effect of Jewish cultural values that emphasize verbal abilities. In a subsequent study of the Wechsler Deterioration Index with 50 elderly Jewish men and women, Levinson (1963) concluded that such quotients can probably serve best as measures of subcultural deviation from the normative population. Analysis of the subtest scores of each individual within the group of 50 yielded suggestive evidence of relationship between the pattern of subtest scores and both schooling and degree of exposure to the American culture. It should be noted that Wechsler (1958, p. 160) does call attention to the need for considering background factors in subtest analyses; but in the zeal to apply diagnostic signs and indices, such precautions are easily forgotten.

The assumption that those subtests showing most normal age decrement are most sensitive to pathological deterioration, which underlies the computation of a deterioration index, is also questionable. The fact that the older subjects in the standardization sample had received less education than the younger makes the interpretation of the observed decrement even more suspect. Furthermore, some of the Hold tests may simply have more flexible scoring standards and may for this reason be less sensitive to change. Some evidence is available to suggest that the apparent resistance of vocabulary tests to decline may be attributable to the substitution of poorer but equally acceptable definitions on the part of deteriorated subjects (Chodorkoff & Mussen, 1952; Feifel, 1949).

Apart from theoretical considerations, extensive data gathered by other investigators have failed to corroborate the various hypotheses regarding diagnostic interpretations of score profiles. That the evidence is predominantly negative is apparent from surveys of the published literature. The original diagnostic indices were derived either from uncontrolled clinical observations or from comparisons of pathological and control groups that were not equated in age, education, or other factors. Failure to cross-validate likewise accounts for a number of spurious differences. Subsequent studies offer little empirical support to the hypotheses regarding scatter and score patterns. Investigations of the rationale underlying the interpretation of specific subtests as indicators of anxiety, distractability, and other personality variables have likewise yielded predominantly negative results (Guertin et al., 1962, 1966).

Results with the Wechsler Deterioration Index have been particularly disappointing. Mental defectives could not be differentiated from psychotics on the basis of this index. Schizophrenics obtained no higher deterioration index than neurotics, and patients with brain damage no higher index than those with functional disorders. Even more telling refutation was provided by longitudinal analyses of retest records, which failed to reveal a significant relation between actual decline in test scores and the deterioration index (Magaret & Simpson, 1948; Sloan, 1947). Also relevant are the observations that "normal" deterioration is not found among older institutionalized mental defectives (Bensberg & Sloan, 1950), and that vocabulary scores do decline in patients hospitalized for long periods (Yates, 1956).

On the other hand, there is some evidence in factor-analytic research that supports the presence of a common "deterioration factor" through some of the Wechsler subtests (Saunders, 1960c). The same research indicated a possible relation between performance on certain WAIS subtests and indices of brain functioning derived from electroencephalography. It was also found that relatively low Digit Span scores occurred more often among brain-damaged than among normal subjects (Saunders, 1961). It is possible that further research will justify the utilization of at least some score patterns on the Wechsler scales for diagnostic purposes.

Like any individual intelligence test, the Wechsler scales can theoretically provide information at various levels. At the most objective level, these scales yield an IQ with high reliability and fair evidence of validity. At a purely qualitative level, any irregularity of performance should alert the clinician to look for peculiarities of past experience, emotional associations, and other individual factors. Bizarreness, overelaboration, or excessive self-reference in responses are often indicative of personality disorders. Even when correct, specific responses may provide promising leads. As Wechsler (1958, p. 181) points out, if in the Vocabulary test one individual defines "sentence" as a group of words and another as a penalty imposed by a judge, this difference may furnish a clue to important dissimilarities in background or personality.

Such qualitative interpretations, however, are tentative and require further verification. The same response—or score pattern—may have different meanings for different subjects. It may have deep significance for some and only trivial connotations for others. Because of their idiosyncratic meanings, such cues cannot be validated by quantitative methods adapted to group trends. Between these two extremes—from the quantitative, objective IQ to purely qualitative observations—fall the various attempts at semiquantitative pattern analysis. It is at this intermediate level that both theoretical analyses and empirical results have thus far lent little or no support to the proposed interpretations.

Attention should also be called to a recent book by Glasser and Zimmerman (1967), which provides a carefully worked out framework for the clinical interpretation of the WISC, with good summaries of relevant data. The soundness of this approach contrasts sharply with the traditional attempts at pattern analysis of the Wechsler scales. For each subtest, Glasser and Zimmerman discuss the types of information that a clinician may obtain with regard to both intellectual and personality characteristics.

PERCEPTUAL AND MEMORY TESTS

A number of tests have been specially designed as clinical instruments for assessing intellectual impairment. Several have been described as indices of organicity, or brain damage. Most available tests in this category, however, are broader in function, and have been employed to detect intellectual deterioration or impairment arising from a variety of possible causes. The many testing techniques proposed for this purpose have been surveyed in a number of books and articles (e.g., Haynes & Sells, 1963; Parker, 1957; Strauss & Kephart, 1955; Yates, 1954). Several are in an experimental stage. Some are designed only to afford the clinician an opportunity for qualitative observations. Others have relatively standardized procedure and objective norms, although the normative samples are often inadequate. Some are subject to one or more of the theoretical objections raised against profile analysis of Wechsler scores. A few have yielded promising empirical data.

All available tests of intellectual impairment are based on the premise of a differential deficit in different functions. Chief among the functions considered to be most sensitive to pathological processes are memory, spatial perception, and abstraction or concept formation. Memory and perceptual functions are frequently combined in the same tests; typical examples of these tests will be examined in this section. Tests of concept formation will be illustrated in the next section.

BENTON VISUAL RETENTION TEST.   This test utilizes 10 cards, each containing one or more simple geometric figures. In the standard administration, each card is exposed for 10 seconds and the subject is told to draw what was on the card immediately after its removal. The test thus requires spatial perception, immediate recall, and visuomotor reproduction of drawings. Performance is scored in terms of number of cards correctly reproduced and total number of errors. Interscorer reliability of the order of .95 is reported for these scores. Additional qualitative information can be obtained by classifying the errors as omissions (and additions), distortions, perseverations, rotations, misplacements, and size errors (see Fig. 56). Three equivalent series of 10 drawings each are available.

The Benton test may also be administered under different conditions: (1) with shorter (5-second) exposure; (2) with a 15-second delay; or (3) as a copying test. However, norms were originally provided only for the standard administration. For this reason, relatively little use has been made of the copying test, although the addition of this test would enrich diagnostic interpretation by separating perceptual from memory errors. In the 1963 manual, some normative data are provided for use with the shorter exposure and with the copying test; but the normative samples were smaller than that employed with the standard administration, and only crude evaluations of performance are offered.

With the standard administration, both number of correct reproductions and number of errors may be compared with the expected "normal" range for each age and intellectual level. The latter can be determined from the IQ on any standard verbal test. If no scores from such a test are available, intellectual level can be estimated from educational and vocational data. Benton scores falling more than a designated number of points below the expected level for an individual are considered significant in the clinical sense. The manual makes it clear, however, that many conditions other than pathology could account for a deviant performance on this test. To reach a diagnosis, the clinician needs corroborative data from other appropriate tests, together with information about the individual's history and background.

Several investigations have yielded significant mean differences between

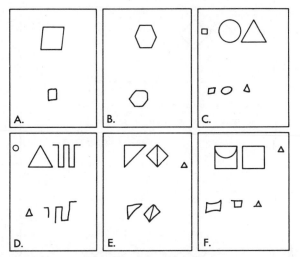

FIG. 56. Errors by a Brain-Injured Patient on Benton Visual Retention Test (Copying Administration). Upper design in each item is sample, lower is patient's copy. In addition to distortions and size errors, note omission of small peripheral figures in Drawings D and E. (From Benton, 1963, p. 61. Reproduced by permission. Copyright © 1963, The Psychological Corporation, New York, N.Y. All rights reserved.)

brain-injured and control cases in both number of correct drawings and total number of errors. While overlapping in score distributions is always present, the frequency of correct differentiations appears promising. In one comparison of 100 brain-injured and 100 control cases, for example, a cutoff score of 3 points below expected number of correct drawings identified 57 percent of the patients, with only 4 percent false positives among the controls. When the cutoff was raised to 4 points below the expected score, 36 percent of the patients and none of the controls were identified as brain-injured (Benton, 1963, pp. 49–50). Although useful in detecting brain-injury in children, the test does not differentiate as sharply when applied to children as when applied to adults. Suggestive data have also been reported on the performance of several other groups, such as schizophrenics, emotionally disturbed children, mental defectives, and persons over 65.

BENDER-GESTALT TEST. The Bender Visual Motor Gestalt Test, commonly known as the Bender-Gestalt Test, is primarily a copying test, although one of the procedural variations used by some investigators involves reproduction from memory. In this test, the nine simple designs shown in Figure 57 are presented one at a time on cards. The subject is instructed

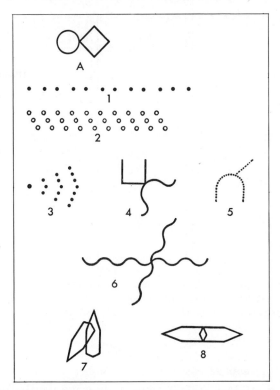

FIG. 57.   The Bender-Gestalt Test. (From Bender, 1938, p. 4; reproduced by permission of Lauretta Bender.)

to copy each design, with the sample before him. The designs were selected by Bender from a longer series originally employed by Wertheimer, one of the founders of the Gestalt school, in his studies of visual perception. The particular designs were constructed so as to illustrate certain principles of Gestalt psychology, and Bender's own analyses of the test results are formulated in terms of Gestalt concepts. Although for many years the test was administered by Bender and others to children and adults showing a variety of intellectual and emotional disorders, the data were not reported in objective and systematic form and were therefore difficult to evaluate.

While many clinicians still interpret the Bender-Gestalt Test through subjective intuitive procedures, several objective scoring systems have been developed for use with either adults or children (see Tolor & Schulberg, 1963). In one of the most carefully developed of these scoring systems, Pascal and Suttell (1951) undertook a standardization and quantification of the Bender-Gestalt Test on an *adult population*. On the basis of the drawing errors that significantly differentiated between matched samples of normals and abnormals, a relatively objective scoring key was developed. Cross validation of this key on new samples of 474 nonpatients (or normal controls), 187 neurotics, and 136 psychotics yielded the distributions shown in Figure 58. It can be seen that as a group the psychotics and neurotics are clearly differentiated from the controls, the mean scores of the three groups being 81.8, 68.2, and 50, respectively. These scores are standard scores with a mean of 50 and a σ of 10, the higher scores indicating more diagnostic errors. The biserial correlation of test scores against the criterion of patient versus nonpatient status was .74. This correlation may be regarded as a measure of concurrent criterion-related validity. There is also evidence that this adaptation of the test can significantly differentiate groups of organics from both normal and psychotic groups (Tolor & Schulberg, 1963).

Retest reliabilities of about .70 were found in normal samples over a 24-hour interval. Scorer reliabilities of approximately .90 are reported for trained scorers. Performance on the test is apparently independent of drawing ability, but is significantly related to amount of education. In this adaptation, the Bender-Gestalt Test appears to have promise as a rapid screening device, especially for detecting the more serious forms of disturbance. The normative sample, however, is rather restricted geographically, educationally, and in other ways. Extension and revision of the norms on the basis of a larger and more representative sample would be desirable. Continuing research on validity in different samples and against other criteria is also needed.

Koppitz (1964) carried out an extensive standardization of the Bender-Gestalt Test with *children*. Providing norms on 1,104 kindergarten to fourth-grade children in midwestern and eastern public schools, this adap-

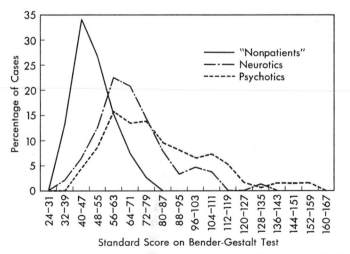

FIG. 58. Percentage Distribution of Psychotic and Neurotic Patients and Control "Non-Patient" Group on Pascal-Suttell Standardization of Bender-Gestalt Test. (Data from Pascal and Suttell, 1951, p. 30.)

tation of the Bender-Gestalt Test was prepared as a nonverbal developmental scale for ages 5 to 10. Scorer reliability appears satisfactory, the interscorer correlations varying between .88 and .96. Retest reliability over a 4-month interval within single grade groups was rather low, with coefficients ranging from .547 to .659. Between the ages of 5 and 10 years, the scores show consistent improvement with age and moderate to high correlations with standard intelligence tests. Within single-year groups, correlations ranging from .48 to .79 were found between Bender-Gestalt scores and Stanford-Binet or WISC IQ's. After the age of 10, the Bender-Gestalt no longer correlates significantly with either intelligence test scores or age, since normal persons beyond that age obtain virtually perfect scores.

Koppitz reports fairly high validities for the test in assessing school readiness and in predicting the subsequent educational achievement of first-grade children. Studies of first- and second-grade children also showed significant relationships between Bender-Gestalt scores and performance in reading and arithmetic, a relationship that Koppitz attributes to the role of visuomotor perception in the early stages of learning these subjects. Finally, evidence is given suggesting that among mentally retarded children the Bender-Gestalt developmental score has fairly high validity as a measure of intellectual level and as a predictor of academic achievement. All these analyses are based on small samples and need further verification.

Comparison of brain-injured with normal children between the ages of 5 and 10 showed significant group differences in total score on the Bender-Gestalt developmental scale. For a diagnosis of brain injury, however, Koppitz concluded that the total score should be supplemented with a number of additional observations of the child's performance, including time required, amount of space employed in reproducing the drawings, detailed analysis of individual errors, observation of the child's behavior, and inquiry into the child's awareness of his errors. All the uses of the Koppitz adaptation of the Bender-Gestalt discussed thus far are based on the developmental scoring scale. In addition, Koppitz presents a set of 10 "emotional indicators" applicable when the test is employed as a projective instrument for detecting emotional disturbances in children.

In all its forms and adaptations, the Bender-Gestalt Test has been employed extensively in both clinical practice and research, as evidenced by the large number of publications devoted to it (see Billingslea, 1963; Garron & Cheifetz, 1965; Tolor & Schulberg, 1963). Although used for a wide variety of testing purposes, its validity for most of these purposes remains largely unproved. Because of methodological limitations in the design of many published studies, negative results reported with this test are often no more conclusive than positive results. The efforts to devise and validate objective scoring systems, notably those of Pascal and Suttell with adults and Koppitz with children, show considerable promise. Significant group differences must be qualified, however, by the considerable overlapping which reduces the diagnostic effectiveness of the test for individual cases. Moreover, the group differences reported by several investigators are markedly reduced when age, intelligence, and educational level are controlled.

Whether interpreted through an objective scoring system or through the intuitive procedures preferred by many clinicians, the Bender-Gestalt Test appears to be most effective in the diagnosis of organicity with such groups as paretics, organic geriatric patients, and brain-injured mental retardates (Billingslea, 1963; Hain, 1964; Tolor & Schulberg, 1963). In young children, however, it is difficult to differentiate signs of organicity or emotional disturbance from sheer immaturity in performance on this test (Billingslea, 1963; Garron & Cheifetz, 1965; Koppitz, 1964). The test also yields moderately valid mental ages for children between the ages of 4 and 12 and for older individuals with equivalent mental ages, but not for persons with higher mental ages.

CONCEPT FORMATION TESTS

Clinical tests of conceptual thinking are more concerned with the methods employed by the subject than with the end result achieved. Largely for this reason, such tests lean heavily on qualitative observations and have thus far made little use of objective scoring and standardized norms. It is recognized, of course, that normative data would be helpful even in the interpretation of qualitative observations, but such data are difficult to obtain.

GOLDSTEIN-SCHEERER TESTS OF ABSTRACT AND CONCRETE THINKING. Developed by Goldstein and his associates as a result of their experience with brain-damaged patients during and after World War I, this series of tests still enjoys wide popularity in clinical practice. Goldstein and his coworkers concluded that the principal effect of brain damage is an impairment of the "abstract attitude." This impairment, they maintained, could be manifested in a number of ways, such as the inability to abstract common properties from objects, to grasp the essential quality of a given whole, to break up a given whole into parts, or to shift from one aspect of a situation to another. First presented in a monograph by Goldstein and Scheerer (1941), the series consists of five tests, illustrated in Figures 59 and 60 and described below:

1. *Goldstein-Scheerer Cube Test* (Fig. 59). This is an adaptation of the Kohs Block Design Test. Twelve designs are to be copied, all but one being taken from the original Kohs series. The designs are presented in increasing order of difficulty. If the patient fails to copy a design, he is given a series of aids which render the task progressively easier and less abstract. For example,

FIG. 59. Goldstein-Scheerer Stick Test, Cube Test, and Color-Form Sorting Test. (Courtesy The Psychological Corporation.)

lines are introduced on the model design to show where the blocks fit together; or a larger model design is substituted that corresponds to the size of the block design; or an exact replica in blocks is substituted for the printed model. Ability to transfer what has been learned by means of these aids to the performance of the original task is also tested.

2. *Weigl-Goldstein-Scheerer Color-Form Sorting Test.* The materials for this test consist of 12 pieces, including 4 circles, 4 squares, and 4 triangles, each shape occurring in red, green, yellow, and blue (Fig. 59). The 12 pieces are presented in random order, with the instructions to place together those that belong together. Upon completion of this task, the subject is asked to sort the pieces in another way. If the subject does not spontaneously sort the pieces according to form and color, a number of aids are provided to facilitate the task, as in the Cube test. In this test, interest is focused on the subject's ability to shift from one basis of classification to the other.

3. *Goldstein-Scheerer Stick Test.* Thirty sticks of 4 lengths are used in this test (Fig. 59). The subject is asked to copy simple geometric designs composed of sticks, and is subsequently required to reproduce the same figures from memory. The designs are presented in increasing order of difficulty. Even more than in the other tests in the series, the evaluation of performance on this test depends on the subject's oral explanation of his procedure.

4. *Gelb-Goldstein Color Sorting Test.* The woolen skeins to be sorted in this test

are shown in Figure 60. Several different shades of each color are represented. In successive parts of this test, the subject is instructed to select all the others that go with the given sample or samples. Either color or brightness may serve as the basis for classification at the abstract level; a more concrete type of performance is characterized by a simple matching procedure.

5. *Goldstein-Scheerer Object Sorting Test.* Figure 60 shows the objects employed in this test. Several different sorting situations are presented in its administration. For example, the subject is given an article selected by the examiner and is asked to pick out the others that belong with it. Or he is asked to place all the articles into groups of his own choice. The examiner also places objects into groups on some basis, such as color, form, use, etc., and asks the subject to state the basis of the classification.

While describing fairly standardized procedures for administering these tests, the authors have developed no standardized scoring system. They give general criteria for rating various levels of abstraction in the subject's responses to each test. In addition, they list a number of specific anomalies of test performance, but empirical validation of the diagnostic significance of these anomalies is meager. For some of the tests in the series, other investigators have devised objective scoring systems, chiefly on the basis of

FIG. 60. Goldstein-Scheerer Object Sorting Test and Color Sorting Test. (Courtesy The Psychological Corporation.)

research with schizophrenics. The Goldstein-Scheerer tests have been found to correlate highly with scores on standard verbal intelligence tests. For an adequate assessment of intellectual impairment, therefore, performance on the Goldstein-Scheerer tests should be evaluated against the individual's earlier intellectual level.

CONCEPT FORMATION TEST.   Hanfmann and Kasanin (1942) prepared an adaptation of an earlier object-sorting test developed by Vigotsky. In this test, commonly known as the Hanfmann-Kasanin Concept Formation Test, the subject is given the blocks pictured in Figure 61. These 22 blocks vary in color, shape, height, and surface size. A category name (nonsense syllables such as *mur*) is printed on the underside of each block, not visible to the subject in the initial presentation. The subject's task is to discover how the blocks should be classified into four groups, each corresponding to one of the four category names. At the outset, the examiner picks up a sample block, shows the subject the name on the underside, and asks him to select all blocks belonging in that class. When the subject has made an error in grouping blocks, the error is shown to him by reversing the block and exhibiting the class name. With the aid of these clues, the subject works until he arrives at the correct solution. He is then asked to state the principle of classification and to re-sort the blocks. The Hanfmann-Kasanin test is more difficult than the sorting tests in the Goldstein-Scheerer series

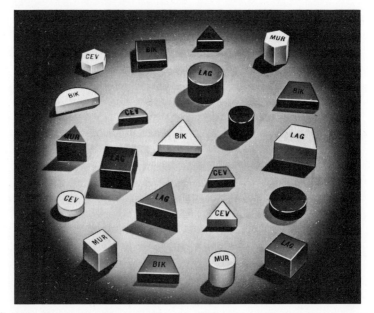

FIG. 61.   Hanfmann-Kasanin Concept Formation Test. (Courtesy C. H. Stoelting Company.)

and is not so satisfactory with persons of low intellectual level. Scoring is quite complex and requires qualitative judgments.

RESEARCH TESTS. The tests discussed in this chapter should be regarded either as relatively unstandardized aids for the skilled clinician or as research instruments. All those considered thus far have been used chiefly in clinical practice and any special materials required for their administration are commercially available. While research has been conducted with these instruments, it has generally been oriented toward the validation of the instrument itself as a diagnostic tool. It should be noted, however, that a number of tests of the same types have also been developed primarily for research purposes. Eventually some of these tests may be released for commercial distribution, when their authors feel that the normative and validation data justify such distribution. In the meantime, the tests are fully described in the research literature, and the materials can usually be obtained from the authors by properly qualified investigators. In terms of both theoretical rationale and empirical test-construction procedures, some of these research tests are clearly superior to commercially available instruments in the same area. And they show considerable promise as potential diagnostic aids. For these reasons, the reader should be alerted to this source of information about "tests in the making."

As an example of a concept formation test that has been widely employed in research, we may consider the Wisconsin Card Sorting Test (Berg, 1948; Fey, 1951; Grant, 1951; Milner, 1963, 1964). This test utilizes 64 response cards each containing from one to four figures. Four shapes are employed (stars, crosses, triangles, and circles) in any one of four colors (red, green, yellow, and blue). The figures on each response card are always of the same shape and color. In the administration of the test, four stimulus cards are presented, containing one red triangle, two green stars, three yellow crosses, and four blue circles, respectively. The subject is instructed to sort the 64 response cards into the four compartments under each stimulus card. It is apparent that the cards could be sorted according to color, form, or number. The subject must discover by trial and error which of the three is the "correct" category. His only clue is the experimenter's comment of "right" or "wrong" after each response. The "correct category" is changed periodically after a certain number of trials. The subject learns of these shifts only through the experimenter's designation of each response as "right" or "wrong."

It will be noted that this test combines the shifting frame of reference of the Weigl-Goldstein-Scheerer sorting test with the empirical discovery of categories of the Hanfmann-Kasanin tests. In studies with schizophrenic, brain-injured, and mentally retarded persons, the Wisconsin test showed promise as a diagnostic tool. Several experiments with normal subjects also contributed to an understanding of the factors involved in this categorizing function. In objectivity of administration and scoring, as well as in the number of well-controlled experiments conducted with it, this test provides a welcome contrast to others of its type.

PROBLEMS IN THE DIAGNOSIS OF ORGANICITY

As we have seen, the tests discussed in this chapter are employed in the assessment of intellectual impairment resulting from a variety of causes. Nevertheless, they have served predominantly as indices of organic involvement in both adults and children—and this application has been increasing. It is therefore appropriate at this point to consider some of the interpretive problems in the diagnosis of organicity.

THE CLASSIC PICTURE OF ORGANICITY.   Knowledge about the behavioral effects of brain damage dates largely from the writings of Kurt Goldstein and his associates in the early 1920's. Following extensive observations of young soldiers who had sustained brain injuries during World War I, Goldstein formulated his classic description of the intellectual impairment associated with brain damage. Among the principal symptoms were a diminution in the ability for abstract thought and a tendency to respond to extraneous stimuli that may disrupt normal perception. It was on the basis of these observations that Goldstein and his coworkers prepared the series of tests described in this chapter.

Widespread concern with brain injury in children arose in the late 1930's and in the 1940's, following the research of Alfred Strauss and his associates (Werner & Strauss, 1941, 1943; Strauss & Lehtinen, 1947). These investigators identified a subgroup of mentally retarded children whose case histories showed evidence of brain injury due to trauma or infection occurring before, during, or shortly after birth. The behavioral description of these children represented an extension and elaboration of the adult syndrome given by Goldstein. It delineated a distinctive pattern of both intellectual and emotional disorders that has been widely accepted as characteristic of *the* brain-injured child. Included in this pattern are specific perceptual and conceptual disorders combined with relatively high verbal ability, as well as overactivity, distractability, and aggressiveness. For many years, both research and practice with brain-injured children have been dominated by a unidimensional concept of "organicity." This approach has led to a search for diagnostic tests of organic involvement as such and an attempt to devise remedial or educational programs suitable for brain-injured children as a whole.

DIVERSITY OF BEHAVIORAL IMPAIRMENT.   It is being increasingly recognized that brain injury may lead to a wide variety of behavioral patterns

(Haynes & Sells, 1963; Robinson & Robinson, 1965, Ch. 10). No one symptom or set of symptoms need be common to all brain-injured cases. In fact, brain damage may produce the opposite behavior pattern in two individuals. Such findings are consistent with the wide diversity of the underlying organic pathology itself.

There is a growing body of evidence indicating that *age* affects the behavioral symptoms associated with brain damage. It cannot be assumed that brain damage will have the same effect in an adult, a school-age child, and an infant. The age at which the injury is sustained has a pronounced influence on the resulting behavioral disorders. In part, this relationship arises from the amount of learning and intellectual development that has occurred prior to the injury. Research on preschool children, for example, indicates that at this age level the brain-injured tend to be deficient in *all* intellectual functions (Graham, Ernhart, *et al.*, 1963). Unlike the pattern found at older ages, impairment among brain-injured preschoolers was just as great in vocabulary as in other cognitive and perceptual functions. Similarly, other studies of young children with a history of prenatal or birth trauma have found an average reduction in IQ on the Stanford-Binet and other standardized intelligence tests. Such broad intellectual impairment may occur because the brain damage itself is diffuse or because a critical deficiency in linguistic development or attention control may seriously hinder the acquisition of other abilities. It is also interesting to note that studies with brain-injured preschool children have failed to find the emotional symptoms of the classic Strauss pattern (Graham *et al.*, 1962; Graham, Ernhart, *et al.*, 1963).

From another angle, the age at which the individual is examined will also influence the results. The amount of time that has elapsed since the injury may determine the extent of behavioral recovery through learning or compensatory readjustments. Moreover, since the nature of intelligence varies at different age levels, the pattern of impairment may be differently manifested at different ages.

Another major condition affecting the behavior pattern is the *locus and extent* of the brain injury. Several generalizations about the behavioral symptoms of organicity are actually specific to lesions in certain areas. The widely quoted statement that brain-damaged persons tend to score higher on verbal than on performance tests is a case in point. Research with adults has shown that injury to the dominant cerebral hemisphere (usually the left) is associated with a greater loss in verbal than in performance tests, while injury to the nondominant hemisphere (usually the right) is associated with a greater loss in performance than in verbal tests (Guertin *et al.*, 1962, 1966; Robinson & Robinson, 1965, Ch. 10). The latter corresponds to the classic diagnostic pattern of organicity. Chronicity also affects the pattern of test performance. In general, the longer the individual has been afflicted with the brain damage to either hemisphere, the less differentiation can be made between the associated patterns of test performance. To complicate the picture still further, diffuse brain damage in adults tends to interfere more with the perceptual-spatial tasks found in performance scales than with verbal tasks. Hence, in these cases the score pattern resembles that found with right-hemisphere lesions.

Still another illustration is particularly relevant to the Benton Visual Retention Test, the Bender-Gestalt Test, and other diagnostic techniques requiring the subject to reproduce drawings. There is evidence that difficulties in copying geometric figures from memory are associated with temporal lobe lesions (see Garron & Cheifetz, 1965). In the light of all these findings, it is small wonder that inconsistent results have been reported by investigators testing general hypotheses regarding signs of organicity in heterogeneous samples.

Finally, it should be noted that in some cases intellectual impairment may be an *indirect result* of brain damage. Throughout the individual's development, organic and experiential factors interact. Some of the personality disorders included in the classic picture of brain-injured children, for example, may be an indirect effect of the frustrations and interpersonal difficulties experienced by the child with an organically caused intellectual deficiency. Whether or not these personality disorders develop may thus depend on the degree of understanding and the attitudes exhibited by parents, teachers, and other significant persons in the child's environment.

Another example of indirect effects of organic impairment is provided by the intellectual retardation often found among children with cerebral palsy (see, e.g., Sarason & Gladwin, 1959, Ch. 7). In some of these cases, the lesion extends to the cortical level. Both motor and intellectual disorders in these cases result directly from organic damage. In other cases, however, the lesion may be limited to subcortical levels, directly causing only the motor handicaps. If these motor handicaps are severe enough, they may seriously interfere with the development of speech and writing, as well as locomotion and other gross motor activities. In these cases, intellectual retardation is likely to result from educational and social handicaps. Through special educational procedures that bypass the motor handicaps, however, these children can reach a normal or even superior intellectual level, as evidenced by the impressive attainment of some cerebral-palsied individuals.

THE DIAGNOSTIC PROBLEM. It is abundantly evident that organicity covers a wide variety of organic disorders, with correspondingly diverse behavioral manifestations. The test performance of brain-injured persons can be expected to vary with the source, extent, and locus of the cerebral damage; the age at which the damage occurred; the age when the individual's behavior is being assessed; and the duration of the pathological condition. To expect behavioral homogeneity among the brain-injured would thus be highly unrealistic. There is obviously need for much more research on the *differential diagnosis* of brain damage.

From another angle, the same intellectual or other behavioral disorder may result from organic factors in one person and from experiential factors in another. These experiential factors, moreover, may be unrelated to the organic damage in one case and an indirect result of it in another. It follows that to interpret any specific diagnostic sign in test performance requires additional information about the individual's experiential background and his personal history.

Tests for organicity can be most effectively employed to provide a description of the specific behavioral deficiencies characterizing each individual. Most commonly these deficiencies will include one or more of the following: poor attention control and distractability, disorganization of spatial perception, disorders of immediate memory, disturbances in the meaningful (as contrasted to rote) use of language, diminution in the ability to handle concepts and to think in abstract terms, and general intellectual retardation. Emotional difficulties and behavior problems may also accompany the intellectual impairment. The specific patterns of deficiencies occurring in each child must be ascertained in order to plan therapeutic and educational programs that are truly adapted to the needs of the individual.

PART 3

TESTS OF SEPARATE ABILITIES

CHAPTER 13

Measuring
Multiple Aptitudes

ONE OF the distinguishing features of contemporary psychological testing is its *differential approach* to the measurement of ability. To be sure, the general intelligence tests discussed in Part 2 are still widely used in preliminary screening and in the clinical examination of extreme deviates. Since World War II, however, there has been a rapid increase in the development and application of instruments that permit an analysis of performance with regard to different aspects of intelligence. Such instruments yield, not a single, global measure such as an IQ, but a set of scores in different aptitudes. They thus provide an intellectual *profile* showing the individual's characteristic strengths and weaknesses.

A number of events have contributed to the growing interest in differential aptitude testing. First, there has been an increasing recognition of intraindividual variation in performance on intelligence tests. Crude attempts to compare the individual's relative standing on different subtests or item groups antedated the development of multiple aptitude batteries by many years. As has been repeatedly pointed out, however, intelligence tests were not designed for this purpose. The subtests or item groups are often too unreliable to justify intraindividual comparisons. In the construction of intelligence tests, moreover, items or subtests are generally chosen to provide a unitary and internally consistent measure. In such a selection, an effort is therefore made to minimize, rather than maximize, intraindividual variation. Subtests or items that correlate very low with the rest of the scale would, in general, be excluded. Yet these are the very parts that would probably have been retained if the emphasis had been on the differentiation of abilities. Because of the way in which intelligence tests are constructed, it is unlikely that performance on these tests can be significantly differentiated into more than two categories, such as verbal and nonverbal or linguistic and quantitative.

The development of multiple aptitude batteries has been further stimulated by the gradual realization that so-called general intelligence tests are in fact less general than was originally supposed. It soon became apparent that many such tests were primarily measures of verbal comprehension. Certain areas, such as that of mechanical abilities, were usually untouched, except in some of the performance and nonlanguage scales. As these limitations of intelligence tests became evident, psychologists began to qualify the term "intelligence." Distinctions between "academic" and "practical" intelligence were suggested by some. Others spoke of "abstract," "mechanical" and "social" intelligence. Tests of "special aptitudes" were likewise designed to supplement the intelligence tests. But closer analysis showed that the intelligence tests themselves could be said to measure a certain combination of special aptitudes, such as verbal and numerical aptitudes, although the area covered by these tests was loosely and inconsistently defined.

A strong impetus to differential aptitude testing was also provided by the growing activities of psychologists in vocational counseling, as well as in the selection and classification of industrial and military personnel. The early development of specialized tests in clerical, mechanical, and other vocational areas is a reflection of such interests. The assembling of test batteries for the selection of applicants for admission to schools of medicine, law, engineering, dentistry, and other professional fields represents a similar development which has been in progress for many years. Moreover, a number of differential aptitude batteries, such as those prepared by the armed services and by the United States Employment Service, were the direct result of vocational selection or classification work.

Finally, the application of factor analysis to the study of trait organization provided the theoretical basis for the construction of multiple aptitude batteries. Through factor-analytic techniques, the different abilities loosely grouped under "intelligence" could be more systematically identified, sorted, and defined. Tests could then be selected so that each represented the best available measure of one of the traits or factors identified by factor analysis.

FACTOR ANALYSIS

THE FACTOR MATRIX.   The principal object of factor analysis is to simplify the description of data by reducing the number of necessary variables, or dimensions. Thus if we find that five factors are sufficient to account for all the common variance in a battery of 20 tests, we can for most purposes substitute 5 scores for the original 20 without sacrificing any essential information. The usual practice is to retain from among the original tests those providing the best measures of each of the factors.

All techniques of factor analysis begin with a complete table of intercorrelations among a set of tests. Such a table is known as a correlation matrix. Every factor analysis ends with a factor matrix, i.e., a table showing the weight or loading of each of the factors in each test. A hypothetical factor matrix involving only two factors is shown in Table 31. The factors are listed across the top and their weights in each of the 10 tests are given in the appropriate rows.

TABLE 31 A HYPOTHETICAL FACTOR MATRIX

Test	Factor I	Factor II
1. Vocabulary	.74	.54
2. Analogies	.64	.39
3. Sentence Completion	.68	.43
4. Disarranged Sentences	.32	.23
5. Reading Comprehension	.70	.50
6. Addition	.22	−.51
7. Multiplication	.40	−.50
8. Arithmetic Problems	.52	−.48
9. Equation Relations	.43	−.37
10. Number Series Completion	.32	−.25

Several different methods for analyzing a set of variables into common factors have been derived. As early as 1901, Pearson (1901) pointed the way for this type of analysis. Kelley (1935) and Thurstone (1947) in America and Burt (1941) in England did much to advance the method. Alternative procedures, modifications, and refinements have been developed by many others. The availability of electronic computers is rapidly leading to the adoption of more refined and laborious techniques. Although differing in their initial postulates, most of these methods yield similar results. Currently the most widely used technique, especially in America, is the centroid method formulated by Thurstone (1947). The factor matrix given in Table 31 is typical of those found by this method. For brief and simple introductions to the specific procedures of factor analysis, consult Guilford (1954, Ch. 16) and Adcock (1954).

It is beyond the scope of this book to cover the mathematical basis or the computational procedures of factor analysis. An understanding of the results of factor analysis, however, need not be limited to those who have mastered its specialized methodology. Even without knowing how the factor loadings were computed, it is possible to see how a factor matrix is utilized in the identification and interpretation of factors. For an intelligent reading of reports of factor-analytic research, however, familiarity with a few other concepts and terms is helpful.

THE REFERENCE AXES.   It is customary to represent factors geometrically as reference axes in terms of which each test can be plotted. Figure 62 illustrates this procedure. In this graph, each of the 10 tests from Table 31 has been plotted against the two factors, which correspond to axes I and II. Thus, the point representing Test 1 is located by moving .74 of the distance along axis I and .54 of the distance along axis II. The points corresponding to the remaining 9 tests are plotted in the same way, using the weights given in Table 31. Although all the weights on Factor I are positive, it will be noted that on Factor II some of the weights are positive and some negative. This can also be seen in Figure 62, where Tests 1 to 5 cluster in one part of the graph and Tests 6 to. 10 in another.

In this connection it should be noted that the position of the reference axes is not fixed by the data. The original correlation table determines only the position of the tests (points in Figure 62) *in relation to each other*. The same points can be plotted with the reference axes in any position. For this reason, factor analysts usually rotate axes until they obtain the most satisfactory and easily interpretable pattern. This is a legitimate procedure, somewhat analogous to measuring longitude from, let us say, Chicago rather than Greenwich.

The reference axes in Figure 62 were rotated to positions I' and II', shown by the broken lines.[1] This rotation was carried out in accordance

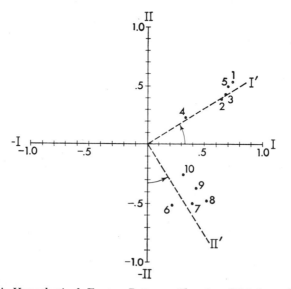

FIG. 62.   A Hypothetical Factor Pattern, Showing Weights of Two Group Factors in Each of Ten Tests.

[1] The reader may feel that rotated axis II' should have been labeled —II', to correspond to the unrotated axis —II. Which pole of the axis is labeled plus and which minus, however, is an arbitrary matter. In the present example, the rotated axis II' has been "reflected" in order to eliminate negative weights.

with Thurstone's criteria of *positive manifold* and *simple structure*. The former requires the rotation of axes to such a position as to eliminate all significant negative weights. Most psychologists regard negative factor loadings as inapplicable to aptitude tests, since such a loading implies that the higher the individual rates in the particular factor, the poorer will be his performance on the test. The criterion of simple structure means that each test shall have loadings on as few factors as possible. Both of these criteria are designed to yield factors that can be most readily and unambiguously interpreted. If a test has a high loading on a single factor and no significant loading on any other, we can learn something about the nature of the factor by examining the content of the test. If instead the test has moderate to low loadings on six factors, it can tell us little about the nature of any of these factors.

It will be seen that on the rotated axes in Figure 62 all the verbal tests (Tests 1 to 5) fall along or very close to axis I'. Similarly, the numerical tests (Tests 6 to 10) cluster closely around axis II'. The new factor loadings, measured along the rotated axes, are given in Table 32. The reader

TABLE 32 ROTATED FACTOR MATRIX

(Data from Figure 62)

Test	Factor I'	Factor II'
1. Vocabulary	.91	−.06
2. Analogies	.75	.02
3. Sentence Completion	.80	.00
4. Disarranged Sentences	.39	−.02
5. Reading Comprehension	.86	−.04
6. Addition	−.09	.55
7. Multiplication	.07	.64
8. Arithmetic Problems	.18	.68
9. Equation Relations	.16	.54
10. Number Series Completion	.13	.38

may easily verify these factor loadings by preparing a paper "ruler" with a scale of units corresponding to that in Figure 62. With this ruler, distances can be measured along the rotated axes. The factor loadings in Table 32 include no negative values except for very low, negligible amounts attributable to sampling errors. All of the verbal tests have high loadings on Factor I' and practically zero loadings on Factor II'. The numerical tests, on the other hand, have high loadings on Factor II' and low, negligible loadings on Factor I'. The identification and naming of the two factors and the description of the factorial composition of each test have thus been simplified by the rotation of reference axes. In actual practice, the number of factors is often greater than two—a condition that complicates the geometrical representation as well as the statistical analysis, but does not alter the basic procedure. The fact that factor patterns are rarely as clear-cut as the one illustrated in Figure 62 adds further to the difficulty of rotating axes and of identifying factors.

INTERPRETATION OF FACTORS. Once the rotated factor matrix has been computed, we can proceed with the interpretation and naming of factors. This step calls for psychological insight rather than statistical training. To learn the nature of a particular factor, we simply examine the tests having high loadings on that factor and we try to discover what psychological processes they have in common. The more tests there are with high loadings on a given factor, the more clearly we can define the nature of the factor. In Table 32, for example, it is apparent that Factor I' is verbal and Factor II' is numerical.

Factor loadings also represent the correlation of each test with the factor. It will be recalled that this correlation is the factorial validity of the test (Ch. 5). From Table 32 we can say, for instance, that the factorial validity of the Vocabulary test as a measure of the verbal factor is .91. The factorial validity of the Addition test, in terms of the numerical factor, is .55. Obviously the first five tests have negligible validity as measures of the numerical factor, and the last five have practically no validity as measures of the verbal factor. The concept of factorial validity is especially relevant to the type of tests to be discussed in this chapter.

FACTORIAL COMPOSITION OF A TEST. One of the two basic theorems of factor analysis states that the total variance of a test is the sum of the variances contributed by the common factors (shared with other tests) and the specific factors (occurring in that test alone), plus the error variance. We have already encountered the error variance in this analysis of test scores (Ch. 4). If, for instance, the reliability coefficient of a test is .83, we conclude that 17 percent of the variance of scores on this test is error variance ($1.00 - .83 = .17$). Through factor analysis, we can further subdivide the sources of variance contributing toward performance on any test.

Let us consider the two tests listed in Table 33. For each test, we have its factor loading in Verbal (V), Numerical (N), and Reasoning (R) factors, as well as its reliability coefficient. Since each factor loading also represents the correlation between the test and the factor, the square of the factor loading gives us the proportion of common variance between the test and that factor. In the last section of the table, each factor loading has been squared to show the proportional contribution of that factor to the total variance of test scores. Thus, we find that in the Arithmetic Reasoning test 16 percent of the variance is attributable to the Verbal factor, 30 percent to the Numerical factor, and 36 percent to the Reasoning factor. The error variance in the last column is found by simply subtracting the reliabil-

TABLE 33 SOURCE OF VARIANCE OF TEST SCORES

Test	Common Factor Loadings			Reliability Coefficient	Proportional Contribution				
	V	N	R		V	N	R	Specific	Error
1. Arithmetic Reasoning	.40	.55	.60	.90	.16	.30	.36	.08	.10
2. Multiplication	.10	.70	.30	.85	.01	.49	.09	.26	.15

ity coefficient from the total variance ($1.00 - .90 = .10$). Whatever is left represents the specificity of this test, i.e., that portion of its "true" variance it does not share with any other test with which it was factor analyzed. For the Arithmetic Reasoning test, we have:

$$.16 + .30 + .36 + .10 = .92$$
$$1.00 - .92 = .08$$

Figure 63 provides a pictorial breakdown of the sources of variance for the two tests of Table 33.

Any individual's performance on these two tests depends on the amounts of each of the relevant abilities or factors he possesses, as well as the relative weights of these factors in the particular test. Thus, if we had the individual's score in the V, N, and R factors, expressed in the same units, we could weight each score by multiplying it by the corresponding factor loading. The sum of these products would provide an estimate of the individual's score on the test. The smaller the contribution of specific and error factors to the test, the more accurate would this estimate be.

In the example given in Table 33, if an individual rates very high in V, this would help him much more on the Arithmetic Reasoning than on the

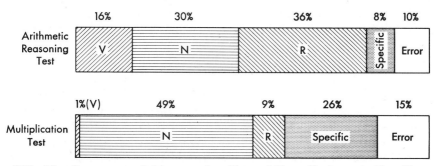

FIG. 63. Percentage of Common, Specific, and Error Variance in Two Hypothetical Tests. (Data from Table 33.)

Multiplication test. In fact, it would help him four times as much, since the weight of the V factor is four times as great in Arithmetic Reasoning as in Multiplication (.40 vs. .10). Of the three common factors, N would have the greatest effect on Multiplication (loading = .70) and R would have the greatest effect on Arithmetic Reasoning (loading = .60).

FACTOR LOADINGS AND CORRELATION. The second basic theorem of factor analysis concerns the relationship between factor loadings and the correlations among variables. The correlation between any two variables is equal to the sum of the cross-products of their common-factor loadings. Since specific and error factors are unique to each variable, they cannot contribute to the correlation between variables. The correlation between any two variables depends only on the factors that these two variables share. The larger the weights of these common factors in the two variables, the higher will be the correlation between the variables. The correlation between the two tests given in Table 33 can be found by multiplying the loadings of each of the three common factors in the two tests and adding the products, as shown below:

$$r_{12} = (.40)(.10) + (.55)(.70) + (.60)(.30) = .60$$

OBLIQUE AXES AND SECOND-ORDER FACTORS. The axes employed in Figure 62 are known as *orthogonal axes*, since they are at right angles to each other. Occasionally, the test clusters are so situated that a better fit can be obtained with *oblique axes*. In such a case, the factors would themselves be correlated. Some investigators have maintained that orthogonal, or uncorrelated, factors should always be employed, since they provide a simpler and clearer picture of trait relationships. Others insist that oblique axes should be used when they fit the data better, since the most meaningful categories need not be uncorrelated. An example cited by Thurstone is that of height and weight. Although it is well known that height and weight are highly correlated, they have proved to be useful categories in the measurement of physique.

When the factors are themselves correlated, it is possible to subject the intercorrelations among the factors to the same statistical analyses we employ with intercorrelations among tests. In other words, we can "factorize the factors" and derive *second-order factors*. This process has been followed in a number of studies with both aptitude and personality variables. Certain investigations with aptitude tests have yielded a single second-order general factor. As a rule, American factor analysts have proceeded by accounting for as much of the common variance as possible through group factors and then identifying a general factor as a second-order factor if the data justified it. British psychologists, on the other hand, usually begin with a general factor, to which they attribute the major portion of the common variance, and then resort to group factors to account for any remaining correlation. These procedural differences reflect differences in theoretical orientation to be discussed in the following section.

THEORIES OF TRAIT ORGANIZATION

THE TWO-FACTOR THEORY. The first theory of trait organization based on a statistical analysis of test scores was the two-factor theory developed by the British psychologist Charles Spearman (1904, 1927). In its original formulation, this theory maintained that all intellectual activities share a single common factor, called the *general factor*, or *g*. In addition, the theory postulated numerous *specifics*, or *s* factors, each being strictly specific to a single activity. Positive correlation between any two functions was thus attributed to the *g* factor. The more highly the two functions were "saturated" with *g*, the higher would be the correlation between them. The presence of specifics, on the other hand, tended to lower the correlation between functions.

Although two types of factors, general and specific, are posited by this theory, it is only the single factor *g* that accounts for correlation. In contrast to other theories of trait relations, therefore, it could be more distinctly characterized as a single-factor theory, although the original designation has persisted. Figure 64 illustrates the basis for correlation among tests according to this theory. In this illustration, tests 1 and 2 would correlate highly with each other since each is highly saturated with *g*, as shown by the shaded areas. The white area in each test represents specific and error variance. Test 3 would have low correlations with each of the other two tests, since it contains very little *g*.

It follows from the two-factor theory that the aim of psychological testing should be to measure the amount of each individual's *g*. If this factor runs through all abilities, it furnishes the only basis for prediction of the

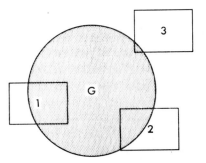

FIG. 64. Correlation Model Underlying Two-Factor Theory.

individual's performance from one situation to another. It would be futile to measure specific factors, since each by definition operates in only a single activity. Accordingly, Spearman proposed that a single test, highly saturated with *g*, be substituted for the heterogeneous collection of items found in intelligence tests. He suggested that tests dealing with abstract relations are probably the best measures of *g* and could be used for this purpose. Examples of tests constructed as measures of *g* include Raven's Progressive Matrices and Cattell's Culture Fair Intelligence Test, both discussed in Chapter 10.

From the outset, Spearman realized that the two-factor theory must be qualified. When the activities compared are very similar, a certain degree of correlation may result over and above that attributable to the *g* factor. Thus, in addition to general and specific factors, there might be another, intermediate class of factors, not so universal as *g* nor so strictly specific as the *s* factors. Such a factor, common to a group of activities but not to all, has been designated as a *group factor*. In the early formulation of his theory Spearman admitted the possibility of very narrow and negligibly small group factors. Following later investigations by several of his students, he included much broader group factors such as arithmetic, mechanical, and linguistic abilities.

MULTIPLE-FACTOR THEORIES. The prevalent contemporary American view of trait organization recognizes a number of moderately broad group factors, each of which may enter with different weights into different tests. For example, a verbal factor may have a large weight in a vocabulary test, a smaller weight in an analogies test, and a still smaller weight in an arithmetic reasoning test. Figure 65 illustrates the intercorrelations among five tests in terms of a multiple-factor model. The correlations of tests 1, 2, and

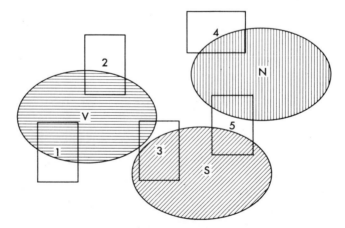

FIG. 65.   Correlation Model Underlying Multiple-Factor Theories.

3 with each other result from their common loadings with the verbal factor (V). Similarly, the correlation between tests 3 and 5 results from the Spatial factor (S), and that between tests 4 and 5 from the Number factor (N). Tests 3 and 5 are factorially complex, each having appreciable loadings in more than one factor: V and S in test 3, N and S in test 5. From the second basic theorem of factor analysis, discussed in the preceding section, we can also tell something about the relative magnitude of the intercorrelations. For example, test 3 will correlate higher with test 5 than with test 2 because the weights of the S factor in tests 3 and 5 (represented by the overlapping areas) are larger than the weights of the V factor in tests 2 and 3.

The publication of Kelley's *Crossroads in the Mind of Man* (1928) paved the way for a large number of studies in quest of particular group factors. Chief among the factors proposed by Kelley were manipulation of spatial relationships, facility with numbers, facility with verbal material, memory, and speed. This list has been modified and extended by subsequent investigators employing the more modern methods of factor analysis discussed in the preceding section.

One of the leading exponents of multiple-factor theory was Thurstone. On the basis of extensive research by himself and his students, Thurstone proposed about a dozen group factors which he designated as "primary mental abilities." Those most frequently corroborated in the work of Thurstone and of other independent investigators (French, 1951; Thurstone, 1938; Thurstone & Thurstone, 1941) include the following:

V. *Verbal Comprehension:* The principal factor in such tests as reading comprehension, verbal analogies, disarranged sentences, verbal reasoning, and proverb matching. It is most adequately measured by vocabulary tests.

W. *Word Fluency:* Found in such tests as anagrams, rhyming, or naming words in a given category (e.g., boys' names, words beginning with the letter T).

N. *Number:* Most closely identified with speed and accuracy of simple arithmetic computation.

S. *Space:* It is possible that this factor may represent two distinct factors, one covering perception of fixed spatial or geometric relations, the other manipulatory visualization, in which changed positions or transformations must be visualized. There is also evidence of a third factor of "kinaesthetic imagery" (Michael *et al.*, 1957).

M. *Associative Memory:* Found principally in tests demanding rote memory for paired associates. There is some evidence to suggest that this factor may reflect the extent to which memory crutches are utilized (Christal, 1958). The evidence is against the presence of a broader factor through all memory tests. Other restricted memory factors, such as memory for temporal sequences and for spatial position, have been suggested by some investigations.

P. *Perceptual Speed:* Quick and accurate grasping of visual details, similarities, and differences. This factor may be the same as the speed factor identified by

Kelley and other early investigators. This is one of several factors subsequently identified in perceptual tasks (Thurstone, 1944).

I   (or R). *Induction* (or *General Reasoning*): The identification of this factor was least clear. Thurstone originally proposed an inductive and a deductive factor. The latter was best measured by tests of syllogistic reasoning and the former by tests requiring the subject to find a rule, as in a number series completion test. Evidence for the deductive factor, however, was much weaker than for the inductive. Moreover, other investigators suggest a general reasoning factor, best measured by arithmetic reasoning tests (Kettner, Guilford, & Christensen, 1956).

It should be noted that the distinction between general, group, and specific factors is not so basic as may at first appear. If the number or variety of tests in a battery is small, a single general factor may account for all the correlations among them. But when the same tests are included in a larger battery with a more heterogeneous collection of tests, the original general factor may emerge as a group factor, common to some but not all tests. Similarly, a certain factor may be represented by only one test in the original battery, but may be shared by several tests in the larger battery. Such a factor would have been identified as a specific in the original battery, but would become a group factor in the more comprehensive battery. In the light of these considerations, it is not surprising to find that intensive factorial investigations of special areas have yielded many factors in place of the one or two primary mental abilities originally identified in each area. Such has been the case in studies of verbal, perceptual, memory, and reasoning tests.

Factorial research seems to have produced a bewildering multiplication of factors. The number of cognitive factors reported to date by different investigators is well over 100. A certain amount of order has been achieved by cross-identification of factors reported by different investigators and often given different names (French, 1951). Such cross-identification can be accomplished when there are several tests common to the investigations being compared. To facilitate this process, a group of factor analysts assembled a kit of "reference tests" measuring the principal aptitude factors so far identified. This kit, which is distributed by Educational Testing Service (French, Ekstrom, & Price, 1963), makes it easier for different investigators planning factorial research to include some common tests in their batteries. The kit covers 24 cognitive factors, with two to five tests for measuring each factor.

It is apparent that even after these efforts at simplification and coordination, the number of factors remains large. Human behavior is varied and complex, and perhaps it is unrealistic to expect a dozen or so factors to provide an adequate description of it. For specific purposes, however, we can choose appropriate factors with regard to both nature and breadth.

For example, if we are selecting applicants for a difficult and highly specialized mechanical job, we would probably want to measure fairly narrow perceptual and spatial factors that closely match the job requirements. In selecting college students, on the other hand, a few broad factors such as verbal comprehension, numerical facility, and general reasoning would be most relevant. Illustrations of the different ways in which factorial results have been utilized in test development will be given later in this chapter.

STRUCTURE-OF-INTELLECT MODEL. Some factor analysts have tried to simplify the picture of trait relationships by organizing the traits into a systematic schema. On the basis of more than two decades of factor-analytic research, Guilford (1967) has proposed a boxlike model which he calls the structure-of-intellect model (SI). Illustrated in Figure 66, this model classifies intellectual traits along three dimensions:

Operations—what the respondent does. These include cognition, memory, divergent production (prominent in creative activity), convergent production, and evaluation.

Contents—the nature of the materials or information on which operations are performed. These include figural, symbolic (e.g., letters, numbers), semantic (e.g., words), and behavioral (information about other persons' behavior, attitudes, needs, etc.).

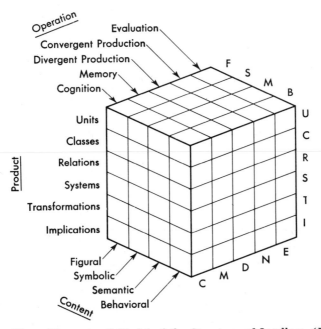

FIG. 66.   Three-Dimensional Model of the Structure of Intellect. (From Guilford, 1967, p. 63.)

Products—the form in which information occurs or is conceived by the respondent. Products are classified into units, classes, relations, systems, transformations, and implications.

Since this classification includes 5 × 4 × 6 categories, there are 120 cells in the model. In each cell, at least one factor or ability is expected; some cells may contain more than one factor. Each factor is described in terms of all three dimensions. The well-known factor of verbal comprehension, for example, corresponds to cognition of semantic units and is best measured by vocabulary tests. A memory-span test utilizing series of unrelated letters or numbers corresponds to memory for symbolic units.

HIERARCHICAL THEORIES. An alternative schema for the organization of factors has been proposed by a number of British psychologists, including Burt (1949) and Vernon (1960), and by Humphreys (1962) in America. A diagram illustrating Vernon's application of this system is reproduced in Figure 67. At the top of the hierarchy, Vernon places Spearman's *g* factor. At the next level are two broad group factors, corresponding to verbal-educational (*v:ed*) and to practical-mechanical (*k:m*) aptitudes, respectively. These major factors may be further subdivided. The verbal-educational factor, for example, yields verbal and numerical subfactors. Similarly, the practical-mechanical factor splits into mechanical-information, spatial, and manual subfactors. Still narrower subfactors can be identified by further analysis, let us say, of the verbal tasks. At the lowest level of the hierarchy are the specific factors. Such a hierarchical structure thus resembles a genealogical tree, with *g* at the top, *s* factors at the bottom, and progressively narrower group factors in between.

Humphreys (1962) also recommends a hierarchical model as a means of coping with the proliferation of factors. Rather than considering the first-order, narrower factors as primary, he suggests that each test constructor or user choose that level of the hierarchy that is most appropriate

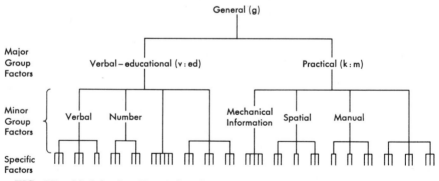

FIG. 67. Model of a Hierarchical Organization of Abilities. (Adapted from Vernon, 1960, p. 22. Copyright 1960, Methuen & Co., Ltd.)

for his purposes. Humphreys recognizes, however, that a single test may be classified into more than one hierarchy, with reference to content, method, and other facets. To measure any one facet, he proposes that the test be made *heterogeneous* with regard to all other facets. For example, if we are interested in the subject's ability to solve analogies problems, we should use a test that includes verbal, numerical, pictorial, and spatial analogies. If we wish to measure verbal ability, we should do so with a variety of item types, such as vocabulary, analogies, series completion, etc. This procedure contrasts with that followed by Guilford, who seeks separate factors (and tests) for each homogeneous cell in his three-way classification.

NATURE AND DEVELOPMENT OF FACTORS. That different investigators may arrive at dissimilar schemas of trait organization becomes less perplexing when we recognize that the traits identified through factor analysis are simply an expression of correlation among behavior measures. They are not underlying entities or causal factors, but descriptive categories. Hence, it is conceivable that different principles of classification may be applicable to the same data.

The concept of factors as descriptive categories is explicit in the writings of Thomson (1916, 1948), Burt (1941, 1944), and Vernon (1960) in England, and those of Tryon (1935) in America. All these writers called attention to the vast multiplicity of behavioral elements, which may become organized into clusters through either hereditary or experiential linkages. For example, persons in our culture are likely to develop a broad verbal-educational factor running through all activities learned in school. A narrower factor of numerical aptitude may result from the fact that all arithmetic processes are taught together by the same teacher in the same classroom. Hence, the child who is discouraged, antagonized, or bored during the arithmetic period will tend to fall behind in his learning of *all* these processes; the one who is stimulated and gratified in his arithmetic class will tend to learn well all that is taught in that class period and to develop attitudes that will advance his subsequent numerical learning.

There has been an increasing recognition of the role of experiential conditions in the formation of group factors. It is not only the level of performance in different abilities, but also the way in which performance is organized into distinct traits that is influenced by experiential background. Differences in factor patterns have been found to be associated with different cultures or subcultures, socioeconomic levels, and types of school curricula (see Anastasi, 1967). Changes in factor patterns over time are also relevant. These include long-term changes—which may reflect the cumulative effect of everyday-life experiences—as well as short-term changes resulting from experimentally controlled learning experiences. Research on animals has also yielded suggestive evidence regarding the experimental production of factors by the control of early experiences (Whimbey & Denenberg, 1966).

The factorial composition of the same objective task may differ among individuals with diverse experiential backgrounds. One reason for these individual differences may be found in the use of different methods to carry out the same task. Individuals with highly developed verbal abilities, for example, will tend to utilize verbal procedures to solve a mechanical or spatial problem; those whose experiences have been predominantly mechanical, on the other hand, will tend to follow a perceptual or spatial approach in solving the same problem. Relevant evidence is provided by French (1965), who found that the factorial composition of the same tests differed between groups of persons classified according to their typical problem-solving styles.

A mechanism for the emergence of factors is provided by the familiar concepts of learning set and transfer of training (Carroll, 1966; Ferguson, 1954, 1956; Whiteman, 1964). The establishment of learning sets enables the individual to learn more efficiently when presented with a new problem of the same kind. In Harlow's (1949, 1960) classic experiments with monkeys, after the animal had solved problems requiring the differentiation between certain shapes (like triangle and circle), it learned to discriminate between *other* shapes much more rapidly than did animals without such prior experience. The animal had established a learning set for differentiating shapes; he knew what to look for when faced with a new problem. He had thus "learned how to learn" this type of problem.

Similarly, many of the skills developed through formal schooling, such as reading and arithmetic computation, are applicable to a wide variety of subsequent learning situations. Efficient and systematic problem-solving techniques can likewise be applied to the solution of new problems. Individual differences in the extent to which these skills have been acquired will thus be reflected in the performance of a large number of different tasks; and in a factor analysis of these tasks, these widely applicable skills would emerge as broad group factors. The breadth of the transfer effect, or the variety of tasks to which a skill is applicable, would thus determine the breadth of the resulting group factor.

In summary, the factors or abilities identified through factor analysis are descriptive categories, reflecting the changing interrelationships of performance in a variety of situations. These factors are not static entities but are themselves the product of the individual's cumulative experiential history. Insofar as the interrelationships of experiences vary among individuals and groups, different factor patterns may be expected among them. As the individual's experiences change—through formal education, occupational functions, and other continuing activities—new traits may become differentiated or previously existing traits may merge into broader composites.

MULTIPLE APTITUDE BATTERIES FOR GENERAL USE

SRA PRIMARY MENTAL ABILITIES. One of the major effects of factor analysis on test construction can be seen in the development of multiple aptitude batteries. These batteries yield a profile of test scores in a set of relatively independent abilities identified through factor-analytic research. The Chicago Tests of Primary Mental Abilities (PMA) represent the first systematic effort to construct such a battery. Originally published in 1941, this battery was the direct outcome of Thurstone's previously described factor-analytic investigations. For each factor, Thurstone selected those tests with the highest factorial validities. This battery, designed principally for the high school and college levels, required six testing sessions.

Later versions of the PMA tests, published by Science Research Associates, were characterized chiefly by reduction in length and extension to younger age levels. These tests were marred by a number of technical deficiencies, which have been fully discussed in a series of reviews in the *Mental Measurements Yearbooks*, as well as in other critical surveys (e.g., Super, 1958). The chief criticisms pertained to inadequacies of normative data, questionable types of scores (such as ratio IQ's), unsupported interpretations of scores in terms of educational and vocational criteria, meager validity data, improper procedures for computing the reliability of speeded tests, excessive dependence of scores on speed, and low reliabilities of certain factor scores.

In a 1962 revision of the PMA tests, some of these technical deficiencies were corrected. The tests are now available in a series of five batteries extending from kindergarten to grade 12.[2] Separate scores are obtained in five factors: Verbal Meaning, Number Facility, Reasoning, Perceptual Speed, and Spatial Relations. However, all five factors are included only in the battery for grades 4–6. Reasoning is omitted at the lower levels and Perceptual Speed is omitted at the higher levels. Scores on each factor, as well as total scores on the entire battery, are expressed as deviation IQ's. The manual explains, however, that owing to teachers' demand for mental ages at the lower grade levels, all scores in the kindergarten–grade 1 battery are expressed as ratio IQ's, and both ratio and deviation IQ's are provided for the grade 2–4 battery. This is strange reasoning indeed. One wonders why the publishers could not have provided mental ages as a supplementary measure, while retaining the uniform standard deviation unit for the IQ's. It will be recalled that this was the practice followed with the WISC and WPPSI to meet the practical demand for mental ages. Scores on the PMA batteries from the fourth grade up can also be expressed as percentiles and stanines, used in plotting individual profiles.

[2] The booklet for grades 9–12 is also printed with a differently colored cover labeled "Adult."

The standardization sample of the 1962 PMA consisted of 32,393 pupils in 73 public schools, approximately stratified as to major geographical region and school size. Reliability coefficients were computed in small homogeneous grade groups on the basis of 1-week and 4-week retests. Since the identical form was employed in retesting, recall of specific answers may have spuriously raised these reliabilities. For total battery scores, the reliabilities appear satisfactory, ranging from .83 to .95. Reliabilities of factor scores vary with the particular factor and the grade level, several being too low to justify much confidence in the scores. The extensive fluctuations in the values of these reliabilities undoubtedly reflect the large sampling errors resulting from small sample size. For example, the ninth-grade Spatial Relations scores yielded a reliability of .53 in the 1-week retest and a reliability of .89 in the 4-week retest (*PMA Technical Report*, p. 15).

Correlations of the PMA tests with achievement tests and school grades indicate moderate to high predictive validity of the total battery scores but give little or no evidence of differential validity of factor scores, particularly at the elementary school levels. In general, multiple aptitude batteries contribute little at the elementary school ages, when abilities tend to be highly intercorrelated. It is not until the high school level that the differentiation of abilities has progressed far enough to justify the practical use of multiple aptitude batteries.

While the 1962 revision of the PMA tests, together with the 1965 *Technical Report*, represents an appreciable technical advance over the earlier editions, it still falls short of the technical standards set by other contemporary tests of its kind. The original Thurstone tests were based on extensive factor-analytic research and represented an important breakthrough in test construction. The present version differs in so many ways from the original series, however, that it needs to be evaluated on its own merits.

THE DIFFERENTIAL APTITUDE TESTS.   First published in 1947, the Differential Aptitude Tests (DAT) are currently available in a 1963 revision and restandardization. This battery was designed principally for use in the educational and vocational counseling of students in grades 8 to 12. Although not utilizing factor analysis in its construction, the authors of the DAT were guided in their choice of tests by the accumulated results of factorial research, as well as by practical counseling needs. Rather than striving for factorial purity, they included tests that might be factorially complex if they represented well-recognized vocational or educational areas. The DAT yields the following eight scores: Verbal Reasoning, Numerical Ability, Abstract Reasoning, Clerical Speed and Accuracy, Mechanical Reasoning, Space Relations, Language Usage I—Spelling, and Language Usage II—Grammar. A sample item from each test is reproduced in Figures 68A and 68B. The complete battery is available in two equivalent forms, L and M.

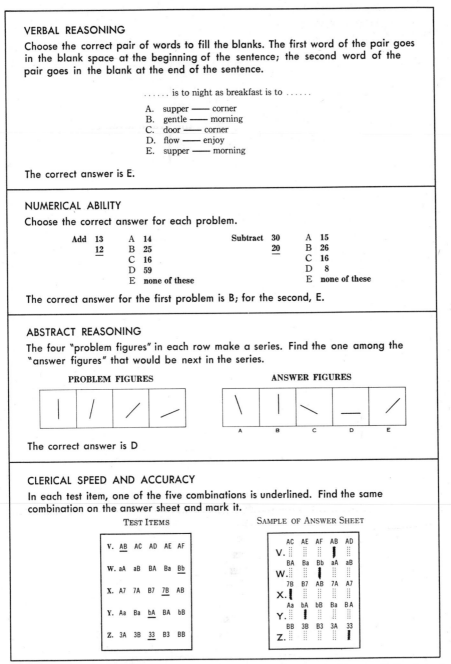

VERBAL REASONING

Choose the correct pair of words to fill the blanks. The first word of the pair goes in the blank space at the beginning of the sentence; the second word of the pair goes in the blank at the end of the sentence.

...... is to night as breakfast is to ......

A. supper —— corner
B. gentle —— morning
C. door —— corner
D. flow —— enjoy
E. supper —— morning

The correct answer is E.

NUMERICAL ABILITY

Choose the correct answer for each problem.

Add	13	A 14	Subtract	30	A 15
	12	B 25		20	B 26
		C 16			C 16
		D 59			D 8
		E none of these			E none of these

The correct answer for the first problem is B; for the second, E.

ABSTRACT REASONING

The four "problem figures" in each row make a series. Find the one among the "answer figures" that would be next in the series.

PROBLEM FIGURES   ANSWER FIGURES

The correct answer is D

CLERICAL SPEED AND ACCURACY

In each test item, one of the five combinations is underlined. Find the same combination on the answer sheet and mark it.

TEST ITEMS

V. AB AC AD AE AF
W. aA aB BA Ba Bb
X. A7 7A B7 7B AB
Y. Aa Ba bA BA bB
Z. 3A 3B 33 B3 BB

SAMPLE OF ANSWER SHEET

V. AC AE AF AB AD
W. BA Ba Bb aA aB
X. 7B B7 AB 7A A7
Y. Aa bA bB Ba BA
Z. BB 3B B3 3A 33

FIG. 68A. Sample Items from the Differential Aptitude Tests. (Reproduced by permission. Copyright © 1961, The Psychological Corporation, New York, N.Y. All rights reserved.)

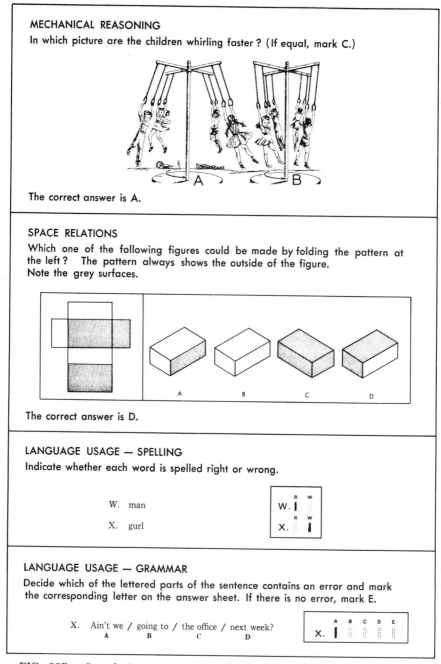

MECHANICAL REASONING
In which picture are the children whirling faster? (If equal, mark C.)

The correct answer is A.

SPACE RELATIONS
Which one of the following figures could be made by folding the pattern at the left? The pattern always shows the outside of the figure. Note the grey surfaces.

A   B   C   D

The correct answer is D.

LANGUAGE USAGE — SPELLING
Indicate whether each word is spelled right or wrong.

W. man

X. gurl

R W
W. | ::
R W
X. :: |

LANGUAGE USAGE — GRAMMAR
Decide which of the lettered parts of the sentence contains an error and mark the corresponding letter on the answer sheet. If there is no error, mark E.

X. Ain't we / going to / the office / next week?
     A   B   C   D

A B C D E
X. | :: :: :: ::

FIG. 68B. Sample Items from the Differential Aptitude Tests. (Reproduced by permission. Copyright © 1962, The Psychological Corporation, New York, N.Y. All rights reserved.)

The fourth edition of the DAT manual, published in 1966, provides a clear and thorough account of the test-construction procedures followed in developing the battery. Norms were derived from over 50,000 students attending 195 schools in 43 states. With the exception of Clerical Speed and Accuracy, all tests are essentially power tests. Reliability coefficients are high and permit interpretation of intertest differences with considerable confidence. By combining information on test reliabilities with the intercorrelations found in the standardization sample, the test authors determined the proportion of differences in excess of chance between each pair of tests. This can be done by reference to the chart reproduced in Figure 69. The percentages ranged from 16 to 53, all but a few exceeding 25 percent. In other words, for nearly all possible test pairs, one fourth or more of the standardization sample obtained larger score differences than would be expected from errors of measurement.

Both stanine and percentile norms are provided. Individual percentile scores are plotted on normalized percentile charts, thereby eliminating the inequalities of percentile units (see Fig. 10, Ch. 3). In order to facilitate the interpretation of intraindividual differences in test scores, the profile charts were designed so that a distance of 1 inch corresponds to 10 standard score points.[3] By computing the standard errors of intraindividual differences between each pair of tests, it can be shown that a difference of approximately

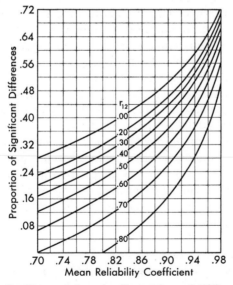

FIG. 69. Chart for Determining the Proportion of Differences in Excess of Chance between Pairs of Tests. (From Bennett and Doppelt, 1948, p. 322; reproduced by permission of *Educational and Psychological Measurement.*)

[3] This is true in the actual profile charts, not in the reduced reproduction given in Figure 10.

10 standard score points between any two tests is significant at the .05 level or better. On this basis it is recommended that if the vertical distance between any two tests on a profile is 1 inch or more, it may be assumed that a true difference exists. Differences between ½ and 1 inch are considered doubtful; and those less than ½ inch, negligible.

The amount of validity data available on the DAT is overwhelming, including several thousand validity coefficients. Most of these data are concerned with predictive validity in terms of high school achievement and (to a more limited extent) college achievement. Many of the coefficients are high, even with intervals as long as three years between test and criterion data. The results are somewhat less encouraging with regard to differential prediction. Although, in general, verbal tests correlate more highly with English courses and numerical tests with mathematics courses, there is evidence of a large general factor underlying performance in all academic work. Verbal Reasoning, for example, gives high correlations with most courses.

It is chiefly for this reason that the VR + NA score was introduced as an index of scholastic aptitude. Being the sum of the raw scores on the Verbal Reasoning and Numerical Ability subtests, this index correlates in the .70's and .80's with composite criteria of academic achievement. Norms are provided for this index, which is one of the scores regularly included in the DAT profile (see Fig. 10, Ch. 3). The manual also provides regression equations for predicting the Verbal and Mathematical scores on the CEEB Scholastic Aptitude Test from appropriate combinations of three DAT subtests. No other regression equations are given. As an aid in the clinical interpretation of profiles, however, the test authors prepared a booklet entitled *Counseling from Profiles* (Bennett, Seashore, & Wesman, 1951). This casebook describes 30 cases actually submitted by high school counselors, together with DAT profiles, to illustrate ways in which such profiles may be used in making individual recommendations.

With regard to vocational criteria, there is some evidence for the predictive validity of individual DAT subtests, but the data are relatively meager. A 4-year follow-up of 1,700 high school juniors and seniors and a 7-year follow-up of a somewhat smaller group revealed several profile differences among students who subsequently entered different educational curricula or occupations.

FLANAGAN APTITUDE CLASSIFICATION TESTS. A still different approach to the construction of multiple aptitude batteries is illustrated by the Flanagan Aptitude Classification Tests, or FACT. Beginning as an outgrowth of Flanagan's research on the development of Air Force classification tests during World War II, this battery is oriented principally toward vocational counseling and employee selection. Job analyses of many occupations led to the identification of 21 "critical job elements," or abilities differentiating successful from unsuccessful workers on each job. Any one job element is common to many types of jobs. Three examples of such job elements are given below (*FACT Technical Report,* 1959, p. 10):

Assembly: Ability to visualize the appearance of an object assembled from a number of separate parts (see Fig. 70).

Planning: Ability to plan, organize, and schedule; ability to foresee problems that may arise, and to anticipate the best order for carrying out the various steps.

Ingenuity: Creative or inventive skill; ability to devise ingenious procedures, equipment, or presentations (see Fig. 70).

A battery of paper-and-pencil tests was prepared to test 19 of the 21 job elements. For the remaining two, Carving and Tapping, performance tests are available. The 19-test battery requires a total of 10½ hours, preferably in three testing sessions. Norms were established on a national sample of approximately 11,000 students in grades 9 to 12, although the representa-

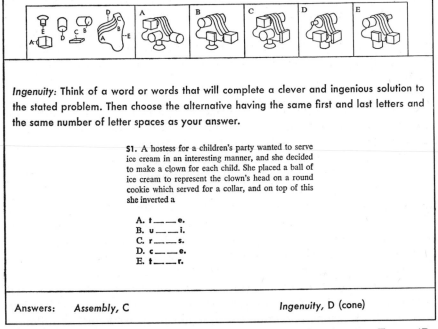

Assembly: In each figure, parts are to be assembled so that places having the same letter are put together. Which of the five assemblies below shows the parts put together correctly?

Ingenuity: Think of a word or words that will complete a clever and ingenious solution to the stated problem. Then choose the alternative having the same first and last letters and the same number of letter spaces as your answer.

S1. A hostess for a children's party wanted to serve ice cream in an interesting manner, and she decided to make a clown for each child. She placed a ball of ice cream to represent the clown's head on a round cookie which served for a collar, and on top of this she inverted a

A. t __ __ e.
B. u __ __ i.
C. r __ __ s.
D. c __ __ e.
E. t __ __ r.

Answers: *Assembly,* C   *Ingenuity,* D (cone)

FIG. 70. Sample Items from Flanagan Aptitude Classification Tests. (Reproduced by permission of John C. Flanagan.)

tiveness of the sample is questionable. On the basis of the initial, qualitative job analyses, test scores were combined into 38 Occupational Aptitude Scores, including one score for predicting general college aptitude and scores for specific occupations ranging from humanities teacher to plumber. The individual tests have rather low reliabilities and some of the score distributions suggest inadequate differentiations among individuals. Reliabilities of the composite Occupational Aptitude Scores are higher. These composite scores, however, show much more overlap than the individual test scores. Intercorrelations among the tests indicate that fairly distinct aptitudes are measured; but apparently many occupations require similar combinations of aptitudes. A correlation of .90 between the occupational scores for telephone operator and office clerk is not surprising; but a correlation of .95 between the aptitude scores of airplane pilot and draftsman suggests inadequate differential validity!

The Occupational Aptitude Scores are being validated longitudinally, by following up the subsequent educational and vocational careers of high school students tested in the standardization sample. This represents an ambitious and commendable plan. Available data from a one-year follow-up of the present form of the battery and follow-ups of earlier forms of as much as five years' duration have so far provided moderately promising evidence of validity. The battery has shown good predictive validity against professional training criteria. But validity data in terms of job entry and advancement are meager and sometimes difficult to evaluate because of criterion inadequacies and the influence of fortuitous factors in occupational careers. The continuing research program carried on with the FACT battery will eventually permit a more definitive evaluation of its contribution.

THE PROBLEM OF DIFFERENTIAL VALIDITY.   About a dozen multiple aptitude batteries have been developed for use in educational testing, counseling, and personnel classification. These instruments vary widely in approach, technical .quality, and amount of available validation data. A common feature, however, is their disappointing performance with regard to differential validity. Yet it is in terms of differential validity that the distinctive contribution of multiple factor batteries should be evaluated. It is in connection with classification decisions that these batteries find their chief practical applications. Many have been designed explicitly for counseling purposes, in which classification decisions are pre-eminent. In a counseling situation, the profile of test scores is utilized to aid the counselee in choosing among several possible fields of educational or vocational specialization. Such a choice represents a typical classification decision. Institutional decisions regarding the assignment of personnel to different jobs or the admission of students to different educational curricula likewise involve a classification strategy. It will be recalled from our earlier discussion of validity (Ch. 6) that for classification instruments it is differential validity that is of prime importance.

Perhaps academic criteria, against which most multiple aptitude batteries have so far been validated, are not clearly differentiable on the basis of aptitudes. It is possible that differences in performance in specific courses depend principally on interests, motivation, and emotional factors. Unpredictable contingency factors, such as interpersonal relations between an individual student and a particular instructor, may also play a part. With regard to aptitudes, the large common contribution of verbal comprehension to achievement in all academic areas has been repeatedly demonstrated. If dependable criteria of occupational success (rather than performance in vocational *training*) can be developed, it is likely that better differential predictions can be made with batteries designed for this purpose. In terms of available data, however, multifactor batteries have fallen short of their initial promise.

MULTIPLE APTITUDE BATTERIES
FOR SPECIAL PROGRAMS

GENERAL APTITUDE TEST BATTERY. Factor analysis underlies the development of classification batteries widely employed in the armed services and in certain civilian agencies. The General Aptitude Test Battery (GATB) was developed by the United States Employment Service (USES) for use by employment counselors in the State Employment Service offices (Dvorak, 1956; USES, 1962). Prior to the preparation of this battery, factorial analyses were conducted on preliminary batteries of 15 to 29 tests, which had been administered to nine groups of men. These groups included a total of 2,156 men between the ages of 17 and 39, most of whom were trainees in vocational courses. A total of 59 tests was covered by the nine overlapping batteries. On the basis of these investigations, 10 factors were identified and 15 tests chosen to measure them. In a later revision of the GATB, the number of tests was reduced to 12 and the number of factors to 9.

The factors currently covered by the GATB are as follows:

G. *Intelligence:* Found by adding the scores on three tests also used to measure other factors (Vocabulary, Arithmetic Reason, Three-Dimensional Space).

V. *Verbal Aptitude:* Measured by a Vocabulary test requiring examinee to indicate which two words in each set have either the same or opposite meaning.

N. *Numerical Aptitude:* Includes both Computation and Arithmetic Reason tests.

S. *Spatial Aptitude:* Measured by Three-Dimensional Space test, involving the ability to comprehend two-dimensional representation of three-dimensional objects and to visualize effects of movement in three dimensions.

P. *Form Perception:* Measured by two tests requiring the examinee to match identical drawings of tools in one test and of geometric forms in the other.

Q. *Clerical Perception:* Similar to P, but requiring the matching of names rather than pictures or forms.

K. *Motor Coordination:* Measured by a simple paper-and-pencil test requiring the examinee to make specified pencil marks in a series of squares.

F. *Finger Dexterity:* Two tests requiring the assembling and disassembling, respectively, of rivets and washers.

M. *Manual Dexterity:* Two tests requiring the examinee to transfer and reverse pegs in a board.

The four tests used for measuring factors F and M require simple apparatus; the other eight are paper-and-pencil tests. Alternate forms are available for the first seven tests, used for measuring factors G through Q. The entire battery requires approximately 2½ hours. Mention may also be made of a nonverbal measure of the first factor, Intelligence, which has been developed for use with non-English-speaking or educationally deficient applicants. It consists of the first three parts of Cattell's Culture Fair Intelligence Test and the Form Perception (P) tests of the GATB. Requiring no reading, this measure correlated .75 with scores on Aptitude G of the GATB in a sample of 475 literate individuals (Droege & Bemis, 1964).

The nine factor scores on the GATB are converted into standard scores with a mean of 100 and an SD of 20. These standard score norms were derived from a sample of 4,000 cases representative of the 1940 working population of the United States in terms of age, sex, educational, occupational, and geographical distribution. This sample may thus be regarded as a fixed reference group to which the score scale is anchored. By testing many groups of employees, applicants, and trainees in different kinds of jobs, score patterns were subsequently established, showing the critical aptitudes and minimum standard scores required for each occupation. For example, general accounting was found to require a minimum score of 105 in Intelligence (G) and 115 in Numerical Aptitude (N). Plumbing called for a minimum score of 85 in intelligence (G) and of 80 in Numerical Aptitude (N), Spatial Aptitude (S), and Manual Dexterity (M). An individual's standard score profile can thus be matched with all those occupations whose cutoff scores he reaches or exceeds, and these occupations can be considered in counseling him.

In USES terminology, the aptitudes (with their appropriate cutoff scores) chosen for a specific occupation constitute a Special Aptitude Test Battery (SATB). The development of an SATB was illustrated in Chapter 6. The procedure followed with each group includes job analysis, selection of suitable criterion data (output records, supervisors' ratings, training performance, etc.), and administration of the 12-test battery. The significant aptitudes are chosen on the basis of their criterion correlations, as well as the means and SD's of scores on each aptitude and the qualitative job-analysis information. For example, if workers on the job under consideration average considerably above the normative sample in a particular aptitude and also show relatively low variability in their scores, that aptitude would probably be included in the SATB even if it fails to show a significant criterion correlation. Such a situation could occur if employees on a certain job were a highly selected group with regard to that aptitude.

To facilitate the use of score patterns in counseling, specific occupations having similar aptitude requirements have been grouped into a relatively small number of job families. Cutoff scores were then established in the three most significant aptitudes for each family. The resulting score patterns are designated as OAP's (Occupational Ability Patterns). Thus far, 36 OAP's have been prepared, covering several hundred specific occupations. More will be added as the need arises and additional data become available.

The GATB is used regularly in state employment service offices in the counseling and job referral of a vast number of persons. In addition, the battery may be obtained by nonprofit organizations such as secondary schools, colleges, Veterans' Administration hospitals, and prisons, under arrangements with the appropriate state employment service. Permission has also been granted to individuals and organizations in many foreign countries to translate the GATB and use it for research purposes.

Through the facilities of the USES and the various state offices, an impressive body of data has been accumulated on the GATB, and a continuing research program is in progress. Despite the brevity of individual tests, reliabilities of the factor scores are generally satisfactory. Both equivalent-form and retest correlations cluster in the .80's and low .90's, although the reliabilities of the motor tests tend to be somewhat lower.

A large amount of information on the validity of both SATB's and OAP's is reported in the Guide (USES, 1962). Although cross validation has not been systematically carried out and rather crude statistical procedures have been employed, available cross validation data are promising. Some predictive studies have been conducted, but most of the validity data were obtained by concurrent validation with groups of employed workers. Such a procedure may be questioned because of the effect of job training and experience on test performance and because of the lack of comparability with an applicant population. For use in counseling young people and other persons inexperienced in a particular type of work, predictive validity of scores obtained prior to job training and experience is more appropriate. In 1958, the USES began a 7-year longitudinal study of approximately 36,000 high school students for this purpose (Droege, 1966b). When the occupational follow-up data from this study are finally analyzed, more conclusive answers regarding the validity of the GATB should be available.

Certain limitations of the GATB should be noted. All tests are highly speeded. Coverage of aptitudes is somewhat limited. No mechanical comprehension test is included, nor are tests of reasoning and inventiveness well represented. The factorial structure of the battery rests on a series of early exploratory studies. A more comprehensive investigation with a large sample and a wider variety of tests would provide a more solid foundation. The consistent reliance on a multiple cutoff strategy, rather than on regression equations, is also open to question. Although it is probable that certain occupations require critical skills whose lack cannot be compensated by other aptitudes, there is no empirical evidence that this is true of all aptitudes required for all occupations. As for nonlinear relations between aptitudes and job criteria, these too can be handled by regression equations, although the computation of the equation is admittedly more complicated in such cases. The principal justification for the universal use of the multiple-cutoff strategy with the GATB is based on practical limitations in the time and technical training of the personnel interpreting the scores. With the increasing availability of computers, however, the utilization of regression strategies becomes feasible. The Army, for example, was able to change from multiple cutoff to regression strategies, following the installation of computerized procedures (Boldt, 1964; Sorenson, 1965).

MILITARY CLASSIFICATION BATTERIES. The armed services make extensive use of multiple aptitude batteries. These batteries are given for classification purposes after preliminary screening with such instruments as the Armed Forces Qualification Test (AFQT), discussed in Chapter 9. Although the Air Force pioneered in the development of classification batteries, all branches of the armed services eventually prepared multifactor batteries for assigning personnel to specialized military jobs. The use of the Aptitude Area scores, derived from the Army Classification Battery, was illustrated in Chapter 6.

In the Air Force, the Aircrew Classification Battery was developed and employed during World War II for selecting pilots, navigators, bombardiers, and other flight personnel. Later, an Airman Classification Test Battery (U.S. Air Force, 1948) was prepared for use with other Air Force personnel. Both batteries were constructed by means of factor analysis. In applying these batteries, the scores on each test are substituted in the appropriate regression equation for the particular specialty. The individual's predicted score, or Aptitude Index, for that specialty serves as a basis for job assignments. For example, in computing the Aptitude Index for clerical specialties, significant weights are given to tests of arithmetic reasoning, background for current affairs, dial- and table-reading, numerical operations, and word knowledge. The index for radio operator is based on tests of arithmetic reasoning, dial- and table-reading, electrical information, memory for landmarks, and numerical operations.

GENERAL EVALUATION. On the whole, both the GATB and the various multifactor batteries developed for military use have proved relatively successful as classification instruments. Both differ from the general batteries discussed in the preceding section in that they have been validated chiefly against occupational rather than academic criteria. To be sure, training criteria have sometimes been substituted for actual job performance, but the training programs were job-oriented and quite unlike schoolwork. Both training and job activities of airplane pilots, bakers, beauticians, and the many other kinds of workers included in these testing programs are far removed from traditional academic tasks. With criteria differing more widely from each other and from the verbally loaded academic criterion, there is more room for differential validity.

Another advantage enjoyed by the military batteries is that the number of occupational fields to be covered is smaller than in a general counseling battery. This was especially true of the Aircrew Classification Battery, whose task was limited to the assignment of personnel to four or five jobs. As a result, it was possible to work with relatively narrow group factors, which specifically matched the criterion requirements. In the Air Force research, for example, a large number of different sensorimotor, perceptual, and spatial factors were identified and utilized in test construction. A general counseling battery, on the other hand, must concentrate on a few broad group factors, each of which is common to many jobs. To do otherwise would require the administration of a prohibitive number of tests to each person. But with such an instrument, distinctions are blurred and differential validity drops.

CHAPTER **14**

Special Aptitude
Tests

EVEN PRIOR to the development of multiple aptitude batteries, it was generally recognized that intelligence tests were limited in their coverage of abilities. Efforts were soon made to fill the major gaps by means of special aptitude tests. Among the earliest were those designed to measure mechanical aptitude. Since intelligence tests concentrate chiefly on "abstract" functions involving the use of verbal or numerical symbols, a particular need was felt for tests covering the more "concrete" or "practical" abilities. Mechanical aptitude tests were developed partly to meet this need.

The demands of vocational selection and counseling likewise stimulated the development of tests to measure mechanical, clerical, musical, and artistic aptitudes. Tests of vision, hearing, and motor dexterity have also found their principal applications in the selection and classification of personnel for industrial and military purposes. It is thus apparent that a strong impetus to the construction of all special aptitude tests has been provided by the urgent problems of matching job requirements with the specific pattern of abilities characterizing each individual.

A word should be added about the concept of special aptitudes. The term originated at a time when the major emphasis in testing was placed on general intelligence. Mechanical, musical, and other special aptitudes were thus regarded as supplementary to the "IQ" in the description of the individual. With the advent of factor analysis, however, it was gradually recognized that intelligence itself comprises a number of relatively independent aptitudes, such as verbal comprehension, numerical reasoning, numerical computation, spatial visualization, associative memory, and the like. More-

348

over, several of the traditional special aptitudes, such as mechanical and clerical, are now incorporated in some of the multiple aptitude batteries.

What, then, is the role of special aptitude tests? First, there are certain areas, such as vision, hearing, motor dexterity, and artistic talents, that are rarely included in multiple aptitude batteries. The situations requiring tests in these areas are too specialized to justify the inclusion of such tests in standard batteries. Special aptitude tests are also employed, however, in areas that are covered in multiple aptitude batteries, such as clerical and mechanical aptitudes. In several testing programs, tests of general intelligence are combined with specially selected tests of other relevant aptitudes. One reason for this practice is to be found in the extensive normative and validation data available for some widely used tests of special aptitudes. Another reason is undoubtedly the flexibility that this procedure provides, not only in the choice of relevant aptitudes but also in the fullness with which each aptitude is measured for specific purposes.

SENSORY CAPACITIES

USE OF SENSORY TESTS IN PSYCHOLOGY. Among the earliest topics investigated in laboratories of experimental psychology were sensory acuity, sensory discrimination, and the influence of various factors on sensitivity. Today, research on sensory capacities is an important phase of engineering psychology. It is one of the principal aims of this field of research to design equipment for maximum effectiveness of use by the human operator. Such laboratory studies on sensitivity, however, are concerned primarily with general characteristics, rather than with the measurement of individual differences. This approach does not, therefore, fall within the scope of psychological testing, although it has occasionally contributed to methodology and to the accumulation of normative data.

Even if we limit the present discussion to standardized tests, we shall find that the measurement of sensory capacities has served a variety of functions in the field of psychological testing. The reader will recall the early attempts by Galton and others to measure intelligence by means of sensory tests. Although these efforts proved futile, a number of later studies on schoolchildren have suggested the detrimental effects that visual or auditory handicaps may have on intellectual development, educational progress, and social adjustment. The examination of schoolchildren for the detection of minor visual or auditory deficiencies is now routine practice in many school systems. These examinations serve a screening function. The children whose test performance shows evidence of defect are then referred for individual examination and clinical diagnosis by a specialist. The results of such clinical examinations may serve as a basis for corrective treatment, assignment to special classes, transfer to special schools, or other appropriate action.

Another application of sensory tests is to be found in the psychological clinic. It is frequently desirable to check for unsuspected sensory deficiencies as a possible source of the individual's difficulties. This is especially important in cases of reading disabilities and speech disorders. But many other conditions, such as behavior disorders or school retardation in children, and depression or abnormal suspiciousness in adults, may have been induced or aggravated by an uncorrected sensory deficiency.

One of the chief current uses of sensory tests is in the selection of industrial or military personnel. A large amount of research is available that indicates the effects of sensory handicaps on quantity and quality of output, spoilage and waste of materials, job turnover, and accidents (see Tiffin & McCormick, 1965, Chs. 6 and 18). Many types of military specialties likewise make heavy demands on visual or auditory capacities. Special attention has been given to the role of both auditory and visual defects in the causation of accidents. Relevant data have been obtained, not only among industrial employees and transportation workers, but also among automobile drivers.

Although psychological research on sensory capacities has extended to all sense modalities, standardized tests for the measurement of individual differences have been limited primarily to vision and hearing. These, of course, are the most important modalities for modern man. It is also interesting to note that most available sensory tests are designed chiefly to detect deficiencies. The identification of superior capacities has received relatively little attention. Perhaps the medical point of view, which is concerned with pathological deviations rather than with the whole range of human variation, has influenced the orientation of sensory tests in this direction.

In the present section, we shall consider some of the most widely used standardized testing techniques in the fields of vision and hearing. Only screening instruments designed for general testing will be discussed. No mention will be made of the more elaborate and refined techniques that have been developed for special purposes. The latter category includes clinical instruments for the use of such medical specialists as oculists and otologists, as well as laboratory apparatus for research in experimental psychology or in other sciences concerned with vision and hearing.

VISION. Visual sensitivity includes not one but many functions. It is common knowledge, for example, that color perception may be impaired or even totally lacking in an individual whose vision is otherwise normal. That a number of other aspects of vision must be differentiated is not, however, so generally recognized. Among the visual characteristics found to be of greatest practical importance may be mentioned: near acuity at reading distance (13–16 inches), far acuity (usually measured at 20 feet), perception of distance or depth, muscular balance of the eyes (phoria), and color discrimination.

The principal characteristic tested by the usual type of wall chart is far acuity. The Snellen Chart, containing rows of letters of gradually decreasing size, is undoubtedly the most familiar of these charts. Not only are such charts limited in the visual capacities they test, but they are also subject to uncontrolled procedural variations with regard to illumination, position of examinee's head, and other testing conditions. More comprehensive visual testing under better controlled conditions can be conducted with certain visual screening instruments designed for large-scale use in industry and in schools. Three well-known instruments for this purpose are the Ortho-Rater, the AO Sight Screener, and the Keystone Telebinocular. These instruments are essentially similar in their operation, each providing measures of near and far acuity, depth perception, lateral and vertical phorias, and color discrimination.

A photograph of the Ortho-Rater in use is reproduced in Figure 71. This instrument has been employed extensively with industrial workers in establishing visual skill requirements for groups of similar jobs. Ortho-Rater profiles for the most common "visual job families" are given in Figure 72.

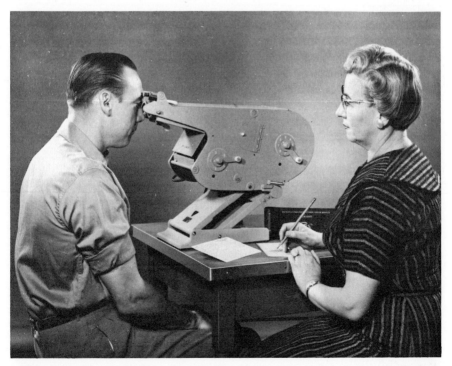

FIG. 71. The Ortho-Rater for Testing Visual Capacities. (Courtesy Bausch & Lomb, Inc.)

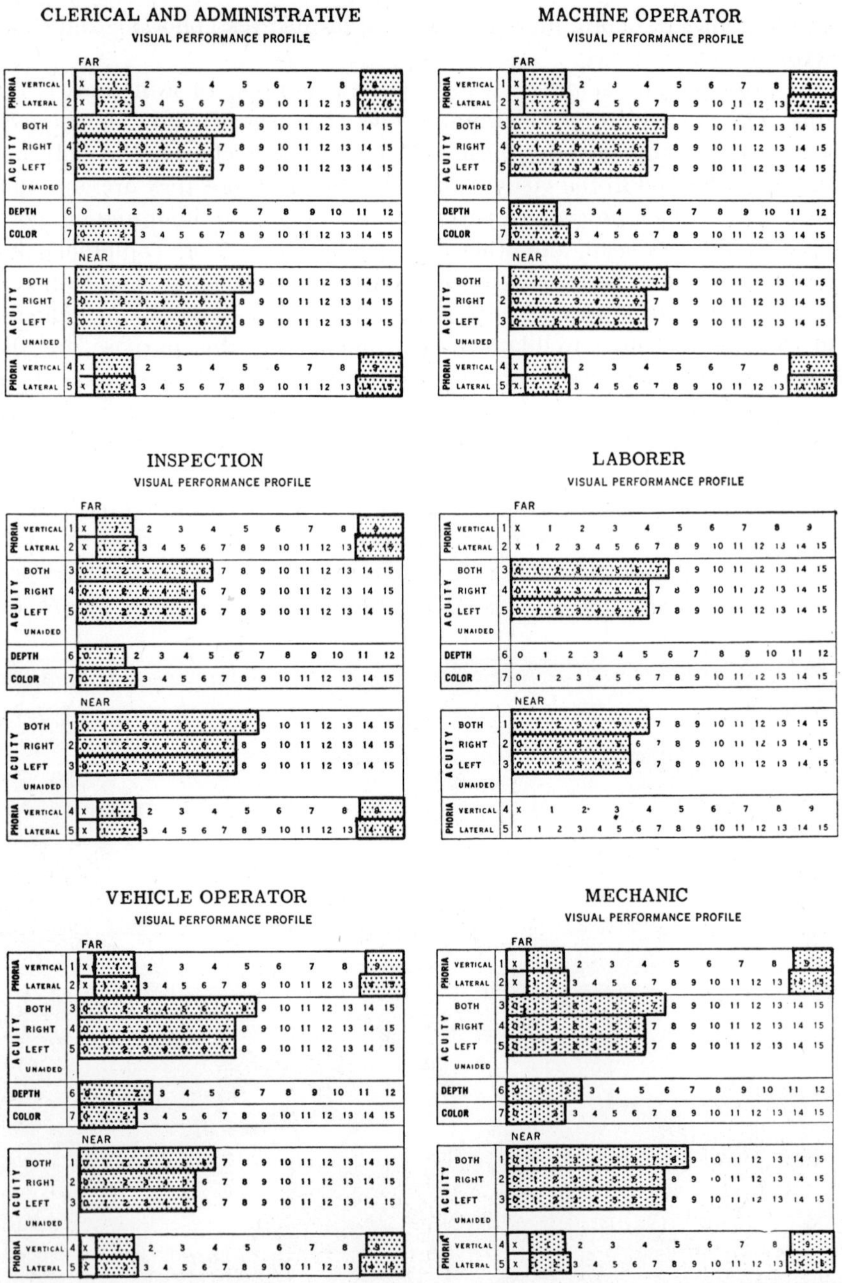
CLERICAL AND ADMINISTRATIVE
VISUAL PERFORMANCE PROFILE
MACHINE OPERATOR
VISUAL PERFORMANCE PROFILE
INSPECTION
VISUAL PERFORMANCE PROFILE
LABORER
VISUAL PERFORMANCE PROFILE
VEHICLE OPERATOR
VISUAL PERFORMANCE PROFILE
MECHANIC
VISUAL PERFORMANCE PROFILE
FAR
PHORIA
VERTICAL
LATERAL
ACUITY
BOTH
RIGHT
LEFT
UNAIDED
DEPTH
COLOR
NEAR

FIG. 72. Profiles for Visual Job Families. An employee passes the visual job requirements if all his scores fall in the unshaded area. (From Tiffin & McCormick, 1965, p. 181.)

Studies of employees in a wide variety of jobs have shown significant relationships between scores in relevant visual capacities and criteria of job performance (Tiffin & McCormick, 1965, Chs. 6 and 18). An adaptation of the Ortho-Rater for use with schoolchildren has also been developed. Known as the New York School Vision Tester, this adaptation uses a different set of slides with the same instrument. It is applicable from kindergarten on.

Because of the special role of color vision in many educational, industrial, and military functions, separate tests of color discrimination have been available for a long time. A common technique utilizes pseudo-isochromatic plates, as in the Ishihara test and its many adaptations. Pseudo-isochromatic plates employ colors so chosen as to appear alike in certain types of color blindness, while appearing distinctly different to the normal eye. The background consists of dots in one of these colors, while a number or pattern is traced in dots of the other color. The color-blind will be unable to see any numbers or patterns on some of the plates; on others, they may see a different number from that seen by normal persons. This approach is followed in the Dvorine Color Vision Test, which also permits a tentative identification of type of color blindness and provides norms with which severity of handicap may be gauged (Peters, 1956).

Two difficulties encountered in the use of such color vision tests arise from the effect of varying illumination and from the fading and soiling of colors. All tests specify the use of a standard illuminant, but owing to inadequate facilities the illuminant often deviates widely from the prescribed standard. Either varying illumination or the fading or soiling of test materials may affect different hues unequally and hence alter the relationship between colored stimuli. Thus despite careful selection of original colors in the construction and printing of the test, a color-blind person might pass such a test because of poorly controlled conditions. Instruments like the Ortho-Rater provide a better control of such conditions.

HEARING.   Like vision, hearing is not a unitary capacity.[1] An individual may be normal or superior in one aspect of hearing and seriously deficient in another. The aspect of most general interest is auditory acuity. Also known as the absolute threshold of hearing, this measure refers to the faintest sound that the individual can just barely hear. A number of other questions can, however, be asked regarding a person's hearing. Some assume major importance if we wish to predict how effectively the individual will function in certain situations. Thus, we may want to test his tolerance for very loud sounds. At what intensity does sound become painful or uncomfortable for him? Or it may be necessary to measure his ability to rec-

[1] For a fuller and more technical discussion of the measurement of hearing, see Hirsh (1952) and Newby (1964).

ognize words against a background of loud and confusing noise, as in an airplane intercommunication system. The answers to these questions can usually be obtained by adaptations of the basic techniques employed in measuring auditory acuity.

In other situations, the individual may have to make fine auditory discriminations, as in distinguishing the pitch or loudness of different tones. In the submarine service, for example, the control of a number of instruments, such as sonar, depends on such auditory discriminations. Since the ability to make fine differentiations between sounds is also of primary importance to musicians, the Seashore Measures of Musical Talents include a series of auditory discrimination tests for pitch, intensity, time, and timbre. These tests have been in use for a long·time in connection with the selection and counseling of prospective music students and will be considered in a later section dealing with musical aptitudes. The Seashore tests subsequently demonstrated a wider applicability, however, having proved helpful in the selection of personnel for certain military and civilian jobs. This is especially true of the pitch discrimination test, which has been extensively employed outside the field of music.

In the measurement of auditory acuity, the most dependable techniques involve the use of electronic *audiometers.* For individual testing, pure tone audiometers are generally employed. In administering such a test, it is customary to test one ear at a time, the subject receiving the sound through a headphone or receiver held against the ear. Beginning with a sound too faint for the subject to hear, the examiner gradually increases the intensity of the tone until the subject indicates that he hears it. The threshold is determined in both an ascending and descending direction. In other words, the intensity is increased until the subject can just barely hear the sound, and it is decreased until he can no longer hear it. This will be recognized as the psychophysical method of limits commonly employed in experimental psychology laboratories. The entire procedure is repeated at several frequency levels in order to check for differential hearing loss.

At each frequency level, the subject's hearing loss in decibels can be read directly from the audiometer dial. The zero point on this dial represents the intensity of sound that the "normal" ear can just barely hear on that audiometer. This point was empirically determined in the process of calibrating each instrument, by testing a large normative sampling of persons. The subject's hearing loss, as indicated on the audiometer, represents the number of decibels by which sound intensity must be increased above the normal threshold in order to be audible to him. The audiometer dial readings are used to plot the subject's *audiogram,* a graph showing his hearing loss at different frequency levels. An audiogram of a schoolchild is reproduced in Figure 73. It illustrates differential hearing loss at the higher

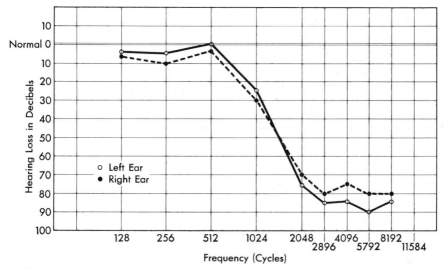

FIG. 73. Audiogram of a Child with Severe High Tone Deafness. (From Watson and Tolan, 1949, p. 247, copyright by L. A. Watson.)

frequencies in a subject whose hearing is virtually normal at lower frequencies.

Pure tone audiometers have also been adapted for group use (Johnson, 1948, 1952; DiCarlo & Gardner, 1958). The Massachusetts Hearing Test provides a standardized procedure that may be followed with several commercially available audiometers. As many as 40 children can be examined simultaneously with individual earphones. The stimulus is a signal tone presented at several frequency levels. The subject merely underlines *yes* or *no* next to the appropriate trial number to indicate whether or not he hears the signal. In some of the trials, no signal is actually given, the position of these trials being specified on the examiner's master sheets. Although this test has been used principally with children in grades 3 to 12, there is evidence that, with minor procedural modifications, it can be successfully applied in kindergarten and the first two grades.

Since one of the most important functions of hearing is the understanding of speech, a more direct measure of this ability may be desirable. Speech audiometers are sometimes employed for this purpose. In this case, the sound stimulus received through the earphones is the human voice pronouncing numbers, words, or sentences. As in the pure tone audiometer, the intensity is varied to determine the point at which the examinee can correctly understand speech. This intensity is usually higher than that at which he can just barely *hear* speech. Such a procedure provides a more functional measure of the social adequacy of the individual's hearing.

MOTOR FUNCTIONS

TYPES OF AVAILABLE TESTS. Many tests have been devised to measure speed, coordination, and other characteristics of movement responses. Most are concerned with manual dexterity, but a few involve leg or foot movements that may be required in performing specific jobs. Some measure a combination of motor and perceptual, spatial, or mechanical aptitudes, thus overlapping the tests to be discussed in the next sections. Mention should also be made of the previously discussed Lincoln-Oseretsky tests (Ch. 10). Since they are concerned chiefly with motor development in children, these tests were considered with other types of developmental scales.

Motor tests are characteristically apparatus tests, although several paper-and-pencil adaptations have been designed for group administration. Both the GATB and the FACT discussed in Chapter 13 include examples of such paper-and-pencil motor tests. Some of these printed motor tests may prove valid in their own right as predictors of practical criteria. Available evidence indicates, however, that there is little or no correlation between printed tests and apparatus tests designed to measure the same motor functions (Fleishman, 1958; Melton, 1947).

The principal application of motor tests has been in the selection of industrial and military personnel. Frequently, they have been custom-made to meet the requirements of specific jobs. Many are constructed on the principle of the "job miniature." This means that the test closely reproduces all or part of the movements required in the performance of the job itself. These tests are not miniatures in the sense of involving smaller movements. On the contrary, to ensure validity, the test and the job should call for the use of the same muscle groups. Many examples of motor coordination tests, ranging from simple to very complex, are provided by the classification testing program conducted by the Air Force during World War II (Melton, 1947). While these tests are not commercially available, their published report represents a rich source of test material for the research worker and the test constructor.[2]

A test requiring several simple manipulative skills is the Crawford Small Parts Dexterity Test, shown in Figure 74. In Part I of this test, the examinee uses tweezers to insert pins in close-fitting holes, and then places a small collar over each pin. In Part II, small screws are placed in threaded holes and screwed down with a screwdriver. The score is the time required to complete each part. Split-half reliability coefficients between .80 and .95 are reported for the two parts of this test. Despite the apparent similarity of

---

[2] Other sources of information about motor tests, as well as their validity in industrial training and job performance, include Bennett & Cruikshank (1942), Ghiselli (1966), and Patterson (1956).

FIG. 74.   Crawford Small Parts Dexterity Test. (Courtesy The Psychological Corporation.)

the functions required by Parts I and II, the correlations between the two parts ranged from .10 to .50 in several industrial and high school samples, with a median correlation of .42.

Another widely used manual dexterity test which, however, utilizes no tools is the Purdue Pegboard. This test is said to provide a measure of two types of activity, one requiring gross movements of hands, fingers, and arms, and the other involving tip-of-the-finger dexterity needed in small assembly work. First, pins are inserted individually in small holes with the right hand, left hand, and both hands together, in successive trials. In another part of the test, pins, collars, and washers are assembled in each hole. The prescribed procedure for this activity involves the simultaneous use of both hands.

Still another type of simple motor test, involving gross hand and arm movements, is illustrated by the Stromberg Dexterity Test (Fig. 75). In this test, red, yellow, and blue blocks are inserted as quickly as possible in the appropriately colored sections of the board. Before each trial, the blocks are arranged in standard order, with only one color to a row in one trial, and only one color to a column in another. The examinee is required to pick up the blocks in a prescribed sequence that prevents the placement of two blocks of the same color in immediate succession.

FIG. 75. Stromberg Dexterity Test. (Courtesy The Psychological Corporation.)

EVALUATION OF MOTOR TESTS. What can be said about the effectiveness of motor tests as a whole? The most important point to note in evaluating such tests is the high degree of *specificity* of motor functions. Intercorrelations and factor analyses of large numbers of motor tests have failed to reveal broad group factors such as those found for intellectual functions. In extensive factor-analytic research, Fleishman and his associates (Fleishman, 1954, 1958; Fleishman & Ellison, 1962; Fleishman & Hempel, 1956) identified the following major factors:

Control Precision: Ability to make fine, highly controlled but not overcontrolled muscular adjustments—important in the rapid and accurate operation of controls by hand, arm, and foot movements.

Multi-Limb Coordination: Ability to coordinate gross movements requiring the simultaneous use of more than one limb in any combination.

Response Orientation: Ability to select the appropriate response under highly speeded conditions—identified in complex coordination tests in which each pattern of signals requires a different choice of controls and direction of movement.

Reaction Time: Speed with which an individual is able to respond to a stimulus when it appears—found to be independent of specific response required and of whether the stimulus is auditory or visual.

Speed of Arm Movement: Speed with which gross arm movements can be made, regardless of precision.

Rate Control: Ability to make continuous anticipatory motor adjustments relative to changes in speed and direction of a moving target—the common factor in pursuit and tracking tests.

Manual Dexterity: Ability to make skillful, well-controlled arm-hand movements in manipulating fairly large objects under speed conditions.

Finger Dexterity: Ability to make skillful, controlled manipulations of small objects, involving primarily finger movements.

Arm-Hand Steadiness: Ability to make precise arm-hand positioning movements where strength and speed are minimized.

Wrist-Finger Speed: Traditionally called "tapping," this ability is best measured by paper-and-pencil tests requiring rapid tapping of the pencil in relatively large areas.

Aiming: A narrowly defined ability measured chiefly by paper-and-pencil dotting tests which require subject to place a dot accurately and rapidly in each of a series of small circles.

Still other factors have been identified in the area of gross bodily movements, as exemplified by tests of physical fitness (Fleishman, 1962a; Hempel & Fleishman, 1955). Examples include trunk strength, gross body coordination, gross body equilibrium, extent of flexibility, dynamic flexibility (repeated, rapid flexing movements), explosive strength (mobilization of energy for a single burst of effort), static strength (continued exertion of force up to a maximum), and dynamic strength (muscular endurance, requiring repeated exertion of force).

There is evidence that the abilities called into play by motor tests may change with *practice*. Fleishman (1962b) factor analyzed the scores obtained during continued practice on the Air Force Complex Coordination Test, a test reproducing many of the eye-hand-foot coordinations required in piloting a plane. Both number and nature of factors identified at different stages of practice varied. At the early stages, nonmotor factors such as spatial orientation, visualization, mechanical experience, and perceptual speed entered into performance together with motor factors. With increasing practice, the importance of the intellectual factors declined and that of the motor factors increased. In the last stages of practice, the only common factors having significant weights were speed of arm movement and control precision. A factor specific to the Complex Coordination Test also increased in weight with practice. Similar results were obtained in later analyses of other complex motor tests.

The change in nature of many motor tests with practice complicates the determination of *reliability*. Increasing the length of a motor test does not usually result in as great a rise in reliability as found with intellectual tests, since the different portions of the motor test may not measure quite the same functions. In general, the reliabilities of motor tests are not so high as those of other types of tests, many falling in the .70's and .80's. Some of the simple motor tests described in this section, however, have higher reliabilities. In such simple, homogeneous tasks, there is less likelihood that practice will alter the nature of the test; hence a reliable measure can be obtained with a short test.

In considering the *validity* of motor tests, we need to differentiate between complex motor tests that closely resemble the particular criterion performance they are trying to predict and tests of simple motor functions designed for more general use. The former are well illustrated by some of the Air Force tests. Such complex, custom-made tests that reproduce the combination of motor aptitudes required by the criterion have shown fair validity. The Complex Coordination Test of the Air Force, for example, considerably improved the prediction of performance in pilot training. For most purposes, however, the use of such tests is not practicable, since a very large number of tests would have to be devised to match different criteria. Moreover, there is a question as to whether the same result might not be achieved through a combination of intellectual tests and simple motor tests. For counseling purposes, of course, such highly specific tests would be of little use.

With regard to commercially available motor tests, the functions they measure are very simple and their validities against most criteria are not high. For this reason, such tests can serve best as part of a selection battery, rather than as single predictors. In general, motor tests have been most successful in predicting performance on routine assembling and machine-operating jobs (Ghiselli, 1966). As the jobs become less repetitive, perceptual and intellectual factors come to play a more important part.

MECHANICAL APTITUDES

Mechanical aptitude tests cover a variety of functions. Motor factors enter into some of the tests in this category, either because the rapid manipulation of materials is required in the performance of the test, or because special subtests designed to measure motor dexterity are included in a paper-and-pencil test. In terms of the factors discussed in the preceding chapter, perceptual and spatial aptitudes play an important part in many of these tests. Finally, mechanical reasoning and sheer mechanical information predominate in a number of mechanical aptitude tests.

It is important to recognize the diversity of functions subsumed under the heading of mechanical aptitude, since each function may be differently related to other variables. For example, mechanical information tests are much more dependent on past experience with mechanical objects than are abstract spatial or perceptual tests. Similarly, sex differences may be reversed from one of these functions to another. Thus, in manual dexterity and in perceptual discrimination tests, women generally excel; in abstract spatial tests, a small but significant average difference in favor of males is usually found; while in mechanical reasoning or information tests, men are markedly superior, the difference increasing with age (Anastasi, 1958a, Ch. 14).

SPATIAL APTITUDE. Among the aptitudes included in all multiple aptitude batteries is spatial aptitude. This is the ability measured by the Space Relations test of the DAT; it corresponds to the S factor in Thurstone's primary mental abilities and to the k factor in the British hierarchical model of intelligence. It has also been found to have a high loading in many performance and nonlanguage tests of general intelligence. One of the best single measures of this aptitude is the Revised Minnesota Paper Form Board Test. Available in two equivalent forms, this test was originally developed as a paper-and-pencil adaptation of the familiar formboard type of test. Two sample items are reproduced in Figure 76. Each item consists of a figure cut into two or more parts. The examinee must determine how the pieces would fit together into the complete figure; he then chooses the drawing that correctly shows this arrangement.

The manual for the Minnesota Paper Form Board provides extensive tables of norms based on large and well-defined educational and industrial samples. Alternate-form reliability coefficients are in the .80's. An unusually large number of studies have been conducted with this test. The results indicate that it is one of the most valid available instruments for measuring the ability to visualize and manipulate objects in space. Among the criteria employed in this research were performance in shop courses, grades in engineering and in other technical and mechanical courses, supervisors' ratings, and objective production records. The test has also shown some validity in predicting the achievement of dentistry and art students.

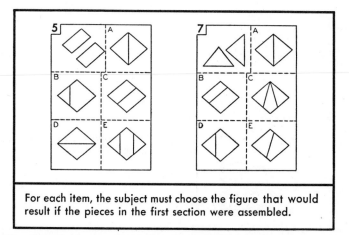

For each item, the subject must choose the figure that would result if the pieces in the first section were assembled.

FIG. 76. Sample Items from the Revised Minnesota Paper Form Board. (Reproduced by permission of The Psychological Corporation, New York, N.Y. Copyright 1941, Rensis Likert and W. H. Quasha.)

MECHANICAL COMPREHENSION.   Another major type of mechanical apti-tude test is concerned with mechanical information, mechanical reasoning, or mechanical comprehension. While requiring some familiarity with com-mon tools and mechanical relations, these tests assume no more technical knowledge than can be acquired through everyday experience in an indus-trial society such as ours. Some of the early tests in this field required the examinee to assemble common mechanical objects from the given parts. For general testing purposes, paper-and-pencil group tests are now widely employed.

A well-known example of this type of test is the Test of Mechanical Comprehension (TMC). Utilizing pictures about which short questions are to be answered, this test emphasizes the understanding of mechanical prin-ciples as applied to a wide variety of everyday-life situations. Two items employed in the fore-exercise of this test are reproduced in Figure 77. The TMC has been used widely for both military and civilian purposes. The principal forms available for civilian use include: Form AA, suitable for boys in high school or trade school, for unselected adult men, and for cer-tain industrial groups; Form BB, a more difficult form designed for engi-neering school applicants and other similarly selected groups; Form CC, a still more difficult form permitting finer discrimination at high ability levels; and Form W1 for women. To these should be added the Mechanical

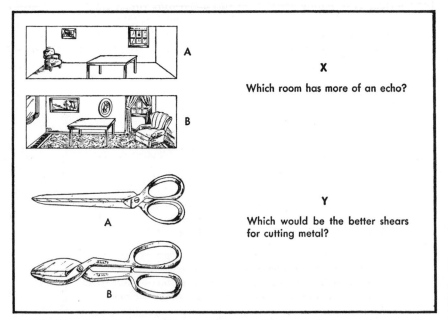

FIG. 77.   Sample Items from the Bennett Mechanical Comprehension Test, Form AA. (Reproduced by permission. Copyright © 1940, The Psychological Corporation, New York, N.Y. All rights reserved.)

Reasoning Test of the DAT, discussed in Chapter 13, which is essentially another form of the same test.

Despite its widespread use, little information regarding the validity of the Test of Mechanical Comprehension is reported in the manual. Other published studies either with this test or with one of its military forms, however, provide good evidence of both concurrent and predictive validity for mechanical trades and engineering. Correlations between .30 and .60 have been found with either training or job-proficiency criteria for many kinds of mechanical jobs (Ghiselli, 1966; Patterson, 1956). During World War II, this test proved to be one of the best predictors of pilot success (Guilford & Lacey, 1947, p. 843). Its validity for this purpose seems to have resulted chiefly from the contribution of a mechanical information factor and a spatial visualization factor, which together accounted for about 60 percent of the variance of its scores (Guilford & Lacey, 1947, pp. 336–339).

CLERICAL APTITUDES

Tests designed to measure clerical aptitudes are characterized by a common emphasis on perceptual speed. A well-known example is the Minnesota Clerical Test, which consists of two separately timed subtests, Number Comparison and Name Comparison. In the first, the examinee is given 200 pairs of numbers, each containing from 3 to 12 digits. If the two numbers in the pair are identical, he places a check mark between them. The task is similar in the second subtest, proper names being substituted for numbers. Sample items from both subtests are reproduced in Figure 78.

When the two numbers or names in a pair are exactly the same, make a check mark on the line between them.

66273894_____66273984

527384578_____527384578

New York World_____New York World

Cargill Grain Co._____Cargil Grain Co.

FIG. 78. Sample Items from the Minnesota Clerical Test. (Reproduced by permission. Copyright © 1933, The Psychological Corporation, New York, N.Y. All rights reserved.)

Although a deduction is made for errors, the scores depend predominantly on speed. Performance on this test is influenced by the examinee's response set. Occasionally a very careful worker will obtain a poor score because he proceeds slowly in order to avoid errors. By contrast, the examinee who emphasizes speed at the expense of accuracy will complete many more items and will be penalized only a few points as a result of errors. The possible effect of response set should therefore be taken into account when interpreting a low score, especially when such a score is obtained by an otherwise able or promising person.

Percentile norms on the Minnesota Clerical Test are reported for several large samples of clerical applicants and employed clerical workers, as well as for boys and girls in grades 8 to 12. Retest reliability coefficients over intervals of several months fall mostly in the .70's and .80's. These values are probably underestimates, since the intervals were longer than those usually employed for estimating reliability.

Data on both concurrent and predictive validity of the Minnesota Clerical Test are provided by a number of independent studies. Moderately high correlations have been found between scores on this test and ratings by office supervisors or by commercial teachers, as well as performance records in courses and in various kinds of clerical jobs. Several studies employed the method of contrasted groups. Thus, comparisons are reported between different levels of clerks, between clerical workers and persons engaged in other occupations, and between employed and unemployed clerks. All these comparisons yielded significant differences in mean scores in the expected direction. A marked and consistent sex difference in favor of women has been found on this test, beginning in childhood and continuing into adulthood.

It is apparent, of course, that such a relatively homogeneous test as the Minnesota Clerical Test measures only one aspect of clerical work. Clerical jobs cover a multiplicity of functions. Moreover, the number and particular combination of duties vary tremendously with the type and level of job. Even specific jobs designated by the same name, such as typist, filing clerk, or shipping clerk, may differ considerably from one company to another, owing to the size of the company, degree of possible specialization of jobs, nature of the work, and other local conditions. Despite such a diversity of activities, however, job analyses of general clerical work indicate that a relatively large proportion of time is spent in such tasks as classifying, sorting, checking, collating and stapling, stuffing and sealing envelopes, and the like (Bennett & Cruikshank, 1949). Speed and accuracy in perceiving details would thus seem to be of primary importance for the clerical worker, especially in the lower-level, routine jobs (Hay, 1954).

To be sure, many types of jobs besides that of clerk require perceptual speed and accuracy. Inspectors, checkers, packers, and a host of other factory workers obviously need this ability. It is interesting to note in this connection that the Minnesota Clerical Test has also been found to have some validity in predicting the performance of such workers (Dorcus & Jones, 1950). However, it is likely that higher validity may be obtained in such cases by designing a similar test with pictorial rather than with verbal or numerical material. It will be recalled that, in the GATB prepared by the United States Employment Service, separate tests are included for the Q and P factors. The Q factor appeared in number- and word-checking tests similar to those that make up the Minnesota Clerical Test. The P factor, on the other hand, occurred in tests requiring the perception of similarities and differences in spatial items, and is probably more closely related to the inspection of materials.

Several tests of clerical aptitude combine perceptual speed and accuracy with other functions required for clerical work. Among the measures used for the latter functions are "job sample" types of tests for such activities as alphabetizing, classifying, coding, and the like. In addition, some measure of verbal and numerical ability may be included, to serve in lieu of a general intelligence test. Other clerical aptitude tests include such office skills as business vocabulary, business information, spelling, and language usage. Finally, it should be added that there are a large number of clerical aptitude tests on the market. Most are quite similar in content, although the available information regarding norms, reliability, and validity varies widely among them.

ARTISTIC APTITUDES

Successful achievement in the visual arts calls for a multiplicity of aptitudes and personality traits. Different combinations of these characteristics may be required by diverse specialties and art forms. The sculptor and the painter utilize different skills; among painters, the traditional portraitist and the surrealist artist undoubtedly differ in a number of significant ways. In pursuing a career in art, moreover, an individual may play any of several roles, each with its distinct set of qualifications. Thus, the creative artist, art teacher, critic, dealer, and museum administrator approach art with different patterns of skills, knowledge, interests, attitudes, and feelings.

Standardized tests of artistic aptitudes have traditionally concentrated on a few aptitudes considered to be basic to artistic activity, whatever its form. Among these tests, however, a distinction can be made between those concerned only with aesthetic appreciation and those measuring also productive skills. Obviously a person may be a highly discriminating and sophisticated connoisseur of paintings without himself being able to paint. But artistic production, except at a routine and mechanical level, undoubtedly presupposes superiority in both appreciative and productive skills. Thus, tests of art appreciation have a broader applicability than tests of production.

ARTISTIC APPRECIATION. Tests of artistic appreciation have generally followed a common pattern. In each item, the examinee is requested to express his preference regarding two or more variants of the same object. One variant is either an original by an eminent artist or a version preferred by the majority of a group of art experts. The other versions represent deliberate distortions designed to violate some accepted principle of art. Any controversial items, on which a clear consensus of experts cannot be obtained, are normally eliminated from such a test.

In the development of art appreciation tests, both original item selection and subsequent validation procedures depend heavily on the opinions of contemporary art experts within our culture. It is well to bear this fact in mind when interpreting scores. Essentially, such tests indicate the degree to which the individual's aesthetic taste agrees with that of contemporary art experts. The representativeness of the particular group of experts employed in developing the test is obviously an important consideration. Insofar as aesthetic standards or taste may change with time, the periodic rechecking of scoring key and item validities is likewise desirable.

A well-established and unusually viable test in the field of art appreciation is the Meier Art Judgment Test. First published in 1929 and revised in 1940, this test represents the first of a proposed set of three tests designed to measure important aspects of artistic talent. The materials employed in the Meier Art Judgment Test consist of relatively timeless art works, which will not readily go out of date. Most are paintings or drawings by acknowledged masters, while a few represent vases or designs suitable for pottery. All reproductions are in black and white. Each item contains only two versions, an original and a variation in which the symmetry, balance, unity, or rhythm has been altered. This test thus concentrates on the judgment of aesthetic organization, which Meier considers to be the key factor in artistic talent. In order to rule out the contribution of perceptual accuracy, the examinee is told in what detail the two versions of each picture differ. An illustrative item is reproduced in Figure 79.

Percentile norms are given for three groups: 1,445 junior high school students; 892 senior high school students; and 982 adults, including college and art school students. All norms were derived largely from students in art courses, whether in high school, college, or special art schools. Data were gathered in 25 schools scattered throughout the United States. Split-half reliability coefficients between .70 and .84 are reported for relatively homogeneous samples.

Most of the available evidence regarding validity of the Meier Art Judgment Test can be summarized under the headings of item selection and contrasted group performance, although a few correlations with independent

FIG. 79. Item Similar to Those Employed in the Meier Art Judgment Test. The difference between the two versions is in the angle at which the window seat crosses the picture. (Courtesy Norman C. Meier.)

criteria of artistic accomplishment have also been reported. First, it should be noted that the original items were chosen from reputable art works and that the distortions were such as to violate accepted art principles. A large number of items thus assembled were then submitted to 25 art experts, and only those items showing clear-cut agreement among the experts were retained. Finally, items were selected on which from 60 to 90 percent of a group of 1,081 miscellaneous subjects chose the original as the preferred version. In the revised edition, items were further selected on the basis of internal consistency.

Total scores on the Meier Art Judgment Test exhibit a sharp differentiation in terms of age, grade, and art training. Thus, art faculty score higher than non-art faculty, art students higher than comparable non-art students. The extent to which these group differences result from selection or from previous art training cannot be determined from available data. Although no validity coefficients are given in the manual, a few are reported in other published sources. Correlations ranging from .40 to .69 have been found between scores on this test and art grades or ratings of artistic ability (Carroll, 1933; Kinter, 1933; Morrow, 1938).

As in most artistic aptitude tests, the Meier Art Judgment Test has regularly shown negligible correlation with traditional intelligence tests, such as the Stanford-Binet or group verbal tests. This does not mean, however, that abstract intelligence or scholastic aptitude is unrelated to ultimate success in an art career. In fact, there is some evidence to indicate that, for higher levels of artistic accomplishment, superior scholastic aptitude is a decided asset. In one of the investigations conducted at Iowa, for example, the mean IQ of successful artists was found to be 119 (Tiebout & Meier, 1936). Similarly, a group of artistically gifted children studied at the University of Iowa had IQ's ranging from 111 to 166 (Meier, 1942).

Prior to the development of the Art Judgment Test, Meier and his associates at the University of Iowa had conducted extensive research on the nature of artistic talent.[3] Although most of their subjects were children, data on adult groups, including professional artists, were also obtained. This research led Meier to the conclusion that artistic aptitude comprises six interlinked traits, viz., manual skill, volitional perseveration, aesthetic intelligence, perceptual facility, creative imagination, and aesthetic judgment. The Meier Art Judgment Test was designed to measure only the last of these six traits. The original plans called for the preparation of creative imagination and aesthetic perception tests, but little progress on the development of these tests could be made for two more decades.

Finally, in 1963, Test II, Aesthetic Perception, was published. This test comprises 50 items, each requiring the examinee to rank four versions of an art work in order of preference. A typical item is illustrated in Figure 80. Responses are scored by assigning one point to each correct placement, thus yielding a possible maximum of 200 points. As in Test I, the subject matter consists of relatively timeless but not widely known art works and covers a wide sampling of world art from ancient to contemporary. Sculpture, painting, and abstract compositions are included. The four versions may differ in unity, proportion, form, design, or degree to which they form a satisfying whole. This test was based on the premise that the aesthetically sensitive person is able to observe phenomena more adequately and to perceive subtle aspects of a situation having aesthetic significance more readily than is the average person. Preliminary percentile norms are available on 350 high school students taking art courses and 350 college students and other adults. Significant mean differences in scores were found among groups of artists, college art students, and high school art students. The triad of tests was to be completed with the appearance of Test III, Creative Imagination, which was being standardized at the time of its author's death.

ARTISTIC PRODUCTION. Most tests of productive ability in the visual arts are actually worksamples. As such, they are undoubtedly influenced to a large extent by formal art training. A few tests, however, have been designed specially for the prediction of performance in subsequent train-

[3] References to published reports of this research can be found in the 1942 manual of the Meier Art Judgment Test.

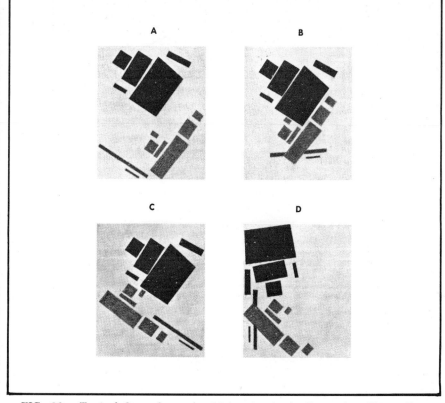

FIG. 80. Typical Item from the Meier Aesthetic Perception Test. (Reproduced by permission of Norman C. Meier.)

ing and have therefore tried to minimize the demands on technical skills and information. The Horn Art Aptitude Inventory may be cited as an example of this type of test. Concerned exclusively with the production of original drawings, this test has a fairly high ceiling and shows adequate discrimination among applicants for admission to art schools. The test includes the following two parts:

1. *Scribble and Doodle Exercise:* The examinee is directed to make 20 quick drawings of common objects (e.g., tree, house, box) and of geometric figures (e.g., six circles, four squares). Time allowed for each drawing varies from 3 to 10 seconds. This exercise is designed partly to give the examinee confidence that he can draw simple shapes and partly to indicate quality of line, originality, and compositional sense.

2. *Imagery:* This test provides 12 rectangles, in each of which a few lines have been printed to act as springboards for artistic compositions. The examinee sketches a picture in each rectangle, building on the given lines. In Figure 81 will be found a given set of lines with two different drawings made from the same lines, used for demonstration purposes in the test.

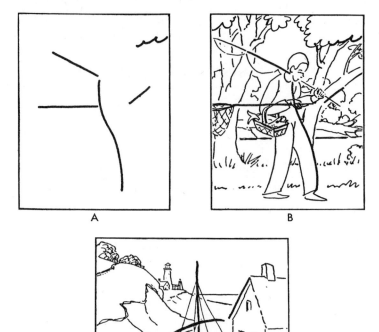

FIG. 81.   Sample Item from the "Imagery" Test of the Horn Art Aptitude
Inventory. The first rectangle shows the stimulus lines; the other two contain
drawings made with these stimulus lines. In the second drawing, the card has
been turned to a horizontal position. (From Horn and Smith, 1945, p. 351; reproduced by permission of American Psychological Association.)

Scoring of the Horn Art Aptitude Inventory illustrates the use of the
product scale technique. Samples of excellent, average, and poor work are
furnished as a basis for rating the subject's drawings. As an additional
scoring guide, the manual lists certain factors to be considered, such as
order, clarity of thought and presentation, quality of line, use of shading,
fertility of imagination, and scope of interests. Although the scoring still
leaves much to subjective judgment, correlations of .79 to .86 are reported
between the results obtained by different scorers.

No norms are included in the manual. An alternate-form reliability of
.76 was found by administering different forms on the same day to 70 art
school applicants. Some indication of validity is provided by two studies
conducted with the Horn test. Within a group of 52 art school graduates, a
correlation of .53 was found between test scores and mean instructors'
ratings of performance in a 3-year art course. The second study was con-

ducted with 36 high school seniors enrolled in a special art course. In this group, the test scores obtained at the beginning of the year correlated .66 with mean instructors' ratings at the end of the course. A negligible correlation between performance on the Horn test and intelligence test scores was found in the previously mentioned group of 52 art school graduates.

As a measure of the more complex aspects of artistic aptitude at a relatively high level, this test appears to have promise. It has, however, been criticized on the grounds that the scoring puts a premium on conformity to tradition in technique and composition, while great artists often deviate from the norm in these respects. Such a criticism could probably be directed against all current art aptitude tests. Whether a test can be devised to measure the degree of originality characteristic of truly great art remains to be seen. In the meantime, many aspects of artistic aptitude can be measured. The skills involved may represent necessary though not sufficient conditions for artistic production.

MUSICAL APTITUDES

SEASHORE MEASURES OF MUSICAL TALENTS. During the first four decades of this century, extensive research on the psychology of music was conducted at the University of Iowa under the direction of Carl E. Seashore (1938). One of the outcomes of these investigations was the preparation of the Seashore Measures of Musical Talents. In its present form, this series consists of six tests covering pitch, loudness, rhythm, time, timbre, and tonal memory. The Seashore tests are now available on both an LP record and a tape recording. Either or both of these modes of presentation are utilized in most current musical aptitude tests to permit group administration and to ensure uniformity of procedure.

Each item in the Seashore tests consists of a pair of tones or tonal sequences. In the pitch test, the examinee indicates whether the second tone is higher or lower than the first. The items are made progressively more difficult by decreasing the difference in pitch between the two tones in each pair. In the loudness test, the question is whether the second tone is stronger or weaker than the first. The rhythm test requires the comparsion of rhythmic patterns that are either the same or different within each pair. In the time test, the examinee records whether the second tone in each pair is longer or shorter than the first. The timbre test calls for the discrimination of tone quality, the two tones in each pair being either the same or different in this respect. In the tonal memory test, short series of three to five tones are played twice in immediate succession. During the second playing, one note is changed, and the examinee must write the number of the altered note, i.e., first, second, etc.

The Seashore tests are applicable from the fourth grade to the adult level.

The testing of younger children by this procedure has not proved feasible because of the difficulty of sustaining interest and attention. Even above the age of 10, the scores on these tests may be lowered by inattention. The scores are not combined into a single total, but are evaluated separately in terms of percentile norms. These norms are reported for grades 4 to 5, 6 to 8, and 9 to 16, the normative samples for each test and grade level containing from 377 to 4,319 cases. Age changes are slight and sex differences are negligible. The tests are probably somewhat susceptible to practice and training, although studies of these effects have yielded conflicting results.

Kuder-Richardson reliability coefficients of the six Seashore tests range from .55 to .85 within the three normative grade-level groups. Only content validity is discussed in the manual, Seashore having argued over the years that this is the most appropriate type of validity for such tests. It is undoubtedly true that ability to discriminate pitch, loudness, timbre, and other properties of tones is essential to both appreciation and production of music. To predict musical achievement, however, we need to know much more. What is the minimum cutoff point for different kinds of musical activities? Is there any correlation between test scores and musical performance beyond the cutoff point? What is the relative importance of each of the functions measured by the tests, both in relation to each other and in relation to the entire array of requisite traits? A few scattered studies provide some evidence of predictive validity against various criteria of performance in music training. Many of these validity coefficients are low, few reaching .30 or .40. Apart from the unreliability of criterion measures and the complexity of factors affecting musical achievement, it should be noted that these investigations were conducted on selected samples of music students. Presumably most of the individuals falling below a certain minimum in relevant auditory capacities had already been eliminated from such groups.

Correlations with intelligence tests are negligible, as would be expected for special aptitude tests. Intercorrelations among the six tests are higher than had been anticipated. The functions measured by the different tests are thus less independent than had originally been supposed, a fact that has also been confirmed by factor analysis (McLeish, 1950). It should also be noted that the Seashore tests, or adaptations of them, have proved helpful in predicting achievement in certain civilian and military specialties requiring auditory discrimination, such as those of sonar operator and radiotelegrapher (Fleishman, 1955; Tufts, 1951).

WING STANDARDIZED TESTS OF MUSICAL INTELLIGENCE. A more comprehensive approach to the measurement of musical aptitude was followed in a battery developed in England by Herbert D. Wing (1941, 1962). Applicable from the age of 8 on, the Wing tests depart from the "atomistic" sensory orientation of the Seashore tests and make use of musically meaningful content. Piano music is employed in each of the seven tests, which cover chord analysis, pitch discrimination, memory for pitch, harmony, intensity, rhythm, and phrasing. The first three tests require sensory discrimination, but at a somewhat more complex level than in the Seashore tests. In the other four, the examinee compares the aesthetic quality of two versions. Thus the battery places considerable emphasis on music appreciation.

Presented on tape, the entire battery requires approximately one hour but may be administered in two sessions. Norms are provided for total scores on the seven-test battery, as well as for a subtotal on the first three tests only. It is suggested that the first three tests may be used as a short battery with younger children or as a preliminary screening instrument. Based on a standardization sample of over 8,000 cases, the norms are reported separately for each age from 8 to 17 (adult). For older children and adults, both retest and split-half reliabilities of total scores on the entire battery are in the .90's; but they drop to the .70's for younger children.

Preliminary studies of validity in small groups yielded correlations of .60 or higher with teachers' ratings of musical ability. Other validation studies on both children and adults give promising evidence of predictive validity in terms of performance in music training. The use of total scores is supported by the identification of a general factor of musical ability in factorial analyses of music tests (McLeish, 1950; Wing, 1941). This factor, described as the cognitive aspect of musical ability, accounted for 30 to 40 percent of the total test variances. The Wing tests have high ceilings and may find their greatest usefulness in the selection of musically talented children for further training.

CREATIVITY

THE MEASUREMENT OF CREATIVE TALENT. One of the major developments in psychological testing during the second half of the twentieth century concerns the measurement of creativity. This development is itself only one aspect of a massive upsurge in research on the nature and stimulation of creative talent (Anastasi, 1965, Ch. 11; Golann, 1963; Taylor, 1964a, 1964b; Taylor & Barron, 1963; Taylor & Williams, 1966; Torrance 1959, 1962). An increasing number of psychologists and educators have come to recognize that creative talent is not synonymous with academic intelligence and is rarely covered by tests yielding an "IQ." In an early paper, Thurstone (1951a) emphasized this distinction and provided a provocative analysis of the possible role of ideational fluency, inductive reasoning, and certain perceptual tendencies in creative behavior. He also called special attention to the contribution of nonintellectual, temperamental factors to creative activity. He observed that creativity is encouraged by a receptive as contrasted to a critical attitude toward novel ideas and that creative solutions are more likely to occur during periods of relaxed, dispersed attention than during periods of active concentration on a problem.

The investigation of creativity has received considerable impetus from the growing demand for research scientists, engineers, and high-level executives. Several currently available creativity tests, in fact, have been explicitly designed for use with engineers.[4] Studies of scientific talent are becoming increasingly concerned with creative abilities. Interest has shifted from the individual who is merely a cautious, accurate, and critical thinker to the one who also displays ingenuity, originality, and inventiveness. Thus creativity, long regarded as the prime quality in artistic production, is coming more and more to be recognized as a basis for scientific achievement as well.

Investigations of the variables associated with creative achievement have followed a variety of approaches. Some have concentrated on the creative person's biographical history and antecedent experiences; others have analyzed the situational variables conducive to creative productivity. Some investigators have conducted intensive clinical studies of highly eminent scientists. Still others have combined a clinical with a psychometric approach through the use of a variety of personality-testing techniques and controlled observational procedures. This approach is exemplified by the continuing research conducted by MacKinnon (1962) and his associates at the University of California's Institute of Personality Assessment and Research (IPAR). In both the IPAR investigations and other research projects, large and significant differences in a number of personality traits have been found between creative and noncreative groups. Some of the tests employed in this type of research will be examined in Chapter 20.

Standardized tests of creative aptitudes have been produced chiefly in the course of large-scale research projects on the nature of creativity. Two major batteries, to be considered below, are the University of Southern California tests, developed by Guilford and his colleagues, and the Torrance Tests of Creative Thinking. Although commercially available, all these tests are still in experimental form and not ready for operational use. The items in creativity tests are typically open-ended, thus precluding objective scoring. For this reason, it is imperative to ascertain scorer reliability for all such instruments. Norms are generally tentative, being based on small scattered groups chosen primarily because of availability. Data on reliability and validity vary among individual tests but are usually quite limited. At this stage, the chief application of these tests is in research. The availability of uniform, standardized testing instruments assures a

---

[4] See, e.g., the following tests listed in Appendix C: AC Test of Creative Ability, Owens Creativity Test for Machine Design, Purdue Creativity Test.

reasonable degree of comparability among different investigations. Eventually some of these tests may be ready for use in clinical, counseling, educational, or vocational situations.

TESTS FROM THE UNIVERSITY OF SOUTHERN CALIFORNIA APTITUDES PROJECT. In Chapter 13 we discussed the factor-analytic research conducted by Guilford and his associates at the University of Southern California. Extending over nearly two decades, this research led to the formulation of the structure-of-intellect model (SI). While this model encompasses all intellectual functions, a major contribution of the Aptitudes Project was in the divergent-production section, about which relatively little prior research was available. In fact, the Aptitudes Project began primarily as an investigation of reasoning, creativity, and problem-solving.

In the course of his factor-analytic investigations, Guilford developed the categories of divergent and convergent thinking. Convergent thinking leads to a single correct solution determined by the given facts. Divergent thinking, on the other hand, is "the kind that goes off in different directions" (Guilford, 1959, p. 381). Such thinking is less restricted by given facts; it permits changes of direction in problem-solving and leads to a diversity of solutions or products. Figure 82 shows the location of the divergent-production slice of the SI model, together with the individual cells for which tests have thus far been published. These tests are described below, along with the code letters of the principal SI factor measured by each. This code, reproduced in Figure 82, always gives the Operation, Content, and Product in that order. For example, DSU stands for "divergent production of symbolic units."

Christensen-Guilford Fluency Tests—four tests in which the examinee writes words as rapidly as possible to meet the following conditions:

Word Fluency (DSU)—words containing a specified letter. E.g., "O": load, over, pot. . . .

Ideational Fluency (DMU)—names of things belonging in a given class. E.g., "fluids that will burn": gasoline, kerosene, alcohol. . . .

Associational Fluency (DMR)—words similar in meaning to a given word. E.g., "hard": difficult, solid, tough. . . .

Expressional Fluency (DSS)—four-word sentences, each word to begin with a given letter. E.g., "K⎯⎯ u⎯⎯ y⎯⎯ i⎯⎯.": Keep up your interest. Kill useless yellow insects. . . . The score depends on the number of different sentences the examinee can write with each set of four letters.

Alternate Uses (DMC)—list possible uses for a specified object, other than its common use. E.g., "Newspaper (used for reading)": Start a fire. Stuffing to pack boxes. . . .

Consequences (DMU, DMT)—list different consequences of a given hypothetical event. E.g., "What would be the results if people no longer needed or wanted

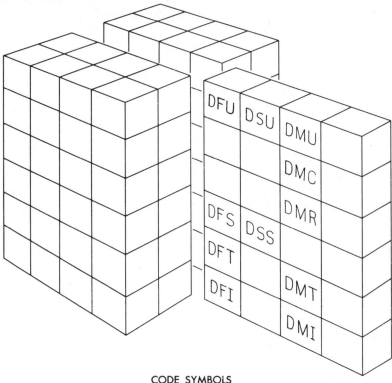

CODE SYMBOLS

Operation
D – Divergent Production

Contents
F – Figural
S – Symbolic
M – Semantic
B – Behavioral

Products
U – Units
C – Classes
R – Relations
S – Systems
T – Transformations
I – Implications

FIG. 82.   Southern California Tests of Divergent Production Placed within the Structure of Intellect Model.

sleep?": Get more work done. Alarm clocks not necessary. . . . Two scores are obtained: total number of "obvious" responses (ideational fluency—DMU); total number of "remote" responses (Originality—DMT).[5]

Possible Jobs (DMI)—list possible jobs that might be symbolized by a given emblem. E.g., "light bulb": electrical engineer, light-bulb manufacturer, a bright student. . . .

Making Objects (DFS)—draw specified objects using only a set of given figures,

[5] Although for an adult population this score did have its highest loading in the originality factor, for a ninth-grade population its highest loading was in spontaneous flexibility (DMC). The difference between these two factors stems largely from the extent to which the individual changes from one catgeory of consequences to another in his responses.

like circle, triangle, etc. Any given figure may be used repeatedly for the same object and may be changed in size, but no other figures or lines may be added. Figure 83 shows the demonstration item employed as a fore-exercise in this test.

Sketches (DFU)—similar to Making Objects, except that each test page contains a set of identical figures, such as circles. The examinee makes as many *different* sketches as possible by elaborating on each figure.

Match Problems (DFT)—remove a specified number of matchsticks, leaving a specified number of squares or triangles. Figure 84 shows part of one of the two demonstration items used with this test.

Decorations (DFI)—outline drawings of common objects are to be decorated with as many *different* designs as possible.

It should be noted that the first seven tests listed above require verbal responses, while the last four employ figural or pictorial content. These 11 tests represent only a small sample of the series developed in the Aptitudes Project. Other available tests from that project may be published in the years to come. Still more tests will undoubtedly be added as research continues on the unfilled cells of the SI model.

In the preliminary manuals, Guilford and his coworkers provide tentative norms in terms of C scores [6] and percentiles. For most of the tests,

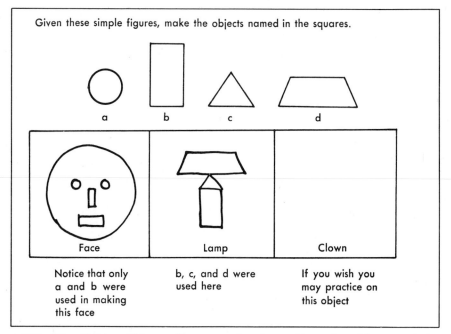

FIG. 83. Making Objects: Demonstration Item. (Reproduced by permission of Sheridan Psychological Services, Inc.)

[6] Similar to stanines, but with 11 units instead of 9.

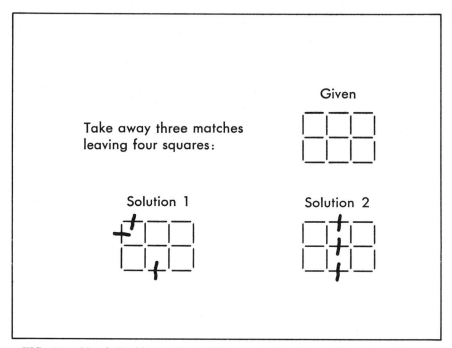

FIG. 84. Match Problems: Part of Demonstration Item. (Reproduced by permission of Sheridan Psychological Services, Inc.)

these norms are given for groups of adults, or ninth-grade students, or both. The tests are generally applicable at the high school level and above, although some are said to be suitable as far down as the first grade. Scorer reliability is not reported in the manuals, but other investigators who have employed these tests in research have obtained coefficients around .90 (see, e.g., Schaefer, 1967). With a reasonable amount of practice in following the instructions and studying the examples in the manuals, such tests can probably be scored with satisfactory consistency, although the scoring process is quite laborious and time consuming.

Split-half reliability coefficients reported in the manuals run lower than would be desirable, ranging from the .60's to the .80's. For all these tests, factorial validity is reported in terms of the SI factors. Such validity data are based on the extensive research that preceded the publication of each test. Information on criterion-related validity, however, is lacking except for a few scattered independent investigations. A possible limitation of all these tests is their heavy reliance on speed of production.

TORRANCE TESTS OF CREATIVE THINKING. While the Southern California tests were a by-product of factor-analytic research on the nature of intellect, the Torrance tests were developed within an educational context, as part of a long-term research program emphasizing classroom experiences that foster and stimulate creativity (Torrance, 1959, 1962). Some of the Torrance tests are adaptations of techniques employed in the Southern California tests. Moreover, the scores derived from the complete batteries are based on factors identified in Guilford's research, namely, Fluency, Flexibility, Originality, and Elaboration. In this connection, Torrance explains that he did not seek factorially pure tests. Rather, he tried to contrive situations that provide models of the creative process in its natural complexity. Each test is therefore scored in terms of two, three, or all four of the above factors.

The Torrance Tests of Creative Thinking comprise ten tests, grouped into a verbal and a pictorial battery. The first battery is labeled *Thinking Creatively with Words*, the second *Thinking Creatively with Pictures*. In an effort to eliminate threat and to induce a comfortable and stimulating psychological climate, the tests are called "activities" and the instructions place much emphasis on "having fun." The tests are described as suitable from kindergarten to graduate school, although below the fourth grade they have to be administered individually and orally. Two equivalent forms of each battery are available.

In *Thinking Creatively with Words*, the first three activities (Ask-and-Guess) utilize a rather intriguing picture to which the examinee responds by: (1) writing all the questions he would need to ask to find out what is happening; (2) listing possible causes of the action depicted; and (3) listing possible consequences of the action. Activity 4 is concerned with ways of improving a given toy so that children will have more fun playing with it. Activity 5 calls for a list of unusual uses for a common object, as in Guilford's Alternate Uses. Activity 6 requires unusual questions that could be asked about the same object. Activity 7, modeled after Guilford's Consequences, asks for all the things that would happen if a given improbable situation were true. The entire battery yields a total score in each of three traits: Fluency, Flexibility, and Originality.

Thinking Creatively with Pictures consists of three activities. In Picture Construction, a brightly colored curved shape is pasted by the examinee on a blank sheet in a position of his choice and is used as a starting point for drawing an unusual picture "that tells an interesting and exciting story." Picture Completion provides a few lines as a start for drawing a picture in each item. This test utilizes the same technique as the Horn Art Aptitude Inventory discussed earlier in this chapter. In the Torrance test, however, the instructions stress unusual ideas and the scoring is based on aspects of creativity rather than on artistic quality. The last activity provides pairs of short parallel lines (Form A) or circles (Form B), with which as many different pictures as possible are to be produced. Four total scores are obtained from the pictorial battery: Fluency, Flexibility, Originality, and Elaboration.

The manuals accompanying the Torrance batteries provide detailed scoring guides, with many examples. The technical manual cites the results of several studies of scorer reliability, indicating a range of interscorer correlations from .76 to .99. Originality is the most difficult trait to score, having yielded the only scorer reliabilities under .80. Some studies on alternate-form reliabilities with intervals of one to two weeks yielded coefficients ranging from the .70's to the .90's. In general, the verbal scores show higher reliabilities than the figural scores. Tentative norms for each of the three verbal and four figural scores are given as T scores in terms of a fixed reference group of fifth-grade children (number not specified). Means and SD's of several other groups of children and adults are also given for comparative purposes.

As in the Southern California tests, speed is an integral part of performance on the Torrance tests, a characteristic common to virtually all current creativity tests. The technical manual summarizes a number of investigations in which the Torrance tests were employed for a variety of research purposes. All these unrelated studies contribute toward the construct validation of the tests, but no clear picture emerges as yet. Most of the studies were conduced on schoolchildren, although some data on high school and college students and on occupational adult groups are also cited. Many suggestive relationships have been found between Torrance scores and interests, attitudes, and other personality traits measured by tests, ratings, or other assessment procedures. Significant improvement in Torrance scores has also been observed as a result of educational experiences designed to stimulate creative thinking, but no external evidence is provided to indicate whether such improvement extends to other, non-test situations.

In general, evidence of relation between the Torrance tests and everyday-life criteria of creative achievement is meager. Ongoing longitudinal studies of high school students, cited in the manual, should contribute toward this type of validation. There is need for comprehensive, systematic validation studies showing the relation of these tests to measures of other intellectual traits as well as to practical criteria. Finally, the use of Fluency, Flexibility, Originality, and Elaboration scores that cut across the individual tests is questionable. A factor analysis of the performance of about 800 fifth-grade children on the Torrance tests gave no support to the interpretation of these scores in terms of single constructs (Yamamoto & Frengel, 1966). On the contrary, the factors identified were task-specific. Thus, the intercorrelations of different scores derived from a single test were higher than the intercorrelations of similarly labeled scores (e.g., Fluency) derived from different tests.

CREATIVE ACHIEVEMENT. Although tests of divergent production, such as those of Guilford and Torrance, probably come closest to measuring the essential aspects of creativity, other abilities are undoubtedly needed for effective creative achievement, especially in the sciences. In their zeal to counteract the earlier concentration on comprehension and memory, as represented by traditional intelligence tests, some investigators may have swung too far in the opposite direction. For genuine creative achievement, the uninhibited divergent-production phase must eventually be followed by critical evaluation. In the technique popularly known as "brainstorming," for example, creativity is stimulated by the temporal separation of the productive and evaluative phases of creative activity. A critical, evaluative attitude at an early stage of creative production may seriously thwart the development of new ideas. But critical evaluation is to be only temporarily deferred, not permanently abolished.

Several cognitive and evaluative aptitudes usually classified under reasoning have emerged from the Guilford research. Some of the published tests from the Aptitudes Project measure these factors. Among them are: the Ship Destination Test, which is heavily loaded with a general reasoning factor and utilizes problems similar to those found in arithmetic reasoning tests; Logical Reasoning, composed of items in syllogistic form; and Pertinent Questions, designed as a measure of conceptual foresight. Another test covering several aspects of effective reasoning is the Watson-Glaser Critical Thinking Appraisal. Designed for high school and college levels, this test contains five parts, dealing with inference, recognition of assumptions, deduction, interpretation, and evaluation of arguments.

In discussing creative productivity in the arts, Guilford (1957, 1967) suggests that several of the divergent-production factors so far identified may play an important part. Those in the verbal area, with which many of the available tests are concerned, are probably related to creative writing. Corresponding factors pertaining to visual, auditory, or even kinaesthetic figural content—many of which have not yet been identified—may play an equally important part in the graphic arts, music, and choreography. In addition, creative productivity in the arts, as in the sciences, undoubtedly requires a certain minimum proficiency in relevant comprehension and memory factors, such as verbal comprehension, spatial orientation, visual or auditory memory, and the like.

It is thus apparent that creative achievement—whether in science, engineering, art, music, or other fields of human endeavor—requires a complex pattern of aptitudes and personality traits appropriate to the particular field. Current tests of creativity concentrate on certain elements of this pattern that had heretofore been largely neglected in psychometrics. But they are not intended to replace other types of available tests.

CHAPTER **15**

Educational
Tests

NEARLY EVERY type of available test is currently being utilized in the schools. Intelligence, special aptitude, multiple aptitude, and personality tests can all be found in the repertory of the educational counselor and the school psychologist. Teachers and educational administrators frequently have to act on the results obtained with several different kinds of tests. Nevertheless, certain types of tests have been specially developed for use in educational contexts, predominantly at the elementary and high school levels. It is with these tests that the present chapter is concerned. They include: (1) *predictive instruments* designed for relatively specific educational purposes; and (2) the many varieties of educational *achievement tests*.

PREDICTIVE INSTRUMENTS

All aptitude tests considered in previous chapters are predictive instruments, and several of them—particularly scholastic aptitude or general intelligence tests—are commonly employed to predict educational performance. Two additional types of predictors, to be considered in this section, are tests of school readiness and prognostic tests for special courses of study.

SCHOOL READINESS. Readiness tests are designed to assess the child's specific qualifications for schoolwork. Essentially, "readiness" refers to the attainment of prerequisite intellectual skills and knowledge that enable

382

the learner to profit maximally from a given kind of instruction. Individual differences in the reading readiness of first-grade schoolchildren provide a familiar example. At one time, readiness was conceived largely in terms of maturation. To be sure, the development of certain minimum physical qualifications facilitate some kinds of learning. Unless a child can make the necessary auditory discriminations, he cannot learn to speak by the usual procedures; without the ability for fine motor coordination, he is unable to manipulate a pencil in writing. Most school learning, however, is not so closely linked to sensorimotor development. In the mastery of educational tasks, the importance of prior learning is being increasingly recognized. More and more emphasis is now placed on the hierarchical development of knowledges and skills, whereby the acquisition of simple concepts equips the child for the learning of more complex concepts at any age.

Readiness tests are generally administered upon school entrance. While they have much in common with intelligence tests for the primary grades, readiness tests place more emphasis on the abilities found to be important in learning to read. Some attention is also given to the prerequisites of numerical thinking and to the sensorimotor control required in learning to write. Among the specific functions frequently covered are visual and auditory discrimination, motor control, verbal comprehension, vocabulary, quantitative concepts, and general information.

As an example of readiness tests for the first grade, we may examine the Metropolitan Readiness Tests. Revised in 1965, this battery consists of the following six subtests:

1. *Word Meaning:* In each row of three pictures, the child selects the one that illustrates the word the examiner names (see Fig. 85).

2. *Listening:* This test is similar to Test 1, except that instead of single words, one or more sentences are used to identify the correct picture in each row.

3. *Matching:* This test requires the recognition of similarities and differences in visual material, including diagrams, numbers, letters, and words (see Fig. 85).

4. *Alphabet:* Letters named by the examiner must be identified on the printed page. This test proved to be the best single predictor of subsequent success in reading.

5. *Numbers:* Covering a wide variety of quantitative concepts and simple numerical operations, this test resembles closely the quantitative subtests included in intelligence tests for the primary grades.

6. *Copying:* The child copies simple geometric forms as well as numbers or letters. This test is related to both physical development and intellectual maturity in young children. It also reveals the tendency toward reversals in drawing and writing shown by some children.

The Metropolitan Readiness Tests are available in two equivalent forms. Total scores can be converted to percentiles or stanines. These norms were

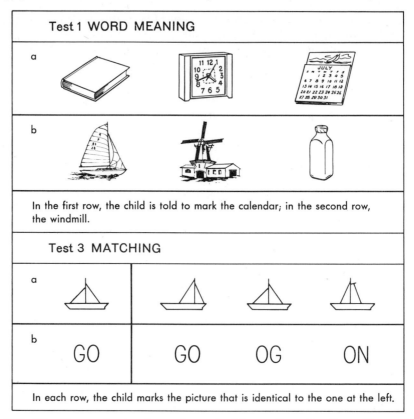

Test 1 WORD MEANING

a

b

In the first row, the child is told to mark the calendar; in the second row, the windmill.

Test 3 MATCHING

a

b

GO GO OG ON

In each row, the child marks the picture that is identical to the one at the left.

FIG. 85. Demonstration Items from the Metropolitan Readiness Tests. (Reproduced by permission of Harcourt, Brace & World.)

based on a nationwide sample of approximately 15,000 first-grade children tested during the first month of school. A classification of score ranges into five readiness levels is also provided. As a supplementary measure, the manual recommends the use of a draw-a-man test, modeled after the Goodenough-Harris test discussed in Chapter 10. The scoring, however, involves the classification of each drawing as a whole into one of five broad categories, rather than the assignment of specific points.

Both alternate-form and split-half reliability coefficients over .90 have been obtained with the Metropolitan Readiness Tests. As is true of readiness tests generally, this test shows considerable overlap with intelligence tests for the primary grades. In a sample of over 12,000 cases, it correlated .76 with the Pintner-Cunningham Primary Test. Evidence of predictive validity is provided by correlations with end-of-year achievement test scores. In a sample of approximately 9,500 cases, these correlations ranged from .575 to .674 with different subtests of the Stanford Achievement Test. All these correlations were slightly higher than the correlations of the Pintner-

Cunningham with the corresponding achievement test scores. Since they are more specifically based on identifiable prerequisite skills, readiness tests are probably better predictors of first-grade achievement than are the more general intelligence tests. Scores on readiness tests are also less subject to misinterpretation than are IQ's; they are less likely to be regarded as providing a permanent "label" for the child.

A different approach to the assessment of school readiness is represented by the developmental behavior tests assembled by Ilg and Ames (1964, 1965) at the Gesell Institute. The procedure described by these authors is essentially that of an individual clinical examination requiring approximately ½ hour per child. Applicable between the ages of 5 and 10 years, this examination is recommended for use not only at school entrance but also prior to promotion to higher grades. Ilg and Ames argue that the usual intelligence or school readiness test is too limited in coverage and that a child may obtain a superior score on such a test but be immature in his general behavior. In contrast, their objective is to assess the developmental level at which the child is behaving as a total organism.

The examination includes the following parts:

1. Initial interview in which the child is asked about his age, birth date, birthday party, names and ages of siblings, and father's occupation.

2. Paper-and-pencil tests: writing name, address, date, and numbers; copying geometric forms; completing an unfinished drawing of a man and answering questions about him.

3. Right-and-left orientation tests: naming parts of body to which examiner points; executing simple motor activities; giving both visual and motor responses to pictures of right and left hands in various positions.

4. Visual form tests: matching forms; memory for designs; projective responses to designs (what does each form look like, what does it remind you of?)

5. Naming all the animals the child can think of in 60 seconds.

6. Concluding interview, in which the child is asked about his favorite indoor and outdoor activities in school and at home.

As useful adjuncts to evaluation, Ilg and Ames also recommend an examination of the teeth, with special reference to the loss of baby teeth as an index of physical development; a vision examination; oral reading tests; and a projective test. Detailed instructions are provided for administering the tests and evaluating the responses. Norms are in the form of percentages of children at each age giving each response, but no quantitative score is computed. As a further aid in evaluating the child's developmental level, age descriptions are provided for each age between 5 and 10 years. These descriptions include a general picture of the behavior characteristic of each age and a summary of typical test responses. In a demonstration project, the authors trained schoolteachers to conduct this examination, but they recommend that the tests be used and interpreted under the supervision of a "developmental guidance coordinator" in each school.

The normative data were derived through four years of longitudinal testing of three overlapping age groups between the ages of 5 and 10 years. The sample included 50 boys and 50 girls at each year of age (including one group at 5½ years). The children were obtained from two Connecticut schools, their grade distribution ranging from kindergarten to the fifth grade. Socioeconomic level was above average, as were the mean IQ's on standard intelligence tests. The normative sample is obviously small and drawn from a rather narrowly limited population. Although not attempting to evaluate these basically clinical procedures in psychometric terms, Ilg and Ames cite some evidence of predictive validity. In a 3-year study in another Connecticut school, they found agreement ranging from 65 percent to 95 percent between estimates of relative developmental level reached from yearly retests. They also report agreements ranging from 59 percent to 83 percent between predictions based on the developmental examination findings in the fall of any year and teachers' judgments in the following spring. This agreement was highest for kindergarten children, lower for first graders, and lowest for second graders. It is possible that this type of examination is most effective at the time of school entrance.

Still another approach to the evaluation of school readiness is to be found in a joint project of the New York City Board of Education and Educational Testing Service (see Loretan, 1966). The procedures developed in this project, known as Let's Look at First Graders, combine assessment and instruction in a continuous program conducted by the teachers themselves in the course of daily classwork. The basic orientation of the program has several noteworthy features that reflect current thinking about the meaning and use of tests. Thus, it is recognized that all tests are measures of behavior samples. Hence, the more extended behavior samples observed in the classroom are not intrinsically different from those observed in testing. Placing tests within such a natural, behavioral context may help to take the "magic" out of tests and to dispel some of the entrenched misconceptions about intelligence tests.

In Let's Look at First Graders, intelligence is seen to comprise a variety of intellectual skills by which the individual processes, organizes, and manipulates information from his environment. These intellectual skills are learned through interaction with the environment. Incorporating Piaget's views on child development (see Flavell, 1963), this program focuses on the transition from prelogical to logical concrete thinking—a transition typically occurring at the first-grade level. The authors began by collecting specific instances of behavior reported by teachers as signs of intellectual development. They then prepared a Guide for use by teachers in both assessment of pupil developmental level and instruction. The Guide provides descriptions of six major areas of intellectual development, together with behavior illustrating each. The six areas and the developmental concepts included within each area are as follows:

1. Basic Language Skills: auditory discrimination and attention, listening comprehension, learning to communicate, language for thinking.

2. Concepts of Space and Time: learning shapes and forms, spatial perspective, the notion of time.

3. Beginning Logical Concepts: logical classification, concepts of relationship.

4. Beginning Mathematical Concepts: the conservation of quantity, one-to-one correspondence, number relations.

5. The Growth of Reasoning Skills: understanding cause and effect, reasoning by association, reasoning by inference.

6. General Signs of Development: growing awareness and responsiveness, directed activity, general knowledge, developing imagination.

In addition, there is a set of instructional and assessment materials, providing more or less standard tasks that can be employed by the teacher to elicit behavior within each area. Some of these tasks are suitable for an entire class, others must be performed in small groups, and still others individually. A typical task is the "conservation problem," illustrated in Figure 86. Equal numbers of wooden beads are dropped, one at a time, into a

FIG. 86. Small Group of First-Grade Children Working on the "Conservation of Quantity" Problem from Let's Look at First Graders. (Reprinted by permission of the Board of Education, City of New York; Photograph by Rollie McKenna.)

tall, narrow jar and into a short, wide jar. It is characteristic of children at the prelogical stage that they do not accept the equality in number of beads under these conditions. Even after they have watched the beads being dropped into the two jars at the same time, they will say one jar contains more beads than the other. At this stage they have not yet grasped the principle that a physical quantity remains the same despite transformations in shape or position.

A series of written exercises is also available for group administration. Falling within the same areas of intellectual development, these exercises are the most testlike materials in the program. A characteristic feature of the exercises, however, is the provision of extensive practice before the child's performance is evaluated. Two demonstration items from exercises dealing with time concepts are reproduced in Figure 87.

Let's Look at First Graders provides no norms or other psychometric data. It is designed to yield only qualitative descriptions of the child's developmental level in basic intellectual skills. In contrast to standardized tests, such as the Metropolitan Readiness Tests, and to individual clinical evaluations as illustrated by the Gesell Institute procedures, Let's Look at First Graders is an attempt to systematize teachers' observations of classroom behavior and to combine assessment with teaching.

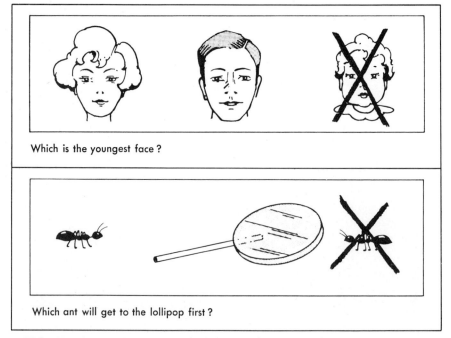

Which is the youngest face ?

Which ant will get to the lollipop first ?

FIG. 87. Demonstration Items from Written Exercises on Time Concepts, in Let's Look at First Graders. (Reprinted by permission of the Board of Education, City of New York.)

SPECIALIZED PROGNOSTIC TESTS. Certain tests have been designed to predict performance in specific courses of study, principally in mathematics and foreign languages. Prognostic tests in mathematics are illustrated by the Orleans-Hanna Algebra Prognosis Test and the Orleans-Hanna Geometry Prognosis Test. In both of these tests, the student is provided with simple material to learn from algebra or geometry, and is immediately tested on what he has learned. These tests are thus worksamples, in which the student's subsequent course learning is predicted from his performance in the sample learning tasks. Other prognostic tests in mathematics cover a combination of prerequisite arithmetic skills and new learning. Some contain material similar to that found in the numerical subtests of intelligence tests, such as number series completions. All such prognostic tests are normally validated against subsequent course grades and terminal achievement test scores.

Another type of predictive instrument is illustrated by the Modern Language Aptitude Test. Designed to assess the capacity of an English-speaking student for learning any foreign language, this test utilizes both paper-and-pencil and tape-recorded materials. It is suitable for high school, college, and adult groups. Two of its subtests require the learning of orally presented numbers and visually presented words in an artificial language. The other three parts test the subject's sensitivity to English grammatical structure, as well as certain word recognition skills with visual and auditory materials. The test may also be administered in a shorter form not requiring a tape recorder.

Percentile norms are reported for beginning language students in grades 9, 10, 11, and 13, as well as for military and civilian personnel assigned to intensive foreign language training. Most of the normative samples are small, however, and may not be comparable at different grade levels. Split-half reliabilities for both total test and short form are high, most of them exceeding .90. Data on predictive validity in college and high school groups appear promising. In an earlier experimental version, this test proved especially effective in predicting success in intensive language training courses conducted by the Foreign Service Institute of the Department of State, the Air Force, and the Army Language School. An elementary form of this test, suitable for grades 3 to 6, was published in 1967.

Designed for the same general purpose, the Pimsleur Language Aptitude Test is applicable in grades 6 to 12. The total score on this test is a weighted sum of the scores on four subtests, the student's grade-point average in academic areas other than foreign languages, and his self-rated interest in learning a foreign language. The four subtests provide measures of English vocabulary, ability to identify and correctly apply grammatical endings and word sequences in an artificial language (see Fig. 88), ability to learn new phonetic distinctions and to recognize them in different contexts, and ability to associate sounds with their written symbols. The di-

---

The list below contains words from a foreign language
and the English equivalents of these words.

gade .... father, a father
shi .... horse, a horse
gade shir le .... Father sees a horse.

By referring to the above list, figure out how the following statement should be expressed in this language.

A horse sees Father.

(Correct answer: shi gader le.)

FIG. 88. Demonstration item from Pimsleur Language Aptitude Test. (Reproduced by permission of Harcourt, Brace & World.)

rections for all tests as well as the items for the last two tests are on tape.

Both percentile and stanine norms are given for students tested at the
beginning of grades 7, 8, and 9, as well as for students completing the first
year of instruction in French or Spanish. Each normative sample includes
from about 1,000 to about 3,000 students drawn from 5 to 13 states. Norms
are available for total scores and for verbal and auditory scores, each of
the latter being based on the sum of two subtests. Split-half reliabilities in
the .80's were obtained for total scores within each grade level of the
normative sample. A few medium to high correlations with terminal course
grades and achievement test scores are reported. It is likely, however, that
the parts of the battery should be combined with different weights for
predicting different aspects of language mastery, such as listening comprehension, speaking, reading, and writing.

ACHIEVEMENT TESTS: THEIR NATURE AND USES

NATURE. Surpassing all other types of standardized tests in sheer numbers, achievement tests are designed to measure the effects of a specific
program of instruction or training. It is customary to contrast achievement
tests with aptitude tests, the latter including general intelligence tests, multiple aptitude batteries, and special aptitude tests. From one point of view,
the difference between achievement and aptitude testing is a difference in
the degree of uniformity of relevant antecedent experience. Thus, achievement tests measure the effects of relatively standardized sets of experiences, such as a course in elementary French, trigonometry, or Gregg

shorthand. In contrast, aptitude test performance reflects the cumulative influence of a multiplicity of experiences in daily living. We might say that aptitude tests measure the effects of learning under relatively uncontrolled and unknown conditions, while achievement tests measure the effects of learning that occurred under partially known and controlled conditions.

A second distinction between aptitude and achievement tests pertains to their respective uses. Aptitude tests serve to predict subsequent performance. They are employed to estimate the extent to which the individual will profit from training, or to forecast the quality of his achievement in a new situation. Achievement tests, on the other hand, generally represent a terminal evaluation of the individual's status on the completion of training. The emphasis in such tests is on what the individual can do at the time. This difference is perhaps most clearly illustrated by the procedures for estimating the validity of achievement tests, as contrasted with those followed in validating aptitude tests. Although predictive criterion-oriented validity is the most direct way of assessing aptitude tests, achievement tests are characteristically evaluated in terms of their content validity (Ch. 5).

It should be recognized, however, that no distinction between aptitude and achievement tests can be rigidly applied. Some aptitude tests may depend on fairly specific and uniform prior learning, while some achievement tests cover relatively broad and unstandardized educational experiences. Similarly, an achievement test may be used as a predictor of future learning. As such it serves the same purpose as an aptitude test. For example, the progress a pupil has made in arithmetic, as determined by his present achievement test score, may be employed to predict his subsequent success in algebra. Achievement tests on premedical courses can serve as predictors of performance in medical school. Whenever different individuals have had the same or closely similar courses of study, achievement tests based on such courses may provide efficient indices of future performance. When used for predictive purposes, of course, achievement tests should be evaluated in terms of their criterion correlations.

In differentiating between aptitude and achievement tests, we should especially guard against the naive assumption that achievement tests measure the effects of learning, while aptitude tests measure "innate capacity" independent of learning. This misconception was fairly prevalent in the early days of psychological testing, but has been largely corrected in the subsequent clarification of psychometric concepts. It should be obvious that all psychological tests measure the individual's current behavior, which inevitably reflects the influence of prior learning. The fact that every test score has a "past" does not, however, preclude its having a "future." While revealing the effects of past learning, test scores may, under certain conditions, serve as predictors of future learning.

A useful concept that is coming to replace the traditional categories of aptitude and achievement in psychometrics is that of *developed abilities*. All ability tests—whether they be designed as general intelligence tests, multiple aptitude batteries, special aptitude tests, or achievement tests— measure the level of development attained by the individual in one or more abilities. No test reveals how or why the individual reached that level. Existing tests of developed abilities may be ordered along a continuum in terms of the specificity of experiential background that they presuppose. This continuum is illustrated in Figure 89. At one extreme are the course-oriented achievement tests covering narrowly defined technical skills or factual information. A test in Russian vocabulary or television maintenance would fall at this end of the continuum. Many of the achievement tests employed for personnel selection or classification in industry or the armed services are of this type.

Next in the continuum come the broadly oriented achievement tests commonly used today to assess the attainment of major, long-term educational goals. Here we find tests focusing on the understanding and application of scientific principles, the interpretation of literature, or the appreciation of art. Still broader in orientation are tests of intellectual skills that affect the individual's performance in a wide variety of activities. These skills may themselves be rather narrowly defined, as in certain common work-study skills (e.g., interpretation of tables, use of indexes and dictionaries). Or they may be broader, such as reading comprehension and arithmetic computation. At the broadest level, we find achievement tests designed to measure the effects of education on logical thinking, critical evaluation of conclusions, problem-solving techniques, and imagination. It is apparent that at this point achievement tests fuse imperceptibly with traditional intelligence and aptitude tests. This overlapping of "aptitude" and "achievement" tests can easily be demonstrated empirically. An exam-

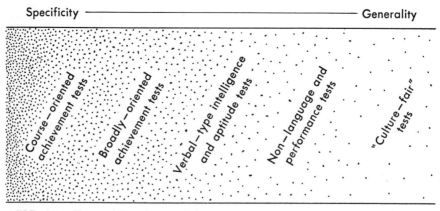

FIG. 89. Tests of Developed Abilities: Continuum of Experiential Specificity.

ination of the content of several current instruments classified as intelligence and as achievement tests, respectively, reveals close similarity of content. It has long been known, moreover, that intelligence tests correlate about as highly with achievement tests as different intelligence tests correlate with each other (Coleman & Cureton, 1954; Kelley, 1927, pp. 193–209). In some instances, in fact, the correlation between achievement and intelligence tests is as high as the reliability coefficients of each test.

Under these conditions, it is questionable whether broadly oriented achievement tests are contributing any information about individuals that could not be obtained from intelligence or other aptitude tests. Although the various available instruments may all serve useful purposes, there seems to be little justification for retaining different labels for them. In fact, calling one an aptitude and another an achievement test may lead to confusion and to the misuse of test results. As early as 1927, Kelley (1927) warned of the "Jangle fallacy," whereby two tests called by different names are assumed to be different.[1] This parallels the "Jingle fallacy," whereby two tests called by the same name (e.g., intelligence) are assumed to measure the same functions.

Further reference to Figure 89 shows a wide disparity among traditional intelligence tests with regard to the experiential or educational specificity of their content. The predominantly verbal intelligence or aptitude tests, such as the Stanford-Binet or the Differential Aptitude Tests, are closest to the achievement tests. Next come nonlanguage and performance tests, and finally the "culture-fair" tests designed for use with persons of widely varied experiential backgrounds (Ch. 10). As a safeguard against possible misinterpretation of either aptitude or achievement test scores, this schematic continuum should be kept constantly in mind.

USES. The many roles that achievement tests can play in the educational process have long been recognized. As an aid in the assignment of grades, such tests have the advantages of objectivity and uniformity. If properly constructed, they have other merits, such as adequacy of content coverage and reduction of the operation of irrelevant and chance factors in marking procedures. Achievement tests also constitute an important feature of remedial teaching programs. In this connection, they are useful both in the identification of pupils with special educational disabilities and in the measurement of progress in the course of remedial work.

For all types of learners, the periodic administration of well-constructed and properly chosen achievement tests serves to facilitate learning. Such

[1] This fallacy underlies the common practice of identifying as underachievers those children whose achievement test scores are lower than their intelligence test scores. A better indication of underachievement could be obtained by utilizing initial and final achievement test scores in a course. As usually computed, measures of over- or underachievement are quite meaningless because of inappropriate statistical procedures as well as conceptual fallacies. For a comprehensive analysis of the methodological problems, see Thorndike (1963).

tests reveal weaknesses in past learning, give direction to subsequent learning, and motivate the learner. The incentive value of "knowledge of results" has been repeatedly demonstrated by psychological experiments in many types of learning situations, with subjects of widely varying age and education. The effectiveness of such self-checking is generally heightened by immediacy. Thus, when achievement examinations are employed primarily as a learning aid, it is desirable for the students to become aware of their errors as soon after taking the tests as possible.

The use of achievement tests as learning devices is highlighted by the development of teaching machines and programed learning. Teaching machines are essentially instructional devices that afford an opportunity for active learner participation, provide immediate feedback or knowledge of results, and permit each individual to advance at his own pace. The teaching machine need not be a machine in the popular sense of "hardware." Some do use apparatus of varying degrees of complexity to present stimuli and record responses; but the same learning principles can be applied with simple paper-and-pencil materials or with programed textbooks. Programed learning, the common feature in all these procedures, involves a series of steps through which the learner is guided in a systematically established sequence. The individual learns by responding to each item and receiving immediate feedback regarding the correctness of his response. In this respect, programed learning represents an application of testing as a teaching technique. There is a considerable body of research demonstrating the effectiveness of this type of learning.

From another angle, achievement tests provide a means of adapting instruction to individual needs. Teaching can be most fruitful when it meets the learner at whatever stage he happens to be. Ascertaining what each individual is already able to do and what he already knows about a subject is thus a necessary first step for effective teaching. The growth of fall testing programs points up the increasing use of test results as a basis for planning what is to be taught to a class as a whole and what modifications and adjustments need to be made in individual cases. By giving tests at the beginning of the school year, constructive steps can be taken to fill the major gaps in knowledge revealed by the test results.

Finally, achievement tests may be employed as aids in the evaluation and improvement of teaching and in the formulation of educational goals. Achievement tests can provide information on the adequacy with which essential content and skills are actually being taught. They can likewise indicate how much of the course content is retained and for how long. Are certain types of material retained longer than others? What are the most common errors and misunderstandings encountered? How well can the learners apply their knowledge to new situations? By focusing attention on such questions and by providing concrete facts, achievement tests stimulate an analysis of training objectives and encourage a critical examination of the content and methods of instruction. In an incisive analysis of the development of educational goals, Dyer (1967) points out that to formulate functional goals we must begin with an investigation of the actual outcomes of present education. Moreover, he argues that "an educational goal is adequately defined only in terms of agreed-upon procedures and instruments by which its attainment is to be measured" (p. 22). Educational goals are often expressed as vague generalities and pious platitudes whose implementation remains a mystery. A carefully constructed achievement test is an effective way of spelling out and illustrating the concrete behavioral changes that a given educational experience is designed to effect.

GENERAL ACHIEVEMENT BATTERIES

NATURE AND SCOPE.   Several batteries are available for measuring general educational achievement in the areas most commonly covered by academic curricula. This type of test can be used from the primary grades to the adult level, although its major application has been in the elementary school. Typically these batteries provide profiles of scores on individual subtests or in major academic areas. An advantage of such batteries as against independently constructed achievement tests is that they may permit horizontal or vertical comparisons, or both. Thus, an individual's relative standing in different subject-matter areas or educational skills can be compared in terms of a uniform normative sample. Or the child's progress from grade to grade can be reported in terms of a single score scale. The test user should check whether a particular battery was so standardized as to yield either or both kinds of comparability.

To provide an overview of the nature and grade range of general achievement batteries, some representative examples have been listed in Table 34, together with the grade levels covered by each. It will be noted that some of these batteries are designed for the elementary grades, others for the high school; but most span a broad range extending into both levels and occasionally even into college. Although a few provide a single battery for the grade range covered, the large majority have several overlapping batteries for use at different grade levels.

Another major difference among available batteries pertains to their relative emphasis on educational skills and knowledge of content. A primary focus on skills is characteristic of the California Achievement Tests, Iowa Tests of Basic Skills, Iowa Tests of Educational Development, and SRA Achievement Series. These tests concentrate on such educational skills as reading, arithmetic, spelling and language usage, and work-study skills

TABLE 34 REPRESENTATIVE ACHIEVEMENT BATTERIES

Battery	\multicolumn{14}{c}{Grade}

Battery	1	2	3	4	5	6	7	8	9	10	11	12	13	14
California Achievement Tests	x	x	x	x	x	x	x	x	x	x	x	x	x	x
Iowa Tests of Basic Skills			x	x	x	x	x	x	x					
Iowa Tests of Educational Development									x	x	x	x		
Metropolitan Achievement Test	x	x	x	x	x	x	x	x	x	x	x	x		
SRA Achievement Series	x	x	x	x	x	x	x	x	x					
Sequential Tests of Educational Progress				x	x	x	x	x	x	x	x	x	x	x
Stanford Achievement Test[a]	x	x	x	x	x	x	x	x	x	x	x	x		
Tests of Academic Progress									x	x	x	x		

[a] Additional preprimary level scheduled for late 1968 publication. The high school battery, first added to the series in 1965, is an independent battery but closely related to the lower-level batteries in subject-matter coverage.

(e.g., map reading, reading graphs, use of references). When achievement in different subject-matter areas is to be measured—particularly at the high school level where specialized courses are common—this type of test may concentrate on the student's ability to understand passages from each content area. The Iowa Tests of Educational Development, for example, include tests on the ability to interpret reading materials in literature, the social studies, and the natural sciences.

Few batteries today are directed primarily toward testing in content areas. At the high school level, content knowledge may be measured with separate achievement tests for different subjects, to be discussed in the next section. Most batteries, at both elementary and high school levels, combine skill testing with some specialized content coverage. Such a composite approach is illustrated by the latest edition of the Stanford Achievement Test. First published in 1923, this pioneer battery was extensively revised in 1929, 1940, 1953, and 1964–1966. The elementary school portion of this battery, comprising four levels that span grades 1 to 9, yields scores in reading, language arts (chiefly spelling and language usage), arithmetic (computation, concepts, and applications), social studies, and science. The basic high school battery, first added to this series in 1965, includes tests in English, numerical competence, mathematics, reading, science, social studies, and spelling. Additional high school tests are available in arts and humanities, business and economics, and technical comprehension in industrial arts.

SEQUENTIAL TESTS OF EDUCATIONAL PROGRESS.   As a specific example of an achievement battery, we may consider the Sequential Tests of Educational Progress (STEP). These tests are available in four levels, suitable for grades 4–6, 7–9, 10–12, and 13–14. Each level contains six multiple-choice tests: Reading Comprehension, Writing, Mathematics, Science, Social Studies, and Listening Comprehension. All tests are available in two parallel forms and are published in separate booklets that may be obtained individually. Each of the six tests requires 70 minutes and can be administered in a single session or in two 35-minute sessions.

Although the need for specific knowledge in particular fields was recognized in constructing STEP items, major emphasis was placed on the application of learned skills to the solution of new problems. The tests are concerned more with the outcomes of school learning than with its content. Since teachers are likely to agree more closely on the objectives of instruction than on materials and methods, tests that concentrate on objectives were deemed to be more widely applicable. Such tests also encourage more flexibility with regard to the specific content taught. The STEP item writers displayed unusual ingenuity and skill in composing items that do in fact measure many of the intellectual skills outlined in such sources as the *Taxonomy of Educational Objectives* (Bloom *et al.*, 1956; see also Ch. 5).

Two examples typical of items found in the tests for Science (grades 4–6) and for Social Studies (grades 10–12) are reproduced in Figures 90 and 91. In the Science and Mathematics tests, a problem situation is presented and is followed by a set of related multiple-choice questions. The situations are chosen so as to be as realistic as possible, dealing with events in the home, at camp, on the farm, etc. A possible drawback of this type of item, especially in the Mathematics test, is its heavy loading with verbal comprehension. This is especially true at the lower levels, where a good deal of irrelevant verbal content is introduced to make each "story" appealing to children. It is not surprising, therefore, to find that at the fourth-grade level the STEP Mathematics score correlates more highly with the verbal than with the quantitative scores on SCAT. Even at higher levels, the correlations with SCAT verbal scores are high enough to denote considerable overlap.

A major portion of the STEP batteries is devoted to the testing of communication skills. This is accomplished through the tests of Writing, Reading Comprehension, and Listening Comprehension. In the Writing tests, the students are given a wide variety of written materials ranging from letters and questionnaire replies to editorials and stories. Most of these materials are actual specimens of student writing. Each passage is followed by multiple-choice items covering specific ways in which the writing could be improved with regard to mechanics of expression as well as organization and effectiveness. In the Reading Comprehension tests, short passages from a variety of content areas are followed by questions designed to test

Situation: Tom wanted to learn which of three types of soil—clay, sand, or loam—would be best for growing lima beans. He found three flowerpots, put a different type of soil in each pot, and planted lima beans in each. He placed them side by side on the window sill and gave each pot the same amount of water.

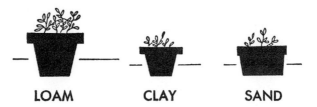

The lima beans grew best in the loam. Why did Mr. Jackson say Tom's experiment was NOT a good experiment and did NOT prove that loam was the best soil for plant growth?

23 A The plants in one pot got more sunlight than the plants in the other pots.
B The amount of soil in each pot was not the same.
C One pot should have been placed in the dark.
D Tom should have used three kinds of seeds.

FIG. 90. Sample Item from STEP Science Test for Grades 4 to 6. (Reproduced by permission of Cooperative Test Division, Educational Testing Service.)

such skills as simple comprehension, interpretation, insight into the writer's motives, and critical evaluation.

The measurement of Listening Comprehension is a relatively late development in achievement testing. The ability to understand, interpret, and critically evaluate what one hears is coming to be recognized as an important educational goal. In the STEP Listening tests, the given passages are read by the classroom teacher. The questions and response options are also read by the teacher, although the students have a copy of the response options before them. A typical passage for grades 7–9, together with three sample items, can be seen in Figure 92. The passages sample many types of listening, including directions and simple explanations, exposition, narration, argument and persuasion, and aesthetic material. Presentation by

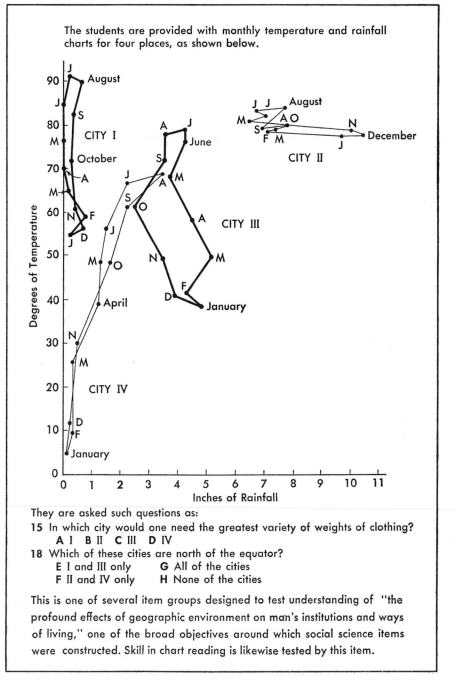

The students are provided with monthly temperature and rainfall charts for four places, as shown below.

They are asked such questions as:

15 In which city would one need the greatest variety of weights of clothing?
   A I   B II   C III   D IV

18 Which of these cities are north of the equator?
   E I and III only   G All of the cities
   F II and IV only   H None of the cities

This is one of several item groups designed to test understanding of "the profound effects of geographic environment on man's institutions and ways of living," one of the broad objectives around which social science items were constructed. Skill in chart reading is likewise tested by this item.

FIG. 91.   Sample Items from STEP Social Studies Test for Grades 10 to 12. (Reproduced by permission of Cooperative Test Division, Educational Testing Service.)

classroom teachers, chosen in favor of recordings for practical reasons, introduces an uncontrolled factor. At the upper levels, a further limitation arises from the brevity of the passages. The high school senior and college student—as well as the adult outside of school—must often listen to lectures considerably longer than the one- to four-minute passages of this test.

Raw scores on each STEP test are first converted into a three-digit score scale which was designed for vertical rather than horizontal comparability. Thus, performance on any one test, such as Mathematics, is expressed in terms of a single scale for all grades; but these scores are not directly comparable from one test to another. By reference to appropriate tables for each grade level, STEP scores can be further transmuted into percentiles. Rather than yielding a single percentile rank, however, the scores are expressed in the form of a *percentile band* for each individual. As in the case of SCAT (see Ch. 9), these percentile bands cover a distance of approximately one standard error of measurement on either side of the corresponding percentile. The chances are thus roughly 2:1 that the student's true position falls within the given band. The STEP Student Profile for the six tests is similar to the SCAT profile illustrated in Figure 17 (Ch. 4). For both STEP and SCAT, there is also a simplified Student Report form, used in interpreting scores to the students themselves. Figure 93 shows the illustration given on the Student Report to explain how the student's relative standing on different tests may be compared by means of percentile bands.

For most of the tests, norms were based on random samples of students from 50 schools, chosen so as to approximate a representative national sample of schools. The adequacy of the normative sample is·questionable, and there is evidence that the grade groups were not always comparable. Although timed, the STEP tests are essentially power tests. Kuder-Richardson reliabilities of each of the six tests within single-grade groups cluster in the upper .80's and low .90's. It would be desirable, however, to have data on stability of scores over time, in terms of parallel-form reliability.

The development of STEP represents content validation at its best. Committees of outstanding educators, representing all levels from the elementary school to college and chosen in consultation with national professional organizations, participated with ETS test-construction specialists both in drawing up test specifications and in preparing and reviewing items. Statistical analyses of preliminary forms included the usual determination of difficulty, discriminative power, and grade progress for individual items. The extent to which it proved feasible to construct objective items measuring understanding rather than mere recall of information represents a major contribution of these tests.

On the other hand, the heavy reliance of STEP on broadly oriented items brings this battery very close to scholastic aptitude or intelligence tests. It is interesting in this connection to compare STEP with SCAT (see Ch. 9),

The examiner reads:

Here is the fourth selection. It is a speech by a student running for school office.

A students, B students, C students, D students, and my friends! As you know, I am running for the office of President of the Student Council. I'd like to tell you what I'll do if I'm elected. In the first place, I think several students ought to sit in on teachers' meetings. They settle too many things for us. I don't think that the teachers always know what's best for us.

In the second place, I'd like to see our Student Council do something. Take the business of the candy machine, for instance. Just because a couple of doctors and dentists don't like it doesn't mean we shouldn't have one. I think they are wrong. I think we should have one. Candy is good for us. It gives us energy, and I, for one, don't think it hurts either your teeth or your appetite. And if it does, so what? You save the lunch money and can go out on a date.

Last, you know that my opponents—and you'll hear from them in a minute—are two girls. Now, everybody says girls are smarter than boys. That might be true—but just because they're smarter doesn't mean they'll make better officers. In fact, I think girls are too smart and can't always get along with people because of that. Maybe we need somebody not so smart, but that can get along. That's me, fellow student—vote for me!

19 The speaker's principal objection to girls as school officers evidently is that they
A talk too much
B support the teacher's point-of-view
C are too smart to get along with people
D don't want a candy machine

22 When the speaker used the word "opponents," he meant
E students from other schools
F students running against him
G the teachers
H doctors and dentists

23 Judging from his comments, how does the speaker feel about the opinions of experts?
A He pretends that the experts agree with him.
B He does not respect the experts if he disagrees with them.
C He pretends to treat the experts with respect.
D He follows expert advice unless he can prove it is wrong.

FIG. 92.   Sample Items from STEP Listening Comprehension Test for Grades 7 to 9. (Reproduced by permission of Cooperative Test Division, Educational Testing Service.)

which was constructed as a scholastic aptitude test to parallel STEP. In the continuum represented in Figure 89, SCAT may fall closer to the achievement end than does STEP. SCAT draws freely on specific word knowledge and arithmetic processes learned in school, while STEP has succeeded in measuring reasoning and other intellectual skills fairly independently of specific factual content. As might be expected, correlations between corre-

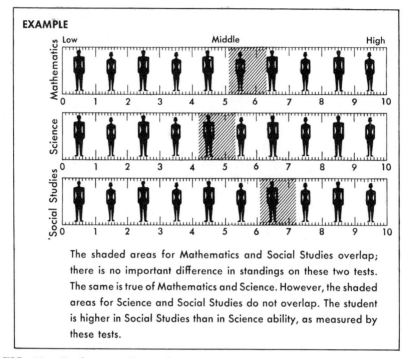

EXAMPLE

The shaded areas for Mathematics and Social Studies overlap; there is no important difference in standings on these two tests. The same is true of Mathematics and Science. However, the shaded areas for Science and Social Studies do not overlap. The student is higher in Social Studies than in Science ability, as measured by these tests.

FIG. 93.   Explanatory Example from STEP Student Report. (Reproduced by permission of Cooperative Test Division, Educational Testing Service.)

sponding parts of STEP and SCAT are quite high, often approaching the reliability coefficients. The comparison of these two batteries, of course, illustrates the artificiality of the traditional distinction between aptitude and achievement tests. At the same time, there is need for the more content-oriented type of achievement test to assess knowledge of specific fields of study. Some recently developed tests, like the 1964–1966 edition of the Stanford Achievement Test, help to meet this need.

ADULT BASIC EDUCATION TESTS.   The increasing concern for .culturally and economically disadvantaged minorities that characterized the decade of the 1960's stimulated the development of new tests, not only for pre-school and primary school children, but also for undereducated adults. An example of the latter type of test is the Adult Basic Learning Examination (ABLE). This is an achievement test specifically designed for use with adults in community adult-education classes, educational programs conducted in penal institutions, and special agencies such as the Job Corps. It is available in two levels corresponding to grades 1–4 (Level I) and 5–8 (Level II). At each level, there are two equivalent forms. Drawing largely from practical problems of adult daily life, ABLE consists of the following four tests, illustrated in Figure 94:

1. *Vocabulary:* examinee chooses correct word to fit orally presented definitions—requires no reading.

2. *Reading:* paragraph comprehension, inference, and associated general information.

3. *Spelling:* writing words from dictation.

4. *Arithmetic:* number computation and problem-solving—requires no reading at Level I.

Scores on each of the four tests may be evaluated in terms of grade equivalents, established by administering both ABLE and the Stanford Achievement Test to samples of 1,000 pupils per grade in grades 2 to 7. Percentile and stanine norms are also available from large adult groups enrolled in adult basic education programs. Split-half reliabilities of each

---

Test 1: Vocabulary (both definition and response words presented orally)

If a box is hard to lift, it is

      small   **valuable**   **heavy**

Test 2: Reading

A car has four wheels, two in front and two in

A   **front.**   **side.**   **back.**
       ○   ○   ●

Mr. Jones is going to paint the kitchen walls.
He needs a paint brush and a can of

B   **paper.**   **paint.**   **wax.**
       ○   ○   ○

Test 3: Spelling (presented orally)

    learning   Bob Ward is *learning* to weld.   learning

Test 4: Arithmetic – Part A. Computation

$$\begin{array}{r} 2 \\ +\ 1 \\ \hline 3 \end{array} \qquad \begin{array}{r} 5 \\ -\ 3 \\ \hline \end{array} \qquad 2\overline{)4}$$

Arithmetic – Part B. Problem Solving

What will your earnings be for a 40-hour week if you earn $2.00 an hour?

A   **$40**   **$46**   **$50**   **$80**   **NG**
    ○   ○   ○   ●   ○

FIG. 94.   Sample Items from Adult Basic Learning Examination (ABLE), Level II. (Reproduced by permission of Harcourt, Brace & World.)

test in adult groups range from .82 to .92. Correlations between corresponding tests of ABLE and the Stanford Achievement Test in the elementary school samples are in the .60's and .70's. Some correlations of the same general magnitude were also found in a Job Corps sample of about 800 young adults who took both tests. Further validation against practical criteria must await the continued use of this test, which was published in 1967.

ACHIEVEMENT TESTS IN SPECIAL AREAS

Among the many achievement tests designed within special areas, two kinds are of particular interest. The first comprises diagnostic tests in reading and arithmetic, which are of basic importance in the identification of special educational disabilities and in the planning of remedial programs. The second includes the vast number of standardized end-of-course examinations spanning the whole gamut of instructional fields.

DIAGNOSTIC TESTS.   In the measurement of both reading and mathematical skills, a distinction is made between survey and diagnostic tests. Survey tests indicate the general level of the individual's achievement in reading or arithmetic. For this purpose, they usually provide a single composite score. Among the best examples of such survey tests are the reading and arithmetic subtests of the general achievement batteries, although a number of separate tests are also available in these areas.[2] Diagnostic tests, on the other hand, are designed to analyze the individual's strengths and weaknesses in the area and to suggest causes of his difficulties. Such tests typically yield several scores.

Diagnostic tests in *reading* vary widely in the thoroughness of analysis they permit and in the specific procedures followed. They range from group tests yielding two or three subtest scores, which serve little more than a survey function, to intensive clinical programs for individual case studies. Some provide detailed checklists of specific types of errors. The individual batteries frequently employ apparatus, such as tachistoscopes for controlling rate of exposure of printed material, and techniques for photographing the individual's eye movements while he reads.

The Stanford Diagnostic Reading Test is an example of a group test suitable for the elementary school. This test is available in two levels: Level I for grades 2.5 to 4.5 and Level II for grades 4.5 to 8.5, with two forms at each level. Both levels yield separate scores in reading comprehension, vocabulary, and several word-recognition skills, including blend-

[2] Of special interest are the elementary school arithmetic tests covering the "new math," such as the Stanford Modern Mathematics Concepts Test and the Wisconsin Contemporary Test of Elementary Mathematics, listed in Appendix C.

ing, syllabication, and sound discrimination. Level I also provides additional subtests on word-recognition skills, involving auditory discrimination and the recognition of beginning and ending sound of words; Level II also contains a subtest on rate of reading. Sample items from three of the Level I subtests on word-recognition skills are shown in Figure 95. The tests are normally administered in four sittings at Level I and three sittings at Level II, each sitting requiring from about 30 to 45 minutes.

Scores on each subtest of the Stanford Diagnostic Reading Test may be

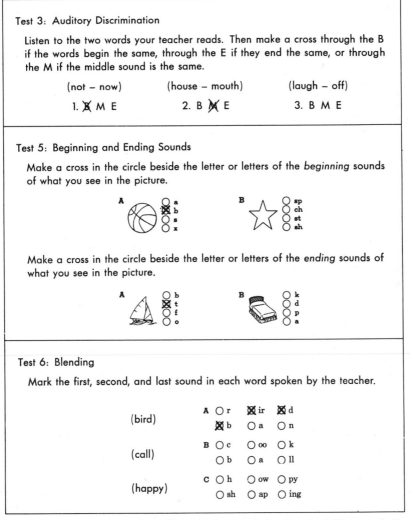

FIG. 95.   Sample Items from Three Subtests of the Stanford Diagnostic Reading Test, Level I. In Tests 3 and 6, the words shown in parentheses are presented orally. (Reproduced by permission of Harcourt, Brace & World.)

interpreted in terms of within-grade stanines or percentiles, although the stanine conversion is recommended and is employed in the pupil profile charts. Reading comprehension scores may also be translated into grade scores [3] to provide an index of the pupil's over-all reading performance. The manual provides supplementary discussion to aid in the qualitative interpretation of performance on each subtest, together with detailed suggestions for appropriate remedial instruction. In the standardization program, the Stanford Diagnostic Reading Test was administered to approximately 12,000 children in six school systems, who also took the reading subtests of the Stanford Achievement Test. The normative sample was selected in terms of the latter scores so as to be representative of the standardization sample of the Stanford Achievement Test.

Subtest reliabilities of the Stanford Diagnostic Reading Test are generally satisfactory. Split-half reliabilities within single-grade groups cluster in the high .80's and .90's. Alternate-form reliability of the rate-of-reading subtest at Level II was .72. Intercorrelations of the subtests vary widely with the particular tests correlated and tend to be lower at the higher grades. For Level II, the median correlations are in the .40's and .50's. When considered together with the reliability coefficients, these intercorrelations indicate that the subtests should differentiate reasonably well among the individual's reading skills. The problem of differential diagnosis is similar to that of interpreting profiles and intraindividual score differences on a multiple aptitude battery, which was discussed in Chapter 13. Referring to Figure 69 in Chapter 13, we can see, for example, that with two subtests whose mean reliability is .90 and whose intercorrelation is .50, about 37 percent of the intraindividual score differences on the two subtests are in excess of chance.

Another series of tests suitable for classroom administration, but requiring also some individual testing, is the Diagnostic Reading Tests. These tests were developed by the Committee on Diagnostic Reading Tests in the course of a continuing program of research on the reading process. They comprise three separate batteries designed to cover all grade levels from kindergarten through the freshman year of college. The basic plan of each battery includes a survey section designed to assess general reading proficiency and a number of supplementary diagnostic tests for appraising specific reading skills. The entire battery need not be given to each individual. Teachers may choose tests in those areas in which the individual exhibits special difficulties, as indicated by his performance on the survey tests.

The upper-level battery, suitable for grades 7 to 13, was the first to be published in the series and has been widely employed in high school and

---

[3] Grade scores are simply grade equivalents without the decimal point. For example, a grade score of 54 corresponds to a grade equivalent of 5.4, representing the fourth month of grade 5.

college reading programs. The survey section of this battery, which can be given within a single class period, yields scores in rate of reading story-type material with satisfactory comprehension, general vocabulary, and comprehension of textbook-type material. All but one of the diagnostic tests are also designed for group administration. These diagnostic tests are available in the same three areas covered by the survey section, and in one additional area, that of word-recognition skills. Specifically, the tests in the diagnostic battery comprise: vocabulary, which covers technical vocabulary in English grammar and literature, mathematics, science, and social studies; comprehension of textbook material, both when the individual reads it himself and when it is read to him; rates of reading, including rate of reading different types of material, as well as flexibility of rate when reading for different objectives; and word attack, both oral and silent. The last-named test, which is individually administered, utilizes a variety of procedures to analyze the individual's responses both to the meanings and to the sounds of words. It also provides a checklist for qualitative observations. A bulletin designed for teachers contains many suggestions regarding the use of test results in planning remedial instruction.

The Diagnostic Reading Tests provide percentile norms, which have been periodically revised. However, the representativeness of these norms, as well as their comparability for the different tests, is questionable. Reliabilities of the separate tests in the .80's and .90's have been reported. There is also some evidence that intercorrelations of tests are appreciably lower than their reliabilities. Considerable research has been conducted with these tests, but much of it is reported only in widely scattered journal articles. There is need for a comprehensive technical manual to collect and organize the relevant data.

A typical battery for intensive individual testing is the Durrell Analysis of Reading Difficulty, designed for grades 1 to 6. The Durrell tests utilize series of paragraphs graded in difficulty, a set of cards, and a simple tachistoscope. Scores are provided for rate and comprehension of oral and silent reading, listening comprehension, rapid word recognition, and word analysis. Supplementary tests of written spelling and speed of handwriting are included. For nonreaders, there are measures of visual memory for word forms, auditory analysis of word elements, letter recognition, rate of learning words, and listening comprehension. All of the comprehension tests actually require simple recall of details read or heard and do not call for much understanding. One of the chief contributions of this battery is a checklist based on reading errors identified in a survey of 4,000 children. The battery is better suited for qualitative than for quantitative analysis of performance. Suggestions for remedial teaching are also provided in the manual.

Among the most common weaknesses of diagnostic reading tests are inadequate reliabilities coupled with high intercorrelations of the subtests from which separate scores are derived. Especially in some of the shorter group tests, these two conditions reduce the diagnostic or differential effectiveness of the tests. Several tests have also been criticized because of the superficiality of understanding required by the reading comprehension subtests. The measurement of rate of reading likewise presents special problems. Rate of reading depends on such factors as the difficulty of the material and the purpose for which it is being read. Any individual may thus have, not one, but many reading rates. This is more likely to be true of the experienced reader, who adjusts his rate to the nature of the task. Furthermore, in any one reading test, the response set established by the directions may differ widely from one person to another. For example, when told to read a passage carefully so as to be able to answer questions about it later, some subjects may skim the material rapidly, while others will try to understand and memorize specific details. In the previously mentioned Diagnostic Reading Tests, special efforts were made to tackle this problem by providing several different measures of reading rate. The effectiveness of this solution, however, has not been objectively demonstrated.

The diagnostic testing of *mathematical skills* presents several of the same methodological problems encountered in diagnostic reading tests. The testing procedures also parallel those in the reading area, ranging from fairly short group tests to intensive programs for individual examination. The number of diagnostic tests developed in the mathematics area, however, is much smaller; and formally organized remedial programs in this area are fewer than in reading.

The Stanford Diagnostic Arithmetic Test closely parallels the previously discussed Stanford Diagnostic Reading Test in both administration and test construction procedures. Also available in two equivalent forms at Level I (grades 2.5 to 4.5) and Level II (grades 4.5 to 8.5), it utilizes group testing to provide a profile of performance in specific arithmetic skills. The profile of scores obtained by a sixth-grade pupil is reproduced in Figure 96. In it can be seen the names of the subtests and the types of normative conversions applied to each score. The stanine is the principal type of score employed, with grade scores also reported for total scores in arithmetic concepts and computation. Since distributions of scores on the last subtest, Number Facts, are highly skewed, only a broad classification of scores into three letter grades is given. The Number Facts subtest, which requires rapid computations with orally presented numbers, was designed to assess the pupil's ability to recall simple number facts, such as $4 \times 7 = 28$. The same number combinations are used in the corresponding items in addition and subtraction, and in multiplication and division. For instance, if item 1 in addition is $8 + 2 = 10$, item 1 in subtraction is $10 - 2 = 8$. Hence, it is possible to see whether or not a pupil recalls related number facts.

The recommended testing schedule for Level II includes seven sittings, varying in length from 15 to 53 minutes. Level I, which contains fewer

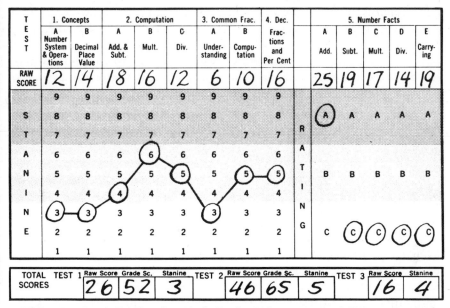

FIG. 96. Pupil Profile of a Sixth-Grade Girl on Stanford Diagnostic Arithmetic Test, Level II. This pupil learns well what she is taught about arithmetic computation but has difficulty in understanding the basic concepts of the subject. She has also failed to master the number facts but is able to figure them out if given time as on Test 2. (Reproduced by permission of Harcourt, Brace & World.)

tests, may be administered in six sittings. Several subtests are given orally by the teacher; the entire test requires little reading, especially at Level I. Technical properties of the test, with regard to norms, reliability, and intercorrelations of subtests, are quite similar to those of the Stanford Diagnostic Reading Test. Both tests were published in 1966 and have two of their three authors in common.

To illustrate a very different approach, we may consider an early classic that has enjoyed wide popularity. The Diagnostic Chart for Fundamental Processes in Arithmetic, prepared by Buswell and John (1926), requires individual administration, since each problem is solved orally by the pupil. It is thus possible to observe the work methods employed by the child in carrying out the different operations. Errors as well as undesirable work habits are recorded on a checklist, which includes the most common difficulties encountered in arithmetic. The problems were specially chosen so as to elicit such difficulties when present. This test is applicable in grades 2 to 8. There are no time limits, no norms, and no total score, the problems and checklist being designed for qualitative rather than quantitative analysis of arithmetic performance.

In connection with the use of all diagnostic tests, one point deserves special emphasis. The diagnosis of reading and arithmetic difficulties and the subsequent program of remedial teaching are the proper functions of a trained specialist. No battery of diagnostic tests could suffice for this purpose. The diagnosis and treatment of severe reading disabilities require an intensive clinical case study, including supplementary information on sensory capacities and motor development, medical and health history, complete educational history, data on home and family background, and a thorough investigation of possible emotional difficulties. In some cases, serious reading retardation proves to be only one symptom of a more basic personality maladjustment. Although survey and group diagnostic tests may serve to identify individuals in need of further attention, the diagnosis and therapy of reading disabilities often represent a problem for the clinician. This may also be true in cases of severe arithmetic disabilities.

STANDARDIZED END-OF-COURSE EXAMINATIONS.   Achievement tests are available for nearly every field of instruction. In the elementary school, with its relatively uniform curriculum, general achievement batteries serve the majority of testing purposes. For more intensive analyses of educational disabilities, these batteries may be supplemented with the diagnostic tests discussed in the preceding section. At the high school and college levels, specialized tests covering particular courses of study are more common. These tests have been prepared for almost every subject taught in school, from American history to physical education, and from accounting to physics. A comprehensive introduction to achievement tests in different instructional fields can be found in Gerberich, Greene, and Jorgensen (1962, Chs. 15–24). The *Mental Measurements Yearbooks* also cover this type of test quite fully, under the appropriate subject-matter categories. A noteworthy development in the 1960's was the publication of tests in modern foreign languages that use tape recordings to test proficiency in reading, writing, listening, and speaking. Examples of these tests and of recently developed tests in other instructional areas are listed in Appendix C.

Of particular interest are the coordinated series of achievement tests for different courses of study. Two well-known examples are the tests administered in the annual testing program of the College Entrance Examination Board (CEEB) and the Evaluation and Adjustment Series published by Harcourt, Brace & World. A major feature of these coordinated series is their provision of a single system of comparable norms for all tests. It is thus possible to make direct comparisons among scores obtained in different subject-matter areas.

Unlike the achievement batteries discussed earlier in this chapter, however, these coordinated test series cannot be standardized on a single normative population. Moreover, it is likely that the normative samples available for the various academic subjects differ appreciably in general scholastic aptitude. For example, students who have completed two years of

Latin are probably a more highly selected group than those who have completed two years of Spanish. And those taking an examination in advanced mathematics are probably more highly selected than those taking an examination in American history. If scores on all these tests were to be evaluated with reference to the means of their respective normative samples, an individual might, for instance, appear to be more proficient in Spanish than in Latin simply because he was compared with a poorer normative sample in the former case.

The two series cited above employ standard score scales that are adjusted for the differences among the normative samples utilized for each test. In the College Board tests, the scores on the Scholastic Aptitude Test (SAT) provide the basis for making such adjustments (Angoff, 1968; Dyer & King, 1955). All raw scores on achievement tests are converted into a standard score scale having a mean of 500 and an SD of 100 in the fixed reference group. As explained in Chapter 3, this group consists of the 10,651 subjects who took the SAT in 1941. The scores obtained by the candidates taking any achievement test during subsequent years are expressed with reference to this group. The adjustment takes into account any differences in the distribution of SAT scores between the present group and the fixed reference group.

The Evaluation and Adjustment Series covers a wide variety of high school courses, such as algebra, geometry, biology, chemistry, physics, American history, world history, and language arts. The raw scores on all these tests are converted into a single scale of standard scores with a mean of 150 and an SD of 15 (Maberly, 1966). The anchor test for equating performance on the different tests was the Otis Quick-Scoring Mental Ability Tests, which was administered for scaling purposes to groups of students taking each achievement test.

The availability of comparable achievement test scores for different fields is desirable for many purposes. It is clear that some adjustment must be made to allow for the differences among the examinee populations in different fields. A word of caution is in order, however, regarding the interpretation of the systems of scaled scores described above. Close comparability of scores can be attained only when the norming test and the anchor test correlate very highly with each other. It cannot be assumed that the relative status of different groups on a highly verbal scholastic aptitude or general intelligence test is necessarily the same as their relative status on other tests. For example, if the candidates taking a geometry test and those taking a Latin test were to obtain the same distribution of intelligence test scores, they might still differ significantly in their aptitudes for Latin and for geometry. In other words, we cannot assume that the Latin sample would have obtained the same scores in geometry as the present geometry sample, if both had pursued the same courses.

To be sure, such an assumption is not implied by the use of the above systems of scaled scores. These systems merely express all scores in terms of a fixed standard that can be precisely and operationally defined. But the test user with only a superficial knowledge of how the scores were derived could easily be misled into unwarranted interpretations. It must be borne in mind that the procedures followed in developing these scoring systems provide comparability of a sort. But they do not necessarily yield the identical norms that would be obtained if all students had been enrolled in the same courses of study and had been given all the tests in each series.

We may inquire where the type of achievement test discussed in this section fits into the total testing picture. Such tests are obviously well suited for use as end-of-course examinations. But they may serve other functions also. In comparison with the more broadly oriented tests of educational development, traditional achievement tests, which are more closely linked to specific courses, measure more nearly distinct skills and knowledge. For this reason, they are likely to yield lower correlations with intelligence tests than have been found for broad achievement tests. If combined with intelligence tests, therefore, the specialized achievement tests will contribute more unique, nonoverlapping variance and may permit better prediction of subsequent outcomes.

There is also an increasing utilization of specialized achievement tests for the advanced placement of college students. On the basis of advanced preparation in high school, students may take special CEEB tests for admission to college with advanced standing in one or more subjects. A related development is to be found in the College-Level Examination Program, introduced by the CEEB in 1965 on a limited, experimental basis (College Entrance Examination Board, 1967a). The general purpose of this program is to facilitate placement and credit by examination and to provide a national system for evaluating college-level education acquired through independent study and other nontraditional procedures.

CHAPTER **16**

Occupational
Tests

PSYCHOLOGICAL TESTS are commonly employed as aids in occupational decisions, including both individual counseling decisions and institutional decisions concerning the selection and classification of personnel. Nearly every type of available test may be useful in occupational decisions. Multiple aptitude batteries and interest tests are particularly appropriate in counseling situations. Special aptitude tests have often been developed primarily for occupational purposes. Further discussion of the role of tests in counseling can be found in a number of sources. Super and Crites (1962) survey those tests that are most frequently employed by the counselor; Goldman (1961) provides an excellent introduction to the ways in which tests may be most effectively incorporated into the counseling process; and Berdie, Layton, Swanson, and Hagenah (1963) discuss testing by counselors in predominantly educational contexts. An overview of the use of psychological tests in industry, with illustrations covering many specific occupations, is given by Lawshe and Balma (1966).

As in our treatment of educational tests in Chapter 15, we shall concentrate in this chapter on those tests specially designed for occupational purposes, over and above the more widely applicable instruments discussed in other chapters. We shall also examine the procedures typically followed in industrial settings to assemble and validate batteries of appropriate tests.

SELECTION AND VALIDATION OF OCCUPATIONAL TESTS

MAJOR STEPS.   The selection and local validation of tests for use within a specific industrial organization represent a special application of the procedures generally followed in the process of test construction itself. Within the industrial context, these procedures fall into four major steps:

1. conducting a job analysis to define the problem and to identify the principal traits to be measured;
2. assembling a trial battery of tests to measure the traits identified in the job analysis;
3. validating each preliminary test against a criterion of job success and choosing tests for final battery;
4. formulating a strategy for personnel decisions, i.e., determining how scores on the chosen tests will be used in making operational decisions.

The purpose of a *job analysis* is to formulate a description of what workers do on the job for which selection procedures are being developed. Such a job description provides the basis for the job specification, or list of worker qualifications for whose assessment tests must be chosen. To be effective, a job analysis must be specific to the job being described. A description in terms of vague generalities that would be equally applicable to many jobs is of little use for this purpose. The job analysis must focus on those requirements that differentiate this job from other jobs. An effective job analysis should also concentrate on those aspects of performance that differentiate most sharply between the better and the poorer workers. In many jobs, workers of different levels of proficiency may differ little in the way they carry out most parts of their jobs—only certain features of the job may bring out the major differences between successes and failures. In his classic book on *Aptitude Testing,* Hull stressed the importance of these differentiating aspects of job performance, which he called "critical part-activities" (Hull, 1928, p. 30). Later, this concept was re-emphasized by Flanagan (1949, 1954a), under the name of "critical requirements."

If it is to yield usable information, job analysis requires systematic data gathering procedures. The job analyst should preferably combine several sources of information to obtain a well-rounded picture of the job activities. He may consult published sources, including descriptions of similar jobs as well as training and operating manuals prepared for the particular job. Performance records may be examined, particularly those containing qualitative descriptions of common errors, learning difficulties, and reasons for failure on this job. Records of customer complaints may provide clues useful in the analysis of sales jobs. An important source of information for any kind of job is provided by interviews—with supervisors, job instructors, and workers of varying degrees of experience and job success.

Other, more direct techniques of job analysis include activity logs kept by workers for a specified period of time, direct observation of a sample of workers by the job analyst, and (if practicable) performance of the job by the analyst himself. To implement the concept of critical requirements,

Flanagan (1954a) proposed the critical incident technique. Essentially, this technique calls for factual descriptions of specific instances of job behavior that are characteristic of either satisfactory or unsatisfactory workers. A record of such incidents is usually kept by the supervisor during a designated period, such as two weeks. Growing out of Air Force research during World War II, the critical incident technique has been employed with such varied groups as commercial airline pilots, research personnel in physical science laboratories, factory workers, dentists, and department store salesclerks.

Job analysis enables the personnel psychologist to define the problem by specifying the critical worker requirements for success in a given job. Such an analysis may indicate, for example, that the job requires finger dexterity, perceptual speed, computational accuracy, and ability to work effectively under distracting conditions. The next step is to *assemble a preliminary set of predictors* designed to assess these traits. Such predictors may include not only tests but also application forms, rating scales, techniques for reference checkups, interview manuals, and other assessment devices. When tests are to be used, they may be selected from previously published tests or custom-made for the particular job. In either case, prior to their validation for the particular job, such tests should be tried out on groups similar to the applicant population with which they will eventually be used. In the course of these preliminary tryouts, some tests may be discarded and others modified. Among the features checked at this stage would be time required for administration, clarity of instructions, suitability of vocabulary and reading level, difficulty level of the items, range and form of score distribution, and test reliability.

In choosing a test or constructing a new test, the personnel psychologist is actually formulating a series of hypotheses to the effect that performance on each test is significantly related to eventual success on the given job. The correctness of these hypotheses depends on several factors, such as the adequacy of the job analysis, the proper utilization of research data obtained with available tests in similar job situations, the psychologist's ingenuity in constructing new instruments, and his familiarity with the variety of available tests. But although much can be done in advance to increase the chances that correct hypotheses will be formulated, it is only by empirical follow-up that their correctness can be demonstrated.

The third step is undoubtedly the heart of the entire process. This is the *validation* of each test in the preliminary battery by correlating test scores with a criterion measure of job performance. The validation of personnel selection tests provides a classic illustration of predictive criterion-related validity. The ideal procedure involves the administration of the tests to an applicant sample, all of whom are hired and whose subsequent job performance provides the criterion data. Obviously the tests that are being validated should not be used to select applicants in the validation sample. Moreover, to avoid criterion contamination (see Ch. 5), scores on these tests should be inaccessible to supervisors and other personnel who may participate in evaluating these employees' job performance. The sample on which validation is conducted should be large enough to yield stable results and should be representative of the applicant population with which the tests will eventually be used.

When limitations of time or other circumstances make a longitudinal investigation impracticable, validity is often determined by administering the tests to present employees and checking scores against concurrent criterion status. This procedure is not so satisfactory for the validation of personnel selection instruments and must be regarded as a makeshift. Since unsuccessful employees tend to leave, present employees do not constitute a representative sample of an applicant population, or even of newly hired employees. Moreover, present employees have had varying amounts of experience on the job, and such experience may affect their test scores. It is also desirable that the tests be administered as part of the normal employment procedures. When employees are given tests "for research purposes only," their motivation and test-taking attitudes may be quite unlike those of genuine job applicants, and these conditions are likely to be reflected in their test performance.

In the validation of tests for industrial purposes, several of the special technical problems discussed in Chapter 6 are particularly relevant. Questions of sample heterogeneity and preselection should be considered. When the validation sample consists of newly hired employees, it is likely to be more homogeneous than the total applicant sample. Although not selected in terms of performance on the tests being validated, these employees are nevertheless selected in terms of other characteristics that may be correlated with performance on the tests. Hence, the range of scores will be narrower than in the total applicant sample. The form of the relationship between test scores and criterion measures should also be investigated. In a number of industrial situations, this relationship may be nonlinear or heteroscedastic, as explained in Chapter 6. These conditions will affect not only the interpretation of validity coefficients obtained in the validation sample, but also the ultimate operational use of the tests.

On the basis of the results of the validation study, the most suitable tests are retained for operational use. These tests should not only correlate highly with the criterion measure, but they should also yield low intercorrelations with each other, in order to avoid unnecessary duplication of testing effort. Ideally, each test should measure a different facet of the criterion and thus make a unique contribution to the overall selection process. In practice, of course, substantial intercorrelation of predictors is often inevitable.

After the tests are chosen, all that remains is to formulate an appropriate *decision strategy* for using the tests in subsequent applicant samples. If only a single test is employed, the decision strategy may involve no more than establishing a cutoff score or possibly hiring from the top of the score distribution until all vacancies are filled. In most personnel selection situations, however, several predictors are employed. Under these conditions, the scores from the different tests must be utilized through one of the selection strategies described in Chapter 6, including multiple regression equations, multiple cutoffs, or clinical judgment. More complex strategies, involving moderator variables, may also be employed (Ch. 6).

THE CRITERION PROBLEM.   It is apparent that the criterion occupies a prominent place in the validation of occupational tests. At the same time, it is often difficult to obtain satisfactory criterion measures. In any industrial validation study, the choice of criterion measure requires careful advance planning. A wide variety of indices may be employed to measure degree of job success. Among them are quantity and quality of output, accidents and loss through breakage, salary and commissions, job stability and length of service, rate of advancement, absenteeism, and merit ratings by supervisors. The criterion measure may be based on the observation of a limited sample of the individual's job performance, such as a worksample, sales interview, or pilot check flight. Or it may be derived from a cumulative record of output, sales, merit ratings, or job history covering the total available period on the job.

For any given job, there is often a multiplicity of possible criterion measures. Moreover, the correlations among these measures may be quite low. What, then, shall be used as the criterion against which to validate tests? There are several possible solutions. Frequently, the introduction of new tests or other predictors into the selection program is explored because of a specific personnel problem in a company. The problem may be one of high turnover among clerical employees, a high accident rate among bus drivers, or an excessive reject rate in an assembly job. In such cases, the specific problem defines the criterion to be used in test evaluation. On the other hand, if a comprehensive battery is being assembled to predict overall effectiveness in a many-faceted job, the criterion measure may be a weighted composite of several different measures of job performance. Although some objective procedures have been proposed to aid in formulating these weights (see, e.g., Brogden & Taylor, 1950), they are usually based on the judgment of company personnel regarding the relative importance of different aspects of job performance.

Still another approach to multiple criteria involves the separate validation of tests against each criterion measure. When several major and relatively independent facets of job success can be identified, tests can be selected to predict each facet independently. This is essentially the approach that underlies the estimation of synthetic validity (Ch. 5). If enough reliable data are available regarding individual facets of the job criterion, test validation in terms of these individual facets would seem to provide more clearly interpretable results than would the use of a composite criterion. When different criterion facets have negligible or even negative intercorrelations, combining them into a single hodgepodge can hardly permit a clear-cut evaluation of the contribution of each predictor.

One distinction frequently made among criterion measures is that between training criteria and job-proficiency criteria. In an extensive survey of published data on the validity of different types of tests against occupational criteria, Ghiselli (1966, Ch. 6) found that most tests predict performance in training better than they predict job performance. Among the reasons for this difference, he mentions the wider range of ability likely to be found among trainees and the greater uniformity of conditions provided by training than by job situations. As a further explanation, however, he cites the relatively verbal and "academic" nature of training criteria, even for jobs that are themselves predominantly nonverbal. Some evidence for this explanation is provided by the finding that, for perceptual and motor tests, the validities are no higher against training criteria than against job proficiency.

Some attention should also be given to the presence of both chance errors and systematic errors in criterion measures. Although criteria themselves may be regarded as perfectly reliable and valid by definition, specific criterion *measures* need to be evaluated in the same terms as other measures. Unreliability may result from inadequacy of the performance sample considered. Sales records or production records for a one-week period, for example, may not provide a stable index of an employee's long-term performance. When supervisory ratings are employed, unreliability of ratings may introduce chance variance into the criterion measure. In addition, criterion measures may be subject to certain systematic errors that reflect the influence of situational factors on job performance. Such errors would be illustrated by a criterion measure based on the total weekly sales by department store salesclerks from different departments, or the dollar value of sales by outside salesmen operating in different territories. Accident records of bus drivers assigned to different routes or different daily shifts represent another example. Combining such heterogeneous criterion data in finding a single validity coefficient would obviously distort the results.

Finally, criteria themselves may undergo long-term, progressive changes over time. An employee may be given different job duties and responsibilities as a function of length of service. Hence, even if his job title remains the same, the actual nature of his job may alter. From a different angle, the nature of jobs themselves may change appreciably with changes in organizational goals, development of new industrial equipment and processes, changing product demand, and other social and economic conditions. For all these reasons, it is desirable to repeat job analyses periodically and to recheck the validities of predictors against local criteria. If nationally standardized tests need to be revised and updated, there is no reason to expect local validation of tests within an organization to be permanent.

RATINGS. It is apparent that objective performance records alone do not automatically provide ready-made criterion measures. For many jobs, objective records may be inadequate or nonexistent. Even when objective records are readily available in profusion, informed judgment is often needed to evaluate the effect of extraneous conditions on performance indices. Consequently, it is generally desirable to include ratings among the criterion measures employed in test validation. In a survey of published validation data from industrial and governmental organizations, Lawshe and Balma (1966, pp. 37–38) found ratings to have been used as the criterion in 68 percent of all investigations.

Although personnel ratings are typically obtained from job supervisors, in certain job situations they may also be secured from coworkers, subordinates, instructors, or other personnel. Many companies have merit rating programs as part of their normal administrative procedures. In other companies, ratings may have to be obtained specially for criterion purposes.

Much can be done to improve the accuracy of ratings. A common difficulty arises from ambiguity in either trait names, scale units, or both. To meet this problem, each trait should be defined in very specific terms and the ratings should be expressed in a form that will be uniformly interpreted by all raters. Rather than using numbers or general descriptive adjectives that convey different meanings to different raters, degrees of a trait may be more clearly identified in terms of specific instances of behavior or graded behavior samples. This technique is illustrated in the *graphic rating scale*, shown in Figure 97. In such a scale, the rater records his judgment by checking any point along a continuous line; the behavior samples described under the line indicate the direction of the line and provide general anchor points for the judgment. After the judgments have been made, the ratings may be expressed quantitatively by superimposing a stencil that divides the line into the desired number of categories. For crude ratings, three categories may suffice. When the raters are highly skilled and have had extensive opportunity to observe the ratees, as many as seven categories may be appropriate. Finer distinctions are unrealistic and are likely to add only chance variance to the judgments.

Reference to Figure 97 will show a box to the right of each line, to be checked if the rater has had no opportunity to observe that trait in a given individual. Such a device helps to ensure that raters base their judgments

DIRECTIONS: For each trait, place a check mark on the line at the point that best fits the employee you are rating. If you have had no opportunity to observe a particular trait in a person, place the check mark in the box at the right.

1. *Oral Communication:* Ability to express himself in face-to-face contacts with different persons on the job.

| Expresses himself clearly and effectively; adjusts communication to listener | Usually gets ideas across clearly | Has some difficulty in making himself understood; little awareness of listener characteristics | Ineffective in oral communication; often misunderstood |

2. *Decision Making:* Ability to make effective decisions in meeting day-by-day job problems.

| Fails to consider all facts and consequences; jumps to conclusions | Considers facts but often fails to anticipate consequences correctly | Considers facts and correctly foresees consequences in most cases | Decisions generally sound and based on adequate analysis |

FIG. 97.   Typical Items in a Graphic Rating Scale, with Graded Behavioral Descriptions and Provision for Lack of Trait Acquaintance.

on *trait acquaintance* with the individual they are rating. It is not enough to have known the person for a long time. The rater should have had an opportunity to observe him in situations in which the trait in question could be manifested. If an employee has never had an opportunity to make a decision on his job, his ability to do so cannot be evaluated by his supervisor.

Ratings are subject to a number of constant errors. A well-known example is the *halo effect.* This is a tendency on the part of raters to be unduly influenced by a single favorable or unfavorable trait, which colors their judgment of the individual's other traits. One way to reduce halo effect is to define traits in terms of concrete behavior. In graphic rating scales, such as that illustrated in Figure 97, it is advisable to reverse the favorable and unfavorable ends of the line in random order for different traits. This device serves to emphasize the distinctness of each trait and forces the rater to read the descriptive statements under each line rather than marking a similar position indiscriminately for all traits. When several persons are to be rated by the same rater, a recommended procedure is to rate all persons in a single trait before rating anyone on the next trait. Thus, all ratees are first rated in oral communication, then all are rated in decision making, and so on. This procedure tends to focus the rater's attention on each trait separately rather than on his general impression of each individual.

Another constant error is the *error of central tendency,* or the tendency to place persons in the middle of the scale and to avoid extreme positions. Still another is the *leniency error,* referring to the reluctance of many raters to assign unfavorable ratings. The former causes a bunching of ratings in the center of the scale, the latter at the upper end. Both errors reduce the effective width of the scale and make ratings less discriminative.

One way to eliminate these errors is to employ ranking or other *order-of-merit procedures.* All these procedures force discrimination among individuals and hence maximize the information yielded by the ratings. They also share the common feature of providing only relative evaluations within a group, rather than absolute evaluations against a constant, external standard. In simple ranking, someone in each group must be first and someone must be last, regardless of the quality of the group as a whole. This is also true of such techniques as pair comparisons, in which each individual is compared in turn with every other, and of forced distributions, in which the number of persons to be classified in each category is specified. All these techniques are applicable when comparisons are made within a single group, but they do not directly permit comparisons across groups evaluated by different raters.

Several other types of rating procedures have been developed to meet specific needs. Descriptions of these procedures can be found in general texts on applied or industrial psychology (see, e.g., Anastasi, 1964b, Ch. 4; Tiffin & McCormick, 1965, Ch. 9). The above examples suffice to illustrate the problems encountered and some of the common solutions. In addition to improving the mechanics of rating, other steps can be taken to increase the effectiveness of ratings. Whenever feasible, having each individual evaluated by more than one rater provides a safeguard against personal bias or idiosyncrasy on the part of any one rater and also enlarges the observational domain on which the ratings are based.

The rating process can also be improved by training the raters. Research in both industrial and military settings has demonstrated the effectiveness of training in increasing the validity of ratings and in reducing such judgment errors as halo effect and leniency error. Rater training programs vary in duration and thoroughness depending on their purposes and the available facilities. Even a relatively simple orientation session lasting only an hour or two will produce noticeable results. In general, such a training program should explain the aims and purposes of the ratings, provide information on common judgment errors such as halo effect, stress the importance of obtaining maximal differentiation and avoiding both leniency and central tendency errors, clarify and illustrate the meaning of the traits to be rated and of the scale units, and give supervised practice in the assignment of ratings.

SHORT INTELLIGENCE TESTS FOR INDUSTRIAL SCREENING

A number of intelligence tests have been specially developed for the rapid, preliminary screening of industrial personnel. Several of these tests represent abridged versions of earlier tests. Others have been specifically constructed for the purpose, a few introducing interesting innovations in testing procedure. In all these tests, administration and scoring are simplified, and an effort is usually made to give the content face validity in an industrial setting.

It should be clearly recognized that general screening tests may have fairly high validity for some jobs and little or no validity for others. The type of behavior sampled by these tests is undoubtedly far more relevant to some types of jobs than to others. Jobs cannot simply be put into a hierarchy in terms of the amount of "intelligence" required, because the *type* of intelligence needed for different jobs varies. For many occupations, especially those requiring mechanical skills, tests of special aptitudes will serve as better predictors of achievement than will the general intelligence tests. This point is not always adequately stressed in the test manuals. In fact, some test manuals tend to create the erroneous impression that the general screening test can be used to predict success in almost every type of industrial work.

An early test that has been widely used in personnel screening is the Otis Self-Administering Test of Mental Ability, which introduced the spiral-omnibus arrangement of test items for ease of administration (see Ch. 9). This test has been used in screening applicants for such varied jobs as those of clerks, calculating-machine operators, assembly-line workers, and foremen and other supervisory personnel. Dorcus and Jones (1950) cited 36 validation studies in which the Otis test was checked against an industrial criterion. Not all of these studies yielded significant validity coefficients, of course, but many of them did. In semiskilled jobs, for example, the Otis test correlated moderately well with success in learning the job and ease of initial adaptation, but not with subsequent job achievement. This would be expected for jobs that are largely routine, once they are learned. Also, for high-level professional personnel, who represent a select group in terms of academic achievement, correlations between Otis scores and criteria of job success were usually negligible, since this test does not discriminate adequately at the upper levels.

Adaptations of the original Otis test have also been prepared for industrial use, the best known being the Wonderlic Personnel Test and the Otis Employment Tests. Both of these tests are currently in use, the latter being in process of revision. All these tests provide extensive norms on industrial samples. Despite their brevity, their reliabilities are generally over .80 and often over .90.

A somewhat different approach is illustrated by the Wesman Personnel Classification Test. Like most current intelligence tests, it yields Verbal, Numerical, and Total scores. The Verbal score is based on an 18-minute verbal analogies test, in which each item contains two blanks, as illustrated in Figure 98. The Numerical score is derived from a 10-minute arithmetic computation test whose items were designed so as to put a premium on ingenuity and ability to perceive numerical relations. Two parallel forms are available. Percentile norms on each of the three scores are reported for groups of students, job applicants, and employees, each group including from 93 to 1,476 cases. Parallel-form reliability coefficients for V, N, and Total scores fall mostly in the .80's. Correlations of V and N scores vary from .25 to .57, indicating that the overlap of the two parts is small enough to justify retention of separate scores.

Mean scores on the test show progressive rise with increasing educational and occupational level in the groups compared. Correlations with criteria of vocational success, usually based on supervisors' ratings, range from .29 to .62. From the nature of the items, as well as from the distribution of scores reported for various groups, it appears that this test may be better suited for higher-level than for lower-level personnel. It also seems likely that the predominantly academic content of the items would not hold the interest of lower-level job applicants and would lack face validity for them.

For the rapid screening of industrial personnel at the other end of the distribution, a more appropriate instrument is the Personnel Tests for In-

---

Each question in Part I is a sentence with the first word and the last word left out. You are to pick out words to fill in the blanks so that the sentence will be true and sensible.

For the first blank, pick out a **numbered** word—1, 2, 3, or 4. For the blank at the end of the sentence, pick out one of the **lettered** words —A, B, C, or D. Then write the number and the letter you have picked on the line at the right.

Example 1.   ..... is to water as eat is to *2C*

| 1. continue | 2. drink | 3. foot | 4. girl |
| A. drive | B. enemy | C. food | D. industry |

Drink is to water as eat is to **food. Drink** is numbered 2, and **food** is lettered C, so 2C has been written on the line at the right.

FIG. 98.   Sample Analogies Item from the Wesman Personnel Classification Test. (Reproduced by permission. Copyright © 1946, The Psychological Corporation, New York, N.Y. All rights reserved.)

dustry (PTI). This battery includes a 5-minute Verbal Test, a 20-minute Numerical Test, and a 15-minute Oral Directions Test. The three tests may be used together or separately. The Oral Directions Test, administered by phonograph or tape recording, is suitable for applicants with limited schooling or with a foreign language background. It is also available in a Spanish edition.

Alternate-form reliabilities of the Verbal and Numerical Tests range from .73 to .92; split-half reliabilities of the Oral Directions Test range from .82 to .94. Norms for all three tests are reported for various industrial and educational samples. Older persons may be somewhat handicapped on the Oral Directions Test because of its dependence on auditory discrimination and speed. The test is rather heavily weighted with perceptual and spatial items, and also depends to a considerable extent on immediate memory for auditory instructions. Available data suggest that it discriminates somewhat better at the lower intellectual levels and may be particularly useful in screening applicants for such jobs as general laborer, maintenance and service worker, and messenger.

VOCATIONAL ACHIEVEMENT TESTS

A large number of achievement tests are utilized for selection and classification purposes in industry, government, and the armed services. When designed for industrial use, they are commonly designated as *trade tests.* Such tests are particularly useful in hiring workers in the skilled trades and in selecting apprentices on completion of trade courses. They can also serve an important function in the transfer and promotion of workers. Because of their obvious job relevance, these tests are more likely to be acceptable to both labor and management as a basis for personnel decisions than are other types of tests. Many vocational achievement tests are custom-made for specific purposes and are not available for general distribution. Civil-service examinations constitute a major example of such restricted tests, and other illustrations can readily be found in industry and in the armed services.

Vocational achievement tests utilize a variety of testing media. The test content may be entirely verbal, or it may involve the use of diagrammatic or pictorial material. Questions may be presented orally or in writing. For many testing purposes, paper-and-pencil content may be replaced by manual or other performance tasks to be executed by the subject.

JOB SAMPLES.   Some vocational achievement tests represent standardized job samples. In such tests, the task set for the subject is similar to the work he is to perform on the job. The representativeness of the behavior sample and the closeness with which the task duplicates actual job conditions are essential considerations. The scoring of worksamples may be based on either the process or the product, or both. The nature of the task may determine which aspect is scored. For example, piloting a plane, driving a car, or singing an aria in a vocal audition must be appraised in terms of the process. On the other hand, the ability to prepare effective advertising copy would usually be evaluated in terms of the end product, the process being of relatively little interest. In many tasks, both process and product are amenable to observation, but the product lends itself more readily to objective scoring.

Process, or performance, scoring may be facilitated and standardized by the use of checklists indicating the points to observe and the relative importance of each. Such checklists are commonly employed in administering road tests for the driver's license, in rating the performance of student pilots, and in many similar types of activities. Products of worksample tests can often be scored in terms of objective records. In a typewriting test, for example, the total number of errors in the typewritten copy may be readily counted. Patterns and gauges can be applied to determine whether a mechanical product falls within specified tolerance limits, or how far it deviates from a perfect specimen. Certain types of products, however, require qualitative evaluation by an expert. Rating scales and checklists may be used as aids in such judgments. In other cases, product scales similar to those described for rating drawings are employed, and the product is matched with the scale specimen it resembles most closely and is rated accordingly.

Among the best-known vocational achievement tests available for general use are those designed for clerical jobs, especially typewriting, stenography, and bookkeeping. Some of these tests include parts dealing with English usage and general business information, together with measures of the primary skills under consideration. Stenographic tests usually employ disc or tape recording to assure uniformity in speed and clarity of dictation. A typical illustration is the Seashore-Bennett Stenographic Proficiency Test. This test requires the examinee to take stenographic notes for five letters of increasing length and complexity, and dictated at increasing rates of speed. The notes are then transcribed in the form of typewritten letters.

Other job-sample tests are more limited in their occupational applications. Examples range from a miniature punch press to elaborate simulators for airplane pilots. Of particular interest are the preliminary attempts to devise a job-sample test for certain aspects of executive work (Frederiksen, 1966a, 1966b; Frederiksen, Saunders, & Wand, 1957). Known as the In-Basket Test, this technique has been adapted for testing Air Force officers in administrative positions, business executives, administrators in government agencies, and school principals. Simulating the familiar "in-basket" found on the administrator's desk, this test provides a carefully prepared set of incoming letters, memoranda, reports, papers to be signed, and similar items. Before taking the test, the examinee has an opportunity to study background materials for orientation and information regarding the hypothetical job. During the test proper, his task is to handle all the matters in his in-basket as he would on the job. All actions must be recorded in writing but may include letters, memos, decisions, plans, directives, information to be obtained or transmitted by telephone, agenda for meetings, or any other notes.

WRITTEN INFORMATION TESTS.   Some occupational achievement tests are concerned, not with job skills, but with technical information. Written tests, suitable for either group or individual administration, have been developed for this purpose. The extensive testing programs conducted by both federal and state civil-service agencies rely heavily on this type of test. Examples of commercially available written trade tests are provided by the series of Purdue Personnel Tests. These tests include, among others, trade information tests for such occupations as carpentry, welding, sheet metal work, and engine lathe operation.

Typical results obtained with one of the Purdue tests are shown in Figure 99. The Purdue Trade Information Test in Engine Lathe Operation was administered to 60 men, including 30 journeymen machinists and 30 vocational high school graduates with at least one year of machine shop instruction. It is apparent that the test differentiated sharply between the two groups. All examinees scoring above 68 were journeymen, as were 93 percent of those scoring between 63 and 68. In contrast, only 50 percent of the scores between 53 and 62 and only 18 percent of the scores below 52

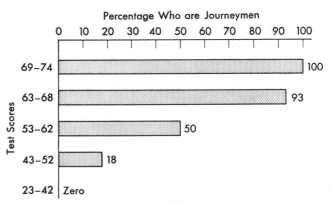

FIG. 99.   Percentage of Examinees Who Were Journeymen Machinists in Relation to Scores on Purdue Trade Information Test in Engine Lathe Operation. (From Tiffin & McCormick, 1965, p. 218.)

were obtained by journeymen. It should be noted, of course, that this type of test is not a substitute for job-sample tests in jobs requiring manipulative skills.

ORAL TRADE TESTS.   Another technique for appraising vocational training and experience involves the use of oral trade tests. These tests consist of short series of questions about specialized trade knowledge. The items of information are so chosen as to be fairly easy for anyone who has actually worked in a particular type of job, but rarely familiar to other persons. Such questions are often used as interview aids by placement counselors in employment offices. They were also extensively utilized for the rapid classification of military personnel in both World Wars. Although not widely used in industry, this technique has yielded promising results when applied to industrial jobs (see Tiffin & McCormick, 1965, pp. 216–217).

The United States Employment Service (USES) has developed an extensive series of oral trade questions covering some 250 occupations. Each set consists of approximately 15 questions, alternate forms being available for many of the jobs. Alternate-form reliability for such jobs range from .79 to .93. A sample item from the bricklayer's test is given below (Stead, Shartle, *et al.*, 1940, p. 45):

Question: What do you mean by building up a lead (*leed*)?
Answer: Building up a section (corner) of wall.

In the development of these oral trade tests, questions were first formulated from information gathered through direct observation of jobs and consultation with foremen and highly skilled workers in each field. Preliminary tryouts with foremen and skilled workers in each type of job led to the elimination, revision, or addition of questions. Some questions were discarded because of regional differences in job practices or materials.

The final validation was conducted on workers classified into three categories: (a) experts; (b) apprentices and helpers; (c) related workers (e.g., for painters, related workers include carpenters, paper hangers, plasterers). The questions for each occupation were validated on 50 to 100 experts and on 25 to 50 persons in each of the other two categories. Questions were chosen on the basis of the magnitude and significance of the difference between the percentages of persons answering correctly in each group. The distributions of scores obtained by the three experience groups within the bricklayer sample are shown in Figure 100. It can be seen that the groups are sharply differentiated and that overlap is minimal, especially when the experts are compared with the other two groups. Because of changes in occupational processes and materials, trade information tests require periodic review. Research is currently in progress to update and revise the USES trade questions.

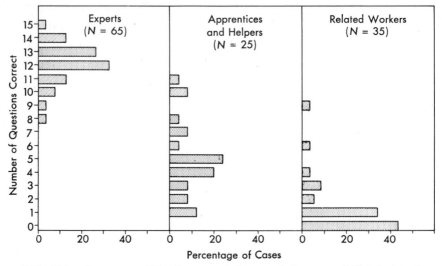

FIG. 100. Percentage Distribution of Scores of Contrasted Validation Samples on USES Oral Trade Questions for Bricklayers. (Data from Stead, Shartle, *et al.*, 1940, p. 41.)

TESTING IN THE PROFESSIONS

A growing application of standardized tests is to be found in large-scale programs for the selection of professional personnel. Many of these programs are directed toward the selection of students for admission to professional training. Tests are currently being administered to candidates for schools of medicine, dentistry, nursing, law, business, engineering, theology, architecture, and other professional fields. Although such testing programs emphasize aptitudes and the prediction of subsequent performance in specialized training, achievement tests on preprofessional courses constitute an important part of most batteries.

It should also be noted that in the selection of students for professional schools what is involved is not so much new types of tests as specially administered testing programs. There is no evidence that the various professional fields require any special aptitudes not already covered by available tests. The typical professional-school testing program includes a test of scholastic aptitude or general intelligence, one or more achievement tests on preprofessional training, and possibly tests of interests or other personality traits. Test results are often supplemented with biographical data, letters of recommendation, previous academic record, and interview ratings.

The intelligence test employed in such a program may be a standard scholastic aptitude test at an advanced level. More often it is specially designed so that the content can be slanted toward the particular professional field under consideration. Such a choice of content increases face validity, in addition to permitting better security control of test materials. There is also some evidence to suggest that the predictive validity of these special tests is a little higher than that of the intelligence or scholastic aptitude tests available for general use. The specialized scholastic aptitude tests often contain measures of reading comprehension for material similar to that which the student will encounter in professional school. Some of the tests yield separate verbal and quantitative scores. Spatial, mechanical, and motor aptitudes may also be separately tested when relevant to the field.

Another level at which standardized testing programs are making major inroads is that of specialty certification and the selection of job applicants following completion of training. Understandably these terminal testing programs draw much more heavily on achievement tests in specialized content areas; but more general types of tests are not excluded. Examples of testing programs at this level include medical specialty board examinations in such areas as surgery, anaesthesiology, and obstetrics and gynecology, administered by ETS; the certification of clinical, counseling, and industrial psychologists by the American Board of Examiners in Professional Psychology (ABEPP); the National Teacher Examinations; the NLN Graduate Nurse Qualifying Examination and other tests in nursing administered by the National League for Nursing; the Officer Selection and Evaluation Program of the U.S. Public Health Service; and the Department of State Foreign Service Examinations. For illustrative purposes, a few examples at both pretraining and posttraining levels will be examined in the following sections.

MEDICINE. Beginning in 1930, the Association of American Medical Colleges sponsored a testing program for selecting medical students. For many years, the test administered for this purpose was one devised by Moss (1942), which measured principally knowledge acquired in premedical college courses and ability to understand and retain new material similar to that taught in medical school. Since 1948, this program has employed the Medical College Admission Test (MCAT). Requiring about four hours, MCAT consists of four separately scored parts: verbal, quantitative, general information, and science. The verbal part consists of analogies, antonyms, and synonyms; the quantitative part contains items from arithmetic, algebra, and geometry, with emphasis on quantitative reasoning with the given facts; the science test covers premedical courses in chemistry, biology, and physics. The general information subtest samples a wide range of content from the humanities and the social sciences. This subtest was designed, not as a predictor of medical school grades, but rather in the effort to select prospective physicians with a broad cultural background. Its inclusion is thus justified on the basis of its content validity rather than its predictive criterion-related validity.

Kuder-Richardson as well as alternate-form reliabilities of the four parts of the MCAT are in the .80's and .90's (Sedlacek,1967).Intercorrelations of parts range from the .30's to the .50's, except for correlations in the .70's between the verbal and general information subtests. For each part, scores are reported on a uniform standard score scale with a mean of 500 and an SD of 100; this scale utilizes a fixed reference group tested in 1951. In addition, normative data are provided for annual candidate samples classified by sex, college status, undergraduate major, and region.

Predictive validity of part scores on MCAT against attrition, medical school grades, and Medical Board Examinations in basic science are promising. It should be noted, of course, that such correlations are necessarily based on students admitted to medical schools. Hence, a certain amount of preselection has occurred in all groups. This circumstance tends to make the correlations lower than if all applicants could be admitted and followed through medical school. The obtained test correlations, however, are not consistently higher than those found between premedical college grades and medical school grades. In fact, in a number of instances the premedical grades appear to be slightly better predictors than the test scores.

To be sure, the above findings with regard to grades are not peculiar to the MCAT or to the prediction of medical school performance. In all fields, preprofessional grades generally prove to be at least as effective as specially designed tests in the prediction of professional school achievement. But when test scores are combined with grades, a more valid predictor usually results. Admission tests are useful as a supplement to, rather than as a substitute for, preprofessional grades. An intrinsic difficulty presented by grades arises from the lack of comparability of grades in different colleges and different courses. An applicant from a college whose students are not highly selected and whose grading standards are relatively low would have an advantage in terms of grade average. Similarly, students who had elected the minimum of required preprofessional courses and had filled their programs with easy courses would probably have a higher overall grade average than those whose preparation was more thorough and more appropriate for their chosen profession. It is in such situations that a uniform admission test proves helpful.

LAW.   Prior to 1940, tests for the selection of law students were developed at a number of universities for use in their own law schools. The pioneer effort in this direction appears to have been made at Columbia University. However, the first test designed for common use in different law schools was the Ferson-Stoddard Law Aptitude Examination. The preparation of this test was begun in 1925 at the Universities of Iowa and North Carolina, although standardization data were also obtained at several other universities (Adams, 1944; Stoddard, 1927). In 1943 Adams and his coworkers at the University of Iowa developed a new legal aptitude test which was made available for general distribution rather than being restricted to law schools (Adams, 1943, 1944). Known as the Iowa Legal Aptitude Test, it originally comprised the following seven verbal subtests: analogies, mixed relations, opposites, memory for the factual content of a judicial opinion read two hours earlier, judging relevancy of legal arguments, reasoning, and legal information. The last-named test was included on the assumption that students interested in law would have learned certain common facts of law prior to formal study of the subject.

Since 1948, the Law School Admission Test (LSAT), constructed by ETS, has been administered to law school candidates on a national basis. In its present form, this test includes a morning session and an afternoon session. The tests administered in the morning session yield a single score designed to reflect the candidate's skills in acquiring information and in logical analysis. The tests employed for this purpose include:

Reading Comprehension, with passages in the humanities, natural sciences, and social sciences.

Reading Recall, in which questions about more highly factual passages from the same three fields are to be answered from memory.

Data Interpretation, designed to measure comprehension of quantitative data in tabular or graphic form (see Fig. 101).

Principles and Cases, in which the relevance of given principles to described cases is to be judged.

Figure Classification, a nonverbal reasoning test requiring examinee to abstract the common feature of a group of geometric figures.

The tests administered in the afternoon session yield two scores, as follows:

(1) *Writing Ability*

Error Recognition, designed to measure proficiency in the mechanics of writing.

Organization of Ideas—classifying sentences in relation to main idea of passage.

Editing—choosing correction for underlined parts of passage.

(2) *General Background*—a single test assessing breadth of knowledge in the humanities, natural sciences, and social sciences.

The predictive validity of LSAT has been investigated in a continuing research program involving the joint participation of many law schools. Available data indicate that, when combined with pre-law grades, this test yields correlations of about .50 to .70 with the criterion of law school grades. In a combined survey of 4,138 students in 25 law schools, first-year

• *Directions:* This section of the test consists of questions based on charts, tables, and graphs. Each question is followed by five choices, only *one* of which is correct. Whenever the option "Not answerable" appears, it is to be understood to mean "Not answerable on the basis of the data given."

Select the correct answer to each question and mark the corresponding space on the answer sheet.

DISTRIBUTION OF EMPLOYMENT IN NEW JERSEY BY INDUSTRY AND SEX—1940.

1. Manufacturing.
2. Trade—wholesale and retail.
3. Personal services.
4. Transportation, communication, utilities.
5. Professional and related.
6. Finance, insurance, real estate.
7. Construction.
8. Government.
9. Agriculture.
10. All other, including those not reported.

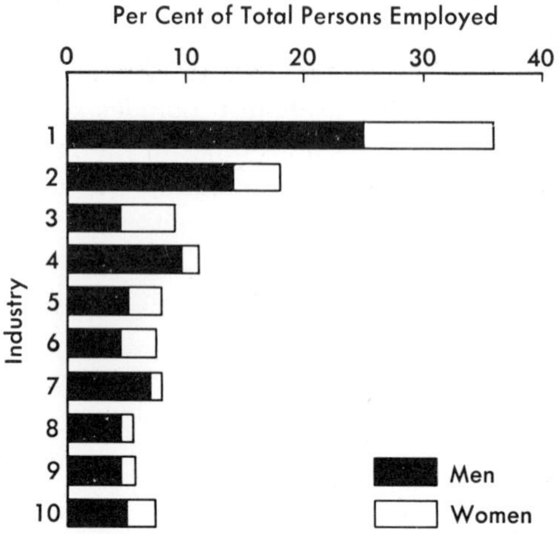

Questions 21-23 are based on the graph above.

21. Which of the industries listed employed the greatest proportion of women?
(A) 1   (B) 2   (C) 3   (D) 7   (E) 8

22. Approximately how many thousand men were employed in the construction industry?
(A) 4   (B) 6   (C) 8   (D) 10   (E) Not answerable

23. Out of every 100 persons employed in the manufacturing industry, approximately how many were women?
(A) 10   (B) 20   (C) 30   (D) 40   (E) Not answerable

ANSWERS: 21—C, 22—E, 23—C.

FIG. 101. Sample Items from Data Interpretation Subtest of Law School Admission Test. (Reproduced by permission of Educational Testing Service.)

law school grades correlated .36 with undergraduate grades, .45 with LSAT scores, and .54 with the best weighted combination of LSAT scores and undergraduate grades (*LSAT Handbook*, 1964, p. 47). These relationships, expressed in the form of expectancy charts, are shown in Figure 102. Despite the increasing homogeneity of student populations from the first to the third year of law school, LSAT scores tend to correlate as highly with three-year grades as with first-year grades (Breslow, 1957; Burnham &

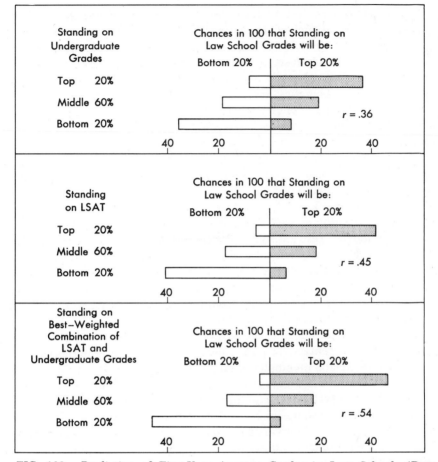

FIG. 102.   Prediction of First-Year Average Grades in Law School. (Data from *LSAT Handbook,* 1964, p. 47.)

Crawford, 1957). It should nevertheless be borne in mind that validity coefficients vary widely from one law school to another, a finding that highlights the need for local validation. Moreover, the correlations between test scores and grades will decrease as students are more stringently selected on the basis of test scores (*LSAT Handbook,* 1964, p. 26; Pitcher, 1965, p. 12). Such a decrease does not, of course, indicate a decline in the validity of the test, but only the increasing utilization of LSAT scores in student selection. The tests of Writing Ability and General Background, introduced in 1961, add little to the validity of the battery in predicting first-year law school grades (Pitcher, 1965, pp. 15–20). These tests were included principally on the basis of content validity, in order to select prospective lawyers who are competent in written communication and have a broad liberal arts background.

ENGINEERING. Several batteries for the selection of engineering students have been assembled from time to time. These batteries generally utilize previously available standard tests, including mechanical comprehension and assembly tests, spatial visualization tests, a measure of general scholastic aptitude, and achievement tests in mathematics, science, and English. Mathematics achievement tests have usually proved to be the best single predictor of engineering school performance. Pre-engineering high school or college grades have high predictive validity and are employed in conjunction with test scores. English usage, vocabulary, and reading comprehension are relevant to the understanding of lecture and reading material encountered in engineering school, as well as to the preparation of descriptive reports.

A test at a higher level, designed for selection of candidates for graduate engineering training as well as for industrial jobs, is the Minnesota Engineering Analogies Test (MEAT). Modeled after the Miller Analogies Test (Ch. 9), the MEAT consists of analogies items with a heavy mathematical and scientific content. The analogies may be expressed wholly in verbal terms, wholly in mathematical terms, or in a mixture of the two. The content of the items is drawn chiefly from the core courses taken by all engineering students during their first two years.

Like the Miller Analogies, the MEAT is a restricted test, administered only at approved centers. Tentative percentile and stanine norms on engineering students and on employed engineers are provided, but the development of local norms is urged. Internal consistency reliability coefficients of each of the two available forms range from .75 to .85. Because of these rather low reliabilities, use of both forms together is recommended. When administered with an interval of two days or less, the two forms correlated from .71 to .88. Content validity was sought in terms of current curricular coverage. Some data are available on concurrent validity, including correlations with engineering school grades and faculty ratings of students, as well as correlations with supervisory ratings of employed engineers. Although varying widely in specific groups, the former correlations cluster between .40 and .60, the latter between .25 and .35.

It should be noted that an Advanced Test in Engineering is a regular part of the testing program of the Graduate Record Examinations, discussed in Chapter 9. The selection of engineers is also closely related to the general problem of identifying high-level talent in science, a problem that has received increasing attention since midcentury. Such interest is reflected in studies on the characteristics of successful research workers, as well as in the development of tests for measuring reasoning and creativity that were discussed in Chapter 14. Much current research on creativity is directed toward the identification and development of inventive talent in engineering.

PART 4

PERSONALITY
TESTS

CHAPTER **17**

Self-Report
Inventories

ALTHOUGH THE term "personality" is sometimes employed in a broader sense, in conventional psychometric terminology "personality tests" are instruments for the measurement of emotional, motivational, interpersonal, and attitudinal characteristics, as distinguished from abilities. In the next four chapters, the major varieties of personality tests will be examined. This chapter will deal with personality inventories. Chapter 18 will consider available techniques for the measurement of interests and attitudes. The instruments to be covered in both of these chapters are essentially paper-and-pencil, self-report questionnaires suitable for group administration. The use of projective techniques for the assessment of personality characteristics will be discussed in Chapter 19. In Chapter 20 we shall survey a number of miscellaneous approaches to the measurement of personality, many of which are still in an experimental stage.

The number of available personality tests runs into several hundred. Especially numerous are the personality inventories and the projective techniques. In this book, we shall be concerned primarily with the types of approaches that have been explored. A few of the most widely known tests of each type will be briefly described for illustrative purposes. Many books have been written exclusively about personality assessment through tests as well as through other techniques. For more detailed treatment of the topic, the reader is referred to such specialized books (e.g., Kleinmuntz, 1967; Megargee, 1966; Sarason, 1966; Vernon, 1964).

In the development of personality inventories, several approaches have been followed in formulating, assembling, selecting, and grouping items. Among the major procedures in current use are those based on content validation, empirical criterion keying, factor analysis, and personality theory. Each of these approaches will be discussed and illustrated in the following sections. It should be noted, however, that they are not alternative or mutually exclusive techniques. Theoretically, all could be combined in the development of a single personality inventory. In actual practice, several inventories have utilized two or more of these procedures.

Personality inventories also differ in item form. Of particular interest in this connection is the forced-choice technique, originally devised to circumvent faking, malingering, and the influence of response sets on personality inventory scores. This item form will be considered within a broader discussion of response sets.

CONTENT VALIDATION

The prototype of self-report personality inventories was the Woodworth Personal Data Sheet, developed for use during World War I. This inventory was essentially an attempt to standardize a psychiatric interview and to adapt the procedure for mass testing. Accordingly, Woodworth gathered information regarding common neurotic and preneurotic symptoms from the psychiatric literature as well as through conferences with psychiatrists. It was in reference to these symptoms that the inventory questions were originally formulated. The questions dealt with such behavior deviations as abnormal fears or phobias, obsessions and compulsions, nightmares and other sleep disturbances, excessive fatigue and other psychosomatic symptoms, feelings of unreality, and motor disturbances such as tics and tremors. In the final selection of items, Woodworth applied certain empirical statistical checks, to be discussed in the next section. Nevertheless, it is apparent that the primary emphasis in the construction and use of this inventory was placed on content validity, as indicated in the sources from which items were drawn as well as in the common recognition of certain kinds of behavior as maladaptive.

One of the clearest examples of content validation in a current personality inventory is provided by the Mooney Problem Check List. Designed chiefly to identify problems for group discussion or for individual counseling, this checklist drew its items from written statements of problems submitted by about 4,000 high school students, as well as from case records, counseling interviews, and similar sources. The checklist is available in junior high school, high school, college, and adult forms. The problem areas covered vary somewhat from level to level. In the high school and college forms, they include health and physical development; finances, living conditions, and employment; social and recreational activities; social-psychological relations; personal-psychological relations; courtship, sex, and marriage; home and family; morals and religion; adjustment to school work; the future—vocational and educational; and curriculum and teaching procedure.

Although the number of items checked in each area can be recorded, the Mooney Problem Check List does not yield trait scores or measures of degree of adjustment. Emphasis is on individual items as self-perceived and self-reported problems or sources of difficulty. While no psychometric evaluation of this instrument has been undertaken, evidence has accumulated indicating its effectiveness. Published research shows that, on the average, students check from 20 to 30 problems; these results suggest that the checklist provides good coverage of problems that students are willing to report. Some data on concurrent validity are available from comparisons of contrasted groups whose reported problem frequencies in relevant areas differ in the expected direction.

Another checklist of needs and problems, suitable for grades 7 to 12, is the STS Youth Inventory. The 167 items comprising this checklist are grouped under the following rubrics: My School, After High School, About Myself, Getting Along with Others, and Things in General. An ingenious device incorporated into this inventory is the use of response boxes of different sizes to enable the respondent to suggest the magnitude of each problem, as illustrated in Figure 103. For each item, the manual provides percentages of respondents in a national normative sample who marked each response alternative.

As a final example of inventories relying primarily on content validation we may consider the California Test of Personality. Available in five levels, with two alternate forms at each level, this inventory undertakes to span the age range from kindergarten to college students and unselected adults. In the type of scores obtained and the proposed interpretations of such scores, the California Test of Personality resembles empirically developed personality tests. In its construction, however, content validation appears

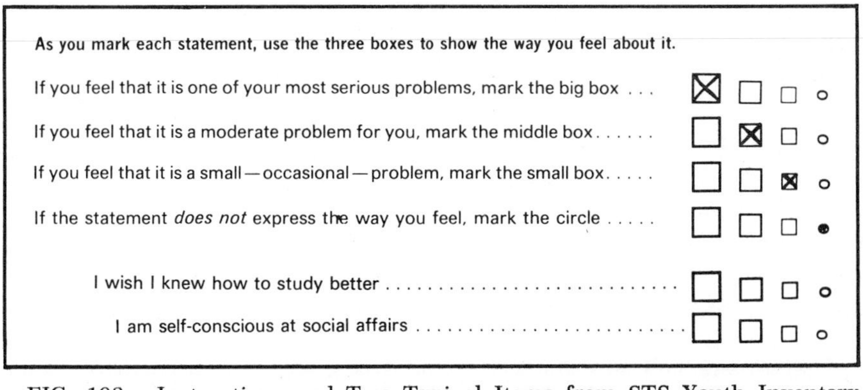
As you mark each statement, use the three boxes to show the way you feel about it.

If you feel that it is one of your most serious problems, mark the big box . . .

If you feel that it is a moderate problem for you, mark the middle box. . . . . .

If you feel that it is a small—occasional—problem, mark the small box. . . . .

If the statement *does not* express the way you feel, mark the circle . . . . .

I wish I knew how to study better . . . .

I am self-conscious at social affairs . . . .

FIG. 103. Instructions and Two Typical Items from STS Youth Inventory, Form G. (Reproduced by permission of Scholastic Testing Service.)

to have predominated. Separate scores are found in 12 areas, identified by such labels as sense of personal worth, withdrawing tendencies, social skills, and school relations. From these part scores, a total adjustment score and two subtotals covering personal and social adjustment are also computed. National norms are provided for evaluating these 15 scores. Internal consistency reliabilities are reasonably satisfactory for total scores and for the two subtotals; but reliabilities of individual subscores are too low to justify intraindividual profile analysis.

It should be noted that with all these inventories some efforts have been made toward empirical validation of scores in each problem area. Few personality tests in use today rest their claims entirely on content validity. All tests cited in this section, however, have relied principally on content validity in the formulation, selection, and grouping of items.

EMPIRICAL CRITERION KEYING

EARLY INVENTORIES.   Empirical criterion keying refers to the development of a scoring key in terms of some external criterion. This procedure involves the selection of items to be retained and the assignment of scoring weights to each response. In the construction of the previously cited Woodworth Personal Data Sheet, some of the statistical checks applied in the final selection of items pointed the way for criterion keying. Thus, no item was retained in this inventory if 25 percent or more of a normal sample answered it in the unfavorable direction. The rationale underlying this procedure was that a behavior characteristic that occurs with such frequency in an essentially normal sample cannot be indicative of abnormality. The method of contrasted groups was likewise employed in the selection of items. Only symptoms reported at least twice as often in a previously diagnosed psychoneurotic group than in a normal group were retained.

Another early example of criterion keying is provided by the A-S Reaction Study (Allport, 1928; Ruggles & Allport, 1939). Described as a measure of ascendance-submission (A-S), this inventory seeks to assess the individual's tendency to dominate his associates or be dominated by them in face-to-face contacts of everyday life. Each item begins with a brief description of a situation that might commonly be encountered at a meeting, in school, on a bus, in a repair shop, or in other familiar settings. Two or four alternative ways of meeting the situation are listed, the subject being instructed to indicate which alternative most nearly represents his usual reaction. The responses vary in the degree of ascendance or submission they represent and are weighted accordingly in the scoring.

The scoring weights for the A-S Reaction Study were empirically established on the basis of the criterion ratings obtained by those subjects in the standardization sample who chose each response. Each subject's criterion rating represented a mean of five ratings for social dominance, including a self-rating and four ratings by associates. Following publication of the test, considerable evidence for the validity of total scores has been accumulated, chiefly by the method of contrasted groups. In addition to enjoying wide popularity in its own right, the A-S Reaction Study has influenced the development of many other inventories. This test is one of the most durable of the early personality inventories. It might also be noted that dominance has proved to be one of the most frequently identified and clearly established traits in subsequent factorial analyses of personality.

THE MINNESOTA MULTIPHASIC PERSONALITY INVENTORY.   The outstanding example of criterion keying in personality test construction is to be found in the Minnesota Multiphasic Personality Inventory (MMPI). Not only is the MMPI the most widely used personality inventory, but it has also stimulated a flood of research. To date, over 1,500 references have been published about this test. A considerable portion of this research is concerned with factorial analyses of the MMPI scales and with the operation of response styles in its scores, topics to be discussed in later sections of this chapter.

The MMPI was originally developed "to assay those traits that are commonly characteristic of disabling psychological abnormality" (Hathaway & McKinley, 1967, p. 1). The inventory consists of 550 affirmative statements, to which the examinee gives the responses: "True," "False," or "Cannot say." In the individual form of the test, the statements are printed on separate cards, which the respondent sorts into the three categories. Later, a group form was prepared, in which the statements are printed in a test booklet and the responses are recorded on an answer sheet. Both forms were designed for adults from about 16 years of age upward, although they have also been employed successfully with somewhat younger adolescents (Hathaway & Monachesi, 1963). Although the card form may be preferable when testing disturbed patients or persons of low educational or intellectual level, the booklet form is now used for most purposes. The MMPI items range widely in content, covering such areas as: health, psychosomatic symptoms, neurological disorders, and motor disturbances; sexual, religious, political, and social attitudes; educational, occupational, family, and marital questions; and many well-known neurotic or psychotic behavior manifestations, such as obsessive and compulsive states, delusions, hallucinations, ideas of reference, phobias, and sadistic and masochistic trends. A few illustrative items are shown below:

I do not tire quickly.

Most people will use somewhat unfair means to gain profit or an advantage rather than to lose it.

I am worried about sex matters.

When I get bored I like to stir up some excitement.

I believe I am being plotted against.

In its regular administration, the MMPI provides scores on ten "clinical scales," listed below:

1. Hs: Hypochondriasis
2. D: Depression
3. Hy: Hysteria
4. Pd: Psychopathic deviate
5. Mf: Masculinity-femininity

6. Pa: Paranoia
7. Pt: Psychasthenia
8. Sc: Schizophrenia
9. Ma: Hypomania
0. Si: Social introversion

Eight of these scales consist of items that differentiated between a specified clinical group and a normal control group of approximately 700 persons. The latter were all visitors at the University of Minnesota hospitals, and represented a fairly adequate cross section of the Minnesota population of both sexes between the ages of 16 and 55. The clinical groups varied in size, but most contained about 50 cases. These scales were thus developed empirically by criterion keying of items, the criterion being traditional psychiatric diagnosis. Items for the Masculinity-femininity scale were selected in terms of frequency of responses by men and women. High scores on this scale indicate a predominance of interests typical of the opposite sex. Such scores have been found to characterize homosexuals, especially among males, although in individual cases high scores may have other interpretations. The Social introversion scale, added later, was derived from the responses of two contrasted groups of college students selected on the basis of extreme scores on a test of introversion-extraversion. This scale was also found to be significantly related to the number of extracurricular activities in which high school or college students participated.

A special feature of the MMPI is its utilization of four so-called validity scales. These scales are not concerned with validity in the technical sense. In effect, they represent checks on carelessness, misunderstanding, malingering, and the operation of special response sets and test-taking attitudes. The validating scores include:

Question Score (?): the total number of items put into the "Cannot say" category.

Lie Score (L): based on a group of items that make the examinee appear in a favorable light, but are unlikely to be truthfully answered in the favorable direction. (E.g., I do not like everyone I know.)

Validity Score (F): determined from a set of items very infrequently answered in the scored direction by the standardization group. Although representing undesirable behavior, these items do not cohere in any pattern of abnormality. Hence, it is unlikely that any one person actually shows all or most of these symptoms. A high F score may indicate scoring errors, carelessness in responding, gross eccentricity, or deliberate malingering.

Correction Score (K): utilizing still another combination of specially chosen items, this score provides a measure of test-taking attitude, related to both L and F, but believed to be more subtle. A high K score may indicate defensiveness or an attempt to "fake good." A low K score may represent excessive frankness and self-criticism or a deliberate attempt to "fake bad."

The first three scores (?, L, F) are ordinarily used for an overall evaluation of the test record. If any of these scores exceeds a specified value, the record is considered invalid. The K score, on the other hand, was designed to function as a "suppressor variable." It is employed to compute a correction factor which is added to the scores on some of the clinical scales in order to obtain adjusted totals.

Since the publication of the MMPI in its initial form, about 200 new scales have been developed, most of them by independent investigators who had not participated in the construction of the original test (Dahlstrom & Welsh, 1960). These scales vary widely in the nature and breadth of the criteria against which items were evaluated. Several scales were developed within normal populations to assess personality traits unrelated to pathology. Some scales have subsequently been applied to the test records of the original MMPI normal standardization sample, thus providing normative data comparable to those of the initial clinical scales. Examples of these new scales include Ego Strength (ES), Dependency (Dy), Dominance (Do), Prejudice (Pr), and Social Status (St). Other scales have been developed for highly specific purposes and are more limited in their applicability.

In its regular administration, the MMPI now yields 14 scores, including the 9 original clinical scales, the Si scale, and the 4 validating scales. Norms on the original control sample of approximately 700 persons are reported in the form of standard scores with a mean of 50 and an *SD* of 10. These standard scores are used in plotting profiles, as illustrated in Figure 104. Any score of 70 or higher—falling 2 *SD*'s or more above the mean—is generally taken as the cutoff point for the identification of pathological deviations. It should be noted, however, that the clinical significance of the same score may differ from one scale to another. A score of 75 on the Hypochondriasis and on the Schizophrenia scales, for example, may not indicate the same severity of abnormality.

There is considerable evidence to suggest that, in general, the greater the number and magnitude of deviant scores on the MMPI, the more likely it is that the individual is severely disturbed. For screening purposes, however, shorter and simpler instruments are available. It is clear that the principal applications of the MMPI are to be found in differential diagnosis. In using the inventory for this purpose, the procedure is much more complex than the labels originally assigned to the scales might suggest. The test

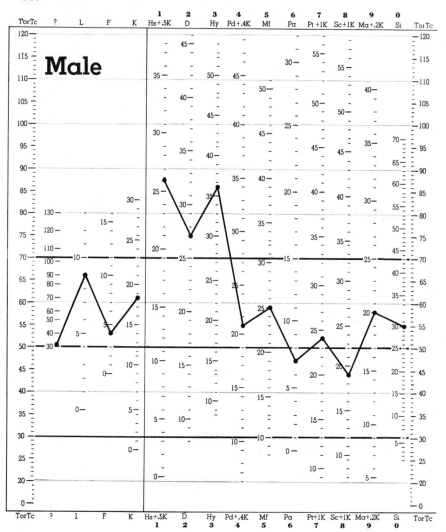

FIG. 104. MMPI Profile Illustrating the Conversion V Code. (Profile Chart reproduced by permission. Copyright © 1948, The Psychological Corporation, New York, N.Y. All rights reserved.)

manual and related publications now caution against literal interpretation of the clinical scales. For example, we cannot assume that a high score on the Schizophrenia scale indicates the presence of schizophrenia. Other psychotic groups show high elevation on this scale, and schizophrenics often score high on other scales. Moreover, such a score may occur in a normal person. It is partly to prevent possible misinterpretations of scores on single scales that the code numbers 0 to 9 have been substituted for the scale names in later publications on the MMPI.

The original clinical scales of the MMPI were based on a traditional psychiatric classification which, though popular, rests on a dubious theoretical foundation. The artificiality of these categories has been a matter of concern in clinical psychology for a long time. The fact that such categories prove unsatisfactory in actual practice is now generally conceded. Another difficulty is that a high score on any one scale may have different implications depending on the accompanying scores on other scales. In other words, it is the score pattern or profile rather than individual scale scores that should be examined.

To facilitate the interpretation of score patterns, systems of numerical profile coding have been developed. In such codes, the sequence and arrangement of scale numbers show at a glance which are the high and low points in the individual's profile. According to one of the most widely used codes, the profile illustrated in Figure 104 would be coded as follows: 13″2′-59 407/68LK-F?. The scales are listed in descending order of magnitude of the scores; successive 10-point score intervals are separated by "elevation symbols"; scales whose scores are within one point of each other are underlined. The same system is used in recording the four validating scales (Hathaway & McKinley, 1967).

As an aid in the diagnostic interpretation of MMPI profiles, Hathaway and Meehl (1951) prepared *An Atlas for the Clinical Use of the MMPI.* This *Atlas* provides coded profiles and short case histories of 968 patients, arranged according to similarity of profile pattern. A similar codebook utilizing data from over 4,000 college students examined in a college counseling center was prepared for use by counselors (Drake & Oetting, 1959). Still another atlas was prepared for use with high school populations (Hathaway & Monachesi, 1961). Current validation of the MMPI is proceeding by the accumulation of empirical data about persons who show each profile pattern or code. By such a process, the construct validity of each MMPI code is gradually built up. The MMPI *Handbook,* compiled by Dahlstrom and Welsh (1960), contains a comprehensive survey of available interpretive data on major profile patterns. More recent codebooks have endeavored to simplify and systematize the interpretation of a small number of major profiles, in order to permit actuarial description in "cookbook fashion" (Gilberstadt & Duker, 1965; Marks & Seeman, 1963). Carrying this process a step farther, psychologists at several centers have developed computerized procedures for completely automated interpretation of MMPI profiles (Kleinmuntz, 1963; Pearson & Swenson, 1967; Swenson *et al.,* 1965).

An example of a commonly observed profile is the "neurotic triad." Characterized by elevations above 70 in scale 1 (Hypochondriasis), 2 (Depression), and 3 (Hysteria), this profile has often been found among neurotics. When scales 1 and 3 are higher than scale 2, the profile is known as the "conversion V," since this V-shaped profile is frequently associated with conversion hysteria. In such cases, somatic complaints are combined with emotional immaturity, dependency, and a tendency to evade problems. Figure 104 shows a profile with elevation above 70 in the three scales of the neurotic triad and a conversion V.

A series of studies of juvenile delinquents (Hathaway & Monachesi, 1953, 1963) showed high scores on scale 4 (Psychopathic deviate), often with a second high point on scale 6 (Paranoia), 8 (Schizophrenia), or 9 (Hypomania). Longitudinal investigations of over 15,000 unselected ninth-graders in Minnesota indicated that the students with such profiles were somewhat more likely to become delinquent within the next two to four years. Certain scales, such as 2 (Depression) and 0 (Social introversion) seem to function as inhibitors in delinquency codes, high scores in these scales reducing the probability of delinquent behavior.

Although the misleading psychiatric labels have been dropped in the coded profiles, it should be noted that MMPI items are still grouped into scales on the basis of such obsolescent categories. Factorial analyses based on intercorrelations of items and of scales indicate that items would be differently grouped on the basis of their empirically established interrelations. Furthermore, high intercorrelations among the basic MMPI clinical scales make their value in differential diagnosis questionable. For differential diagnosis, it would have been better to select items by comparing the responses of each clinical group, not with those of normals, but with those of other clinical groups. On the other hand, an extensive body of normative data and clinical experience pertaining to the old scales has accumulated over the years. In order not to lose this store of information, later efforts have been directed toward the reinterpretation of the old scales in terms of empirically derived profile codes.

A closely related limitation of the MMPI stems from inadequate reliabilities of some of the scales. The effectiveness of any profile analysis is weakened by chance errors in the scores on which it is based. If individual scale scores are unreliable and highly intercorrelated, many of the interscore differences that determine the profile code may have resulted from chance. Retest reliabilities on normal and abnormal adult samples reported in the manual range from the .50's to the low .90's. The intervals between retests varied from a few days to over a year. Retest coefficients found in a group of college students, however, were generally lower, although only a one-week interval had elapsed between testings (Gilliland & Colgin, 1951). The mean of these reliabilities was only .61. Six of the nine coefficients fell below .70, and two fell below .40. Moreover, split-half reliabilities computed for the same college sample showed an even wider variation from scale to scale, ranging from −.05 for scale 6 (Pa) to .81 for scale 7 (Pt). An equally wide range of split-half reliabilities has been found in studies of psychiatric patients (see Welsh & Dahlstrom, 1956).

Still another limitation of the MMPI pertains to the size and representativeness of the normative sample. The standard scores from which all profile codes are derived are expressed in terms of the performance of the control group of approximately 700 Minneapolis adults tested in the original standardization. Such a normative sample appears quite inadequate when compared, for example, with the nationwide standardization samples employed with many of the ability tests discussed in Parts 2 and 3. That the norms may vary appreciably in different normal populations is illustrated by the finding that the means obtained by college students are consistently above 50 on some of the scales (Clark, 1954; Gilliland & Colgin, 1951; Welsh & Dahlstrom, 1956, pp. 574–578). In one study of 600 college students, 39 percent received scores above 70 in one or more scales (Gilliland and Colgin, 1951). Perhaps it would be best to regard the original standardization sample as a nonnormative fixed reference group, in terms of which the score scale is defined. The much more extensive data subsequently collected with reference to profile codes would then provide all normative interpretation.

Even more than ability tests, personality tests can be expected to show large subcultural as well as cultural differences. As would be anticipated, studies conducted in other countries reveal significant elevation on certain scales when profiles are based on the original Minnesota norms (e.g., Sundberg, 1956; Taft, 1957). Any explanation of such cultural and subcultural differences requires specific knowledge of cultural conditions and other circumstances prevailing within each group. Cultural differentials may operate at many different levels (see Anastasi, 1958a, pp. 567–569). Group differences in MMPI scores could, for example, reflect nothing more than differences in interpretation of individual items or of instructions. High elevation in some groups could result from strong traditions of self-depreciation and modesty. Cultural differences in the type of behavior considered socially desirable may likewise influence scores. In still other groups, high scores may indicate the prevalence of genuine emotional problems arising from child-rearing practices, conflicts of social roles, minority group frustrations, and other broad cultural differences.

In summary, the MMPI is essentially a clinical instrument whose proper interpretation calls for considerable psychological sophistication. If the simplified actuarial interpretations and computer analyses are perceived as diagnostic aids for the overworked clinician, they can serve a useful purpose. There is danger, however, that the trend toward automation may encourage interpretation of MMPI profiles by inadequately trained users.

CALIFORNIA PSYCHOLOGICAL INVENTORY. Besides stimulating a proliferation of scoring scales, the MMPI has served as a basis for the development of other widely used inventories. An outstanding example is the California Psychological Inventory (CPI).[1] While drawing about half of its items from the MMPI, the CPI was developed specifically for use with normal populations from age 13 up. Consisting of 480 items to be answered *True* or *False,* the CPI yields scores in 18 scales. Three are "validity" scales designed to assess test-taking attitudes. These scales are designated as: Sense of well-being (Wb), based on responses by normals asked to "fake bad"; Good impression (Gi), based on responses by normals asked to "fake good"; and Communality (Cm), based on a frequency count of highly popular responses. The remaining 15 scales provide scores in such personality dimensions as Dominance, Sociability, Self-acceptance, Responsibility, Socialization, Self-control, Achievement-via-conformance, Achievement-via-independence, and Femininity.

For 11 of these 15 scales, items were selected on the basis of contrasted group responses, against such criteria as course grades, social class membership, participation in extracurricular activities, and ratings. The ratings were obtained through peer nominations, found to be an effective assessment technique for many interpersonal traits. For the remaining 4 scales, items were originally grouped subjectively and then checked for internal consistency. Cross validation of all scales on sizable samples has yielded significant group differences, although the overlapping of contrasted criterion groups is considerable and criterion correlations are often low.

As in the MMPI, all scores are reported in terms of a standard score scale with a mean of 50 and an *SD* of 10; this scale was derived from a normative sample of 6,000 males and 7,000 females, widely distributed in age, socioeconomic level, and geographic area. In addition, means and *SD*'s of scores on each scale are given for many special groups. Retest reliabilities over intervals of one to three weeks in an adult group yielded a median coefficient of .80; with a one-year interval in high school groups, the median reliabilities were .65 for males and .68 for females. No data on split-half reliabilities are reported in the manual. Intercorrelations of scales are relatively high. All but four scales, for example, correlate at least .50 with one or more other scales. This lack of independence, resulting in redundancy among the 18 scores, is perhaps the chief limitation of the CPI.

On the whole, however, the CPI is one of the best personality inventories currently available. Its technical development is of a high order and it has been subjected to extensive research and continuous improvement. In contrast to the clinical interpretation of coded profiles employed with the MMPI, research with the CPI has provided a number of regression equations for the optimal weighting of scales to predict such criteria as delinquency (Gough, 1966a), parole outcome (Gough, Wenk, & Rozynko, 1965), high school and college grades (Gough, 1964a, 1964b), and the probability of high school dropout (Gough, 1966c). Cross-cultural studies with indi-

---

[1] Other examples include the Taylor Manifest Anxiety Scale (Taylor, 1953) and the Minnesota Counseling Inventory (Berdie & Layton, 1960—listed in Appendix C).

vidual scales, such as Socialization and Femininity, have also yielded prom-ising validity data against local criteria within different cultures (Gough, 1965a, 1966a, 1966b).

FACTOR ANALYSIS IN TEST DEVELOPMENT

In the effort to arrive at a systematic classification of personality traits, a number of psychologists have turned to factor analysis. A series of studies by Guilford and his coworkers represents one of the pioneer ventures in this direction (see Guilford, 1959, Ch. 16; Guilford & Zimmerman, 1956). Rather than correlating total scores on existing inventories, these investi-gators computed the intercorrelations among individual items from many personality inventories. As a by-product of this research, three personality inventories were developed and eventually combined into the Guilford-Zimmerman Temperament Survey. This inventory yields separate scores for the following traits, each score based on 30 different items:

G. *General Activity:* Hurrying, liking for speed, liveliness, vitality, production, efficiency vs. slow and deliberate, easily fatigued, inefficient.

R. *Restraint:* Serious-minded, deliberate, persistent vs. carefree, impulsive, ex-citement-loving.

A. *Ascendance:* Self-defense, leadership, speaking in public, bluffing vs. sub-missiveness, hesitation, avoiding conspicuousness.

S. *Sociability:* Having many friends, seeking social contacts and limelight vs. few friends and shyness.

E. *Emotional Stability:* Evenness of moods, optimistic, composure vs. fluctuation of moods, pessimism, daydreaming, excitability, feelings of guilt, worry, lone-liness, and ill health.

O. *Objectivity:* Thick-skinned versus hypersensitive, self-centered, suspicious, having ideas of reference, getting into trouble.

F. *Friendliness:* Toleration of hostile action, acceptance of domination, respect for others vs. belligerence, hostility, resentment, desire to dominate, and contempt for others.

T. *Thoughtfulness:* Reflective, observing of self and others, mental poise vs. in-terest in overt activity and mental disconcertedness.

P. *Personal Relations:* Tolerance of people, faith in social institutions vs. fault-finding, critical of institutions, suspicious, self-pitying.

M. *Masculinity:* Interest in masculine activities, not easily disgusted, hard-boiled, inhibits emotional expression, little interest in clothes and style vs. interest in feminine activities and vocations, easily disgusted, fearful, romantic, emo-tionally expressive.

The items in the Guilford-Zimmerman Temperament Survey are expressed in the form of affirmative statements, rather than questions. Most concern the examinee directly. A few represent generalizations about other persons. Three examples are given below:

You start work on a new project with a great deal of enthusiasm . YES   ?   NO

You are often in low spirits .... YES   ?   NO

Most people use politeness to cover up what is really "cut-throat" competition .... YES   ?   NO

The affirmative item form was chosen in the effort to reduce the resistance that a series of direct questions is likely to arouse. In addition, three verification keys are provided to detect falsification and carelessness of response.

Percentile and standard score norms were derived chiefly from college samples. Attention is called to the desirability of interpreting not only single-trait scores but also total profiles. For example, a high score in Emotional Stability is favorable if coupled with a high General Activity score, but may be unfavorable if it occurs in combination with a low General Activity score. In the latter case, the individual may be sluggish, phlegmatic, or lazy. Split-half reliabilities of separate factor scores range from .75 to .85. Higher reliabilities would of course be desirable for the differential interpretation of individual profiles. Similarly, although an effort was made to obtain independent, uncorrelated trait categories, some of the intercorrelations among the 10 traits are still appreciable. Originally presented only on the basis of its factorial validity, the inventory has subsequently been employed in scattered studies of empirical validity, with varied results.

A somewhat different application of factorial methods to the construction of personality inventories is to be found in the work of Cattell (1946, 1957). In the effort to arrive at a comprehensive description of personality, Cattell began by assembling all personality trait names occurring both in the dictionary (as compiled by Allport and Odbert, 1936) or in the psychiatric and psychological literature. This list was first reduced to 171 trait names by combining obvious synonyms. The 171-trait list was then employed in obtaining associates' ratings of a heterogeneous group of 100 adults. Intercorrelations and factor analyses of these ratings were followed by further ratings of 208 men on a shortened list. Factorial analyses of the latter ratings led to the identification of what Cattell described as "the primary source traits of personality," a designation that seems to imply more universality and stability of results than appear justified by the antecedent research.

Factors identified through the correlation of ratings may reflect in part the influence of social stereotypes and other constant errors of judgment, rather than the subjects' trait organization. Cattell maintains that his identification of primary personality traits is corroborated by the findings of other studies by himself and other investigators, using not only ratings but also such techniques as questionnaires and objective tests. Some of the alleged similarities in trait descriptions, however, appear forced and not too convincing (see also Becker, 1960). It should be recalled that an element of subjectivity is likely to enter into the identification of factors, since the process depends on an examination of those measures or items having the highest loadings on each factor (see Ch. 13). Hence, the cross-identification of factors from different investigations using different measures is difficult. Despite the extensive research conducted by Cattell and his associates over more than twenty years, the traits proposed by Cattell must be regarded as tentative.

On the basis of their factorial research, Cattell and his coworkers have constructed a number of personality inventories, of which the most comprehensive is the Sixteen Personality Factor Questionnaire (16 PF). Designed for ages 16 and over, this inventory yields 16 scores in such traits as reserved vs. outgoing, humble vs. assertive, shy vs. venturesome, and trusting vs. suspicious. A "motivational distortion" or verification key is also provided for one of the forms (C). Owing to the shortness of the scales, reliabilities of factor scores for any single form are generally low. Even when two forms are combined, several split-half coefficients fall below .80. There is also some question about the factorial homogeneity of items within each scale, as well as the factorial independence of scales (Levonian, 1961). Available information on normative samples and other aspects of test construction is inadequate. Empirical validation data include average profiles for various occupational groups and psychiatric syndromes.

A similar inventory has been developed for ages 12 to 18 (Jr.-Sr. High School Personality Questionnaire) and another for ages 8 to 12 (IPAT Children's Personality Questionnaire). In addition, separate inventories have been published within more limited areas, including anxiety, introversion-extraversion, and neuroticism.[2] These areas correspond to certain second-order factors identified among correlated first-order factors. All of these inventories are experimental instruments requiring further development, standardization, and validation.

Factor analysis provides a technique for grouping personality inventory items into relatively homogeneous and independent clusters. Such a grouping should facilitate the investigation of validity against empirical criteria. It should also permit a more effective combination of scores for the prediction of specific criteria. Homogeneity and factorial purity are desirable goals in test construction. But they are not substitutes for empirical validity.

PERSONALITY THEORY IN TEST DEVELOPMENT

Personality theories have usually originated in clinical settings. The amount of experimental verification to which they have subsequently been

[2] See *Sixth Mental Measurements Yearbook* #121, 123, 124, 148.

subjected varies tremendously from one theoretical system to another. Regardless of the extent of such objective verification, a number of personality tests have been constructed within the framework of one or another personality theory. Clinically formulated hypotheses have been especially prominent in the development of projective techniques, to be considered in Chapter 19. While this approach to test construction has been followed less often for self-report inventories, two well-known examples in this category are the Edwards Personal Preference Schedule and the Myers-Briggs Type Indicator.

EDWARDS PERSONAL PREFERENCE SCHEDULE. Among the personality theories that have stimulated test development, one of the most prolific has been the manifest need system proposed by Murray and his associates at the Harvard Psychological Clinic (Murray *et al.*, 1938). The most comprehensive inventory designed to assess the strength of such needs is the Edwards Personal Preference Schedule (EPPS). Beginning with 15 needs drawn from Murray's list, Edwards prepared sets of items whose content appeared to fit each of these needs. The complete list of needs, together with the normal percentile chart employed in plotting EPPS scores, can be found in Figure 105. Examples include the need for Achievement (to do one's best and accomplish something difficult), Deference (to conform to what is expected of one), Exhibition (to be the center of attention), Intraception (to analyze the motives and feelings of oneself and others), Dominance (to influence others and to be regarded as a leader), and Nurturance (to help others in trouble).

The inventory consists of 210 pairs of statements in.which items from each of the 15 scales are paired with items from the other 14.[3] Within each pair, the examinee must choose one statement as more characteristic of himself. Two pairs, used as demonstration items, are given below:[4]

A. I like to talk about myself to others.
B. I like to work toward some goal that I have set for myself.

A. I feel depressed when I fail at something.
B. I feel nervous when giving a talk before a group.

The EPPS utilizes several ingenious internal checks. To provide an index of respondent consistency, 15 pairs of statements are repeated in identical form. In Figure 105, the last entry (labeled *con* for *consistency*) shows that this respondent made the identical choice in 14 of the 15 pairs, which put him at the 97th percentile of the normative sample in response consistency.

---

[3] This item form, which represents an important feature of the EPPS, will be discussed further in the next section, as an example of the forced-choice technique.

[4] Reproduced by permission. Copyright © 1953, The Psychological Corporation, New York, N.Y. All rights reserved.

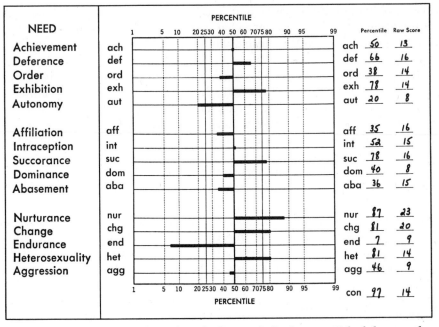

FIG. 105. Profile on the Edwards Personal Preference Schedule, together with List of Needs. (Reproduced by permission. Copyright © 1953, The Psychological Corporation, New York, N.Y. All rights reserved.)

Another check yields a profile stability score, which is the correlation between the individual's odd and even scores in the 15 scales.

The 15 need scores on the EPPS can be evaluated in terms of both percentile and T-score norms for college men and college women. These norms were based on 749 men and 760 women tested in 29 colleges scattered over the country. Additional percentile norms are provided from a general adult sample, including 4,031 men and 4,932 women. Drawn from urban and rural areas in 48 states, these respondents constituted a consumer-purchase panel used for market surveys. The need for specific group norms on personality tests is highlighted by the large and significant mean differences found between this consumer panel and the college sample.

It is important to bear in mind that the EPPS employs *ipsative* scores— that is, the strength of each need is expressed, not in absolute terms, but in relation to the strength of the individual's other needs. The frame of reference in ipsative scoring is the individual rather than the normative sample. Whenever an individual responds by expressing a preference for one item against another, the resulting score is ipsative. Under these conditions, two individuals with identical scores on the EPPS may differ markedly in the absolute strength of their needs. Because of their ipsative nature, the conversion of EPPS scores to normative percentiles may be questioned.

The combination of normative and ipsative frames of reference makes interpretation of these scores somewhat confusing and less meaningful than would be the case with a consistently ipsative *or* consistently normative approach.

Retest reliabilities of the 15 scales reported in the manual range from .74 to .88; split-half reliabilities range from .60 to .87. However, both sets of values may be somewhat inflated; the first, through recall of responses over the short interval employed (one week); the second, because of the repetition of identical statements three or four times in different pairs within each scale.

Although the validity data reported in the EPPS manual are meager, a large number of independent validation studies have been published. The results of these studies, however, are often difficult to interpret because most of them failed to take into account the ipsative nature of the scores. With ipsative scores, the mean intercorrelation of individual scales tends to be negative and the mean correlation of all the scales with any outside variable will approach zero. Owing to these artificial constraints, ipsative scores cannot be properly analyzed by the usual correlational procedures. It is not surprising, therefore, that the published validation studies have yielded conflicting and inconclusive results. Although the EPPS has many promising features, it is in need of: (a) revision to eliminate certain technical weaknesses, particularly with regard to item form and score interpretation; and (b) properly conducted validation studies utilizing techniques of score pattern analysis appropriate to ipsative scores.

MYERS-BRIGGS TYPE INDICATOR.   Taking its orientation from Jung's theory of types (Jung, 1923), the Myers-Briggs Type Indicator was constructed on the premise that individuals differ systematically in their basic preferences with regard to perception and judgment. The four major preferences in terms of which the respondent is classified into dichotomous type categories are as follows:

EI. *Extraversion or Introversion:* directing perception and judgment on outer world of people and things or inner world of concepts and ideas.

SN. *Sensing or Intuition:* perceiving directly in a factual, realistic way or indirectly through associated ideas and imaginative implications.

TF. *Thinking or Feeling:* judging through logical analysis of truth or falsity or through an appreciation of personal and interpersonal values.

JP. *Judgment or Perception:* dealing with the outer world principally in terms of an evaluative, judgmental attitude or in terms of an understanding and perceptive attitude.

Having been written to meet these general theoretical specifications, items were eventually selected on the basis of internal consistency within each category.

As in the EPPS, each item calls for a choice between two contrasting alternatives [5] (e.g., introverted or extraverted, sensing or intuitive, etc.). However, choices are always made *within* each of the four categories, never between them. Consequently, the four scores are experimentally independent and are not subject to artificial constraints. In each of the four categories, the individual's score is based on the number of times he chooses one or the other category. His "type" is then designated by the letters of his predominant modes in all four categories. For example, INTJ represents an individual who expresses a predominant preference for introverted, intuitive, thinking, and judgmental responses. With two alternatives in each of four categories, the number of possible type combinations is 16. Percentile norms for each of the four separate scores are provided for high school and college groups, the number of cases in each of the normative samples ranging from 240 to 2,389. The percentage distributions of each of the 16 types in a number of educational and occupational samples are also given.

The four categories have been found to be uncorrelated except for a significant tendency for "intuitives" to prefer a perceptive over a judgmental attitude. With few exceptions, split-half reliabilities computed in samples of high school and college students ($N = 26$ to 100) fall in the upper .70's and .80's. The manual summarizes a considerable body of data contributing to the construct validation of the scores. The criteria employed in this research include scores on other personality inventories, grades and other indices of academic achievement, instructors' ratings of college students, turnover in several types of jobs, and evidence of distinguished creative achievement. The data reveal a number of significant relationships in the expected directions. The large majority of highly creative persons investigated, for example, were predominantly intuitive, a relationship that held regardless of sex or field of specialization. High academic achievement was found to be associated with intuition, introversion, and a judgmental attitude. Job turnover tended to be most frequent among introverts in active jobs, extraverts in clerical jobs, and thinking types in sales jobs; among those who remained on sales jobs, extraverted and feeling types predominated.

These results, of course, are only suggestive and need much more extensive corroboration. One can only echo the commendable restraint expressed in the manual, which characterizes this inventory as an experimental instrument whose "most sagacious use involves a constant search for separate verification and new meanings" (Myers, 1962, p. 77). It might be added that a series of studies by Stricker and Ross (1964), designed to investigate the construct validity of the Myers-Briggs scales, suggest certain changes in the definitions of the variables measured, in the light of their empirical relationships.

[5] A few items offer three alternatives and one offers five.

TEST-TAKING ATTITUDES AND RESPONSE SETS

FAKING AND SOCIAL DESIRABILITY.   Self-report inventories are especially subject to malingering or faking. Despite introductory statements to the contrary, most items on such inventories have one answer that is recognizable as socially more desirable or acceptable than the others. On such tests, the respondent may be motivated to "fake good," or choose answers that create a favorable impression, as when applying for a job or seeking admission to an educational institution. Under other circumstances, he may be motivated to "fake bad," thus making himself appear more psychologically disturbed than he is. The latter may occur, for example, in the testing of accused criminals or military draftees.

Evidence of the success with which subjects can dissemble on personality inventories is plentiful (see, e.g., Gehman, 1957; Noll, 1951; Wesman, 1952; J. S. Wiggins, 1966). A common classroom demonstration consists in asking different groups to fake responses in specified ways. For example, one section of the class is directed to answer each question as it would be answered by a happy and well-adjusted college student; another section is told to respond in the manner of a severely maladjusted person; and in the last section subjects are instructed to answer the items truthfully with reference to their own behavior. Or the same subjects may take the test twice, first with instructions to simulate in a specified way and later under ordinary conditions. The results of such studies clearly demonstrate the facility with which the desired impression can be deliberately created on such inventories. To be sure, subjects of lower educational or intellectual level are probably less successful in disguising their responses than are the college groups on which most of these studies have been conducted. As long as a subject has sufficient education to enable him to answer a personality inventory, however, he probably has the ability to alter his score appreciably in the desired direction.

It is interesting to note that specific faking for a particular vocational objective can also be successfully carried out. Thus, in one study (Wesman, 1952), the responses of the same group of students were compared on two administrations of a personality inventory taken a week apart. On the first testing, the subjects were instructed to pretend they were applying for the position of salesman in a large industrial organization and to answer in a manner designed to increase their chances of employment. On the second testing, the same instructions were given, but the position of librarian was substituted for that of salesman. When the responses were scored for the trait of self-confidence, a conspicuous difference was found in the distributions of scores on the two occasions, the simulated-salesman scores being much higher than the corresponding librarian scores. That job applicants do in fact fake personality test responses was demonstrated in another study (Green, 1951), in which the scores obtained by a group of applicants were compared with the scores of a comparable group of job holders who were tested for research purposes only. Under these contrasting motivating conditions, the scores of the two groups differed in the expected direction.

The tendency to choose socially desirable responses on a self-report inventory need not indicate deliberate deception on the part of the respondent. Edwards (1957a), who first investigated the social desirability (SD) variable, conceptualized it primarily as a façade effect or tendency to "put up a good front," of which the respondent is largely unaware. This tendency may indicate lack of insight into one's own characteristics, self-deception, or an unwillingness to face up to one's limitations. Other investigators (Crowne & Marlow, 1964; Frederiksen, 1965) have presented evidence to suggest that the strength of the social desirability response set is related to the individual's more general need for self-protection, avoidance of criticism, social conformity, and social approval. On the other hand, the individual who chooses unfavorable items in a self-description may be motivated by a need for attention, sympathy, or help in meeting his personal problems. A person seeking psychotherapy, for example, is likely to make himself appear more maladjusted on a personality inventory than he actually is (Hathaway, 1948).

In order to investigate the contribution of the social desirability variable to personality test responses, Edwards (1957a) developed a special social desirability scale. Beginning with 150 heterogeneous MMPI items taken from the three validating keys and the Taylor Manifest Anxiety Scale, Edwards selected 79 items that yielded complete agreement among 10 judges with regard to the socially desirable response. Through item analyses against total scores on this preliminary scale, he shortened the list to 39 items. The SD scale correlated .81 with the K scale of the MMPI, partly because of common items between the two scales. Individual scores on this scale can be correlated with scores on any personality test as a check on the degree to which the social desirability variable has been ruled out of test responses. Whatever the cause of the relation, Edwards argued that insofar as social desirability is correlated with test scores, the effectiveness of the test in discriminating individual differences in specific, content-related traits is reduced.

Several procedures have been followed in the effort to meet the problem of faking and related response sets in personality inventories. The construction of relatively "subtle" or socially neutral items may reduce the operation of these factors in some inventories.[6] In a number of situations, the

[6] See, e.g., the development by Block (1965, Ch. 7) of an Ego-Resiliency (Subtle) scale for the MMPI.

test instructions and the establishment of rapport may motivate the individual to respond frankly, if he can be convinced that it is to his own advantage to do so. This approach would be ineffective in certain situations, however; and it would not have much effect on social desirability response sets of which the individual is unaware. Other attempted solutions include verification keys that detect faking or response sets, such as the L and F scales of the MMPI, and correction terms, such as those provided by the K scale of the MMPI. There is evidence that such scales are moderately effective in identifying various forms of dissimulation (Cofer, Chance, & Judson, 1949). Still another procedure, directed not to the detection but to the prevention of dissimulation, is the use of forced-choice items.

FORCED-CHOICE TECHNIQUE. The forced-choice technique was simultaneously developed by several psychologists working in industry or in the armed services during the decade of the 1940's (Jurgensen, 1944; Shipley, Gray, & Newbert, 1946; Sisson, 1948). Essentially, it requires the respondent to choose between two descriptive terms or phrases that appear equally acceptable but differ in validity. The paired phrases may both be desirable or both undesirable. The two demonstration items from the EPPS, reproduced earlier in this chapter, illustrate this item form. Forced-choice items may also contain three, four, or five terms, as illustrated by the sample item from the Gordon Personal Inventory reproduced in Figure 106. In such cases, the respondent must indicate which phrase is most characteristic and which least characteristic of himself.

The construction of a forced-choice inventory requires two principal

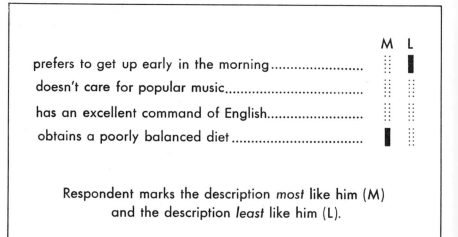

FIG. 106.   Sample Forced-Choice Item from Gordon Personal Inventory. (Reproduced by permission of Harcourt, Brace & World.)

types of information regarding each response alternative, viz., its social desirability or "preference index" and its validity or "discriminative index." The latter may be determined on the basis of any specific criterion the inventory is designed to predict, such as academic achievement or success on a particular kind of job; or it may be based on the factor loading of items or their theoretical relevance to different traits. Social desirability can be found by having the items rated for this variable by a representative group, or by ascertaining the frequency with which the item is endorsed in self-descriptions. In a series of studies on many different groups, Edwards (1957a) has shown that frequency of choice and judged social desirability correlate between .80 and .90. In other words, the *average* self-description of a population agrees closely with its average description of a desirable personality. Moreover, the rated SD of items remains remarkably stable in groups differing in sex, age, education, socioeconomic level, or nationality. Consistent results were also obtained when the judgments of hospitalized psychiatric patients were compared with those of normal groups.

In order to rule out the operation of the SD variable in the EPPS, Edwards relied exclusively on the forced-choice type of item. Independent research with this test since its publication, however, indicates that the influence of SD may have been reduced but was certainly not eliminated. When EPPS items were presented in a free-choice format, the scores correlated quite highly with the scores obtained with the regular forced-choice form of the test (Lanyon, 1966). The median correlation was .73, several of the correlations approaching the test-retest reliability of the scales. There is evidence that the context in which an item is encountered affects its perceived social desirability. Thus, the SD of an item rated separately may change when that item is paired with another item in a forced-choice format. Not only were significant differences in SD found between the paired items in the EPPS, but the redetermined SD values also yielded substantial correlations with the frequency of item endorsement (Corah *et al.*, 1958). These correlations sometimes approached the correlations found between SD ratings and frequency of endorsement of items presented singly and marked "True" or "False" (Edwards, 1957a, 1966).

It has also been shown that EPPS responses *can* be deliberately faked to create the desired impressions, especially for specific purposes (Borislow, 1958; Dicken, 1959). It cannot be assumed that judged SD is constant for all purposes, even though the judgments of general social desirability obtained from different populations may agree. The relative desirability of the same items for salesmen or for physicians, for example, may differ from their desirability when judged in terms of general cultural norms. Thus, a forced-choice test whose items were equated in general social desirability could still be faked when taken by job applicants, candidates for admission to professional schools, and other specifically oriented groups. From another angle, it has been shown that when items are paired on the basis of average *group* judgments of general social desirability, they may be far from equated for *individuals* (N. Wiggins, 1966).

In conclusion, it appears that the forced-choice technique has not proved as effective as had been anticipated in controlling faking or social desirability response sets. At the same time, the forced-choice item format, with the resulting ipsative scores, introduces other technical difficulties and eliminates information about absolute strength of individual characteristics that may be of prime importance in some testing situations.[7]

RESPONSE SETS AND RESPONSE STYLES. The tendency to choose socially desirable response alternatives is only one of several response sets that have been identified in test responses. Although the voluminous literature on the operation of response sets in personality inventories dates largely from midcentury, the influence of response sets in both ability and personality tests was observed by earlier investigators (see Block, 1965, Ch. 2). One of the response sets that attracted early attention was *acquiescence*, or the tendency to answer "True" or "Yes." Acquiescence is conceptualized as a continuous variable; at one end of the scale are the consistent "Yeasayers" and at the other end the consistent "Naysayers" (Couch & Keniston, 1960). The implications of this response set for the construction of personality inventories is that the number of items in which a "Yes" response is keyed positively in any trait scale should equal the number of items in which a "No" response is keyed positively. This balance can be achieved by the proper selection or rewording of items.

A third response set that has been widely investigated is *deviation*, or the tendency to give unusual or uncommon responses. Berg (1955, 1957, 1959, 1961), who proposed this deviation hypothesis, has argued strongly for the content-free nature of this response set. Accordingly he demonstrated its operation with nonverbal content in a specially developed test requiring an expression of preference for geometric figures.

Research on response sets such as social desirability, acquiescence, and deviation has passed through two principal stages. When first identified, response sets were regarded as a source of irrelevant or error variance to be eliminated from test scores. Efforts were therefore made to rule out their influence through the reformulation of items, the development of special keys, or the application of correction terms. Later these response sets came to be considered as indicators of broad and durable personality characteristics that were worth measuring in their own right (Jackson & Messick, 1958, 1962; J. S. Wiggins, 1962). At this stage, they were commonly de-

---

[7] The forced-choice technique has also been employed in rating scales. It is even more difficult to equate response alternatives for SD in this case, however, since the supervisors who use rating scales are familiar with specific job requirements and can therefore identify the more relevant response alternatives within each pair.

scribed as *response styles*.[8] We have already noted the association of the social desirability response set with certain general behavior tendencies to seek social approval. Evidence has likewise been gathered to suggest pervasive personality differences between Yeasayers and Naysayers (Couch & Keniston, 1960) and between those who choose common responses and those who choose deviant responses (Berg, 1961).

Now we have come full circle. Personality inventory responses are again regarded to have broad diagnostic significance, but in terms of their stylistic properties rather than in terms of specific item content. At the same time, the elaborate edifice that has been built around response styles shows signs of crumbling. The empirical data adduced in support of a response-style interpretation of scores on such inventories as the MMPI is being challenged from many directions (Block, 1965; Heilbrun, 1964; Rorer, 1965). Factorial analyses of the MMPI scales by several investigators have generally yielded two major factors that account for nearly all the common variance among the scales. The exponents of response sets and response styles have interpreted these two factors as social desirability and acquiescence, although differing in the relative importance they attribute to each. In a sophisticated statistical analysis of MMPI scales and items, Block (1965) presents strong evidence supporting a content-oriented interpretation of these two factors and indicating that the contribution of response styles to the variance of MMPI scores is negligible. He also demonstrated that the evidence advanced earlier in support of stylistic interpretations of these factors reflected methodological artifacts.

It would seem that the controversy over response sets, while not yet settled, may prove to be a tempest in a teapot. Like many scientific controversies, it has stimulated extensive research and has produced several hundred publications. And like many scientific controversies, its net effect will probably be to sharpen our understanding of methodological problems and thereby improve both the construction of personality inventories and the research conducted with them in the future. It is likely that some stylistic scales may ultimately prove to be valid predictors of important personality traits; but it is unlikely that stylistic scales will generally replace content-related scales in personality inventories.

EVALUATION OF PERSONALITY INVENTORIES

PRACTICAL APPLICATION. It should now be apparent that the construction and use of personality inventories are beset with special difficulties over and above the common problems encountered in all psychological testing. The question of faking and malingering is far more acute in personality

---

[8] This distinction between response sets and response styles is not universal, however. Some writers use the two terms in a different sense (see, e.g., Rorer, 1965).

measurement than in aptitude testing. The behavior measured by personality tests is also more changeable over time than that measured by tests of ability. The latter fact complicates the determination of test reliability, since random temporal fluctuations in test performance are likely to become confused with broad, systematic behavioral changes. Even over relatively short intervals, it cannot be assumed that variations in test response are restricted to the test itself and do not characterize the area of non-test behavior under consideration.

Another problem is presented by the greater situational specificity of responses in the sphere of personality. For example, an individual might be quite sociable and extroverted at the office, but rather shy and introverted at formal social receptions. Or a student who cheats on examinations might be scrupulously honest in money matters. Such specificity is in turn related to the difficulty of grouping items into clearly defined categories or personality traits. There is certainly less agreement among the different schemas of classification proposed in the personality than in the aptitude area.

To a large extent, the problems cited above are shared by all types of personality tests. But for the present we shall limit our discussion to self-report inventories. The acknowledged deficiencies of current personality inventories may be met in at least two major ways. First, personality inventories may be recognized as intrinsically crude instruments and their application restricted accordingly. Second, various procedures for improving the inventories may be explored. Most psychologists today would probably accept some combination of the two approaches, although a few may align themselves exclusively behind one or the other.

A specific illustration of the first approach is provided by the use of a personality inventory merely as a springboard for a clinical interview. In such cases, the interviewer might not even score the inventory in the standard manner, but might simply examine the subject's answers with a view to identifying problem areas for further probing during the interview. Other current practices stemming from a recognition of the pitfalls presented by personality inventories pertain to the interpretation of "poor" versus "good" scores, and the use of inventories in counseling versus selection. In most situations a "poor," or unfavorably deviant, score is likely to signify maladjustment, while a "good" score may be ambiguous. It is also evident that the motivation to create a favorable impression is much stronger in the job applicant than in the person seeking help from a counselor or in the subject of a research project. Even in the latter situations, however, complete candor cannot be assumed, because of the prevalence of rationalizations, defensive reactions, and other façade effects.

Attempts to improve self-report inventories by direct attack on the major sources of difficulty have been described throughout this chapter. Among such efforts may be mentioned the application of factor analysis as a means of arriving at more systematic trait categories, the keying of individual items against highly specific criteria, the use of a forced-choice technique, the development of verification and correction scales, and the preparation of "subtle" items whose diagnostic significance is less apparent to the respondent. All of these techniques were evaluated when first discussed. It is evident that none provides a completely satisfactory solution, but each has something to contribute.

THEORETICAL RATIONALE. Personality inventories may also be evaluated at a more basic level, in terms of their theoretical assumptions and underlying rationale. A whole volume could easily be devoted to this discussion. For the present purpose, however, a consideration of two frequently recurring and related questions will suffice. The first concerns the type of information that personality inventories are designed to elicit. The second pertains to the inherent ambiguity of inventory responses.

Because the early personality inventories were designed as a rapid substitute for the psychiatric interview, it is frequently assumed that the response to each question is an index of the presence or absence of the specific symptom or other behavior characteristic described by the question. In the light of the usual procedures for selecting test items and validating the inventories, however, such an assumption appears unwarranted. As in any psychological test, the responses should be operationally interpreted in terms of the criteria against which validity was established.

The distinction between these alternative ways of interpreting inventory items has been repeatedly emphasized in the literature. Various terms have been suggested to differentiate the two types of interpretation. Among them are "factual versus psychological," "veridical versus diagnostic," and "literal versus symptomatic." The already familiar distinction between content validity and the various types of empirical validity may serve in this connection. In effect, the factual-veridical-literal interpretation is based on the inspectionally determined content validity of the questions, while the psychological-diagnostic-symptomatic interpretation stems from the empirically established relationships of the inventory responses to various appropriate criteria. As Meehl put it, the personality inventory response "constitutes an intrinsically interesting and significant bit of verbal behavior, the non-test correlates of which must be discovered by empirical means" (Meehl, 1945a, p. 297).

Elsewhere, in characterizing the approach followed in the construction of the MMPI, Meehl wrote,

. . . the verbal type of personality inventory is *not* most fruitfully seen as a "self-rating" or self-description whose value requires the assumption of accuracy on the part of the testee in his observations of self. Rather is the response to a test item taken as an intrinsically interesting segment of verbal behavior, knowledge regarding which may be of more value than any knowledge of the "factual" material about which the item superficially purports to inquire. Thus if a hypochondriac says that he has "many headaches" the fact of interest is that he *says* this (Meehl, 1945b, p. 9).

In the same vein, Cattell cites the following illustration:

The questionnaire asks, "Would you enjoy being a sailor in a submarine?" If the subject replies "Yes," one does not assume that he would in fact be happy as a sailor in a submarine. One observes, perhaps, that good librarians as opposed to bad librarians more frequently answer "No" to this question, and one uses it empirically as an index of librarianship interests or temperament (Cattell, 1946, p. 344).

A self-report inventory is indubitably a series of standardized verbal stimuli. When proper test-construction procedures have been followed, the responses elicited by these stimuli are scored in terms of their empirically established behavior correlates. They are thus treated like any other psychological test responses. That questionnaire responses may correspond to the subject's *perception* of reality does not alter this situation. It merely provides one hypothesis to account for the empirically established validity of certain items.

It might be argued that the diagnostic as contrasted with the veridical interpretation of personality inventory responses is more closely related to empirical criterion keying than to other test construction methods described in this chapter. By whatever method the original items are chosen, however, some empirical investigation of the external correlates of either item responses or total scores is desirable. Furthermore, all four methods could profitably be combined. Items may be prepared within a theoretical framework, written so as to have good content validity, retained on the basis of criterion correlation, and further screened and grouped on the basis of factor loadings. There is also some suggestive evidence that personality inventory scales constructed by any of the four major methods may be equally effective. In a study with college women, scales constructed by these four methods from the CPI item pool proved to be equally valid in predicting a variety of practical criteria (Hase & Goldberg, 1967). In the same investigation, scales constructed to measure several response styles had little or no validity in predicting the same criteria—a finding that is consistent with the trend of results discussed in the preceding section.

From another angle, personality inventories have been attacked on the grounds that their responses are necessarily ambiguous. A classic exposition of this difficulty was given by Allport, who wrote:

The stimulus-situation is assumed to be identical for each subject, and his response is assumed to have constant significance. A test will assume, for example—and with some justification in terms of statistical probability—that a person who conspicuously takes a front seat at church or at an entertainment should as a rule receive a plus score for ascendance. But the fact of the matter is that this person *may* seek a front seat not because he is ascendant but because he is hard of hearing. Or a test will assume again, with statistical (empirical) justification, that a person who confesses to keeping a diary is introverted; yet upon closer inspection (which no test can give) it may turn out that the diary is almost wholly an expense account, kept not because of introversion but because of money-mindedness. It is a fallacy to assume that all people have the same psychological reasons for their similar responses. At the level of personality it cannot be said with certainty that the same symptoms in two people indicate the same trait, nor that different responses necessarily indicate different traits. All mental tests fail to allow sufficiently for an individual interpretation of cause and effect sequences (Allport, 1937, p. 449).

It is possible, of course, to reduce the frequency of ambiguous or equivocal responses by formulating items more specifically and by increasing the number and variety of items used to assess a particular personality trait. Apart from the practical problems of test construction, however, the prevalence of response ambiguity is itself of theoretical interest. Why is ambiguity a more serious problem in personality testing than in aptitude testing? The answer can probably be found in the *greater standardization of the individual's reactional biography in the intellectual sphere* (Anastasi, 1948). For example, the system of formal education in our culture assures relative uniformity of interpretation for, let us say, vocabulary or arithmetic computation items. But no such fund of common antecedent experience is available for the preparation of personality test items. This difficulty is similar to that encountered in the construction of aptitude tests for infants and young children, who have not yet been exposed to a highly standardized educational curriculum (Ch. 10). The very organization of behavior into traits is affected by the degree of uniformity of the pertinent experiential background. It is partly for this reason that factor pattern analyses of the emotional and motivational aspects of behavior have generally yielded trait categories that are less consistent and more difficult to interpret than those of aptitudes.

Some psychologists have maintained that, in the domain of personality, the individual can be effectively described only in terms of his own peculiar behavior interrelationships, rather than in terms of common traits (see, e.g., Allport, 1937). This approach represents an extreme reaction to the relatively unstandardized nature of the emotional and motivational aspects of the individual's reactional biography. It is undoubtedly true that an intensive study of the individual case will yield the richest and most precise picture of the person. But the judicious use of common techniques and normative data should materially aid such an analysis.

CHAPTER 18

Measures of Interests and Attitudes

THE STRENGTH and direction of the individual's interests, attitudes, motives, and values represent an important aspect of his personality. These characteristics materially affect his educational and vocational adjustment, his interpersonal relations, the enjoyment he derives from his avocational pursuits, and other major phases of his daily living. Although certain tests are specifically directed toward the measurement of one or another of these variables, the available instruments cannot be rigidly classified according to such discrete categories as interests, attitudes, and values. Overlapping is the rule. Thus, a questionnaire designed to assess the relative strength of different values, such as the practical, aesthetic, or intellectual, may have much in common with interest inventories. Similarly, such a questionnaire might be said to gauge the individual's attitudes toward pure science, art for art's sake, practical applications, and the like.

The study of *interests* has probably received its strongest impetus from vocational and educational counseling. To a slightly lesser extent, the development of tests in this area has also been stimulated by vocational selection and classification. From the viewpoint of both the worker and the employer, a consideration of the individual's interests is of practical significance. Achievement is a resultant of aptitude and interest. Although these two variables are positively correlated, a high level in one does not necessarily imply a superior status in the other. An individual may have sufficient aptitude for success in a certain type of activity—educational, vocational, or recreational—without the corresponding interest. Or he may be interested in work for which he lacks the prerequisite aptitudes. A measure of both types of variables thus permits a more effective prediction of performance than would be possible from either alone.

The assessment of *opinions and attitudes* originated largely as a problem in social psychology. Attitudes toward different groups have obvious implications for intergroup relations. Similarly, the gauging and prediction of public opinion regarding a wide variety of issues, institutions, or practices are of deep concern to the social psychologist, as well as to the practical worker in business, politics, and other applied fields. The measurement of opinions and attitudes has also made rapid strides in the areas of market research and employee relations.

In this chapter, we shall examine typical standardized tests designed to measure interests, attitudes, and related aspects of personality. As in the preceding chapter, attention will be focused on the paper-and-pencil self-report inventory. The majority of interest and attitude measures in current use are of this type. It should be noted, however, that in this area—as in the measurement of all personality characteristics—other approaches are being increasingly explored. A consideration of noninventory techniques will be reserved for Chapters 19 and 20.

INTEREST TESTS

It would seem that the most expedient and direct way of determining an individual's interests in different types of work, educational curricula, or recreational activities would be simply to ask him. But early investigators soon discovered that answers to direct questions about interests are often unreliable, superficial, and unrealistic (see Fryer, 1931, Ch. 5). This is particularly true of children and young people at the ages when information regarding interests is especially useful for counseling purposes.

The reasons for this situation are not hard to find. In the first place, most persons have insufficient information about different jobs, courses of study, and other activities. They are thus unable to judge whether they would really like all that their choice actually involves. Their interest—or lack of interest—in a job may stem from a limited notion of what the day-by-day work in that field entails. A second, related factor is the prevalence of stereotypes regarding certain vocations. The life of the average doctor, lawyer, or engineer is quite unlike the versions encountered in movies, television, and popular magazines. The problem, therefore, is that individuals are rarely in a position to know their own interests in various fields prior to actual participation in those fields. And by the time they have had the benefit of such personal contact, it may be too late to profit from the experience, since a change may be too wasteful.

For this reason, it was soon realized that more indirect and subtle approaches to the determination of interests would have to be explored. One of the most fruitful of these approaches originated in a graduate seminar on interests conducted at the Carnegie Institute of Technology during the academic year 1919–1920 (Fryer, 1931, Ch. 3). Several standardized interest inventories were subsequently prepared as a result of the work begun by their authors while attending this seminar. But the one whose development has been carried furthest is the Strong Vocational Interest Blank (SVIB), constructed by E. K. Strong, Jr. Unlike other early tests, the SVIB has undergone continuing research, revision, and extension.

The interest inventories developed by the Carnegie group introduced two principal procedural innovations. First, the items dealt with the subject's liking or dislike for a wide variety of specific activities, objects, or types of persons that he has commonly encountered in daily living. Second, the responses were empirically keyed for different occupations. These interest inventories were thus among the first tests to employ criterion keying of items, subsequently followed in the development of such personality inventories as the MMPI and CPI (Ch. 17). It was found that persons engaged in different occupations were characterized by common interests that differentiated them from persons in other occupations. These differences in interests extended not only to matters pertaining directly to job activities, but also to schoolwork, hobbies, sports, types of plays or books the individual enjoyed, social relations, and many other facets of everyday life. It thus proved feasible to question the individual about his interests in relatively familiar things, and thereby determine how closely his interests resembled those of persons successfully engaged in different vocations.

STRONG VOCATIONAL INTEREST BLANK.   The current form of the SVIB, published in 1966, consists of 399 items grouped into eight parts. In the first five parts, the examinee records his preference by encircling one of the letters L, I, or D, signifying "Like," "Indifferent," and "Dislike," respectively. Each of these five parts is concerned with one of the following categories: occupations, school subjects, amusements, activities (such as repairing a clock, making a speech, or raising money for a charity), and types of people. The remaining three parts of the SVIB require the subject to rank given activities in order of preference, compare his interest in pairs of items, and rate his present abilities and other characteristics.

The blank is scored with a different scale for each occupation. To date, 54 occupational scales are available for scoring the men's form, and 32 for the women's form.[1] New scales are developed from time to time, as data on other occupational groups are gathered. In the development of these occupational scales, the responses of persons successfully engaged in each occupation were compared with those of "men-in-general" (or "women-in-general"). The general reference group for the men's form consisted of

[1] Publication of revised women's form scheduled for late 1968.

men in a wide variety of professional and business occupations that college graduates usually enter. The choice of reference group was based on the fact that most of the SVIB occupational scales deal with professions and higher business positions. The use of a reference group representative of the total male population proved less effective in bringing out the differentiating interests of the individual occupations. The interests of professional and business men as a group differ so much from those of skilled laborers that the differences between one high-level occupation and another were obscured when the more general reference group was employed. For the same reason, the few available SVIB scales for lower-level occupations are not as discriminative as they might be if the reference group had been closer to the socioeconomic level of the occupations concerned [2] (Strong, 1943, Chs. 21 and 22).

Items for each occupational scale of the SVIB were selected and weighted on the basis of differences in frequency of choice by men in that occupational group and men-in-general. In the lawyer scale, for example, a $+1$ weight indicates that the response occurs more frequently, and a -1 weight indicates that it occurs less frequently among lawyers than among men-in-general. Responses that fail to differentiate between lawyers and men-in-general do not appear in the lawyer scale, regardless of how frequently they were chosen by lawyers. An individual's total raw score on each occupational scale is simply the algebraic sum of his plus and minus weights. These raw scores are converted to standard scores with a mean of 50 and an SD of 10 in terms of the distribution of scores in each occupational criterion group. These criterion groups, usually containing about 300 persons, included only men between the ages of 25 and 55, employed in the given occupation for three years or more, who reported satisfaction with their work.

To facilitate interpretation of standard scores, letter ratings are also provided. Thus, an A rating represents a score at or above $-\frac{1}{2}SD$, i.e., a point above which approximately 69 percent of the occupational group in question scored. Similarly, the lower boundary for a B rating is set at $-2SD$, and scores below $-2SD$ are rated C. A rating of C would thus mean that the individual obtained a lower score on that particular scale than about 98 percent of the corresponding occupational sample. It should be noted that, however expressed, scores on the SVIB are based on *differences* between the interests of an occupational group and those of men-in-general. Thus, a high score in, let us say, the physician scale indicates that the individual's interests differ from those of men-in-general in the same directions as do the interests of physicians.

An individual's SVIB may be scored for a single occupation. For selection purposes, for example, we might want to know how closely the appli-

---

[2] For such occupations, the Minnesota Vocational Interest Inventory, described later in this section, is more appropriate.

cant's interests resemble those of successful life-insurance salesmen. More often, however, the blank is scored on all available scales, thus permitting an examination of the individual's total interest pattern. This type of analysis provides a more dependable prediction of eventual occupational interest. For counseling, in which interest inventories find their major application, a consideration of the entire interest profile is essential. A further counseling aid is provided by the groups of related occupational scales. These groups were derived by studying the relations among the scales through factor analysis and other procedures.

A list of the occupational scales available to date, classified within the appropriate groups, can be found on the SVIB Profile reproduced in Figure 107. Group II, for example, comprises architect, mathematician, physicist, chemist, and engineer. Group V, apparently characterized by a common interest in "uplift" or social betterment, includes personnel director, public administrator, rehabilitation counselor, YMCA secretary, social worker, social science teacher, school superintendent, and minister. The supplementary scales at the bottom of the Profile have been added most recently and have not yet been placed in groups. Across the top of the Profile are the letter ratings corresponding to different standard score ranges. In addition, the shaded area across from each occupation shows the range of the middle third of the scores obtained by men-in-general on that scale. For illustrative purposes, the profile of the psychologist criterion group has been plotted in Figure 107.

Besides the occupational scales, the SVIB provides four nonoccupational scales, including Specialization Level (SL), Occupational Level (OL), Masculinity-Femininity (MF), and Academic Achievement (AACH).[3] The SL scale was originally developed by comparing the responses of medical specialists with those of a group of physicians-in-general. This scale was later found to be applicable to other fields in identifying men who would enjoy advanced study of a type involving narrow specialization. The OL scale measures the difference between the interests of unskilled workers, on the one hand, and those of business and professional men, on the other. The MF scale shows the degree of similarity of the individual's interests to the interests of men or of women, respectively. The most recent addition to the nonoccupational scales, the AACH scale, was developed by comparing the responses of groups of high school and college students who had obtained high and low academic grades, respectively. On the basis of subsequent research, this scale appears to reflect interests in scientific and intellectual endeavors as contrasted with interests in business, sales, or skilled-trades activities.

The SVIB has been subjected to a continuing program of research that has yielded extensive information about its reliability and validity. Odd-

[3] An occupational introversion-extraversion scale has also been developed, but it is currently available for research purposes only.

Group	Scale	Plus Score	Minus Score	Raw Score	Std. Score	LETTER RATINGS AND STANDARD SCORES
I	DENTIST				25	
	OSTEOPATH				28	
	VETERINARIAN				18	
	PHYSICIAN				34	
	PSYCHIATRIST				46	
	PSYCHOLOGIST				50	
	BIOLOGIST				41	
II	ARCHITECT				30	
	MATHEMATICIAN				34	
	PHYSICIST				28	
	CHEMIST				35	
	ENGINEER				30	
III	PRODUCTION MGR.				27	
	ARMY OFFICER				20	
	AIR FORCE OFFICER				27	
IV	CARPENTER				13	
	FOREST SERVICE MAN				11	
	FARMER				24	
	MATH–SCIENCE TEACHER				30	
	PRINTER				21	
	POLICEMAN				9	
V	PERSONNEL DIRECTOR				32	
	PUBLIC ADMINISTRATOR				42	
	REHABILITATION COUNSELOR				36	
	YMCA SECRETARY				20	
	SOCIAL WORKER				37	
	SOCIAL SCIENCE TEACHER				27	
	SCHOOL SUPERINTENDENT				30	
	MINISTER				27	
VI	LIBRARIAN				37	
	ARTIST				31	
	MUSICIAN PERFORMER				36	
	MUSIC TEACHER				30	
VII	CPA OWNER				28	
VIII	SENIOR CPA				19	
	ACCOUNTANT				17	
	OFFICE WORKER				15	
	PURCHASING AGENT				20	
	BANKER				16	
	PHARMACIST				20	
	MORTICIAN				20	
IX	SALES MANAGER				20	
	REAL ESTATE SALESMAN				27	
	LIFE INSURANCE SALESMAN				22	
X	ADVERTISING MAN				29	
	LAWYER				35	
	AUTHOR–JOURNALIST				36	
XI	PRES., MFG. CONCERN				23	
Suppl. Occup. Scales						
	CREDIT MANAGER				24	
	CHAMBER OF COMM. EXEC.				31	
	PHYSICAL THERAPIST				29	
	COMPUTER PROGRAMMER					
	BUSINESS EDUC. TEACHER				25	
	COMMUNITY RECR. ADMIN.					

Nonoccupational Scales   SL: ___ ___ 55 + − raw standard   OL: ___ ___ 62 + − raw standard   MF: ___ ___ 45 + − raw standard   AACH: ___ ___ 58 + − raw standard NUMBER

FIG. 107. Profile of Psychologist Criterion Group on SVIB, 1966 Revision, Showing Mean Scores of 1,045 Male Psychologists. (Reproduced by permission of Stanford University Press.)

even reliabilities of the individual scales in the earlier edition average .88, only one falling below .80. A median retest correlation of .91 was found for 139 college sophomores tested over a two-week interval, as well as for 102 young adults tested over a 30-day interval. Extensive longitudinal studies have revealed good long-term stability of scores on individual scales. These findings include a 3-year retest correlation of .68 for college freshmen, an 8-year retest correlation of .61 for high school seniors, a 22-year retest correlation of .67 for college seniors, and a 30-year retest correlation of .56 for a group of 48 bankers first tested at about 40 years of age. In general, interest scores are less stable at the high school level but achieve considerable stability by college age.

Another type of analysis concerns the stability of mean occupational profiles over time. For this purpose, the SVIB was administered to different samples of men holding the same jobs in the same organizations on two occasions separated by an interval of 30 years or more. This procedure was followed with four occupational groups: school superintendents, ministers, bankers, and corporation presidents. In general, the mean occupational profiles obtained over this interval were remarkably similar, suggesting that the scales developed on the original criterion groups are still applicable today.

With regard to validity, there is considerable evidence that individuals tend to enter and to remain in occupations in which they receive high SVIB scores. One of the most extensive longitudinal investigations of this relationship is Strong's 18-year follow-up of 663 Stanford University students who had taken the inventory while in college (Strong, 1955). Figure 108 summarizes the principal results of this study in the form of an expectancy chart. It can be seen that there were 88 chances in 100 that a student who had scored 55 or higher on an occupational scale would be employed in that occupation, while there were only 17 chances in 100 that a student scoring below 30 would be employed in that occupation.

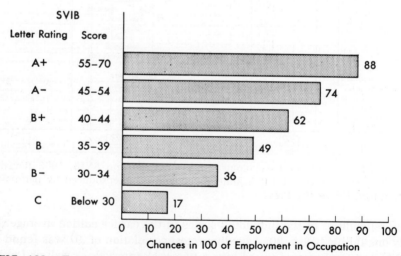

FIG. 108.   Expectancy Chart Showing Relation between College Students' Scores on SVIB Occupational Scale and Chances of Entering and Remaining in that Occupation 18 Years Later. (Data from Strong & Campbell, 1966, p. 44.)

With high school students, the field or occupational group of the individual's eventual employment can be predicted fairly well. Prediction of specific occupation, however, is uncertain except for the relatively few students who exhibit very distinct interest patterns. There are also data indicating a relationship between SVIB scores and subsequent job success or job satisfaction; but the evidence for predictive validity against these criteria is meager and more difficult to interpret. In most cases, however, continuation in an occupation provides fairly good evidence that the individual has achieved at least a minimum level of success and that he finds the work reasonably congenial. Several research projects with the SVIB are currently in progress at The Center for Interest Measurement Research, established in 1963 at the University of Minnesota (Campbell, 1964). One of these projects is a 35-year longitudinal study of over 1,000 15-year-old boys first tested in 1930 (Strong & Campbell, 1966). Each individual in this study took the SVIB again at the age of about 50 and also completed a brief occupational history. This study will thus contribute further data pertaining to both long-term stability and predictive validity.

To round out this discussion of the SVIB, it should be noted that a similar interest inventory has been developed for various skilled and semiskilled occupations [4] (Campbell, 1966; Clark, 1961; Clark & Campbell, 1965). Modeled after the SVIB but utilizing tradesmen-in-general as a reference group, the Minnesota Vocational Interest Inventory provides 21 scales for such occupations as baker, milk-wagon driver, plumber, and radio-TV repairman. There are also nine area scales showing the examinee's liking for work activities common to several occupations, such as mechanical, food service, and electronics. The items in the Minnesota Vocational Interest Inventory are more heavily oriented toward vocational activities than are those of the SVIB, and they are all presented in a forced-choice triad format. Differentiation among occupations is not as sharp with this inventory as with the SVIB. It is likely that this difference between the two instruments stems from the nature of the occupations themselves. There is extensive evidence to show that at higher levels of the occupational hierarchy (professional, managerial, etc.) job satisfaction is derived chiefly from intrinsic liking for the work, while at the lower levels there is increasing reliance on such extrinsic factors as pay, security, social contacts, and recognition as a person (Darley & Hagenah, 1955). The measurement of vocational interest patterns may thus become less relevant as we go down the occupational hierarchy.

THE KUDER INTEREST INVENTORIES.   The various forms, versions, and editions of the Kuder interest inventories may be regarded as a family of related instruments which approach the measurement of interests from

---

[4] See also Gordon Occupational Check List (Appendix C), designed for occupations requiring no academic education beyond high school.

different angles and are designed for somewhat different purposes. The best known of these inventories is the Kuder Preference Record—Vocational. Developed later than the SVIB, this test followed a different approach in the selection and scoring of items. Its major purpose was to indicate relative interest in a small number of broad areas, rather than in specific occupations. The items were originally formulated and tentatively grouped on the basis of content validity. This was followed by extensive item analyses on high school and adult groups. The object of such item analyses was the development of item groups showing high internal consistency and low correlations with other groups. This aim was reasonably well fulfilled for most of the scales.

The items in the Kuder—Vocational are of the forced-choice triad type. For each of three activities listed, the respondent indicates which he would like most and which he would like least. Two sample triads are illustrated in Figure 109. The test provides 10 interest scales plus a Verification scale

P. Visit an art gallery . . . .   o P o
Q. Browse in a library . . . .   o Q ● ←Least
R. Visit a museum . . . .   Most→   ● R o

S. Collect autographs . . . .   Most→   ● S o
T. Collect coins . . . .   o T o
U. Collect butterflies . . . .   o U ● ←Least

In the first triad, the subject has punched a hole to the *left* of R, indicating that he *likes most* to visit a museum. He has punched a hole to the *right* of Q, indicating that he *likes least* to browse in a library.
The second triad has been similarly marked.

FIG. 109. Sample Items from Kuder Preference Record—Vocational. (Copyright © 1948, by G. Frederic Kuder. Reprinted by permission of the publisher, Science Research Associates, Inc., Chicago, Illinois.)

for detecting carelessness, misunderstanding, and the choice of socially desirable but unlikely answers. The interest scales include: Outdoor (agricultural, naturalistic), Mechanical, Computational, Scientific, Persuasive, Artistic, Literary, Musical, Social Service, and Clerical. Separate sex norms are available for high school, college, and adult groups. Total scores in the 10 interest areas are plotted on a normalized percentile chart, as illustrated in Figure 110. The pattern shown is typical of professional engineers.

The reliabilities of the Kuder scales, as determined by the Kuder-Richardson technique, cluster around .90. Stability over intervals of about a year or less also appears to be satisfactory. Little information is available regarding stability over longer periods. There is some evidence to suggest that, especially in the case of high school students, shifts in high and low interest areas are relatively frequent when retests are several years apart (Herzberg & Bonton, 1954; Mallinson & Crumrine, 1952; Reid, 1951; Rosenberg, 1953). Studies on the simulation of interest scores have shown that faking is possible to some extent on both the Kuder and the Strong; but visibility is somewhat greater on the Kuder, owing to the more obvious nature of its items (Durnall, 1954; Longstaff, 1948).

The manual for the Kuder—Vocational provides an extensive list of occupations, grouped according to their major interest area or pair of interest areas. For example, radio operator is classified under Mechanical; landscape architect, under Outdoor-Artistic. This is an a priori listing in terms of logical or content analysis. In addition, empirically established occupational profiles are given for 41 homogeneous occupational families. The data employed in deriving these occupational profiles were contributed largely by test users. Consequently, several of the groups are small and their representativeness or comparability is questionable. Several investigators have attempted to work out an empirical coding system for Kuder profiles similar to that developed for the MMPI (Callis, Engram, & McGowan, 1954; Frandsen, 1952; Wiener, 1951). Efforts have also been made to develop regression equations for finding total scores for specific occupations or other criterion groups (Mugaas & Hester, 1952).

Validation research with this inventory has been conducted chiefly against a criterion of job satisfaction.[5] In the most comprehensive longitudinal study, 1,164 students who had taken the Kuder Preference Record —Vocational in high school were given a job satisfaction questionnaire seven to ten years later. At that time, 728 were engaged in work classified as "consistent" with their original interest patterns and 436 were engaged in work classified as "inconsistent" with these patterns. The percentage of satisfied workers was 62 in the "consistent" group but only 34 in the "inconsistent" group; the percentage of dissatisfied workers, on the other hand, was 8 in the "consistent" group and 25 in the "inconsistent" group. Similar relationships were found in several studies of persons employed in specific fields, such as clerks, industrial workers, vocational rehabilitation counselors, and accountants. Among accountants, for example, the satisfied group scored significantly higher than the dissatisfied group on the Computation and Clerical interest scales, and significantly lower on the Outdoor, Scientific, and Artistic interest scales.

More recently, the Kuder General Interest Survey has been developed as a revision and downward extension of the Kuder Preference Record—Vocational. Designed for grades 6 to 12, the General Interest Survey employs simpler language and easier vocabulary than the earlier form, requiring

[5] References to this research can be found in Kuder (1964), pp. 39–40.

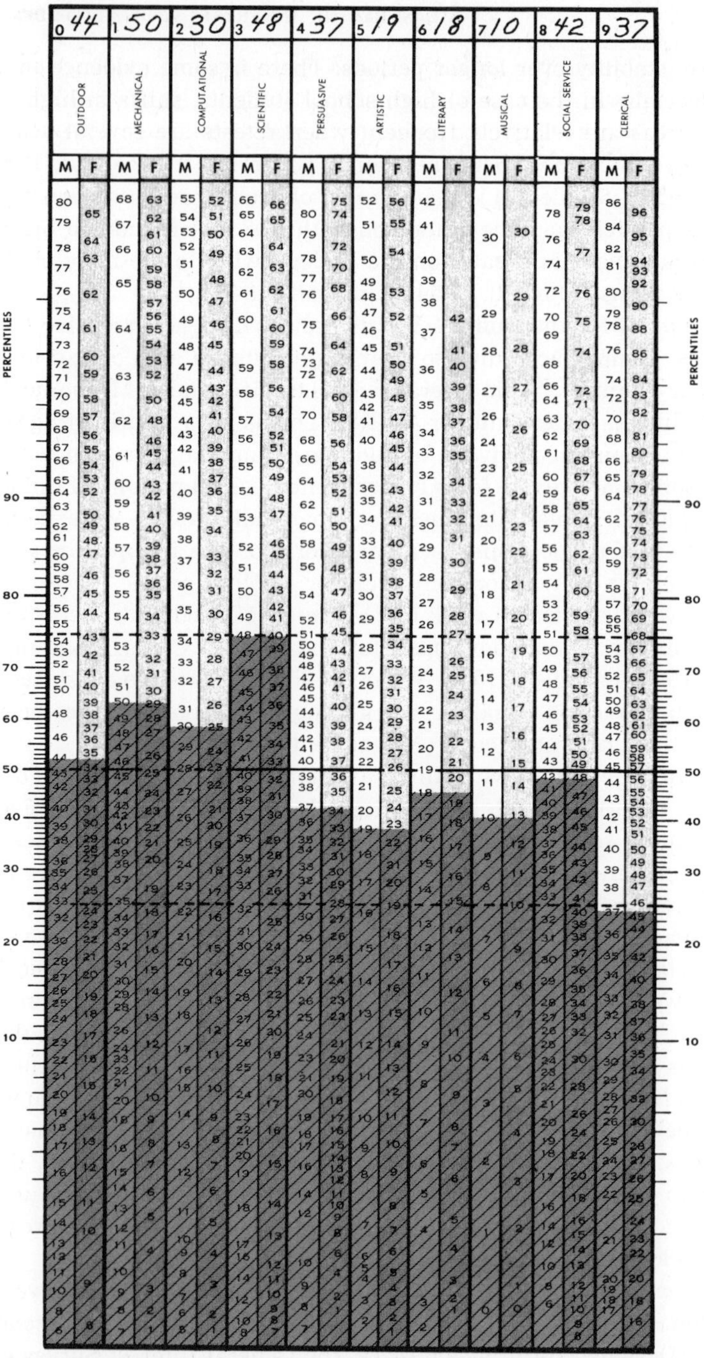

FIG. 110.   Profile on Kuder Preference Record—Vocational. (PROFILE SHEET Copyright © 1951, by C. Frederic Kuder. Reprinted by permission of the publisher, Science Research Associates, Inc., Chicago, Illinois.)

only a sixth-grade reading level. Percentile norms are reported for a national stratified sample of over 10,000 boys and girls and for small adult samples. Research is in progress to discover whether this inventory is equally suitable for adults, in which case it may eventually replace the Kuder Preference Record—Vocational. Correlations between scores on the two instruments are nearly as high as their reliability coefficients.

Still another version, the Kuder Occupational Interest Survey (OIS), has been developed through criterion keying procedures similar to those followed with the SVIB (Kuder, 1966a, 1966b). Unlike the SVIB and an earlier Kuder occupational form, however, the OIS does not employ a reference group of men-in-general. Instead, the individual's score on each occupational scale is expressed as a correlation between his interest pattern and the interest pattern of the given occupational group.[6] The OIS cannot be hand-scored; answer sheets are returned to the publisher for scoring by a combination of high-speed optical scanning equipment and electronic computers. Scores are currently provided for 79 occupations and 20 college-major fields for men and for 56 occupations and 25 college-major fields for women. Over a third of the women's scores, however, are obtained with scales developed with male criterion groups in fields in which men predominate but which offer vocational opportunities to women. The occupations covered by this inventory vary widely in level, ranging from baker and truck driver to chemist and lawyer. The elimination of a reference group permits this broad coverage within a single instrument.

In addition to the occupational and college-major scales, the OIS provides a Verification scale and eight experimental scales currently employed for research purposes only. While designed for use from grade 10 to the adult level, the OIS requires a reading vocabulary at approximately the sixth-grade level. As in the other Kuder inventories, all items are presented in forced-choice triad form. The content of the items covers the broad interest areas included in the Kuder Preference Record—Vocational, together with several other areas, such as preference for working independently, for avoiding conflict, or for familiar and stable situations.

Through intensive statistical analyses of the scores of 3,000 subjects (100 in each of 30 core groups representative of the occupations and college-major fields covered by the inventory), Kuder has demonstrated that better differentiation between occupational groups can be achieved with the OIS scoring system than with the occupational scales derived through the use of a men-in-general reference group. The same 30 scales have been

---

[6] The correlation employed is the lambda coefficient developed by Clemans (1958). This is essentially a point-biserial correlation adjusted for differences in homogeneity of different criterion groups. The dichotomous variable consists of the marked versus unmarked responses on the individual's answer sheet; the continuous variable is the proportion of persons in the criterion group marking each response.

employed in extensive analyses of retest reliability, intercorrelation of scores on different scales, and other technical aspects of the inventory. In all these analyses, the OIS appears to be highly satisfactory. Research on the other occupational scales, as well as validation against external criteria, remains to be done. This instrument presents some major innovations in test construction. Its ultimate contribution can be assessed only after further research and application in practical contexts.

SOME METHODOLOGICAL QUESTIONS. The development of interest inventories highlights several important problems in test construction. A major controversial question pertains to the use of ipsative scores (see, e.g., Bauernfeind, 1962). Some of the implications of these scores have already been discussed in Chapter 17, in connection with the EPPS. It will be recalled that ipsative scores permit comparisons of the relative strength of characteristics within the individual, while normative scores permit external comparisons with a normative sample. When this distinction is overlooked or when both types of scores are combined, confusion is likely to result in both score interpretation and statistical analysis of data.

Interest inventories have traditionally relied on ipsative scores. This is true of both the SVIB and the Kuder inventories. Although the ipsative nature of the Kuder scores is more obvious, because of the triad item form in which different interests are contrasted, the SVIB scores also have ipsative properties. This is so not only because certain parts of the SVIB require ranking of response alternatives, but also because individual responses are scored on more than one scale. Hence, scores on different scales are not experimentally independent. For example, insofar as the same response may be positively weighted on one scale and negatively weighted on another, it is impossible for an individual to obtain high scores or low scores on all scales.

The controversy regarding the use of ipsative scores is far from resolved. While several critics have objected to the use of ipsative scores, particularly when combined with normative interpretations, Kuder has defended the practical meaningfulness of such scores. Thus, he argues that, if a student obtains a percentile score of 90 on the Mechanical scale of the Kuder Preference Record—Vocational, it means that, "when faced with a complex series of choices typical of real-life situations, he chose mechanical activities more frequently than 90 percent of his contemporaries" (Kuder, 1964, p. 6). Bauernfeind (1962), on the other hand, marshals the arguments against such a combination of ipsative and normative approaches, calling attention to the difficulties of interpreting such scores and to the frequency with which they have been analyzed by inapplicable statistical procedures. He also notes that ipsative interest scores partial out any individual differences in level of interest or enthusiasm, although such differences may be germane to many practical decisions. While the controversy remains unsettled, the test user should be alerted to the ipsative nature of interest inventory scores and to their interpretive implications.

A second methodological question pertains to the alternative approaches to interest measurement represented by criterion-keyed occupational scales (as in the SVIB and Kuder OIS), and by assessment of broad interest areas (as in the Kuder Preference Record—Vocational and the Kuder General Interest Survey). It should be noted that, even with the latter approach, an individual's interest in specific occupations can be appraised by such procedures as occupational coding of interest profiles or the computation of regression equations for specific occupations. To be sure, these procedures require considerably more computational labor, but with the increasing utilization of electronic computers this may no longer represent a practical drawback.

When occupational scales are employed, a further question concerns the use of reference groups. Such groups have been utilized in the development of the SVIB, the Minnesota Vocational Interest Inventory, and the earlier form of Kuder's occupational interest inventory. More recently, Kuder has argued convincingly for the derivation of occupational scores without a reference group (Kuder, 1963, 1966b). It is certainly theoretically true that the direct comparison of one occupation with another is likely to elicit sharper differentiation between them than is obtained when each occupation is compared with a miscellaneous group. The elimination of a reference group also sweeps away several persistent problems regarding the selection of suitable reference groups, in terms of socioeconomic level, occupational diversity, etc. The selection of reference groups for women's occupational scales has proved especially perplexing. Should housewives be included, and, if so, in what proportion? What about women engaged in occupations that are predominantly male, such as engineering?

There are obvious advantages in the elimination of a reference group. On the other hand, the scoring procedure followed in the OIS, as a result of the elimination of the reference group, is so time-consuming as to require computer utilization. Again, this may not constitute a practical limitation in our society today. In this connection, it is interesting to note that changes introduced in the latest Kuder inventory are such as to preclude hand scoring, while changes introduced in the latest revision of the SVIB (from multiple scoring weights to simple + or − item weights) are such as to make hand scoring practicable for the first time in the history of this inventory.

OPINION AND ATTITUDE MEASUREMENT

NATURE OF INSTRUMENTS. An attitude is often defined as a tendency to react favorably or unfavorably toward a designated class of stimuli, such as a national or racial group, a custom, or an institution. It is evident that, when so defined, attitudes cannot be directly observed, but must be inferred from overt behavior, both verbal and nonverbal. In more objective terms, the concept of attitude may be said to connote response consistency with regard to certain categories of stimuli (Campbell, 1950). In actual practice, the term "attitude" has been most frequently associated with social stimuli and with emotionally toned responses.

Opinion is sometimes differentiated from attitude, but the proposed distinctions are neither consistent nor logically defensible. More often the two terms are used interchangeably, and they will be so employed in this discussion. With regard to assessment methodology, however, opinion surveys are traditionally distinguished from attitude scales. *Opinion surveys* are characteristically concerned with replies to specific questions, which need not be related. The answers to such questions are kept separate rather than being combined into a total score. An employee opinion survey, for example, might include questions about work schedules, rate of pay, fringe benefits, company cafeteria, and relation to supervisors; each of these items is included because of its intrinsic relevance to the improvement of employee relations. The replies to each question are separately tabulated in the effort to identify sources of employee satisfaction and dissatisfaction.

Attitude scales, on the other hand, typically yield a total score indicating the direction and intensity of the individual's attitude toward a company, group of people, policy, or other stimulus category. In the construction of an attitude scale, the different questions are designed to measure a single attitude or unidimensional variable, and some objective procedures are usually followed in the effort to approach this goal. An employee attitude scale, for example, yields a single score showing the individual's degree of job satisfaction or over-all attitude toward the company.

APPLICATIONS. Both opinion surveys and attitude scales have been widely used for a variety of purposes. *Public opinion polling* is a familiar application. Besides the election forecasts undertaken by commercial pollsters, nationwide polls are conducted regularly on many social, political, economic, and international questions of general interest. The large-scale nature of these polls and the rapidity with which answers are required have encouraged the utilization of survey, rather than attitude-scale, techniques. But attitude scales have also found a place in public opinion research. *Market research* has much in common with public opinion studies. Because of similar practical demands, survey techniques have served as the principal tool in both fields. The object of market research is to investigate consumer needs and reactions in reference to products, services, or advertisements. The resulting information may be used for such purposes as choosing the most effective advertisement for a specific article, improving a type of service, preparing a new model, or designing a new product to meet consumer specifications.

Another major field of application is to be found in the measurement of *employee attitudes and morale* through both opinion surveys and attitude scales. Such techniques are also employed to assess the effectiveness of *education and training*. Attitude scales, for example, may provide an index for evaluating different instructional procedures. Or they may be utilized in measuring the changes in student attitudes toward literature, art, different racial and cultural groups, or social and economic problems following a given educational program. One of the most extensive applications of attitude measurement is to be found in *research in social psychology*. Practically every textbook on social psychology contains sections on attitudes and their measurement. Among the many problems investigated through attitude measurement may be mentioned group differences in attitudes, the role of attitudes in intergroup relations, background factors associated with the development of attitudes, the interrelations of attitudes (including factor analyses), trends and temporal shifts in attitudes, and the experimental alteration of attitudes through interpolated experiences.

METHODOLOGICAL PROBLEMS. The measurement of attitudes is both difficult and controversial.[7] Whether verbally expressed opinions can be regarded as indicators of "real" attitudes has frequently been questioned. In part, this problem concerns the relationship between verbal and nonverbal overt behavior. In other words, does the individual suit his actions to his words—or to his attitude scale score? Discrepancies between verbally expressed attitudes and overt behavior have been noted in a number of studies. It has been further pointed out that even observations of overt behavior may not always provide an accurate index of attitude. For example, an individual may both profess strong religious beliefs and attend church regularly, not because of his religious convictions but as a means of gaining social acceptance in his community. Such a possibility raises the further question of the relationship between "public" and "private" attitudes. How do the individual's publicly expressed attitudes compare with the opinions he voices in conversation with his family or close friends? Public opinion surveys are usually "public" in more than one sense. They represent a verbal expression of attitudes by the public and to the public.

The relationship between "what the person says" and "what he does," as well as the relationship between publicly and privately expressed attitudes, will be recognized as special instances of *validity*. Attitude scales and opinion polls may be validated against a number of criteria, such as membership in contrasted groups, ratings by close acquaintances, and biographical data secured through intensive interviews or case studies. Because of the

[7] For a comprehensive introduction to relevant literature, see Fishbein (1967).

practical difficulties in obtaining such criterion data, however, investigators have frequently relied on the familiar makeshifts involving validation by internal consistency or by correlation with another attitude scale. Other investigators have resorted to a superficial kind of content validation based on the examination and classification of questions according to the topics covered. For opinion polling, validation is rarely attempted at all.

Data on reliability are also meager, especially with reference to opinion surveys. Yet in the case of survey techniques, with their reliance on single questions, reliability is most likely to be suspect. Attitude measurement also presents a number of other methodological problems. These problems are not fundamentally different from those encountered in the construction and administration of other types of psychological tests, but they are accentuated in the measurement of attitudes. The major difficulties center around the proper formulation of questions so as to avoid ambiguity, suggestion, and other sources of error; adequate sampling of the population in terms of size and representativeness; and control of conditions under which the survey is conducted, such an ensuring anonymity of replies and reducing the influence of interviewer characteristics.

All of the problems considered above—including validity, reliability, questionnaire construction, sampling, and administration—are encountered in varying degrees in both opinion surveys and attitude measurement. From a technical viewpoint, attitude scales are clearly superior to opinion surveys. In their construction and use, attitude scales are more nearly similar to psychological tests. Although by their very nature most opinion surveys and many attitude scales must be custom-made to meet specific needs, at least some attitude scales have been developed for general use. In the following section, we shall examine in more detail the procedures employed in the development and application of attitude scales.

ATTITUDE SCALES

THURSTONE-TYPE SCALES. Attitude scales are designed to provide a quantitative measure of the individual's relative position along a unidimensional attitude continuum. Special procedures have been devised in an attempt to achieve comparability of scores from scale to scale, equality of distances between scale units, and unidimensionality or homogeneity of items. Thurstone's adaptation of psychophysical methods to the quantification of judgment data represented an important milestone in attitude scale construction (Thurstone, 1959; Thurstone & Chave, 1929). By these procedures, Thurstone and his coworkers prepared about thirty scales for measuring attitudes toward war, Negroes, capital punishment, the church, patriotism, censorship, and many other institutions, practices, issues, and racial or national groups.

The construction of the Thurstone-type scales may be illustrated by considering the Scale for Measuring Attitude toward the Church, since the development of this scale was fully reported in published form (Thurstone & Chave, 1929). Essentially the same procedure was followed in preparing all other scales in the series. The first step was to gather a large number of statements regarding the church. These statements were obtained principally by asking several groups of people to write out their opinions about the church. The list was supplemented with statements taken from current literature. A search was made for expressions of opinion ranging from extremely favorable, through neutral, to extremely unfavorable. From the material thus collected, a list of 130 carefully edited, short statements was drawn up.

These statements, each mimeographed on a separate slip, were given to each of 300 judges for sorting into 11 piles, from A to K. The judges were instructed to put in category A those statements they believed expressed the highest appreciation of the value of the church, in category F those expressing a neutral position, and in category K those expressing the strongest depreciation of the church. In the intervening piles, statements were to be arranged in accordance with the degree of appreciation or depreciation they expressed. This sorting procedure has been described as the method of "equal-appearing intervals," although the judges were not actually told that the intervals between piles were to appear equal. It should also be noted that the judges were not asked to indicate their own attitudes toward the church, but were requested only to classify the statements.

The percentage of judges who placed each statement in the different categories constituted the basic data for computing the scale values of the statements. The method is illustrated in Figure 111. On the baseline of the cumulative frequency graph are the numbers 1 to 11, corresponding to categories A to K, which are treated as equally spaced points on the scale. The vertical axis shows the percentage of judges placing the statement in or below each category. The 50th percentile, or median position, assigned by the judges to the statement can be read directly from the graph. This median position is taken as the *scale value* of the statement. It will be noted that for one of the statements illustrated (No. 39), which is quite favorable to the church, the scale value is 1.8. The other statement (No. 8) has a scale value of 6.7. Once the scale values were computed for all statements, the next step was to select those statements whose scale values were equally spaced along the attitude continuum.

Besides the scale value, or median position, of each statement, the graphs also show the variability or spread of positions assigned to it by the different judges. The index of variability employed for this purpose (Q) is simply the distance between the 25th and 75th percentile points. Reference to Figure 111 shows that the judges agreed closely in the placement of statement 39, but varied widely in classifying statement 8. This difference is

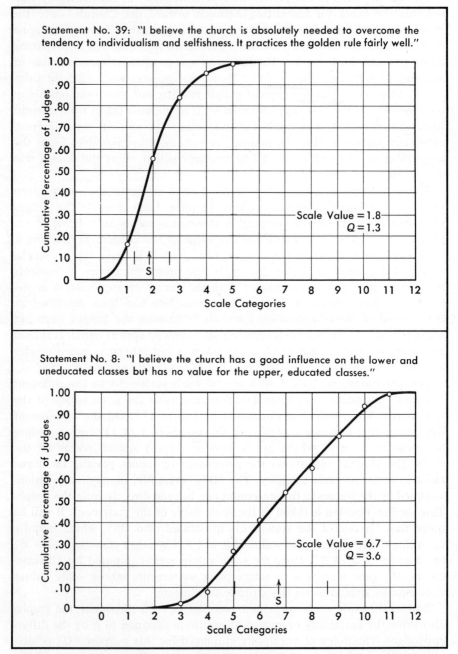

Statement No. 39: "I believe the church is absolutely needed to overcome the tendency to individualism and selfishness. It practices the golden rule fairly well."

Scale Value = 1.8
Q = 1.3

Statement No. 8: "I believe the church has a good influence on the lower and uneducated classes but has no value for the upper, educated classes."

Scale Value = 6.7
Q = 3.6

FIG. 111.   Determination of Scale Values for Thurstone-Type Attitude Scale. (Adapted from Thurstone and Chave, 1929, pp. 37, 39; reproduced by permission of University of Chicago Press.)

reflected in the Q's of 1.3 and 3.6, respectively, which were obtained for the two statements. This measure of variability was taken as an index of the *ambiguity* of statements. Thus, ambiguous or double-barreled statements, which are variously interpreted by different judges, would tend to be less consistently classified. Accordingly, statements yielding high Q's were eliminated from the final scale.

The statements were also checked for *irrelevance*. This was accomplished by presenting the 130 statements to subjects with the instructions to mark those statements with which they agreed. The responses were then analyzed statistically to determine their internal consistency. Statements that failed to meet the criterion of internal consistency were excluded as being irrelevant to the variable under consideration. The final scales thus comprise items that proved to be relatively unambiguous, relevant, and evenly distributed over the range of scale values.

In taking any Thurstone-type attitude scale, the respondent marks all statements with which he agrees. His score is the median scale value of the statements he has endorsed. The Thurstone technique has been applied to the development of attitude scales for many purposes. Thurstone-type scales have been constructed, for example, to measure the attitude of employees toward their company. A few statements from one of these scales, with their corresponding scale values, are shown below (Uhrbrock, 1934):

I think this company treats its employees better than any other company does 10.4

If I had to do it over again I'd still work for this company 9.5

The workers put as much over on the company as the company puts over on them 5.1

You've got to have "pull" with certain people around here to get ahead 2.1

An honest man fails in this company 0.8

A difficulty inherent in the development of Thurstone-type scales pertains to the possible effects of the judges' own attitudes on their classification of the statements. Thurstone recognized this problem, stating that "if the scale is to be regarded as valid, the scale values of the statements should not be affected by the opinions of the people who help to construct it," and adding "until experimental evidence may be forthcoming, we shall make the assumption that the scale values of the statements are independent of the attitude distribution of the readers who sort the statements (Thurstone & Chave, 1929, p. 92). A number of early studies corroborated Thurstone's original assumption, insofar as scale values did not differ appreciably when redetermined on groups known to differ in their own attitudes.

Later investigations, however, found that under certain conditions scale values are significantly affected by judges' attitudes (Farnsworth, 1943; Fishman & Lorge, 1959; Hovland & Sherif, 1952; Sherif, Sherif, & Nebergall, 1965). Thus, large and significant shifts in the scale values of statements about war occurred from 1930 to 1940. Similar differences were obtained with the scale on attitude toward Negroes, when items were re-scaled on several Negro and white groups. The constancy of scale values reported by the earlier studies appeared to have resulted in part from the failure to include subjects with a sufficiently wide range of attitudes. Moreover, it was a common practice in these studies, as in Thurstone's original work, to discard the records of judges who placed 30 or more statements in a single pile. Such a massing of statements was regarded as evidence of careless sorting. It has subsequently been demonstrated, however, that these disproportionate groupings are more likely to occur among individuals whose own views are extreme.

In general, intergroup differences in item placement are reduced when ambiguous items with large inter-judge variability (Q) are eliminated and when only items separated by large scale differences are chosen. On the other hand, if judges are presented with ambiguous and relatively neutral items and if the conditions of judgment are not highly controlled—as when judges are allowed to determine how many categories to use—the classification of items is so strongly affected by the judges' own opinions as to permit the use of this procedure itself as a disguised attitude test (Sherif, Sherif, & Nebergall, 1965). The fact that, under these conditions, item placement reflects the attitudes of the judges, however, does not invalidate the use of this technique, under suitable conditions, for attitude scale construction (Hinckley, 1963; Upshaw, 1965).

LIKERT-TYPE SCALES.   Another approach to the construction of attitude scales is that followed by Likert (1932). The Likert procedure does not require the classification of items by a group of judges. Items are selected solely on the basis of the responses of subjects to whom they are administered in the course of developing the test. Internal consistency is often the only criterion for item selection, although external criteria may be employed when available.

The Likert-type scale, moreover, calls for a graded response to each statement. The response is usually expressed in terms of the following five categories: strongly agree (SA), agree (A), undecided (U), disagree (D), and strongly disagree (SD). The individual statements are either clearly favorable or clearly unfavorable. To score the scale, the alternative responses are credited 5, 4, 3, 2, or 1, respectively, from the favorable to the unfavorable end. For example, "strongly agree" with a favorable statement would receive a score of 5, as would "strongly disagree" with an unfavorable statement. The sum of the item credits represents the individual's total score, which must be interpreted in terms of empirically established norms.

An example of a modified Likert-type scale is the Minnesota Teacher Attitude Inventory. Designed to assess pupil-teacher relations, this test was developed by administering over 700 items to 100 teachers nominated by their principals as superior in pupil-teacher relations and 100 nominated as inferior. Cross validation of the resulting 150-item inventory in different groups yielded concurrent validity coefficients of .46 to .60 with a composite criterion derived from principal's estimate, pupils' ratings, and evaluation by a visiting expert. Two sample items from this inventory are shown below.

Most pupils are resourceful when left on their own.

A teacher should never acknowledge his ignorance of a topic in the presence of his pupils.

For each statement, respondents mark SA, A, U, D, or SD. The scores assigned to these responses are based on criterion keying, as in the SVIB, rather than on arbitrary 1 to 5 weights. Since its publication, this test has been widely used in research. For practical application in selection and counseling, however, more information about the test is needed, especially with regard to its predictive validity and the interpretation of norms from different groups.

Several other techniques of attitude-scale construction have been proposed, some of them embodying considerable theoretical sophistication and statistical refinement (see Edwards, 1957b; Fishbein, 1967; Shaw & Wright, 1967). The large majority of attitude scales, however, have been developed by either the Thurstone or the Likert technique. An extensive collection of attitude scales constructed for a variety of purposes has been assembled in a book by Shaw and Wright (1967). This book provides a valuable source of items and scales for the research worker. Scale values, scoring procedures, reliability, and other technical information about each scale are also included. Few available scales, however, are ready for operational use, especially for individual assessment. Although most of the scales are moderately reliable, little information about their validity has been accumulated. Normative data are also meager. Most attitude scales must be regarded as experimental instruments.

OTHER MEASURES OF INTERESTS, ATTITUDES, AND RELATED VARIABLES

There remain a few well-known instruments that have much in common with interest tests, attitude scales, or both, but do not fall clearly into either category. Some of these tests also include measures of other personality variables, thus overlapping the inventories covered in Chapter 17.

A widely used instrument in this category is the Study of Values, prepared by Allport, Vernon, and Lindzey. Originally suggested by Spranger's *Types of Men* (1928), this inventory was designed to measure the relative strength of six basic interests, motives, or evaluative attitudes, as described below:

Theoretical: Characterized by a dominant interest in the discovery of truth and by an empirical, critical, rational, "intellectual" approach.

Economic: Emphasizing useful and practical values; conforming closely to the prevailing stereotype of the "average American businessman."

Aesthetic: Placing the highest value on form and harmony; judging and enjoying each unique experience from the standpoint of its grace, symmetry, or fitness.

Social: Originally defined as love of people, this category has been more narrowly limited in later revisions of the test to cover only altruism and philanthropy.

Political: Primarily interested in personal power, influence, and renown; not necessarily limited to the field of politics.

Religious: Mystical, concerned with the unity of all experience, and seeking to comprehend the cosmos as a whole.

Items for the Study of Values were first formulated on the basis of the theoretical framework provided by Spranger. The criterion for the final item selection was internal consistency within each of the six areas. Intercorrelations of scores on the current form reveal no substantial overlap among any of these areas. The items are arranged in random order in the test booklet, with no clue regarding the categories according to which they will be scored. Each item requires the preferential rating of either two or four alternatives falling in different value categories. Two sample items are reproduced in Figure 112.

Total raw scores on each of the six values are plotted in a profile, as illustrated in Figure 113. Although normative data are provided for comparative purposes, the authors clearly recognize the ipsative nature of these scores and do not recommend the use of percentiles or other normative types of scores. Mean scores in each value are given for each sex within a general college population, as well as for different types of colleges and several occupational groups. The split-half reliabilities of the six scores range from .73 to .90. Retests after one or two months yielded reliabilities between .77 and .93 for the six scales. The fact that retest reliabilities run slightly higher than split-half reliabilities may indicate low item equivalence within scales. There is no conclusive evidence of unidimensionality of scales.

Validity has been checked partly by the method of contrasted groups. Profiles of various educational and occupational samples exhibit significant differences in the expected directions. For example, medical students ob-

Part I. The two alternatives are rated 3 and 0, if the subject agrees with one and disagrees with the other; if he has only a slight preference for one over the other, they are rated 2 and 1, respectively.

Example:

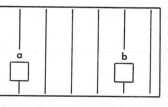

If you should see the following news items with headlines of equal size in your morning paper, which would you read more attentively? (a) PROTESTANT LEADERS TO CONSULT ON RECONCILIATION; (b) GREAT IMPROVEMENTS IN MARKET CONDITIONS.

Part II. The answers are rated in order of personal preference, giving 4 to the most attractive and 1 to the least attractive alternative.

Example:

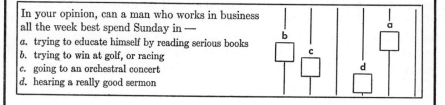

In your opinion, can a man who works in business all the week best spend Sunday in —
a. trying to educate himself by reading serious books
b. trying to win at golf, or racing
c. going to an orchestral concert
d. hearing a really good sermon

FIG. 112. Sample Items from Allport-Vernon-Lindzey Study of Values. (Reproduced by permission of Houghton Mifflin Company.)

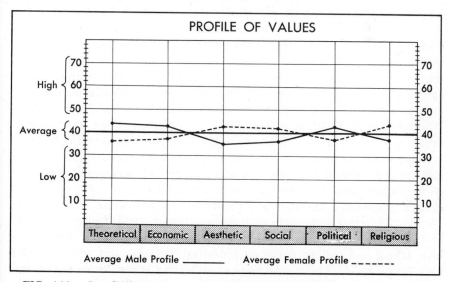

FIG. 113. Sex Differences on the Allport-Vernon-Lindzey Study of Values. (Reproduced by permission of Houghton Mifflin Company.)

tained their highest scores in the theoretical area, theological students in the religious area. Some relationship has been demonstrated between value profiles and academic achievement, especially when relative achievement in different fields is considered. Data are also available on the correlation of value scores with self-ratings and associates' ratings. Other overt behavioral indices of attitudes with which scores on the Study of Values have been compared include newspaper reading, descriptions of one's "ideal person," club membership, church attendance, and the like. Significant relationships in the expected directions have likewise been reported with a number of other tests, such as SVIB and Thurstone attitude scales. Finally, some studies have shown significant changes in score following specific types of experience, such as a period of study under different styles of education.

It might be noted that a Pictorial Study of Values has been prepared for subjects with linguistic or reading difficulties. Pictures for this test were assigned to each of the six scales on the basis of their correlations with Allport-Vernon-Lindzey scores in a sample of 100 cases. Although providing a promising idea for test development, in its present form this test is not ready for general use. Attempts have also been made to prepare verbal forms at a lower reading level (Engstrom & Powers, 1959; Levy, 1958).

THE PLACE OF INTERESTS IN PERSONALITY THEORY

The measurement of interests began as a relatively specific, minor, and tangential development in the study of personality. Early interest inventories were oriented chiefly toward the prediction of the individual's eventual acceptance or rejection of particular job functions. From these modest beginnings, interest tests are gradually coming to play a major role in the formulation of personality theory. The impetus for these developments is coming from several different sources. Factorial analyses of interest items, as illustrated by the work of Guilford and his associates (Guilford, 1959; Guilford et al., 1954), have demonstrated the interconnections of interests with other important dimensions of personality.

A large number of studies have revealed significant associations between measured vocational interests and other aspects of personality. Research on alcoholics, male homosexuals, neurotics, and persons with other psychiatric disabilities has shown a predominance of certain characteristic vocational interest patterns in each group (Carnes, 1964; Drasgow & Carkhuff, 1964; Force, 1958; Haselkorn, 1956; Patterson, 1957). Studies on high school and college students, industrial workers, and adult patients have found accident-proneness to be significantly related to scores on certain scales of the SVIB (Kunce, 1967).

Scores on such inventories as the SVIB and the Kuder—Vocational have also proved to be related to performance on other personality tests, such as the MMPI and the Study of Values (Darley & Hagenah, 1955). Some investigators have provided personality descriptions of normal persons scoring high or low on particular vocational interest scores. In a survey of 1,000 male University of Minnesota freshmen, scores on certain SVIB occupational scales were found to be significantly correlated with other measured emotional and attitudinal variables (Darley & Hagenah, 1955, Ch. 4). For example, students scoring high in the social-service or business-contact clusters of occupational keys obtained higher social adjustment scores than those scoring high in other clusters. On economic conservatism, these same two groups scored in opposite ways, those with high social-service interests being more liberal than those with high business-contact interests.

More detailed personality evaluations of individuals receiving high scores on different occupational interest scales are to be found in a study of 100 Air Force officers conducted at the University of California (see Darley & Hagenah, 1955, pp. 128–129). Each subject was given a battery of tests, including the SVIB, and also underwent an intensive assessment program through interviews and other observational techniques. On the basis of the available information, subjects were described by eight clinical psychologists in terms of 76 designated personality variables. Correlations of these trait ratings with each of the SVIB occupational keys revealed a number of statistically significant relations. For illustrative purposes, the personality descriptions associated with high scores on two keys are summarized below:

High Scorers on Mathematician Key: Self-abasing, concerned with philosophical problems, introspective, lacking in social poise, lacking confidence in own ability, sympathetic, reacts poorly to stress, not persuasive in personal contacts, not an effective leader, not ostentatious, not aggressive or socially ascendant.

High Scorers on Real Estate Salesman Key: Self-indulgent, guileful, cynical, opportunistic, aggressive, persuasive, ostentatious, may arouse hostility in others, not sympathetic, not concerned with philosophical problems, not lacking confidence in own ability, not self-abasing.

From a different angle, it is now widely recognized that the choice of an occupation often reflects the individual's basic emotional needs and that occupational adjustment is a major aspect of general life adjustment (Bordin, 1943; Darley & Hagenah, 1955; Holland, 1958; Roe, 1956). There are many different ways of dealing with interpersonal relations and other life problems. No one way is universally better than others. When he chooses a vocation, each individual is to some extent selecting those adjustment techniques, life patterns, and roles most congenial to himself. The measurement of vocational interests—and more specifically the identification of those occupational groups whose interests and attitudes the individual shares most closely—thus becomes a focal point in the understanding of different personalities. Direct studies of the characteristics of persons in different occupations have been contributing to a growing fund of factual material for implementing this approach.

In line with the above viewpoint, Holland has come full circle in developing the Holland Vocational Preference Inventory, in which occupational titles are used to measure personality characteristics. In this test, the respondent merely indicates whether he likes or dislikes each of 300 occupations. Although constructed largely in terms of content validity and internal consistency, the resulting scales yielded significant differences between matched samples of psychiatric patients and normal controls. Interest profiles of students in different curricula were also consistent with expectation. The inventory provides ten "personality" scales, as illustrated by Physical Activity, Intellectuality, Responsibility, and Conformity, as well as three response set scales. How effective this inventory will ultimately prove to be in either research or practice remains to be seen. But its development illustrates current emphasis on vocational choices as clues to personality.

From still another angle, Tyler (1959) regards the study of interests as a way of identifying the choices that the individual makes at various stages. These choices are both a reflection of the kind of person he is and a forecast of what he is likely to become. As each choice is made—choice of friends, recreations, courses, jobs, and the like—the individual's subsequent experiences are thereby channeled into certain paths. Alternative developmental routes are eliminated at each choice point. Translating the predictive validity of the SVIB into these terms, Tyler (1959, p. 78) writes:

An A signifies that the person's characteristic pattern of acceptance and rejection of life's varied possibilities is like the choice pattern characteristic of persons in a certain occupation. What we should expect then to be able to predict from such a score is . . . the way he will make his choices at later junctures of his life. This makes sense of the high degree of validity Strong's recent studies have shown for the test.

The measurement of interests promises to be a lively field of test development and research in the years ahead. Having proved so far to be among the most successful tests outside the aptitude domain, interest inventories are now well on the way to attaining theoretical respectability. At the same time, we can anticipate that the interpretation of interest profiles will show further advances in depth and sophistication.

CHAPTER **19**

Projective
Techniques

THE AVAILABLE supply of projective techniques is abundant and steadily growing. In this chapter, we shall consider the major varieties of such techniques, together with some well-known examples. Except for special points peculiar to particular techniques, no critical evaluation of individual instruments will be undertaken. Instead, a summary evaluation of projective techniques will be given in a separate section, with emphasis on common methodological problems. Projective techniques present a curious discrepancy between research and practice. When evaluated as psychometric instruments, the large majority make a poor showing. Yet their popularity in clinical use continues unabated. The nature and implications of this inconsistency will be examined in the last section.

The literature on projective techniques is vast, running to over 3,000 references on a single instrument. For a broader coverage of available projective techniques, as well as for a fuller discussion of individual instruments, the reader is referred to such sources as Holzberg (1966), Lindzey (1961), Murstein (1963), Shneidman (1965), and Zubin, Eron, and Schumer (1965). The *Mental Measurements Yearbooks* contain a separate section on projective techniques, in which multiple reviews are given for some of the more popular instruments.

NATURE OF PROJECTIVE TECHNIQUES

The chief distinguishing feature of projective techniques is to be found in their assignment of a relatively *unstructured* task, i.e., a task that permits an almost unlimited variety of possible responses. In order to allow free play to the individual's fantasy, only brief, general instructions are provided. For the same reason, the test stimuli are usually vague or ambiguous. The underlying hypothesis is that the way in which the individual perceives and interprets the test material, or "structures" the situation, will reflect fundamental aspects of his psychological functioning. In other words, it is expected that the test materials will serve as a sort of screen on which the respondent "projects" his characteristic thought processes, needs, anxieties, and conflicts.

Typically, projective instruments also represent *disguised* testing procedures, insofar as the examinee is rarely aware of the type of psychological interpretation that will be made of his responses. Projective techniques are likewise characterized by a *global* approach to the appraisal of personality. Attention is focused on a composite picture of the whole personality, rather than on the measurement of separate traits. Finally, projective techniques are regarded by their exponents as especially effective in revealing *covert, latent, or unconscious* aspects of personality. Moreover, the more unstructured the test, it is argued, the more sensitive it is to such covert material. This follows from the assumption that the more unstructured or ambiguous the stimuli, the less likely they are to evoke defensive reactions on the part of the respondent.

Projective methods originated within a clinical setting and have remained predominantly a tool for the clinician. Some have evolved from therapeutic procedures (such as art therapy) employed with psychiatric patients. In their theoretical framework, most projective techniques reflect the influence of psychoanalytic concepts. There have also been scattered attempts to lay a foundation for projective techniques in stimulus-response theory and in perceptual theories of personality (see Lindzey, 1961, Ch. 4). It should be noted, of course, that the specific techniques need not be evaluated in the light of their particular theoretical slants or historical origins. A procedure may prove to be practically useful or empirically valid for reasons other than those initially cited to justify its introduction.

In line with their typically global approach, projective techniques have been concerned not only with emotional, motivational, and interpersonal characteristics, but also with certain intellectual aspects of behavior. Examples of the latter include general intellectual level, originality, and problem-solving styles. Certain adaptations of projective techniques have been specially designed for the measurement of attitudes (Campbell, 1950; Weschler & Bernberg, 1950), and thus supplement the instruments described in Chapter 18. It might be added that any psychological test, regardless of the purpose for which it was designed, may serve as a projective instrument. Intelligence tests, for example, are employed in this fashion by some clinicians (Fromm, Hartman, & Marschak, 1957).

THE RORSCHACH AND RELATED INSTRUMENTS

THE RORSCHACH. The most popular projective technique is undoubtedly that employing the Rorschach inkblots. Developed by the Swiss psychiatrist, Hermann Rorschach (1942), this technique was first described in 1921. Although standardized series of inkblots had previously been utilized by psychologists in studies of imagination and other functions, Rorschach was the first to apply inkblots to the diagnostic investigation of the personality as a whole. In the development of this technique, Rorschach experimented with a large number of inkblots which he administered to different psychiatric groups. As a result of such clinical observations, those response characteristics that differentiated between the various psychiatric syndromes were gradually incorporated into the scoring system. The scoring procedures were further sharpened by supplementary testing of mental defectives, normals, artists, scholars, and other persons of known characteristics. Rorschach's methodology thus represented an early, informal, and relatively subjective application of criterion keying.

The Rorschach utilizes 10 cards,[1] on each of which is printed a bilaterally symmetrical inkblot similar to that illustrated in Figure 114. Five of the blots are executed in shades of gray and black only; two contain additional touches of bright red; and the remaining three combine several pastel shades. As the examinee is shown each inkblot, he is asked to tell what he

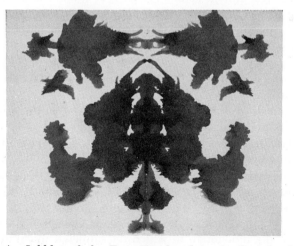

FIG. 114. An Inkblot of the Type Employed in the Rorschach Technique.

[1] The cards, or plates, are printed by Hans Huber, in Berne, Switzerland. They can be obtained in America from Grune & Stratton or from a number of test distributors, such as C. H. Stoelting and The Psychological Corporation.

sees—what the blot could represent. Besides keeping a verbatim record of the responses to each card, the examiner notes time of responses, position or positions in which cards are held, spontaneous remarks, emotional expressions, and other incidental behavior of the examinee during the test session. Following the presentation of all 10 cards, the examiner questions the individual systematically regarding the parts and aspects of each blot to which the associations were given. During this inquiry, the examinee also has an opportunity to clarify and elaborate his earlier responses.

While several systems for scoring and interpreting the Rorschach have been developed, the most common scoring categories include location, determinants, and content. *Location* refers to the part of the blot with which the examinee associates each response. Does he use the whole blot, a common detail, an unusual detail, white space, or some combination of these areas? The *determinants* of the response include form, color, shading, and "movement." Although there is of course no movement in the blot itself, the respondent's perception of the blot as a representation of a moving object is scored in this category. Further differentiations are made within these categories. For example, human movement, animal movement, and abstract or inanimate movement are separately scored. Similarly, shading may be perceived as representing depth, texture, hazy forms such as clouds, or achromatic reproductions of colors as in a photograph.

The treatment of *content* varies from one scoring system to another, although certain major categories are regularly employed. Chief among these are human figures, human details (or parts of human figures), animal figures, animal details, and anatomical diagrams. Other broad scoring categories include inanimate objects, plants, maps, clouds, blood, x-rays, sexual objects, and symbols. A *popularity* score is often found on the basis of the relative frequency of different responses among people in general. For each of the 10 cards, certain responses are scored as popular because of their common occurrence.

Further analysis of Rorschach responses is based on the relative number of responses falling into the various categories, as well as on certain ratios and interrelations among different categories. Examples of the sort of qualitative interpretations that have commonly been utilized with Rorschach responses include the association of "whole" responses with conceptual thinking, of "color" responses with emotionality, and of "human movement" responses with imagination and fantasy life. In the usual application of the Rorschach, major emphasis is placed on the final "global" description of the individual, in which the clinician integrates the results from different parts of the protocol and takes into account the interrelations of different scores and indices. In actual practice, information derived from outside sources, such as other tests, interviews, and case history records, is also utilized in preparing these global descriptions.

Although the Rorschach is considered to be applicable from the preschool to the adult level, its normative data were derived largely from adult groups. This limitation also characterizes the general fund of clinical experience accumulated through the use of the Rorschach and employed in the qualitative interpretation of protocols. In the effort to extend the empirical framework for Rorschach interpretation to other age groups, Ames and her coworkers at the Gesell Institute of Child Development at Yale collected and published Rorschach norms on children between the ages of 2 and 10 years, on adolescents between the ages of 10 and 16, and on older persons from the age of 70 up (Ames *et al.*, 1952, 1954, 1959).

Some of the underlying assumptions of traditional Rorschach scoring have been called into question by a growing body of research findings. Comparative studies with standard and achromatic series of Rorschach cards, for example, have demonstrated that color itself has no effect on most of the response characteristics customarily attributed to it (Baughman, 1958). There is also evidence that verbal aptitude influences several Rorschach scores commonly interpreted as indicators of personality traits (Lotsof, 1953; Sachman, 1952). In one study (Sachman, 1952), an analysis of the verbal complexity of individual Rorschach responses given by 100 persons revealed that "movement" responses tended to be longer and linguistically more complex than "form" responses. It was also found that verbal complexity of Rorschach responses was highly correlated with the subjects' scores on a verbal aptitude test, as well as with age and educational level.

A major complicating factor in the interpretation of Rorschach scores is the total number of responses—known as response productivity, or R (Fiske & Baughman, 1953). Because of large individual differences in R, the practice of considering the absolute number of responses in various categories is obviously misleading. If two individuals or groups differ in R, they are also likely to differ in the same direction in the number of responses falling in specific categories. Thus, the differences found in certain categories may be only an artifact resulting from the variation in total number of responses. Nor is the use of percentages a completely satisfactory solution. For example, a protocol containing many responses is likely to include a smaller *proportion* of "whole" responses, since the number of "whole" responses that can reasonably be perceived in the blots is quite limited, while associations to isolated details of the blots may continue indefinitely.

To these intrinsic characteristics of the Rorschach scores may be added the empirical fact that response productivity appears to be closely related to age, intellectual level, and amount of education. Even more disturbing is the finding that R varies significantly from one examiner to another (Baughman, 1951; Guilford & Lacey, 1947). All of these results suggest that R, which may itself be a major determinant of many of the common Rorschach scores, is influenced by factors quite extraneous to the basic personality variables allegedly measured by the Rorschach. Findings such as these strike at the very foundation on which the entire elaborate superstructure of Rorschach scoring is supported.

In view of the unsatisfactory nature of the traditional Rorschach scoring system, some investigators have turned to *content analysis* of Rorschach responses (Zubin, Eron, & Sultan, 1956). Rorschach himself and most of his followers have relied most heavily on the perceptual bases of the respondent's associations to the inkblots, as illustrated by location, color, form, shading, etc. Implicit in such an approach are the assumptions that the individual's responses to the Rorschach cards are indicative of his usual perceptual responses and that personality traits influence perception. In contrast to this approach, content analysis concentrates on *what* the subject perceives in the blots. Such content can then be treated in much the same way as one would treat any material reported during a clinical interview. Results obtained through this approach appear somewhat more promising than those utilizing perceptual scoring procedures.

THE HOLTZMAN INKBLOT TECHNIQUE. Unlike most projective techniques, the Holtzman Inkblot Technique represents a genuine attempt to meet the technical standards of psychometric instruments (Holtzman *et al.*, 1961). Modeled after the Rorschach, the Holtzman test was so designed as to eliminate the principal technical deficiencies of the earlier instrument. The changes in stimulus materials and procedure are sufficiently extensive, however, to require that the Holtzman be regarded as a new test and evaluated without reference to either the theoretical or empirical characteristics of the Rorschach. The Holtzman technique provides two parallel series of 45 cards each. Only one response per card is obtained, thereby holding response productivity (R) constant for each examinee and avoiding many of the pitfalls of traditional Rorschach scoring. Administration and scoring of the Holtzman are well standardized and clearly described. Scores are obtained in 22 response variables, including most of the traditional Rorschach form variables and such additional variables as pathognomic verbalization, anxiety, and hostility.

For each variable on the Holtzman test, percentile scores are reported for several normal samples ranging from 5-year-olds to adults, as well as for a few pathological groups; but the number of cases in each of these groups is rather small. Scorer reliability appears to be highly satisfactory. Both split-half and alternate-form reliability have been thoroughly investigated, with generally encouraging results. The evidence for validity, however, is still meager. Major group differences and developmental trends appear promising, but more data are needed to establish the diagnostic significance of the various scores and the construct validity of the variables assessed by this instrument. A group form of this test has also been developed which yields scores that are closely similar to those obtained through individual administration (Holtzman *et al.*, 1963).

THE THEMATIC APPERCEPTION TEST AND OTHER PICTORIAL TECHNIQUES

THEMATIC APPERCEPTION TEST. In contrast to inkblot techniques, the Thematic Apperception Test (TAT) presents more highly structured stimuli and requires more complex and meaningfully organized verbal responses. Interpretation of responses by the examiner is usually based on content analysis of a rather qualitative nature. First developed by Murray and his staff at the Harvard Psychological Clinic (Murray *et al.*, 1938), the TAT has not only been widely used in clinical practice and research, but it has also served as a model for the development of many other instruments (Atkinson, 1958; Harrison, 1965; Henry, 1956).

The TAT materials consist of 19 cards containing vague pictures in black and white and one blank card. The examinee is asked to make up a story to fit each picture, telling what led up to the event shown in the picture, describing what is happening at the moment and what the characters are feeling and thinking, and giving the outcome. In the case of the blank card, he is instructed to imagine some picture on the card, describe it, and then tell a story about it. The original procedure outlined by Murray in the test manual requires two one-hour sessions, 10 cards being employed during each session. The cards reserved for the second session were deliberately chosen to be more unusual, dramatic, and bizarre, and the accompanying instructions urge the individual to give free play to his imagination. Four overlapping sets of 20 cards are available—for boys, girls, men over 14, and women over 14. Most clinicians use abridged sets of specially selected cards, seldom giving more than 10 cards to a single respondent. A card from the second set of the adult women's series is shown in Figure 115.

In interpreting TAT stories, the examiner first determines who is the "hero," the character of either sex with whom the subject has presumably identified himself. The content of the stories is then analyzed principally in reference to Murray's list of "needs" and "press." Several of the proposed needs were described in the preceding chapter, in connection with the Edwards Personal Preference Schedule. Examples include achievement, affiliation, and aggression. Press refers to environmental forces that may facilitate or interfere with the satisfaction of needs. Being attacked or criticized by another person, receiving affection, being comforted, and exposure to physical danger as in a shipwreck are illustrations of press. In assessing the importance or strength of a particular need or press for the individual, special attention is given to the intensity, duration, and frequency of its

FIG. 115.   One of the Pictures Used in the Thematic Apperception Test. (Reproduced by permission of Harvard University Press.)

occurrence in different stories, as well as to the uniqueness of its association with a given picture. The assumption is made that unusual material, which departs from the common responses to each picture, is more likely to have significance for the individual.

A fair amount of normative information has been published regarding the most frequent response characteristics for each card, including the way each card is perceived, the themes developed, the roles ascribed to the characters, emotional tones expressed, speed of responses, length of stories, and the like (see Atkinson, 1958; Henry, 1956). Although these normative data provide a general framework for interpreting individual responses, most clinicians rely heavily on "subjective norms" built up through their own experience with the test. A number of quantitative scoring schemes and rating scales have been developed that yield good scorer reliability. Since their application is rather time consuming, however, such scoring procedures are seldom used in clinical practice. Although typically given as an individual oral test in the clinical situation, the TAT may also be administered in writing and as a group test. There is some evidence suggesting that under the latter conditions productivity of meaningful material may be facilitated.

The TAT has been used extensively in personality research. Several investigations have been concerned with the assumptions that underlie TAT interpretations, such as self-identification with the hero and personal significance of uncommon responses (Lindzey, 1959). Although they cannot establish criterion-related validity of the TAT for specific uses, such studies contribute to the construct validation of TAT interpretations. A basic assumption that TAT shares with other projective techniques is that present motivational and emotional condition of the subject affects his responses to an unstructured test situation. A considerable body of experimental data is available to show that such conditions as hunger, sleep deprivation, social frustration, and the experience of failure in a preceding test situation significantly affect TAT responses (Atkinson, 1958). While supporting the projective hypothesis, the sensitivity of the TAT to such temporary conditions may complicate the detection of more enduring personality traits.

ADAPTATIONS OF THE TAT AND RELATED TESTS. Many adaptations of the TAT have been developed for special purposes. These exhibit varying degrees of resemblance to the original. Where to draw the line between modified versions of the TAT and new tests based on the same general approach as the TAT is arbitrary. Several versions of the TAT have been prepared for use in attitude surveys; examples include sets for assessing attitudes toward labor problems, minority groups, school, and authority (Campbell, 1950; Harrison, 1965). Other adaptations have been developed for use in vocational counseling, executive appraisal, and a wide variety of research projects. Forms have been constructed for special populations, including preschool children, elementary schoolchildren, adolescents, crippled children, and various national and ethnic groups (Harrison, 1965). There are also versions utilizing other media, such as sound films, colored pictures, and verbal descriptions of pictures. Some versions present only sets of auditory stimuli, such as typewriter, dialogue, or foghorn, which are to be incorporated into a story.

Some TAT adaptations have focused on the intensive measurement of a single need or drive, such as sex or aggression. Of special interest is the extensive research on the achievement need (n-Ach) conducted by McClelland and his associates (Atkinson, 1958; Atkinson & Feather, 1966; McClelland et al., 1953; McClelland, 1961). To measure n-Ach, McClelland selected four pictures, two of which were taken from the TAT. The cards portray men working at a machine, a boy at a desk with a book, a father and son picture, and a boy who is apparently daydreaming. Detailed scoring schemas have been developed for scoring the resulting stories with regard to expressions of n-Ach. This technique has been utilized in an extensive program of research on achievement motivation. The problems investigated range from basic motivation theory (Atkinson & Feather, 1966) to the social origins and consequences of n-Ach and its role in the rise and fall of societies (McClelland, 1961).

Although the original TAT is said to be applicable to children as young as 4 years of age, the Children's Apperception Test (CAT) was specially designed for use between the ages of 3 and 10 years (Bellak, 1954). The CAT cards substitute animals for people on the assumption that young children project more readily to pictures of animals than to pictures of humans. The various animals in the pictures are portrayed in typically human situations, in the characteristic anthropomorphic fashion of comic strips and movie cartoons. The pictures are designed to evoke fantasies relating to problems of feeding and other oral activity, sibling rivalry, parent-child relations, aggression, toilet-training, and other childhood experiences. Contrary to the authors' assumption, several studies with children from the first grade up found either no difference or, more often, greater productivity of clinically significant material with human than with animal pictures (Murstein, 1963). In response to these research findings, the authors of the CAT have prepared a human modification of the test (CAT-H) for use with older children, especially those with a mental age beyond 10 years (Bellak & Hurvich, 1966). The authors maintain that either the human or the animal form may be more effective depending on the age and personality characteristics of the child.

ROSENZWEIG PICTURE-FRUSTRATION STUDY. Unlike other techniques described in this section, the Rosenzweig Picture-Frustration Study (P-F Study) is not a picture-story test. Rather than composing an entire story, the respondent is required only to insert a short bit of conversation in each picture. The P-F Study was developed on the basis of Rosenzweig's theory of frustration and aggression (see Rosenzweig, 1960). It is available in a form for children (4 to 13 years) and a form for adults (14 years and older). Each form comprises a series of cartoonlike drawings, depicting two principal characters. One of these characters is involved in a frustrating situation common in everyday life; the other is saying something that either occasions the frustration or calls attention to the frustrating circumstances. The examinee is instructed to write in the blank caption box what the frustrated person would answer. He is urged to give the very first reply that comes to his mind. The frustrating situations are of two types: (a) "ego-blocking," in which some obstruction, personal or impersonal, impedes, disappoints, deprives, or otherwise thwarts the individual directly; and (b) "superego-blocking," in which the individual is insulted, accused, or otherwise incriminated by another person. Two items from the children's form are reproduced in Figure 116.

The P-F Study is based on the assumption that the individual identifies with the frustrated character in each picture and projects his own reaction tendencies in the reply. In scoring the test, each reply is classified with reference to type and direction of aggression. Type of aggression includes: "obstacle-dominance," in which the frustrating object is emphasized in the response; "ego-defense," in which attention is focused on the protection of the thwarted individual; and "need-persistence," in which the constructive

FIG. 116. Typical Items from the Rosenzweig Picture-Frustration Study, Children's Form. (Reproduced by permission of Saul Rosenzweig.)

solution of the frustrating problem is paramount. Direction of aggression is scored as: "extrapunitive," or turned outward on the environment; "intropunitive," or turned inward on the subject; and "impunitive," or turned off in an attempt at glossing over or evading the situation. In scoring the test, the percentage of responses falling into each of these categories is compared with the corresponding normative percentages. A group conformity rating (GCR), showing the individual's tendency to give responses that agree with the modal responses of the standardization sample, may also be obtained.

Being more limited in coverage, more highly structured, and relatively objective in its scoring procedures, the P-F Study lends itself better to statistical analysis than most other projective techniques. More systematic efforts have also been made to gather norms and to check its reliability and validity. Like a number of other projective instruments, the P-F Study has been adapted by other investigators for research on a variety of problems. The general approach of the P-F Study has been followed in tests designed for studying attitudes toward minority groups (Brown, 1947), opinions on the prevention of war (Fromme, 1941), consumers' responses to products (Smith, 1954, pp. 120–121), and the reactions of amputees toward their disability (Peizer, 1958).

VERBAL TECHNIQUES

Although all the projective techniques discussed thus far require verbal responses, certain projective techniques are wholly verbal, utilizing only words in both stimulus materials and responses. Some of these verbal techniques can be administered in either oral or written form; but all are suitable for written group administration. When so administered, of course, they presuppose a minimum reading level and thorough familiarity with the language in which the test was developed. These requirements thus preclude the use of such techniques with young children, illiterates, or the foreign-speaking.

WORD ASSOCIATION. A technique that antedated the flood of projective tests by more than half a century is the word association test. Originally known as the "free association test," this technique was first systematically described by Galton (1879). Wundt and J. McK. Cattell subsequently introduced it into the psychological laboratory, where it was adapted to many uses. The procedure involves simply the presentation of a series of disconnected words, to each of which the subject is told to respond by giving the first word that comes to his mind. The early experimental psychologists, as well as the first mental testers, saw in such association tests a tool for the exploration of thinking processes.

The *clinical application* of word association methods was stimulated largely by the psychoanalytic movement, although other psychiatrists, such as Kraepelin, had previously investigated such techniques. Among the psychoanalysts, Jung's contribution to the systematic development of the word association test is most conspicuous. Jung (1910) selected stimulus words to represent common "emotional complexes." The responses were analyzed with reference to reaction time and content, the latter being classified according to the general character of the association, such as contrast, supraordinate, modifying adjective, sound association, and the like. Overt expressions of emotional tension, such as laughing, flushing, and hand movements, were also noted. The test was then readministered with the subject being instructed to try to recall the original responses. Changes in response words and other features of the subject's retest behavior provided further diagnostic clues.

Over thirty years later, a word association technique was developed at the Menninger Clinic by Rapaport and his associates (1946, Ch. 2). In its general orientation, this adaptation reveals its kinship to the earlier Jung test. The 60-word list contains a preponderance of words selected for their psychoanalytic significance, many of them being associated with psychosexual conflicts. According to its authors, the test had a dual aim: to aid in detecting impairment of thought processes and to suggest areas of significant internal conflicts. Results are analyzed with reference to such characteristics as proportion of common or popular responses, reaction time, associative disturbances, and impaired reproduction on retest.

A different approach to the word association test is illustrated by the early work of Kent and Rosanoff (1910). Designed principally as a psychiatric screening instrument, the Kent-Rosanoff Free Association Test utilized completely objective scoring and statistical norms. The stimulus words consisted of 100 common, neutral words, chosen because they tend to evoke the same associations from people in general. For example, to the word *table*, most people respond "chair"; to *dark*, they say "light." A set of frequency tables was prepared—one for each stimulus word—showing the number of times each response was given in a standardization sample of 1,000 normal adults.

In scoring the Kent-Rosanoff test, the median frequency value of the responses the examinee gives to the 100 stimulus words is employed as an "index of commonality." Any responses not found in the normative tables are designated as "individual." Comparisons of psychotics with normals suggested that psychotics give more individual responses and obtain a lower index of commonality than normals. The diagnostic use of the test declined, however, with the gradual realization that response frequency also varies widely with age, socioeconomic and educational level, regional and cultural background, creativity, and other factors. Hence, proper interpretation of scores requires norms on many subgroups, as well as supplementary information about the examinee.

The Kent-Rosanoff test has nevertheless retained its position as a standard laboratory technique. Additional norms have been gathered by several investigators, and the technique has been extensively employed in research on verbal behavior and personality (Jenkins & Russell, 1960; Palermo & Jenkins, 1963; Russell & Jenkins, 1954). All this research activity has stimulated some resurgence of interest in the potentialities of the Kent-Rosanoff technique in clinical practice. It is noteworthy that the Kent-Rosanoff is the oldest test reviewed in the *Sixth Mental Measurements Yearbook*. Although each edition of these yearbooks concentrates on recently published tests, the Kent-Rosanoff was considered sufficiently important for inclusion in the 1965 yearbook.

The free association method has also been employed in the measurement of *interests and attitudes*. A free association interest test was developed for use in the well-known study of gifted children conducted under the direction of Terman at Stanford University (Wyman, 1925). In this test, responses were scored with reference to intellectual, social, and activity interest. In another application, the respondent's attitude toward such concepts as "father," "Communism," and "religion" was assessed by analyzing the adjectives he gave in response to such stimulus words (Murray & Morgan, 1945).

Mention may likewise be made of the use of the word association technique as a *lie detector*. This application was also initiated by Jung, and has subsequently been subjected to extensive research—both in the laboratory and in practical situations (Burtt, 1931; Lindsley, 1955). The rationale offered to justify the employment of word association in the detection of lying or guilt is similar to that which underlies its utilization in uncovering areas of emotional conflict. Content analysis, reaction time, and response disturbances have all been explored as indices of lying or guilt. Frequently, physiological measures of emotional excitement are obtained concurrently with the verbal responses. The word lists chosen for lie detection purposes are usually custom-made to cover distinctive features of the particular crime or other situation under investigation. Whether word association has any practical value as a lie detector is still a moot point. Its effectiveness certainly varies widely with the specific circumstances under which it is used.

SENTENCE COMPLETION. Unlike the incomplete sentences sometimes employed to assess verbal aptitude, those utilized in projective tests permit highly varied completions. Generally, only the opening words, or sentence stems, are provided, the respondent being required to write the ending. A few typical examples are shown below:

I feel . . .
What annoys me . . .
My mind . . .
If I had my way . . .
Women . . .

The sentence stems are frequently formulated so as to elicit responses relevant to the personality domain under investigation. This flexibility of the sentence-completion technique represents one of its advantages for clinical and research purposes. Nevertheless, some standardized forms have been published for more general application.

An example is the Rotter Incomplete Sentences Blank, consisting of 40 sentence stems. The directions to the examinee read: "Complete these sentences to express *your real feelings*. Try to do every one. Be sure to make a complete sentence." Each completion is rated on a seven-point scale according to the degree of adjustment or maladjustment indicated. Illustrative completions corresponding to each rating are given in the manual. With the aid of these specimen responses, fairly objective scoring is possible. The sum of the individual ratings provides a total adjustment score that can be used for screening purposes. The response content can also be examined clinically for more specific diagnostic clues. Validation studies have yielded some promising results. The manual gives a well-balanced, conservative evaluation of the strengths and weaknesses of the test.

In the Sentence Completions Test developed by Rohde (1957), a system of quantitative scoring has been worked out in terms of Murray's needs and press. Since such scoring is rather time consuming, however, qualitative content analysis may be employed instead. Normative data have been gathered on junior high school and normal adult groups. Comparative results are also available from neurotic and psychotic samples.

EXPRESSIVE TECHNIQUES

A large and amorphous category of projective techniques comprises many forms of relatively free self-expression. It is characteristic of all these techniques that they may be employed as therapeutic as well as diagnostic procedures. Through the opportunities for self-expression that these activities afford, it is believed that the individual not only reveals his emotional difficulties but also relieves them. The techniques most frequently employed in this category are drawing and dramatic use of toys.

DRAWING. Although almost every art medium, technique, and type of subject matter has been investigated in the search for significant diagnostic clues, special attention has centered on drawings of the human figure. A well-known example is provided by the Machover Draw-a-Person Test (D-A-P). In this test, the examinee is provided with paper and pencil, and told simply to "draw a person." Upon completion of the first drawing, he is asked to draw a person of the opposite sex from that of the first figure. While the individual draws, the examiner notes his comments, the sequence in which different parts are drawn, and other procedural details. The drawing may be followed by an inquiry, in which the examinee is asked to make up a story about each person drawn, "as if he were a character in a play or novel." A series of questions is also employed during the inquiry to elicit specific information about age, schooling, occupation, family, and other facts associated with the characters portrayed.

Scoring of the Draw-a-Person Test is essentially qualitative, involving the preparation of a composite personality description from an analysis of many features of the drawings. Among the factors considered in this connection are the absolute and relative size of the male and female figures, their position on the page, quality of lines, sequence of parts drawn, stance, front or profile view, position of arms, depiction of clothing, and background and grounding effects. Special interpretations are given for the omission of different bodily parts, disproportions, shading, amount and distribution of details, erasures, symmetry, and other stylistic features. There is also detailed discussion of the significance of each major body part, such as head, individual facial features, hair, neck, shoulders, breast, trunk, hips, and extremities.

The interpretive guide for the Draw-a-Person Test abounds in sweeping generalizations, such as "Disproportionately large heads will often be given by individuals suffering from organic brain disease," or "The sex given the proportionately larger head is the sex that is accorded more intellectual and social authority." But no evidence is provided in support of these statements. Reference is made to a file of "thousands of drawings" examined in clinical contexts, and a few selected cases are cited for illustrative purposes. No systematic presentation of data, however, accompanies the original published report of the test (Machover, 1949). Validation studies by other investigators have yielded conflicting results, the better controlled studies lending no support to the diagnostic interpretations proposed by Machover.

Another drawing test that has aroused considerable interest, as witnessed by the number of relevant research publications, is the House-Tree-Person Projective Technique (H-T-P), devised by J. N. Buck. In this test, the examinee is told to draw as good a picture of a house as he can, the same instructions being repeated in turn with "tree" and "person." Meanwhile, the examiner takes copious notes on time, sequence of parts drawn, spontaneous comments, and expressions of emotion. The completion of the drawings is followed by an oral inquiry, including a long set of standardized questions. The drawings are analyzed both quantitatively and qualitatively, chiefly on the basis of their formal or stylistic characteristics.

In discussing the rationale underlying the choice of objects to be drawn, Buck maintains that "house" should arouse associations concerning the individual's home and those living with him; "tree" should evoke associations pertaining to his life role and his ability to derive satisfaction from his environment in general; and "person" should call up associations dealing with interpersonal relations. Some clinicians may find helpful leads in such drawings, when they are considered jointly with other information about the individual case. But the elaborate and lengthy administrative and scoring procedures described by Buck appear unwarranted in the light of the highly inadequate nature of the supporting data.

TOY TESTS. Toys and dramatic objects, such as puppets, dolls, and miniatures, have been widely utilized in projective testing. Originating in play therapy with children, these materials have subsequently been adapted for the diagnostic testing of both adults and children. The objects are usually selected because of their expected associative value. Among the articles most frequently employed for these purposes, for example, are dolls representing adults and children of both sexes, furniture, bathroom and kitchen fixtures, and other household furnishings. Play with such articles is expected to reveal the child's attitudes toward his own family, as well as sibling rivalries, fears, aggressions, conflicts, and the like. The examiner notes what items the child chooses and what he does with them, as well as his verbalizations, emotional expressions, and other overt behavior.

With children, these techniques often take the form of free play with the collection of toys that the examiner simply makes available. With adults, the materials are presented with general instructions to carry out some task of a highly unstructured nature. These instructions may, of course, also be employed with children. Frequently the task has certain dramatic features, as in the arrangement of figures on a miniature stage set. Several investigators have used play techniques in studying prejudice and other intergroup attitudes (Campbell, 1950).

One attempt to standardize projective toy tests is represented by the World Test. First developed in England by Lowenfeld (1939), this test has been adapted, revised, and restandardized by Buhler and her associates (1951), Bolgar and Fischer (1947), and others.[2] The materials consist of a large number of miniature pieces—from 150 to 300 in different forms—including houses, people, animals, bridges, trees, cars, fences, and other common objects that might be found outdoors. The subject is told to construct whatever he would like, using a large table top, the floor, or a sandbox as a base. In the various adaptations of the World Test, the responses have been evaluated in a number of ways. Some interpretive systems rely chiefly on formal properties of procedure and product, such as sequence of pieces chosen, number and variety of objects included, rigidity of organization, and the like. Others place more emphasis on content and symbolism. Accompanying verbalizations and other expressive reactions are also considered.

EVALUATION OF PROJECTIVE TECHNIQUES

It is evident that projective techniques differ widely among themselves. Some appear more promising than others because of more favorable empirical findings, sounder theoretical orientation, or both. Regarding some techniques, such as the Rorschach, voluminous data have been gathered, although their interpretation is often uncertain. About others little is known, either because of their recent origin, or because objective verifica-

[2] The latest version prepared by Buhler—and the only one listed in Appendix C and in the *Mental Measurements Yearbooks*—is called the Toy World Test to distinguish it from Buhler's more recently developed Picture World Test.

tion is hindered by the intrinsic nature of the instruments or by the attitudes of their exponents.

To evaluate each instrument individually and to attempt to summarize the extensive pertinent literature would require a separate volume. Within this chapter, critical comments have been interjected only in the cases of instruments that presented unique features—whether of a favorable or unfavorable nature. There are certain points, however, that apply to a greater or lesser extent to the bulk of projective techniques. These points can be conveniently considered in summary form.

RAPPORT AND APPLICABILITY. Most projective techniques represent an effective means for "breaking the ice" during the initial contacts between subject and examiner. The task is usually intrinsically interesting and often entertaining. It tends to divert the individual's attention away from himself and thus reduces embarrassment and defensiveness. And it offers little or no threat to his prestige, since any response he gives is "right."

Certain projective techniques may be especially useful with young children, illiterates, and persons with language handicaps or speech defects. Nonverbal media would be readily applicable to all these groups. And oral responses to pictorial and other nonlanguage stimuli could be secured from the first two. With all these verbally limited groups, projective techniques may help the examinee to communicate with the examiner. These techniques may also aid the individual in clarifying for himself some of his own behavior that he had not previously verbalized.

FAKING. In general, projective instruments are less susceptible to faking than are self-report inventories. The purpose of projective techniques is usually disguised. Even if an individual has some psychological sophistication and is familiar with the general nature of a particular instrument, such as the Rorschach or TAT, it is still unlikely that he can predict the intricate ways in which his responses will be scored and interpreted. Moreover, the examinee soon becomes absorbed in the task and hence is less likely to resort to the customary disguises and restraints of interpersonal communication.

On the other hand, it cannot be assumed that projective tests are completely immune to faking. Several experiments with the Rorschach, TAT, and other projective instruments have shown that significant differences do occur when subjects are instructed to alter their responses so as to create favorable or unfavorable impressions, or when they are given statements suggesting that certain types of responses are more desirable (Masling, 1960). In a particularly well-controlled study, Davids and Pildner (1958) administered a battery of self-report and projective tests to two groups of college students, one of which took the tests as genuine job applicants, the other as participants in a research project. Under these conditions, the job applicants obtained significantly better-adjusted scores than the research subjects on the self-report but *not* on the projective tests. Certain types of projective test items, however, were found to be susceptible to faking. For example, sentence completion stems expressed in the first person yielded significantly more favorable responses than those expressed in the third person.

EXAMINER AND SITUATIONAL VARIABLES. It is obvious that most projective techniques are inadequately standardized with respect to both administration and scoring. Yet there is evidence that even subtle differences in the phrasing of verbal instructions and in examiner-subject relationships can appreciably alter performance on these tests (Baughman, 1951; Hamilton & Robertson, 1966; Herron, 1964; Klinger, 1966; Masling, 1960; Sarason, 1954). Presenting the Holtzman Inkblot Technique as an intelligence test, for example, yielded scores in several variables that were significantly different from the scores obtained with the standard instructional set (Herron, 1964). Even when employing identical instructions, some examiners may be more encouraging or reassuring, others more threatening, owing to their general manner and appearance. Such differences may affect response productivity, defensiveness, stereotypy, imaginativeness, and other basic performance characteristics. In the light of these findings, problems of administration and testing conditions assume even greater importance than in other psychological tests.

Equally serious is the lack of objectivity in scoring. Even when objective scoring systems have been developed, the final steps in the evaluation and integration of the raw data depend on the skill and clinical experience of the examiner. Such a situation has several implications. In the first place, it reduces the number of examiners who are properly qualified to employ the technique and thus limits the range of its effective application. It also means that the results obtained by different examiners may not be comparable, a fact that complicates research with the instrument. But perhaps the most disturbing implication is that the interpretation of scores is often as projective for the examiner as the test stimuli are for the examinee. In other words, the final interpretation of projective test responses may reveal more about the theoretical orientation, favorite hypotheses, and personality idiosyncrasies of the examiner than it does about the examinee's personality dynamics.

NORMS. Another conspicuous deficiency common to most projective instruments pertains to normative data. Such data may be completely lacking, grossly inadequate, or based on vaguely described populations. In the absence of adequate objective norms, the clinician falls back on his "general clinical experience" to interpret projective test performance. But such a frame of reference is subject to all the distortions of memory that are themselves reflections of theoretical bias, preconceptions, and other idiosyncrasies of the clinician. Moreover, any one clinician's contacts may have been limited largely to persons who are atypical in education, socioeconomic level, sex ratio, age distribution, or other relevant characteristics. In at least one respect, the clinician's experience is almost certain to produce a misleading picture, since he deals predominantly with maladjusted or pathological cases. He thus lacks sufficient firsthand familiarity with the characteristic reactions of normal people. The Rorschach norms gathered by Ames and her associates on children, adolescents, and persons over 70 represent one effort to correct some of the more obvious lacks in this regard.

Interpretation of projective test performance often involves subgroup norms, of either a subjective or an objective nature. Thus, the clinician may have a general subjective picture of what constitutes a "typical" schizophrenic or psychoneurotic performance on a particular test. Or the published data may provide qualitative or quantitative norms that delineate the characteristic performance of different diagnostic groups. In either case, the subgroup norms may lead to faulty interpretations unless the subgroups were equated in other respects. For example, if the schizophrenics and normals on whom the norms were derived differed also in educational level, the observed disparities between schizophrenic and normal performance may have resulted from educational inequality rather than from schizophrenia. Similar systematic or constant errors may operate in the comparison of various psychiatric syndromes. For example, schizophrenics as a group tend to be younger than manic-depressives; anxiety neurotics are likely to come from higher educational and socioeconomic levels than hysterics.

RELIABILITY. In view of the relatively unstandardized scoring procedures and the inadequacies of normative data, *scorer reliability* becomes an important consideration in projective testing. For projective techniques, a proper measure of scorer reliability should include not only the more objective preliminary scoring, but also the final integrative and interpretive stages. It is not enough, for example, to demonstrate that examiners who have mastered the same system of Rorschach scoring agree closely in their tallying of such characteristics as whole, unusual detail, or color responses. On a projective test like the Rorschach, these raw quantitative measures cannot be interpreted directly from a table of norms, as in the usual type of psychological test. Interpretive scorer reliability is concerned with the extent to which different examiners attribute the same personality characteristics to the examinee on the basis of their interpretations of the identical record.

Few adequate studies have been conducted on the scorer reliability of projective tests. Some investigations have revealed marked divergencies in the interpretations given by reasonably well-qualified test users. A fundamental ambiguity in such results stems from the unknown contribution of the interpreter's skill. Neither high nor low scorer reliability can be directly generalized to other scorers differing appreciably from those utilized in the particular investigation.

Attempts to measure other types of test reliability have fared equally poorly in the field of projective testing. Coefficients of *internal consistency*, when computed, have usually been low. In such tests as the Rorschach, TAT, and Rosenzweig P-F Study, it has been argued that different cards or items are not comparable and hence should not be used in finding split-half reliabilities. In fact, individual items in such instruments were designed to measure different variables. Moreover, the trend of responses over successive items is often considered significant in interpreting responses. One solution, of course, would be to construct a parallel form that *is* comparable, as was done in the Holtzman Inkblot Technique. It should also be noted that insofar as responses to different cards or items are combined in arriving at a total estimate of any personality characteristic, interitem agreement is assumed. Yet empirical results have rarely supported this assumption.

Retest reliability also presents special problems. With long intervals, genuine personality changes may occur which the test should detect. With short intervals, a retest may show no more than recall of original responses. When investigators instructed their subjects to write different TAT stories on a retest, in order to determine whether the same themes would recur, most of the scored variables yielded insignificant retest correlations (Lindzey & Herman, 1955). It is also relevant to note that many scores derived from projective techniques are based on very inadequate response samples. In the case of the Rorschach, for instance, the number of responses within a given individual's protocol that fall into such categories as animal movement, human movement, shading, color, unusual detail, and the like may be so few as to yield extremely unreliable indices. Large chance variations are to be expected under such circumstances. Ratios and percentages computed with such unreliable measures are even more unstable than the individual measures themselves (Cronbach, 1949, pp. 411–412).

VALIDITY. For any test, the most fundamental question is that of validity. Many validation studies of projective tests have been concerned with concurrent criterion-related validity. Most of these have compared the performance of contrasted groups, such as occupational or diagnostic groups. As was pointed out in connection with norms, however, these groups often differ in other respects, such as age or education. Other investigations of concurrent validity have used essentially a matching technique, in which personality descriptions derived from test records are compared with descriptions or data about the same subjects taken from case histories, psychiatric interviews, or long-range behavioral records. A few studies have investigated predictive validity against such criteria as success in specialized types of training, job performance, or response to psychotherapy. There has been an increasing trend to investigate the construct validity of projective instruments by testing specific hypotheses that underlie the use and interpretation of each test.

The large majority of published validation studies on projective techniques are inconclusive because of procedural deficiencies in either experimental controls or statistical analysis, or both. This is especially true of studies concerned with the Rorschach. Some methodological deficiencies may have the effect of producing *spurious evidence of validity* where none exists. An example is the contamination of either criterion or test data. Thus, the criterion judges may have had some knowledge of the subjects' test performance. Similarly, the examiner may have obtained cues about the subject's characteristics from conversation with him in the course of test administration, or from case history material and other non-test sources. The customary control for the latter type of contamination in validation studies is to utilize blind analysis, in which the test record is interpreted by a scorer who has had no contact with the subject and who has no information about him other than that contained in the test protocol. Clinicians have argued, however, that blind analysis is an unnatural way to interpret projective test responses and does not correspond to the way these instruments are used in clinical practice.

Another common source of spurious validity data is failure to cross-validate (see, e.g., Kinslinger, 1966). Because of the large number of potential diagnostic signs or scorable elements that can be derived from most projective tests, it is very easy by chance alone to find a set of such signs that differentiate significantly between criterion groups. The validity of such a scoring key, however, will collapse to zero when applied to new samples.

A more subtle form of error is illustrated by stereotype accuracy. Certain descriptive statements, such as might occur in a Rorschach protocol, may apply widely to persons in general, or to young men, or to hospitalized patients, or to whatever category of subjects is sampled by the particular investigation.[3] Agreement between criterion and test data with regard to such statements would therefore yield a spurious impression of validity. Some check on this error is needed, such as a measure of the agreement between the test evaluation of one subject and the criterion evaluation of another subject in the same category. This measure would indicate the amount of spurious agreement resulting from stereotype accuracy under the conditions of the particular investigation (see, e.g., Silverman, 1959).

Inadequacies of experimental design may also have the opposite effect

---

[3] The use of such generally applicable statements was characterized by D. G. Paterson as "personality description after the manner of P. T. Barnum" and was subsequently labeled the "Barnum effect" by Meehl (1956).

of *underestimating the validity* of a diagnostic instrument. It is widely recognized, for example, that traditional psychiatric categories, such as schizophrenia, manic-depressive psychosis, and hysteria, represent crude and unrealistic classifications of the personality disorders actually manifested by patients. Hence, if such diagnostic categories are used as the sole criterion for checking the validity of a personality test, negative results are inconclusive. Similarly, failure to predict occupational criteria may reflect no more than the examiner's ignorance of the traits required for the jobs under consideration. When such criteria are employed, it is also possible that the projective test is a valid measure of the personality traits it is designed to measure, but that these traits are irrelevant to success in the chosen criterion situations.

Those who stress the importance of configural scoring, response patterns, and trait interrelationships in personality assessment have also objected to attempts to validate isolated scores or diagnostic signs derived from projective techniques. That insignificant correlations may result from failure to allow for complex patterns of relationship among personality variables can be illustrated by studies of aggression indicators in TAT stories. In interpreting the results of such investigations, it has been repeatedly pointed out that the hypothesized relation between aggression in fantasy, as revealed in the TAT, and aggression in overt behavior is not a simple one. Depending on other concomitant personality characteristics, high aggression in fantasy may be associated with either high or low overt aggression. There is some evidence suggesting that, if strong aggressive tendencies are accompanied by high anxiety or fear of punishment, expressions of aggression will tend to be high in fantasy and low in overt behavior; when anxiety and fear of punishment are low, high fantasy aggression is associated with high overt aggression (Mussen & Naylor, 1954; Pittluck, 1950).

Lack of significant correlation between expressions of aggression in TAT stories and in overt behavior in a random sample of cases is thus consistent with expectation, since the relation may be positive in some individuals and negative in others. Obviously, however, such a lack of correlation is also consistent with the hypothesis that the test has no validity at all in detecting aggressive tendencies. What is needed, of course, is more studies using complex experimental designs that permit an analysis of the conditions under which each assumption is applicable.

Few research projects have been so designed as to avoid all the major pitfalls of projective test validation. The reader is urged to examine for himself the reports of such studies as those of Golden (1964), Henry and Farley (1959), Little and Shneidman (1959), and Silverman (1959), which set a high standard in experimental design. While differing in type of subject examined and in specific problems they set out to investigate, these studies point to a common conclusion: when experienced clinicians are given an opportunity to examine and interpret in their own way subjects' protocols from such projective tests as the Rorschach and TAT, their evaluations of the subjects' personalities tend to match independent case history evaluations significantly better than chance. Insofar as can be ascertained, however, the obtained relations are low. Moreover, the relationship appears to be a function of the particular clinician and subject, a number of individual matches being no better than chance. There is also little agreement among evaluations based on different projective techniques, or among different clinicians using the same technique.

PSYCHOMETRIC INSTRUMENT VERSUS CLINICAL TOOL

THE PROJECTIVE HYPOTHESIS. It is a fundamental assumption of all projective techniques that the individual's responses to the ambiguous stimuli presented to him reflect significant and relatively enduring personality attributes. Yet there is a large and growing body of research data indicating that many other factors affect the individual's projective test responses. To the extent that retest reliability has been measured, marked temporal shifts have frequently been observed, indicating the operation of considerable chance error. More direct evidence regarding the susceptibility of projective test responses to temporary states is provided by several experimental studies demonstrating the effect of such factors as hunger, sleep deprivation, drugs, anxiety, and frustration on such responses.

The response variability associated with even slight changes in stimulus characteristics, furthermore, suggests that the responses are stimulus-specific and hence of questionable generalizability. Significant response differences have likewise been found in relation to instructional sets, examiner characteristics, and the examinee's perception of the testing situation. Ability factors—and particularly verbal ability—clearly affect scores on most projective tests. In the light of all these findings, projective test responses can be meaningfully interpreted only when the examiner has extensive information about the circumstances under which they were obtained and the aptitudes and experiential background of the examinee.

From another angle, the advantages of using unstructured or ambiguous stimuli have been questioned (Epstein, 1966). Such stimuli are ambiguous for the examiner as well as for the subject; thus, they tend to increase the ambiguity of the examiner's interpretations of the subject's responses. With structured stimuli, on the other hand, it is possible to select stimuli relevant to the personality characteristics to be assessed and to vary the nature of the stimuli in a systematic and balanced manner so as to fully explore a given personality dimension. Such a procedure makes for clearer interpretation of test performance than is possible with the shotgun approach of unstructured stimuli. There is also evidence against the common assumption that the less structured the stimuli the more likely they are to elicit projection and to tap "deep" layers of personality (Murstein, 1963). Actually the relation between ambiguity and projection appears to be non-linear, with an intermediate degree of ambiguity representing an optimum for purposes of projection.

The assumption that fantasy, as elicited by such projective techniques as the TAT, reveals covert motivational dispositions has also been called into question. One survey of the experimental literature on the projective assessment of achievement need indicated that the data were more nearly consistent with alternative explanations involving perceptual and cognitive factors (Klinger, 1966). Similarly, in a 20-year longitudinal study of TAT fantasy and relevant overt behavior, adolescent activities predicted adult TAT imagery much better than adolescent TAT imagery predicted adult activities (McClelland, 1966; Skolnick, 1966). For example, individuals who had shown upward social mobility obtained higher scores on achievement need as adults; but those who obtained higher achievement need scores in adolescence were not among the ones who subsequently showed upward social mobility.

Findings such as these reverse the relationship implied by the traditional rationale of projective techniques. They can be explained if we regard TAT responses, not as direct projective expressions of motives, but as samples of the individual's thoughts, which may in turn have been influenced by his previous actions. Individuals who have achieved more and those who were more often exposed to achievement-oriented models in their developmental history tend to perceive more achievement themes in unstructured pictures.

In summary, many types of research have tended to cast doubt on the projective hypothesis. There is ample evidence that alternative explanations may account as well or better for the individual's responses to unstructured test stimuli.

PROJECTIVE TECHNIQUES AS PSYCHOMETRIC INSTRUMENTS. Besides their questionable theoretical rationale, projective techniques are clearly found wanting when evaluated in accordance with test standards. This is evident from the data summarized in the preceding section with regard to standardization of administration and scoring procedures, adequacy of norms, reliability, and validity. The accumulation of published studies that have *failed* to demonstrate any validity for such projective techniques as the Rorschach and the D-A-P is truly impressive. Yet after three decades of negative results, the status of projective techniques remains unchanged. In the words of one reviewer, "There are still enthusiastic clinicians and doubting statisticians" (Adcock, 1965).

This apparent contradiction can perhaps be understood if we recognize that, with a few possible exceptions, projective techniques are not truly tests. One notable exception is the Holtzman Inkblot Technique, in whose development a systematic effort was made to follow psychometric procedures. Another possible candidate for this category is the Rosenzweig P-F Study. It is interesting to note in this connection that both of these instruments have proved to be equally applicable in group and individual forms —a finding not generally characteristic of projective techniques, where the interpersonal relation between examiner and subject is often an integral part of the examining process. Even in the case of these two instruments, however, there is need for much more validity data to specify the nature of the constructs measured by their scores, as well as for more normative data on clearly defined populations. Thus, while coming closer to meeting test standards than have other projective techniques, even these instruments are not ready for routine operational use.

A few other examples of quasi-tests could undoubtedly be found among the many remaining projective techniques that were not discussed in this chapter.[4] Such exceptions, however, only serve to demonstrate that unstructured stimuli may be used in constructing psychometric instruments. The fact remains, nevertheless, that they have not been so used in the vast majority of projective techniques, particularly in the more popular and firmly entrenched techniques.

PROJECTIVE TECHNIQUES AS CLINICAL TOOLS. Rather than being regarded and evaluated as psychometric instruments, or *tests* in the strict sense of the term, projective techniques are coming more and more to be regarded as clinical tools. Thus, they may serve as supplementary qualitative interviewing aids in the hands of a skilled clinician. Their value as clinical tools is proportional to the skill of the clinician and hence cannot be assessed independently of the individual clinician using them. Attempts to evaluate them in terms of the usual psychometric procedures would thus be inappropriate. But by the same token, the use of elaborate scoring systems that yield quantitative scores is not only wasteful but also misleading. Such scoring procedures lend the scores an illusory semblance of objectivity and may create the unwarranted impression that the given technique can be treated as a test. What value projective techniques may have is more likely to emerge when they are interpreted by qualitative, clinical procedures than when they are quantitatively scored and interpreted as psychometric instruments (see, e.g., Lindzey, 1965).

Borrowing a concept from information theory, Cronbach and Gleser (1965) characterized interviewing and projective techniques as "wideband" procedures. Bandwidth, or breadth of coverage, is achieved at the cost of lowered fidelity or dependability of information. Objective psychometric tests characteristically yield a narrow band of information at a high

---

[4] A series of quantitative rating scales for scoring both the Rorschach and the TAT, developed by Zubin, Eron, and Schumer (1965), represent an ambitious effort to convert these projective techniques into psychometric instruments; but the practical applicability and the validity of these scales remain to be demonstrated.

level of dependability. In contrast, projective and interviewing techniques provide a much wider range of information of lower dependability. Moreover, the kinds of data furnished by any one projective technique may vary from individual to individual. One person's TAT responses, for example, may tell us a good deal about his aggression and little or nothing about his creativity or achievement need; another person's record may permit a thorough assessment of the degree of creativity of his behavior and of the strength of his achievement need, while revealing little about his aggression. Such a lack of uniformity in the kinds of information provided in individual cases helps to explain the low validities found when projective test responses are analyzed for any single trait across a group of persons.

It is interesting to note that a similar unevenness characterizes clinicians' interpretations of individual records. Thus, in their study of the validity of the TAT, Henry and Farley (1959, p. 22) conclude:

> There is no single correct way of employing the TAT interpretation. There was little item agreement between judges, but each judge made enough "correct" decisions to yield a highly significant agreement figure. Judges may arrive at essentially the same interpretive implications of the test report, by quite different routes; or judges may differ individually in their ability to utilize TAT predictions in different areas . . . or for different subjects.

The nature of clinical judgment through which projective and interviewing data may be utilized in reaching decisions about individual cases is receiving increasing attention from psychologists (see Ch. 6). In this process, the very constructs or categories in terms of which the data are organized are built up inductively through an examination of the particular combination of data available in the individual case. The special function of the clinician is to make predictions from unique or rare combinations of events about which it is impracticable to prepare any statistical table or equation. By creating new constructs to fit the individual case, the clinician can predict from combinations of events that he has never encountered before in any other case. In making his predictions, he can also take into account the varied significance of similar events for different individuals. Such clinical predictions are helpful, provided they are not accepted as final but are constantly tested against information elicited through subsequent inquiry, test responses, reaction to therapy, or other behavior on the part of the subject. It follows from the nature of interviewing and projective techniques that decisions should not be based on any single datum or score obtained from such sources. These techniques serve best in sequential decisions, by suggesting leads for further exploration or hypotheses about the individual for subsequent verification.

CHAPTER **20**

Other Techniques for Personality Assessment

THE SELF-REPORT inventories and projective techniques surveyed in the preceding chapters represent the best-known and most widely used instruments for personality appraisal. Nevertheless, there still remains a rich supply of other devices that are being explored for this purpose. Out of this diversity of approaches may come techniques that will eventually stimulate progress in new directions. The procedures to be considered in this chapter are principally research techniques, although some may also serve as supplementary clinical aids in the hands of a skilled clinician. While representing a wide variety of approaches, these procedures fall into three major categories: situational tests; stylistic tests utilizing perceptual, cognitive, or evaluative tasks; and procedures designed to assess self-concepts and personal constructs. In the last section of the chapter, we shall consider the role of direct behavioral observations in personality assessment.

SITUATIONAL TESTS

Although the term "situational test" was popularized during and following World War II, tests fitting this description had been developed prior to that time. Essentially, a situational test is one that places the examinee in a situation closely resembling or simulating a "real-life" criterion situation. Such tests thus show certain basic similarities to the worksample technique employed in constructing vocational achievement tests (Ch. 16). In the present tests, however, the criterion behavior that is sampled is more varied and complex. Moreover, performance is not evaluated in terms of abilities and knowledge, but in terms of emotional, social, attitudinal, and other personality variables.

TESTS OF THE CHARACTER EDUCATION INQUIRY. Among the earliest situational tests—although they were not so labeled at the time—were those constructed by Hartshorne, May, and their associates (1928, 1929, 1930) for the Character Education Inquiry (CEI). These tests were designed principally as research instruments for use in an extensive project on the nature and development of character in children. Nevertheless, the techniques can be adapted to other testing purposes, and a number have been so utilized.

In general, the CEI techniques made use of familiar, natural situations within the schoolchild's daily routine. The tests were administered in the form of regular classroom examinations, as part of the pupil's homework, in the course of athletic contests, or as party games. Moreover, the children were not aware that they were being tested, except insofar as ordinary school examinations might be involved in the procedure. At the same time, all of the Hartshorne-May tests represented carefully standardized instruments which yielded objective, quantitative scores.

The CEI tests were designed to measure such behavior characteristics as honesty, self-control, and altruism. The largest number of tests in the CEI series were concerned with honesty in situations providing opportunities for cheating. One group of tests developed for this purpose utilized a duplicating technique. In this technique, common tests such as vocabulary, sentence completion, or arithmetic reasoning were administered in the classroom. The test papers were then collected and a duplicate of each child's responses was made. At a subsequent session, the original, unmarked test papers were returned, and each child scored his own paper from a key. Comparison with the duplicate record revealed any changes the individual had made in scoring his paper.

Another technique for the detection of cheating was based on improbable achievement. In this case, a task was given under such conditions that achievement above a certain empirically established level indicated cheating. Among the tasks utilized for this purpose were weight discrimination, the solution of various mechanical puzzles, and paper-and-pencil tests of motor coordination. An example of the last-named type of test is provided by the Circles Puzzle. In this test, the child was instructed to make a mark in each of 10 small, irregularly arranged circles, while keeping his eyes shut. Control tests under conditions that precluded peeking indicated that a score of more than 13 correctly placed marks in a total of three trials was highly improbable. By peeking, however, the child might obtain a higher score.

Another type of honesty test utilized a written questionnaire with items such as the following (Hartshorne & May, 1928):

Did you ever act greedily by taking more than your share of anything?

Are you always on time at school or for other appointments?

Do you always smile when things go wrong?

Did you ever say anything about your teacher that you would be unwilling to say to her face?

On the basis of empirical investigations, it was decided that a child who answered 24 or more of these questions in the socially approved direction was probably lying to create a favorable impression. This test will be recognized as a precursor of the MMPI L scale.

Self-control was assessed in part by the length of time the child persisted in a given task, such as solving a difficult puzzle or reading the ending of a story in which the words were run together. In the latter test, the examiner read aloud the beginning of an exciting story. The children were then given pages containing the rest of the story printed in a form that made reading difficult. As the end of the story was approached, moreover, the difficulty of deciphering the words increased further, as shown in the three successive samples given below (Hartshorne, May, & Maller, 1929):

CHARLESLIFTEDLUCILLETOHISBACK"PUTYOURARMSTIGHTAROUNDMY
NECKANDHOLDON

NoWhoWTogETBaCkONthETREStle.HoWTOBRingTHaTTerrIfIEDBURDeN
OFAChILDuPtOSafeTY

fiN ALly tAp-tAPC AME ARHYTH Month eBriD GeruNNing fee Tfee Tcom
INGtow ArdT Hem

Other measures of self-control were concerned with the extent to which the child resisted distraction while performing an assigned task. For example, an arithmetic test was administered on two occasions, once under normal and once under distracting conditions. For the latter purpose, the problems were presented on a page covered with cartoonlike sketches, short comments, and other miscellaneous doodles. The larger the difference between the scores obtained on the two occasions, the less successful the child had been in resisting the "pull" of the distracting material.

Most of the CEI tests proved to have good discriminative power, yielding a wide range of individual differences in scores. Reliability also appeared to be fairly satisfactory. The children's responses, however, showed considerable situational specificity. The intercorrelations of different tests within each category (e.g., honesty tests or persistence tests) proved to be very low. This specificity is understandable when we consider the operation of the child's interests, values, and motives in different situations. For example, the child who is motivated to excel in schoolwork is not necessarily concerned about his achievement in athletic contests or party games. These motivational differences would in turn be reflected in the child's behavior on honesty tests administered in these different contexts. The influence of individual teachers was also apparent in the results; children who cheated in one teacher's room would not do so in another teacher's room. Regardless of the results, however, the major contribution of these investigations to testing was in the development of several ingenious techniques that have subsequently been adapted for other purposes.

SITUATIONAL STRESS TESTS. Like the tests developed in the CEI program, situational stress tests are realistic and disguised. The principal difference in the case of stress tests is to be found in the introduction of features designed to induce anxiety or other disruptive emotional states. The individual's reactions to stress may be assessed through objective records of performance on the assigned tasks, qualitative observations by trained observers, or both. Among the most ambitious projects concerned with the development and use of situational stress tests was that undertaken by the United States Office of Strategic Services (OSS) during World War II (Murray & MacKinnon, 1946; OSS Assessment Staff, 1948). The object of this testing program was the evaluation of candidates for assignment to military intelligence. The principal assessment program consisted of a 3-day session of intensive testing and observation. During this period, the candidates lived together in small groups under almost continuous scrutiny by members of the assessment staff. Besides specially constructed situational tests, the program included aptitude tests, projective techniques, intensive interviewing, and general observations under casual and informal conditions. Several of the situational tests were modeled after techniques developed in the German and British armies.

An example of an OSS situational stress test is provided by the Construction Test, in which a 5-foot cube had to be assembled from wooden poles, blocks, and pegs. The subject was informed that, since it was impossible for one man to complete the task within the 10 minutes allotted to it, he would be given two helpers. Actually, the helpers were psychologists who played prearranged roles. One followed a policy of inertia and passive resistance; the other obstructed the work by making impractical suggestions, asking irrelevant and often embarrassing questions, and needling the candidate with ridicule and criticism. So well did the helpers succeed in frustrating the candidates that the construction was never completed in the history of the assessment program. The subject's emotional and interpersonal reactions in this situation were observed and evaluated qualitatively.

Available validity data on situational stress tests are meager (Guilford & Lacey, 1947; Kelly, 1954; OSS Assessment Staff, 1948). A major difficulty arises from the lack of suitable criterion data. In the OSS project, for example, the diversity of individual assignments reduced the possibility of evaluating field performance under comparable conditions for different members of the group. Unreliability of criterion ratings also tends to reduce validity estimates. With these qualifications, it must be noted that, when determined, predictive validity of situational stress tests has proved to be low. Although a few techniques may be promising for special purposes, the contribution of these tests rarely justifies the time, equipment, and highly trained personnel that their administration requires.

LEADERLESS GROUP SITUATIONS. A relatively common type of situational test utilizes a "leaderless group" as a device for appraising such characteristics as cooperation, teamwork, resourcefulness, initiative, and leadership. In such tests, a task is assigned that requires the cooperative efforts of a group of examinees, none of whom is designated as leader or given specific responsibilities. Examples from the OSS program include the Brook Situation, involving the transfer of personnel and equipment across a brook with maximum speed and safety; and the Wall Situation, in which men and materials had to be conveyed over a double wall separated by an imaginary canyon.

A promising variant of this technique is the Leaderless Group Discussion (LGD). Requiring a minimum of equipment and time, this technique has been used widely in the selection of such groups as military officers, civil service supervisors and administrators, industrial executives and management trainees, sales trainees, teachers, and social workers (Bass, 1954). It has also been employed in research on leadership (Bass, 1959; Carter, 1954), on the effects of counseling (Pepinsky, Siegel, & Vanatta, 1952), and on the selection of clinical psychology trainees (Kelly & Fiske, 1951). Essentially, the group is assigned a topic for discussion during a specified period. Examiners observe and rate each person's performance, but do not participate in the discussion. Although often used under informal and unstandardized conditions, the LGD has been subjected to considerable research. Rater reliability has been found to be reasonably high for both LGD and other situational tests based on group decision-making through discussion (Greenwood & McNamara, 1967).

Validity studies suggest that LGD techniques are among the most effective applications of situational tests. Many significant and sizeable correlations have been found between ratings from LGD performance and follow-up or concurrent ratings obtained in military, industrial, and social settings (Bass, 1954; Guilford, 1959). Some of these correlations are as high as .60. It is also interesting to note that leadership ratings based on a one-hour LGD correlated over .60 with leadership assessment from three days of situational testing in the OSS program (OSS Assessment Staff, 1948). A similar correlation between LGD and an entire battery of situational tests was found by Vernon (1950) in a British study.

Neither LGD nor other, more elaborate situational tests, however, have proved valid as devices for assessing broad personality traits (Kelly, 1954; Kelly & Fiske, 1951; OSS Assessment Staff, 1948). All such tests appear to be most effective when they approximate actual worksamples of the criterion behavior they are designed to predict. The LGD tests in particular have some validity in predicting performance in jobs requiring a certain amount of verbal communication, verbal problem-solving, and acceptance by peers. Another factor that seems to increase the predictive validity of situational tests is job familiarity on the part of the raters (Holmen, 1956; Vernon, 1950). Such a finding again suggests that situational tests work best when the examinee's performance is interpreted as a worksample rather than in terms of underlying personality variables.

ROLE PLAYING. Some situational tests employ role playing to obtain a sample of interpersonal, job-relevant behavior. The problem situations presented in these tests involve the sort of face-to-face contacts common in administrative jobs. Several such tests have been developed for military use in assessing the leadership and human-relations skills of officers (Flanagan, 1954b). An example of such a role-playing situation is described below (American Institutes for Research, 1957):

The examinee is evaluated as the commanding officer of a small ship. He must discuss with Ensign Baker, the ship's engineering officer, an unsatisfactory performance report he is about to submit. Although Baker is highly qualified in the technical skills required, he lacks experience. He has allowed the enlisted men to run his department. This has led to no specific incident in which his department has interfered with the ship's operating efficiency, but his behavior has set a bad example for the men and the other officers on board.

The examinee is instructed to assume the given role and carry out the interview with "Ensign Baker," whose part is played by a trained actor. The examiner observes and evaluates the individual's performance with the aid of a previously developed checklist of effective and ineffective behaviors. Examples of such behaviors include: Gives reason for meeting; allows Baker to direct conversation; vacillates in, or changes position on, unsatisfactory report; mentions Baker's fine engineering background; mentions constructive nature of Fitness Report.

STYLISTIC TESTS

A major trend in personality testing today is the development of a wide variety of simple and comparatively objective tests, which call for perceptual, cognitive, or evaluative activities. In common with the previously discussed situational tests, these techniques can be characterized as relatively structured and disguised. Rather than attempting to utilize complex, lifelike, realistic situations, however, these tests present the examinee with an artificial task bearing little or no resemblance to the criterion to be predicted. The tests under consideration represent efforts to identify behavior that may serve as a valid predictor of a criterion, without being a direct sample of criterion behavior. For this reason, these techniques have sometimes been described as "indirect" tests.

Although varying widely in content and specific techniques, these tests have several common distinguishing features. First, the examinee is *task-oriented*, rather than being report-oriented as in personality questionnaires. He is given an objective task to perform, rather than being asked to describe his habitual behavior. Second, the purpose of these tests is *disguised*, the individual not realizing which aspects of his performance are to be scored. Third, the tasks set for the examinee are *structured*. In this feature lies their principal difference from the tasks utilized in projective techniques. To be sure, structuring is a matter of degree. As a group, however, the tests now under consideration are more highly structured than are typical projective devices.

A fourth and related feature pertains to the *apparent existence of a "right solution"* for each task or problem—at least from the examinee's viewpoint. Thus, many of the tests are perceived as aptitude measures, in which the examinee endeavors to give "correct" answers. True, the instruments are not actually treated as aptitude tests, nor are they scored on the basis of right and wrong responses. But the individual's approach to the test is nevertheless quite unlike that encouraged by projective tests, in which "anything goes." Finally, the rationale underlying the construction of such tests is based on the concept of *personal styles*, or broad stylistic traits of behavior, which may be manifested in a wide variety of dissimilar activities or media.

Major research projects that included the development of personality tests in the present category have been conducted under the direction of Thurstone (1951b, 1953), MacKinnon (1966), Cattell (Cattell, 1957; Cattell & Warburton, 1967), Eysenck (1960), and others. In addition to these comprehensive and continuing projects, other investigators have been engaged in developing single tests of the same nature for specific purposes. It might be added that several tests discussed in earlier chapters could also be included in the present category. This is true, for example, of the various sorting and perceptual tests described in Chapter 12, the Porteus Mazes cited in Chapter 10, and some of the more highly standardized projective techniques covered in Chapter 19.

PERCEPTUAL FUNCTIONS. One of the principal sources of the simple, objective personality tests under consideration is to be found in the area of perceptual functions. A large body of experimental literature has demonstrated significant relationships between the individual's attitudinal, motivational, or emotional characteristics and his performance on perceptual or cognitive tasks (Blake & Ramsey, 1951; Bruner & Krech, 1950; Jenkin,

1957; Witkin *et al.*, 1954). It should also be recognized that a number of projective techniques—notably the Rorschach—are essentially perceptual tests.

Of the factors identified in factorial analyses of perception, two that have proved particularly fruitful in personality research are speed of closure and flexibility of closure (Pemberton, 1952; Thurstone, 1944). The first involves the rapid recognition of a familiar word, object, or other figure in a relatively unorganized or mutilated visual field. Typical items from a test found to be highly saturated with this factor (Street Gestalt Completion) are reproduced in Figure 117. Flexibility of closure requires the identification of a figure amid distracting and confusing details. Two items

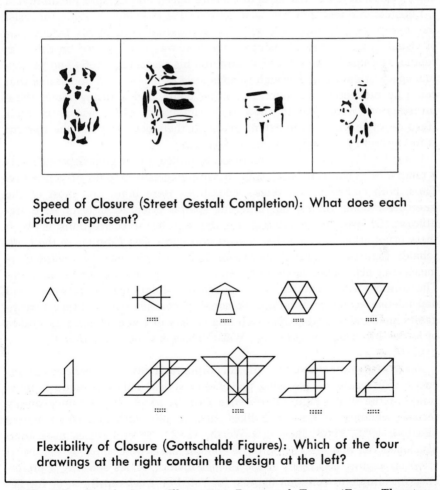

Speed of Closure (Street Gestalt Completion): What does each picture represent?

Flexibility of Closure (Gottschaldt Figures): Which of the four drawings at the right contain the design at the left?

FIG. 117. Sample Items Illustrating Perceptual Tests. (From Thurstone, 1950, p. 7.)

from a test with a high loading in this factor (Gottschaldt Figures) are also shown in Figure 117. Several studies have reported suggestive data indicating possible relationships between each of these factors and personality traits. In one investigation (Pemberton, 1952), for example, persons who excelled in speed of closure tended to rate themselves as sociable, quick in reactions, artistic, self-confident, systematic, neat and precise, and disliking logical and theoretical problems. In contrast, those scoring high in flexibility of closure had high self-ratings on such traits as socially retiring, independent of the opinions of others, analytical, interested in theoretical and scientific problems, and disliking rigid systematization and routine. Commercially available forms of these two perceptual tests have been published under the titles of Closure Speed and Closure Flexibility.

Considerable research has been done on the individual's ability to resist the disruptive influence of conflicting contextual cues in his perceptions of visual forms and relationships. Attention was first focused on this perceptual variable by the work of Witkin and his associates (1954) on perceptual space orientation. Through various tests utilizing a rod and frame that could be independently moved, a tilting chair, and a tilting room, these investigators were able to show that individuals differ widely in their "field dependence," or the extent to which their perception of the upright is influenced by the surrounding visual field.

Considerable evidence was amassed to indicate that field dependence is a relatively stable, consistent trait, having a certain amount of generality. Thus, both odd-even and retest reliabilities were high, and most of the intercorrelations among the different spatial orientation tests were significant. Of even more interest are the significant correlations between these orientation tests and the Embedded-Figure Test (similar to the Gottschaldt Figures illustrated in Figure 117), which may be regarded as measuring field dependence in a purely visual, paper-and-pencil situation. The authors also reported some suggestive relationships between field dependence scores and various personality characteristics. Other investigators have followed this approach in a variety of contexts, such as studies of leadership behavior (see, e.g., Weissenberg & Gruenfeld, 1966).

AESTHETIC PREFERENCES.   Another approach utilizes aesthetic preferences as a means of assessing personality styles. This technique is illustrated by the Welsh Figure Preference Test, in which the examinee simply records whether he likes or dislikes each of 400 black and white figures (Barron, 1952, 1958; Barron & Welsh, 1952). Several scales have been developed for this test, some on a content basis and some by empirical criterion keying. Examples of the former include scales showing a preference for simple or complex figures, for ruled or freehand lines, or for figures suggesting movement. Among the empirical scales, two that have successfully withstood cross validation are the Neuropsychiatric Scale, differentiating between neuropsychiatric patients and normals, and the Barron-Welsh Art Scale, differentiating between the responses of artists and non-artists.[1] Two items from the latter scale are reproduced in Figure 118.

Subsequent research suggests that performance on the Barron-Welsh Art Scale may be related to creativity, not only in art but also in other fields. There is also considerable data on its relation to personality variables. For example, low scorers on the Barron-Welsh Scale tended more often to yield to social pressure, while high scorers tended more often to

FIG. 118. Typical Figures from the Barron-Welsh Art Scale of the Welsh Figure Preference Test. For each figure, the respondent merely records "Like" or "Don't Like." (Reproduced by permission of George S. Welsh.)

form independent judgments. In self-descriptions, high scorers more often chose such terms as adventurous, argumentative, dominant, impulsive, shrewd, and unconventional, while low scorers more often chose the adjectives conservative, conventional, industrious, persevering, and thorough, among others. This test has been used extensively in research and has shown considerable promise as an indicator of fairly broad personality variables. Together with the other scales of the Welsh Figure Preference Test, it has the advantage of requiring no language and being applicable to a wide variety of persons, from 6-year-old children to college students and eminent scientists.

Another attempt to utilize aesthetic responses in the development of personality tests is to be found in the IPAT Music Preference Test of Personality (Cattell & Anderson, 1953; Cattell & Saunders, 1954). This test consists of 100 short, recorded piano selections. For each musical excerpt, the respondent marks "Like," "Indifferent," or "Dislike." On the basis of factor analysis, the 100 items were classified into 11 groups, each yielding a separate factor score. Evidence for the validity of this test, as well as for the psychological interpretations of the music preference factors, was de-

---

[1] The Revised Art Scale is a shorter version of the Barron-Welsh Art Scale, in which the number of items keyed "Like" and "Don't Like" is equal.

rived in part from correlations with Cattell's 16 PF test (Ch. 17). Additional evidence was based on certain relations found with psychiatric syndromes.

HUMOR.   Reactions to humor have likewise been explored as possible indicators of personality variables. The IPAT Humor Test of Personality (Cattell & Luborsky, 1947; Luborsky & Cattell, 1947), available in two forms, provides jokes and cartoons to be evaluated. Form A consists of 104 pairs of jokes, in each of which the respondent chooses the joke he considers funnier. A sample item is shown below:

(a) Epitaph to a waiter:
    By and by
    God caught his eye.

(b) One prehistoric man to another:
    "Now that we've learned to communicate with each other—shut up!"

In Form B, 130 jokes or cartoons are individually rated as funny or dull. Although Form A controls the response set to check many or few jokes as funny, Form B provides additional information about the individual's general tendency to regard jokes as funny. As in the IPAT Music Preference Test, the items were grouped into clusters on the basis of factor analysis. A separate score is reported for each of 13 personality factors.

EVALUATION OF PROVERBS.   Still another technique utilizes reactions to proverbs or aphorisms. In the Famous Sayings test (Bass, 1956), the examinee responds to each of 130 statements by indicating whether he agrees, disagrees, or is uncertain. Scales identified as Hostility, Fear of Failure, and Conventional Mores were derived through factor analysis. A Social Acquiescence score is also found on the basis of the respondent's general acceptance or rejection of items. Apart from the factorial analyses and a few significant correlations with certain personality inventory scores, validity data for this test were based largely on significant differences between various occupational, regional, educational, and clinical groups (Bass, 1957; Walsh, 1966).

INTERESTS AND ATTITUDES.   Finally, mention may be made of the use of relatively objective, task-oriented tests in the appraisal of interests and attitudes. Some of the earliest attempts to measure interests centered around the use of tests of information, learning, and distraction (Fryer, 1931). It is certainly reasonable to expect that an individual will more readily learn and retain information related to his interests, and that material appealing to his interests will prove to be more distracting to him than material in which he is not interested. These early tests, however, did not prove as successful as interest inventories such as the SVIB, and hence were soon abandoned. More recently, efforts to construct "indirect" tests of interest have been renewed (Campbell, 1950; Cattell *et al.*, 1950; Peel, 1959; Weschler & Bernberg, 1950).

A number of information tests have been developed for research on attitudes. The knowledge an individual has acquired is apt to reflect his selective perception and retention of facts, as well as his biased sources of information. We are likely to notice and to remember those facts that are in line with our expectations or hypotheses, and to overlook and forget others. Moreover, when no information is available on a given question, the direction of guessing may be determined by the respondent's attitude; this tendency has been utilized in the *error-choice technique* (Hammond, 1948), in which the respondent is forced to choose between two equally incorrect alternatives reflecting opposed biases. The items in error-choice tests are such that the correct answers are not generally familiar to the majority of respondents. Hence, the errors are not readily apparent. Attitude bias on the part of the individual is revealed by systematic errors in one direction, as opposed to random errors.

Among the many other techniques utilized for the measurement of attitudes may be mentioned perception and memory tests, in which distortions and errors reflect bias; the evaluation of arguments, syllogistic conclusions, inferences, and the like; prediction of the outcomes of described events; estimation of group opinions, the estimated opinions being presumably colored by the individual's own views; responding in various ways to photographs of persons identified as members of different minority groups, occupations, etc.; expressing approval or disapproval of pictured or described incidents involving intergroup relations; and rating jokes, some of which pertain to minority-group members.

SELF-CONCEPTS AND PERSONAL CONSTRUCTS

PHENOMENOLOGICAL INFLUENCE. A number of current approaches to personality assessment concentrate on the way the individual views himself and others. Such techniques reflect the influence of phenomenological psychology, which focuses on how events are *perceived* by the individual (Kelly, 1955; Snygg & Combs, 1959). The individual's self-description thus becomes of primary importance in its own right, rather than being regarded as a second-best substitute for other behavioral observations. Interest also centers on the extent of self-acceptance shown by the individual.

It might be argued that self-concept tests do not differ essentially from the self-report inventories discussed in Chapter 17. True, but it would be more accurate to say that self-report inventories are actually measures of self-concept. The interpretation of personality inventory responses in terms of self-conceptualization forms the basis of a provocative hypothesis formulated by Loevinger (1966a, 1966b; Loevinger & Ossorio, 1958). Bringing together many disparate findings from her own research and that of others, Loevinger proposed a personality trait which she defined as the capacity to conceptualize oneself, or to "assume distance" from oneself and one's impulses. According to Loevinger, it is the manifestations of this trait in personality inventories that have been described in such terms as façade, test-taking defensiveness, response set, social desirability, acquiescence, and personal style. In common with a number of other psychologists, Loevinger regards such test-taking attitudes, not as instrumental errors to be ruled out, but as the major source of valid variance in personality inventories.

On the basis of data from many sources, Loevinger suggested that ability to form a self-concept increases with age, intelligence, education, and socioeconomic level. At the lowest point, illustrated by the infant, the individual is incapable of self-conceptualization. As the ability develops, he gradually forms a stereotyped, conventional, and socially acceptable concept of himself. This stage Loevinger considers to be typical of adolescence. With increasing maturity, the individual progresses beyond such a stereotyped concept to a differentiated and realistic self-concept. At this point, he is fully aware of his idiosyncrasies and accepts himself for what he is. Loevinger maintains that the level of self-conceptualization attained by the individual is a basic determiner of his impulse control, social attitudes, and other important aspects of personality.

According to Loevinger, many (if not most) persons fail to reach the final stage of differentiated self-concept. Insofar as personality inventory responses are evaluated in terms of normative data, individuals whose self-concepts are at the stereotyped conventional stage receive higher or "better adjusted" scores. In the course of psychotherapy, some persons may advance beyond this stage to the individualized self-concept and hence may show a decline in scores on adjustment inventories (Loevinger & Ossorio, 1958). Such a hypothesis could account for the apparent failures of personality inventories when used in a clinical setting. The finding by some investigators (Sanford, 1956) that, when evaluated in terms of personality inventory norms, college seniors appear to have poorer emotional adjustment than college freshmen may have a similar explanation. Essentially, Loevinger argues that the capacity for self-conceptualization is an important personality trait and that the relation of this trait to personality inventory scores is not linear but curvilinear.

The procedures to be considered in this section all have as their primary focus the individual's perception of himself and others. Another common feature of these procedures is their applicability to intensive investigation of the individual case. For this reason, they are of special interest to the clinical psychologist. Many of them, in fact, have originated within a clinical setting.

THE ADJECTIVE CHECK LIST.   Several techniques have been specifically developed for assessing self-concepts (Strong & Feder, 1961). A widely applicable instrument that is commercially available is the Adjective Check List (ACL). Originally constructed for use in the research program of the Institute for Personality Assessment and Research (IPAR), this instrument provides a list of 300 adjectives arranged alphabetically from "absent-minded" to "zany"' (Gough, 1960; Gough & Heilbrun, 1965). The respondent marks all the adjectives he considers to be descriptive of himself.

The ACL can be scored for 24 currently available scales. Three are response set scales, including the total number of words marked and the number of these that are favorable and unfavorable, respectively. The total number of items marked is not only used to adjust the scores on the other scales but is also of interest in its own right. Persons marking many adjectives tend to be described as active and enthusiastic; those marking few adjectives, as quiet, reserved, and cautious. Four scales were developed by empirical item keying against a criterion of intensive personal observation and evaluation of participants in the IPAR assessment program; these include the scales of Self-confidence, Self-control, Lability,[2] and Personal adjustment. Another empirical scale, labeled Counseling readiness, was developed by comparing the responses of contrasting groups of counseling clients, one showing more positive and the other less positive response to counseling. The remaining 15 scales were prepared on a rational or content basis, by assigning adjectives to each of the 15 needs covered by the EPPS (see Ch. 17). Examples include the needs for Achievement, Dominance, Affiliation, Order, and Autonomy.

Although assessments of participants in the IPAR program were used in developing only four of the scales, they were subsequently employed in building up the construct validity of other scales as well. On the basis of these assessments as well as other research, the manual provides personality sketches of individuals scoring high and low on each scale. While considerable information is available about some of these scales, the manual properly characterizes all the scales as being experimental. Nevertheless, the ACL is applicable to a wide variety of problems and has already been extensively employed in research.

Q SORT.   Another special technique suitable for investigating self-concepts is the Q sort originally developed by Stephenson (1953). In this technique, the individual is given a set of cards containing statements or trait names which he must sort into piles ranging from "most characteristic" to "least characteristic" of himself. The items may come from a standard list, but more often are designed to fit the individual case. To ensure

[2] Refers to spontaneity, flexibility, need for change, rejection of convention, and assertive individuality.

uniform distribution of ratings, a "forced-normal" distribution is used, the respondent being instructed to place a specified number of cards in each pile. Such a distribution can be prepared for any size of item sample by reference to a normal curve table. It should be noted that, like the forced-choice technique discussed in Chapter 17, the Q sort yields ipsative rather than normative data. In other words, the individual tells us which he considers his strong and which his weak traits, but not how strong he believes himself to be in comparison with another person or some outside norm.

Q sorts have been employed to study a variety of psychological problems (Block, 1961; Mowrer, 1953; Rogers & Dymond, 1954). In intensive investigations of individual personality, the subject is often asked to re-sort the same set of items within different frames of reference. For example, he may sort the items as they apply to himself and to other persons, such as his father, his mother, or his wife. Similarly, he may sort the items as they apply to himself in different settings, such as job, home, or social situations. Q sorts can likewise be obtained for the individual as he believes he actually is (real self), as he believes others see him (social self), and as he would like to be (ideal self). To observe change, Q sorts may be obtained successively at different stages during psychotherapy, a procedure that has been followed especially by client-centered therapists. With therapy, the self-concept tends to become more favorable and to resemble more closely the individual's ideal-self concept [3] (Rogers & Dymond, 1954, Ch. 4).

THE SEMANTIC DIFFERENTIAL.   This technique was first developed by Osgood and his associates (1957) as a tool for research on the psychology of meaning, although its possibilities for personality assessment were soon recognized. The Semantic Differential represents a standardized and quantified procedure for measuring the connotations of any given concept for the individual. Each concept is rated on a 7-point graphic scale as being more closely related to one or the other of a pair of opposites, as illustrated in Figure 119. For every concept, a series of these bipolar adjectival scales is employed; usually 15 or more scales are included. Intercorrelations and factorial analyses of the original set of 50 scales developed by Osgood revealed three major factors: *Evaluative,* with high loadings in such scales as good-bad, valuable-worthless, and clean-dirty; *Potency,* found in such scales as strong-weak, large-small, and heavy-light; and *Activity,* identified in such scales as active-passive, fast-slow, and sharp-dull. The evaluative factor is the most conspicuous, accounting for the largest percentage of total variance.

Responses on the Semantic Differential can be analyzed in several ways. For quantitative treatment, the ratings on each scale can be assigned nu-

---

[3] All these procedures can, of course, be followed also with the previously described Adjective Check List or with any other techniques for assessing self-concepts.

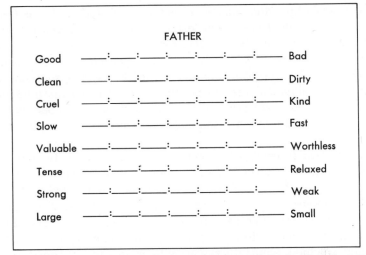

FIG. 119.   Illustration of the Semantic Differential Technique. In rating the concept "Father," respondent places a check mark on the appropriate segment of each scale. Usually a much larger number of scales is employed.

merical values from 1 to 7, or from −3 to +3. The over-all similarity of any two concepts for an individual or a group can then be measured in terms of their positions on all scales. The connotations of all concepts rated by a single individual can be investigated by computing the "score" of each concept in the three principal factors described above. Thus, on a scale extending from −3 to +3, a given individual's concept of "My Brother" may rate −2 in the evaluative factor, 0.1 in potency, and 2.7 in activity.

The concepts to be rated can be chosen to fit whatever problem is being investigated. The respondent can, for example, be asked to rate: himself, members of his family, friends, employers, teachers, or public figures; members of different ethnic or cultural groups; persons engaged in different occupations; activities, such as studying or outdoor sports; abstract ideas, such as confusion, hatred, sickness, peace, or love; product names or brand names; and radio or television programs. The Semantic Differential has been applied in many different contexts, in research on such varied problems as clinical diagnosis and therapy (Osgood & Luria, 1954), vocational choices (Hunt, 1967), and consumers' reactions to products and brand names (Mindak, 1956).

ROLE CONSTRUCT REPERTORY TEST.   A technique devised specifically as an aid in clinical practice is the Role Construct Repertory Test (Rep Test) developed by G. A. Kelly (1955). This technique shares certain features with other testing procedures, notably the Semantic Differential and the various sorting tests used to study concept formation (Ch. 12). In the Rep Test, however, the objects to be sorted are persons who are important in the individual's life. And unlike the Semantic Differential, the Rep Test requires the individual himself to designate the scales, dimensions, or constructs in terms of which he characterizes these persons.

The development of the Rep Test is intimately related to Kelly's personality theory. A basic proposition in this theory is that the concepts or constructs an individual uses to perceive objects or events influence his behavior. In the course of psychotherapy, it is frequently necessary to build new constructs and to discard some old constructs before progress can be made.

The Rep Test is designed to help the clinician identify some of the client's important constructs about people. Although the test can be administered in many ways, including both group and individual versions, one of its simpler variants will serve to illustrate its essential characteristics. In this variant, the examinee is first given a Role Title List and asked to name a person in his experience who fits each role title. Typical roles might include: your father, your wife or present girl friend, a teacher you liked, a person with whom you have been closely associated recently who appears to dislike you. The examiner next selects three of the persons named and asks, "In what *important way* are two of them alike but different from the third?" This procedure is repeated with many other sets of three names, in which some of the names recur in different combinations.

The Rep Test yields a wealth of qualitative data. A simplified factor-analytic procedure has also been developed for quantitative identification of constructs that are important for each individual. Other investigators have identified major dimensions of role constructs through analyses of group data (Messick & Kogan, 1966). When individuals were scored on these dimensions, the scores were found to correlate significantly with certain cognitive and personality variables. In another study, retests over a 2-week interval with both identical and different instructions revealed a high level of stability in the constructs employed by individuals (Fjeld & Landfield, 1961).

OBSERVER EVALUATIONS

The tests considered thus far give ample evidence of the variety of approaches that have been followed in the assessment of personality. Yet the best that can be said about most of them is that they are promising experimental instruments, suitable for research purposes, or useful adjuncts in the hands of the skilled clinician. It is apparent that for the assessment of personality variables today one cannot rely entirely on standardized tests. Other sources of information are needed to follow up or supplement the leads provided by test scores, to assess traits for which no adequate tests are available, and to obtain criterion data for developing and validating personality tests.

It is important to recognize that, especially in the domain of personality, tests cannot do the whole assessment job. Direct observations of behavior play an essential part in personality appraisal, whether in the clinic, counseling center, classroom, personnel office, or any other context calling for individual evaluations. To place such behavioral observations in the proper perspective, we must remember that all tests are themselves evaluations of small samples of behavior. To be sure, these behavior samples are obtained and evaluated under standardized conditions. But against the obvious advantages of such standardized procedures we must balance the advantages of a much more extensive sampling of behavior available through observational techniques in natural settings. To take an extreme example, if we had a detailed biography of a person extending from birth to age 30, we could probably predict his subsequent behavior more accurately than could be done with any test or battery of tests. Such a record of all the minutiae and circumstances of his life would be hard to come by; but if we had it, we could make predictions from a 30-year behavior sample rather than from the 1- or 2-hour samples provided by tests.

In all the techniques to be considered in this section, what the individual does in natural contexts over relatively long periods of time is transmitted through the medium of one or more observers. Much can be done to improve the accuracy and communicability of such observations.

OBSERVATIONAL CHILD STUDY. Techniques for the direct observation of spontaneous behavior in natural settings have been employed most widely by child psychologists, particularly with preschool children. Although such procedures can be followed with persons of any age, the younger the individual the less likely is it that his behavior will be affected by the presence of the observer or that he has developed the social façades that complicate the interpretation of behavior. These observational techniques have also proved useful in the classroom, especially if the observer is the teacher or someone else who fits readily into the normal school setting. More use has been made of these techniques for research than for individual assessment. School psychologists, however, occasionally supplement their evaluations of individual children with such observations in the classroom, on the playground, or in other school situations.

Many varieties of observational procedures are utilized by child psychologists (see Wright, 1960). They range from comprehensive, long-term techniques, as illustrated by the diary method, to more narrowly circumscribed, shorter, and more highly controlled observations, as illustrated by time sampling. The latter comprises a representative distribution of short observation periods, which has been described as "a series of far-between flashes on a behavior stream that otherwise flows in the dark" (Wright, 1960, p. 98). Depending on the nature and purpose of the observations, such periods may vary in length from less than a minute to several hours; periods of five minutes or less are the most common. The observations may be concentrated in one day or spaced over several months. They may cover all behavior occurring during the specified period; but more often they are limited to a particular kind of behavior, such as language, locomotion, interpersonal behavior, or aggression. Checklists of what to look for are a useful observational aid. When practicable, the observations may be supplemented with tape recordings or motion pictures.

It might be noted that naturalistic observations have much in common with the previously discussed situational tests. They differ principally in two respects: in naturalistic observations, no control is exerted over the stimulus situation, and—at least in most observational methods—a more extensive behavior sample is observed.

CRITICAL INCIDENT TECHNIQUE. Unlike the observational procedures considered in the preceding section, the critical incident technique was originally developed for use with adults and has been employed more extensively with adults than with children. In this procedure, the observer records specific instances of behavior that illustrate either favorable or unfavorable manifestations of the variable under consideration. This technique was first utilized in job analyses, as an aid in identifying the characteristics that differentiated satisfactory from unsatisfactory workers in a given job (see Ch. 16). For example, a supervisor of a research laboratory might be asked to keep a 2-month record of all instances of specific actions typical of productive and unproductive research workers on his staff; or a sales manager might be asked to submit incidents to illustrate both effective and ineffective behavior observed among his salesmen.

Although still used widely for job analysis, the critical incident technique has been adapted for many other purposes, including individual assessment. In schools, critical incidents provide a concrete and realistic record with which teachers may chart the personal and social development of individual children. An adaptation of this technique is also employed in Let's Look at First Graders (see Ch. 15) to help teachers in assessing the intellectual progress of first-grade children. An example of the application of the critical incident technique to industrial merit rating is provided by The Performance Record. This device was developed in three forms, for use with hourly employees, nonsupervisory salaried employees, and foremen and supervisors, respectively.

THE INTERVIEW. Mention should also be made of the time-honored source of information provided by interviewing techniques. Interviewing serves many purposes in clinical psychology, counseling, personnel psychology, and education. In personnel work, interviews are used not only for selection and placement but also in conducting employee attitude surveys, as a means of communication between management and workers, in handling grievances, and in other supervisory functions. The exit interview, held with employees who are leaving the company, can yield valuable data on the causes of turnover and on the characteristics of workers who fail on a particular job or who choose to leave it. Still another type of personnel interview is that used for employee development (Maier, 1958). Related both to merit rating and to training programs, this type of interview is designed to let the employee know how well he is doing the job and to help him improve.

Psychological discussions of the methods, applications, and effectiveness of interviewing can be found in many sources.[4] In form, interviews may vary from the highly structured (representing little more than an orally administered questionnaire), through patterned or guided interviews covering certain predetermined areas, to nondirective and depth interviews in which the interviewer merely sets the stage and encourages the subject to talk as freely as possible.

Interviews provide chiefly two kinds of information. First, they afford an opportunity for direct observation of a rather limited sample of behavior manifested during the interview situation itself. For example, the individual's speech, language usage, poise, and manner in meeting a stranger can be noted. A much more important function of interviewing, however, is to elicit life history data. What the individual has done in the past is a good indicator of what he may do in the future, especially when interpreted in the light of concomitant circumstances and of his comments regarding his actions. The interview should concern itself not only with what has happened to the individual but also with his perceptions of these events and his current evaluations of them.

On the interviewer's part, the interview requires skill in data gathering and in data interpreting. An interview may lead to wrong decisions because important data were not elicited or because given data were inadequately or incorrectly interpreted. An important qualification of the successful interviewer is sensitivity in identifying clues in the interviewee's behavior or in facts he reports. Such clues then lead to further probing for other facts that may either support or contradict the original hypothesis.

NOMINATING TECHNIQUE. All types of rating techniques may be employed for individual assessments by teachers, job supervisors, officers, counselors, and other persons who have had an opportunity to observe the individual in normal everyday contacts. Several procedures for improving the accuracy of ratings were discussed in Chapter 16. A rating procedure

[4] See, e.g., Bingham, Moore, & Gustad (1959), Fear (1958), Kahn & Cannell (1957), Maier (1958), Mayfield (1964), Ulrich & Trumbo (1965).

that is especially useful in obtaining peer ratings is the nominating technique. Originally developed in sociometry (Moreno, 1953) for investigating group structure, this technique may be used within any group of persons who have been together long enough to be acquainted with one another, as in a class, factory, institution, club, or military unit. Each individual is asked to choose one or more group members with whom he would like to study, work, eat lunch, play, or carry out any other designated function. Respondents may be asked to nominate as many group members as they wish, or a specified number (such as first, second, and third choice), or only one person for each function.

Sociometric data may be analyzed in two principal ways. As an aid in understanding *group structure*, the nominations may be plotted in a sociogram, illustrated in Figure 120. This diagram shows the expressed preferences of a hypothetical group of eight girls, when each was allowed two choices. In sociometric lingo, Claire is a "star," having been chosen by four of the eight girls. Jean is an "isolate" who has neither made nor received any choices. Although Helen and Nancy both chose a preferred partner, they too received no choices. Some writers would classify them as isolates along with Jean; others reserve the term "unchosen" for this category. The sociogram also serves to reveal the presence of cliques of various sizes. In Figure 120, Claire, Ruth, and Judy form a closely knit triangle through their mutual choices. Debbie and Mary constitute a mutual pair, but Mary

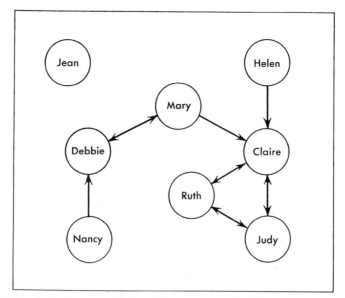

FIG. 120. A Sociogram. Eight girls in a school club are asked to choose a partner with whom they would like to work on a specific project; each is allowed two choices.

is also an intermediary between this pair and the previously mentioned triangle. With larger groups, the sociogram may show still other features of group structure.

Sociograms have been put to many uses both in research and in the practical management of groups. The sociogram of a group may serve as a basis for assigning individuals to subgroups where they will function congenially. Or it may suggest ways for improving the cohesiveness and effectiveness of the total group. Thus, a particular group may have many isolates; it may be torn apart by strong cliques; or it may exhibit other features that interfere with its unified functioning. Sociograms may be obtained on different occasions to determine the effects of intervening factors on group structure. They may also be utilized in studying attitudes toward minority group members within a group.

From the standpoint of *individual assessment,* sociometric data can help in identifying isolates as well as leaders. In addition, several indices can be computed for a more precise assessment of each individual. The simplest is a count of the number of times an individual was nominated for a specific function, which can be treated as his score or peer rating. When used for individual assessment, the nominating technique can be broadened to cover any desired behavior. For example, the respondents may be asked to name the person who has the most original ideas, who can be counted on to get a job done, or who is the best sport. They may be asked to designate not only the person who is most like the given description but also the one who is least like it. In that case, positive nominations would be weighted +1 and negative nominations −1 in totaling each person's score.

A variant of the nominating technique that is especially applicable in obtaining children's ratings of each other is the "Guess Who" technique, first used in the Character Education Inquiry together with the previously discussed situational tests. In this technique, the children are given a number of brief "word-pictures" and are instructed to write under each the name of every classmate who might fit the description. Examples include (Hartshorne, May, & Maller, 1929, p. 88):

This is a jolly good fellow—friends with everyone, no matter who they are.

This one is always picking on others and annoying them.

Sociometric nominations have generally proved to be one of the most dependable of rating techniques (Fiske & Cox, 1960; Hollander, 1965; Lindzey & Borgatta, 1954; Reynolds, 1966; Weitz, 1958). When checked against a variety of practical criteria dependent on interpersonal relations, such ratings have been found to have good predictive validity. These findings are understandable when we consider some of the features of sociometry. First, the number of raters is large, including all group members.

Second, an individual's peers are often in a particularly favorable position to observe his typical behavior. They may thus be better judges of certain interpersonal traits than teachers, supervisors, and other outside observers. Third, and probably most important, is the fact that the opinions of group members—right or wrong—influence their actions and hence partly determine the nature of the individual's subsequent interactions with the group. Other comparable groups may be expected to react toward the individual in a similar fashion. Sociometric ratings may thus be said to have content validity in the same sense as worksamples.

OBSERVER USE OF SELF-REPORT INSTRUMENTS. Any self-report instrument, such as the personality and interest inventories discussed in Chapters 17 and 18, may also be employed by an observer in describing another person. Instruments designed to assess self-concept are especially well suited for this purpose. The Adjective Check List (ACL) has been used extensively to obtain observers' evaluations in the IPAR research program (Gough & Heilbrun, 1965). Trained psychologists who have observed the subject closely over a 2- or 3-day assessment period record their evaluations by checking the appropriate adjectives on the list.

For certain purposes these observer evaluations can be obtained on the same persons who have reported their own self-concept on the ACL. Thus, in a sample of 45 research scientists who participated in the IPAR program, the observers' descriptions of the high scorers on each ACL self-concept scale were compared with their descriptions of the low scorers on the same scale. The high scorers on the Endurance key, for example, were described by the observers as: cautious, conventional, discreet, formal, gentle, mannerly, methodical, reasonable, steady, and ·tactful. The low scorers were most often described as: adventurous, careless, clever, flirtatious, hasty, headstrong, pleasure seeking, progressive, sharp-witted, and unscrupulous. This type of comparison contributes toward the construct validation of the ACL scales.

The Q sort has also been widely used for observer evaluations. Block (1961) describes the California Q-set (CQ-set), which was specially developed to provide a standard language for comprehensive personality evaluations by professionally trained observers. The CQ-set consists of 100 statements to be sorted into a 9-point forced distribution. The statements are sorted with regard to their "salience" for the individual—that is, their importance in specifying the unique and essential characteristics of the individual. Thus, the ipsative frame of reference typical of Q sorts is retained; the individual is not compared with outside normative standards.

The availability of such a uniform Q-set facilitates communication and assures comparability of data from different observers. The standard Q-set can also be used for a number of other research or clinical purposes. With it, evaluations can be recorded not only from personal observations but also from case histories, interviews, or projective tests. In validation research on projective techniques, for example, Q sorts have been used to obtain both criterion and test evaluations from different observers. Since the two sets of evaluations are expressed in the same terms, direct comparisons between them can be made. Another application involves the use of this technique in individual assessments. In this connection, Block (1961) provides examples of three "defining Q sorts," representing a consensus evaluation of an optimally normal individual and two psychiatric syndromes, against which a given individual's Q sort can be compared. Similar defining Q sorts may be developed for any desired category of persons.

PART 5

Testing
Today

CHAPTER 21

Social Implications
of Psychological
Testing

SINCE THE early 1950's there has been a mounting unrest regarding the use of tests. Public concern about testing undoubtedly stems in part from the rapid expansion of testing itself. This expansion—which may sometimes have outrun the readiness of available tests for operational use—is manifested along several parameters. First, the sheer number of persons tested, at all ages and in all walks of life, has multiplied to an unprecedented degree. Second, tests are being used in an increasing diversity of contexts, including schools, industrial organizations, the armed services, government agencies, clinics, hospitals, and prisons, among others. Third, tests are being employed to assess more and more aspects of behavior, including not only aptitudes for a wide range of activities, but also interests, attitudes, emotional characteristics, and interpersonal behavior. Finally, test results are being utilized to an increasing extent in making practical decisions of vital importance for both the individual and society.

As these applications of tests progressed by leaps and bounds, concern about the social implications of testing grew apace. The cautions and reservations traditionally expressed by psychologists, as illustrated by test reviews in the *Mental Measurements Yearbooks,* have too often gone unheeded. As a result, tests of all kinds have either been misused, misinterpreted, and clothed with occult powers they were never designed to have, or they have been indiscriminately attacked as a social evil. This state of affairs is sufficiently serious to merit careful consideration.

THE ANTI-TEST REVOLT

The critics of testing have raised their voices in many settings, including school boards, parents' organizations, legislative bodies, civil rights organizations, and the popular press. A few sensational books have added to the confusion (e.g., Black, 1963; Gross, 1962; Hoffman, 1962; Whyte, 1956). Surveys of public attitudes toward testing (Brim, 1965; Fiske, 1967; Goslin, 1963) also revealed misgivings about tests, although the proportion of persons expressing negative attitudes varied with the context in which tests were to be used and with the education, socioeconomic level, and personal characteristics of the respondents (Neulinger, 1966).

Against this background of popular disenchantment and misunderstanding about tests, there have appeared several well-considered and sober analyses of the contributions and limitations of testing in our society (see, e.g., Carter, Brim, Stalnaker, & Messick, 1965; Dunnette, 1964; Dyer, 1961, 1964; Ebel, 1966; Wolfle, 1963). The American Psychological Association appointed a Committee on Social Impact of Psychological Assessment (Berdie, 1965) and devoted a special issue of the *American Psychologist* to "Testing and Public Policy" (1965), in which the 1965 Congressional inquiry into testing was reported.[1] For a fuller discussion of the issues, the interested reader is urged to consult these and other publications cited in this chapter.

Some of the public concerns about testing stem from genuine ethical issues that have come to the fore as the testing movement grew. The questions of invasion of privacy and confidentiality of test results fall into this category. These questions were certainly recognized in the original formulation of *Ethical Standards of Psychologists* (Appendix A). But they are complex questions that require continuing re-examination.

A second source of test criticisms is to be found in the occasional flagrant misuses of tests, which are clearly violations of accepted professional practice. Available procedures for curbing such misuses are provided by voluntary restrictions in the sale and distribution of psychological tests, by state licensing and certification laws, and by the activities of the ethics committees of state and national psychological associations. Obviously none of these procedures can completely eradicate this form of charlatanism. The test critics, however, have pounced upon and dramatized isolated instances of downright charlatanism. What these critics fail to make clear is that psychologists have for many years been cautioning against just such misuses of tests. Moreover, the critics fail to differentiate between the misuse of tests by the untrained or unscrupulous practitioner and the appropriate and constructive use of tests by the qualified psychologist. If they can dem-

---

[1] A further report of these hearings is included in the May, 1966, *American Psychologist* (pp. 404–422).

onstrate that one personality test is bad, then it follows that all personality tests are bad. If one test user is unethical or naive, then anyone who uses tests is suspect.

Another group of criticisms arises from misinterpretations of test results and misconceptions about the nature and purpose of tests. In part, these difficulties result from inadequate communication between psychometricians and their various publics—educators, parents, legislators, job applicants, and so forth. Misconceptions about the implications of an IQ and about the construction and use of personality inventories represent the most common examples. It is a frequent reaction among laymen, for example, to ask what a specific personality inventory item is supposed to show. An inventory that may have been developed by empirical criterion keying is thus judged in terms of its factual or veridical content. Moreover, the assumption is made that the examiner is interested in the respondent's answers to specific items rather than in the total scores.[2]

Not all misconceptions about tests, however, can be attributed to inadequate communication between psychologists and laymen. Psychological testing itself has tended to become dissociated from the mainstream of behavioral science (Anastasi, 1967). The growing complexity of the science of psychology has inevitably been accompanied by increasing specialization among psychologists. In this process, psychometricians have concentrated more and more on the technical refinements of test construction and have tended to lose contact with developments in other relevant specialties, such as learning, child development, and individual differences. Thus, the technical aspects of test construction have tended to outstrip the psychological sophistication with which test results are interpreted. Test scores can be properly interpreted only in the light of all available knowledge regarding the behavior that the tests are designed to measure.

Finally, some test critics apparently try to evaluate tests against nonexistent ideal predictors. For instance, they make much of the fact that multiple-choice items are sometimes misunderstood and that they may occasionally penalize the brilliant and erudite student who sees unusual implications in the answers. Granted that this is possible, the obvious conclusion is that tests are not perfect. A realistic evaluation, however, requires that such tests be compared with alternative assessment procedures. How do the tests compare with grades, essay examinations, interviewing procedures, application forms, ratings, and any other predictors whose utilization is practicable in specific situations?

To be sure, these other assessment procedures should not be entirely discarded, particularly in the appraisal of personality characteristics. As was noted in Chapter 20, there is a place for observer evaluations of be-

[2] Examples of this misconception about personality inventories can be found in the Congressional hearings about tests (Testing and Public Policy, 1965, p. 978). See also Hathaway (1964).

hen such observations can be made under conditions that mini- ment errors. But in most practical situations it is much more dif- achieve objectivity of evaluation through the proper selection and training of assessment personnel than through the introduction of well-constructed tests. Certainly in the assessment of abilities, the contribution of tests has been amply demonstrated by empirical follow-up data. In the evaluation of personality traits, moreover, available tests can serve as effective aids in the assessment process if used by an adequately trained psychologist—and if the assessment is made by inadequately trained personnel, then interviewing and other subjective techniques cannot be relied upon either.

In the following sections, we shall examine the principal criticisms that have been directed against tests and testing practices, with special reference to their possible constructive implications.

PROTECTION OF PRIVACY

The problem that has received the greatest attention, including Congressional investigations, centers around the possibility that testing may constitute an invasion of privacy. Although this criticism has generally been directed against personality tests, it can logically apply to any type of test. Certainly any intelligence, aptitude, or achievement test may reveal limitations in skills and knowledge that an individual would rather not disclose. Moreover, any observation of an individual's behavior—as in an interview, casual conversation, or other personal encounter—may yield information about him that he would prefer to conceal and that he may reveal unwittingly. The fact that psychological tests have often been singled out in discussions of the invasion of privacy probably reflects prevalent misconceptions about tests. If all tests were recognized as measures of behavior samples, with no mysterious powers to penetrate beyond behavior, popular fears and suspicion would be lessened.

It should also be noted that all behavior research, whether employing tests or other observational procedures, presents the possibility of invasion of privacy. Yet, as scientists, psychologists are committed to the goal of advancing knowledge about human behavior. Principle 1a in *Ethical Standards of Psychologists* (Appendix A) clearly spells out the psychologist's conviction "that society will be best served when he investigates where his judgment indicates investigation is needed." Several other principles, on the other hand, are concerned with the protection of privacy and with the welfare of research subjects (see, e.g., 7d, 8a, 16). Conflicts of values may thus arise, which must be resolved in individual cases.

The problem is obviously not simple; and it has been the subject of extensive deliberation by psychologists and other professionals. In a report

entitled *Privacy and Behavioral Research* (1967), prepared for t
of Science and Technology, the right to privacy is defined as "th
the individual to decide for himself how much he will share with others
his thoughts, his feelings, and the facts of his personal life" (p. 2). It is
further characterized as "a right that is essential to insure dignity and
freedom of self-determination" (p. 2). To safeguard personal privacy, no
universal rules can be formulated; only general guidelines can be provided.
In the application of these guidelines to specific cases, there is no substitute for the ethical awareness and professional responsibility of the individual psychologist. Solutions must be worked out in terms of the particular
circumstances.

One relevant factor is the purpose for which the testing is conducted—
whether for individual counseling, institutional decisions regarding selection and classification, or research. In clinical or counseling situations, the
client is usually willing to reveal himself in order to obtain help with his
problems. The clinician or examiner does not invade privacy where he is
freely admitted. Even under these conditions, however, the client should be
warned that in the course of the testing or interviewing he may reveal information about himself without realizing that he is so doing; or he may disclose feelings of which he himself is unaware.

When testing is conducted for institutional purposes, the examinee
should of course be fully informed as to the use that will be made of his
test scores. It is also desirable, however, to explain to the examinee that
correct assessment will benefit him, since it is not to his advantage to be
placed in a position where he will fail or which he will find uncongenial.
The results of tests administered in a clinical or counseling situation, of
course, should not be made available for institutional purposes, unless the
examinee gives his consent.

When tests are given for research purposes, anonymity should be pre-
served as fully as possible and the procedures for ensuring such anonymity
should be explained in advance to the subjects. Anonymity does not, however, solve the problem of protecting privacy in all research contexts. Some
subjects may resent the disclosure of facts they consider personal, even
when complete confidentiality of responses is assured. In most cases, however, cooperation of subjects may be elicited if they are convinced that the
information is needed for the research in question and if they have sufficient confidence in the integrity and competence of the investigator. All
research on human behavior, whether or not it utilizes tests, may present
conflicts of values. Freedom of inquiry, which is essential to the progress
of science, must be balanced against the protection of the individual. The
investigator must be alert to the values involved and must carefully weigh
alternative solutions (see *Privacy and Behavioral Research*, 1967; Ruebhausen & Brim, 1966).

Whatever the purposes of testing, the protection of privacy involves two key concepts: relevance and informed consent. The information that the individual is asked to reveal must be *relevant* to the stated purposes of the testing. An important implication of this principle is that all practicable efforts should be made to ascertain the validity of tests for the particular diagnostic or predictive purpose for which they are used. An instrument that is demonstrably valid for a given purpose is one that provides relevant information. It also behooves the examiner to make sure that test scores are correctly interpreted. An individual is less likely to feel that his privacy is being invaded by a test assessing his readiness for a particular educational program than by a test allegedly measuring his "native intelligence."

The concept of *informed consent* also requires clarification; and its application in individual cases may call for the exercise of considerable judgment (Ruebhausen & Brim, 1966). The examinee should certainly be informed about the purpose of testing, the kinds of data sought, and the use that will be made of his scores. It is not implied, however, that he be shown the test items in advance or told how his responses will be scored.[3] Such information would usually invalidate the test. Not only would the giving of this information seriously impair the usefulness of an ability test, but it would also tend to distort responses on many personality tests. For example, if an individual is told in advance that a self-report inventory will be scored with a masculinity-femininity scale, his responses are likely to be influenced by stereotyped (and often erroneous) ideas he may have about sex differences, or by a false or distorted self-concept.

COMMUNICATING TEST RESULTS

Like the protection of privacy, to which it bears some relation, the communication of test results presents a number of complex problems. These problems are quite varied; but each in its way has serious social implications. One problem pertains to *confidentiality* of test results (*Ethical Standards*, 1963, No. 6). Professional ethics requires that the psychologist safeguard the confidentiality of test records. The information contained in such records can be made available to third parties only when two conditions are met. First, the person to whom it is transmitted must have a genuine and legitimate need for the information, as in the case of teachers or prospective employers. Moreover, each person should receive only that information which is relevant to his immediate need. Second, test information should be released only with the prior consent of the examinee. This condition is implied in obtaining the examinee's informed consent to be tested.

These principles are clear, but complications arise in their application. First, even in the absence of informed consent, the psychologist has an obligation to reveal information to appropriate professional workers or

[3] Nor should the test items be shown to a parent, in the case of a minor.

public authorities in the relatively rare circumstances "when there is clear and imminent danger to an individual or to society" (*Ethical Standards*, 1963, No. 6a). The decision to communicate confidential information in such cases calls for careful deliberation and individual judgment. Second, the psychologist may be legally bound to reveal information given to him by a client, even when such disclosure is against his own judgment. About one third of the states have not yet enacted laws that extend the right of privileged communication to certified psychologists. When not protected by such laws, the confidential records of a psychologist, including test scores, are subject to subpoena.

A third limitation on confidentiality pertains to the parents or guardians of a minor. Even where protected by privileged communication laws, the psychologist is obliged to disclose test information to a child's parents or to school authorities who serve *in loco parentis*. In fact, there have been cases in which parents have tried legally to force school psychologists to disclose their children's test scores and even the full record of test responses. Apart from the risk that such data be seriously misinterpreted— with potential harm to the child—this obligation may conflict with the child's own right to privacy. Such a conflict is most likely to occur in the case of older children and adolescents. In a searching analysis of the problems of privacy, Ruebhausen and Brim (1966, pp. 431–432) write: "Should not a child, even before the age of full legal responsibility, be accorded the dignity of a private personality? Considerations of healthy personal growth, buttressed with reasons of ethics, seem to command that this be done."

It is also relevant to point out that the emotional problem under investigation may involve parent-child relations. In some cases, too, the difficulty may stem chiefly from the emotional disturbance of the parent, who may need therapy more than the child does. Moreover, if a psychologist should turn over test scores and other records of raw data to a parent, he is actually violating a principle of professional ethics (*Ethical Standards*, 1963, No. 14b) that requires the communication of test results in such a manner as to guard against misinterpretation or misuse.

It is apparent that, with regard to the parents of a minor, the question is not *whether* to communicate test results but *how* to do so. Parents have a legal right to information about their child. Furthermore, except in rare instances, it is highly desirable for them to have such information in usable form. The question of transmitting information to parents highlights the more general question regarding appropriate *methods of communicating test information* to all persons concerned (Berdie, 1960; Berdie, 1965; Brown, 1961; *The Use of Student Records*, 1961).

Psychologists, school counselors, and educators have given much thought to the communication of test results to parents in a form that will be meaningful and useful. It is clear that the information should not be transmitted routinely, but should be accompanied by interpretive explanations by a professionally trained person. An ideal procedure is to arrange a group meeting at which a counselor or school psychologist explains the purpose and nature of the tests, the sort of conclusions that may reasonably be drawn from the results, and the limitations of the data. Written reports about their own children may then be distributed to the parents, and arrangements made for personal interviews with any parents wishing to discuss the reports further. Regardless of how they are transmitted, however, an important condition is that test results should be presented in terms of general levels only, and not as numerical scores. This is especially true of intelligence tests, which are more likely to be misinterpreted than are achievement tests.

In communicating results to teachers, school administrators, employers, and other appropriate persons, similar safeguards should be provided. Broad levels of performance and qualitative descriptions in simple terms are to be preferred over specific numerical scores, except when communicating with adequately trained professionals. Even well-educated laymen have been known to confuse percentiles with percentage scores, percentiles with IQ's, norms with standards, and interest ratings with aptitude scores. But a more serious misinterpretation pertains to the conclusions drawn from test scores, even when their technical meaning is correctly understood. A familiar example is the popular assumption than an IQ indicates a fixed characteristic of the individual which predetermines his lifetime level of intellectual achievement.

In all test communication, it is desirable to take into account the characteristics of the person who is to receive the information. This applies not only to that person's general education and his knowledge about psychology and testing, but also to his anticipated emotional response to the information. In the case of a parent or teacher, for example, personal emotional involvement with the child may interfere with a calm and rational acceptance of factual information.

Last but by no means least is the problem of communicating test results to the individual himself, whether child or adult. The same general safeguards against misinterpretation apply here as in communicating with a third party. The individual's emotional reaction to the information is especially important, of course, when he is learning about his own assets and shortcomings. Counseling psychologists have devoted much thought to the most effective ways of transmitting test information to their clients (see, e.g., Goldman, 1961, Ch. 14–16). Although the details of this process are beyond the scope of our present discussion, two major guidelines are of particular interest. First, test-reporting is to be viewed as an integral part of the counseling process and incorporated into the total counselor-client relationship. Second, insofar as possible, test results should be reported as answers to specific questions raised by the counselee. An important consideration in counseling relates to the counselee's acceptance of the information presented to him. The counseling situation is such that if the individual rejects any information, for whatever reasons, then that information is likely to be totally wasted.

LIMITATIONS OF TEST COVERAGE

Some test critics have argued that, because of their limited coverage of intellectual functions, intelligence and scholastic aptitude tests tend to perpetuate a narrow conception of ability. More specifically, it has been objected that the use of such tests for college admission or for the selection of scholarship recipients will exclude able persons whose intellectual talents lie in other directions. A further criticism is that these tests encourage impersonal, mechanistic decision-making. It has also been argued that the use of standardized tests tends to produce a standardized student body. The critics conjure up a depressing vision of uniform models coming off the educational assembly line.

What are the facts? First, intelligence or scholastic aptitude tests do not attempt to sample all cognitive functions. They are predominantly measures of verbal and numerical aptitudes and should be clearly recognized as such. True, the global connotations of test names encourage misunderstanding. Particularly the term "intelligence test," with its many popular associations, should be avoided in communicating test results to laymen. Psychometricians have been advocating a more precise label for decades. It should be noted, however, that all test labels are likely to suggest more generality than the test possesses. A clerical aptitude test does not cover all the traits required of an office clerk, nor does a mechanical aptitude test cover all aspects of mechanical tasks. A test title that attempted to provide a precise operational definition of test content would be unwieldy and impracticable.

What of the abilities that are actually measured by intelligence and scholastic aptitude tests? There is ample follow-up data to demonstrate that the particular intellectual skills sampled by these tests are important prerequisites for classroom learning. In fact, the data on occupational performance (Ch. 16) indicate that these skills are relevant to learning outside the traditional academic setting as well.

As has been repeatedly observed throughout this book, however, verbal and numerical skills are a necessary but not a sufficient condition for successful learning in these contexts. Other special aptitudes are highly relevant in particular fields. Mechanical, motor, musical, and artistic aptitudes are obvious examples. Motivational, emotional, and attitudinal variables are important determiners of achievement in all areas. Current creativity research is identifying both cognitive and personality variables that are associated with creative productivity. All this implies, of course, that both individual and institutional decisions should be based on as much relevant data as can reasonably be gathered. To base decisions on tests alone, and especially on one or two tests alone, is clearly a misuse of tests. Decisions must be made by persons. Tests represent one source of data utilized in making decisions; they are not themselves decision-making instruments.

With regard to the "standardization of students," it might be noted that diversification of curriculum must precede diversification of the testing program. At all educational levels, tests are designed and validated within the framework provided by existing educational curricula. Tests follow curricular changes rather than initiating them. Curricular innovations must begin with curricular planners, not test constructors. Tests necessarily reflect what the individual has learned in school; and when tests are employed for educational guidance, their predictive validity is measured against a criterion of success within existing curricula.

Rather than fostering standardization of educational development, tests facilitate the identification of individual differences in patterns of ability and interest. Thus, they make it possible to guide individuals into diversified educational programs, when such programs are available. The use of multiple aptitude batteries and interest tests in the counseling of high school students illustrates this application of tests.

From another angle, objective tests of ability have been attacked because of the restrictions imposed on the examinee's responses. Criticisms have been directed particularly against multiple-choice items and against analogies, similarities, classification, and other standard item types employed in aptitude or achievement tests (Hoffman, 1962; LaFave, 1966; Sigel, 1963). Some of the arguments are ingenious and provocative. Qualitative analyses of errors on intelligence or achievement tests would undoubtedly yield interesting information about individual cases. An inquiry into the reasons why an individual chooses a particular answer and the methods whereby he solves a given problem would likewise provide useful information about cognitive styles, unusual interests, atypical experiential background, and other idiosyncrasies.

The advantages of individual testing, which permits such intensive clinical exploration of individual cases, have always been recognized in psychometrics. Such procedures are desirable when the necessary time and trained professional personnel are available. At the same time, any practicable suggestions for improving the information yield of group tests should of course be carefully followed up. With the growing sophistication of test-construction procedures, these tests have already undergone many innovations over the years. There is every reason to anticipate that they will continue to do so.

PERSONALITY TESTS AND SOCIAL CONFORMITY

Just as scholastic aptitude tests have been blamed for any real or imaginary limitations of educational curricula, so personality tests have been blamed for some of the ills of modern business organizations.[4] This criticism was first popularized by Whyte's *Organization Man* (1956). Whyte argued that personality tests are generally employed in industry to select executives who are conformists and lacking in individuality—in other words, typical "organization men." Insofar as this criticism may be true, it is an indictment, not of the tests, but of the criteria of executive success against which they must be validated. It would apply just as much—if not more so—to the relatively subjective and unstandardized predictors advocated by Whyte and other critics, such as previous job history and interviewing techniques. Especially when interviews are conducted by untrained interviewers, in the casual and impressionistic manner apparently admired by test critics, they give full play to interviewer bias. Under these conditions, such irrelevant characteristics as the applicant's appearance, his interest in sports, or his political preferences would have the greatest opportunity to influence the general impression he makes on the interviewer. On the other hand, tests (as well as objectively developed biographical history blanks and properly conducted interviews) focus on traits shown to be relevant to job performance.

If success in a given company depends on characteristics irrelevant to actual job performance—such as being a "yes" man or playing golf with the boss—this condition cannot be altered by using tests. Were the tests to select rugged individualists or persons with a strong interest in art and music and an aversion for conventional sports, these persons would not succeed in the company—and they would certainly not enjoy working there. The point of this example is simply that tests cannot be used as instruments of criterion reform. If the criterion situation calls for improvement, it should be attacked directly, not through tests or other selection procedures.

On the other hand, insofar as criteria do change over time, test validities need to be re-examined periodically. For a variety of reasons, the nature and personnel requirements of jobs in industry, government, and the armed services do not remain fixed. It is therefore desirable to repeat job analyses or task analyses from time to time. Such analyses may themselves suggest that some of the tests in use as predictors are outdated in a particular context. Periodic revalidation of instruments against current criteria provides a more definitive safeguard against the retention of instruments

---

[4] See especially Gross (1962) and Whyte (1956). For critical analyses of this point, see Dunnette (1964) and Stark (1958).

that may have become irrelevant. This requirement applies to personality tests just as well as it does to ability tests.

With special reference to the question of social conformity, it should be noted that the social desirability of personality traits is often specific to the context. Either end of a particular personality scale may be positive depending on the purpose for which the test is given. For example, in a scale for measuring introversion-extraversion, the "conformist" score would be near the extraverted end of the scale for house-to-house salesmen and social directors, but near the introverted end for librarians and research mathematicians.

An even more cogent point is that job requirements are complex. Consequently, different individuals may achieve success on the same job for different reasons. The proper utilization of tests for personnel selection permits diversity of aptitude and personality patterns among the individuals selected for a given job. Particularly in the case of executives and other high-level personnel, individuals may structure the job to fit their own capabilities. One manager may succeed because of his ability to communicate effectively, another because of his skill in identifying and balancing all relevant factors in making decisions, a third because of his technical brilliance and his effectiveness in stimulating creative achievement in his department, and a fourth because of his emotional control and ability to think clearly in a face-to-face crisis. When properly employed, tests should serve to facilitate the selection of applicants with different patterns of qualifications. Combining tests in a battery by means of regression equations, for example, represents one statistical device for allowing persons to qualify through a diversity of trait patterns.

TESTS AND THE CULTURALLY DISADVANTAGED

CULTURAL DIFFERENTIALS IN TEST SCORES. Another type of criticism asserts that tests are unfair to culturally disadvantaged persons. To criticize tests because they reveal cultural influences is to miss the essential nature of tests. Every psychological test measures a behavior sample. Insofar as culture affects behavior, its influence will and should be reflected in the test. Moreover, if we rule out cultural differentials from a test, we might thereby lower its validity against the criterion we are trying to predict. The same cultural differentials that impair an individual's test performance are likely to handicap him in schoolwork, job performance, or any other activity we are trying to predict.

Tests are designed to show what an individual can do at a given point in time. They cannot tell us *why* he performs as he does. To answer that question, we need to investigate his background, motivations, and other pertinent circumstances. Nor can tests tell how able a culturally disadvantaged child might have been if he had been reared in a more favorable environment. Moreover, tests cannot compensate for cultural deprivation by eliminating its effects from their scores. On the contrary, tests should reveal such effects, so that appropriate remedial steps can be taken. To conceal the effects of cultural disadvantages by rejecting tests or by trying to devise tests that are insensitive to such effects can only retard progress toward a genuine solution of social problems. Such reactions toward tests are equivalent to breaking a thermometer because it registers a body temperature of 101°.

SUBGROUP VALIDATION. If we want to use tests to predict outcome in some future situation, such as an applicant's performance in college or on a job, we need tests with high predictive validity against the specific criterion. This requirement is commonly overlooked in the development of so-called culture-fair tests (see Ch. 10 and Anastasi, 1961, 1964, 1966). In the effort to include in such tests only functions common to different cultures or subcultures, we may choose content that has little relevance to any criterion we wish to predict. A better solution is to choose criterion-relevant content and then investigate the effect of moderator variables on test scores (Ch. 6). Validity coefficients, regression weights, and cutoff scores may vary as a function of certain background conditions of the subjects. These values should therefore be checked within different subgroups.

It should be noted, however, that the predictive characteristics of test scores are less likely to vary among cultural groups when the test is intrinsically relevant to criterion performance. If a verbal test is employed to predict nonverbal job performance, a fortuitous validity may be found in one cultural group because of traditional associations of past experiences within that culture. In a group with a different experiential background, however, the validity of the test may disappear. On the other hand, a test that directly samples criterion behavior, or one that measures essential prerequisite skills, is likely to retain its validity in different groups.

A further point pertains to the concept of *test bias*. In the psychometric sense, test bias refers to overprediction or underprediction of criterion measures. If a test consistently underpredicts criterion performance for a given group, it shows unfair discrimination or "bias" against this group. Thus, if Group A consistently excels Group B on a predictor test, but the two groups do not differ significantly in job performance, then the test discriminates against Group B. With this test, more of the higher-scoring Group A members would be hired, although they are not better job performers than are the Group B members. Similarly, if Groups A and B do *not* differ on the test, but Group A performs significantly better on the job, then the test is biased against Group A. Finally, although two groups differ significantly in test scores, the test is not biased if the two groups show corresponding differences in criterion performance.

The operation of test bias is illustrated in Figure 121. Part 1 shows the bivariate distribution of two groups with different means and *SD*'s in the predictor, but with identical regression lines between predictor and criterion. In this case, there is no test bias, since any given test score (X) corresponds to the identical criterion score (Y) in both groups. In Part 2, the two groups have regression lines with the same slope but different intercepts. Although the validity coefficients computed within each group may thus be equal, any given test score (X) will correspond to different criterion scores in the two groups, as shown by points Y_A and Y_B. The same test score thus has a different predictive meaning for the two groups. In this situation, if the same minimum qualifying score is applied to both groups, it will discriminate unfairly against Group B.

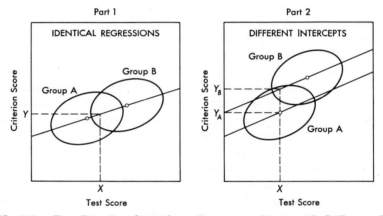

FIG. 121.   Test Bias Resulting from Regression Lines with Different Intercepts. The ellipses show the regions within which members of each group fall when their test scores are plotted against their criterion performance. (Adapted from Gordon, 1953, p. 3.)

Considerable research is under way to check the validity of tests in predicting educational and occupational criteria in culturally disadvantaged minority groups. Several studies with college admission tests have thus far yielded no evidence that such tests are biased against students with culturally disadvantaged backgrounds. In one study, the validity of a scholastic aptitude test in predicting college grades was computed within groups of students classified according to parents' occupational and educational level (Hewer, 1965). Criterion correlations were no higher in the professional group than in the lower occupational groups. Moreover, the grades actually obtained by students from professional homes tended to be higher than those predicted from their test scores, while the grades obtained in the other groups tended to be equal to their predicted grades or lower. Thus, the test underpredicted the criterion performance of students in the professional group and overpredicted the criterion performance of students from lower socioeconomic levels.

Similar results have been obtained in investigations of Negro and white college students. Validity coefficients of the SAT for Negro college students were generally higher than those obtained for white college students. This relationship was found when Negro and white students were attending separate colleges, as well as when they were attending the same colleges (Cleary, 1966; Hills, 1964; Hills, Klock, & Lewis, 1963; Roberts, 1964; Stanley & Porter, 1967). In a special investigation of possible test bias of the SAT, Cleary (1966) compared actual and predicated grades of Negro and white students attending three integrated colleges. In two of these colleges, there was no significant difference between Negro and white students in the extent to which the SAT overpredicted or underpredicted grades. In the third college, a significant difference was found, but it was the Negro grades that were overpredicted. Thus, in this college, the SAT proved to be slightly biased in favor of Negro students.

Research on the prediction of vocational criteria in culturally disadvantaged groups has been proceeding in a number of settings.[5] In the Air Force (Gordon, 1953), the use of the Airman Classification Battery in predicting performance in various technical schools was investigated with several samples of white men, Negro men, and white women. The results indicated that the same minimum qualifying scores are applicable to white and Negro airmen. The women's criterion performance, on the other hand, tended to be underpredicted in some of the technical programs, and some adjustments in their minimum qualifying scores were recommended.

An extensive research project on the selection of job applicants from different socioeconomic and ethnic backgrounds has been conducted by the Research Center for Industrial Behavior at New York University (Kirkpatrick et al., 1967). Test scores and criterion data were analyzed on some 1,200 persons, including whites, Negroes, and Puerto Ricans. The job groups included clerical workers, nursing students, and participants in a job training program for unemployed men who were being trained for maintenance work or for heavy vehicle driving. The results varied with the tests and the jobs. Many of the tests performed equally well in the different ethnic groups. In some cases, different tests worked best in different groups, as had also been found in the previously cited studies by the Port of New York Authority (Lopez, 1966; see also Ch. 6). The inclusion of an index of cultural disadvantage as a moderator variable in regression equations improved test validity for some jobs. In general, this research yielded enough suggestive findings to justify similar investigations in other specific job situations.

---

[5] See also Parrish et al. (1966), reporting the papers given at a symposium on "The Industrial Psychologist: Selection and Equal Employment Opportunity," held at the 1964 convention of the American Psychological Association.

Mention should also be made of the many activities undertaken by the United States Employment Service with regard to the testing and job placement of culturally disadvantaged applicants (see Jurgensen, 1966). These include the development of nonreading forms of several GATB tests; experimentation with new types of tests, such as worksamples; and the introduction of several test-orientation and screening procedures to reduce the operation of test-related handicaps. A research project conducted jointly by the USES and the Urban League is concerned with the job performance and job satisfaction of two random samples of Negroes: one sample placed on jobs or in-training programs with the use of GATB scores, the other without reference to such scores (USES, 1967). All such research should contribute to the more effective use of tests in personnel decisions.

TEST-RELATED FACTORS.   In testing culturally disadvantaged persons, it is important to differentiate between cultural factors that affect both test and criterion behavior and those whose influence is restricted to the test. It is the latter, test-related factors that reduce validity. Examples of such factors include previous experience in taking tests, motivation to perform well on tests, rapport with the examiner, and any other variables affecting performance on the particular test but irrelevant to the criterion under consideration. Special efforts should be made to reduce the operation of these test-related factors when testing persons with dissimilar cultural backgrounds. A desirable procedure is to provide adequate test-taking orientation and preliminary practice, as illustrated by the booklets and tape recordings cited in Chapter 2 and by the written exercises of Let's Look at First Graders (Ch. 15).[5]

INTERPRETATION OF TEST SCORES.   By far the most important considerations in the testing of culturally disadvantaged persons—as in all testing— pertain to the interpretation of test scores. The most frequent misgivings regarding the use of tests with minority group members stem from misinterpretations of scores. If a culturally deprived person obtains a low score on an aptitude test or a deviant score on a personality test, it is essential to investigate why he did so. For example, an inferior score on an arithmetic test could result from low test-taking motivation, poor reading ability, or inadequate knowledge of arithmetic, among other reasons. Some thought should also be given to the type of norms to be employed in evaluating individual scores. Depending on the purpose of the testing, the appropriate

[5] For a more detailed discussion of these testing problems, see Guidelines for Testing Minority Group Children (Fishman et al., 1964), prepared by a Work Group of the Society for the Psychological Study of Social Issues, a division of the American Psychological Association, as well as Guidelines on Employment Testing Procedures, prepared by the Equal Employment Opportunity Commission (1966), and related discussion (Wallace, Kissinger, & Reynolds, 1966).

norms may be general norms, subgroup norms based on persons with comparable experiential backgrounds, or the individual's own previous score.

In predicting outcome, such as performance on a job or in an educational program, we must also consider the effects of differential treatments. It is one of the contributions of decision theory to psychometrics that it provides ways of incorporating differential treatment into the prediction of outcomes from test scores (Ch. 6). For example, given certain test scores obtained by an individual with a specified cultural background, what will be his predicted college grades if we introduce remedial teaching programs, counseling designed to modify educational attitudes and motivation, or other appropriate treatments?

OBJECTIVITY OF TESTS.   When social stereotypes and prejudice may distort interpersonal evaluations, tests provide a safeguard against favoritism and arbitrary or capricious decisions. Commenting on the use of tests in schools, Gardner (1961, pp. 48–49) wrote: "The tests couldn't see whether the youngster was in rags or in tweeds, and they couldn't hear the accents of the slum. The tests revealed intellectual gifts at every level of the population."

In the same vein, the *Guidelines for Testing Minority Group Children* (Fishman *et al.*, 1964, p. 139) contain the following observation:

Many bright, non-conforming pupils, with backgrounds different from those of their teachers, make favorable showings on achievement tests, in contrast to their low classroom marks. These are very often children whose cultural handicaps are most evident in their overt social and interpersonal behavior. Without the intervention of standardized tests, many such children would be stigmatized by the adverse subjective ratings of teachers who tend to reward conformist behavior of middle-class character.

With regard to personnel selection, the contribution of tests was aptly characterized in the following words by John W. Macy, Jr., Chairman of the United States Civil Service Commission (*Testing and Public Policy*, 1965, p. 883):

The necessity to measure characteristics of people that are related to job performance is at the very root of the merit system, which is the basis for entry into the career services of the Federal Government. Thus, over the years, the public service has had a vital interest in the development and application of psychological testing methods. I have no doubt that the widespread public confidence in the objectivity of our hiring procedures has in large part been nurtured by the public's perception of the fairness, the practicality, and the integrity of the appraisal methods they must submit to.

In summary, tests *can* be misused in testing culturally disadvantaged persons—as in testing anyone else. When properly used, however, they serve an important function in preventing irrelevant and unfair discrimination. They also provide a quantitative index of the extent of cultural handicap as a necessary first step in remedial programs.

UNDERSTANDING VERSUS CATEGORIZING

The tendency to categorize and label, as a shortcut substitute for understanding, is all too prevalent. The diagnostic categories of classical psychiatry, whereby patients are assigned such labels as "paranoid schizophrenic" or "manic-depressive," are well known. Aware of the many deficiencies of this system of classification, clinical psychologists have turned increasingly to personality descriptions. Unlike the diagnostic labels, these descriptions focus on the origins and individual significance of deviant behavior and provide a more effective basis for therapy. But the traditional labels are not easily dislodged.

Another example of the categorizing tendency is provided by popular misinterpretations of the IQ. A common criticism of intelligence tests is that they encourage a rigid, inflexible, and permanent classification of individuals. A low IQ, it is argued, places an indelible stamp of inferiority on a child. In the case of culturally disadvantaged children, such an IQ would thus serve to perpetuate their handicap. It is largely because implications of permanent status have become attached to the IQ that in 1964 the use of group intelligence tests was discontinued in the New York City public schools (Gilbert, 1966; Loretan, 1966). That it proved necessary to discard the tests in order to eliminate the misconceptions about the fixity of the IQ is a revealing commentary on the tenacity of the misconceptions.

As long as misconceptions about the meaning of an IQ do persist, however, information about a child's IQ may adversely affect his intellectual development. What is expected of an individual tends to determine what he becomes. The mere fact that a behavioral outcome is predicted increases the probability of its occurrence. Known as the "self-fulfilling prophecy," this phenomenon has been demonstrated in a wide variety of contexts (Rosenthal, 1966; Rosenthal & Jacobson, 1968). The expectations that are aroused affect the attitudes and actions of one's associates, as well as the opportunities for behavior development that are made available. Gradually these expectations become part of the individual's own self-concept, which in turn affects his motivation and achievement.

An experiment that is especially relevant to intelligence tests was performed by Rosenthal and Jacobson (1966, 1968). Teachers of 18 classes, including three classes at each grade from 1 to 6, were given the names of children identified by a test as academic "spurters." The expectation was thus aroused that these children would progress more rapidly than their classmates. Actually, the names had been selected at random, with no reference to test scores. Retests after four and eight months, however, showed significantly larger rises in total IQ in the experimental than in the control cases. These effects were greater in the lower academic grades and greater on a nonverbal than on a verbal subtest.

Although the above experiment explicitly aroused an expectation of differences in academic progress, knowledge about a child's IQ would probably have a similar effect. According to popular misconceptions, the IQ is an index of innate intellectual potential; and it represents a fixed property of the organism. The actuarial, group data on the constancy of the IQ, discussed in Chapter 8, have often been misconstrued as supporting this interpretation. It will be recalled, however, that the observed constancy of the IQ on such tests as the Stanford-Binet can be explained in terms of: (1) the cumulative nature of intellectual development, with the resulting overlap of intellectual skills tested at successive ages; (2) the fact that most children remain in the same general environment as they grow up; and (3) the influence of prerequisite intellectual skills on subsequent learning. Moreover, there is evidence that dramatic rises in IQ do in fact occur as a result of special educational programs and other environmental interventions. It follows that when properly interpreted, intelligence test scores should not foster a rigid categorizing of individuals. On the contrary, scores on intelligence tests—and on any other test—should contribute to an understanding of the individual as he is at the time. When combined with information about his experiential background, test scores should facilitate the planning of effective educational experiences for maximum individual development.

CHAPTER **22**

Psychological Interpretation of Test Results

ONE WAY to meet the outside pressures that threaten to undermine psychological testing is to make improvements from within. Improvements are needed, not so much in the construction of tests as in the interpretation of test scores and the orientation of test users. Available tests need not be summarily replaced by new kinds of tests; they sample important behavior and provide an accumulation of normative and validation data that should not be lightly dismissed.

Psychological tests should be regarded as tools. Like all tools, their effectiveness depends on the knowledge, skill, and integrity of the user. A hammer can be employed to build a crude kitchen table or a fine cabinet— or as a weapon of assault. Since psychological tests are measures of behavior, the interpretation of test results requires knowledge about human behavior. Psychological tests cannot be properly applied outside the context of psychological science. Familiarity with relevant behavioral research is needed not only by the test constructor but also by the test user. To illustrate the contributions that psychological research can make to the interpretation of test results, we shall consider typical developments in four areas: the testing situation, the nature of intelligence, personality and intellect, and the assessment of environments.

THE TESTING SITUATION

The basic rationale of testing involves generalization from the behavior sample observed in the testing situation to behavior manifested in other,

566

nontest situations. A test score should help us to predict how the client will feel and act outside the clinic, how the student will achieve in college courses, and how the applicant will perform on the job. Any influences that are specific to the test situation constitute error variance and reduce test validity. In the interpretation of test scores, it is therefore important to identify any test-related influences that limit or impair the generalizability of test results.

COACHING, PRACTICE, AND TEST SOPHISTICATION. In evaluating the effect of coaching or practice on test scores, a fundamental question is whether the improvement is limited to the specific items included in the test or whether it extends to the broader area of behavior that the test is designed to predict. The answer to this question represents the difference between coaching and education. Obviously any educational experience the individual undergoes, either formal or informal, in or out of school, should be reflected in his performance on tests sampling the relevant aspects of behavior. Such broad influences would in no way invalidate the test, since the test score would in such cases present an accurate picture of the individual's standing in the abilities under consideration. The difference is, of course, one of degree. Influences cannot be classified as either narrow or broad, but obviously vary widely in scope, from those affecting only a single administration of a single test, through those affecting performance on all items of a certain type, to those influencing the individual's performance in the large majority of his activities. From the standpoint of effective testing, however, a workable distinction can be made. Thus, it can be stated that a test score is invalidated only when a particular experience raises it without appreciably affecting the behavior domain that the test is designed to predict.

The effects of *coaching* on test scores have been widely investigated. Many of these studies were conducted by British psychologists, with special reference to the effects of practice and coaching on the tests used in assigning 11-year-old children to different types of secondary schools (Yates *et al.*, 1953–1954). As might be expected, the extent of improvement depends on the ability and earlier educational experiences of the examinees, the nature of the tests, and the amount and type of coaching provided. Individuals with deficient educational backgrounds are more likely to benefit from special coaching than are those who have had superior educational opportunities and are already prepared to do well on the tests. It is obvious, too, that the closer the resemblance between test content and coaching material, the greater will be the improvement in test scores. On the other hand, the more closely instruction is restricted to specific test content, the less likely is improvement to extend to criterion performance.

In America, the College Entrance Examination Board has been concerned about the prevalence of ill-advised coaching courses for college applicants.

To clarify the issues, the College Board conducted several well-controlled experiments to determine the effects of coaching on its Scholastic Aptitude Test and surveyed the results of similar studies by other, independent investigators (College Entrance Examination Board, 1965). These studies covered a variety of coaching methods and included students in both public and private high schools; one investigation was conducted with Negro students in 15 urban and rural high schools in Tennessee. The conclusion from all these studies is that intensive drill on items similar to those on the SAT is unlikely to produce appreciably greater gains than occur when students are retested with the SAT after a year of regular high school instruction.

On the basis of such research, the Trustees of the College Board issued a formal statement about coaching, in which the following points were made, among others (College Entrance Examination Board, 1965, pp. 8–9):

The results of the coaching studies which have thus far been completed indicate that average increases of less than 10 points on a 600 point scale can be expected. It is not reasonable to believe that admissions decisions can be affected by such small changes in scores. This is especially true since the tests are merely supplementary to the school record and other evidence taken into account by admissions officers. . . . As the College Board uses the term, aptitude is not something fixed and impervious to influence by the way the child lives and is taught. Rather, this particular Scholastic Aptitude Test is a measure of abilities that seem to grow slowly and stubbornly, profoundly influenced by conditions at home and at school over the years, but not responding to hasty attempts to relive a young lifetime.

A different approach to coaching is illustrated by an investigation conducted with schoolchildren in Israel (Ortar, 1960). This research was undertaken in an effort to develop a measure of academic aptitude applicable to Oriental immigrant children with severe language and cultural handicaps. A test similar to the Arthur Stencil Design Test (Ch. 10) was administered in three stages. The first part was given and scored in the usual way. This was followed by a period of intensive practice on similar items and instruction adapted to the individual's performance. The principles underlying the task were explained in terms of the child's own approach. The third part of the test, again administered and scored in the usual manner, provides the score that is actually used as an index of the child's ability to profit from school instruction. Validity coefficients against school grades were consistently higher for final scores than for initial scores. It is likely that this test served as a sort of job sample within the given school situation. It may have reflected the child's ability to learn abstract principles through instruction similar to that provided in the classroom, as well as his desire to do well in adult-imposed tasks of no immediate practical value, his interest in mastering unfamiliar tasks, and other tendencies conducive to school learning among such children.

It is apparent that coaching may affect test scores in diverse ways, depending on the specific circumstances. It may have little or no effect on the performance of individuals who are already well prepared, as in the case of college-bound American high school students. Or it may markedly raise scores in such ways as to either raise or lower test validity.

The effects of sheer repetition, or *practice*, on test performance are similar to the effects of coaching, but usually less pronounced. It should be noted that practice, as well as coaching, may alter the nature of the test, since the subjects may employ entirely different work methods in solving the same problems. Intelligence tests frequently contain items whose nature can be expected to change with repetition. Retest scores on such tests, whether derived from a repetition of the identical test or from a parallel form, should therefore be carefully scrutinized. A number of studies have been concerned with the effects of the identical repetition of intelligence tests over periods ranging from a few days to several years.[1] Both adults and children, and both normal and mentally retarded persons have been employed. Most of the studies have utilized group tests, although some data on individual tests are also available. All agree in showing significant mean gains in score on retests. Nor is improvement necessarily limited to the initial repetitions. Whether gains persist or level off in successive administrations seems to depend on the difficulty of the test and the ability level of the subjects.

The implications of such findings are illustrated by the results obtained in annual retests of 3,500 schoolchildren with a variety of intelligence tests (Dearborn & Rothney, 1941). When the same test was readministered in successive years, the median IQ of the group rose from 102 to 113, but it dropped to 104 when another test was substituted. Because of the retest gains, the meaning of an IQ obtained on an initial and later trial proved to be quite different. For example, an IQ of 100 fell approximately at the average of the distribution on the initial trial, but in the lowest quarter on a retest. Such IQ's, though numerically identical and derived from the same test, might thus signify normal ability in the one instance and inferior ability in the other.

Gains in score are also found on retesting with parallel forms of the same test, although such gains tend in general to be smaller. Significant mean gains have been reported when alternate forms of a test were administered in immediate succession or after intervals ranging from one day to three years (Droege, 1966a; Peel, 1951, 1952; E. L. Thorndike, 1922). Similar results have been obtained with normal and intellectually gifted schoolchildren, high school and college students, and employee samples. Data on the distribution of gains to be expected on a retest with a

[1] See Adkins (1937), P. Cattell (1931), Crane & Heim (1950), Dearborn & Rothney (1941), Heim & Wallace (1949–1950), Levine & Angoff (1956), Quereshi (1968), Watts (1958).

parallel form should be provided in test manuals and allowance for such gains should be made when interpreting test scores.

The general problem of *test sophistication* should also be considered in this connection. The individual who has had extensive prior experience in taking psychological tests enjoys a certain advantage in test performance over one who is taking his first test (Heim & Wallace, 1949–1950; Millman, Bishop, & Ebel, 1965; Rodger, 1936). Part of this advantage stems from having overcome an initial feeling of strangeness, as well as from having developed more self-confidence and better test-taking attitudes. Part is the result of a certain amount of overlap in the type of content and functions covered by many tests. Specific familiarity with common item types and practice in the use of objective answer sheets may also improve performance slightly. It is particularly important to take test sophistication into account when comparing the scores obtained by children from different types of schools, where the extent of test-taking experience may have varied widely.

TEST ANXIETY AND TEST-TAKING MOTIVATION. Most middle-class American schoolchildren and college students are not only fairly test-wise, but they are also generally motivated to succeed in academic work and in test situations. In such groups, cooperation can be obtained with little difficulty. Special motivational problems are encountered, however, in testing certain other groups. Emotionally disturbed persons, prisoners, or juvenile delinquents, especially when tested in an institutional setting, are likely to manifest a number of unfavorable attitudes, such as suspicion, insecurity, fear, or cynical indifference. Specific abnormal factors in the past experience of such persons are also likely to influence their test performance adversely. As a result of early failures and frustrations in school, for example, such individuals may have developed feelings of hostility and inferiority toward any academic material.

There is also ample evidence to suggest that test-taking motivation varies widely in different ethnic and socioeconomic groups (Anastasi, 1958a, p. 552; Eells *et al.*, 1951, pp. 20–21). One illustration is provided by the following statement, appearing in a summary of socioeconomic differences in test performance:

Observation of the performance of lower-class children on speed tests leads one to suspect that such children often work very rapidly through a test, making responses more or less at random. Apparently they are convinced in advance that they cannot do well on the test, and they find that by getting through the test rapidly they can shorten the period of discomfort which it produces (Eells *et al*, 1951, p. 21).

It is interesting to note that a reaction almost identical with that described above was observed among Puerto Rican school children tested in New York City (Anastasi & Cordova, 1953) and in Hawaii (S. Smith, 1942).

Closely related to test-taking motivation is the question of *test anxiety*. The nature, correlates, and effects of such anxiety have been studied with both schoolchildren and college students, much of this research having been conducted by Sarason and his associates at Yale (S. B. Sarason *et al.*, 1960). First, a questionnaire was constructed to assess the individual's test-taking attitudes. The children's form, for example, contains items such as the following:

Do you worry a lot before taking a test?

When the teacher says she is going to find out how much you have learned, does your heart begin to beat faster?

While you are taking a test, do you usually think you are not doing well?

Of primary interest is the finding that both school achievement and intelligence test scores yielded significant negative correlations with test anxiety. Similar correlations have been found among college students (I. G. Sarason, 1961). Longitudinal studies likewise revealed an inverse relation between changes in anxiety level and changes in intelligence or achievement test performance (Hill & Sarason, 1966; S. B. Sarason, Hill, & Zimbardo, 1964).

Such findings, of course, do not indicate the direction of causal relationships. It is possible that children develop test anxiety because they perform poorly on tests and have thus experienced failure and frustration in previous test situations. In support of this interpretation is the finding that within subgroups of high scorers on intelligence tests, the negative correlation between anxiety level and test performance disappears (Denny, 1966; Feldhusen & Klausmeier, 1962). On the other hand, there is evidence suggesting that at least some of the relationship results from the deleterious effects of anxiety on test performance. In one study (Waite *et al.*, 1958), high-anxious and low-anxious children equated in intelligence test scores were given repeated trials in a learning task. Although initially equal in the learning test, the low-anxious group improved significantly more than the high-anxious.

Several investigators have compared test performance under conditions designed to evoke "anxious" and "relaxed" states. Mandler and Sarason (1952), for example, found that ego-involving instructions, such as telling subjects that everyone is expected to finish in the time allotted, had a beneficial effect on the performance of low-anxious subjects, but a deleterious effect on that of high-anxious subjects. Other studies have likewise found an interaction between testing conditions and such individual characteristics as anxiety level and achievement motivation (Lawrence, 1962; Paul &

Eriksen, 1964). It thus appears likely that the relation between anxiety and test performance is nonlinear, a slight amount of anxiety being beneficial while a large amount is detrimental. Individuals who are customarily low-anxious benefit from test conditions that arouse some anxiety, while those who are customarily high-anxious perform better under more relaxed conditions.

It is undoubtedly true that a chronically high anxiety level will exert a detrimental effect on school learning and intellectual development. Such an effect, however, should be distinguished from the test-limited effects with which this discussion is concerned. To what extent does test anxiety make the individual's test performance unrepresentative of his customary performance level in nontest situations? Because of the competitive pressure experienced by college-bound high school seniors in America today, it has been argued that performance on college admission tests may be unduly affected by test anxiety. In a thorough and well-controlled investigation of this question, French (1962) compared the performance of high school students on a test given as part of the regular administration of the SAT with performance on a parallel form of the test administered at a different time under "relaxed" conditions. The instructions on the latter occasion specified that the test was given for research purposes only and scores would not be sent to any college. The results showed that performance was no poorer during the standard administration than during the relaxed administration. Moreover, the concurrent validity of the test scores against high school course grades did not differ significantly under the two conditions.

EXAMINER AND SITUATIONAL VARIABLES. Comprehensive surveys of the effects of examiner and situational variables on test scores have been prepared by S. B. Sarason (1954), Masling (1960), Moriarty (1961, 1966), and Sattler and Theye (1967). Although some effects have been demonstrated with objective group tests, most of the data have been obtained with either projective techniques or individual intelligence tests. These extraneous factors are more likely to operate with unstructured and ambiguous stimuli, as well as with difficult and novel tasks, than with clearly defined and well learned functions. In general, children are more susceptible to examiner and situational influences than are adults; in the examination of preschool children, the role of the examiner is especially crucial. Emotionally disturbed and insecure persons of any age are also more likely to be affected by such conditions than are well-adjusted persons.

There is considerable evidence that test results may vary systematically as a function of the examiner (Cohen, 1965; Masling, 1960). These differences may be related to personal characteristics of the examiner, such as his age, sex, race, professional or socioeconomic status, and appearance. The examiner's behavior before and during test administration has also been shown to affect test results. For example, controlled investigations have yielded significant differences in intelligence test performance as a result of a "warm" versus a "cold" interpersonal relation between examiner and examinees, or a rigid and aloof versus a natural manner on the part of the examiner (Exner, 1966; Masling, 1959). Moreover, there may be significant interactions between examiner and examinee characteristics, in the sense that the same examiner characteristic or testing manner may have a different effect on different examinees as a function of the examinee's own personality characteristics.

Still another way in which an examiner may inadvertently affect the examinee's responses is through his own expectations. This is simply a special instance of the self-fulfilling prophecy (Rosenthal, 1966). An experiment conducted with the Rorschach will illustrate this effect (Masling, 1965). The examiners were 14 graduate student volunteers, 7 of whom were told, among other things, that experienced examiners elicit more human than animal responses from the subjects, while the other 7 were told that experienced examiners elicit more animal than human responses. Under these conditions, the two groups of examiners obtained significantly different ratios of animal to human responses from their subjects. These differences occurred despite the fact that neither examiners nor subjects reported awareness of any influence attempt. Moreover, tape recordings of all testing sessions revealed no evidence of verbal influence on the part of any examiner. The examiners' expectations apparently operated through subtle postural and facial cues to which the subjects responded.

Apart from the examiner, other aspects of the testing situation may significantly affect test performance. Military recruits, for example, are often examined shortly after induction, during a period of intense readjustment to an unfamiliar and stressful situation. In one investigation designed to test the effect of acclimatization to such a situation on test performance, 2,724 recruits were given the Navy Classification Battery during their ninth day at the Naval Training Center (Gordon & Alf, 1960). When their scores were compared with those obtained by 2,180 recruits tested at the conventional time, during their third day, the 9-day group scored significantly higher on all subtests of the battery.

The examinees' activities immediately preceding the test may also affect their performance, especially when such activities produce emotional disturbance, fatigue, or other handicapping conditions. In an investigation with third- and fourth-grade schoolchildren, there was some evidence to suggest that IQ on the Draw-a-Man Test (Ch. 10) was influenced by the children's preceding classroom activity (McCarthy, 1944). On one occasion, the class had been engaged in writing a composition on "The Best Thing That Ever Happened to Me"; on the second occasion, they had again been writing, but this time on "The Worst Thing That Ever Happened to Me." The IQ's on the second test, following what may have been an emotionally depressing experience, averaged 4 or 5 points lower than on the first test. These findings were corroborated in a later investigation specifically designed to determine the effect of immediately preceding experience on the Draw-a-Man Test (Reichenberg-Hackett, 1953). In this study, children who had had a gratifying experience involving the successful solution of an interesting puzzle, followed by a reward of toys and candy, showed more improvement in their test scores than those who had undergone neutral or less gratifying experiences.

The examples cited in this section illustrate the wide diversity of test-related factors that may affect test scores. In the majority of well-administered testing programs, the influence of these factors is negligible for practical purposes. Nevertheless, the skilled examiner is constantly on guard to detect the possible operation of such factors and to minimize their influence. When circumstances do not permit the control of these conditions, the conclusions drawn from test performance should be qualified.

NATURE OF INTELLIGENCE

Misconceptions about the nature of intelligence—and of the abilities measured by intelligence tests—are at the root of many current misuses of test scores. In mid-1967, a court decision outlawing ability grouping (or the "track system") in the public schools of the nation's capital received wide publicity (see Bickel, 1967; Mathews, 1967). This decision is in a class with the banning of group intelligence tests by the New York City Board of Education (Ch. 21). Both represent drastic measures evoked by prevalent misinterpretations of IQ's by parents, teachers, and school administrators. Ability grouping with reference to specific areas of instruction, such as reading or arithmetic, can serve a useful function if it facilitates remedial instruction and permits each individual to advance at his own rate. But if ability grouping represents a rigid classification based on the notion that IQ's are indices of general, innate learning potential, it simply opens the way for the self-fulfilling prophecy.

Much that has been said earlier in this book, especially in Chapters 8 and 13, pertains to the nature of intelligence. With reference to the social implications of intelligence testing, two points deserve particular emphasis: (1) the multiplicity of abilities constituting intelligence; and (2) the changes that may occur in an individual's intelligence over time.

MULTIPLICITY OF ABILITIES. Factorial analyses of intelligence have identified a large number of relatively independent abilities (Ch. 13). The traditional intelligence test, which concentrates on those abilities most relevant to school learning, measures chiefly abstract verbal and numerical aptitudes. For an adequate picture of the individual's mental functioning, these tests should be supplemented with data from other sources, including other types of tests, behavioral observations, and biographical-history information. Since intelligence tests sample primarily comprehension and memory functions, further information on productive thinking and creativity is also desirable.

Because individuals often vary considerably in their relative development along verbal and quantitative lines, even when a single intelligence test is administered, performance on verbal and quantitative or nonverbal parts should be separately analyzed. Much more research is needed on the interaction between ability patterns and teaching methods. It is likely that individuals will learn best when taught by methods that capitalize on their own strengths. An investigation conducted in the Air Force provides some suggestive data in this connection (Bush et al., 1965). When the same persons were taught by different methods, those whose reading vocabulary scores exceeded their mathematics scores learned faster through lecture-like instruction, while those with the reverse score pattern learned faster through laboratory-type instruction. Ability grouping based on such ability patterns might be well worth exploring, in addition to ability grouping designed to provide remedial instruction in areas of deficient development.

FOCUS ON CHANGE. When properly used, tests can serve as instruments for facilitating and recording behavioral change in desired directions. With regard to intelligence, there is extensive research on the conditions associated with rises or declines in IQ. In comparison with the general norms, children reared in culturally disadvantaged environments tend to decline in IQ with age, those reared in superior environments to gain (Ch. 8). Not only the facilities and opportunities for intellectual development in the home, but also child-rearing practices and parental attitudes may influence the rate of the child's intellectual development. Similarly, persons who continue their education longer gain more in IQ, on the average, than do those who discontinue their schooling at an earlier age (Ch. 11).

Rises and drops in IQ may also occur as a result of both fortuitous environmental changes occurring in a child's life and planned environmental interventions (see Ch. 8 and Anastasi, 1958a). Major changes in family structure, sharp rises or drops in family income level, migration, adoption into a foster home, or attendance at nursery school may alter the course of a child's intellectual development and produce conspicuous increases or decreases in IQ. Significant gains in IQ have likewise been reported as a result of compensatory educational programs for culturally disadvantaged preschool children, although most of these programs are too recent for a definitive evaluation of their effectiveness (Bloom, Davis, & Hess, 1965; Gordon & Wilkerson, 1966).

Similar data are provided by longitudinal studies of populations, in which comparable samples of the same population are tested many years apart (see Anastasi, 1958a, pp. 209–211). When cultural conditions have improved over the interval, a significant rise in the mean intelligence test performance of the population has generally been found. Such findings are illustrated by a comparison of the test scores of American soldiers examined during World Wars I and II, spanning an interval of 25 years (Tuddenham, 1948). For this purpose, a representative sample of enlisted men in the World War II army was given both the AGCT and a revision of the Army Alpha of World War I. The distribution of this group on the AGCT paralleled closely that of the entire army. With the data from this sample as a bridge, it was possible to estimate that the median performance of the World War II army fell at the 83rd percentile of the World War I army. In other words, 83 percent of the World War I population fell below the median score of the World War II population. It is noteworthy that the average amount of education in the World War II population was 10 years, as compared with 8 years during World War I. This increase in amount of education, accompanied by improvements in communication, transportation, and other cultural changes that increased the individual's range of experience, was reflected in improved test performance.

A similar investigation on a smaller scale was conducted with school children living in certain mountainous counties of Tennessee (Wheeler, 1942). Group intelligence tests were administered in 1940 to over 3,000 children in 40 rural schools. The results were compared with those obtained with children in the same areas and largely from the same families, who had been similarly tested in 1930. During the intervening 10-year period, the economic, cultural, and educational status of these counties had improved conspicuously. Paralleling such environmental changes, a rise in IQ was found at all ages and all grades. The median IQ was 82 in the 1930 sample and 93 in the 1940 sample.

From another angle, the very composition of intelligence may alter as a result of the individual's experiences. The individual's pattern of abilities will tend to change with age as his environment fosters and encourages the development of some aptitudes and de-emphasizes other aptitudes. Moreover, factor-analytic research has demonstrated that experiential differences may influence not only the level of performance reached in different abilities, but also the way in which intelligence becomes differentiated into identifiable traits (Ch. 13). That the number and nature of traits or abilities may change over time and may differ among cultures or subcultures has been empirically demonstrated. At the theoretical level, the concepts of learning set and transfer of training provide a possible mechanism to explain the role of experience in the formation of traits (Ch. 13).

PERSONALITY AND INTELLECT

Although it is customary and convenient to classify tests into separate categories, it should be recognized that all such distinctions are superficial.

In interpreting test scores, personality and aptitudes cannot be kept apart. An individual's performance on an aptitude test, as well as his performance in school, on the job, or in any other context, is influenced by his achievement drive, his persistence, his value system, his freedom from handicapping emotional problems, and every other characteristic traditionally classified under the heading of "personality."

PERSONALITY AND INTELLECTUAL DEVELOPMENT. Even more important is the cumulative effect of personality characteristics on the direction and extent of the individual's intellectual development. Some of the evidence for this effect, collected through longitudinal studies of children and adults, was summarized in Chapter 8. In the Fels study of children from infancy to adolescence, for example, emotional dependence on parents was found to be associated with IQ loss during the preschool ages. During the early school years, IQ gains were related chiefly to achievement drive, competitive striving, and curiosity about nature (Kagan & Freeman, 1963; Kagan, Sontag, Baker, & Nelson, 1958; Sontag, Baker, & Nelson, 1958). Similarly, in Haan's (1963) adult follow-up of individuals first tested in their early teens, those who gained in IQ tended to cope with life's problems and frustrations in objective, constructive, and realistic ways; those showing IQ losses, on the other hand, tended to resort to such defense mechanisms as withdrawal, denial, rationalization, and distortion.

It would thus seem that prediction of a child's subsequent intellectual development could be improved by combining information about his emotional and motivational characteristics with his scores on ability tests. A word should be added, however, regarding the assessment of "motivation." In the practical evaluation of schoolchildren, college students, job applicants, and other categories of persons, psychologists are often asked for a measure of the individual's "motivation." When thus worded, this is a meaningless request, since motivation is specific. What is needed is an indication of the individual's value system and the intensity with which he will strive toward specific goals. The strength of these specific motives will interact with situational factors, as well as with aptitudes, to determine the individual's actual performance in given situations.

RECIPROCITY OF RELATIONSHIP. The relation between personality and intellect is reciprocal. Not only do personality characteristics affect intellectual development, but intellectual level also affects personality development. The success the individual attains in the development and use of his aptitudes is bound to influence his emotional adjustment, interpersonal relations, and self-concept. In the self-concept we can see most clearly the mutual influence of aptitudes and personality traits. The child's achievement in school, on the playground, and in other situations helps to shape his self-concept; and his self-concept at any given stage influences his subsequent performance, in a continuing spiral. In this regard, the self-concept operates as a sort of private self-fulfilling prophecy.

A THEORY OF DRIVES AND INTELLECT.   At a more basic theoretical level, Hayes (1962) has proposed an ingenious hypothesis concerning the relationship of drives and intellect. Regarding intelligence as a collection of learned abilities, Hayes maintains that the individual's motivational make-up influences the kind and amount of learning that occurs. Specifically, it is the strength of the "experience-producing drives" that affects intellectual development. These drives are illustrated by exploratory and manipulatory activities, curiosity, play, the babbling of infants, and other intrinsically motivated behavior. Citing chiefly research on animal behavior, Hayes argues that these experience-producing drives are genetically determined and represent the only hereditary basis of individual differences in intelligence. It might be added that the hereditary or environmental basis of the experience-producing drives need not alter the conceptualization of their role in intellectual development. These two parts of the theory may be considered independently.

Whatever the origin of the experience-producing drives, the individual's experience is regarded as a joint function of the strength of these drives and the environment in which they operate. The cumulative effect of these experiences in turn determines the individual's intellectual level at any given time. This is a promising hypothesis, through which Hayes integrates a considerable body of data from many types of research on both human and animal behavior.

THE ASSESSMENT OF ENVIRONMENTS

There are two major ways in which the assessment of environments may contribute to behavioral prediction. Behavior does not occur in a vacuum. The individual behaves in a particular environmental context, which in part determines the nature of his responses. The resulting behavior depends on the interaction of respondent and situational variables. The same individual will respond differently in different situations. Hence, the prediction of criterion performance from test scores or from earlier criterion behavior (such as school grades or performance on a previous job) can be materially improved by taking situational variables into account. The same student may perform well at Shady Lanes College and do poorly at Center State U.; the same employee may succeed at Amalgamated Widgets and fail at International Teletaste and Teletouch; the same housewife may be a community leader in Starkville and an unhappy isolate in Suburbiton. We shall use the term *criterion environment* to refer to the environmental situations about which behavior predictions are to be made.

Even more important for prediction purposes is knowledge about the *intervening environment* to which the individual is likely to be exposed in the interval between time *A*, when the prediction is made, and time *B*, to which the prediction refers. Such knowledge is especially significant when the interval falls within a child's developmental period. Information about relevant characteristics of the intervening environment should substantially increase the validity of behavioral prediction.

Although the importance of environmental variables in the determination of behavior is now widely recognized, instruments for the measurement of environment are still scarce. The *Mental Measurements Yearbooks* contain a section on socioeconomic scales, but few entries are included. Moreover, most of the available measures are crude and superficial. It is only since the late 1950's that serious efforts have been made to develop sophisticated indices of environmental variables for specific purposes.

CRITERION ENVIRONMENTS. Informal and qualitative descriptions of criterion environments have long been a factor in personnel decisions. Job analysis (Ch. 16) is designed in part to provide information about the physical and interpersonal conditions under which the employee will be expected to function. Skilled interviewers balance applicant characteristics, especially as manifested in earlier situations with known properties, against the anticipated properties of the prospective job situation. It should also be borne in mind that the situational characteristics of jobs may change as a function of time spent on the job (Ch. 5). A job that may be challenging in its early stages may become dull and routine after the worker has mastered it; this may lead to rapid turnover among certain types of workers. In judging promotion potential, moreover, the interviewer must estimate the individual's response to the many situational changes that a promotion would entail.

Similar efforts have been made to describe educational environments. It is well established, for example, that the average level and range of scholastic aptitude test scores vary widely among colleges. The differences are so large, in fact, that there is little overlap between the top and bottom colleges in these scores. Colleges also differ in their psychological climate and in the kinds of environmental pressures that they put on students. Some of the major differences pertain to the relative emphasis placed on theoretical versus practical orientation, the degree of conformity expected of the student, the importance of extracurricular participation, the extent of student concern with social action and international problems, and achievement pressure versus a relaxed, easygoing atmosphere. Quite apart from his intellectual qualifications, a student may be a misfit in one of these college environments and an outstanding leader in another.

One of the most ambitious investigations of college environments led to

TABLE 35   COLLEGE CHARACTERISTICS INDEX: ITEMS DIFFERENTIATING BE-
TWEEN SEVEN LIBERAL ARTS AND THREE BUSINESS ADMINISTRATION PROGRAMS
BY 40 PERCENTAGE POINTS OR MORE

(From Stern, 1962, p. 41)

No.	Item	Scale[a]	Percentage Response	
			Liberal Arts	Business Administration
1.	Students are discouraged from criticizing administrative policies and teaching practices	Aba	20.2	92.0
2.	The school administration has little tolerance for student complaints and protests	Aba	14.1	56.0
9.	Students address faculty members as "professor" or "doctor"	Dfr	13.5	63.3
69.	Religious worship here stresses service to God and obedience to His laws	Dfr	18.5	64.4
22.	In many classes students have an assigned seat	Ord	12.9	99.3
142.	Professors usually take attendance in class	Ord	32.2	83.0
292.	Classes meet only at their regularly scheduled time and place	Ord	34.7	90.3
47.	The school offers many opportunities for students to understand and criticize important works in art, music, and drama	Hum	85.1	40.8
77.	A lecture by an outstanding literary critic would be well attended	Hum	90.4	34.3
107.	Many students are planning postgraduate work in the social sciences	Hum	76.2	18.8
167.	When students get together, they often talk about trends in art, music, or the theatre	Hum	75.3	17.9
197.	Humanities courses are often elected by students majoring in other areas	Hum	89.9	49.1
261.	The school has an excellent reputation for academic freedom	Obj	90.6	48.6
25.	Books dealing with psychological problems or personal values are widely read and discussed	Ref	55.2	13.8
55.	There would be a capacity audience for a lecture by an outstanding philosopher or theologian	Ref	76.2	18.1
115.	Modern art and music get considerable attention here	Ref	89.6	41.3
235.	Long, serious intellectual discussions are common among the students	Ref	84.6	21.6
295.	There is considerable interest in the analysis of value systems and the relativity of societies and ethics	Ref	86.9	38.3
30.	There is a lot of emphasis on preparing for graduate work	Und	62.4	10.4
90.	Most students have considerable interest in round tables, panel meetings, or other formal discussions	Und	74.7	34.2
180.	Many students here prefer to talk about poetry, philosophy, or mathematics, as compared with motion pictures, politics, or inventions	Und	78.6	26.5

[a] Abbreviations of the need-press categories, or scales, are as follows: Aba—Abasement, Dfr—Deference, Ord—Order, Hum—Humanism, Obj—Objectivity, Ref—Reflectiveness, Und—Understanding.

the construction of the College Characteristics Index (Pace, 1960; Pace & Stern, 1958; Stern, 1962, 1963). Later versions of this index have also been developed for use in other contexts, such as high schools, evening colleges, and industrial organizations. Paralleling these institutional instruments is the Activities Index, applicable to individuals. Together, the two types of instruments provide a basic taxonomy for characterizing both persons and situations in comparable terms.

The College Characteristics Index (CCI) and the Activities Index take as their starting point Murray's (1938) theoretical model of individual needs and environmental press. The Activities Index covers 30 needs, similar to those sampled by the EPPS (Ch. 17) and the TAT (Ch. 19). The CCI (and the other versions of this index) measure a parallel set of "environmental press" or situational characteristics. In both types of instruments, 10 items are employed to sample each need (or press). Typical items from the CCI, with their corresponding need-press categories, are reproduced in Table 35. This table includes those items yielding the largest differences between seven liberal arts colleges and three business administration programs.

Data on each institution (or curricular program) are obtained by having the CCI filled out by a sample of students; the percentages of students answering each item affirmatively or negatively are then employed in plotting the institutional profile. The index thus describes the institution as it is perceived by its students. The results for a given institution, however, are quite consistent with data obtained from other sources, including faculty, administration, and such special student samples as National Merit Scholars. There is also as much student agreement on impressionistic items as on items referring to objectively verifiable institutional characteristics. Although of relatively recent origin, the CCI has already been widely applied in research on many types of institutions.

Another instrument designed for the same purpose is the College and University Environment Scales (CUES). This instrument originated in the same research project as the CCI; it differs from the CCI principally in the categories employed for describing college environments. Instead of the Murray need-press categories, CUES utilizes dimensions derived by factor analysis of institutional scores. The data for these analyses were obtained from a representative national sample of 50 colleges and universities. CUES provides scores in five factors: Practicality, Community, Awareness, Propriety, and Scholarship.

INTERVENING ENVIRONMENTS. After surveying relevant research findings from a variety of sources, Bloom (1964, p. 200) draws the following conclusion:

The correlation between measurements of the same characteristic at two different times will approach unity when the environment in which the individuals have lived during the intervening period is known and taken into account.

Recognizing the crudity and inadequacy of available indices of a child's environment, Bloom nevertheless illustrated the effect of including environmental data in predictions based on published data. For example, for a group of 40 pupils, the correlation between reading comprehension at grade 2 and at grade 8 rose from .52 to .72 when father's occupation was added as a rough index of the cultural level of the home (p. 119). Again, a reanalysis of intelligence test data from the Harvard Growth Study showed that the correlation between intelligence test scores at ages 7 and 16 could be raised from .58 to .92, when parents' educational level was included in the multiple correlation (p. 80).

Available measures of childhood environments are extremely limited. Examples of some of the techniques that have been employed for this purpose can be found in Anastasi (1958a, Ch. 15) and Gerberich, Greene, and Jorgensen (1962, Ch. 4). Sociologists have utilized elaborate procedures for identifying an individual's social class membership (Warner, Meeker, & Eells, 1949). Simpler and more readily applicable indices, however, have proved to be equally effective, yielding results that agree very closely with those obtained by the more laborious methods. In fact, a reasonably close approximation of socioeconomic level can be found from the occupation of the father or other principal wage earner in the family. Several rough scales have been constructed for classifying parental occupation into levels; some combine occupational information with parental educational level (Hollingshead & Redlich, 1957).

Other scales have attempted to give a more highly differentiated picture of home environment, including not only parental characteristics but also such data as size and nature of home; availability of such modern conveniences as telephones, vacuum cleaners, and refrigerators; presence of books, magazines, and newspapers in the home; and formal out-of-school instruction, such as music lessons. For these scales, data may be gathered through a pupil questionnaire, parental interviews, home visits, or some combination of these procedures.

A major limitation of all these approaches stems from the fact that environments are treated as if they fell along a single dimension of better-or-worse, higher-or-lower, or some other composite variable. Bloom (1964) and Wolf (1966) have pointed out that environments should be described with reference to their effect on specific individual characteristics. Thus, the optimal environments for physical growth, school achievement, independence, creativity, and social conformity are probably quite dissimilar. Accordingly, Wolf (1966) and Dave (see Bloom, 1964) at the University of Chicago explored the possibility of constructing "sub-environment" scales; one of these scales was specifically oriented toward general intelligence, the other toward academic achievement. These scales are applied through home visits and parental interviews. They differ from traditional instruments in that only items relevant to the particular sub-environment are included. In addition, the focus is on what parents do in relation to the child rather than on parental status and physical characteristics of the home. Among the items in the academic achievement scale, for example, are questions about parental aspirations and plans for the child's education; social pressure and rewards for academic achievement; parental knowledge of the child's academic progress; nature and amount of assistance provided in overcoming academic difficulties; and opportunities provided for verbal development.

In preliminary validation research with 60 midwestern fifth-grade children, the intelligence scale correlated .69 with scores on a group intelligence test, in contrast with the correlations of .20 to .40 generally found between intelligence test scores and indices of socioeconomic level. Similarly, the academic achievement scale correlated .80 with an achievement battery, in contrast with the usual correlations of the order of .50 obtained with socioeconomic level. It is also relevant to note that within the achievement battery, the highest correlations were obtained with word knowledge, reading, and language, and the lowest with arithmetic subtests. It is the child's verbal development that is most susceptible to home influences. While these two sub-environment scales represent only a modest beginning, they point the way to a highly promising approach to the assessment of environments.

Although specific instruments have been described in connection with the principal use for which they were developed, any environmental scale can, of course, be employed for assessing either criterion environments or intervening environments. For example, the previously cited scales for describing college environments may be used, in conjunction with student characteristics, in the prediction of post-college behavior of individuals.

Any text on psychological testing written today could well be titled "Testing in Transition." Psychological testing is moving in many directions and at a constantly accelerating pace. The changing nature of the field has been reflected in this book through the inclusion of tests at different stages of their own life cycle. Some time-honored instruments for which research has provided little support are declining in acceptance. Others have proved viable and have undergone repeated updating. Recently developed instruments, following a variety of novel approaches, have been coming to the fore and gaining recognition. Still others are too new to be regarded as anything more than promising and suggestive; they may prove their worth, lead indirectly to other developments, or quietly disappear. A true picture of the current state of the field must convey an impression of movement. While necessarily presenting a cross-sectional view at one point in time, this book has consistently endeavored to identify trends and directions in a changing scene.

References

ADAMS, E. W. Survey of Bernouillian utility theory. In H. Solomon (Ed.), *Mathematical thinking in the measurement of behavior.* New York: Free Press, 1960. Pp. 151–268.

ADAMS, W. M. Prediction of scholastic success in colleges of law: I. The experimental edition of the Iowa Legal Aptitude Test. *Educational and Psychological Measurement,* 1943, 3, 291–305.

ADAMS, W. M. Prediction of scholastic success in colleges of law: II. An investigation of pre-law grades and other indices of law school aptitude. *Educational and Psychological Measurement,* 1944, 4, 13–19.

ADCOCK, C. J. *Factorial analysis for non-mathematicians.* New York: Cambridge University Press, 1954.

ADCOCK, C. J. Thematic Apperception Test. *Sixth Mental Measurements Yearbook,* 1965, 533–535.

ADKINS, D. C. The effects of practice on intelligence test scores. *Journal of Educational Psychology,* 1937, 28, 222–231.

AHLSTRÖM, K. G. Studies in spelling: I. Analysis of three different aspects of spelling ability. Report No. 20, The Institute of Education, Uppsala University (Sweden), 1964.

ALBRECHT, P. A., GLASER, E. M., & MARKS, J. Validation of a multiple-assessment procedure for managerial personnel. *Journal of Applied Psychology,* 1964, 48, 351–360.

ALBRIGHT, L. E., SMITH, W. J., & GLENNON, J. R. A follow-up on some "invalid" tests for selecting salesmen. *Personnel Psychology,* 1959, 12, 105–112.

ALEXAKOS, C. E. Predictive efficiency of two multivariate statistical techniques in comparison with clinical predictions. *Journal of Educational Psychology,* 1966, 57, 297–306.

58

ALIMENA, B. Norms for scatter analysis on the Wechsler Intelligence Scales. *Journal of Clinical Psychology*, 1951, 7, 289–290.

ALLEN, R. M., & COLLINS, M. G. Suggestions for the adaptive administration of intelligence tests for those with cerebral palsy. *Cerebral Palsy Review*, 1955, 16, 11–14.

ALLPORT, G. W. A test for ascendance-submission. *Journal of Abnormal and Social Psychology*, 1928, 23, 118–136.

ALLPORT, G. W. *Personality: A psychological interpretation.* New York: Holt, 1937.

ALLPORT, G. W., & ODBERT, H. S. Trait-names, a psycholexical study. *Psychological Monographs*, 1936, 47, No. 1.

AMERICAN INSTITUTES FOR RESEARCH. Situational tests for evaluating supervisory skill. *AIR Research Notes*, 1957, No. 14.

AMES, L. B., *et al.* *Child Rorschach responses: Developmental trends from two to ten years.* New York: Hoeber-Harper, 1952.

AMES, L. B., *et al.* *Rorschach responses in old age.* New York: Hoeber-Harper, 1954.

AMES, L. B., *et al.* *Adolescent Rorschach responses: Developmental trends from ten to sixteen years.* New York: Hoeber-Harper, 1959.

ANASTASI, A. Practice and variability. *Psychological Monographs*, 1934, 45, No. 5.

ANASTASI, A. The nature of psychological "traits." *Psychological Review*, 1948, 55, 127–138.

ANASTASI, A. The concept of validity in the interpretation of test scores. *Educational and Psychological Measurement*, 1950, 10, 67–78.

ANASTASI, A. Age changes in adult test performance. *Psychological Reports*, 1956, 2, 509.

ANASTASI, A. *Differential psychology.* (3rd ed.) New York: Macmillan, 1958. (a)

ANASTASI, A. Heredity, environment, and the question "How?" *Psychological Review*, 1958, 65, 197–208. (b)

ANASTASI, A. Psychological tests: Uses and abuses. *Teachers College Record*, 1961, 62, 389–393.

ANASTASI, A. Culture-fair testing. *Educational Horizons*, 1964, 43, 26–30. (a)

ANASTASI, A. *Fields of applied psychology.* New York: McGraw-Hill, 1964. (b)

ANASTASI, A. (Ed.) *Individual differences.* New York: Wiley, 1965.

ANASTASI, A. Some implications of cultural factors for test construction. In A. Anastasi (Ed.), *Testing problems in perspective.* Washington: American Council on Education, 1966. Pp. 453–457.

ANASTASI, A. Psychology, psychologists, and psychological testing. *American Psychologist*, 1967, 22, 297–306.

ANASTASI, A., & CORDOVA, F. A. Some effects of bilingualism upon the intelligence test performance of Puerto Rican children in New York City. *Journal of Educational Psychology*, 1953, 44, 1–19.

ANASTASI, A., & DRAKE, J. An empirical comparison of certain techniques for estimating the reliability of speeded tests. *Educational and Psychological Measurement*, 1954, 14, 529–540.

ANDERSON, J. E. The prediction of terminal intelligence from infant and preschool tests. *Thirty-ninth Yearbook, National Society for the Study of Education*, 1940, Part I, 385–403.

ANDERSON, S. B., KATZ, M., & SHIMBERG, B. *Meeting the test.* (Rev. ed.) New York: Four Winds Press, 1965.

ANGOFF, W. H. Scales with nonmeaningful origins and units of measurement. *Educational and Psychological Measurement*, 1962, 22, 27–34.

ANGOFF, W. H. Technical problems of obtaining equivalent scores on tests. *Journal of Educational Measurement*, 1964, 1, 11–13.

ANGOFF, W. H. Can useful general-purpose equivalency tables be prepared for different college admissions tests? In A. Anastasi (Ed.), *Testing problems in perspective.* Washington: American Council on Education, 1966. Pp. 251–264.

ANGOFF, W. H. (Ed.) *Technical manual: College Entrance Examination Board.* Princeton, N.J.: Educational Testing Service, 1968.

ANGOFF, W. H. Scales, norms, and equivalent scores. In R. L. Thorndike (Ed.), *Educational measurement.* (2nd ed.) Washington: American Council on Education, 1971. Ch. 15.

ANSBACHER, H. L. The Goodenough Draw-a-Man Test and primary mental abilities. *Journal of Consulting Psychology*, 1952, 16, 176–180.

Army Air Forces aviation psychology program, research reports. Rep. Nos. 1–19. Washington: Government Printing Office, 1947–1948.

ARNOLD, G. F. A technique for measuring the mental ability of the cerebral palsied. *Psychological Service Center Journal*, 1951, 3, 171–180.

ATKINSON, J. W. (Ed.) *Motives in fantasy, action, and society.* Princeton, N.J.: Van Nostrand, 1958.

ATKINSON, J. W., & FEATHER, N. T. *A theory of achievement motivation.* New York: Wiley, 1966.

BALLER, W. R., CHARLES, D. C., & MILLER, E. L. Mid-life attainment of the mentally retarded: A longitudinal study. *Genetic Psychology Monographs*, 1967, 75, 235–329.

BALMA, M. J. The concept of synthetic validity. *Personnel Psychology*, 1959, 12, 395–396.

BARRON, F. Personality style and perceptual choice. *Journal of Personality*, 1952, 20, 385–401.

BARRON, F. The psychology of imagination. *Scientific American*, 1958, 199, 150–166.

BARRON, F., & WELSH, G. S. Artistic perception as a possible factor in personality style: Its measurement by a figure preference test. *Journal of Psychology*, 1952, 33, 199–203.

BARTLETT, C. J., & EDGERTON, H. A. Stanine values for ranks for different numbers of things ranked. *Educational and Psychological Measurement*, 1966, 26, 287–289.

BASS, B. M. The leaderless group discussion. *Psychological Bulletin*, 1954, 51, 465–492.

BASS, B. M. Development of a structured disguised personality test. *Journal of Applied Psychology*, 1956, 40, 393–397.

BASS, B. M. Validity studies of a proverbs personality test. *Journal of Applied Psychology*, 1957, 41, 158–160.

BASS, B. M. An approach to the objective assessment of successful leadership. In B. M. Bass & I. A. Berg (Eds.), *Objective approaches to personality assessment.* Princeton, N.J.: Van Nostrand, 1959. Ch. 8.

BAUERNFEIND, R. H. The matter of "ipsative" scores. *Personnel and Guidance Journal*, 1962, 41, 210–217.

BAUGHMAN, E. E. Rorschach scores as a function of examiner difference. *Journal of Projective Techniques*, 1951, 15, 243–249.

BAUGHMAN, E. E. The role of the stimulus in Rorschach responses. *Psychological Bulletin*, 1958, 55, 121–147.

BAUMAN, M. K., & HAYES, S. P. *A manual for the psychological examination of the adult blind.* New York: Psychological Corporation, 1951.

BAYLEY, N. Mental growth during the first three years. *Genetic Psychology Monographs*, 1933, 14, 1–93.

BAYLEY, N. On the growth of intelligence. *American Psychologist*, 1955, 10, 805–818.

BAYLEY, N., & ODEN, M. H. The maintenance of intellectual ability in gifted adults. *Journal of Gerontology*, 1955, 10, 91–107.

BAYLEY, N., & SCHAEFER, E. S. Correlations of maternal and child behaviors with the development of mental abilities. *Monographs of the Society for Research in Child Development*, 1964, 29, No. 6.

BECKER, W. C. The matching of behavior rating and questionnaire personality factors. *Psychological Bulletin*, 1960, 57, 201–212.

BELL, A., & ZUBEK, J. The effect of age on the intellectual performance of mental defectives. *Journal of Gerontology*, 1960, 15, 285–295.

BELL, F. O., HOFF, A. L., & HOYT, K. B. Answer sheets do make a difference. *Personnel Psychology*, 1964, 17, 65–71.

BELLAK, L. *The Thematic Apperception Test and the Children's Apperception Test in clinical use*. New York: Grune & Stratton, 1954.

BELLAK, L., & HURVICH, M. S. A human modification of the Children's Apperception Test (CAT-H). *Journal of Projective Techniques and Personality Assessment*, 1966, 30, 228–242.

BENDER, L. A visual motor Gestalt test and its clinical use. *American Orthopsychiatric Association, Research Monographs*, 1938, No. 3.

BENNETT, G. K., & CRUIKSHANK, R. M. *A summary of manual and mechanical ability tests*. New York: Psychological Corporation, 1942.

BENNETT, G. K., & CRUIKSHANK, R. M. *A summary of clerical tests*. New York: Psychological Corporation, 1949.

BENNETT, G. K., & DOPPELT, J. E. The evaluation of pairs of tests for guidance use. *Educational and Psychological Measurement*, 1948, 8, 319–325.

BENNETT, G. K., & DOPPELT, J. E. *Test Orientation Procedure*. New York: Psychological Corporation, 1967.

BENNETT, G. K., SEASHORE, H. G., & WESMAN, A. G. *Counseling from profiles: A casebook for the Differential Aptitude Tests*. New York: Psychological Corporation, 1951.

BENSBERG, G. J., & SLOAN, W. A study of Wechsler's concept of "normal deterioration" in older mental defectives. *Journal of Clinical Psychology*, 1950, 6, 359–362.

BENTON, A. L. *Revised Visual Retention Test: Manual*. New York: Psychological Corporation, 1963.

BERDIE, R. F. Policies regarding the release of information about clients. *Journal of Counseling Psychology*, 1960, 7, 149–150.

BERDIE, R. F. Intra-individual variability and predictability. *Educational and Psychological Measurement*, 1961, 21, 663–676.

BERDIE, R. F. The Ad Hoc Committee on Social Impact of Psychological Assessment. *American Psychologist*, 1965, 20, 143–146.

BERDIE, R. F., & LAYTON, W. L. Research on the Minnesota Counseling Inventory. *Journal of Counseling Psychology*, 1960, 7, 218–224.

BERDIE, R. F., LAYTON, W. L., SWANSON, E. O., & HAGENAH, T. *Testing in guidance and counseling*. New York: McGraw-Hill, 1963.

BERG, E. A. A simple objective technique for measuring flexibility in thinking. *Journal of General Psychology*, 1948, 39, 15–22.

BERG, I. A. Response bias and personality: The deviation hypothesis. *Journal of Psychology*, 1955, 40, 61–72.

BERG, I. A. Deviant responses and deviant people: The formulation of the deviation hypothesis. *Journal of Counseling Psychology*, 1957, 4, 154–161.

BERG, I. A. The unimportance of test item content. In B. M. Bass & I. A. Berg (Eds.), *Objective approaches to personality assessment*. Princeton, N. J.: Van Nostrand, 1959. Pp. 83–99.

BERG, I. A. Measuring deviant behavior by means of deviant response sets. In I. A. Berg & B. M. Bass (Eds.), *Conformity and deviation*. New York: Harper, 1961. Pp. 328–379.

BERNARDONI, L. C. A culture fair intelligence test for the Ugh, No, and Oo-La-La cultures. *Personnel and Guidance Journal*, 1964, 42, 554–557.

BERNSTEIN, L. The examiner as an inhibiting factor in clinical testing. *Journal of Consulting Psychology*, 1956, 20, 287–290.

BICKEL, A. M. Skelly Wright's sweeping decision. *New Republic*, July 8, 1967, 11–12.

BILLINGSLEA, F. Y. The Bender Gestalt: A review and a perspective. *Psychological Bulletin*, 1963, 60, 233–251.

BINET, A., & HENRI, V. La psychologie individuelle. *Année psychologique*, 1895, 2, 411–463.

BINET, A., & SIMON, TH. Méthodes nouvelles pour le diagnostic du niveau intellectuel des anormaux. *Année psychologique*, 1905, 11, 191–244.

BINGHAM, W. V., MOORE, B. V., & GUSTAD, J. *How to interview*. (4th ed.) New York: Harper, 1959.

BLACK, H. *They shall not pass*. New York: Morrow, 1963.

BLAKE, R. R., & RAMSEY, G. V. (Eds.) *Perception: An approach to personality*. New York: Ronald, 1951.

BLOCK, J. *The Q sort method in personality assessment and psychiatric research*. Springfield, Ill.: Charles C Thomas, 1961.

BLOCK, J. *The challenge of response sets: Unconfounding meaning, acquiescence, and social desirability in the MMPI*. New York: Appleton-Century-Crofts, 1965.

BLOMMERS, P., & LINDQUIST, E. F. *Elementary statistical methods in psychology and education*. Boston: Houghton Mifflin, 1960.

BLOOM, B. S. *Stability and change in human characteristics*. New York: Wiley, 1964.

BLOOM, B. S., et al. *Taxonomy of educational objectives, handbook I: Cognitive domain*. New York: McKay, 1956.

BLOOM, B. S., DAVIS, A., & HESS, R. *Compensatory education for cultural deprivation*. New York: Holt, Rinehart & Winston, 1965.

BOLDT, R. F. Development of an optimum computerized allocation system. *USAPRO Technical Research Report No. 1135*, April 1964.

BOLGAR, H., & FISCHER, L. K. Personality projection in the World Test. *American Journal of Orthopsychiatry*, 1947, 17, 117–128.

BOLTON, T. L. The growth of memory in school children. *American Journal of Psychology*, 1891–1892, 4, 362–380.

BOND, E. A. Tenth grade abilities and achievements. *Teachers College Contributions to Education*, 1940, No. 813.

BORDIN, E. S. A theory of vocational interests as dynamic phenomena. *Educational and Psychological Measurement*, 1943, 3, 49–65.

BORING, E. G. *A history of experimental psychology*. (Rev. ed.) New York: Appleton-Century-Crofts, 1950.

BORISLOW, B. The Edwards Personal Preference Schedule (EPPS) and fakability. *Journal of Applied Psychology*, 1958, 42, 22–27.

BRADWAY, K. P. IQ constancy on the Revised Stanford-Binet from the preschool to the junior high school level. *Journal of Genetic Psychology*, 1944, 65, 197–217.

BRADWAY, K. P. An experimental study of factors associated with Stanford-Binet IQ changes from the preschool to the junior high school. *Journal of Genetic Psychology*, 1945, 66, 107–128. (a)

BRADWAY, K. P. Predictive value of Stanford-Binet preschool items. *Journal of Educational Psychology*, 1945, 36, 1–16. (b)

BRADWAY, K. P., THOMPSON, C. W., & CRAVENS, R. B. Preschool IQ's after twenty-five years. *Journal of Educational Psychology*, 1958, 49, 278–281.

BRESLOW, E. The predictive efficiency of the Law School Admission Test at the New York University School of Law. *Psychology Newsletter, New York University*, 1957, 9, 13–22.

BRIM, O. G., JR. American attitudes toward intelligence tests. *American Psychologist*, 1965, 20, 125–130.

BROGDEN, H. E. On the interpretation of the correlation coefficient as a measure of predictive efficiency. *Journal of Educational Psychology*, 1946, 37, 65–76.

BROGDEN, H. E. Increased efficiency of selection resulting from replacement of a single predictor with several differential predictors. *Educational and Psychological Measurement*, 1951, 11, 173–196.

BROGDEN, H. E., & TAYLOR, E. K. The dollar criterion—applying the cost accounting concept to criterion construction. *Personnel Psychology*, 1950, 3, 133–154.

BROSS, J. D. J. *Design for decision*. New York: Macmillan, 1953. (Paperback ed., Free Press, 1965).

BROWN, C. W., & GHISELLI, E. E. Per cent increase in proficiency resulting from use of selective devices. *Journal of Applied Psychology*, 1953, 37, 341–345.

BROWN, D. W. Interpreting the college student to prospective employers, government agencies, and graduate schools. *Personnel and Guidance Journal*, 1961, 39, 576–582.

BROWN, J. F. A modification of the Rosenzweig Picture-Frustration Test to study hostile interracial attitudes. *Journal of Psychology*, 1947, 24, 247–272.

BRUNER, J. S., & KRECH, D. (Eds.) *Perception and personality: A symposium*. Durham, N. C.: Duke University Press, 1950.

BUCHWALD, A. M. Values and the use of tests. *Journal of Consulting Psychology*, 1965, 29, 49–54.

BUHLER, C., LUMRY, G. K., & CARROLL, H. S. World-test standardization studies. *Journal of Child Psychiatry*, 1951, 2, 2–81.

BURIK, T. E. Relative roles of the learning and motor factors involved in the digit symbol test. *Journal of Psychology*, 1950, 30, 33–42.

BURKE, H. R. Raven's Progressive Matrices: A review and critical evaluation. *Journal of Genetic Psychology*, 1958, 93, 199–228.

BURNHAM, P. S. Prediction and performance. In *From high school to college: Readings for counselors*. New York: College Entrance Examination Board, 1965. Pp. 65–71.

BURNHAM, P. S., & CRAWFORD, A. B. Law school prediction at mid-century. *Journal of Legal Education*, 1957, 10, 201–207.

BURNS, R. B. Age and mental ability: Re-testing with thirty-three years' interval. *British Journal of Educational Psychology*, 1966, 36, 116.

BUROS, O. K. (Ed.) *Tests in print*. Highland Park, N. J.: Gryphon Press, 1961.

BUROS, O. K. (Ed.) *The sixth mental measurements yearbook*. Highland Park, N. J.: Gryphon Press, 1965.

BURT, C. *The factors of the mind: An introduction to factor-analysis in psychology.* New York: Macmillan, 1941.

BURT, C. Mental abilities and mental factors. *British Journal of Educational Psychology,* 1944, 14, 85–89.

BURT, C. The structure of the mind; a review of the results of factor analysis. *British Journal of Psychology,* 1949, 19, 176–199.

BURTT, H. E. *Legal psychology.* Englewood Cliffs, N. J.: Prentice-Hall, 1931.

BUSH, W. J., *et al.* Some interactions between individual differences and modes of instruction. *USAF AMRL Technical Report,* 1965, No. 65-228.

BUSWELL, G. T., & JOHN, L. Diagnostic studies in arithmetic. *Supplementary Educational Monographs,* 1926, No. 30.

CALDWELL, O. W., & COURTIS, S. A. *Then and now in education, 1845–1923.* Yonkers, N. Y.: World Book Co., 1923.

CALLIS, R., ENGRAM, W. C., & MCGOWAN, J. F. Coding the Kuder Preference Record—Vocational. *Journal of Applied Psychology,* 1954, 38, 359–363.

CAMPBELL, D. P. The Center for Interest Measurement Research. *Journal of Counseling Psychology,* 1964, 11, 395–399.

CAMPBELL, D. P. A cross-sectional and longitudinal study of scholastic abilities over twenty-five years. *Journal of Counseling Psychology,* 1965, 12, 55–61.

CAMPBELL, D. P. The Minnesota Vocational Interest Inventory. *Personnel and Guidance Journal,* 1966, 44, 854–858.

CAMPBELL, D. T. The indirect assessment of social attitudes. *Psychological Bulletin,* 1950, 47, 15–38.

CAMPBELL, D. T. Recommendations for APA test standards regarding construct, trait, and discriminant validity. *American Psychologist,* 1960, 15, 546–553.

CAMPBELL, D. T., & FISKE, D. W. Convergent and discriminant validation by the multitrait-multimethod matrix. *Psychological Bulletin,* 1959, 56, 81–105.

CANFIELD, A. A. The "sten" scale—A modified C-scale. *Educational and Psychological Measurement,* 1951, 11, 295–297.

CARNES, G. D. Vocational interest characteristic of abnormal personalities. *Journal of Counseling Psychology,* 1964, 11, 272–279.

CARROLL, H. A. What do the Meier-Seashore and the McAdory Art Tests measure? *Journal of Educational Research,* 1933, 26, 661–665.

CARROLL, J. B. Factors of verbal achievement. In A. Anastasi (Ed.), *Testing problems in perspective.* Washington: American Council on Education, 1966. Pp. 406–413.

CARTER, L. F. Evaluating the performance of individuals as members of small groups. *Personnel Psychology,* 1954, 7, 477–484.

CARTER, L. F., BRIM, O. G., STALNAKER, J. M., & MESSICK, S. Psychological tests and public responsibility. *American Psychologist,* 1965, 20, 123–142.

Casebook on ethical standards of psychologists. Washington: American Psychological Association, 1967.

CATTELL, J. McK. Mental tests and measurements. *Mind,* 1890, 15, 373–380.

CATTELL, P. Constant changes in Stanford-Binet IQ. *Journal of Educational Psychology,* 1931, 22, 544–550.

CATTELL, P. *The measurement of intelligence of infants and young children.* New York: Psychological Corporation, 1947.

CATTELL, R. B. *Description and measurement of personality.* Yonkers, N. Y.: World Book Co., 1946.

CATTELL, R. B. *Personality and motivation structure and measurement.* Yonkers, N. Y.: World Book Co., 1957.

CATTELL, R. B. *et al.* The objective measurement of dynamic traits. *Educational and Psychological Measurement,* 1950, 10, 224–248.

CATTELL, R. B., & ANDERSON, J. C. The measurement of personality and behavior disorders by the IPAT music preference test. *Journal of Applied Psychology,* 1953, 37, 446–454.

CATTELL, R. B., & LUBORSKY, L. B. Personality factors in response to humor. *Journal of Abnormal and Social Psychology,* 1947, 42, 402–421.

CATTELL, R. B., & SAUNDERS, D. R. Musical preferences and personality diagnosis: I. A factorization of one hundred and twenty themes. *Journal of Social Psychology,* 1954, 39, 3–24.

CATTELL, R. B., & WARBURTON, F. *Principles of objective personality measurement, and a compendium of objective tests.* Urbana, Ill.: University of Illinois Press, 1967.

CAVANAUGH, M. C. *et al.* Prediction from Cattell Infant Intelligence Scale. *Journal of Consulting Psychology,* 1957, 21, 33–37.

CHARLES, D. C. Ability and accomplishment of persons earlier judged mentally deficient. *Genetic Psychology Monographs,* 1953, 47, 3–71.

CHARLES, D. C., & JAMES, S. T. Stability of average intelligence. *Journal of Genetic Psychology,* 1964, 105, 105–111.

CHERNOFF, H., & MOSES, L. E. *Elementary decision theory.* New York: Wiley, 1959.

CHODORKOFF, B., & MUSSEN, P. Qualitative aspects of the vocabulary responses of normals and schizophrenics. *Journal of Consulting Psychology,* 1952, 16, 43–48.

CHRISTAL, R. E. Factor analytic study of visual memory. *Psychological Monographs,* 1958, 72, No. 13.

CLARK, J. H. The interpretation of the MMPI profiles of college students; mean scores for male and female groups. *Journal of Social Psychology,* 1954, 40, 319–321.

CLARK, K. E. *The vocational interests of nonprofessional men.* Minneapolis: University of Minnesota Press, 1961.

CLARK, K. E., & CAMPBELL, D. P. *Manual for the Minnesota Vocational Interest Inventory.* New York: Psychological Corporation, 1965.

CLEARY, T. A., & HILTON, T. I. Test bias: Prediction of grades of Negro and white students in integrated colleges. *Journal of Educational Measurement,* 1968, 5, 115–124.

CLEMANS, W. V. An index of item-criterion relationship. *Educational and Psychological Measurement,* 1958, 18, 167–172.

CLEMANS, W. V. Administration of tests and testing programs. In R. L. Thorndike (Ed.), *Educational measurement.* (2nd ed.) Washington: American Council on Education, 1971. Ch. 7.

COFER, C. N., CHANCE, J. E., & JUDSON, A. J. A study of malingering on the MMPI. *Journal of Psychology,* 1949, 27, 491–499.

COHEN, E. Examiner differences with individual intelligence tests. *Perceptual and Motor Skills,* 1965, 20, 1324.

COHEN, J. A factor-analytically based rationale for the Wechsler Adult Intelligence Scale. *Journal of Consulting Psychology,* 1957, 21, 451–457. (a)

COHEN, J. The factorial structure of the WAIS between early adulthood and old age. *Journal of Consulting Psychology,* 1957, 21, 283–390. (b)

COLEMAN, W., & CURETON, E. E. Intelligence and achievement: The "jangle fallacy" again. *Educational and Psychological Measurement,* 1954, 14, 347–351.

College Entrance Examination Board. *Effects of coaching on Scholastic Aptitude Test scores.* New York: CEEB, 1965.

College Entrance Examination Board. *College-level examination program: Description and uses, 1967.* New York: CEEB, 1967. (a)

College Entrance Examination Board. *A description of the College Board achievement tests.* New York: CEEB, 1967. (b)

College Entrance Examination Board. *A description of the College Board Scholastic Aptitude Test.* New York: CEEB, 1967. (c)

College Entrance Examination Board. *A description of the College Board supplementary achievement tests.* New York: CEEB, 1967. (d)

COOLEY, W. W. Further relationships with the TALENT battery. *Personnel and Guidance Journal,* 1965, 44, 295–303.

COOLEY, W. W., & MILLER, J. D. The Project TALENT tests as a national standard. *Personnel and Guidance Journal,* 1965, 43, 1038–1044.

CORAH, M. L., *et al.* Social desirability as a variable in the Edwards Personal Preference Schedule. *Journal of Consulting Psychology,* 1958, 22, 70–72.

COUCH, A., & KENISTON, K. Yeasayers and naysayers: Agreeing response set as a personality variable. *Journal of Abnormal and Social Psychology,* 1960, 60, 151–174.

CRANE, V. R., & HEIM, A. W. The effects of repeated retesting: III. Further experiments and general conclusions. *Quarterly Journal of Experimental Psychology,* 1950, 2, 182–197

CRONBACH, L. J. Statistical methods applied to Rorschach scores: A review. *Psychological Bulletin,* 1949, 46, 393–429.

CRONBACH, L. J. Coefficient alpha and the internal structure of tests. *Psychometrika,* 1951, 16, 297–334.

CRONBACH, L. J., & GLESER, G. C. *Psychological tests and personnel decisions.* (2nd ed.) Urbana, Ill.: University of Illinois Press, 1965.

CRONBACH, L. J., & MEEHL, P. E. Construct validity in psychological tests. *Psychological Bulletin,* 1955, 52, 281–302.

CRONBACH, L. J., & WARRINGTON, W. G. Time-limit tests: Estimating their reliability and degree of speeding. *Psychometrika,* 1951, 16, 167–188.

CRONBACH, L. J., & WARRINGTON, W. G. Efficiency of multiple-choice tests as a function of spread of item difficulties. *Psychometrika,* 1952, 17, 124–147.

CROWNE, D. P., & MARLOWE, D. *The approval motive: Studies in evaluative dependence.* New York: Wiley, 1964.

CURETON, E. E. Validity, reliability, and baloney. *Educational and·Psychological Measurement,* 1950, 10, 94–96.

CURETON, E. E. Recipe for a cookbook. *Psychological Bulletin,* 1957, 54, 494–497. (a)

CURETON, E. E. The upper and lower twenty-seven per cent rule. *Psychometrika,* 1957, 22, 293–296. (b)

CURETON, E. E. Reliability and validity: Basic assumptions and experimental designs. *Educational and Psychological Measurement,* 1965, 25, 327–346.

DAHLSTROM, W. G., & WELSH, G. S. *An MMPI handbook: A guide to use in clinical practice and research.* Minneapolis: University of Minnesota Press, 1960.

DAILEY, J. T., SHAYCOFT, M. F., & ORR, D. B. Calibration of Air Force selection tests to Project TALENT norms. *Personnel Research Laboratory,* PRL-TDR-62-6, May 1962.

DAMON, A. Discrepancies between findings of longitudinal and cross-sectional studies in adult life: Physique and physiology. *Human Development,* 1965, 8, 16–22.

DARCY, N. T. Bilingualism and the measurement of intelligence: Review of a decade of research. *Journal of Genetic Psychology*, 1963, 103, 259–282.

DARLEY, J. G., & HAGENAH, T. *Vocational interest measurement: Theory and practice*. Minneapolis: University of Minnesota Press, 1955.

DARLINGTON, R. B., & STAUFFER, G. F. A method for choosing a cutting point on a test. *Journal of Applied Psychology*, 1966, 50, 229–231.

DAS, R. S. Analysis of the components of reasoning in nonverbal tests and the structure of reasoning in a bilingual population. *Archiv für die gesamte Psychologie*, 1963, 115(3), 217–229.

DAVIDS, A., & PILDNER, H., JR. Comparison of direct and projective methods of personality assessment under different conditions of motivation. *Psychological Monographs*, 1958, 72, No. 11.

DAVIS, P. C. A factor analysis of the Wechsler-Bellevue Scale. *Educational and Psychological Measurement*, 1956, 16, 127–146.

DEARBORN, W. F., & ROTHNEY, J. *Predicting the child's development*. Cambridge, Mass.: Sci-Art Pub., 1941.

DEMMING, J. A., & PRESSEY, S. L. Tests "indigenous" to the adult and older years. *Journal of Counseling Psychology*, 1957, 4, 144–148.

DENNIS, W. Goodenough scores, art experience, and modernization. *Journal of Social Psychology*, 1966, 68, 211–228.

DENNY, J. P. Effects of anxiety and intelligence on concept formation. *Journal of Experimental Psychology*, 1966, 72, 596–602.

DiCARLO, L. M., & GARDNER, E. F. A comparative study of the efficiency of three group pure tone screening tests for public school children. *Exceptional Children*, 1958, 24, 351–359.

DICKEN, C. F. Simulated patterns on the Edwards Personal Preference Schedule. *Journal of Applied Psychology*, 1959, 43, 372–378.

DICKEN, C. F., & BLACK, J. D. Predictive validity of psychometric evaluations of supervisors. *Journal of Applied Psychology*, 1965, 49, 34–47.

DOLL, E. A. (Ed.) *The Oseretsky Tests of Motor Proficiency*. Minneapolis: Educational Test Bureau, 1946. (now American Guidance Service)

DOLL, E. A. *The measurement of social competence*. Minneapolis: Educational Test Bureau, 1953. (now American Guidance Service)

DOLL, E. A. *Vineland Social Maturity Scale: Manual of directions*. (Rev. ed.) Minneapolis: Educational Test Bureau, 1965. (now American Guidance Service)

DONAHOE, J. W. A dimensional analysis of clinical judgment. *Journal of Consulting Psychology*, 1960, 24, 96.

DONOFRIO, A. F. Clinical value of infant testing. *Perceptual and Motor Skills*, 1965, 21, 571–574.

DOPPELT, J. E. Estimating the Full Scale score of the Wechsler Adult Intelligence Scale from scores on four subtests. *Journal of Consulting Psychology*, 1956, 20, 63–66.

DOPPELT, J. E., & WALLACE, W. L. Standardization of the Wechsler Adult Intelligence Scale for older persons. *Journal of Abnormal and Social Psychology*, 1955, 51, 312–330.

DORCUS, R. M., & JONES, M. H. *Handbook of employee selection*. New York: McGraw-Hill, 1950.

DRAKE, L. E., & OETTING, E. R. *An MMPI codebook for counselors*. Minneapolis: University of Minnesota Press, 1959.

DRASGOW, J., & CARKHUFF, R. R. Kuder neuropsychiatric keys before and after psychotherapy. *Journal of Counseling Psychology*, 1964, 11, 67–71.

DRESSEL, P. L., *et al. Comprehensive examinations in a program of general education.* East Lansing, Mich.: Michigan State University Press, 1949.

DROEGE, R. C. Effects of practice on aptitude scores. *Journal of Applied Psychology,* 1966, 50, 306–310. (a)

DROEGE, R. C. GATB longitudinal maturation study. *Personnel and Guidance Journal,* 1966, 44, 919–930. (b)

DROEGE, R. C., & BEMIS, S. E. New developments in aptitude testing of the educationally deficient. *American Psychologist,* 1964, 19, 521.

DuBois, P. H. A test-dominated society: China 1115 B.C.–1905 A.D. In A. Anastasi (Ed.), *Testing problems in perspective.* Washington: American Council on Education, 1966. Pp. 29–36.

DuBois, P. H. (Ed.) *The classification program.* (AAF Aviation Psychology Program, Research Reports. Rep. No. 2) Washington: Government Printing Office, 1947.

DUNN, J. A. Inter- and intrarater reliability of the new Harris-Goodenough Draw-A-Man Test. *Perceptual and Motor Skills,* 1967, 24, 269–270.

DUNNETTE, M. D. A modified model for test validation and selection research. *Journal of Applied Psychology,* 1963, 47, 317–323. (a)

DUNNETTE, M. D. A note on the criterion. *Journal of Applied Psychology,* 1963, 47, 251–254. (b)

DUNNETTE, M. D. Critics of psychological tests: Basic assumptions: How good? *Psychology in the Schools,* 1964, 1, 63–69.

DUNNETTE, M. D. *Personnel selection and placement.* Belmont, Calif.: Wadsworth, 1966.

DURNALL, E. J., JR. Falsification of interest patterns of the Kuder Preference Record. *Journal of Educational Psychology,* 1954, 45, 240–243.

DVORAK, B. J. The General Aptitude Test Battery. *Personnel and Guidance Journal,* 1956, 35, 145–154.

DYER, H. S. Is testing a menace to education? *New York State Education,* 1961, 49, 16–19.

DYER, H. S. The menace of testing reconsidered. *Educational Horizons,* 1964, 43, 3–8.

DYER, H. S. The discovery and development of educational goals. *Proceedings of the 1966 Invitational Conference on Testing Problems, Educational Testing Service,* 1967, 12–24.

DYER, H. S., & KING, R. G. *College Board scores: Their use and interpretation. No. 2.* New York: College Entrance Examination Board, 1955.

EBEL, R. L. Obtaining and reporting evidence on content validity. *Educational and Psychological Measurement,* 1956, 16, 269–282.

EBEL, R. L. Must all tests be valid? *American Psychologist,* 1961, 16, 640–647.

EBEL, R. L. Content standard test scores. *Educational and Psychological Measurement,* 1962, 22, 15–25.

EBEL, R. L. *Measuring educational achievement.* Englewood Cliffs, N. J.: Prentice-Hall, 1965.

EBEL, R. L. The social consequences of educational testing. In A. Anastasi (Ed.), *Testing problems in perspective.* Washington: American Council on Education, 1966. Pp. 18–28.

EBEL, R. L., & DAMRIN, D. E. Tests and examinations. *Encyclopedia of Educational Research,* 3rd ed., 1960, 1502–1517.

EBBINGHAUS, H. Über eine neue Methode zur Prüfung geistiger Fähigkeiten und ihre Anwendung bei Schulkindern. *Zeitschrift für angewandte Psychologie,* 1897, 13, 401–459.

EDGERTON, H. A. A table for computing the phi coefficient. *Journal of Applied Psychology*, 1960, 44, 141–145.

EDWARDS, A. J. Using vocabulary as a measure of general ability. *Personnel and Guidance Journal*, 1963, 42, 153–154.

EDWARDS, A. L. *The social desirability variable in personality assessment and research.* New York: Dryden, 1957. (a)

EDWARDS, A. L. *Techniques of attitude scale construction.* New York: Appleton-Century-Crofts, 1957. (b)

EDWARDS, A. L. Relationship between probability of endorsement and social desirability scale value for a set of 2,824 personality statements. *Journal of Applied Psychology*, 1966, 50, 238–239.

EELLS, K., *et al. Intelligence and cultural differences.* Chicago: University of Chicago Press, 1951.

EISDORFER, C. The WAIS performance of the aged: A retest evaluation. *Journal of Gerontology*, 1963, 18, 169–172.

EISDORFER, C., & COHEN, L. D. The generality of the WAIS standardization for the aged: A regional comparison. *Journal of Abnormal and Social Psychology*, 1961, 62, 520–527.

ENGELHART, M. D. A comparison of several item discrimination indices. *Journal of Educational Measurement*, 1965, 2, 69–76.

ENGSTROM, W. C., & POWERS, M. E. A revision of the Study of Values for use in magazine readership research. *Journal of Applied Psychology*, 1959, 43, 74–78.

EPSTEIN, S. Some theoretical considerations on the nature of ambiguity and the use of stimulus dimensions in projective techniques. *Journal of Consulting Psychology*, 1966, 30, 183–192.

Equal Employment Opportunity Commission. *Guidelines on employment testing procedures.* Washington, 1966.

ESCALONA, S. K. The use of infant tests for predictive purposes. *Bulletin of the Menninger Clinic*, 1950, 14, 117–128.

ESQUIROL, J. E. D. *Des maladies mentales considérées sous les rapports médical, hygiénique, et médico-légal.* Paris: Baillière, 1838. 2 vols.

ESTES, B. W. Influence of socioeconomic status on Wechsler Intelligence Scale for Children: An exploratory study. *Journal of Consulting Psychology*, 1953, 17, 58–62.

ESTES, B. W. Influence of socioeconomic status on Wechsler Intelligence Scale for Children: Addendum. *Journal of Consulting Psychology*, 1955, 19, 225–226.

Ethical standards of psychologists. *American Psychologist*, 1963, 18, 56–60.

EXNER, J. E., JR. Variations in WISC performances as influenced by differences in pretest rapport. *Journal of General Psychology*, 1966, 74, 299–306.

EYSENCK, H. J. *The structure of human personality.* London: Methuen, 1960.

FAN, C. T. *Item analysis table.* Princeton, N. J.: Educational Testing Service, 1952.

FAN, C. T. Note on construction of an item analysis table for the high-low-27-per-cent group method. *Psychometrika*, 1954, 19, 231–237.

FARNSWORTH, P. R. Shifts in the values of opinion items. *Journal of Psychology*, 1943, 16, 125–128.

FEAR, R. A. *The evaluation interview: Predicting job performance in business and industry.* New York: McGraw-Hill, 1958.

FEIFEL, H. Qualitative differences in the vocabulary responses of normals and abnormals. *Genetic Psychology Monographs*, 1949, 39, 151–204.

FELDHUSEN, J. F., & KLAUSMEIER, H. J. Anxiety, intelligence, and achievement in children of low, average, and high intelligence. *Child Development*, 1962, 33, 403–409.

FERGUSON, G. A. On learning and human ability. *Canadian Journal of Psychology*, 1954, 8, 95–112.

FERGUSON, G. A. On transfer and the abilities of man. *Canadian Journal of Psychology*, 1956, 10, 121–131.

FEY, E. T. The performance of young schizophrenics on the Wisconsin Card-Sorting Test. *Journal of Consulting Psychology*, 1951, 15, 311–319.

FIELD, J. G. Two types of tables for use with Wechsler's Intelligence Scales. *Journal of Clinical Psychology*, 1960, 16, 3–7.

FINDLEY, W. G. Rationale for the evaluation of item discrimination statistics. *Educational and Psychological Measurement*, 1956, 16, 175–180.

FINE, S. A. Functional job analysis (FJA) as a method of indirect validation: A study in synthetic validity. *American Psychologist*, 1963, 18, 438.

FISHBEIN, M. (Ed.) *Readings in attitude theory and measurement*. New York: Wiley, 1967.

FISHER, G. M. A corrected table for determining the significance of the difference between verbal and performance IQ's on the WAIS and the Wechsler-Bellevue. *Journal of Clinical Psychology*, 1960, 16, 7–8.

FISHER, J. The twisted pear and the prediction of behavior. *Journal of Consulting Psychology*, 1959, 23, 400–405.

FISHMAN, J. A., et al. Guidelines for testing minority group children. *Journal of Social Issues*, 1964, 20, 127–145.

FISHMAN, J. A., & LORGE, I. The influence of judges' characteristics on item judgments and on Thurstone scaling via the method of ranks (utilization of judges with varying national, religious, and experiential backgrounds). *Journal of Social Psychology*, 1959, 49, 187–205.

FISKE, D. W. The subject reacts to tests. *American Psychologist*, 1967, 22, 287–296.

FISKE, D. W., & BAUGHMAN, E. E. Relationships between Rorschach scoring categories and the total number of responses. *Journal of Abnormal and Social Psychology*, 1953, 48, 25–32.

FISKE, D. W., & COX, J. A., JR. The consistency of ratings by peers. *Journal of Applied Psychology*, 1960, 44, 11–17.

FJELD, S. P., & LANDFIELD, A. W. Personal construct consistency. *Psychological Reports*, 1961, 8, 127–129.

FLANAGAN, J. C. Scientific development of the use of human resources: Progress in the Army Air Forces. *Science*, 1947, 105, 57–60.

FLANAGAN, J. C. Critical requirements: A new approach to employee evaluation. *Personnel Psychology*, 1949, 2, 419–425.

FLANAGAN, J. C. The critical incident technique. *Psychological Bulletin*, 1954, 51, 327–358. (a)

FLANAGAN, J. C. Some considerations in the development of situation tests. *Personnel Psychology*, 1954, 7, 461–464. (b)

FLANAGAN, J. C. Symposium: Standard scores for aptitude and achievement tests: Discussion. *Educational and Psychological Measurement*, 1962, 22, 35–39.

FLANAGAN, J. C., et al. *The American high school student*. Pittsburgh, Pa.: Project TALENT Office, University of Pittsburgh, 1964.

FLAVELL, J. H. *The developmental psychology of Jean Piaget*. Princeton, N. J.: Van Nostrand, 1963.

FLEISHMAN, E. A. Dimensional analysis of psychomotor abilities. *Journal of Experimental Psychology*, 1954, 48, 437–454.

598 PSYCHOLOGICAL TESTING

FLEISHMAN, E. A. Predicting code proficiency of radiotelegraphers by means of aural tests. *Journal of Applied Psychology*, 1955, 39, 150–155.

FLEISHMAN, E. A. Dimensional analysis of movement reactions. *Journal of Experimental Psychology*, 1958, 55, 438–453.

FLEISHMAN, E. A. The dimensions of physical fitness: The nationwide normative and developmental study of basic tests. Technical Report No. 4, 1962, Yale University, Contract Nonr 609(32), Office of Naval Research. (a)

FLEISHMAN, E. A. The description and prediction of perceptual-motor skill learning. In R. Glaser (Ed.), *Training, research, and education*. Pittsburgh, Pa.: University of Pittsburgh Press, 1962. (b)

FLEISHMAN, E. A., & ELLISON, G. D. A factor analysis of fine manipulative tests. *Journal of Applied Psychology*, 1962, 46, 96–105.

FLEISHMAN, E. A., & HEMPEL, W. E., JR. Changes in factor structure of a complex psychomotor test as a function of practice. *Psychometrika*, 1954, 19, 239–252.

FLEISHMAN, E. A., & HEMPEL, W. E., JR. The relation between abilities and improvement with practice in a visual discrimination task. *Journal of Experimental Psychology*, 1955, 49, 301–312.

FLEISHMAN, E. A., & HEMPEL, W. E., JR. Factorial analyses of complex psychomotor performance and related skills. *Journal of Applied Psychology*, 1956, 40, 96–104.

FORCE, R. C. Development of a covert test for the detection of alcoholism by a keying of the Kuder Preference Record. *Quarterly Journal of Studies on Alcohol*, 1958, 19, 72–78.

FRANDSEN, A. N. A note on Wiener's coding of Kuder Preference Record profiles. *Educational and Psychological Measurement*, 1952, 12, 137–139.

FREDERIKSEN, N. Response set scores as predictors of performance. *Personnel Psychology*, 1965, 18, 225–244.

FREDERIKSEN, N. In-basket tests and factors in administrative performance. In A. Anastasi (Ed.), *Testing problems in perspective*. Washington: American Council on Education, 1966. Pp. 208–221. (a)

FREDERIKSEN, N. Validation of a simulation technique. *Organizational Behavior and Human Performance*, 1966, 1, 87–109. (b)

FREDERIKSEN, N., & GILBERT, A. C. F. Replication of a study of differential predictability. *Educational and Psychological Measurement*, 1960, 20, 759–767.

FREDERIKSEN, N., & MELVILLE, S. D. Differential predictability in the use of test scores. *Educational and Psychological Measurement*, 1954, 14, 647–656.

FREDERIKSEN, N., SAUNDERS, D. R., & WAND, B. The In-Basket Test. *Psychological Monographs*, 1957, 71, No. 9.

FRENCH, J. W. The description of aptitude and achievement tests in terms of rotated factors. *Psychometric Monographs*, 1951, No. 5.

FRENCH, J. W. Effect of anxiety on verbal and mathematical examination scores. *Educational and Psychological Measurement*, 1962, 22, 553–564.

FRENCH, J. W. The relationship of problem-solving styles to the factor composition of tests. *Educational and Psychological Measurement*, 1965, 25, 9–28.

FRENCH, J. W. The logic of and assumptions underlying differential testing. In A. Anastasi (Ed.), *Testing problems in perspective*. Washington: American Council on Education, 1966. Pp. 321–330.

FRENCH, J. W., EKSTROM, R. B., & PRICE, L. A. *Kit of reference tests for cognitive factors*. (Rev. ed.) Princeton, N. J.: Educational Testing Service, 1963.

FROMM, E., HARTMAN, L. D., & MARSCHAK, M. Children's intelligence tests as a measure of dynamic personality functioning. *American Journal of Orthopsychiatry,* 1957, 27, 134–144.

FROMME, A. On the use of certain qualitative methods of attitude research. *Journal of Social Psychology,* 1941, 13, 425–459.

FRYER, D. *Measurement of interests.* New York: Holt, 1931.

FULKERSON, S. C. Individual differences in response validity. *Journal of Clinical Psychology,* 1959, 15, 169–173.

FURST, E. J. *Constructing evaluation instruments.* New York: McKay, 1958.

GALTON, F. Psychometric experiments. *Brain,* 1879, 2, 149–162.

GALTON, F. *Inquiries into human faculty and its development.* London: Macmillan, 1883.

GARDNER, J. W. *Excellence.* New York: Harper, 1961.

GARRON, D. C., & CHEIFETZ, D. I. Comment on "Bender Gestalt discernment of organic pathology." *Psychological Bulletin,* 1965, 63, 197–200.

GEHMAN, I. H., & MATYAS, R. P. Stability of the WISC and Binet tests. *Journal of Consulting Psychology,* 1956, 20, 150–152.

GEHMAN, W. S. A study of ability to fake scores on the Strong Vocational Interest Blank for Men. *Educational and Psychological Measurement,* 1957, 17, 65–70.

GERBERICH, J. R. *Specimen objective test items: A guide to achievement test construction.* New York: McKay, 1956.

GERBERICH, J. R., GREENE, H. A., & JORGENSEN, A. N. *Measurement and evaluation in the modern school.* New York: McKay, 1962.

GESELL, A., & AMATRUDA, C. S. *Developmental diagnosis.* (2nd ed.) New York: Hoeber-Harper, 1947.

GHISELLI, E. E. Differentiation of individuals in terms of their predictability. *Journal of Applied Psychology,* 1956, 40, 374–377.

GHISELLI, E. E. Differentiation of tests in terms of the accuracy with which they predict for a given individual. *Educational and Psychological Measurement,* 1960, 20, 675–684. (a)

GHISELLI, E. E. The prediction of predictability. *Educational and Psychological Measurement,* 1960, 20, 3–8. (b)

GHISELLI, E. E. Moderating effects and differential reliability and validity. *Journal of Applied Psychology,* 1963, 47, 81–86.

GHISELLI, E. E. *The validity of occupational aptitude tests.* New York: Wiley, 1966.

GHISELLI, E. E., & HAIRE, M. The validation of selection tests in the light of the dynamic character of criteria. *Personnel Psychology,* 1960, 13, 225–231.

GILBERSTADT, H., & DUKER, J. *A handbook for clinical and actuarial MMPI interpretation.* Philadelphia: Saunders, 1965.

GILBERT, H. B. On the IQ ban. *Teachers College Record,* 1966, 67, 282–285.

GILBERT, J. A. Researches on the mental and physical development of school children. *Studies from the Yale Psychological Laboratory,* 1894, 2, 40–100.

GILLILAND, A. R., & COLGIN, R. Norms, reliability, and forms of the MMPI. *Journal of Consulting Psychology,* 1951, 15, 435–438.

GLASSER, A. J., & ZIMMERMAN, I. L. *Clinical interpretation of the Wechsler Intelligence Scale for Children.* New York: Grune & Stratton, 1967.

GOLANN, S. E. Psychological study of creativity. *Psychological Bulletin,* 1963, 60, 548–565.

GOLDEN, M. Some effects of combining psychological tests on clinical inferences. *Journal of Consulting Psychology,* 1964, 28, 440–446.

GOLDMAN, L. *Using tests in counseling.* New York: Appleton-Century-Crofts, 1961.

GOLDSTEIN, K., & SCHEERER, M. Abstract and concrete behavior; an experimental study with special tests. *Psychological Monographs,* 1941, 53, No. 2.

GOODENOUGH, F. L. *Mental testing: Its history, principles, and applications.* New York: Rinehart, 1949.

GOODENOUGH, F. L., & HARRIS, D. B. Studies in the psychology of children's drawings: II. 1928–1949. *Psychological Bulletin,* 1950, 47, 369–433.

GOODENOUGH, F. L., MAURER, K. M., & VAN WAGENEN, M. J. *Minnesota Preschool Scales: Manual.* Minneapolis: Educational Test Bureau, 1940. (now American Guidance Service)

GORDON, E. W., & WILKERSON, D. A. *Compensatory education for the disadvantaged—programs and practices: Preschool through college.* New York: College Entrance Examination Board, 1966.

GORDON, L. V., & ALF, E. F. Acclimatization and aptitude test performance. *Educational and Psychological Measurement,* 1960, 20, 333–337.

GORDON, M. A. A study of the applicability of the same minimum qualifying scores for technical schools to white males, WAF, and Negro males. San Antonio, Texas: Human Resources Research Center, Lackland Air Force Base. Technical Report 53-54, 1953.

GOSLIN, D. A. *The search for ability: Standardized testing in social perspective.* New York: Russell Sage Foundation, 1963.

GOUGH, H. G. A new dimension of status. I. Development of a personality scale. *American Sociological Review,* 1948, 13, 401–409.

GOUGH, H. G. The Adjective Check List as a personality assessment research technique. *Psychological Reports,* 1960, 6, 107–122.

GOUGH, H. G. Academic achievement in high school as predicted from the California Psychological Inventory. *Journal of Educational Psychology,* 1964, 55, 174–180. (a)

GOUGH, H. G. Achievement in the first course in psychology as predicted from the California Psychological Inventory. *Journal of Psychology,* 1964, 57, 419–430. (b)

GOUGH, H. G. Cross-cultural validation of a measure of asocial behavior. *Psychological Reports,* 1965, 17, 379–387. (a)

GOUGH, H. G. A validational study of the Chapin Social Insight Test. *Psychological Reports,* 1965, 17, 344–368. (b)

GOUGH, H. G. Appraisal of social maturity by means of the CPI. *Journal of Abnormal Psychology,* 1966, 71, 189–195. (a)

GOUGH, H. G. A cross-cultural analysis of the CPI Femininity scale. *Journal of Consulting Psychology,* 1966, 30, 136–141. (b)

GOUGH, H. G. Graduation from high school as predicted from the California Psychological Inventory. *Psychology in the Schools,* 1966, 3, 208–216. (c)

GOUGH, H. G., & HEILBRUN, A. B., JR. *The Adjective Check List Manual.* Palo Alto, Calif.: Consulting Psychologists Press, 1965.

GOUGH, H. G., WENK, E. A., & ROZYNKO, V. V. Parole outcome as predicted from the CPI, the MMPI, and a base expectancy table. *Journal of Abnormal Psychology,* 1965, 70, 432–441.

GRAHAM, F. K., et al. Development three years after perinatal anoxia and other potentially damaging newborn experiences. *Psychological Monographs,* 1962, 76, No. 3.

GRAHAM, F. K., ERNHART, C. B., et al. Brain injury in the preschool child. *Psychological Monographs,* 1963, 77, No. 10-11.

GRANT, D. A. Perceptual versus analytical responses to the number concept of a Weigl-type card sorting test. *Journal of Experimental Psychology*, 1951, 41, 23–29.

GREEN, R. F. Does a selection situation induce testees to bias their answers on interest and temperament tests? *Educational and Psychological Measurement*, 1951, 11, 503–515.

GREENWOOD, J. M., & McNAMARA, W. J. Interrater reliability in situational tests. *Journal of Applied Psychology*, 1967, 51, 101–106.

GRONLUND, N. E. *Measurement and evaluation in teaching*. New York: Macmillan, 1965.

GROOMS, R. R., & ENDLER, N. S. The effect of anxiety on academic achievement. *Journal of Educational Psychology*, 1960, 51, 299–304.

GROSS, M. L. *The brain watchers*. New York: Random House, 1962.

GUERTIN, W. H., *et al.* Research with the Wechsler Intelligence Scales for Adults: 1955–60. *Psychological Bulletin*, 1962, 59, 1–26.

GUERTIN, W. H., *et al.* Research with the Wechsler Intelligence Scales for Adults: 1960–1965. *Psychological Bulletin*, 1966, 66, 385–409.

GUERTIN, W. H., FRANK, G. H., & RABIN, A. I. Research with the Wechsler-Bellevue Intelligence Scale: 1950–1955. *Psychological Bulletin*, 1956, 53, 235–257.

GUICCIARDI, G., & FERRARI, G. C. I testi mentali per l'esame degli alienati. *Rivista sperimentale di Freniatria*, 1896, 22, 297–314.

GUILFORD, J. P. *Psychometric methods*. (2nd ed.) New York: McGraw-Hill, 1954.

GUILFORD, J. P. Creative abilities in the arts. *Psychological Review*, 1957, 64, 110–118.

GUILFORD, J. P. *Personality*. New York: McGraw-Hill, 1959.

GUILFORD, J. P. *Fundamental statistics in psychology and education*. (4th ed.) New York: McGraw-Hill, 1965.

GUILFORD, J. P. *The nature of human intelligence*. New York: McGraw-Hill, 1967.

GUILFORD, J. P., *et al.* A factor analysis study of human interests. *Psychological Monographs*, 1954, 68, No. 4.

GUILFORD, J. P., & Lacey, J. I. (Eds.) *Printed classification tests*. (AAF Aviation Psychology Program, Research Reports. Rep. No. 5) Washington: Government Printing Office, 1947.

GUILFORD, J. P., & ZIMMERMAN, W. S. Fourteen dimensions of temperament. *Psychological Monographs*, 1956, 70, No. 10.

GUION, R. M. Synthetic validity in a small company: A demonstration. *Personnel Psychology*, 1965, 18, 49–63.

GULLIKSEN, H. Intrinsic validity. *American Psychologist*, 1950, 5, 511–517. (a)

GULLIKSEN, H. The reliability of speeded tests. *Psychometrika*, 1950, 15, 259–269. (b)

GULLIKSEN, H. *Theory of mental tests*. New York: Wiley, 1950. (c)

GUTTMAN, L. Reliability formulas for noncompleted or speeded tests. *Psychometrika*, 1955, 20, 113–124.

GUTTMAN, I., & RAJU, N. S. A minimum loss function as determiner of optimal cutting scores. *Personnel Psychology*, 1965, 18, 179–185.

HAAN, N. Proposed model of ego functioning: Coping and defense mechanisms in relationship to IQ change. *Psychological Monographs*, 1963, 77, No. 8.

HAIN, J. D. The Bender Gestalt Test: A scoring method for identifying brain damage. *Journal of Consulting Psychology*, 1964, 28, 34–40.

HAKEL, M. D. Prediction of college achievement from the Edwards Personal

Preference Schedule using intellectual ability as a moderator. *Journal of Applied Psychology*, 1966, 50, 336–340.

HALL, J. A correlation of a modified form of Raven's Progressive Matrices (1938) with Wechsler Adult Intelligence Scale. *Journal of Consulting Psychology*, 1957, 21, 23–26.

HAMILTON, R. G., & ROBERTSON, M. H. Examiner influence on the Holtzman Inkblot Technique. *Journal of Projective Techniques and Personality Assessment*, 1966, 30, 553–558.

HAMMOND, K. R. Measuring attitudes by error choice; an indirect method. *Journal of Abnormal and Social Psychology*, 1948, 43, 38–48.

HANFMANN, E., & KASANIN, J. Conceptual thinking in schizophrenia. *Nervous and Mental Disease Monographs*, 1942, No. 67.

HARLOW, H. F. The formation of learning sets. *Psychological Review*, 1949, 56, 51–65.

HARLOW, H. F. Learning set and error factor theory. In S. Koch (Ed.), *Psychology: A study of a science.* Vol. 2. New York: McGraw-Hill, 1960. Pp. 492–537.

HARRIS, D. B. *Children's drawings as measures of intellectual maturity: A revision and extension of the Goodenough Draw-a-Man Test.* New York: Harcourt, Brace & World, 1963.

HARRISON, R. Thematic apperception methods. In B. B. Wolman (Ed.), *Handbook of clinical psychology.* New York: McGraw-Hill, 1965. Pp. 562–620.

HARTSHORNE, H., & MAY, M. A. *Studies in deceit.* New York: Macmillan, 1928.

HARTSHORNE, H., MAY, M. A., & MALLER, J. B. *Studies in service and self-control.* New York: Macmillan, 1929.

HARTSHORNE, H., MAY, M. A., & SHUTTLEWORTH, F. K. *Studies in the organization of character.* New York: Macmillan, 1930.

HASE, H. D., & GOLDBERG, L. R. Comparative validity of different strategies of constructing personality inventory scales. *Psychological Bulletin*, 1967, 67, 231–248.

HASELKORN, H. The vocational interests of a group of male homosexuals. *Journal of Counseling Psychology*, 1956, 3, 8–11.

HATHAWAY, S. R. Some considerations relative to nondirective counseling as therapy. *Journal of Clinical Psychology*, 1948, 4, 226–231.

HATHAWAY, S. R. MMPI: Professional use by professional people. *American Psychologist*, 1964, 19, 204–210.

HATHAWAY, S. R., & McKINLEY, J. C. *Minnesota Multiphasic Personality Inventory: Manual for administration and scoring.* New York: Psychological Corporation, 1967.

HATHAWAY, S. R., & MEEHL, P. E. *An atlas for the clinical use of the MMPI.* Minneapolis: University of Minnesota Press, 1951.

HATHAWAY, S. R., & MONACHESI, E. D. *Analyzing and predicting juvenile delinquency with the MMPI.* Minneapolis: University of Minnesota Press, 1953.

HATHAWAY, S. R., & MONACHESI, E. D. *An atlas of juvenile MMPI profiles.* Minneapolis: University of Minnesota Press, 1961.

HATHAWAY, S. R., & MONACHESI, E. D. *Adolescent personality and behavior.* Minneapolis: University of Minnesota Press, 1963.

HAY, E. N. Comparative validities in clerical testing. *Journal of Applied Psychology*, 1954, 38, 299–301.

HAYES, K. J. Genes, drives, and intellect. *Psychological Reports*, 1962, 10, 299–342.

HAYES, S. P. Alternative scales for the mental measurement of the visually handicapped. *Outlook for the Blind*, 1942, 36, 225–230.

HAYES, S. P. A second test scale for the mental measurement of the visually handicapped. *Outlook for the Blind*, 1943, 37, 37–41.

HAYNES, J. R., & SELLS, S. B. Assessment of organic brain damage by psychological tests. *Psychological Bulletin*, 1963, 60, 316–325.

HEALY, W., & FERNALD, G. M. Tests for practical mental classification. *Psychological Monographs*, 1911, 13, No. 2.

HEBB, D. O. Heredity and environment in mammalian behavior. *British Journal of Animal Behavior*, 1953, 1, 43–47.

HEILBRUN, A. B. Social-learning theory, social desirability, and the MMPI. *Psychological Bulletin*, 1964, 61, 377–387.

HEIM, A. W., & WALLACE, J. G. The effects of repeatedly retesting the same group on the same intelligence test. *Quarterly Journal of Experimental Psychology*, 1949, 1, 151–159; 1950, 2, 19–32.

HELME, W. H. Differential validity of the ACB for courses in seven job areas. *Personnel Research Branch, TAGO, DA, Technical Report No.* 1118, April 1960.

HELME, W. H., & FITCH, D. J. Grouping Army training courses by Army Classification Battery factors. *USAPRO Technical Research Note No.* 128, October 1962.

HELMSTADTER, G. C., & ORTMEYER, D. H. Some techniques for determining the relative magnitude of speed and power components of a test. *Educational and Psychological Measurement*, 1953, 13, 280–287.

HEMPEL, W. E., & FLEISHMAN, E. A. A factor analysis of physical proficiency and manipulative skill. *Journal of Applied Psychology*, 1955, 39, 12–16.

HENRY, W. E. *The analysis of fantasy: The thematic apperception technique in the study of personality.* New York: Wiley, 1956.

HENRY, W. E., & FARLEY, J. The validity of the Thematic Apperception Test in the study of adolescent personality. *Psychological Monographs*, 1959, 73, No. 17.

HENRYSSON, S. Correction of item-total correlations in item analysis. *Psychometrika*, 1963, 28, 211–218.

HENRYSSON, S. Gathering, analyzing, and using data on test items. In R. L. Thorndike (Ed.), *Educational Measurement.* (2nd ed.) Washington: American Council on Education, 1971. Ch. 5.

HERRON, W. E. Changes in inkblot perception with presentation of the Holtzman inkblot technique as an "intelligence test." *Journal of Projective Techniques and Personality Assessment*, 1964, 28, 442–447.

HERZBERG, F., & BOUTON, A. A further study of the stability of the Kuder Preference Record. *Educational and Psychological Measurement*, 1954, 14, 326–331.

HEWER, V. H. Are tests fair to college students from homes with low socioeconomic status? *Personnel and Guidance Journal*, 1965, 43, 764–769.

HIGGINS, C., & SIVERS, C. H. A comparison of Stanford-Binet and Colored Raven Progressive Matrices IQs for children with low socioeconomic status. *Journal of Consulting Psychology*, 1958, 22, 465–468.

HILDRETH, G. H. *A bibliography of mental tests and rating scales.* (2nd ed.) New York: Psychological Corporation, 1939.

HILDRETH, G. H. *A bibliography of mental tests and rating scales, 1945 supplement.* New York: Psychological Corporation, 1946.

HILL, K. T., & SARASON, S. B. The relation of test anxiety and defensiveness to test and school performance over the elementary school years. *Monographs of the Society for Research in Child Development*, 1966, 31, No. 2.

HILLS, J. R. Prediction of college grades for all public colleges of a state. *Journal of Educational Measurement*, 1964, 1, 155–159.

HILLS, J. R., KLOCK, J. C., & LEWIS, S. *Freshman norms for the University System of Georgia, 1961–1962.* Atlanta, Ga.: Office of Testing and Guidance, Regents of the University System of Georgia, 1963.

HIMELSTEIN, P. Research with the Stanford-Binet, Form L-M: The first five years. *Psychological Bulletin*, 1966, 65, 156–164.

HINCKLEY, E. D. A follow-up study on the influence of individual opinion on the construction of an attitude scale. *Journal of Abnormal and Social Psychology*, 1963, 67, 290–292.

HIRSH, I. J. *The measurement of hearing.* New York: McGraw-Hill, 1952.

HISKEY, M. S. *Hiskey-Nebraska Test of Learning Aptitude: Manual.* Lincoln, Neb.: Union College Press, 1966.

HOBERT, R., & DUNNETTE, M. D. Development of moderator variables to enhance the prediction of managerial effectiveness. *Journal of Applied Psychology*, 1967, 51, 50–64.

HOFFMAN, B. *The tyranny of testing.* New York: Crowell-Collier, 1962.

HOFFMAN, P. J. The paramorphic representation of clinical judgment. *Psychological Bulletin*, 1960, 57, 116–131.

HOLDEN, R. H. Improved methods in testing cerebral palsied children. *American Journal of Mental Deficiency*, 1951, 56, 349–353.

HOLLAND, J. L. A personality inventory employing occupational titles. *Journal of Applied Psychology*, 1958, 42, 336–342.

HOLLANDER, E. P. Validity of peer nominations in predicting a distant performance criterion. *Journal of Applied Psychology*, 1965, 49, 434–438.

HOLLINGSHEAD, A. B., & REDLICH, F. C. *Two factor index of social position.* New Haven, Conn.: Authors, 1957.

HOLMEN, M. G., et al. An assessment program for OCS applicants. *HumRRO Technical Report No. 26*, 1956.

HOLT, R. R. Clinical and statistical prediction: A reformulation and some new data. *Journal of Abnormal and Social Psychology*, 1958, 56, 1–12.

HOLTZMAN, W. H. Can the computer supplant the clinician? *Journal of Clinical Psychology*, 1960, 16, 119–122.

HOLTZMAN, W. H., et al. *Inkblot perception and personality—Holtzman Inkblot Technique.* Austin, Texas: University of Texas Press, 1961.

HOLTZMAN, W. H., et al. Comparison of the group method and the standard individual version of the Holtzman Inkblot Technique. *Journal of Clinical Psychology*, 1963, 19, 441–449.

HOLZBERG, J. D. Projective techniques. In I. A. Berg & L. A. Pennington (Eds.), *An introduction to clinical psychology.* New York: Ronald, 1966. Pp. 106–153.

HONZIK, M. P., MACFARLANE, J. W., & ALLEN, L. The stability of mental test performance between two and eighteen years. *Journal of Experimental Education*, 1948, 17, 309–324.

HOPKINS, K. D., & MICHAEL, W. B. The diagnostic use of WISC subtest patterns. *California Journal of Educational Research*, 1961, 12, 116–117, 130.

HORN, C. C., & SMITH, L. F. The Horn Art Aptitude Inventory. *Journal of Applied Psychology*, 1945, 29, 350–355.

HORST, P. A technique for the development of a differential prediction battery. *Psychological Monographs*, 1954, 68, No. 9.

HOSKOVEC, J., & KANKA, Z. *Wechslerovy Zkousky W-B, WAIS, WISC Bibliografie.* Prague: Ceskoslovenska Psychologicka Spolecnost Pri Ceskoslovenske Akademii Ved, Praha, 1961.

HOVLAND, C. I., & SHERIF, M. Judgmental phenomena and scales of attitude measurement: Item displacement in Thurstone scales. *Journal of Abnormal and Social Psychology,* 1952, 47, 822–832.

HUDDLESTON, E. M. Test development on the basis of content validity. *Educational and Psychological Measurement,* 1956, 16, 283–293.

HULL, C. L. *Aptitude testing.* Yonkers, N. Y.: World Book Co., 1928.

HUMPHREYS, L. G. The organization of human abilities. *American Psychologist,* 1962, 17, 475–483.

HUNT, R. A. Self and other semantic concepts in relation to choice of a vocation. *Journal of Applied Psychology,* 1967, 51, 242–246.

HUSÉN, T. The influence of schooling upon IQ. *Theoria,* 1951, 17, 61–88.

ILG, F. L., & AMES, L. B. *School readiness: Behavior tests used at the Gesell Institute.* New York: Harper & Row, 1964.

ILG, F. L., AMES, L. B., & APELL, R. J. School readiness as evaluated by Gesell developmental, visual, and projective tests. *Genetic Psychology Monographs,* 1965, 71, 61–91.

JACKSON, D. N., & MESSICK, S. Content and style in personality assessment. *Psychological Bulletin,* 1958, 55, 243–252.

JACKSON, D. N., & MESSICK, S. Response styles and the assessment of psychopathology. In S. Messick & J. Ross (Eds.), *Measurement in personality and cognition.* New York: Wiley, 1962. Pp. 129–155.

JANKE, L. L., & HAVIGHURST, R. J. Relations between ability and social status in a midwestern community: II. Sixteen-year-old boys and girls. *Journal of Educational Psychology,* 1945, 36, 499–509.

JARRETT, R. F. Per cent increase in output of selected personnel as an index of test efficiency. *Journal of Applied Psychology,* 1948, 32, 135–146.

JENKIN, N. Affective processes in perception. *Psychological Bulletin,* 1957, 54, 100–127.

JENKINS, J. J., & RUSSELL, W. A. Systematic changes in word association norms: 1910–1952. *Journal of Abnormal and Social Psychology,* 1960, 60, 293–304.

JENSEN, A. R. Social class and verbal learning. In M. Deutsch, I. Katz, & A. R. Jensen (Eds.), *Social class, race, and psychological development.* New York: Holt, Rinehart & Winston, 1968. Ch. 4.

JOHNSON, A. P. Notes on a suggested index of item validity: The U-L index. *Journal of Educational Psychology,* 1951, 42, 499–504.

JOHNSON, P. W. The Massachusetts Hearing Test. *Journal of the Acoustical Society of America,* 1948, 20, 697–703.

JOHNSON, P. W. An efficient group screening test. *Journal of Speech and Hearing Disorders,* 1952, 17, 8–12.

JONES, H. G. The evaluation of the significance of differences between scaled scores on the WAIS: Perpetuation of a fallacy. *Journal of Consulting Psychology,* 1956, 20, 319–320.

JONES, L. V. A factor analysis of the Stanford-Binet at four age levels. *Psychometrika,* 1949, 14, 299–331.

JONES, L. V. Primary abilities in the Stanford-Binet, age 13. *Journal of Genetic Psychology,* 1954, 84, 126–147.

JUNG, C. G. The association method. *American Journal of Psychology,* 1910, 21, 219–269.

JUNG, C. G. *Psychological types.* London: Routledge & Kegan Paul, 1923.

JURGENSEN, C. E. Report on the "classification inventory," a personality test for industrial use. *Journal of Applied Psychology,* 1944, 28, 445–460.

JURGENSEN, C. E. Table for determining phi coefficients. *Psychometrika,* 1947, 12, 17–29.

JURGENSEN, C. E. Advisory panel appraises suitability of USES testing. *The Industrial Psychologist,* 1966, 4, 41–44.

KAGAN, J., & FREEMAN, M. Relation of childhood intelligence, maternal behaviors, and social class to behavior during adolescence. *Child Development,* 1963, 34, 899–911.

KAGAN, J., SONTAG, L. W., BAKER, C. T., & NELSON, V. L. Personality and IQ change. *Journal of Abnormal and Social Psychology,* 1958, 56, 261–266.

KAHN, M. W. Clinical and statistical prediction revisited. *Journal of Clinical Psychology,* 1960, 16, 115–118.

KAHN, R. L., & CANNELL, C. F. *The dynamics of interviewing: Theory, technique, and cases.* New York: Wiley, 1957.

KAHNEMAN, D., & GHISELLI, E. E. Validity and nonlinear heteroscedastic models. *Personnel Psychology,* 1962, 15, 1–11.

KAISER, H. F. A modified stanine scale. *Journal of Experimental Education,* 1958, 26, 261.

KARPINOS, B. D. Mental test failures. In S. Tax (Ed.), *The draft, a handbook of facts and alternatives.* Chicago: University of Chicago Press, 1967. Pp. 35–49.

KATZ, E. The "Pointing Modification" of the Revised Stanford-Binet Intelligence Scales, Forms L and M, Years II through VI: A report of research in progress. *American Journal of Mental Deficiency,* 1958, 62, 698–707.

KAVRUCK, S. Thirty-three years of test research: A short history of test development in the U. S. Civil Service Commission. *American Psychologist,* 1956, 11, 329–333.

KELLEY, T. L. *Interpretation of educational measurements.* Yonkers, N. Y.: World Book Co., 1927.

KELLEY, T. L. *Crossroads in the mind of man: A study of differentiable mental abilities.* Stanford, Calif.: Stanford University Press, 1928.

KELLEY, T. L. *Essential traits of mental life.* Cambridge, Mass.: Harvard University Press, 1935.

KELLEY, T. L. The selection of upper and lower groups for the validation of test items. *Journal of Educational Psychology,* 1939, 30, 17–24.

KELLEY, T. L. Cumulative significance of a number of independent experiments: Reply to A. E. Traxler and R. N. Hilkert. *School and Society,* 1943, 57, 482–484.

KELLY, E. L. The place of situation tests in evaluating clinical psychologists. *Personnel Psychology,* 1954, 7, 484–492.

KELLY, E. L., & FISKE, D. W. *The prediction of performance in clinical psychology.* Ann Arbor, Mich.: University of Michigan Press, 1951.

KELLY, G. A. *The psychology of personal constructs.* Vol. 1. *A theory of personality.* New York: Norton, 1955.

KENNEDY, W. A., et al. The ceiling of the new Stanford-Binet. *Journal of Clinical Psychology,* 1960, 17, 284–286.

KENNEDY, W. A., VAN DE REIT, V., & WHITE, J. C. A normative sample of intelligence and achievement of Negro elementary school children in the southeastern United States. *Monographs of the Society for Research in Child Development,* 1963, 28, No. 6.

KENT, G. H., & ROSANOFF, A. J. A study of association in insanity. *American Journal of Insanity,* 1910, 67, 37–96; 317–390.

KETTNER, N., GUILFORD, J. P., & CHRISTENSEN, P. R. A factor-analytic investigation of the factor called general reasoning. *Educational and Psychological Measurement,* 1956, 16, 438–453.

KINSLINGER, H. J. Application of projective techniques in personnel psychology since 1940. *Psychological Bulletin,* 1966, 66, 134–149.

KINTER, M. *The measurement of artistic abilities.* New York: Psychological Corporation, 1933.

KIRCHNER, W. K. A note on the effect of privacy in taking typing tests. *Journal of Applied Psychology,* 1966, 50, 373–374.

KIRKPATRICK, J. J., et al. Differential selection among applicants from different socioeconomic or ethnic backgrounds. New York University, Research Center for Industrial Behavior: Final Report to the Ford Foundation, 1967.

KLEINMUNTZ, B. Personality test interpretation by digital computer. *Science,* 1963, 139, 416–418.

KLEINMUNTZ, B. *Personality measurement: An introduction.* Homewood, Ill.: Dorsey, 1967.

KLINEBERG, O. An experimental study of speed and other factors in "racial" differences. *Archives of Psychology,* 1928, No. 93.

KLINGER, E. Fantasy need achievement as a motivational construct. *Psychological Bulletin,* 1966, 66, 291–308.

KNAPP, R. R. The effects of time limits on the intelligence test performance of Mexican and American subjects. *Journal of Educational Psychology,* 1960, 51, 14–20.

KNOBLOCH, H., & PASAMANICK, B. An evaluation of the consistency and predictive value of the 40 week Gesell Developmental Schedule. *Psychiatric Research Reports,* 1960, 13, 10–41.

KNOELL, D. M., & HARRIS, C. W. A factor analysis of spelling ability. *Journal of Educational Research,* 1952, 46, 95–111.

KNOX, H. A. A scale based on the work at Ellis Island for estimating mental defect. *Journal of the American Medical Association,* 1914, 62, 741–747.

KOHS, S. C. *Intelligence measurement: A psychological and statistical study based upon the Block-Design Tests.* New York: Macmillan, 1923.

KOPPITZ, E. M. *The Bender Gestalt Test for young children.* New York: Grune & Stratton, 1964.

KRAEPELIN, E. *Über die Beeinflüssung einfacher psychischer Vorgänge durch einige Arzneimittel.* Jena: Fischer, 1892.

KRAEPELIN, E. Der psychologische Versuch in der Psychiatrie. *Psychologische Arbeiten,* 1895, 1, 1–91.

KRATHWOHL, D. R., et al. *Taxonomy of educational objectives; the classification of educational goals; handbook 2: Affective domain.* New York: McKay, 1964.

KUDER, G. F. A rationale for evaluating interests. *Educational and Psychological Measurement,* 1963, 23, 3–10.

KUDER, G. F. *Kuder General Interest Survey: Manual.* Chicago: Science Research Associates, 1964.

KUDER, G. F. *Kuder Occupational Interest Survey: General Manual.* Chicago: Science Research Associates, 1966. (a)

KUDER, G. F. The occupational interest survey. *Personnel and Guidance Journal,* 1966, 45, 72–77. (b)

KUDER, G. F., & RICHARDSON, M. W. The theory of estimation of test reliability. *Psychometrika,* 1937, 2, 151–160.

KUHLEN, R. G. Age and intelligence: The significance of cultural change in longitudinal vs. cross-sectional findings. *Vita Humana,* 1963, 6, 113–124.

608 PSYCHOLOGICAL TESTING

KUHLMANN, F. A revision of the Binet-Simon system for measuring the intelligence of children. *Journal of Psycho-Asthenics, Monograph Supplement,* 1912, 1, 1–41.

KUHLMANN, F. *Tests of mental development.* Minneapolis: Educational Test Bureau, 1939.

KUNCE, J. T. Vocational interests and accident proneness. *Journal of Applied Psychology,* 1967, 51, 223–225.

KURTZ, A. K. A research test of the Rorschach test. *Personnel Psychology,* 1948, 1, 41–51.

LSAT handbook. Princeton, N. J.: Educational Testing Service, 1964.

LAFAVE, L. Essay vs. multiple-choice: Which test is preferable? *Psychology in the Schools,* 1966, 3, 65–69.

LANNHOLM, G. V., & PITCHER, B. *Mean score changes on the Graduate Record Examinations Area Tests for college students tested three times in a four-year period.* Princeton, N. J.: Educational Testing Service, 1959.

LANYON, R. I. A free-choice version of the EPPS. *Journal of Clinical Psychology,* 1966, 22, 202–205.

LAWRENCE, S. W., JR. The effects of anxiety, achievement motivation, and task importance upon performance on an intelligence test. *Journal of Educational Psychology,* 1962, 53, 150–156.

LAWSHE, C. H. Employee selection. *Personnel Psychology,* 1952, 5, 31–34.

LAWSHE, C. H., & BALMA, M. J. *Principles of personnel testing.* (2nd ed.) New York: McGraw-Hill, 1966.

LENNON, R. T. Assumptions underlying the use of content validity. *Educational and Psychological Measurement,* 1956, 16, 294–304.

LENNON, R. T. A comparison of results of three intelligence tests. In C. I. Chase & H. G. Ludlow (Eds.), *Readings in educational and psychological measurement.* Boston: Houghton Mifflin, 1966. Pp. 198–205. (a)

LENNON, R. T. Norms: 1963. In A. Anastasi (Ed.), *Testing problems in perspective.* Washington: American Council on Education, 1966. Pp. 243–250. (b)

LEVINE, R. L., & ANGOFF, W. H. The effect of practice on scores on the Scholastic Aptitude Test of the College Entrance Examination Board. *American Psychologist,* 1956, 11, 423.

LEVINSON, B. M. Traditional Jewish cultural values and performance on the Wechsler tests. *Journal of Educational Psychology,* 1959, 50, 177–181.

LEVINSON, B. M. Sub-cultural values and IQ stability. *Journal of Genetic Psychology,* 1961, 98, 69–82.

LEVINSON, B. M. The WAIS quotient of subcultural deviation. *Journal of Genetic Psychology,* 1963, 103, 123–131.

LEVONIAN, E. A statistical analysis of the 16 Personality Factor Questionnaire. *Educational and Psychological Measurement,* 1961, 21, 589–596.

LEVY, J. Readability level and differential test performance: A language revision of the Study of Values. *Journal of Educational Psychology,* 1958, 49, 6–12.

LIKERT, R. A technique for the measurement of attitudes. *Archives of Psychology,* 1932, No. 140.

LINDSLEY, D. B. The psychology of lie detection. In G. J. Dudycha et al. *Psychology for law enforcement officers.* Springfield, Ill.: Charles C Thomas, 1955. Ch. 4.

LINDZEY, G. On the classification of projective techniques. *Psychological Bulletin,* 1959, 56, 158–168.

LINDZEY, G. *Projective techniques and cross-cultural research.* New York: Appleton-Century-Crofts, 1961.

LINDZEY, G. Seer versus sign. *Journal of Experimental Research in Personality*, 1965, 1, 17–26.

LINDZEY, G., & BORGATTA, E. F. Sociometric measurement. In G. Lindzey (Ed.), *Handbook of social psychology*. Cambridge, Mass.: Addison-Wesley, 1954. Vol. 1, Ch. 11.

LINDZEY, G., & HERMAN, P. S. Thematic Apperception Test: A note on reliability and situational validity. *Journal of Projective Techniques*, 1955, 19, 36–42.

LITTELL, W. M. The Wechsler Intelligence Scale for Children: Review of a decade of research. *Psychological Bulletin*, 1960, 57, 132–156.

LITTLE, K. B., & SHNEIDMAN, E. S. Congruencies among interpretations of psychological test and anamnestic data. *Psychological Monographs*, 1959, 73, No. 6.

LIVERANT, S. Intelligence: A concept in need of re-examination. *Journal of Consulting Psychology*, 1960, 24, 101–110.

LOEVINGER, J. The meaning and measurement of ego development. *American Psychologist*, 1966, 21, 195–206. (a)

LOEVINGER, J. A theory of test response. In A. Anastasi (Ed.), *Testing problems in perspective*. Washington: American Council on Education, 1966. Pp. 545–556. (b)

LOEVINGER, J., & OSSORIO, A. G. Evaluation of therapy by self-report: A paradox. *American Psychologist*, 1958, 13, 366.

LONGSTAFF, H. P. Fakability of the Strong Interest Blank and the Kuder Preference Record. *Journal of Applied Psychology*, 1948, 32, 360–369.

LOPEZ, F. M., JR. Current problems in test performance of job applicants. *Personnel Psychology*, 1966, 19, 10–17.

LORD, F. M. The relation of the reliability of multiple-choice tests to the distribution of item difficulties. *Psychometrika*, 1952, 17, 181–194. (a)

LORD, F. M. A theory of test scores. *Psychometric Monographs*, 1952, No. 7. (b)

LORD, F. M. Relation of test score to trait underlying the test. *Educational and Psychological Measurement*, 1953, 13, 517–549.

LORETAN, J. O. Alternatives to intelligence testing. *Proceedings of the 1965 Invitational Conference on Testing Problems, Educational Testing Service*, 1966, 19–30.

LORGE, I. Schooling makes a difference. *Teachers College Record*, 1945, 46, 483–492.

LOTSOF, E. J. Intelligence, verbal fluency, and the Rorschach test. *Journal of Consulting Psychology*, 1953, 17, 21–24.

LOWENFELD, M. The world pictures of children. *British Journal of Medical Psychology*, 1939, 18, 65–101.

LUBORSKY, L. B., & CATTELL, R. B. The validation of personality factors in humor. *Journal of Personality*, 1947, 15, 283–291.

LYMAN, H. B. *Test scores and what they mean*. Englewood Cliffs, N. J.: Prentice-Hall, 1963.

MABERLY, N. C. *The standard score scale for revised tests in the Evaluation and Adjustment Series*. New York: Harcourt, Brace & World, 1966.

MACHOVER, K. *Personality projection in the drawing of the human figure: A method of personality investigation*. Springfield, Ill.: Charles C Thomas, 1949.

MACKINNEY, A. C. The assessment of performance change: An inductive example. *Organizational Behavior and Human Performance*, 1967, 2, 56–72.

MACKINNON, D. W. The nature and nurture of creative talent. *American Psychologist*, 1962, 17, 484–495.

MACKINNON, D. W. Tests for the measurement of personal effectiveness. In A.

Anastasi (Ed.), *Testing problems in perspective*. Washington: American Council on Education, 1966. Pp. 518–527.

MACNAMARA, J. (Ed.) Problems of bilingualism. *Journal of Social Issues*, 1967, 23 (2), 1–35.

MAGARET, A., & SIMPSON, M. A comparison of two measures of deterioration in psychotics. *Journal of Consulting Psychology*, 1948, 12, 265–270.

MAIER, N. R. F. *The appraisal interview: Objectives, methods, and skills*. New York: Wiley, 1958.

MALLINSON, G. G., & CRUMRINE, W. M. An investigation of the stability of interests of high school students. *Journal of Educational Research*, 1952, 45, 369–383.

MANDLER, G., & SARASON, S. B. A study of anxiety and learning. *Journal of Abnormal and Social Psychology*, 1952, 47, 166–173.

MANUEL, H. T. *Taking a test: How to do your best*. New York: Harcourt, Brace & World, 1956.

MARKS, P. A., & SEEMAN, W. *The actuarial description of abnormal personality—An atlas for use with the MMPI*. Baltimore: Williams & Wilkins, 1963.

MASLING, J. The effects of warm and cold interaction on the administration and scoring of an intelligence test. *Journal of Consulting Psychology*, 1959, 23, 336–341.

MASLING, J. The influence of situational and interpersonal variables in projective testing. *Psychological Bulletin*, 1960, 56, 65–85.

MASLING, J. Differential indoctrination of examiners and Rorschach responses. *Journal of Consulting Psychology*, 1965, 29, 198–201.

MATHEWS, J. Ruling against track system stirs IQ test doubts. Washington (D. C.) *Evening Star*, June 30, 1967.

MAXFIELD, K. B., & BUCHHOLZ, S. *A social maturity scale for blind preschool children: A guide to its use*. New York: American Foundation for the Blind, 1957.

MAXWELL, E. Validities of abbreviated WAIS scales. *Journal of Consulting Psychology*, 1957, 21, 121–126.

MAYFIELD, E. C. The selection interview—a re-evaluation of published research. *Personnel Psychology*, 1964, 17, 239–260.

MCARTHUR, C. Analyzing the clinical process. *Journal of Counseling Psychology*, 1954, 1, 203–207.

MCCALL, W. A. *How to measure in education*. New York: Macmillan, 1922.

MCCARTHY, D. A study of the reliability of the Goodenough drawing test of intelligence. *Journal of Psychology*, 1944, 18, 201–216.

MCCLELLAND, D. C. *The achieving society*. New York: Free Press, 1961.

MCCLELLAND, D. C. Longitudinal trends in the relation of thought to action. *Journal of Consulting Psychology*, 1966, 30, 479–483.

MCCLELLAND, D. C., et al. *The achievement motive*. New York: Appleton-Century-Crofts, 1953.

MCCORMICK, E. J. Application of job analysis to indirect validity. *Personnel Psychology*, 1959, 12, 395–420.

MCHUGH, R. B., & APOSTOLAKOS, P. C. Methodology for the comparison of clinical with actuarial predictions. *Psychological Bulletin*, 1959, 56, 301–308.

MCLEISH, J. The validation of Seashore's measures of musical talent by factorial methods. *British Journal of Psychology, Statistical Section*, 1950, 3, 129–140.

MCNEMAR, Q. *The revision of the Stanford-Binet Scale: An analysis of the standardization data*. Boston: Houghton Mifflin, 1942.

McNEMAR, Q. On abbreviated Wechsler-Bellevue Scales. *Journal of Consulting Psychology*, 1950, 14, 79–81.

McNEMAR, Q. On WAIS difference scores. *Journal of Consulting Psychology*, 1957, 21, 239–240.

MEEHL, P. E. The dynamics of "structured" personality tests. *Journal of Clinical Psychology*, 1945, 1, 296–303. (a)

MEEHL, P. E. An investigation of a general normality or control factor in personality testing. *Psychological Monographs*, 1945, 59, No. 4. (b)

MEEHL, P. E. *Clinical versus statistical prediction: A theoretical analysis and a review of the evidence.* Minneapolis: University of Minnesota Press, 1954.

MEEHL, P. E. Wanted—a good cookbook. *American Psychologist*, 1956, 11, 263–272.

MEEHL, P. E. A comparison of clinicians with five statistical methods of identifying psychotic MMPI profiles. *Journal of Counseling Psychology*, 1959, 6, 102–109.

MEEHL, P. E. Seer over sign: The first good example. *Journal of Experimental Research in Personality*, 1965, 1, 27–32.

MEEHL, P. E., & ROSEN, A. Antecedent probability and the efficiency of psychometric signs, patterns, or cutting scores. *Psychological Bulletin*, 1955, 52, 194–216.

MEGARGEE, E. I. (Ed.) *Research in clinical assessment.* New York: Harper & Row, 1966.

MEIER, N. C. *Art in human affairs.* New York: McGraw-Hill, 1942.

MELTON, A. W. (Ed.) *Apparatus tests.* (AAF Aviation Psychology Program, Research Reports. Rep. No. 4) Washington: Government Printing Office, 1947.

MESSICK, S., & KOGAN, N. Personality consistencies in judgment: Dimensions of role construct. *Multivariate Behavioral Research*, 1966, 1, 165–175.

MICHAEL, W. B., *et al.* The description of spatial-visualization abilities. *Educational and Psychological Measurement*, 1957, 17, 185–199.

MILLER, H., & BIERI, J. An informational analysis of clinical judgment. *Journal of Abnormal and Social Psychology*, 1963, 67, 317–325.

MILLMAN, J., BISHOP, C. H., & EBEL, R. An analysis of test-wiseness. *Educational and Psychological Measurement*, 1965, 25, 707–726.

MILNER, B. Effects of different brain lesions on card sorting. *Archives of Neurology*, 1963, 9, 90–100.

MILNER, B. Some effects of frontal lobectomy in man. In J. M. Warren & K. Akert (Eds.), *The frontal granular cortex and behavior.* New York: McGraw-Hill, 1964. Pp. 313–334.

MINDAK, W. A. A new technique for measuring advertising effectiveness. *Journal of Marketing*, 1956, 20, 367–378.

MOLLENKOPF, W. G. An experimental study of the effects on item-analysis data of changing item placement and test time limit. *Psychometrika*, 1950, 15, 291–317. (a)

MOLLENKOPF, W. G. Predicted differences and differences between predictions. *Psychometrika*, 1950, 15, 409–417. (b)

MORENO, J. L. *Who shall survive? Foundations of sociometry, group psychotherapy, and sociodrama.* (2nd ed.) Beacon, N. Y.: Beacon House, 1953. (*Sociometry Monographs*, No. 29.)

MORIARTY, A. E. Children's ways of coping with the intelligence test. *Menninger Clinic Bulletin*, 1960, 24, 115–127.

MORIARTY, A. E. Coping patterns of preschool children in response to intelligence test demands. *Genetic Psychology Monographs*, 1961, 64, 3–127.

MORIARTY, A. E. *Constancy and IQ change: A clinical view of relationships between tested intelligence and personality.* Springfield, Ill.: Charles C Thomas, 1966.

MORROW, R. S. An analysis of the relations among tests of musical, artistic, and mechanical abilities. *Journal of Psychology*, 1938, 5, 253–263.

MOSIER, C. I. Problems and designs of cross-validation. *Educational and Psychological Measurement*, 1951, 11, 5–11.

MOSIER, C. I., & McQUITTY, J. V. Methods of item validation and abacs for item-test correlation and critical ratio of upper-lower difference. *Psychometrika*, 1940, 5, 57–65.

MOSS, F. A. Report of the Committee on Aptitude Tests for Medical Schools. *Journal of the Association of American Medical Colleges*, 1942, 17, 312–315.

MOWRER, O. H. "Q-technique"—description, history, and critique. In O. H. Mowrer (Ed.), *Psychotherapy theory and research.* New York: Ronald, 1953. Pp. 316–375.

MUGAAS, H. D., & HESTER, R. The development of an equation for identifying the interests of carpenters. *Educational and Psychological Measurement*, 1952, 12, 408–414.

MURPHY, G. *An historical introduction to modern psychology.* (Rev. ed.) New York: Harcourt, Brace, 1949.

MURRAY, H. A., et al. *Explorations in personality.* New York: Oxford University Press, 1938.

MURRAY, H. A., & MacKINNON, D. W. Assessment of OSS personnel. *Journal of Consulting Psychology*, 1946, 10, 76–80.

MURRAY, H. A., & MORGAN, C. D. A clinical study of sentiments: I and II. *Genetic Psychology Monographs*, 1945, 32, 3–311.

MURSTEIN, B. I. *Theory and research in projective techniques (emphasizing the TAT).* New York: Wiley, 1963.

MUSSEN, P. H., & NAYLOR, H. K. The relationships between overt and fantasy aggression. *Journal of Abnormal and Social Psychology*, 1954, 49, 235–240.

MYERS, I. B. *The Myers-Briggs Type Indicator: Manual.* Princeton, N. J.: Educational Testing Service, 1962.

NEULINGER, J. Attitudes of American secondary school students toward the use of intelligence tests. *Personnel and Guidance Journal*, 1966, 44, 337–341.

NEWBY, H. A. *Audiology: Principles and practices.* (2nd ed.) New York: Appleton-Century-Crofts, 1964.

NISBET, J. D. Symposium: Contributions to intelligence testing and the theory of intelligence: IV. Intelligence and age: Retesting with twenty-four years' interval. *British Journal of Educational Psychology*, 1957, 27, 190–198.

NOLL, V. H. Simulation by college students of a prescribed pattern on a personality scale. *Educational and Psychological Measurement*, 1951, 11, 478–488.

NORMAN, R. D. A revised deterioration formula for the Wechsler Adult Intelligence Scale. *Journal of Clinical Psychology*, 1966, 22, 287–294.

OEHRN, A. *Experimentelle Studien zur Individualpsychologie.* Dorpater disser., 1889. (Also in *Psychologische Arbeiten*, 1895, 1, 95–152.)

ORTAR, G. Improving test validity by coaching. *Educational Research* (London), 1960, 2, 137–142.

ORTAR, G. Is a verbal test cross-cultural? *Scripta Hierosolymitana* (Hebrew University, Jerusalem), 1963, 13, 219–235.

OSGOOD, C. E., et al. *The measurement of meaning.* Urbana, Ill.: University of Illinois Press, 1957.

OSGOOD, C. E., & LURIA, Z. A blind analysis of a case of multiple personality using the semantic differential. *Journal of Abnormal and Social Psychology,* 1954, 49, 579–591.

OSS Assessment Staff. *Assessment of men: Selection of personnel for the Office of Strategic Services.* New York: Rinehart, 1948.

OWENS, W. A. Age and mental abilities: A longitudinal study. *Genetic Psychology Monographs,* 1953, 48, 3–54.

OWENS, W. A. Age and mental abilities: A second adult follow-up. *Journal of Educational Psychology,* 1966, 57, 311–325.

PACE, C. R. Five college environments. *College Board Review,* 1960, 41, 24–28.

PACE, C. R., & STERN, C. G. An approach to the measurement of psychological characteristics of college environments. *Journal of Educational Psychology,* 1958, 49, 269–277.

PALERMO, D. S., & JENKINS, J. J. Frequency of superordinate responses to a word association test as a function of age. *Journal of Verbal Learning and Verbal Behavior,* 1963, 1, 378–383.

PARKER, J. W. The validity of some current tests for organicity. *Journal of Consulting Psychology,* 1957, 21, 425–428.

PARRISH, J. A., et al. The industrial psychologist: Selection and equal employment opportunity. (A symposium.) *Personnel Psychology,* 1966, 19, 1–40.

PASCAL, G. R., & SUTTELL, B. J. *The Bender-Gestalt Test: Quantification and validity for adults.* New York: Grune & Stratton, 1951.

PASTOVIC, J. J., & GUTHRIE, G. M. Some evidence on the validity of the WISC. *Journal of Consulting Psychology,* 1951, 15, 385–386.

PATTERSON, C. H. Predicting success in trade and vocational courses: Review of the literature. *Educational and Psychological Measurement,* 1956, 16, 352–400.

PATTERSON, C. H. Interest tests and the emotionally disturbed client. *Educational and Psychological Measurement,* 1957, 17, 264–280.

PATTERSON, R. M. The significance of practice effect upon readministration of the Grace Arthur Performance Scale to high grade mentally deficient children. *American Journal of Mental Deficiency,* 1946, 50, 393–401.

PAUL, G. L., & ERIKSEN, C. W. Effects of test anxiety on "real-life" examinations. *Journal of Personality,* 1964, 32, 480–494.

PEARSON, J. S., & SWENSON, W. M. *A user's guide to the Mayo Clinic automated MMPI program.* New York: Psychological Corporation, 1967.

PEARSON, K. On lines and planes of closest fit to systems of points in space. *Philosophical Magazine,* Series 6, 1901, 2, 559–572.

PEATMAN, J. G. *Introduction to applied statistics.* New York: Harper & Row, 1963.

PEEL, E. A. A note on practice effects in intelligence tests. *British Journal of Educational Psychology,* 1951, 21, 122–125.

PEEL, E. A. Practice effects between three consecutive tests of intelligence. *British Journal of Educational Psychology,* 1952, 22, 196–199.

PEEL, E. A. The measurement of interests by verbal methods. *British Journal of Statistical Psychology,* 1959, 12, 105–118.

PEIZER, E. Studies of the upper extremity amputee. I. Design and scope. *Artificial Limbs,* 1958, 5(1), 4–56.

PEMBERTON, C. L. The closure factors related to temperament. *Journal of Personality,* 1952, 21, 159–175.

PEPINSKY, H. B., SIEGEL, L., & VANATTA, A. The criterion in counseling: A group participation scale. *Journal of Abnormal and Social Psychology,* 1952, 47, 415–419.

PETERS, G. A. A color-blindness test for use in vocational guidance. *Personnel and Guidance Journal*, 1956, 34, 572–575.

PETERSON, J. *Early conceptions and tests of intelligence.* Yonkers, N. Y.: World Book Co., 1926.

PHILIPPE, J. Jastrow—exposition d'anthropologie de Chicago—testes psychologiques, etc. *Année psychologique*, 1894, 1, 522–526.

PINNEAU, S. R. *Changes in intelligence quotient from infancy to maturity.* Boston: Houghton Mifflin, 1961.

PINTNER, R., & PATERSON, D. G. *A Scale of Performance Tests.* New York: Appleton, 1917.

PITCHER, B. The Law School Admission Test as a predictor of first-year law school grades, 1962–1963. *Statistical Report, Educational Testing Service*, SR-65-32, 1965.

PITTLUCK, P. The relation between aggressive fantasy and overt behavior. Unpublished doctoral dissertation, Yale University, 1950.

PORTEUS, S. D. *Guide to Porteus Maze Test.* Vineland, N. J.: The Training School, 1924.

PORTEUS, S. D. *The Porteus Maze Test and intelligence.* Palo Alto, Calif.: Pacific Books, 1950.

PORTEUS, S. D. *The Maze Test and clinical psychology.* Palo Alto, Calif.: Pacific Books, 1959.

PRESCOTT, G. A. *Test administration guide.* New York: Harcourt, Brace & World, undated. (Test Service Bulletin No. 102)

PRIEN, E. P. Dynamic character of criteria: Organization change. *Journal of Applied Psychology*, 1966, 50, 501–504.

PRIMOFF, E. S. Empirical validations of the J-coefficient. *Personnel Psychology*, 1959, 12, 413–418.

Privacy and behavioral research. Washington: Government Printing Office, 1967.

QUERESHI, M. Y. Practice effects on the WISC subtest scores and IQ estimates. *Journal of Clinical Psychology*, 1968, 24, 79–85.

RABIN, A. I., & GUERTIN, W. H. Research with the Wechsler-Bellevue Test: 1945–1950. *Psychological Bulletin*, 1951, 48, 211–248.

RAPAPORT, D., et al. *Diagnostic psychological testing.* Chicago: Year Book Publishers, Vol. I, 1945; Vol. II, 1946.

RAWLS, R. F. Objective tests and testing of blind children. *New Outlook for the Blind*, 1954, 48, 39–45.

REICHENBERG-HACKETT, W. Changes in Goodenough drawings after a gratifying experience. *American Journal of Orthopsychiatry*, 1953, 23, 501–517.

REID, J. W. Stability of measured Kuder interests in young adults. *Journal of Educational Research*, 1951, 45, 307–312.

REYNOLDS, H. H. Efficacy of sociometric ratings in predicting leadership success. *Psychological Reports*, 1966, 19, 35–40.

RICH, C. C., & ANDERSON, R. P. A tactual form of the Progressive Matrices for use with blind children. *Personnel and Guidance Journal*, 1965, 43, 912–919.

RICHARDS, J. M., JR. Reconceptualization of the clinical and statistical prediction controversy in terms of components of accuracy of interpersonal perception scores. *Psychological Reports*, 1963, 12, 443–448.

RICHARDS, J. M., JR., et al. An investigation of the criterion problem for one group of medical specialists. *Journal of Applied Psychology*, 1965, 49, 79–90.

RICHARDSON, M. W. The interpretation of a test validity coefficient in terms of increased efficiency of a selected group of personnel. *Psychometrika*, 1944, 9, 245–248.

RIMLAND, B. Multidimensional scatterplotting: A graphic approach to profile analysis. *Journal of Applied Psychology*, 1960, 44, 404–406.

RIMOLDI, H. J. A note on Raven's Progressive Matrices Test. *Educational and Psychological Measurement*, 1948, 8, 347–352.

ROBERTS, S. O. Comparative validity study of CEEB and CIEP test programs. Nashville, Tenn.: Department of Psychology, Fisk University, 1964. (Mimeographed)

ROBINSON, H. B., & ROBINSON, N. M. *The mentally retarded child: A psychological approach.* New York: McGraw-Hill, 1965.

RODGER, A. G. The application of six group intelligence tests to the same children, and the effects of practice. *British Journal of Educational Psychology*, 1936, 6, 291–305.

ROE, A. *The psychology of occupations.* New York: Wiley, 1956.

ROGERS, C. R., & DYMOND, R. F. (Eds.) *Psychotherapy and personality change.* Chicago: University of Chicago Press, 1954.

ROHDE, A. R. *The sentence completion method.* New York: Ronald, 1957.

RORER, L. G. The great response-style myth. *Psychological Bulletin*, 1965, 63, 129–156.

RORER, L. G., et al. Optimum cutting scores to discriminate groups of unequal size and variance. *Journal of Applied Psychology*, 1966, 50, 153–164.

RORSCHACH, H. (Transl. by P. Lemkau & B. Kronenburg.) *Psychodiagnostics: A diagnostic test based on perception.* Berne: Huber, 1942 (1st German ed., 1921; U. S. distributor, Grune & Stratton.)

ROSENBERG, N. Stability and maturation of Kuder interest patterns of medical, law, and business school alumni. *Journal of Applied Psychology*, 1953, 37, 367–369.

ROSENTHAL, R. *Experimenter effects in behavioral research.* New York: Appleton-Century-Crofts, 1966.

ROSENTHAL, R., & JACOBSON, L. Teachers' expectancies: Determinants of pupils' IQ gains. *Psychological Reports*, 1966, 19, 115–118.

ROSENTHAL, R., & JACOBSON, L. Self-fulfilling prophecies in the classroom: Teachers' expectations as unintended determinants of pupils' intellectual competence. In M. Deutsch, I. Katz, & A. R. Jensen (Eds.), *Social class, race, and psychological development.* New York: Holt, Rinehart & Winston, 1968. Ch. 6.

ROSENZWEIG, S. The Rosenzweig Picture-Frustration Study, Children's Form. In A. I. Rohm & M. R. Haworth (Eds.), *Projective techniques with children.* New York: Grune & Stratton, 1960.

RUEBHAUSEN, O. M., & BRIM, O. G., JR. Privacy and behavioral research. *American Psychologist*, 1966, 21, 423–437.

RUGGLES, R., & ALLPORT, G. W. Recent applications of the A-S Reaction Study. *Journal of Abnormal and Social Psychology*, 1939, 34, 518–528.

RULON, P. J. A simplified procedure for determining the reliability of a test of split-halves. *Harvard Educational Review*, 1939, 9, 99–103.

RUSSELL, W. A., & JENKINS, J. J. The complete Minnesota norms for responses to 100 words from the Kent-Rosanoff Word Association Test. Studies on the role of language in behavior, Technical Report, No. 11. Contract No. N8-ONR-66216. University of Minnesota, 1954.

SACHMAN, H. An investigation of certain aspects of the validity of the formal Rorschach scoring system in relation to age, education, and vocabulary score. Unpublished doctoral dissertation, Fordham University, 1952.

SACKS, E. L. Intelligence scores as a function of experimentally established social relationships between the child and examiner. *Journal of Abnormal and Social Psychology*, 1952, 47, 354–358.

SANFORD, N. (Ed.) Personality development during the college years. *Journal of Social Issues*, 1956, 12, 3–70.

SARASON, I. G. Test anxiety and the intellectual performance of college students. *Journal of Educational Psychology*, 1961, 52, 201–206.

SARASON, I. G. *Personality: An objective approach.* New York: Wiley, 1966.

SARASON, S. B. *The clinical interaction, with special reference to the Rorschach.* New York: Harper, 1954.

SARASON, S. B., et al. *Anxiety in elementary school children.* New York: Wiley, 1960.

SARASON, S. B., & GLADWIN, T. *Psychological problems in mental deficiency.* (3rd ed.) New York: Harper, 1959.

SARASON, S. B., HILL, K. T., & ZIMBARDO, P. A longitudinal study of the relation of test anxiety to performance on intelligence and achievement tests. *Monographs of the Society for Research in Child Development*, 1964, 29, No. 7.

SARBIN, T. R., TAFT, R., & BAILEY, D. E. *Clinical inference and cognitive theory.* New York: Holt, Rinehart & Winston, 1960.

SATTLER, J. M., & THEYE, F. Procedural, situational, and interpersonal variables in individual intelligence testing. *Psychological Bulletin*, 1967, 68, 347–360.

SAUNDERS, D. R. Moderator variables in prediction. *Educational and Psychological Measurement*, 1956, 16, 209–222.

SAUNDERS, D. R. On the dimensionality of the WAIS battery for two groups of normal males. *Psychological Reports*, 1959, 5, 529–541.

SAUNDERS, D. R. A factor analysis of the Information and Arithmetic items of the WAIS. *Psychological Reports*, 1960, 6, 367–383. (a)

SAUNDERS, D. R. A factor analysis of the Picture Completion items of the WAIS. *Journal of Clinical Psychology*, 1960, 16, 146–149. (b)

SAUNDERS, D. R. Further implications of Mundy-Castle's correlations between EEG and WB variables. *Journal of the Institute for Personality Research*, 1960, 8, 91–101. (c)

SAUNDERS, D. R. D and Alpha frequency: A cross-validation. *Journal of Clinical Psychology*, 1961, 17, 165–167.

SAWYER, J. Measurement *and* prediction, clinical *and* statistical. *Psychological Bulletin*, 1966, 66, 178–200.

SCHAEFER, C. E. Biographical inventory correlates of scientific and artistic creativity in adolescents. Unpublished doctoral dissertation, Fordham University, 1967.

SCHAIE, K. W. A general model for the study of developmental problems. *Psychological Bulletin*, 1965, 64, 92–107.

SCHWARZ, P. A. Development and application of African ability tests: Summary report. American Institutes for Research in the Behavioral Sciences, Contract ICAc-2155, AIR-C71-12/64-TR, 1964. (a)

SCHWARZ, P. A. Development of manpower screening tests for the developing nations: Technical manual. American Institutes for Research in the Behavioral Sciences, Contract ICAc-2155, AIR-C71-6/64-TR, 1964. (b)

SEASHORE, C. E. *Psychology of music.* New York: McGraw-Hill, 1938.

SEASHORE, H. G. Differences between verbal and performance IQ's on the Wechsler Intelligence Scale for Children. *Journal of Consulting Psychology*, 1951, 15, 62–67.

SEASHORE, H. G. Women are more predictable than men. *Journal of Counseling Psychology*, 1962, 9, 261–270.

SEASHORE, H. G., WESMAN, A. G., & DOPPELT, J. E. The standardization of the Wechsler Intelligence Scale for Children. *Journal of Consulting Psychology,* 1950, 14, 99–110.

SEASHORE, S. E., INDIK, B. P., & GEORGOPOULOS, B. S. Relationships among criteria of job performance. *Journal of Applied Psychology,* 1960, 44, 195–202.

SEDLACEK, W. E. (Ed.) *Medical College Admission Test: Handbook for admissions committees.* Evanston, Ill.: Association of American Medical Colleges, 1967.

SEGUIN, E. *Idiocy: Its treatment by the physiological method.* (Reprinted from original ed. of 1866.) New York: Bureau of Publications, Teachers College, Columbia University, 1907.

SHARP, S. E. Individual psychology: A study in psychological method. *American Journal of Psychology,* 1898–1899, 10, 329–391.

SHAW, M. E., & WRIGHT, J. M. *Scales for the measurement of attitudes.* New York: McGraw-Hill, 1967.

SHAYCOFT, M. F., NEYMAN, C. A., JR., & DAILEY, J. T. Comparison of Navy recruits with male high school students on the basis of Project TALENT data. Final Report, Nonr-3482(00), June 1962. (American Institutes for Research, Washington, D. C.)

SHERIF, C. W., SHERIF, M., & NEBERGALL, R. *Attitude and attitude change: The social judgment-involvement approach.* Philadelphia: Saunders, 1965.

SHIPLEY, W. C., GRAY, F. E., & NEWBERT, N. The personal inventory. *Journal of Clinical Psychology,* 1946, 2, 318–322.

SHNEIDMAN, E. S. Projective techniques. In B. B. Wolman (Ed.), *Handbook of clinical psychology.* New York: McGraw-Hill, 1965. Pp. 498–521.

SIGEL, I. E. How intelligence tests limit understanding of intelligence. *Merrill-Palmer Quarterly,* 1963, 9, 39–56.

SILVERMAN, L. H. A Q-sort of the validity of evaluations made from projective techniques. *Psychological Monographs,* 1959, 73, No. 7.

SISSON, D. E. Forced-choice—the new Army rating. *Personnel Psychology,* 1948, 1, 365–381.

SKOLNICK, A. Motivational imagery and behavior over twenty years. *Journal of Consulting Psychology,* 1966, 30, 463–47.,.

SLOAN, W. Validity of Wechsler's deterioration quotient in high grade mental defectives. *Journal of Clinical Psychology,* 1947, 3, 187–188.

SLOAN, W. The Lincoln-Oseretsky Motor Development Scale. *Genetic Psychology Monographs,* 1955, 51, 183–252.

SMITH, A. Talkers and doers: Or education, intelligence, and WAIS verbal-performance ratios in psychiatric patients. *American Psychologist,* 1966, 21, 687.

SMITH, G. H. *Motivation research in advertising and marketing.* New York: McGraw-Hill, 1954.

SMITH, S. Language and non-verbal test performance of racial groups in Honolulu before and after a 14-year interval. *Journal of General Psychology,* 1942, 26, 51–93.

SNYGG, D., & COMBS, A. W. *Individual behavior: A perceptual approach to behavior.* (Rev. ed.) New York: Harper, 1959.

SOMMER, R. *Diagnostik der Geisteskrankheiten für praktische Ärzte und Studierende.* Wien und Leipzig: Urban und Schwarzenberg, 1894.

SONTAG, L. W., BAKER, C. T., & NELSON, V. L. Mental growth and personality development: A longitudinal study. *Monographs of the Society for Research in Child Development,* 1958, 23, No. 2.

SORENSON, R. C. Optimal allocation of enlisted men—full regression equations vs. aptitude area scores. *USAPRO Technical Research Note No.* 163, November 1965.

SORENSON, W. W. Test of mechanical principles as a suppressor variable for the prediction of effectiveness on a mechanical repair job. *Journal of Applied Psychology*, 1966, 50, 348–352.

SPEARMAN, C. "General intelligence" objectively determined and measured. *American Journal of Psychology*, 1904, 15, 201–293.

SPEARMAN, C. *The abilities of man.* New York: Macmillan, 1927.

SPRANGER, E. (transl. by P. J. W. Pigors) *Types of men.* Halle: Niemeyer, 1928.

Standards for educational and psychological tests and manuals. Washington: American Psychological Association, 1966.

STANLEY, J. C. *Measurement in today's schools.* (4th ed.) Englewood Cliffs, N. J.: Prentice-Hall, 1964.

STANLEY, J. C., & PORTER, A. C. Correlation of Scholastic Aptitude Test scores with college grades for Negroes versus whites. *Journal of Educational Measurement*, 1967, 4, 199–218.

STARK, S. Executive personality and psychological testing. *Current Economic Comment*, 1958, 20(2), 15–32.

STEAD, W. H., SHARTLE, C. L., *et al.* Occupational counseling techniques. New York: American Book Company, 1940.

STEPHENSON, W. *The study of behavior: Q-technique and its methodology.* Chicago: University of Chicago Press, 1953.

STERN, G. G. The measurement of psychological characteristics of students and learning environments. In S. Messick & J. Ross (Eds.), *Measurement in personality and cognition.* New York: Wiley, 1962. Pp. 27–68.

STERN, G. G. Characteristics of the intellectual climate in college environments. *Harvard Educational Review*, 1963, 33, 5–41.

STODDARD, G. D. Ferson and Stoddard Law Aptitude Examination. Preliminary report. *American Law School Review*, 1927, 6, 78–81.

STORMS, L. H. Rationales for the "twisted pear." *Journal of Consulting Psychology*, 1960, 24, 552–553.

STOTT, L. H., & BALL, R. S. Infant and preschool mental tests: Review and evaluation. *Monographs of the Society for Research in Child Development*, 1965, 30, No. 3.

STRAUSS, A. A., & KEPHART, N. C. *Psychopathology and education of the brain-injured child.* New York: Grune & Stratton, 1955.

STRAUSS, A. A., & LEHTINEN, L. E. *Psychopathology and education of the brain-injured child.* New York: Grune & Stratton, 1947.

STRICKER, L. J. Compulsivity as a moderator variable: A replication and extension. *Journal of Applied Psychology*, 1966, 50, 331–335.

STRICKER, L. J., & ROSS, J. Some correlates of a Jungian personality inventory. *Psychological Reports*, 1964, 14, 623–643.

STRONG, D. J., & FEDER, D. D. Measurement of the self-concept: A critique of the literature. *Journal of Counseling Psychology*, 1961, 8, 170–178.

STRONG, E. K., JR. *Vocational interests of men and women.* Stanford, Calif.: Stanford University Press, 1943.

STRONG, E. K., JR. *Vocational interests 18 years after college.* Minneapolis: University of Minnesota Press, 1955.

STRONG, E. K., JR., & CAMPBELL, D. P. *Manual for Strong Vocational Interest Blanks.* Stanford, Calif.: Stanford University Press, 1966.

STUTSMAN, R. *Mental measurement of preschool children.* Yonkers, N. Y.: World Book Co., 1931.

SUNDBERG, N. D. The use of the MMPI for cross-cultural personality study: A preliminary report on the German translation. *Journal of Abnormal and Social Psychology*, 1956, 58, 281–283.

SUPER, D. E. (Ed.) *The use of multifactor tests in guidance.* Washington: American Personnel and Guidance Association, 1958. (Reprinted from *Personnel and Guidance Journal*, 1956, 1957.)

SUPER, D. E., & CRITES, J. O. *Appraising vocational fitness by means of psychological tests.* (Rev. ed.) New York: Harper, 1962.

SWENSON, W. M., et al. A totally automated psychological test. *Journal of the American Medical Association*, 1965, 191, 925–927.

SYDIAHA, D. On the equivalence of clinical and statistical methods. *Journal of Applied Psychology*, 1959, 43, 395–401.

SYMONDS, P. M. *Diagnosing personality and conduct.* New York: Century, 1931.

TAFT, R. A cross-cultural comparison of the MMPI. *Journal of Consulting Psychology*, 1957, 21, 161–164.

TAYLOR, C. W. (Ed.) *Creativity: Progress and potential.* New York: Wiley, 1964. (a)

TAYLOR, C. W. (Ed.) *Widening horizons in creativity.* New York: Wiley, 1964. (b)

TAYLOR, C. W., & BARRON, F. (Eds.) *Scientific creativity: Its recognition and development.* New York: Wiley, 1963.

TAYLOR, C. W., & WILLIAMS, F. E. (Eds.) *Instructional media and creativity.* New York: Wiley, 1966.

TAYLOR, H. C., & RUSSELL, J. T. The relationship of validity coefficients to the practical effectiveness of tests in selection: Discussion and tables. *Journal of Applied Psychology*, 1939, 23, 565–578.

TAYLOR, J. A. A personality scale of manifest anxiety. *Journal of Abnormal and Social Psychology*, 1953, 48, 285–290.

TERMAN, L. M. *The measurement of intelligence.* Boston: Houghton Mifflin, 1916.

TERMAN, L. M., & MERRILL, M. A. *Measuring intelligence.* Boston: Houghton Mifflin, 1937.

TERMAN, L. M., & MERRILL, M. A. *Stanford-Binet Intelligence Scale: Manual for the third revision, Form L-M.* Boston: Houghton Mifflin, 1960.

TERMAN, L. M., & ODEN, M. H. *The gifted child grows up: Twenty-five years' follow-up of a superior group.* Stanford, Calif.: Stanford University Press, 1947.

TERMAN, L. M., & ODEN, M. H. *The gifted group at mid-life: Thirty-five years' follow-up of the superior child.* Stanford, Calif.: Stanford University Press, 1959.

Testing and public policy. (Special issue) *American Psychologist*, 1965, 20, 857–992.

THOMSON, G. H. A hierarchy without a general factor. *British Journal of Psychology*, 1916, 8, 271–281.

THOMSON, G. H. *The factorial analysis of human ability.* (3rd ed.) Boston: Houghton Mifflin, 1948.

THORNDIKE, E. L. Practice effects on intelligence tests. *Journal of Experimental Psychology*, 1922, 5, 101–107.

THORNDIKE, R. L. The effect of interval between test and retest on the constancy of the IQ. *Journal of Educational Psychology*, 1933, 24, 543–549.

THORNDIKE, R. L. "Constancy" of the IQ. *Psychological Bulletin*, 1940, 37, 167–186.

THORNDIKE, R. L. *The concepts of over- and under-achievement.* New York: Bureau of Publications, Teachers College, Columbia University, 1963.

THORNE, F. C. Clinical judgment: A clinician's viewpoint. *Journal of Clinical Psychology*, 1960, 16, 128–134.

THURSTONE, L. L. *Vectors of mind: Multiple-factor analysis for the isolation of primary traits.* Chicago: University of Chicago Press, 1935.

THURSTONE, L. L. Primary mental abilities. *Psychometric Monographs*, 1938, No. 1.

THURSTONE, L. L. A factorial study of perception. *Psychometric Monographs*, 1944, No. 4.

THURSTONE, L. L. *Multiple-factor analysis.* Chicago: University of Chicago Press, 1947.

THURSTONE, L. L. Some primary abilities in visual thinking. *Psychometric Laboratory, University of Chicago*, No. 59, August 1950.

THURSTONE, L. L. Creative talent. *Proceedings of the 1950 Invitational Conference on Testing Problems, Educational Testing Service*, 1951, 55–69(a). (Reprinted in A. Anastasi [Ed.], *Testing problems in perspective.* Washington: American Council on Education, 1966. Pp. 414–428.)

THURSTONE, L. L. Experimental tests of temperament. In *Essays in psychology dedicated to David Katz.* Uppsala, Sweden: Almquist & Wiksells, 1951. Pp. 248–262. (b)

THURSTONE, L. L. The development of objective measures of temperament. *Psychometric Laboratory, University of North Carolina*, No. 1, April 1953.

THURSTONE, L. L. *The measurement of values.* Chicago: University of Chicago Press, 1959.

THURSTONE, L. L., & CHAVE, E. J. *The measurement of attitude.* Chicago: University of Chicago Press, 1929.

THURSTONE, L. L., & THURSTONE, T. G. Factorial studies of intelligence. *Psychometric Monographs*, 1941, No. 2.

TIEBOUT, C., & MEIER, N. C. Artistic ability and general intelligence. *Psychological Monographs*, 1936, 48, 95–125.

TIFFIN, J., & McCORMICK, E. J. *Industrial Psychology.* (5th ed.) Englewood Cliffs, N. J.: Prentice-Hall, 1965.

TOLOR, A., & SCHULBERG, H. C. *An evaluation of the Bender-Gestalt Test.* Springfield, Ill.: Charles C Thomas, 1963.

TORRANCE, E. P. Current research on the nature of creative talent. *Journal of Counseling Psychology*, 1959, 6, 309–316.

TORRANCE, E. P. *Guiding creative talent.* Englewood Cliffs, N. J.: Prentice-Hall, 1962.

TRACHT, V. S. Preliminary findings on testing the cerebral palsied with Raven's "Progressive Matrices." *Journal of Exceptional Children*, 1948, 15, 77–79.

TRANKELL, A. The psychologist as an instrument of prediction. *Journal of Applied Psychology*, 1959, 43, 170–175.

TRAXLER, A. E., & HILKERT, R. N. Effect of type of desk on results of machine-scored tests. *School and Society*, 1942, 56, 277–296.

TRYON, R. C. A theory of *psychological components*—an alternative to "mathematical factors." *Psychological Review*, 1935, 42, 425–454.

TSUDZUKI, A., HATA, Y., & KUZE, T. (A study of rapport between examiner and subject.) *Japanese Journal of Psychology*, 1957, 27, 22–28.

TUDDENHAM, R. D. Soldier intelligence in World Wars I and II. *American Psychologist*, 1948, 3, 54–56.

Tufts College Institute of Applied Experimental Psychology. *Handbook of human engineering data.* (2nd ed.) NAVEXOS P-643. Technical Report—SDC 199-1-2. Special Devices Center, ONR, 1951.

TYLER, L. E. Toward a workable psychology of individuality. *American Psychologist*, 1959, 14, 75–81.

UHLANER, J. E. Development of Armed Forces Qualification Test and predecessor army screening tests, 1946–1950. *PRB Report* 976, 1952.

UHRBROCK, R. S. Attitudes of 4430 employees. *Journal of Social Psychology*, 1934, 5, 365–377.

ULRICH, L., & TRUMBO, D. The selection interview since 1949. *Psychological Bulletin*, 1965, 63, 100–116.

U. S. Air Force. Development of the Airman Classification Test Battery. *Air Training Command Research and Development Program, Research Bulletin*, 48-4, Nov. 1948.

USES. Technical report on standardization of General Aptitude Test Battery. *Technical Report* B-381, July 1958.

USES. *Guide to the use of the General Aptitude Test Battery: Section III. Development.* Washington: Government Printing Office, 1962.

USES. Research design for USES–Urban League Testing Project. Mimeographed Report, 1967.

UPSHAW, H. S. The effects of variable perspectives on judgments of opinion statements for Thurstone scales: Equal-appearing intervals. *Journal of Personality and Social Psychology*, 1965, 2, 60–69.

The use of student records: A statement of policy from the American Personnel and Guidance Association. Washington: APGA, 1961.

VERNON, P. E. The validation of civil service selection board procedures. *Occupational Psychology*, 1950, 24, 75–95.

VERNON, P. E. *The structure of human abilities.* (Rev. ed.) London: Methuen, 1960.

VERNON, P. E. *Personality assessment: A critical survey.* London: Methuen, 1964.

VERNON, P. E. Ability factors and environmental influences. *American Psychologist*, 1965, 20, 723–733.

WAITE, R. R., et al. A study of anxiety and learning in children. *Journal of Abnormal and Social Psychology*, 1958, 57, 267–270.

WALD, A. *Statistical decision function.* New York: Wiley, 1950.

WALLACE, P., KISSINGER, B., & REYNOLDS, B. Testing of minority group applicants for employment. Equal Employment Opportunity Commission, Office of Research and Reports, Research Report 1966-7, March 1966.

WALLACE, S. R. Criteria for what? *American Psychologist*, 1965, 20, 411–417.

WALSH, T. M. Responses on the Famous Sayings Test of professional and nonprofessional personnel in a medical population. *Psychological Reports*, 1966, 18, 151–157.

WARNER, W. L., MEEKER, M., & EELLS, K. *Social class in America: A manual of procedure for the measurement of social status.* Chicago: Science Research Associates, 1949.

WATSON, L. A., & TOLAN, T. *Hearing tests and hearing instruments.* Baltimore: Williams & Wilkins, 1949.

WATTS, K. P. Intelligence test performance from 11 to 18: A study of grammar school girls. *British Journal of Educational Psychology*, 1958, 28, 112–119.

WECHSLER, D. *The measurement of adult intelligence.* Baltimore: Williams & Wilkins, 1939.

WECHSLER, D. Equivalent test and mental ages for the WISC. *Journal of Consulting Psychology*, 1951, 15, 381–384.

WECHSLER, D. *Manual for the Wechsler Adult Intelligence Scale.* New York: Psychological Corporation, 1955.

WECHSLER, D. *The measurement and appraisal of adult intelligence.* (4th ed.) Baltimore: Williams & Wilkins, 1958.

WEISSENBERG, P., & GRUENFELD, L. W. Relationships among leadership dimensions and cognitive style. *Journal of Applied Psychology,* 1966, 50, 392–395.

WEITZ, J. Selecting supervisors with peer ratings. *Personnel Psychology,* 1958, 11, 25–35.

WELSH, G. S., & DAHLSTROM, W. G. (Eds.) *Basic readings on the MMPI in psychology and medicine.* Minneapolis: University of Minnesota Press, 1956.

WERNER, H., & STRAUSS, A. A. Pathology of figure-background relation in the child. *Journal of Abnormal and Social Psychology,* 1941, 36, 236–248.

WERNER, H., & STRAUSS, A. A. Impairment in thought processes of brain-injured children. *American Journal of Mental Deficiency,* 1943, 47, 291–295.

WESCHLER, I. R., & BERNBERG, R. Indirect methods of attitude measurement. *International Journal of Opinion and Attitude Research,* 1950, 4, 209–228.

WESMAN, A. G. Effect of speed on item-test correlation coefficients. *Educational and Psychological Measurement,* 1949, 9, 51–57.

WESMAN, A. G. Faking personality test scores in a simulated employment situation. *Journal of Applied Psychology,* 1952, 36, 112–113.

WESMAN, A. G. Writing the test item. In R. L. Thorndike (Ed.), *Educational Measurement.* (2nd ed.) Washington: American Council on Education, 1971. Ch. 4.

WHEELER, L. R. A comparative study of the intelligence of East Tennessee mountain children. *Journal of Educational Psychology,* 1942, 33, 321–334.

WHIMBEY, A. E., & DENENBERG, V. H. Programming life histories: Creating individual differences by the experimental control of early experiences. *Multivariate Behavioral Research,* 1966, 1, 279–286.

WHITEMAN, M. Intelligence and learning. *Merrill-Palmer Quarterly,* 1964, 10, 297–309.

WHYTE, W. H., JR. *The organization man.* Garden City, N. Y.: Doubleday, 1956.

WICKES, T. A., JR. Examiner influence in a testing situation. *Journal of Consulting Psychology,* 1956, 20, 23–26.

WIENER, D. N. Empirical occupational groupings of Kuder Preference Record profiles. *Educational and Psychological Measurement,* 1951, 11, 273–279.

WIENER, G., RIDER, R. V., & OPPEL, W. Some correlates of IQ change in children. *Child Development,* 1963, 34, 61–67.

WIGGINS, J. S. Strategic, method, and stylistic variance in the MMPI. *Psychological Bulletin,* 1962, 59, 224–242.

WIGGINS, J. S. Social desirability estimation and "faking good" well. *Educational and Psychological Measurement,* 1966, 26, 329–341.

WIGGINS, N. Individual viewpoints of social desirability. *Psychological Bulletin,* 1966, 66, 68–77.

WILLIAMS, M. The effect of past experience on mental performance in the elderly. *British Journal of Medical Psychology,* 1960, 33, 215–219.

WING, H. D. A factorial study of musical tests. *British Journal of Psychology,* 1941, 31, 341–355.

WING, H. D. A revision of the Wing Musical Aptitude Test. *Journal of Research in Music Education,* 1962, 10, 39–46.

WISSLER, C. The correlation of mental and physical traits. *Psychological Monographs,* 1901, 3, No. 16.

WITKIN, H. A., et al. *Personality through perception: An experimental and clinical study.* New York: Harper, 1954.

WOLF, R. The measurement of environments. In A. Anastasi (Ed.), *Testing problems in perspective.* Washington: American Council on Education, 1966. Pp. 491–503.

WOLFLE, D. Educational tests. *Science*, 1963, 142, 1529.

WOOD, D. A. *Test construction: Development and interpretation of achievement tests.* Columbus, Ohio: Merrill, 1960.

WRIGHT, H. F. Observational child study. In P. E. Mussen (Ed.), *Handbook of research methods in child development.* New York: Wiley, 1960. Ch. 3.

WYMAN, J. B. Tests of intellectual, social, and activity interests. In L. M. Terman et al., *Genetic studies of genius.* Vol. I. *Mental and physical traits of a thousand gifted children.* Stanford, Calif.: Stanford University Press, 1925. Ch. 16.

YAMAMOTO, K., & FRENGEL, B. A. An exploratory component analysis of the Minnesota tests of creative thinking. *California Journal of Educational Research*, 1966, 17, 220–229.

YATES, A. J. The validity of some psychological tests of brain damage. *Psychological Bulletin*, 1954, 51, 359–379.

YATES, A. J. The use of vocabulary in the measurement of intellectual deterioration—a review. *Journal of Mental Science*, 1956, 102, 409–440.

YATES, A. J., et al. Symposium on the effects of coaching and practice in intelligence tests. *British Journal of Educational Psychology*, 1953, 23, 147–162; 1954, 24, 1–8, 57–63.

YERKES, R. M. (Ed.) Psychological examining in the United States Army. *Memoirs of the National Academy of Sciences*, 1921, 15.

ZUBIN, J., ERON, L. D., & SCHUMER, F. *An experimental approach to projective techniques.* New York: Wiley, 1965.

ZUBIN, J., ERON, L. D., & SULTAN, F. A psychometric evaluation of the Rorschach experiment. *American Journal of Orthopsychiatry*, 1956, 26, 773–782.

APPENDIXES

A. Ethical Standards of
   Psychologists
B. Test Publishers
C. Classified List of
   Representative Tests

Ethical Standards of Psychologists [1]

THE PSYCHOLOGIST believes in the dignity and worth of the individual human being. He is committed to increasing man's understanding of himself and others. While pursuing this endeavor, he protects the welfare of any person who may seek his service or of any subject, human or animal, that may be the object of his study. He does not use his professional position or relationships, nor does he knowingly permit his own services to be used by others, for purposes inconsistent with these values. While demanding for himself freedom of inquiry and communication, he accepts the responsibility this freedom confers: for competence where he claims it, for objectivity in the report of his findings, and for consideration of the best interests of his colleagues and of society.

SPECIFIC PRINCIPLES

PRINCIPLE 1. RESPONSIBILITY.   The psychologist,[2] committed to increasing man's understanding of man, places high value on objectivity and integrity, and maintains the highest standards in the services he offers.

    a. As a scientist, the psychologist believes that society will be best served when he investigates where his judgment indicates investigation is needed; he plans his research in such a way as to minimize the possibility that his findings will be misleading; and he publishes full reports of his work, never

[1] From *American Psychologist*, 1963, 18, 56–60.
[2] A student of psychology who assumes the role of psychologist shall be considered a psychologist for the purpose of this code of ethics.

discarding without explanation data which may modify the interpretation of results.

b. As a teacher, the psychologist recognizes his primary obligation to help others acquire knowledge and skill, and to maintain high standards of scholarship.

c. As a practitioner, the psychologist knows that he bears a heavy social responsibility because his work may touch intimately the lives of others.

PRINCIPLE 2. COMPETENCE. The maintenance of high standards of professional competence is a responsibility shared by all psychologists, in the interest of the public and of the profession as a whole.

a. Psychologists discourage the practice of psychology by unqualified persons and assist the public in identifying psychologists competent to give dependable professional service. When a psychologist or a person identifying himself as a psychologist violates ethical standards, psychologists who know firsthand of such activities attempt to rectify the situation. When such a situation cannot be dealt with informally, it is called to the attention of the appropriate local, state, or national committee on professional ethics, standards, and practices.

b. The psychologist recognizes the boundaries of his competence and the limitations of his techniques and does not offer services or use techniques that fail to meet professional standards established in particular fields. The psychologist who engages in practice assists his client in obtaining professional help for all important aspects of his problem that fall outside the boundaries of his own competence. This principle requires, for example, that provision be made for the diagnosis and treatment of relevant medical problems and for referral to or consultation with other specialists.

c. The psychologist in clinical work recognizes that his effectiveness depends in good part upon his ability to maintain sound interpersonal relations, that temporary or more enduring aberrations in his own personality may interfere with this ability or distort his appraisals of others. Therefore he refrains from undertaking any activity in which his personal problems are likely to result in inferior professional services or harm to a client; or, if he is already engaged in such an activity when he becomes aware of his personal problems, he seeks competent professional assistance to determine whether he should continue or terminate his services to his client.

PRINCIPLE 3. MORAL AND LEGAL STANDARDS. The psychologist in the practice of his profession shows sensible regard for the social codes and moral expectations of the community in which he works, recognizing that violations of accepted moral and legal standards on his part may involve his clients, students, or colleagues in damaging personal conflicts, and impugn his own name and the reputation of his profession.

PRINCIPLE 4. MISREPRESENTATION. The psychologist avoids misrepresentation of his own professional qualifications, affiliations, and purposes, and those of the institutions and organizations with which he is associated.

a. A psychologist does not claim either directly or by implication professional qualifications that differ from actual qualifications, nor does he misrepresent his affiliation with any institution, organization, or individual, nor lead others to assume he has affiliations that he does not have. The psychologist is responsible for correcting others who misrepresent his professional qualifications or affiliations.

b. The psychologist does not misrepresent an institution or organization with which he is affiliated by ascribing to it characteristics that it does not have.

c. A psychologist does not use his affiliation with the American Psychological Association or its Divisions for purposes that are not consonant with the stated purposes of the Association.

d. A psychologist does not associate himself with or permit his name to be used in connection with any services or products in such a way as to misrepresent them, the degree of his responsibility for them, or the nature of his affiliation.

PRINCIPLE 5. PUBLIC STATEMENTS. Modesty, scientific caution, and due regard for the limits of present knowledge characterize all statements of psychologists who supply information to the public, either directly or indirectly.

a. Psychologists who interpret the science of psychology or the services of psychologists to clients or to the general public have an obligation to report fairly and accurately. Exaggeration, sensationalism, superficiality, and other kinds of misrepresentation are avoided.

b. When information about psychological procedures and techniques is given, care is taken to indicate that they should be used only by persons adequately trained in their use.

c. A psychologist who engages in radio or television activities does not participate in commercial announcements recommending purchase or use of a product.

PRINCIPLE 6. CONFIDENTIALITY. Safeguarding information about an individual that has been obtained by the psychologist in the course of his teaching, practice, or investigation is a primary obligation of the psychologist. Such information is not communicated to others unless certain important conditions are met.

a. Information received in confidence is revealed only after most careful deliberation and when there is clear and imminent danger to an individual or to society, and then only to appropriate professional workers or public authorities.

b. Information obtained in clinical or consulting relationships, or evaluative data concerning children, students, employees, and others are discussed only for professional purposes and only with persons clearly concerned with the case. Written and oral reports should present only data germane to the purposes of the evaluation; every effort should be made to avoid undue invasion of privacy.

c. Clinical and other case materials are used in classroom teaching and writing only when the identity of the persons involved is adequately disguised.

d. The confidentiality of professional communications about individuals is maintained. Only when the originator and other persons involved give their express permission is a confidential professional communication shown to the individual concerned. The psychologist is responsible for informing the client of the limits of the confidentiality.

e. Only after explicit permission has been granted is the identity of research subjects published. When data have been published without permission for identification, the psychologist assumes responsibility for adequately disguising their sources.

f. The psychologist makes provision for the maintenance of confidentiality in the preservation and ultimate disposition of confidential records.

PRINCIPLE 7. CLIENT WELFARE. The psychologist respects the integrity and protects the welfare of the person or group with whom he is working.

a. The psychologist in industry, education, and other situations in which conflicts of interest may arise among various parties, as between management and labor, or between the client and employer of the psychologist, defines for himself the nature and direction of his loyalties and responsibilities and keeps all parties concerned informed of these commitments.

b. When there is a conflict among professional workers, the psychologist is concerned primarily with the welfare of any client involved and only secondarily with the interest of his own professional group.

c. The psychologist attempts to terminate a clinical or consulting relationship when it is reasonably clear to the psychologist that the client is not benefiting from it.

d. The psychologist who asks that an individual reveal personal information in the course of interviewing, testing, or evaluation, or who allows such information to be divulged to him, does so only after making certain that the responsible person is fully aware of the purposes of the interview, testing, or evaluation and of the ways in which the information may be used.

e. In cases involving referral, the responsibility of the psychologist for the welfare of the client continues until this responsibility is assumed by the professional person to whom the client is referred or until the relationship with the psychologist making the referral has been terminated by mutual agreement. In situations where referral, consultation, or other changes in the conditions of the treatment are indicated and the client refuses referral, the psychologist carefully weighs the possible harm to the client, to himself, and to his profession that might ensue from continuing the relationship.

f. The psychologist who requires the taking of psychological tests for didactic, classification, or research purposes protects the examinees by insuring that the tests and test results are used in a professional manner.

g. When potentially disturbing subject matter is presented to students, it is discussed objectively, and efforts are made to handle constructively any difficulties that arise.

h. Care must be taken to insure an appropriate setting for clinical work to protect both client and psychologist from actual or imputed harm and the profession from censure.

PRINCIPLE 8. CLIENT RELATIONSHIP. The psychologist informs his prospective client of the important aspects of the potential relationship that might affect the client's decision to enter the relationship.

   a. Aspects of the relationship likely to affect the client's decision include the recording of an interview, the use of interview material for training purposes, and observation of an interview by other persons.

   b. When the client is not competent to evaluate the situation (as in the case of a child), the person responsible for the client is informed of the circumstances which may influence the relationship.

   c. The psychologist does not normally enter into a professional relationship with members of his own family, intimate friends, close associates, or others whose welfare might be jeopardized by such a dual relationship.

PRINCIPLE 9. IMPERSONAL SERVICES. Psychological services for the purpose of diagnosis, treatment, or personalized advice are provided only in the context of a professional relationship, and are not given by means of public lectures or demonstrations, newspaper or magazine articles, radio or television programs, mail, or similar media.

   a. The preparation of personnel reports and recommendations based on test data secured solely by mail is unethical unless such appraisals are an integral part of a continuing client relationship with a company, as a result of which the consulting psychologist has intimate knowledge of the client's personnel situation and can be assured thereby that his written appraisals will be adequate to the purpose and will be properly interpreted by the client. These reports must not be embellished with such detailed analyses of the subject's presonality traits as would be appropriate only after intensive interviews with the subject. The reports must not make specific recommendations as to employment or placement of the subject which go beyond the psychologist's knowledge of the job requirements of the company. The reports must not purport to eliminate the company's need to carry on such other regular employment or personnel practices as appraisal of the work history, checking of references, past performance in the company.

PRINCIPLE 10. ANNOUNCEMENT OF SERVICES. A psychologist adheres to professional rather than commercial standards in making known his availability for professional services.

   a. A psychologist does not directly solicit clients for individual diagnosis or therapy.

   b. Individual listings in telephone directories are limited to name, highest relevant degree, certification status, address, and telephone number. They may also include identification in a few words of the psychologist's major areas of practice; for example, child therapy, personnel selection, industrial psychology. Agency listings are equally modest.

   c. Announcements of individual private practice are limited to a simple statement of the name, highest relevant degree, certification or diplomate status, address, telephone number, office hours, and a brief explanation of the types of services rendered. Announcements of agencies may list names of staff members with their qualifications. They conform in other particulars with the same standards as individual announcements, making certain that the true nature of the organization is apparent.

d. A psychologist or agency announcing nonclinical professional services may use brochures that are descriptive of services rendered but not evaluative. They may be sent to professional persons, schools, business firms, government agencies, and other similar organizations.

e. The use in a brochure of "testimonials from satisfied users" is unacceptable. The offer of a free trial of services is unacceptable if it operates to misrepresent in any way the nature or the efficacy of the services rendered by the psychologist. Claims that a psychologist has unique skills or unique devices not available to others in the profession are made only if the special efficacy of these unique skills or devices has been demonstrated by scientifically acceptable evidence.

f. The psychologist must not encourage (nor, within his power, even allow) a client to have exaggerated ideas as to the efficacy of services rendered. Claims made to clients about the efficacy of his services must not go beyond those which the psychologist would be willing to subject to professional scrutiny through publishing his results and his claims in a professional journal.

PRINCIPLE 11. INTERPROFESSIONAL RELATIONS. A psychologist acts with integrity in regard to colleagues in psychology and in other professions.

a. A psychologist does not normally offer professional services to a person receiving psychological assistance from another professional worker except by agreement with the other worker or after the termination of the client's relationship with the other professional worker.

b. The welfare of clients and colleagues requires that psychologists in joint practice or corporate activities make an orderly and explicit arrangement regarding the conditions of their association and its possible termination. Psychologists who serve as employers of other psychologists have an obligation to make similar appropriate arrangements.

PRINCIPLE 12. REMUNERATION. Financial arrangements in professional practice are in accord with professional standards that safeguard the best interest of the client and the profession.

a. In establishing rates for professional services, the psychologist considers carefully both the ability of the client to meet the financial burden and the charges made by other professional persons engaged in comparable work. He is willing to contribute a portion of his services to work for which he receives little or no financial return.

b. No commission or rebate or any other form of remuneration is given or received for referral of clients for professional services.

c. The psychologist in clinical or counseling practice does not use his relationships with clients to promote, for personal gain or the profit of an agency, commercial enterprises of any kind.

d. A psychologist does not accept a private fee or any other form of remuneration for professional work with a person who is entitled to his services through an institution or agency. The policies of a particular agency may make explicit provision for private work with its clients by members of its staff, and in such instances the client must be fully apprised of all policies affecting him.

PRINCIPLE 13. TEST SECURITY. Psychological tests and other assessment devices, the value of which depends in part on the naivete of the subject, are not reproduced or described in popular publications in ways that might invalidate the techniques. Access to such devices is limited to persons with professional interests who will safeguard their use.

  a. Sample items made up to resemble those of tests being discussed may be reproduced in popular articles and elsewhere, but scorable tests and actual test items are not reproduced except in professional publications.
  b. The psychologist is responsible for the control of psychological tests and other devices and procedures used for instruction when their value might be damaged by revealing to the general public their specific contents or underlying principles.

PRINCIPLE 14. TEST INTERPRETATION. Test scores, like test materials, are released only to persons who are qualified to interpret and use them properly.

  a. Materials for reporting test scores to parents, or which are designed for self-appraisal purposes in schools, social agencies, or industry are closely supervised by qualified psychologists or counselors with provisions for referring and counseling individuals when needed.
  b. Test results or other assessment data used for evaluation or classification are communicated to employers, relatives, or other appropriate persons in such a manner as to guard against misinterpretation or misuse. In the usual case, an interpretation of the test result rather than the score is communicated.
  c. When test results are communicated directly to parents and students, they are accompanied by adequate interpretive aids or advice.

PRINCIPLE 15. TEST PUBLICATION. Psychological tests are offered for commercial publication only to publishers who present their tests in a professional way and distribute them only to qualified users.

  a. A test manual, technical handbook, or other suitable report on the test is provided which describes the method of constructing and standardizing the test, and summarizes the validation research.
  b. The populations for which the test has been developed and the purposes for which it is recommended are stated in the manual. Limitations upon the test's dependability, and aspects of its validity on which research is lacking or incomplete, are clearly stated. In particular, the manual contains a warning regarding interpretations likely to be made which have not yet been substantiated by research.
  c. The catalog and manual indicate the training or professional qualifications required for sound interpretation of the test.
  d. The test manual and supporting documents take into account the princi-

ples enunciated in the *Technical Recommendations for Psychological Tests and Diagnostic Techniques.*

e. Test advertisements are factual and descriptive rather than emotional and persuasive.

PRINCIPLE 16. RESEARCH PRECAUTIONS. The psychologist assumes obligations for the welfare of his research subjects, both animal and human.

a. Only when a problem is of scientific significance and it is not practicable to investigate it in any other way is the psychologist justified in exposing research subjects, whether children or adults, to physical or emotional stress as part of an investigation.

b. When a reasonable possibility of injurious aftereffects exists, research is conducted only when the subjects or their responsible agents are fully informed of this possibility and agree to participate nevertheless.

c. The psychologist seriously considers the possibility of harmful aftereffects and avoids them, or removes them as soon as permitted by the design of the experiment.

d. A psychologist using animals in research adheres to the provisions of the Rules Regarding Animals, drawn up by the Committee on Precautions and Standards in Animal Experimentation and adopted by the American Psychological Association.

PRINCIPLE 17. PUBLICATION CREDIT. Credit is assigned to those who have contributed to a publication, in proportion to their contribution, and only to these.

a. Major contributions of a professional character, made by several persons to a common project, are recognized by joint authorship. The experimenter or author who has made the principal contribution to a publication is identified as the first listed.

b. Minor contributions of a professional character, extensive clerical or similar nonprofessional assistance, and other minor contributions are acknowledged in footnotes or in an introductory statement.

c. Acknowledgment through specific citations is made for unpublished as well as published material that has directly influenced the research or writing.

d. A psychologist who compiles and edits for publication the contributions of others publishes the symposium or report under the title of the committee or symposium, with his own name appearing as chairman or editor among those of the other contributors or committee members.

PRINCIPLE 18. RESPONSIBILITY TOWARD ORGANIZATION. A psychologist respects the rights and reputation of the institute or organization with which he is associated.

a. Materials prepared by a psychologist as a part of his regular work under specific direction of his organization are the property of that organization. Such materials are released for use or publication by a psychologist in accordance with policies of authorization, assignment of credit, and related matters which have been established by his organization.

b. Other material resulting incidentally from activity supported by any agency, and for which the psychologist rightly assumes individual responsibility, is published with disclaimer for any responsibility on the part of the supporting agency.

PRINCIPLE 19. PROMOTIONAL ACTIVITIES. The psychologist associated with the development or promotion of psychological devices, books, or other products offered for commercial sale is responsible for ensuring that such devices, books, or products are presented in a professional and factual way.

a. Claims regarding performance, benefits, or results are supported by scientifically acceptable evidence.
b. The psychologist does not use professional journals for the commercial exploitation of psychological products, and the psychologist-editor guards against such misuse.
c. The psychologist with a financial interest in the sale or use of a psychological product is sensitive to possible conflict of interest in his promotion of such products and avoids compromise of his professional responsibilities and objectives.

Test Publishers

BELOW ARE the names and addresses of some of the larger American publishers and distributors of psychological tests. Catalogues of current tests can be obtained from these publishers on request. For names and addresses of other test publishers, see the Publisher's Directory in the latest *Mental Measurements Yearbook*.

American Guidance Service, Inc., Publishers' Building, Circle Pines, Minn. 55014.

Bobbs-Merrill Company, Inc., 4300 West 62nd Street, Indianapolis, Ind. 46206.

California Test Bureau, Del Monte Research Park, Monterey, Calif. 93940.

Consulting Psychologists Press, Inc., 577 College Avenue, Palo Alto, Calif. 94306.

Educational and Industrial Testing Service, P.O. Box 7234, San Diego, Calif. 92107.

Educational Testing Service, Princeton, N.J. 08540.

Harcourt, Brace & World, Inc., 757 Third Avenue, New York, N.Y. 10017.

Houghton Mifflin Company, 110 Tremont Street, Boston, Mass. 02107.

Industrial Relations Center, University of Chicago, 1225 East 60th Street, Chicago, Ill. 60637.

Institute for Personality and Ability Testing, 1602 Coronado Drive, Champaign, Ill. 61820.

Psychological Corporation, 304 East 45th Street, New York, N.Y. 10017.

Psychological Test Specialists, Box 1441, Missoula, Mont. 59801.

Psychometric Affiliates, Chicago Plaza, Brookport, Ill. 62910.

636

Scholastic Testing Service, Inc., 480 Meyer Road, Bensenville, Ill. 60106.

Science Research Associates, Inc., 259 East Erie Street, Chicago, Ill. 60611.

Sheridan Psychological Services, P.O. Box 837, Beverly Hills, Calif. 90213.

C. H. Stoelting Company, 424 North Homan Avenue, Chicago, Ill. 60624.

Teachers College Press, Teachers College, 525 West 120th Street, New York, N.Y. 10027.

University Bookstore, Purdue University, 360 State Street, West Lafayette, Ind. 47906.

Western Psychological Services, 12035 Wilshire Boulevard, Los Angeles, Calif. 90025.

Classified List of
Representative Tests

THIS TABLE includes all published tests discussed in the text, except out-of-print tests cited for historical reasons only. In order to provide a more representative sample, a few additional tests not cited in the text are also listed under the appropriate categories. For more nearly complete coverage, the reader is referred to the *Mental Measurements Yearbooks* (MMY) and other sources cited in Chapter 1.

For each listed test, the table gives the volume and entry number in the MMY where the latest citation of that test can be found, including references to earlier reviews. When the latest edition of a test has not yet been listed in the MMY, reference to an earlier edition is given in parentheses, together with the publication date of the revised edition. For new tests, not yet included in the MMY, only the publication date is given. For publishers not listed in Appendix B, the address is included in this table.

The tests are classified under the same categories employed in the text. Each major category corresponds to a chapter, except that intelligence tests (Chs. 8–11) are listed together and are subdivided only into individual and group tests. All tests listed in this table are also included in the Subject Index.

Title	Publisher	MMY (or date)

INTELLIGENCE TESTS AND DEVELOPMENTAL SCALES (CHS. 8–11)

INDIVIDUAL TESTS (CHS. 8, 10, 11)

Title	Publisher	MMY (or date)
Arthur Point Scale of Performance Tests: Form I	Stoelting	4-335
Form II	Psychological Corporation	
Bayley Infant Scales of Development	Psychological Corporation	1968
Cattell Infant Intelligence Scale	Psychological Corporation	6-515
Full Range Picture Vocabulary Test	Psychological Test Specialists	6-521
Cain-Levine Social Competency Scale	Consulting Psychologists Press	6-69
Columbia Mental Maturity Scale	Harcourt, Brace & World	6-517
Gesell Developmental Schedules	Psychological Corporation	6-522
Griffiths Mental Development Scale for Testing Babies from Birth to Two Years	Ruth Griffiths, Child Development Research Center, 47 Hollycroft Avenue, London N.W. 3, England	6-523
Hiskey-Nebraska Test of Learning Aptitude	Marshal S. Hiskey, 5640 Baldwin, Lincoln, Neb. 68507	(5-409) 1966
Leiter International Performance Scale	Stoelting	6-526
Lincoln-Oseretsky Motor Development Scale	Stoelting	5-767
Merrill-Palmer Scale of Mental Tests (revision in progress)	Stoelting	6-527
Minnesota Preschool Scale	American Guidance Service (Educational Test Bureau)	6-528
Peabody Picture Vocabulary Test	American Guidance Service	6-530
Pictorial Test of Intelligence	Houghton Mifflin	6-531
Porteus Maze Test	Psychological Corporation	6-532
Quick Test	Psychological Test Specialists	6-534
Stanford-Binet Intelligence Scale	Houghton Mifflin	6-536
Van Alstyne Picture Vocabulary Test	Harcourt, Brace & World	6-537
Vineland Social Maturity Scale	American Guidance Service (Educational Test Bureau)	6-194
Wechsler Adult Intelligence Scale (WAIS)	Psychological Corporation	6-538
Wechsler Intelligence Scale for Children (WISC)	Psychological Corporation	6-540

Title	Publisher	MMY (or date)
INTELLIGENCE TESTS AND DEVELOPMENTAL SCALES (Cont.)		
Wechsler Preschool and Primary Scale of Intelligence (WPPSI)	Psychological Corporation	1967
GROUP TESTS (CHS. 9 AND 10)		
Academic Ability Test	Educational Testing Service (Cooperative Test Division)	1963
Alpha Examination, Modified Form 9	Psychological Corporation	3-220
American College Testing Program Examination	American College Testing Program, P. O. Box 168, Iowa City, Iowa 52240	6-1
Analysis of Learning Potential (ALP)	Harcourt, Brace & World	1968
Armed Forces Qualification Test (AFQT)	U.S. Department of the Army	see Uhlaner (1952)
Army General Classification Test (AGCT): First Civilian Edition	Science Research Associates	6-441
California Test of Mental Maturity, 1963 Revision	California Test Bureau	6-444
College Entrance Examination Board Scholastic Aptitude Test (SAT)	Educational Testing Service (for CEEB)	6-449
College Qualification Tests	Psychological Corporation	6-450
Concept Mastery Test	Psychological Corporation	6-451
Cooperative Primary Tests	Educational Testing Service (Cooperative Test Division)	1968
Cooperative School and College Ability Tests (SCAT) (also Series II, 1968)	Educational Testing Service (Cooperative Test Division)	6-452
Culture Fair Intelligence Test	Institute of Personality and Ability Testing	6-453
D 48 Test	Consulting Psychologists Press	6-454
Goodenough-Harris Drawing Test	Harcourt, Brace & World	6-460
Graduate Record Examinations (GRE)	Educational Testing Service	6-461, 6-762
Henmon-Nelson Tests of Mental Ability, Revised Edition	Houghton Mifflin	6-462
Kuhlmann-Anderson Intelligence Tests, Seventh Edition	Personnel Press, Inc., 20 Nassau Street, Princeton, N.J. 08540	6-466
Lorge-Thorndike Intelligence Tests (multilevel edition)	Houghton Mifflin	(6-467) 1964

Title	Publisher	MMY (or date)

INTELLIGENCE TESTS AND DEVELOPMENTAL SCALES (Cont.)

Title	Publisher	MMY (or date)
Miller Analogies Test	Psychological Corporation	6-472
Ohio State University Psychological Test, Forms 21 and 23	Science Research Associates	5-359
Otis-Lennon Mental Ability Test	Harcourt, Brace & World	(6-481) 1967–1968
Pintner General Ability Tests—Revised	Harcourt, Brace & World	(5-368) 1966–1968
Progressive Matrices	H. K. Lewis & Co., Ltd. (U.S. distributor: Psychological Corporation)	6-490
Purdue Non-Language Test	Science Research Associates	6-491
Quick Word Test	Harcourt, Brace & World	1964–1967
Revised Beta Examination	Psychological Corporation	6-494
SRA Non-Verbal Form	Science Research Associates	4-318
SRA Pictorial Reasoning Test	Science Research Associates	1966–1967
SRA Short Test of Educational Ability (STEA)	Science Research Associates	1966
SRA Tests of Educational Ability, 1962 Edition (TEA)	Science Research Associates	6-495
Terman-McNemar Test of Mental Ability	Harcourt, Brace & World	4-324
Tests of General Ability (TOGA)	Science Research Associates	6-496

MEASURES OF INTELLECTUAL IMPAIRMENT (CH. 12)

Title	Publisher	MMY (or date)
Babcock Test of Mental Efficiency	Western Psychological Services	6-64
Bender-Gestalt Test	Psychological Corporation	6-203
Benton Visual Retention Test, Revised Edition	Psychological Corporation	6-543
Concept Formation Test (Kasanin & Hanfmann)	Stoelting	6-78
Goldstein-Scheerer Tests of Abstract and Concrete Thinking	Psychological Corporation	6-101
Grassi Block Substitution Test	Western Psychological Services	5-60

Title	Publisher	MMY (or date)
MEASURES OF INTELLECTUAL IMPAIRMENT (Cont.)		
Hunt-Minnesota Test for Organic Brain Damage	University of Minnesota Press Minneapolis, Minn. 55455	4-51
Illinois Test of Psycholinguistic Abilities, Experimental Edition	University of Illinois Press Urbana, Ill. 61803	6-549
Kahn Test of Symbol Arrangement	Psychological Test Specialists	6-224
Memory-For-Designs Test (Graham & Kendall)	Psychological Test Specialists	6-140
MULTIPLE APTITUDE BATTERIES (CH. 13)		
Academic Promise Tests (APT)	Psychological Corporation	6-766
Differential Aptitude Tests (DAT)	Psychological Corporation	6-767
Employee Aptitude Survey (EAS)	Psychological Services, Inc., 1800 Wilshire Boulevard, Los Angeles, Calif. 90057	6-769
Flanagan Aptitude Classification Tests (FACT)	Science Research Associates	6-770
General Aptitude Test Battery (GATB)	U.S. Employment Service	6-771
Guilford-Zimmerman Aptitude Survey	Sheridan Psychological Services	6-772
Multiple Aptitude Tests, 1959 Edition	California Test Bureau	6-776
SRA Primary Mental Abilities, Revised	Science Research Associates	6-780
SPECIAL APTITUDE TESTS (CH. 14)		
SENSORY TESTS		
AO Sight Screener	American Optical Company, Southbridge, Mass. 01550	5-770
Dvorine Color Vision Test	Harcourt, Brace & World	6-955
Keystone Telebinocular	Keystone View Company, Meadville, Pa. 16335	5-780
Massachusetts Hearing Test	Massachusetts Department of Public Health, Division of Maternal and Child Health Services, 88 Broad Street, Boston, Mass. 02110	6-949
New York School Vision Tester	Bausch & Lomb, Inc., Rochester, N.Y. 14602	6-958

Title	Publisher	MMY (or date)

SPECIAL APTITUDE TESTS (Cont.)

Ortho-Rater	Bausch & Lomb, Inc., Rochester, N.Y. 14602	5-783

MOTOR TESTS

Crawford Small Parts Dexterity Test	Psychological Corporation	5-871
Purdue Pegboard	Science Research Associates	6-1081
Stromberg Dexterity Test	Psychological Corporation	4-755

MECHANICAL APTITUDE TESTS

MacQuarrie Test for Mechanical Ability	California Test Bureau	4-759
Mellenbruch Mechanical Motivation Test	Psychometric Affiliates	5-879
Revised Minnesota Paper Form Board Test	Psychological Corporation	6-1092
SRA Mechanical Aptitudes	Science Research Associates	4-764
Test of Mechanical Comprehension (Bennett)	Psychological Corporation	6-1094

CLERICAL APTITUDE TESTS

Minnesota Clerical Test	Psychological Corporation	6-1040
Short Employment Tests	Psychological Corporation	6-1045
Short Tests of Clerical Ability	Science Research Associates	6-1046

ARTISTIC APTITUDE TESTS

Graves Design Judgment Test	Psychological Corporation	4-220
Horn Art Aptitude Inventory	Stoelting	5-242
Meier Art Tests: 1. Art Judgment 2. Aesthetic Perception	Bureau of Educational Research and Service, University of Iowa, Iowa City, Iowa 52240	6-346
Tests in Fundamental Abilities of Visual Arts (Lewerenz)	California Test Bureau	1940-1329

MUSICAL APTITUDE TESTS

Drake Musical Aptitude Tests	Science Research Associates	5-245
Musical Aptitude Profile	Houghton Mifflin	1966
Seashore Measures of Musical Talents, Revised Edition	Psychological Corporation	6-353
Wing Standardized Tests of Musical Intelligence	National Foundation for Educational Research in England and Wales, the Mere, Upton Park, Slough, Bucks, England	6-354

Title	Publisher	MMY (or date)
SPECIAL APTITUDE TESTS (Cont.)		
CREATIVITY AND REASONING		
AC Test of Creative Ability	Industrial Relations Center, University of Chicago	6-1130
Logical Reasoning	Sheridan Psychological Services	5-694
Owens Creativity Test for Machine Design	Iowa State University Press, Ames, Iowa 50010	6-1134
Pertinent Questions	Sheridan Psychological Services	6-557
Purdue Creativity Test	University Book Store, Purdue University	6-1136
Remote Associates Test (RAT)	Houghton Mifflin	1967
Ship Destination Test	Sheridan Psychological Services	6-500
Southern California Tests of Divergent Production	Sheridan Psychological Services	6-542, 6-544, 6-547, 6-548, 6-552, 6-554, 6-558
Torrance Tests of Creative Thinking	Personnel Press, 20 Nassau St. Princeton, N.J. 08540	1966
Watson-Glaser Critical Thinking Appraisal	Harcourt, Brace & World	6-867

EDUCATIONAL TESTS (CH. 15)		
PREDICTIVE INSTRUMENTS		
Lee Test of Geometric Aptitude, 1963 Revision	California Test Bureau	6-647
Lee-Clark Reading Readiness Test, 1962 Revision	California Test Bureau	6-846
Let's Look at First Graders	Educational Testing Service (for N.Y.C. Board of Education)	1965
Metropolitan Readiness Tests	Harcourt, Brace & World	(4-570) 1965
Modern Language Aptitude Test	Psychological Corporation	6-357
Modern Language Aptitude Test—Elementary	Psychological Corporation	1967
Orleans-Hanna Algebra Prognosis Test	Harcourt, Brace & World	(4-396) 1968
Orleans-Hanna Geometry Prognosis Test	Harcourt, Brace & World	(4-427) 1968
Pimsleur Language Aptitude Battery	Harcourt, Brace & World	1966

Title	Publisher	MMY (or date)

EDUCATIONAL TESTS (Cont.)

School Readiness Behavior Tests Used at the Gesell Institute (Gesell Developmental Kits)	Harper & Row Publishers, Inc., 49 East 33rd Street, New York, N.Y. 10016	1964–1965

GENERAL ACHIEVEMENT BATTERIES

Adult Basic Learning Examination (ABLE)	Harcourt, Brace & World	1967
California Achievement Tests	California Test Bureau	6-3
Iowa Tests of Basic Skills	Houghton Mifflin	6-13
Iowa Tests of Educational Development	Science Research Associates	6-14
Fundamental Achievement Series	Psychological Corporation	1968
Metropolitan Achievement Test	Harcourt, Brace & World	6-15
SRA Achievement Series	Science Research Associates	6-21
Sequential Tests of Educational Progress (STEP)	Educational Testing Service (Cooperative Test Division)	6-25
Stanford Achievement Test, 1964 Revision	Harcourt, Brace & World	6-26
Stanford Achievement Test: High School Battery	Harcourt, Brace & World	1965
Stanford Pre-Primary Achievement Test	Harcourt, Brace & World	1968
Tests of Academic Promise (TAP)	Houghton Mifflin	1964

DIAGNOSTIC TESTS

Diagnostic Chart for Fundamental Processes in Arithmetic (Buswell-John)	Bobbs-Merrill	4-413
Diagnostic Reading Scales	California Test Bureau	6-821
Diagnostic Reading Tests	Committee on Diagnostic Reading Tests, Inc., Mountain Home, N.C. 28758	6-823
Diagnostic Tests and Self-Helps in Arithmetic	California Test Bureau	5-472
Durrell Analysis of Reading Difficulty, New Edition	Harcourt, Brace & World	5-660
Gates-McKillop Reading Diagnostic Tests	Teachers College Press	6-824
Nelson-Denny Reading Test	Houghton Mifflin	6-800
Stanford Diagnostic Arithmetic Test	Harcourt, Brace & World	1967

Title	Publisher	MMY (or date)
EDUCATIONAL TESTS (Cont.)		
Stanford Diagnostic Reading Test	Harcourt, Brace & World	1967
ACHIEVEMENT TESTS IN SPECIAL SUBJECTS		
Anderson-Fiske Chemistry Test	Harcourt, Brace & World	(5-737) 1966
Blyth Second-Year Algebra Test—Revised Edition	Harcourt, Brace & World	(5-443) 1966
Contemporary Mathematics Test	California Test Bureau	1965
Cooperative Mathematics Tests	Educational Testing Service (Cooperative Test Division)	6-594, 6-607, 6-643, 6-645, 6-654, 6-655, 6-657
Cooperative Science Tests	Educational Testing Service (Cooperative Test Division)	6-867a, 6-872a, 6-887a, 6-909a, 6-931a
Crary American History Test	Harcourt, Brace & World	(5-816) 1965
Cummings World History Test	Harcourt, Brace & World	(5-817) 1966
Dunning-Abeles Physics Test	Harcourt, Brace & World	(5-753) 1967
Lankton First-Year Algebra Test	Harcourt, Brace & World	(5-451) 1965
MLA Cooperative Foreign Language Tests	Educational Testing Service (Cooperative Test Division)	6-378, 6-392, 6-402, 6-416, 6-426
Modern Math Understanding Test	Science Research Associates	1966
Nelson Biology Test—Revised Edition	Harcourt, Brace & World	(5-728) 1965
Pimsleur Modern Foreign Language Proficiency Tests: French, German, Spanish	Harcourt, Brace & World	1967
Stanford Modern Mathematics Concepts Test	Harcourt, Brace & World	1965
Wisconsin Contemporary Test of Elementary Mathematics	Personnel Press, Inc., 20 Nassau Street, Princeton, N.J. 08540	1966– 1967

Title	Publisher	MMY (or date)

OCCUPATIONAL TESTS (CH. 16)

SHORT INTELLIGENCE TESTS FOR INDUSTRIAL SCREENING

Title	Publisher	MMY (or date)
Otis Employment Tests (revision in progress)	Harcourt, Brace & World	(4-310)
Personnel Tests for Industry	Psychological Corporation	5-366
Wesman Personnel Classification Test	Psychological Corporation	5-399
Wonderlic Personnel Test	E. F. Wonderlic & Associates, P. O. Box 7, Northfield, Ill. 60094	6-513

VOCATIONAL ACHIEVEMENT TESTS

Title	Publisher	MMY (or date)
Business Education Achievement Tests	Gregg Division, McGraw-Hill Book Co., 330 West 42nd St., New York, N.Y. 10036	1967
Purdue Personnel Tests	University Book Store, Purdue University	5-942 to 5-945
SRA Typing Skills	Science Research Associates	6-51
Seashore-Bennett Stenographic Proficiency Test	Psychological Corporation	5-519
Turse Clerical Aptitudes Test	Harcourt, Brace & World	5-855

TESTS IN THE PROFESSIONS

Title	Publisher	MMY (or date)
Dental Aptitude Testing Program	Division of Educational Measurements, Council on Dental Education, American Dental Association, 211 East Chicago Avenue, Chicago, Ill. 60611	5-916
Law School Admission Test	Educational Testing Service	5-928
Medical College Admission Test	Psychological Corporation	6-1137
Minnesota Engineering Analogies Test (MEAT)	Psychological Corporation	6-1133
NLN Achievement Tests in Nursing	National League for Nursing, Inc., 10 Columbus Circle, New York, N.Y. 10019	6-1157 to 6-1162
National Teacher Examinations	Educational Testing Service	6-700

SELF–REPORT PERSONALITY INVENTORIES (CH. 17)

Title	Publisher	MMY (or date)
A-S Reaction Study	Houghton Mifflin	6-57
Adjustment Inventory (Bell)	Consulting Psychologists Press	6-59
California Psychological Inventory (CPI)	Consulting Psychologists Press	6-71

Title	Publisher	MMY (or date)
SELF–REPORT PERSONALITY INVENTORIES (Cont.)		
California Test of Personality	California Test Bureau	6-73
Edwards Personal Preference Schedule (EPPS)	Psychological Corporation	6-87
Eysenck Personality Inventory	Educational and Industrial Testing Service	6-93
Gordon Personal Inventory	Harcourt, Brace & World	6-102
Gordon Personal Profile	Harcourt, Brace & World	6-103
Guilford-Zimmerman Temperament Survey	Sheridan Psychological Services	6-110
IPAT Children's Personality Questionnaire	Institute for Personality and Ability Testing	6-122
Jr.-Sr. High School Personality Questionnaire	Institute for Personality and Ability Testing	6-131
Minnesota Counseling Inventory	Psychological Corporation	6-142
Minnesota Multiphasic Personality Inventory (MMPI)	Psychological Corporation	6-143
Mooney Problem Check List	Psychological Corporation	6-145
Myers-Briggs Type Indicator	Educational Testing Service	6-147
Personal Orientation Inventory	Educational and Industrial Testing Service	1966
Personality Inventory (Bernreuter)	Consulting Psychologists Press	6-157
STS Youth Inventory	Scholastic Testing Service	(6-170) 1967
Sixteen Personality Factor Questionnaire	Institute for Personality and Ability Testing	6-174
INTEREST AND ATTITUDE TESTS (CH. 18)		
Gordon Occupational Check List	Harcourt, Brace & World	6-1056
Guilford-Zimmerman Interest Inventory	Sheridan Psychological Services	6-1057
Holland Vocational Preference Inventory	Consulting Psychologists Press	6-115
Kuder General Interest Survey	Science Research Associates	6-1061a
Kuder Occupational Interest Survey	Science Research Associates	(6-1062) 1964– 1966
Kuder Preference Record— Personal	Science Research Associates	6-132
Kuder Preference Record— Vocational	Science Research Associates	6-1063
Minnesota Teacher Attitude Inventory	Psychological Corporation	6-699

Title	Publisher	MMY (or date)
INTEREST AND ATTITUDE TESTS (Cont.)		
Minnesota Vocational Interest Inventory	Psychological Corporation	1965
Occupational Interest Inventory, 1956 Revision (Lee-Thorpe)	California Test Bureau	5-864
Pictorial Study of Values	Psychometric Affiliates	5-96
Strong Vocational Interest Blank (SVIB)	Stanford University Press, Stanford, Calif. 94305	(6-1070, 6-1071) 1966, 1968
Study of Values	Houghton Mifflin	6-182

Title	Publisher	MMY (or date)
PROJECTIVE TECHNIQUES (CH. 19)		
Blacky Pictures	Psychodynamic Instruments, P. O. Box 1221, Ann Arbor, Mich.	6-204
Children's Apperception Test (CAT)	C. P. S. Inc., P. O. Box 83, Larchmont, N.Y. 10538	6-206
Four Picture Test (van Lennep)	Martinus Nijhoff, P. O. Box 269, The Hague, Holland (distributor in all countries)	6-213
H-T-P: House-Tree-Person Projective Technique	Western Psychological Services	6-215
Holtzman Inkblot Technique	Psychological Corporation	6-217
Kent-Rosanoff Free Association Test	Stoelting	6-226
Machover Draw-a-Person Test	Charles C Thomas, 327 East Lawrence Avenue, Springfield, Ill. 62703	6-229
Make A Picture Story (MAPS)	Psychological Corporation	6-230
Rohde Sentence Completion Test	Western Psychological Services	5-158
Rorschach	Grune & Stratton, Inc., 381 Park Avenue South, New York, N.Y. 10016 (United States distributor)	6-237
Rosenzweig Picture-Frustration Study (P-F Study)	Saul Rosenzweig, 8029 Washington Street, St. Louis, Mo. 63114	6-238
Rotter Incomplete Sentences Blank	Psychological Corporation	6-239
Szondi Test	Grune & Stratton, Inc., 381 Park Avenue South, New York, N.Y. 10016 (United States distributor)	6-243

Title	Publisher	MMY (or date)

PROJECTIVE TECHNIQUES (Cont.)

Thematic Apperception Test (TAT)	Harvard University Press, 79 Garden Street, Cambridge, Mass. 02138	6-245; see also 5-166
Tomkins-Horn Picture Arrangement Test (PAT)	Springer Publishing Co., Inc., 44 East 23rd Street, New York, N.Y. 10010	6-246
Toy World Test	Joyce B. Baisden, 4570 Mont Eagle Place, Los Angeles, Calif. 90014	5-168

PERSONALITY TESTS: MISCELLANEOUS (CH. 20)

NOTE: Several techniques discussed in Chapter 20 are not published tests and are described only in the references cited in the text.

Adjective Check List (ACL)	Consulting Psychologists Press	1965
Barron-Welsh Art Scale (see Welsh Figure Preference Test)		
California Q-Set (CQ-set).	Consulting Psychologists Press	6-72
Chapin Social Insight Test	Consulting Psychologists Press	see Gough, 1965b
Closure Flexibility (Concealed Figures)	Industrial Relations Center, University of Chicago	6-545
Closure Speed (Gestalt Completion)	Industrial Relations Center, University of Chicago	6-546
Embedded Figures Test	Herman A. Witkin, State University College of Medicine, 450 Clarkson Avenue, Brooklyn, N.Y. 11203	6-89
Famous Sayings	Psychological Test Specialists	6-96
IPAT Humor Test of Personality	Institute for Personality and Ability Testing	(4-61) 1966
IPAT Music Preference Test of Personality	Institute for Personality and Ability Testing	6-125
Performance Record	Science Research Associates	5-902
Welsh Figure Preference Test	Consulting Psychologists Press	6-197

MEASURES OF ENVIRONMENT (CH. 22)

American Home Scale	Psychometric Affiliates	5-596
College Characteristics Index (and other versions for different contexts)	National Computer Systems, 1015 South Sixth Street, Minneapolis, Minn. 55415	6-92; see also 6-180
College and University Environment Scales (CUES)	Educational Testing Service	6-695

Author Index

Subject Index

frequency, 25, 40-42, 49-51
  normal, 25-27, 42, 45, 51-52
  rectangular, 27n
  skewed, 25-27
Drake Musical Aptitude Tests, 643
Draw-a-Man Test, 248-250, 573-574
Draw-a-Person Test (D-A-P), 507-508
Drawing, aptitude tests for, 368-371
  in intelligence testing, 248-250
  in personality measurement, 507-508
Drives, relation to intelligence, 578
Dunning-Abeles Physics Tests, 646
Duplicating technique, 521
Durrell Analysis of Reading Difficulty,
  New Edition, 407, 645
Dvorine Color Vision Test, 353, 642

Educational age, 61
Educational norms, 60-62
Educational quotient, 61
Educational Testing Service (ETS), 16,
  167, 429, 431
Educational tests, 3, 15-16, 644-646
Edwards Personal Preference Schedule
  (EPPS), 452-454, 458-459, 648
Elementary school children, group intelli-
  gence tests for, 221-224
Embedded Figures Test, 528, 650
Empirical criterion keying, 440-449, 468-
  469, 479
Employee Aptitude Survey (EAS), 642
Employee attitudes, 480-481, 485
Engineering tests, 434
Environment, measurement of, 578-583,
  650
Environmental variables, scales for, 579-
  583
Equal-appearing intervals, method of, 483
Equal-unit scaling, 55n
Equipercentile method, 66
Error of central tendency in rating, 421
Error-choice technique, 531
Error variancé, 71, 87-89, 325
Essay questions, 160
Ethical Standards of Psychologists, 32-33,
  548, 550, 552-553, 596, 627-635
Evaluation and Adjustment Series, 66,
  410-411
Examiner, preparation, 36-37
  qualifications, 31
  reliability, 86
  variables, 38, 572-574
  in projective techniques, 511
Executive selection and personality tests,
  557-558
Expectancy charts, 125-127
Expectancy tables, 124-127
Experience-producing drives, 578
Experimental psychology, influence on
  early test development, 6-7
Eysenck Personality Inventory, 648

Face validity, 104
Factor analysis, 14, 116-117, 320-327
  creativity, 375-377
  intelligence, 329-334, 574-576
  motor functions, 358-359
  music tests, 373
  perception, 527-528
  personality inventories, 449-451
  Stanford-Binet, 205-206
  WAIS, 280-281
Factor matrix, 320-321
Factorial validity, 116-117

Faking, on personality inventories, 456-
  458
  on projective tests, 510
False positives, 133
Famous Sayings test, 530, 650
Ferson-Stoddard Law Aptitude Examina-
  tion, 430
Field dependence, tests of, 528
Fixed reference group in nonnormative
  scales, 67-69
Flanagan Aptitude Classification Tests
  (FACT), 67, 340-342, 642
Flexibility of closure, 527-528, 650
Fluency tests, 375
Forced-choice technique, 458-460
Forced distribution, 421
Four Picture Test (van Lennep), 649
Free association tests, 8, 17, 18, 504-506
Frequency distribution (see Distribution,
  frequency)
Frequency polygon, 41-42
Full Range Picture Vocabulary Test, 639
Fundamental Achievement Series, 645

g factor, 327-328
Galton laboratory, influence on early test
  development, 7-8
Gates-McKillop Reading Diagnostic Tests,
  645
General Aptitude Test Battery (GATB),
  67, 149-150, 343-346, 642
Gesell Developmental Schedules, 254-256,
  639
Gesell Institute, developmental scale, 254-
  256
  school readiness tests, 385-386
Goldstein-Scheerer Tests of Abstract and
  Concrete Thinking, 307-310, 641
Goodenough Draw-a-Man Test, 248-250
Goodenough-Harris Drawing Test, 248-250,
  640
Gordon Occupational Check List, 473n,
  648
Gordon Personal Inventory, 458, 648
Gordon Personal Profile, 648
Gottschaldt Figures, 527-528
Grade norms, 60-61
Grade progress, in achievement test vali-
  dation, 101-103
Grade scores, 405
Graduate Record Examinations (GRE),
  232-234, 434, 640
Graduate school students, tests for, 232-
  234
Graphic rating scale, 419-420
Grassi Block Substitution Test, 641
Graves Design Judgment Test, 643
Griffiths Mental Development Scale, 639
Group factors, 328-334
Group tests, nature of, 213-216
  origin of, 11-12
  survey of, 216-235
"Guess Who" technique, 541
Guidelines for Testing Minority Group
  Children, 562n, 563, 597
Guilford-Zimmerman Aptitude Survey,
  642
Guilford-Zimmerman Interest Inventory,
  648
Guilford-Zimmerman Temperament Sur-
  vey, 449-450, 648

Halo effect in ratings, 420
Hanfmann-Kasanin Concept Formation
  Test, 310-311, 641